AMERICAN POETRY:
THE TWENTIETH CENTURY

VOLUME ONE

American Poetry: The Twentieth Century

VOLUME ONE
Henry Adams to Dorothy Parker

THE LIBRARY OF AMERICA

Some of the material in this volume is reprinted by
permission of the holders of copyright and publication rights.
Acknowledgments will be found on pages 941–45.

The paper used in this publication meets the
minimum requirements of the American National Standard for
Information Sciences—Permanence of Paper for Printed
Library Materials, ANSI Z39.48—1984.

Distributed to the trade in the United States
by Penguin Putnam Inc.
and in Canada by Penguin Books Canada Ltd.

Library of Congress Catalog Number: 99–043721
For cataloging information, see end of Index.
ISBN 1–883011–77–9

First Printing
The Library of America—115

Manufactured in the United States of America

Volume One of
American Poetry: The Twentieth Century
was published with generous financial support
from the National Endowment for the Humanities.

Contents

ANONYMOUS BALLADS

White House Blues

Zolgotz, mean man,
He shot McKinley with his handkerchief on his hand,
In Buffalo, in Buffalo.

Zolgotz, you done him wrong,
You shot McKinley when he was walking along,
In Buffalo, in Buffalo.

The pistol fires, then McKinley falls,
And the doctor says, "McKinley, cain't find the ball,"
In Buffalo, in Buffalo.

They sent for the doctor, the doctor come,
He come in a trot, and he come in a run,
To Buffalo, to Buffalo.

He saddled his horse, and he swung on his mane,
And he trotted the horse till he outrun the train
To Buffalo, to Buffalo.

Forty-four boxes all trimmed in braid,
The sixteen-wheel driver, boys, they couldn't make the grade
To Buffalo, to Buffalo.

Forty-four boxes trimmed in lace,
Take him back to the baggage, boys, where we can't see his
        face,
In Buffalo, in Buffalo.

Mrs. McKinley took a trip, and she took it out west,
Where she couldn't hear the people talk about McKinley's
        death,
In Buffalo, in Buffalo.

The engine whistled down the line,
Blowing every station, McKinley was a-dying,
In Buffalo, in Buffalo.

Seventeen coaches all trimmed in black
Took McKinley to the graveyard, but never brought him
    back,
To Buffalo, to Buffalo.

Seventeen coaches all trimmed in black
Took Roosevelt to the White House, but never brought him
    back,
To Buffalo, to Buffalo.

Casey Jones

Come all you rounders, for I want you to hear,
The story of a brave engineer.
Casey Jones was the rounder's name.
On a big eight wheeler of a mighty fame.

Caller called Casey 'bout half-past four,
He kissed his wife at the station door,
Climbed to the cab with the orders in his hand,
He says, "This is my trip to the holy land."

Out of South Memphis yard on the fly,
Heard the fireman say, "You got a white eye."
Well, the switchmen knew by the engine moan
That the man at the throttle was Casey Jones.

The rain was comin' down five or six weeks.
The railroad track was like the bed of a creek.
They slowed her down to a thirty mile gait
And the south-bound mail was eight hours late.

Fireman says, "Casey, you're runnin' too fast,
You run that block board the last station you passed."
Casey says, "I believe we'll make it though,
For she steams a lot better than I ever know."

Casey says, "Fireman, don't you fret,
Keep knockin' at the fire door, don't give up yet,
I'm going to run her till she leaves the rail,
Or make it on time with the south-bound mail."

Around the curve and down the dump,
Two locomotives was a bound to jump,
Fireman hollered, "Casey, it's just ahead,
We might jump and make it but we'll all be dead."

Around the curve comes a passenger train,
Casey blows the whistle, tells the fireman, "Ring the bell,"
Fireman jumps and says "Good-by,
Casey Jones, you're bound to die."

Well Casey Jones was all right.
He stuck to his duty day and night.
They loved his whistle and his ring number three,
And he came into Memphis on the old I. C.

Fireman goes down the depot track,
Begging his honey to take him back,
She says, "Oranges on the table, peaches on the shelf,
You're a goin' to get tired sleepin' by yourself."

Mrs. Casey Jones was a sittin' on the bed.
Telegram comes that Casey is dead.
She says, "Children, go to bed, and hush your cryin',
'Cause you got another papa on the Frisco line."

Headaches and heartaches and all kinds of pain.
They ain't apart from a railroad train.
Stories of brave men, noble and grand,
Belong to the life of a railroad man.

Claude Allen

Claude Allen he and his dear old pappy
 Have met their fatal doom at last.
Their friends are glad their trouble's ended
 And hope their souls are now at rest.

Claude Allen was that tall and handsome,
 He still had hopes until the end
That he'll some way or other
 Escape his death from the Richmond pen.

The governor being so hard-hearted,
 Not caring what his friends might say,
He finally took his sweet life from him.
 In the cold, cold ground his body lay.

Claude Allen had a pretty sweetheart,
 She mourned the loss of the one she loved.
She hoped to meet beyond the river,
 Her fair young face in heaven above.

Claude's mother's tears was gently flowing,
 All for the one she loved so dear.
It seemed no one could tell her troubles,
 It seemed no one could tell but her.

How sad, how sad, to think of killin'
 A man all in his youthful years,
A-leaving his old mother weepin'
 And all his friends in bitter tears.

Look up on yonder lonely mountain,
 Claude Allen sleeps beneath the clay.
No more you'll hear his words of mercy
 Or see his face till Judgment Day.

Come all young boys, you may take warning.
 Be careful how you go astray,
Or you may be like poor Claude Allen
 And have this awful debt to pay.

Midnight Special

If you evah go to Houston,
You better walk right;
You better not gamble
And you better not fight.
T. Bentley will arrest you,
He'll surely take you down;
Judge Nelson'll sentence you,
Then you're jailhouse bound.

O let the Midnight Special
Shine a light on me,
Let the Midnight Special
Shine a evah lovin' light on me!

Every Monday mawnin',
When the ding-dong rings,
You go to the table,
See the same damn things;
And on the table,
There's a knife an' pan,
Say anything about it,
Have trouble with a man.

Yondah come Miss Rosy;
Oh, how do you know?
By th' umbrella on her shoulder
An' the dress that she woah!
Straw hat on her head,
Piece of paper in her hand,
Says, "Look here, Mr. Jailer,
I want's my life-time man."

The Titanic

It was on one Monday morning just about one o'clock
When the great *Titanic* began to reel and rock.
People began to scream and cry,
Saying, "Oh, Lord, I'm going to die!"
It was sad when that great ship went down.

    Don't you know it was sad when that great ship went
       down,
    It was sad when that great ship went down,
    Husbands and wives, little children lost their lives,
    It was sad when that great ship went down.

People aboard the ship was a long way from home,
With friends standing around didn't know their time had
      come;
But death came riding by, sixteen hundred had to die,
It was sad when that great ship went down.

When Paul he was a sailor, his men all standing around,
God sitting in his Kingdom, not a man should be drowned;
Sixteen hundred and threescore
All got landed on that shore,
It was sad when that great ship went down.

    Don't you know it was sad when that great ship went
       down,
    It was sad when that great ship went down,
    Husbands and wives, little children lost their lives,
    It was sad when that great ship went down.

HENRY ADAMS

Prayer to the Virgin of Chartres

GRACIOUS LADY:—
Simple as when I asked your aid before;
  Humble as when I prayed for grace in vain
Seven hundred years ago; weak, weary, sore
  In heart and hope, I ask your help again.

You, who remember all, remember me;
  An English scholar of a Norman name,
I was a thousand who then crossed the sea
  To wrangle in the Paris schools for fame.

When your Byzantine portal was still young
  I prayed there with my master Abailard;
When Ave Maris Stella was first sung,
  I helped to sing it here with Saint Bernard.

When Blanche set up your gorgeous Rose of France
  I stood among the servants of the Queen;
And when Saint Louis made his penitence,
  I followed barefoot where the King had been.

For centuries I brought you all my cares,
  And vexed you with the murmurs of a child;
You heard the tedious burden of my prayers;
  You could not grant them, but at least you smiled.

If then I left you, it was not my crime,
  Or if a crime, it was not mine alone.
All children wander with the truant Time.
  Pardon me too! You pardoned once your Son!

For He said to you:—"Wist ye not that I
   Must be about my Father's business?" So,
Seeking his Father he pursued his way
   Straight to the Cross towards which we all must go.

So I too wandered off among the host
   That racked the earth to find the father's clue.
I did not find the Father, but I lost
   What now I value more, the Mother,—You!

I thought the fault was yours that foiled my search;
   I turned and broke your image on its throne,
Cast down my idol, and resumed my march
 _ To claim the father's empire for my own.

Crossing the hostile sea, our greedy band
   Saw rising hills and forests in the blue;
Our father's kingdom in the promised land!
   —We seized it, and dethroned the father too.

And now we are the Father, with our brood,
   Ruling the Infinite, not Three but One;
We made our world and saw that it was good;
   Ourselves we worship, and we have no Son.

Yet we have Gods, for even our strong nerve
   Falters before the Energy we own.
Which shall be master? Which of us shall serve?
   Which wears the fetters? Which shall bear the crown?

Brave though we be, we dread to face the Sphinx,
   Or answer the old riddle she still asks.
Strong as we are, our reckless courage shrinks
   To look beyond the piece-work of our tasks.

But when we must, we pray, as in the past
   Before the Cross on which your Son was nailed.
Listen, dear lady! You shall hear the last
   Of the strange prayers Humanity has wailed.

_____

Prayer to the Dynamo

Mysterious Power! Gentle Friend!
   Despotic Master! Tireless Force!
You and We are near the End.
Either You or We must bend
   To bear the martyrs' Cross.

We know ourselves, what we can bear
   As men; our strength and weakness too;
Down to the fraction of a hair;
And know that we, with all our care
   And knowledge, know not you.

You come in silence, Primal Force,
   We know not whence, or when, or why;
You stay a moment in your course
To play; and, lo! you leap across
   To Alpha Centauri!

We know not whether you are kind,
   Or cruel in your fiercer mood;
But be you Matter, be you Mind,
We think we know that you are blind,
   And we alone are good.

We know that prayer is thrown away,
   For you are only force and light;
A shifting current; night and day;
We know this well, and yet we pray,
   For prayer is infinite,

Like you! Within the finite sphere
   That bounds the impotence of thought,
We search an outlet everywhere
But only find that we are here
   And that you are—are not!

What are we then? the lords of space?
   The master-mind whose tasks you do?
Jockey who rides you in the race?
Or are we atoms whirled apace,
   Shaped and controlled by you?

Still silence! Still no end in sight!
   No sound in answer to our cry!
Then, by the God we now hold tight,
Though we destroy soul, life and light,
   Answer you shall—or die!

We are no beggars! What care we
   For hopes or terrors, love or hate?
What for the universe? We see
Only our certain destiny
   And the last word of Fate.

Seize, then, the Atom! rack his joints!
   Tear out of him his secret spring!
Grind him to nothing!—though he points
To us, and his life-blood anoints
   Me—the dead Atom-King!

———

A curious prayer, dear lady! is it not?
   Strangely unlike the prayers I prayed to you!
Stranger because you find me at this spot,
   Here, at your feet, asking your help anew.

Strangest of all, that I have ceased to strive,
   Ceased even care what new coin fate shall strike.
In truth it does not matter. Fate will give
   Some answer; and all answers are alike.

So, while we slowly rack and torture death
   And wait for what the final void will show,
Waiting I feel the energy of faith
   Not in the future science, but in you!

The man who solves the Infinite, and needs
    The force of solar systems for his play,
Will not need me, nor greatly care what deeds
    Made me illustrious in the dawn of day.

He will send me, dethroned, to claim my rights,
    Fossil survival of an age of stone,
Among the cave-men and the troglodytes
    Who carved the mammoth on the mammoth's bone.

He will forget my thought, my acts, my fame,
    As we forget the shadows of the dusk,
Or catalogue the echo of a name
    As we the scratches on the mammoth's tusk.

But when, like me, he too has trod the track
    Which leads him up to power above control,
He too will have no choice but wander back
    And sink in helpless hopelessness of soul,

Before your majesty of grace and love,
    The purity, the beauty and the faith;
The depth of tenderness beneath; above,
    The glory of the life and of the death.

When your Byzantine portal still was young,
    I came here with my master Abailard;
When Ave Maris Stella was first sung,
    I joined to sing it here with Saint Bernard.

When Blanche set up your glorious Rose of France,
    In scholar's robes I waited on the Queen;
When good Saint Louis did his penitence,
    My prayer was deep like his: my faith as keen.

What loftier prize seven hundred years shall bring,
    What deadlier struggles for a larger air,
What immortality our strength shall wring
    From Time and Space, we may—or may not—care;

But years, or ages, or eternity,
    Will find me still in thought before your throne,
Pondering the mystery of Maternity,
    Soul within Soul,—Mother and Child in One!

Help me to see! not with my mimic sight—
    With yours! which carried radiance, like the sun,
Giving the rays you saw with—light in light—
    Tying all suns and stars and worlds in one.

Help me to know! not with my mocking art—
    With you, who knew yourself unbound by laws;
Gave God your strength, your life, your sight, your heart,
    And took from him the Thought that Is—the Cause.

Help me to feel! not with my insect sense,—
    With yours that felt all life alive in you;
Infinite heart beating at your expense;
    Infinite passion breathing the breath you drew!

Help me to bear! not my own baby load,
    But yours; who bore the failure of the light,
The strength, the knowledge and the thought of God,—
    The futile folly of the Infinite!

CHARLES ERSKINE SCOTT WOOD

(1852–1944)

from
The Poet in the Desert

I have entered into the Desert, the place of desolation.
The Desert confronts me haughtily and assails me with
    solitude.
She sits on a throne of light,
Her hands clasped, her eyes solemnly questioning.
I have come into the lean and stricken land
Which fears not God, that I may meet my soul
Face to face, naked as the Desert is naked;
Bare as the great silence is bare:

I will question the Silent Ones who have gone before and are
    forgotten,
And the great host which shall come after,
By whom I also shall be forgot.
As the Desert is defiant unto all gods,
So am I defiant of all gods,
Shadows of Man cast upon the fogs of his ignorance.
As a helpless child follows the hand of its mother,
So I put my hand into the hand of the Eternal.

I have come to lose myself in the wide immensity and know
    my littleness.
I have come to lie in the lap of my mother and be comforted.
I am alone but not alone—I am with myself.
My soul is my companion above all companions.

Behold the signs of the Desert:
A buzzard, afloat on airy seas,
Alone, between the two immensities, as I am alone between
    two immensities;
A juniper-tree on a rocky hillside;

A dark signal from afar off, where the weary may rest in the
    shade;
A monastery for the flocks of little birds which by night hurry
    across the Desert and hide in the heat of the day;
A basaltic-cliff, embroidered with lichens and illuminated by
    the sun, orange and yellow,
The work of a great painter, careless in the splash of his
    brush.
In its shadow lie timid antelope, which flit through the sage-
    brush and are gone;
But easily they become fearless unto love.
The sea of sage-brush, breaking against the purple hills far
    away.
And the white alkali-flats which shimmer in the mirage as
    beautiful blue lakes, constantly retreating.
The mirage paints upon the sky, rivers with cool, willowy
    banks;
You can almost hear the lapping of the water,
But they flee mockingly, leaving the thirsty to perish.
I lie down upon the warm sand of the Desert and it seems to
    me Life has its mirages, also.
I sift the sand through my fingers.

Behold the signs of the Desert:
The stagnant water-hole, trampled with hoofs;
About it shine the white bones of those who came too late.
The whirling dust-pillar, waltz of Wind and Earth,
The dust carried up to the sky in the hot, furious arms of the
    wind, as I also am lifted up.
The glistening black wall of obsidian, where the wild tribes
    came to fashion their arrows, knives, spearheads.
The ground is strewn with the fragments, just as they
    dropped them, the strokes of the maker undimmed
    through the desperate years.
But the hunters have gone forever.

The Desert cares no more for the death of the tribes than for
    the death of the armies of black crawling crickets.
Silence. Invincible. Impregnable. Compelling the soul to
    stand forth to be questioned.

Dazzling in the sun, whiter than snow, I see the bones
Of those who have existed as I now exist. The bones are here;
    where are they who lived?
Like a thin veil, I see a crowd of gnats, buzzing their hour.
I know that they are my brethren, I am less than the shadow
    of this rock,
For the shadow returneth forever.
Night overwhelms me. The coyotes bark to the stars.
Upon the warm midnight sand I lie thoughtfully sifting the
    earth through my fingers. I am that dust.
I look up unto the stars, knowing that to them my life is not
    more valuable than that of the flowers;
The little, delicate flowers of the Desert,
Which, like a breath, catch at the hem of Spring and are
    gone.

LIZETTE WOODWORTH REESE

Crows

Earth is raw with this one note,
This battered making of a song
Narrowed down to a crow's throat,
Above the willow-trees that throng

The crooking field from end to end.
Fixed as the sun, the grass, that sound;
Of what the weather has to spend,
As much a part as sky, or ground.

The primal yellow of that flower,
That tansy making August plain,
And the stored wildness of this hour,
It sucks up like a bitter rain.

Miss it we would, were it not here;
Simple as water, rough as spring,
It hurls us, at the point of spear,
Back to some naked, early thing.

Fog

I had a house; I had a yard
Crammed with marigolds, so high,
So deep in fire, that it was hard
Not to believe, if I went by,

I would be blistered to the bone.
All gone. A square of dripping grass
Each side, and underfoot wet stone,
That sound like click of glass on glass.

This spare, hidden beauty all around,
Is not too little, or too much;
A surfeit had I; now am bound
To a ghost's wealth, too frail for touch.

To a ghost's weather, that or this
Of its old secrecy left untold;
Relinquished, let alone, I miss
House, nor yard, nor a tall marigold.

Wind

Now has the wind a sound
Made out of rain;
A misty, broken secretness,
That drenches road and pane.
It drips and drips; a hush
Falls on the town;
Like golden clods an old tree shakes
Its apples down.

The White Fury of the Spring

Oh, now, now the white fury of the spring
Whirls at each door, and on each flowering plot—
The pear, the cherry, the grave apricot!
The lane's held in a storm, and is a thing
To take into a grave, a lantern-light
To fasten there, by which to stumble out,
And race in the new grass, and hear about
The crash of bough with bough, of white with white.
Were I to run, I could not run so fast,
But that the spring would overtake me still;
Halfway I go to meet it on the stair.
For certainly it will rush in at last,
And in my own house seize me at its will,
And drag me out to the white fury there.

HARRIET MONROE
(1860–1936)

Radio

"I caught a fella last night in the South Pacific—
He was on a freighter way beyond New Zealand.
And what do you think he said to me, that guy?"
The young radio man was talking.

" 'How did the Cubs come out today?' he said—
'How did the Cubs come out?' Nothing he wanted
But that fool game! 'They got it in the neck,'
I answered him—ten thousand miles across—
'The Pirates chewed 'em up.' 'The hell they did!'
'Say, where's the sun out your way?' I ticked off—
'Here it went down an hour or two ago.'
'It'll be coming up in half an hour,' he answered,
'It's Sunday here.' 'Oh, get a move on you!—
Sunday's most over—you're in yesterday.'
'Well, it's the same old sun coming or going—
Yesterdays and tomorrows get all mixed up;
We'll cross the line pretty soon. Where are you, buddy?'
'Oh, near Chicago. So long—see you again.'
So I clicked off and went to bed—and he
To breakfast probably."
                            "Do you often talk
So far?" I asked him, wondering.
                                        "Oh, that's nothing!
I talked with Byrd's Antarctic Expedition
The other night. Say, but it's cold down there!"

EDITH WHARTON

(1862–1937)

Terminus

Wonderful was the long secret night you gave me, my Lover,
Palm to palm, breast to breast in the gloom. The faint red
    lamp
Flushing with magical shadows the common-place room of
    the inn,
With its dull impersonal furniture, kindled a mystic flame
In the heart of the swinging mirror, the glass that has seen
Faces innumerous and vague of the endless travelling
    automata
Whirled down the ways of the world like dust-eddies swept
    through a street,
Faces indifferent or weary, frowns of impatience or pain,
Smiles (if such there were ever) like your smile and mine
    when they met
Here, in this self-same glass, while you helped me to loosen
    my dress,
And the shadow-mouths melted to one, like sea-birds that
    meet in a wave—
Such smiles, yes, such smiles the mirror perhaps has reflected;
And the low wide bed, as rutted and worn as a high-road,
The bed with its soot-sodden chintz, the grime of its brasses,
That has born the weight of fagged bodies, dust-stained,
    averted in sleep,
The hurried, the restless, the aimless—perchance it has also
    thrilled
With the pressure of bodies ecstatic, bodies like ours,
Seeking each other's souls in the depths of unfathomed
    caresses,
And through the long windings of passion emerging again to
    the stars . . .
Yes, all this through the room, the passive and featureless
    room,

Must have flowed with the rise and fall of the human
    unceasing current,
And lying there hushed in your arms, as the waves of rapture
    receded,
And far down the margin of being we heard the low beat of
    the soul,
I was glad as I thought of those others, the nameless, the
    many,
Who perhaps thus had lain and loved for an hour on the
    brink of the world,
Secret and fast in the heart of the whirlwind of travel,
The shaking and shrieking of trains, the night-long shudder
    of traffic;
Thus, like us they have lain and felt, breast to breast in the
    dark,
The fiery rain of possession descend on their limbs while
    outside
The black rain of midnight pelted the roof of the station;
And thus some woman like me waking alone before dawn,
While her lover slept, as I woke and heard the calm stir of
    your breathing,
Some woman has heard as I heard the farewell shriek of the
    trains
Crying good-bye to the city and staggering out into darkness,
And shaken at heart has thought: "So must we forth in the
    darkness,
Sped down the fixed rail of habit by the hand of implacable
    fate—"
So shall we issue to life, and the rain, and the dull dark
    dawning;
You to the wide flair of cities, with windy garlands and
    shouting,
Carrying to populous places the freight of holiday throngs;
I, by waste land and stretches of low-skied marsh,
To a harbourless wind-bitten shore, where a dull town
    moulders and shrinks,
And its roofs fall in, and the sluggish feet of the hours
Are printed in grass in its streets; and between the featureless
    houses
Languid the town-folk glide to stare at the entering train,

The train from which no one descends; till one pale evening
 of winter,
When it halts on the edge of the town, see, the houses have
 turned into grave-stones,
The streets are the grassy paths between the low roofs of the
 dead;
And as the train glides in ghosts stand by the doors of the
 carriages;
And scarcely the difference is felt—yes, such is the life I
 return to . . . !
Thus may another have thought; thus, as I turned, may have
 turned
To the sleeping lips at her side, to drink, as I drank there,
 oblivion.

FRANCES DENSMORE
(1867–1957)

from
Chippewa Music

I Am Walking

Toward calm and shady places
I am walking
On the earth

The Sound Is Fading Away

The sound is fading away
It is of five sounds
Freedom
The sound is fading away
It is of five sounds

The Song of Butterfly

in the coming heat
of the day
I stood there

A Song of Spring

as my eyes
search
the prairie
I feel the summer in the spring

The Sky Will Resound

it will resound finely
the sky
when I come making a noise

My Love Has Departed

A loon
I thought it was
But it was
My love's
Splashing oar

To Sault Ste. Marie
He has departed
My love
Has gone on before me
Never again
Can I see him

I Have Found My Lover

Oh
I am thinking
Oh
I am thinking
I have found
my lover
Oh
I think it is so

MARY AUSTIN
(1868–1934)

The Grass on the Mountain
From the Paiute.

Oh, long, long
The snow has possessed the mountains.

The deer have come down and the big-horn,
They have followed the Sun to the south
To feed on the mesquite pods and the bunch grass.
Loud are the thunder drums
In the tents of the mountains.

Oh, long, long
Have we eaten *chia* seeds
And dried deer's flesh of the summer killing.
We are wearied of our huts
And the smoky smell of our garments.

We are sick with desire of the sun
And the grass on the mountain.

W.E.B. DU BOIS

(1868–1963)

The Song of the Smoke

I am the Smoke King
I am black!
I am swinging in the sky,
I am wringing worlds awry;
  I am the thought of the throbbing mills,
  I am the soul of the soul-toil kills,
  Wraith of the ripple of trading rills;
Up I'm curling from the sod,
I am whirling home to God;
    I am the Smoke King
    I am black.

    I am the Smoke King,
    I am black!
I am wreathing broken hearts,
I am sheathing love's light darts;
  Inspiration of iron times
  Wedding the toil of toiling climes,
  Shedding the blood of bloodless crimes—
Lurid lowering 'mid the blue,
Torrid towering toward the true,
    I am the Smoke King,
    I am black.

    I am the Smoke King,
    I am black!
I am darkening with song,
I am hearkening to wrong!
  I will be black as blackness can—
  The blacker the mantle, the mightier the man!
  For blackness was ancient ere whiteness began.

I am daubing God in night,
I am swabbing Hell in white:
    I am the Smoke King
    I am black.

    I am the Smoke King
    I am black!
I am cursing ruddy morn,
I am hearsing hearts unborn:
  Souls unto me are as stars in a night,
  I whiten my black men—I blacken my white!
  What's the hue of a hide to a man in his might?
Hail! great, gritty, grimy hands—
Sweet Christ, pity toiling lands!
    I am the Smoke King
    I am black.

A Litany at Atlanta

O Silent God, Thou whose voice afar in mist and mystery hath left our ears an-hungered in these fearful days—
    Hear us, good Lord!

Listen to us, Thy children: our faces dark with doubt are made a mockery in Thy Sanctuary. With uplifted hands we front Thy Heaven, O God, crying:
    We beseech Thee to hear us, good Lord!

We are not better than our fellows, Lord; we are but weak and human men. When our devils do deviltry, curse Thou the doer and the deed,—curse them as we curse them, do to them all and more than ever they have done to innocence and weakness, to womanhood and home.
    Have mercy upon us, miserable sinners!

And yet, whose is the deeper guilt? Who made these devils? Who nursed them in crime and fed them on injustice? Who ravished and debauched their mothers and their grand-mothers? Who bought and sold their crime and waxed fat and rich on public iniquity?
    Thou knowest, good God!

Is this Thy Justice, O Father, that guile be easier than innocence and the innocent be crucified for the guilt of the untouched guilty?

Justice, O Judge of men!

Wherefore do we pray? Is not the God of the Fathers dead? Have not seers seen in Heaven's halls Thine hearsed and lifeless form stark amidst the black and rolling smoke of sin, where all along bow bitter forms of endless dead?

Awake, Thou that sleepest!

Thou art not dead, but flown afar, up hills of endless light, through blazing corridors of suns, where worlds do swing of good and gentle men, of women strong and free—far from the cozenage, black hypocrisy, and chaste prostitution of this shameful speck of dust!

Turn again, O Lord; leave us not to perish in our sin!

From lust of body and lust of blood,—

Great God, deliver us!

From lust of power and lust of gold,—

Great God, deliver us!

From the leagued lying of despot and of brute,—

Great God, deliver us!

A city lay in travail, God our Lord, and from her loins sprang twin Murder and Black Hate. Red was the midnight; clang, crack, and cry of death and fury filled the air and trembled underneath the stars where church spires pointed silently to Thee. And all this was to sate the greed of greedy men who hide behind the veil of vengeance!

Bend us Thine ear, O Lord!

In the pale, still morning we looked upon the deed. We stopped our ears and held our leaping hands, but they—did they not wag their heads and leer and cry with bloody jaws: *Cease from Crime!* The word was mockery, for thus they train a hundred crimes while we do cure one.

Turn again our captivity, O Lord!

Behold this maimed and broken thing, dear God; it was an humble black man, who toiled and sweat to save a bit from the pittance paid him. They told him: *Work and Rise!* He worked. Did this man sin? Nay, but someone told how someone said another did—one whom he had never seen nor known. Yet for that man's crime this man lieth maimed and murdered, his wife naked to shame, his children to poverty and evil.

Hear us, O heavenly Father!

Doth not this justice of hell stink in Thy nostrils, O God? How long shall the mounting flood of innocent blood roar in Thine ears and pound in our hearts for vengeance? Pile the pale frenzy of blood-crazed brutes, who do such deeds, high on Thine Altar, Jehovah Jireh, and burn it in hell forever and forever!

Forgive us, good Lord; we know not what we say!

Bewildered we are and passion-tossed, mad with the madness of a mobbed and mocked and murdered people; straining at the armposts of Thy throne, we raise our shackled hands and charge Thee, God, by the bones of our stolen fathers, by the tears of our dead mothers, by the very blood of Thy crucified Christ: What meaneth this? Tell us the plan; give us the sign!

Keep not Thou silent, O God!

Sit not longer blind, Lord God, deaf to our prayer and dumb to our dumb suffering. Surely Thou, too, art not white, O Lord, a pale, bloodless, heartless thing!

Ah! Christ of all the Pities!

Forgive the thought! Forgive these wild, blasphemous words! Thou art still the God of our black fathers and in Thy Soul's Soul sit some soft darkenings of the evening, some shadowings of the velvet night.

But whisper—speak—call, great God, for Thy silence is white terror to our hearts! The way, O God, show us the way and point us the path!

Whither? North is greed and South is blood; within, the coward, and without, the liar. Whither? To death?

Amen! Welcome, dark sleep!

Whither? To life? But not this life, dear God, not this. Let the cup pass from us, tempt us not beyond our strength, for there is that clamoring and clawing within, to whose voice we would not listen, yet shudder lest we must,—and it is red. Ah! God! It is a red and awful shape.

Selah!

In yonder East trembles a star.

Vengeance is Mine; I will repay, saith the Lord!

Thy Will, O Lord, be done!
Kyrie Eleison!
Lord, we have done these pleading, wavering words.
We beseech Thee to hear us, good Lord!
We bow our heads and hearken soft to the sobbing of women and little children.
We beseech Thee to hear us, good Lord!
Our voices sink in silence and in night.
Hear us, good Lord!
In night, O God of a godless land!
Amen!
In silence, O Silent God.
Selah!

EDGAR LEE MASTERS

(1868–1950)

from
Spoon River Anthology

Serepta Mason

My life's blossom might have bloomed on all sides
Save for a bitter wind which stunted my petals
On the side of me which you in the village could see.
From the dust I lift a voice of protest:
My flowering side you never saw!
Ye living ones, ye are fools indeed
Who do not know the ways of the wind
And the unseen forces
That govern the processes of life.

Amanda Barker

Henry got me with child,
Knowing that I could not bring forth life
Without losing my own.
In my youth therefore I entered the portals of dust.
Traveler, it is believed in the village where I lived
That Henry loved me with a husband's love,
But I proclaim from the dust
That he slew me to gratify his hatred.

Constance Hately

You praise my self-sacrifice, Spoon River,
In rearing Irene and Mary,
Orphans of my older sister!
And you censure Irene and Mary
For their contempt for me!
But praise not my self-sacrifice,

And censure not their contempt;
I reared them, I cared for them, true enough!—
But I poisoned my benefactions
With constant reminders of their dependence.

Benjamin Pantier

Together in this grave lie Benjamin Pantier, attorney at law,
And Nig, his dog, constant companion, solace and friend.
Down the gray road, friends, children, men and women,
Passing one by one out of life, left me till I was alone
With Nig for partner, bed-fellow, comrade in drink.
In the morning of life I knew aspiration and saw glory.
Then she, who survives me, snared my soul
With a snare which bled me to death,
Till I, once strong of will, lay broken, indifferent,
Living with Nig in a room back of a dingy office.
Under my jaw-bone is snuggled the bony nose of Nig—
Our story is lost in silence. Go by, mad world!

Mrs. Benjamin Pantier

I know that he told that I snared his soul
With a snare which bled him to death.
And all the men loved him,
And most of the women pitied him.
But suppose you are really a lady, and have delicate tastes,
And loathe the smell of whiskey and onions.
And the rhythm of Wordsworth's "Ode" runs in your ears,
While he goes about from morning till night
Repeating bits of that common thing;
"Oh, why should the spirit of mortal be proud?"
And then, suppose:
You are a woman well endowed,
And the only man with whom the law and morality
Permit you to have the marital relation
Is the very man that fills you with disgust
Every time you think of it—while you think of it
Every time you see him?

That's why I drove him away from home
To live with his dog in a dingy room
Back of his office.

Reuben Pantier

Well, Emily Sparks, your prayers were not wasted,
Your love was not all in vain.
I owe whatever I was in life
To your hope that would not give me up,
To your love that saw me still as good.
Dear Emily Sparks, let me tell you the story.
I pass the effect of my father and mother;
The milliner's daughter made me trouble
And out I went in the world,
Where I passed through every peril known
Of wine and women and joy of life.
One night, in a room in the Rue de Rivoli,
I was drinking wine with a black-eyed cocotte,
And the tears swam into my eyes.
She thought they were amorous tears and smiled
For thought of her conquest over me.
But my soul was three thousand miles away,
In the days when you taught me in Spoon River.
And just because you no more could love me,
Nor pray for me, nor write me letters,
The eternal silence of you spoke instead.
And the black-eyed cocotte took the tears for hers,
As well as the deceiving kisses I gave her.
Somehow, from that hour, I had a new vision—
Dear Emily Sparks!

Emily Sparks

Where is my boy, my boy—
In what far part of the world?
The boy I loved best of all in the school?—
I, the teacher, the old maid, the virgin heart,
Who made them all my children.

Did I know my boy aright,
Thinking of him as spirit aflame,
Active, ever aspiring?
Oh, boy, boy, for whom I prayed and prayed
In many a watchful hour at night,
Do you remember the letter I wrote you
Of the beautiful love of Christ?
And whether you ever took it or not,
My boy, wherever you are,
Work for your soul's sake,
That all the clay of you, all of the dross of you,
May yield to the fire of you,
Till the fire is nothing but light! . . .
Nothing but light!

Trainor, the Druggist

Only the chemist can tell, and not always the chemist,
What will result from compounding
Fluids or solids.
And who can tell
How men and women will interact
On each other, or what children will result?
There were Benjamin Pantier and his wife,
Good in themselves, but evil toward each other:
He oxygen, she hydrogen,
Their son, a devastating fire.
I Trainor, the druggist, a mixer of chemicals,
Killed while making an experiment,
Lived unwedded.

Minerva Jones

I am Minerva, the village poetess,
Hooted at, jeered at by the Yahoos of the street
For my heavy body, cock-eye, and rolling walk,
And all the more when "Butch" Weldy
Captured me after a brutal hunt.
He left me to my fate with Doctor Meyers;

And I sank into death, growing numb from the feet up,
Like one stepping deeper and deeper into a stream of ice.
Will some one go to the village newspaper,
And gather into a book the verses I wrote?—
I thirsted so for love!
I hungered so for life!

"Indignation" Jones

You would not believe, would you,
That I came from good Welsh stock?
That I was purer blooded than the white trash here?
And of more direct lineage than the New Englanders
And Virginians of Spoon River?
You would not believe that I had been to school
And read some books.
You saw me only as a run-down man,
With matted hair and beard
And ragged clothes.
Sometimes a man's life turns into a cancer
From being bruised and continually bruised,
And swells into a purplish mass,
Like growths on stalks of corn.
Here was I, a carpenter, mired in a bog of life
Into which I walked, thinking it was a meadow,
With a slattern for a wife, and poor Minerva, my daughter,
Whom you tormented and drove to death.
So I crept, crept, like a snail through the days
Of my life.
No more you hear my footsteps in the morning,
Resounding on the hollow sidewalk,
Going to the grocery store for a little corn meal
And a nickel's worth of bacon.

Doctor Meyers

No other man, unless it was Doc Hill,
Did more for people in this town than I.
And all the weak, the halt, the improvident

And those who could not pay flocked to me.
I was good-hearted, easy Doctor Meyers.
I was healthy, happy, in comfortable fortune,
Blessed with a congenial mate, my children raised,
All wedded, doing well in the world.
And then one night, Minerva, the poetess,
Came to me in her trouble, crying.
I tried to help her out—she died—
They indicted me, the newspapers disgraced me,
My wife perished of a broken heart.
And pneumonia finished me.

Mrs. Meyers

He protested all his life long
The newspapers lied about him villainously;
That he was not at fault for Minerva's fall,
But only tried to help her.
Poor soul so sunk in sin he could not see
That even trying to help her, as he called it,
He had broken the law human and divine.
Passers by, an ancient admonition to you:
If your ways would be ways of pleasantness,
And all your pathways peace,
Love God and keep his commandments.

"Butch" Weldy

After I got religion and steadied down
They gave me a job in the canning works,
And every morning I had to fill
The tank in the yard with gasoline,
That fed the blow-fires in the sheds
To heat the soldering irons.
And I mounted a rickety ladder to do it,
Carrying buckets full of the stuff.
One morning, as I stood there pouring,
The air grew still and seemed to heave,
And I shot up as the tank exploded,

And down I came with both legs broken,
And my eyes burned crisp as a couple of eggs.
For someone left a blow-fire going,
And something sucked the flame in the tank.
The Circuit Judge said whoever did it
Was a fellow-servant of mine, and so
Old Rhodes' son didn't have to pay me.
And I sat on the witness stand as blind
As Jack the Fiddler, saying over and over,
"I didn't know him at all."

Flossie Cabanis

From Bindle's opera house in the village
To Broadway is a great step.
But I tried to take it, my ambition fired
When sixteen years of age,
Seeing "East Lynne" played here in the village
By Ralph Barrett, the coming
Romantic actor, who enthralled my soul.
True, I trailed back home, a broken failure,
When Ralph disappeared in New York,
Leaving me alone in the city—
But life broke him also.
In all this place of silence
There are no kindred spirits.
How I wish Duse could stand amid the pathos
Of these quiet fields
And read these words.

Margaret Fuller Slack

I would have been as great as George Eliot
But for an untoward fate.
For look at the photograph of me made by Peniwit,
Chin resting on hand, and deep-set eyes—
Gray, too, and far-searching.
But there was the old, old problem:
Should it be celibacy, matrimony or unchastity?

Then John Slack, the rich druggist, wooed me,
Luring me with the promise of leisure for my novel,
And I married him, giving birth to eight children,
And had no time to write.
It was all over with me, anyway,
When I ran the needle in my hand
While washing the baby's things,
And died from lock-jaw, an ironical death.
Hear me, ambitious souls,
Sex is the curse of life!

Justice Arnett

It is true, fellow citizens,
That my old docket lying there for years
On a shelf above my head and over
The seat of justice, I say it is true
That docket had an iron rim
Which gashed my baldness when it fell—
(Somehow I think it was shaken loose
By the heave of the air all over town
When the gasoline tank at the canning works
Blew up and burned Butch Weldy)—
But let us argue points in order,
And reason the whole case carefully:
First I concede my head was cut,
But second the frightful thing was this:
The leaves of the docket shot and showered
Around me like a deck of cards
In the hands of a sleight of hand performer.
And up to the end I saw those leaves
Till I said at last, "Those are not leaves,
Why, can't you see they are days and days
And the days and days of seventy years?
And why do you torture me with leaves
And the little entries on them?

A. D. Blood

If you in the village think that my work was a good one,
Who closed the saloons and stopped all playing at cards,
And haled old Daisy Fraser before Justice Arnett,
In many a crusade to purge the people of sin;
Why do you let the milliner's daughter Dora,
And the worthless son of Benjamin Pantier,
Nightly make my grave their unholy pillow?

Editor Whedon

To be able to see every side of every question;
To be on every side, to be everything, to be nothing long;
To pervert truth, to ride it for a purpose,
To use great feelings and passions of the human family
For base designs, for cunning ends,
To wear a mask like the Greek actors—
Your eight-page paper—behind which you huddle,
Bawling through the megaphone of big type:
"This is I, the giant."
Thereby also living the life of a sneak-thief,
Poisoned with the anonymous words
Of your clandestine soul.
To scratch dirt over scandal for money,
And exhume it to the winds for revenge,
Or to sell papers,
Crushing reputations, or bodies, if need be,
To win at any cost, save your own life.
To glory in demoniac power, ditching civilization,
As a paranoiac boy puts a log on the track
And derails the express train.
To be an editor, as I was.
Then to lie here close by the river over the place
Where the sewage flows from the village,
And the empty cans and garbage are dumped,
And abortions are hidden.

Ralph Rhodes

All they said was true:
I wrecked my father's bank with my loans
To dabble in wheat; but this was true—
I was buying wheat for him as well,
Who couldn't margin the deal in his name
Because of his church relationship.
And while George Reece was serving his term
I chased the will-o'-the-wisp of women,
And the mockery of wine in New York.
It's deathly to sicken of wine and women
When nothing else is left in life.
But suppose your head is gray, and bowed
On a table covered with acrid stubs
Of cigarettes and empty glasses,
And a knock is heard, and you know it's the knock
So long drowned out by popping corks
And the pea-cock screams of demireps—
And you look up, and there's your Theft,
Who waited until your head was gray,
And your heart skipped beats to say to you:
The game is ended. I've called for you.
Go out on Broadway and be run over,
They'll ship you back to Spoon River.

Oscar Hummel

I staggered on through darkness,
There was a hazy sky, a few stars
Which I followed as best I could.
It was nine o'clock, I was trying to get home.
But somehow I was lost,
Though really keeping the road.
Then I reeled through a gate and into a yard,
And called at the top of my voice:
"Oh, Fiddler! Oh, Mr. Jones!"
(I thought it was his house and he would show me the way
    home.)
But who should step out but A. D. Blood,

In his night shirt, waving a stick of wood,
And roaring about the cursed saloons,
And the criminals they made?
"You drunken Oscar Hummel," he said,
As I stood there weaving to and fro,
Taking the blows from the stick in his hand
Till I dropped down dead at his feet.

Archibald Higbie

I loathed you, Spoon River. I tried to rise above you,
I was ashamed of you. I despised you
As the place of my nativity.
And there in Rome, among the artists,
Speaking Italian, speaking French,
I seemed to myself at times to be free
Of every trace of my origin.
I seemed to be reaching the heights of art
And to breathe the air that the masters breathed,
And to see the world with their eyes.
But still they'd pass my work and say:
"What are you driving at, my friend?
Sometimes the face looks like Apollo's,
At others it has a trace of Lincoln's."
There was no culture, you know, in Spoon River,
And I burned with shame and held my peace.
And what could I do, all covered over
And weighted down with western soil,
Except aspire, and pray for another
Birth in the world, with all of Spoon River
Rooted out of my soul?

Harry Wilmans

I was just turned twenty-one,
And Henry Phipps, the Sunday-school superintendent,
Made a speech in Bindle's Opera House.
"The honor of the flag must be upheld," he said,
"Whether it be assailed by a barbarous tribe of Tagalogs

Or the greatest power in Europe."
And we cheered and cheered the speech and the flag he
    waved
As he spoke.
And I went to the war in spite of my father,
And followed the flag till I saw it raised
By our camp in a rice field near Manila,
And all of us cheered and cheered it.
But there were flies and poisonous things;
And there was the deadly water,
And the cruel heat,
And the sickening, putrid food;
And the smell of the trench just back of the tents
Where the soldiers went to empty themselves;
And there were the whores who followed us, full of
    syphilis;
And beastly acts between ourselves or alone,
With bullying, hatred, degradation among us,
And days of loathing and nights of fear
To the hour of the charge through the steaming swamp,
Following the flag,
Till I fell with a scream, shot through the guts.
Now there's a flag over me in Spoon River!
A flag! A flag!

Willie Metcalf

I was Willie Metcalf.
They used to call me "Doctor Meyers"
Because, they said, I looked like him.
And he was my father, according to Jack McGuire.
I lived in the livery stable,
Sleeping on the floor
Side by side with Roger Baughman's bulldog,
Or sometimes in a stall.
I could crawl between the legs of the wildest horses
Without getting kicked—we knew each other.
On spring days I tramped through the country
To get the feeling, which I sometimes lost,

That I was not a separate thing from the earth.
I used to lose myself, as if in sleep,
By lying with eyes half-open in the woods.
Sometimes I talked with animals—even toads
        and snakes—
Anything that had an eye to look into.
Once I saw a stone in the sunshine
Trying to turn into jelly.
In April days in this cemetery
The dead people gathered all about me,
And grew still, like a congregation in silent prayer.
I never knew whether I was a part of the earth
With flowers growing in me, or whether I walked—
Now I know.

Webster Ford

Do you remember, O Delphic Apollo,
The sunset hour by the river, when Mickey M'Grew
Cried, "There's a ghost," and I, "It's Delphic Apollo";
And the son of the banker derided us, saying, "It's light
By the flags at the water's edge, you half-witted fools."
And from thence, as the wearisome years rolled on,
        long after
Poor Mickey fell down in the water tower to his death,
Down, down, through bellowing darkness, I carried
The vision which perished with him like a rocket
        which falls
And quenches its light in earth, and hid it for fear
Of the son of the banker, calling on Plutus to save me?
Avenged were you for the shame of a fearful heart,
Who left me alone till I saw you again in an hour
When I seemed to be turned to a tree with trunk and
        branches
Growing indurate, turning to stone, yet burgeoning
In laurel leaves, in hosts of lambent laurel,
Quivering, fluttering, shrinking, fighting the numbness
Creeping into their veins from the dying trunk and
        branches!

'Tis vain, O youth, to fly the call of Apollo.
Fling yourselves in the fire, die with a song of spring,
If die you must in the spring. For none shall look
On the face of Apollo and live, and choose you must
'Twixt death in the flame and death after years of
    sorrow,
Rooted fast in the earth, feeling the grisly hand,
Not so much in the trunk as in the terrible numbness
Creeping up to the laurel leaves that never cease
To flourish until you fall. O leaves of me
Too sere for coronal wreaths, and fit alone
For urns of memory, treasured, perhaps, as themes
For hearts heroic, fearless singers and livers—
Delphic Apollo!

EDWIN ARLINGTON ROBINSON

(1869–1935)

Isaac and Archibald

(To Mrs. Henry Richards)

Isaac and Archibald were two old men.
I knew them, and I may have laughed at them
A little; but I must have honored them
For they were old, and they were good to me.

I do not think of either of them now,
Without remembering, infallibly,
A journey that I made one afternoon
With Isaac to find out what Archibald
Was doing with his oats. It was high time
Those oats were cut, said Isaac; and he feared
That Archibald—well, he could never feel
Quite sure of Archibald. Accordingly
The good old man invited me—that is,
Permitted me—to go along with him;
And I, with a small boy's adhesiveness
To competent old age, got up and went.
I do not know that I cared overmuch
For Archibald's or anybody's oats,
But Archibald was quite another thing,
And Isaac yet another; and the world
Was wide, and there was gladness everywhere.
We walked together down the River Road
With all the warmth and wonder of the land
Around us, and the wayside flash of leaves,—
And Isaac said the day was glorious;
But somewhere at the end of the first mile
I found that I was figuring to find
How long those ancient legs of his would keep
The pace that he had set for them. The sun
Was hot, and I was ready to sweat blood;

But Isaac, for aught I could make of him,
Was cool to his hat-band. So I said then
With a dry gasp of affable despair,
Something about the scorching days we have
In August without knowing it sometimes;
But Isaac said the day was like a dream,
And praised the Lord, and talked about the breeze.
I made a fair confession of the breeze,
And crowded casually on his thought
The nearness of a profitable nook
That I could see. First I was half inclined
To caution him that he was growing old,
But something that was not compassion soon
Made plain the folly of all subterfuge.
Isaac was old, but not so old as that.

So I proposed, without an overture,
That we be seated in the shade a while,
And Isaac made no murmur. Soon the talk
Was turned on Archibald, and I began
To feel some premonitions of a kind
That only childhood knows; for the old man
Had looked at me and clutched me with his eye,
And asked if I had ever noticed things.
I told him that I could not think of them,
And I knew then, by the frown that left his face
Unsatisfied, that I had injured him.
"My good young friend," he said, "you cannot feel
What I have seen so long. You have the eyes—
Oh, yes—but you have not the other things:
The sight within that never will deceive,
You do not know—you have no right to know;
The twilight warning of experience,
The singular idea of loneliness,—
These are not yours. But they have long been mine,
And they have shown me now for seven years
That Archibald is changing. It is not
So much that he should come to his last hand,
And leave the game, and go the old way down;

But I have known him in and out so long,
And I have seen so much of good in him
That other men have shared and have not seen,
And I have gone so far through thick and thin,
Through cold and fire with him, that now it brings
To this old heart of mine an ache that you
Have not yet lived enough to know about.
But even unto you, and your boy's faith,
Your freedom, and your untried confidence,
A time will come to find out what it means
To know that you are losing what was yours,
To know that you are being left behind;
And then the long contempt of innocence—
God bless you, boy!—don't think the worse of it
Because an old man chatters in the shade—
Will all be like a story you have read
In childhood and remembered for the pictures.
And when the best friend of your life goes down,
When first you know in him the slackening
That comes, and coming always tells the end,—
Now in a common word that would have passed
Uncaught from any other lips than his,
Now in some trivial act of every day,
Done as he might have done it all along
But for a twinging little difference
That nips you like a squirrel's teeth—oh, yes,
Then you will understand it well enough.
But oftener it comes in other ways;
It comes without your knowing when it comes;
You know that he is changing, and you know
That he is going—just as I know now
That Archibald is going, and that I
Am staying. . . . Look at me, my boy,
And when the time shall come for you to see
That I must follow after him, try then
To think of me, to bring me back again,
Just as I was to-day. Think of the place
Where we are sitting now, and think of me—
Think of old Isaac as you knew him then,
When you set out with him in August once

To see old Archibald."—The words come back
Almost as Isaac must have uttered them,
And there comes with them a dry memory
Of something in my throat that would not move.

If you had asked me then to tell just why
I made so much of Isaac and the things
He said, I should have gone far for an answer;
For I knew it was not sorrow that I felt,
Whatever I may have wished it, or tried then
To make myself believe. My mouth was full
Of words, and they would have been comforting
To Isaac, spite of my twelve years, I think;
But there was not in me the willingness
To speak them out. Therefore I watched the ground;
And I was wondering what made the Lord
Create a thing so nervous as an ant,
When Isaac, with commendable unrest,
Ordained that we should take the road again—
For it was yet three miles to Archibald's,
And one to the first pump. I felt relieved
All over when the old man told me that;
I felt that he had stilled a fear of mine
That those extremities of heat and cold
Which he had long gone through with Archibald
Had made the man impervious to both;
But Isaac had a desert somewhere in him,
And at the pump he thanked God for all things
That He had put on earth for men to drink,
And he drank well,—so well that I proposed
That we go slowly lest I learn too soon
The bitterness of being left behind,
And all those other things. That was a joke
To Isaac, and it pleased him very much;
And that pleased me—for I was twelve years old.

At the end of an hour's walking after that
The cottage of old Archibald appeared.
Little and white and high on a smooth round hill
It stood, with hackmatacks and apple-trees

Before it, and a big barn-roof beyond;
And over the place—trees, house, fields and all—
Hovered an air of still simplicity
And a fragrance of old summers—the old style
That lives the while it passes. I dare say
That I was lightly conscious of all this
When Isaac, of a sudden, stopped himself,
And for the long first quarter of a minute
Gazed with incredulous eyes, forgetful quite
Of breezes and of me and of all else
Under the scorching sun but a smooth-cut field,
Faint yellow in the distance. I was young,
But there were a few things that I could see,
And this was one of them.—"Well, well!" said he;
And "Archibald will be surprised, I think,"
Said I. But all my childhood subtlety
Was lost on Isaac, for he strode along
Like something out of Homer—powerful
And awful on the wayside, so I thought.
Also I thought how good it was to be
So near the end of my short-legged endeavor
To keep the pace with Isaac for five miles.

Hardly had we turned in from the main road
When Archibald, with one hand on his back
And the other clutching his huge-headed cane,
Came limping down to meet us.—"Well! well! well!"
Said he; and then he looked at my red face,
All streaked with dust and sweat, and shook my hand,
And said it must have been a right smart walk
That we had had that day from Tilbury Town.—
"Magnificent," said Isaac; and he told
About the beautiful west wind there was
Which cooled and clarified the atmosphere.
"You must have made it with your legs, I guess,"
Said Archibald; and Isaac humored him
With one of those infrequent smiles of his
Which he kept in reserve, apparently,
For Archibald alone. "But why," said he,
"Should Providence have cider in the world

If not for such an afternoon as this?"
And Archibald, with a soft light in his eyes,
Replied that if he chose to go down cellar,
There he would find eight barrels—one of which
Was newly tapped, he said, and to his taste
An honor to the fruit. Isaac approved
Most heartily of that, and guided us
Forthwith, as if his venerable feet
Were measuring the turf in his own door-yard,
Straight to the open rollway. Down we went,
Out of the fiery sunshine to the gloom,
Grateful and half sepulchral, where we found
The barrels, like eight potent sentinels,
Close ranged along the wall. From one of them
A bright pine spile stuck out alluringly,
And on the black flat stone, just under it,
Glimmered a late-spilled proof that Archibald
Had spoken from unfeigned experience.
There was a fluted antique water-glass
Close by, and in it, prisoned, or at rest,
There was a cricket, of the brown soft sort
That feeds on darkness. Isaac turned him out,
And touched him with his thumb to make him jump,
And then composedly pulled out the plug
With such a practised hand that scarce a drop
Did even touch his fingers. Then he drank
And smacked his lips with a slow patronage
And looked along the line of barrels there
With a pride that may have been forgetfulness
That they were Archibald's and not his own.
"I never twist a spigot nowadays,"
He said, and raised the glass up to the light,
"But I thank God for orchards." And that glass
Was filled repeatedly for the same hand
Before I thought it worth while to discern
Again that I was young, and that old age,
With all his woes, had some advantages.

"Now, Archibald," said Isaac, when we stood
Outside again, "I have it in my mind

That I shall take a sort of little walk—
To stretch my legs and see what you are doing.
You stay and rest your back and tell the boy
A story: Tell him all about the time
In Stafford's cabin forty years ago,
When four of us were snowed up for ten days
With only one dried haddock. Tell him all
About it, and be wary of your back.
Now I will go along."—I looked up then
At Archibald, and as I looked I saw
Just how his nostrils widened once or twice
And then grew narrow. I can hear to-day
The way the old man chuckled to himself—
Not wholesomely, not wholly to convince
Another of his mirth,—as I can hear
The lonely sigh that followed.—But at length
He said: "The orchard now's the place for us;
We may find something like an apple there,
And we shall have the shade, at any rate."
So there we went and there we laid ourselves
Where the sun could not reach us; and I champed
A dozen of worm-blighted astrakhans
While Archibald said nothing—merely told
The tale of Stafford's cabin, which was good,
Though "master chilly"—after his own phrase—
Even for a day like that. But other thoughts
Were moving in his mind, imperative,
And writhing to be spoken: I could see
The glimmer of them in a glance or two,
Cautious, or else unconscious, that he gave
Over his shoulder: . . . "Stafford and the rest—
But that's an old song now, and Archibald
And Isaac are old men. Remember, boy,
That we are old. Whatever we have gained,
Or lost, or thrown away, we are old men.
You look before you and we look behind,
And we are playing life out in the shadow—
But that's not all of it. The sunshine lights
A good road yet before us if we look,
And we are doing that when least we know it;

For both of us are children of the sun,
Like you, and like the weed there at your feet.
The shadow calls us, and it frightens us—
We think; but there's a light behind the stars
And we old fellows who have dared to live,
We see it—and we see the other things,
The other things . . . Yes, I have seen it come
These eight years, and these ten years, and I know
Now that it cannot be for very long
That Isaac will be Isaac. You have seen—
Young as you are, you must have seen the strange
Uncomfortable habit of the man?
He'll take my nerves and tie them in a knot
Sometimes, and that's not Isaac. I know that—
And I know what it is: I get it here
A little, in my knees, and Isaac—here."
The old man shook his head regretfully
And laid his knuckles three times on his forehead.
"That's what it is: Isaac is not quite right.
You see it, but you don't know what it means:
The thousand little differences—no,
You do not know them, and it's well you don't;
You'll know them soon enough—God bless you, boy!—
You'll know them, but not all of them—not all.
So think of them as little as you can:
There's nothing in them for you, or for me—
But I am old and I must think of them;
I'm in the shadow, but I don't forget
The light, my boy,—the light behind the stars.
Remember that: remember that I said it;
And when the time that you think far away
Shall come for you to say it—say it, boy;
Let there be no confusion or distrust
In you, no snarling of a life half lived,
Nor any cursing over broken things
That your complaint has been the ruin of.
Live to see clearly and the light will come
To you, and as you need it.—But there, there,
I'm going it again, as Isaac says,
And I'll stop now before you go to sleep.—

Only be sure that you growl cautiously,
And always where the shadow may not reach you."

Never shall I forget, long as I live,
The quaint thin crack in Archibald's voice,
The lonely twinkle in his little eyes,
Or the way it made me feel to be with him.
I know I lay and looked for a long time
Down through the orchard and across the road,
Across the river and the sun-scorched hills
That ceased in a blue forest, where the world
Ceased with it. Now and then my fancy caught
A flying glimpse of a good life beyond—
Something of ships and sunlight, streets and singing,
Troy falling, and the ages coming back,
And ages coming forward: Archibald
And Isaac were good fellows in old clothes,
And Agamemnon was a friend of mine;
Ulysses coming home again to shoot
With bows and feathered arrows made another,
And all was as it should be. I was young.

So I lay dreaming of what things I would,
Calm and incorrigibly satisfied
With apples and romance and ignorance,
And the still smoke from Archibald's clay pipe.
There was a stillness over everything,
As if the spirit of heat had laid its hand
Upon the world and hushed it; and I felt
Within the mightiness of the white sun
That smote the land around us and wrought out
A fragrance from the trees, a vital warmth
And fullness for the time that was to come,
And a glory for the world beyond the forest.
The present and the future and the past,
Isaac and Archibald, the burning bush,
The Trojans and the walls of Jericho,
Were beautifully fused; and all went well
Till Archibald began to fret for Isaac
And said it was a master day for sunstroke.

That was enough to make a mummy smile,
I thought; and I remained hilarious,
In face of all precedence and respect,
Till Isaac (who had come to us unheard)
Found he had no tobacco, looked at me
Peculiarly, and asked of Archibald
What ailed the boy to make him chirrup so.
From that he told us what a blessed world
The Lord had given us.—"But, Archibald,"
He added, with a sweet severity
That made me think of peach-skins and goose-flesh,
"I'm half afraid you cut those oats of yours
A day or two before they were well set."
"They were set well enough," said Archibald,—
And I remarked the process of his nose
Before the words came out. "But never mind
Your neighbor's oats: you stay here in the shade
And rest yourself while I go find the cards.
We'll have a little game of seven-up
And let the boy keep count."—"We'll have the game,
Assuredly," said Isaac; "and I think
That I will have a drop of cider, also."

They marched away together towards the house
And left me to my childish ruminations
Upon the ways of men. I followed them
Down cellar with my fancy, and then left them
For a fairer vision of all things at once
That was anon to be destroyed again
By the sound of voices and of heavy feet—
One of the sounds of life that I remember,
Though I forget so many that rang first
As if they were thrown down to me from Sinai.

So I remember, even to this day,
Just how they sounded, how they placed themselves,
And how the game went on while I made marks
And crossed them out, and meanwhile made some Trojans.
Likewise I made Ulysses, after Isaac,
And a little after Flaxman. Archibald

Was injured when he found himself left out,
But he had no heroics, and I said so:
I told him that his white beard was too long
And too straight down to be like things in Homer.
"Quite so," said Isaac.—"Low," said Archibald;
And he threw down a deuce with a deep grin
That showed his yellow teeth and made me happy.
So they played on till a bell rang from the door,
And Archibald said, "Supper."—After that
The old men smoked while I sat watching them
And wondered with all comfort what might come
To me, and what might never come to me;
And when the time came for the long walk home
With Isaac in the twilight, I could see
The forest and the sunset and the sky-line,
No matter where it was that I was looking:
The flame beyond the boundary, the music,
The foam and the white ships, and two old men
Were things that would not leave me.—And that night
There came to me a dream—a shining one,
With two old angels in it. They had wings,
And they were sitting where a silver light
Suffused them, face to face. The wings of one
Began to palpitate as I approached,
But I was yet unseen when a dry voice
Cried thinly, with unpatronizing triumph,
"I've got you, Isaac; high, low, jack, and the game."

Isaac and Archibald have gone their way
To the silence of the loved and well-forgotten.
I knew them, and I may have laughed at them;
But there's a laughing that has honor in it,
And I have no regret for light words now.
Rather I think sometimes they may have made
Their sport of me;—but they would not do that,
They were too old for that. They were old men,
And I may laugh at them because I knew them.

Calverly's

We go no more to Calverly's,
For there the lights are few and low;
And who are there to see by them,
Or what they see, we do not know.
Poor strangers of another tongue
May now creep in from anywhere,
And we, forgotten, be no more
Than twilight on a ruin there.

We two, the remnant. All the rest
Are cold and quiet. You nor I,
Nor fiddle now, nor flagon-lid,
May ring them back from where they lie.
No fame delays oblivion
For them, but something yet survives:
A record written fair, could we
But read the book of scattered lives.

There'll be a page for Leffingwell,
And one for Lingard, the Moon-calf;
And who knows what for Clavering,
Who died because he couldn't laugh?
Who knows or cares? No sign is here,
No face, no voice, no memory;
No Lingard with his eerie joy,
No Clavering, no Calverly.

We cannot have them here with us
To say where their light lives are gone,
Or if they be of other stuff
Than are the moons of Ilion.
So, be their place of one estate
With ashes, echoes, and old wars,—
Or ever we be of the night,
Or we be lost among the stars.

Shadrach O'Leary

O'Leary was a poet—for a while:
He sang of many ladies frail and fair,
The rolling glory of their golden hair,
And emperors extinguished with a smile.
They foiled his years with many an ancient wile,
And if they limped, O'Leary didn't care:
He turned them loose and had them everywhere,
Undoing saints and senates with their guile.

But this was not the end. A year ago
I met him—and to meet was to admire:
Forgotten were the ladies and the lyre,
And the small, ink-fed Eros of his dream.
By questioning I found a man to know—
A failure spared, a Shadrach of the Gleam.

How Annandale Went Out

"They called it Annandale—and I was there
To flourish, to find words, and to attend:
Liar, physician, hypocrite, and friend,
I watched him; and the sight was not so fair
As one or two that I have seen elsewhere:
An apparatus not for me to mend—
A wreck, with hell between him and the end,
Remained of Annandale; and I was there.

"I knew the ruin as I knew the man;
So put the two together, if you can,
Remembering the worst you know of me.
Now view yourself as I was, on the spot—
With a slight kind of engine. Do you see?
Like this . . . You wouldn't hang me? I thought not."

Miniver Cheevy

Miniver Cheevy, child of scorn,
  Grew lean while he assailed the seasons;
He wept that he was ever born,
  And he had reasons.

Miniver loved the days of old
  When swords were bright and steeds were prancing;
The vision of a warrior bold
  Would set him dancing.

Miniver sighed for what was not,
  And dreamed, and rested from his labors;
He dreamed of Thebes and Camelot,
  And Priam's neighbors.

Miniver mourned the ripe renown
  That made so many a name so fragrant;
He mourned Romance, now on the town,
  And Art, a vagrant.

Miniver loved the Medici,
  Albeit he had never seen one;
He would have sinned incessantly
  Could he have been one.

Miniver cursed the commonplace
  And eyed a khaki suit with loathing;
He missed the mediæval grace
  Of iron clothing.

Miniver scorned the gold he sought,
  But sore annoyed was he without it;
Miniver thought, and thought, and thought,
  And thought about it.

Miniver Cheevy, born too late,
  Scratched his head and kept on thinking;
Miniver coughed, and called it fate,
  And kept on drinking.

For a Dead Lady

No more with overflowing light
Shall fill the eyes that now are faded,
Nor shall another's fringe with night
Their woman-hidden world as they did.
No more shall quiver down the days
The flowing wonder of her ways,
Whereof no language may requite
The shifting and the many-shaded.

The grace, divine, definitive,
Clings only as a faint forestalling;
The laugh that love could not forgive
Is hushed, and answers to no calling;
The forehead and the little ears
Have gone where Saturn keeps the years;
The breast where roses could not live
Has done with rising and with falling.

The beauty, shattered by the laws
That have creation in their keeping,
No longer trembles at applause,
Or over children that are sleeping;
And we who delve in beauty's lore
Know all that we have known before
Of what inexorable cause
Makes Time so vicious in his reaping.

Cassandra

I heard one who said: "Verily,
  What word have I for children here?
Your Dollar is your only Word,
  The wrath of it your only fear.

"You build it altars tall enough
  To make you see, but you are blind;
You cannot leave it long enough
  To look before you or behind.

"When Reason beckons you to pause,
    You laugh and say that you know best;
But what it is you know, you keep
    As dark as ingots in a chest.

"You laugh and answer, 'We are young;
    O leave us now, and let us grow.'—
Not asking how much more of this
    Will Time endure or Fate bestow.

"Because a few complacent years
    Have made your peril of your pride,
Think you that you are to go on
    Forever pampered and untried?

"What lost eclipse of history,
    What bivouac of the marching stars,
Has given the sign for you to see
    Millenniums and last great wars?

"What unrecorded overthrow
    Of all the world has ever known,
Or ever been, has made itself
    So plain to you, and you alone?

"Your Dollar, Dove and Eagle make
    A Trinity that even you
Rate higher than you rate yourselves;
    It pays, it flatters, and it's new.

"And though your very flesh and blood
    Be what your Eagle eats and drinks,
You'll praise him for the best of birds,
    Not knowing what the Eagle thinks.

"The power is yours, but not the sight;
    You see not upon what you tread;
You have the ages for your guide,
    But not the wisdom to be led.

"Think you to tread forever down
    The merciless old verities?
And are you never to have eyes
    To see the world for what it is?

"Are you to pay for what you have
    With all you are?"—No other word
We caught, but with a laughing crowd
    Moved on. None heeded, and few heard.

Hillcrest

(To Mrs. Edward MacDowell)

No sound of any storm that shakes
Old island walls with older seas
Comes here where now September makes
An island in a sea of trees.

Between the sunlight and the shade
A man may learn till he forgets
The roaring of a world remade,
And all his ruins and regrets;

And if he still remembers here
Poor fights he may have won or lost,—
If he be ridden with the fear
Of what some other fight may cost,—

If, eager to confuse too soon,
What he has known with what may be,
He reads a planet out of tune
For cause of his jarred harmony,—

If here he venture to unroll
His index of adagios,
And he be given to console
Humanity with what he knows,—

He may by contemplation learn
A little more than what he knew,
And even see great oaks return
To acorns out of which they grew.

He may, if he but listen well,
Through twilight and the silence here,
Be told what there are none may tell
To vanity's impatient ear;

And he may never dare again
Say what awaits him; or be sure
What sunlit labyrinth of pain
He may not enter and endure.

Who knows to-day from yesterday
May learn to count no thing too strange:
Love builds of what Time takes away,
Till Death itself is less than Change.

Who sees enough in his duress
May go as far as dreams have gone;
Who sees a little may do less
Than many who are blind have done;

Who sees unchastened here the soul
Triumphant has no other sight
Than has a child who sees the whole
World radiant with his own delight.

Far journeys and hard wandering
Await him in whose crude surmise
Peace, like a mask, hides everything
That is and has been from his eyes;

And all his wisdom is unfound,
Or like a web that error weaves
On airy looms that have a sound
No louder now than falling leaves.

Eros Turannos

She fears him, and will always ask
   What fated her to choose him;
She meets in his engaging mask
   All reasons to refuse him;
But what she meets and what she fears
Are less than are the downward years,
Drawn slowly to the foamless weirs
   Of age, were she to lose him.

Between a blurred sagacity
   That once had power to sound him,
And Love, that will not let him be
   The Judas that she found him,
Her pride assuages her almost,
As if it were alone the cost.—
He sees that he will not be lost,
   And waits and looks around him.

A sense of ocean and old trees
   Envelops and allures him;
Tradition, touching all he sees,
   Beguiles and reassures him;
And all her doubts of what he says
Are dimmed of what she knows of days—
Till even prejudice delays
   And fades, and she secures him.

The falling leaf inaugurates
   The reign of her confusion;
The pounding wave reverberates
   The dirge of her illusion;
And home, where passion lived and died,
Becomes a place where she can hide,
While all the town and harbor side
   Vibrate with her seclusion.

We tell you, tapping on our brows,
   The story as it should be,—

As if the story of a house
   Were told, or ever could be;
We'll have no kindly veil between
Her visions and those we have seen,—
As if we guessed what hers have been,
   Or what they are or would be.

Meanwhile we do no harm; for they
   That with a god have striven,
Not hearing much of what we say,
   Take what the god has given;
Though like waves breaking it may be,
Or like a changed familiar tree,
Or like a stairway to the sea
   Where down the blind are driven.

The Unforgiven

When he, who is the unforgiven,
Beheld her first, he found her fair:
No promise ever dreamt in heaven
Could then have lured him anywhere
That would have been away from there;
And all his wits had lightly striven,
Foiled with her voice, and eyes, and hair.

There's nothing in the saints and sages
To meet the shafts her glances had,
Or such as hers have had for ages
To blind a man till he be glad,
And humble him till he be mad.
The story would have many pages,
And would be neither good nor bad.

And, having followed, you would find him
Where properly the play begins;
But look for no red light behind him—
No fumes of many-colored sins,

Fanned high by screaming violins.
God knows what good it was to blind him,
Or whether man or woman wins.

And by the same eternal token,
Who knows just how it will all end?—
This drama of hard words unspoken,
This fireside farce, without a friend
Or enemy to comprehend
What augurs when two lives are broken,
And fear finds nothing left to mend.

He stares in vain for what awaits him,
And sees in Love a coin to toss;
He smiles, and her cold hush berates him
Beneath his hard half of the cross;
They wonder why it ever was;
And she, the unforgiving, hates him
More for her lack than for her loss.

He feeds with pride his indecision,
And shrinks from what will not occur,
Bequeathing with infirm derision
His ashes to the days that were,
Before she made him prisoner;
And labors to retrieve the vision
That he must once have had of her.

He waits, and there awaits an ending,
And he knows neither what nor when;
But no magicians are attending
To make him see as he saw then,
And he will never find again
The face that once had been the rending
Of all his purpose among men.

He blames her not, nor does he chide her,
And she has nothing new to say;
If he were Bluebeard he could hide her,
But that's not written in the play,

And there will be no change to-day;
Although, to the serene outsider,
There still would seem to be a way.

The Poor Relation

No longer torn by what she knows
And sees within the eyes of others,
Her doubts are when the daylight goes,
Her fears are for the few she bothers.
She tells them it is wholly wrong
Of her to stay alive so long;
And when she smiles her forehead shows
A crinkle that had been her mother's.

Beneath her beauty, blanched with pain,
And wistful yet for being cheated,
A child would seem to ask again
A question many times repeated;
But no rebellion has betrayed
Her wonder at what she has paid
For memories that have no stain,
For triumph born to be defeated.

To those who come for what she was—
The few left who know where to find her—
She clings, for they are all she has;
And she may smile when they remind her,
As heretofore, of what they know
Of roses that are still to blow
By ways where not so much as grass
Remains of what she sees behind her.

They stay a while, and having done
What penance or the past requires,
They go, and leave her there alone
To count her chimneys and her spires.
Her lip shakes when they go away,

And yet she would not have them stay;
She knows as well as anyone
That Pity, having played, soon tires.

But one friend always reappears,
A good ghost, not to be forsaken;
Whereat she laughs and has no fears
Of what a ghost may reawaken,
But welcomes, while she wears and mends
The poor relation's odds and ends,
Her truant from a tomb of years—
Her power of youth so early taken.

Poor laugh, more slender than her song
It seems; and there are none to hear it
With even the stopped ears of the strong
For breaking heart or broken spirit.
The friends who clamored for her place,
And would have scratched her for her face,
Have lost her laughter for so long
That none would care enough to fear it.

None live who need fear anything
From her, whose losses are their pleasure;
The plover with a wounded wing
Stays not the flight that others measure;
So there she waits, and while she lives,
And death forgets, and faith forgives,
Her memories go foraging
For bits of childhood song they treasure.

And like a giant harp that hums
On always, and is always blending
The coming of what never comes
With what has past and had an ending,
The City trembles, throbs, and pounds
Outside, and through a thousand sounds
The small intolerable drums
Of Time are like slow drops descending.

Bereft enough to shame a sage
And given little to long sighing,
With no illusion to assuage
The lonely changelessness of dying,—
Unsought, unthought-of, and unheard,
She sings and watches like a bird,
Safe in a comfortable cage
From which there will be no more flying.

The Mill

The miller's wife had waited long,
    The tea was cold, the fire was dead;
And there might yet be nothing wrong
    In how he went and what he said:
"There are no millers any more,"
    Was all that she had heard him say;
And he had lingered at the door
    So long that it seemed yesterday.

Sick with a fear that had no form
    She knew that she was there at last;
And in the mill there was a warm
    And mealy fragrance of the past.
What else there was would only seem
    To say again what he had meant;
And what was hanging from a beam
    Would not have heeded where she went.

And if she thought it followed her,
    She may have reasoned in the dark
That one way of the few there were
    Would hide her and would leave no mark:
Black water, smooth above the weir
    Like starry velvet in the night,
Though ruffled once, would soon appear
    The same as ever to the sight.

Souvenir

A vanished house that for an hour I knew
By some forgotten chance when I was young
Had once a glimmering window overhung
With honeysuckle wet with evening dew.
Along the path tall dusky dahlias grew,
And shadowy hydrangeas reached and swung
Ferociously; and over me, among
The moths and mysteries, a blurred bat flew.

Somewhere within there were dim presences
Of days that hovered and of years gone by.
I waited, and between their silences
There was an evanescent faded noise;
And though a child, I knew it was the voice
Of one whose occupation was to die.

Mr. Flood's Party

Old Eben Flood, climbing alone one night
Over the hill between the town below
And the forsaken upland hermitage
That held as much as he should ever know
On earth again of home, paused warily.
The road was his with not a native near;
And Eben, having leisure, said aloud,
For no man else in Tilbury Town to hear:

"Well, Mr. Flood, we have the harvest moon
Again, and we may not have many more;
The bird is on the wing, the poet says,
And you and I have said it here before.
Drink to the bird." He raised up to the light
The jug that he had gone so far to fill,
And answered huskily: "Well, Mr. Flood,
Since you propose it, I believe I will."

Alone, as if enduring to the end
A valiant armor of scarred hopes outworn,
He stood there in the middle of the road
Like Roland's ghost winding a silent horn.
Below him, in the town among the trees,
Where friends of other days had honored him,
A phantom salutation of the dead
Rang thinly till old Eben's eyes were dim.

Then, as a mother lays her sleeping child
Down tenderly, fearing it may awake,
He set the jug down slowly at his feet
With trembling care, knowing that most things break;
And only when assured that on firm earth
It stood, as the uncertain lives of men
Assuredly did not, he paced away,
And with his hand extended paused again:

"Well, Mr. Flood, we have not met like this
In a long time; and many a change has come
To both of us, I fear, since last it was
We had a drop together. Welcome home!"
Convivially returning with himself,
Again he raised the jug up to the light;
And with an acquiescent quaver said:
"Well, Mr. Flood, if you insist, I might.

"Only a very little, Mr. Flood—
For auld lang syne. No more, sir; that will do."
So, for the time, apparently it did,
And Eben evidently thought so too;
For soon amid the silver loneliness
Of night he lifted up his voice and sang,
Secure, with only two moons listening,
Until the whole harmonious landscape rang—

"For auld lang syne." The weary throat gave out,
The last word wavered; and the song being done,
He raised again the jug regretfully
And shook his head, and was again alone.

There was not much that was ahead of him,
And there was nothing in the town below—
Where strangers would have shut the many doors
That many friends had opened long ago.

The Sheaves

Where long the shadows of the wind had rolled,
Green wheat was yielding to the change assigned;
And as by some vast magic undivined
The world was turning slowly into gold.
Like nothing that was ever bought or sold
It waited there, the body and the mind;
And with a mighty meaning of a kind
That tells the more the more it is not told.

So in a land where all days are not fair,
Fair days went on till on another day
A thousand golden sheaves were lying there,
Shining and still, but not for long to stay—
As if a thousand girls with golden hair
Might rise from where they slept and go away.

Karma

Christmas was in the air and all was well
With him, but for a few confusing flaws
In divers of God's images. Because
A friend of his would neither buy nor sell,
Was he to answer for the axe that fell?
He pondered; and the reason for it was,
Partly, a slowly freezing Santa Claus
Upon the corner, with his beard and bell.

Acknowledging an improvident surprise,
He magnified a fancy that he wished
The friend whom he had wrecked were here again.
Not sure of that, he found a compromise;
And from the fulness of his heart he fished
A dime for Jesus who had died for men.

Why He Was There

Much as he left it when he went from us
Here was the room again where he had been
So long that something of him should be seen,
Or felt—and so it was. Incredulous,
I turned about, loath to be greeted thus,
And there he was in his old chair, serene
As ever, and as laconic and as lean
As when he lived, and as cadaverous.

Calm as he was of old when we were young,
He sat there gazing at the pallid flame
Before him. "And how far will this go on?"
I thought. He felt the failure of my tongue,
And smiled: "I was not here until you came;
And I shall not be here when you are gone."

GEORGE STERLING

(1869–1926)

The Black Vulture

Aloof upon the day's immeasured dome,
    He holds unshared the silence of the sky.
    Far down his bleak, relentless eyes descry
The eagle's empire and the falcon's home—
Far down, the galleons of sunset roam;
    His hazards on the sea of morning lie;
    Serene, he hears the broken tempest sigh
Where cold sierras gleam like scattered foam.

And least of all he holds the human swarm—
    Unwitting now that envious men prepare
        To make their dream and its fulfilment one,
When, poised above the caldrons of the storm,
    Their hearts, contemptuous of death, shall dare
        His roads between the thunder and the sun.

ARTHUR GUITERMAN

(1871–1943)

On the Vanity of Earthly Greatness

The tusks that clashed in mighty brawls
Of mastodons, are billiard balls.

The sword of Charlemagne the Just
Is ferric oxide, known as rust.

The grizzly bear whose potent hug
Was feared by all, is now a rug.

Great Caesar's dead and on the shelf,
And I don't feel so well myself!

JAMES WELDON JOHNSON

(1871–1938)

Lift Every Voice and Sing

Lift every voice and sing
Till earth and heaven ring,
Ring with the harmonies of Liberty;
Let our rejoicing rise
High as the listening skies,
Let it resound loud as the rolling sea.
Sing a song full of the faith that the dark past has taught us,
Sing a song full of the hope that the present has brought us.
Facing the rising sun of our new day begun,
Let us march on till victory is won.

Stony the road we trod,
Bitter the chastening rod,
Felt in the days when hope unborn had died;
Yet with a steady beat,
Have not our weary feet
Come to the place for which our fathers sighed?
We have come over a way that with tears has been watered,
We have come, treading our path through the blood of the
        slaughtered,
Out from the gloomy past,
Till now we stand at last
Where the white gleam of our bright star is cast.

God of our weary years,
God of our silent tears,
Thou who hast brought us thus far on the way;
Thou who hast by Thy might
Led us into the light,
Keep us forever in the path, we pray.
Lest our feet stray from the places, our God, where we met
        Thee,

Lest, our hearts drunk with the wine of the world, we forget
 Thee;
Shadowed beneath Thy hand,
May we forever stand.
True to our God,
True to our native land.

O Black and Unknown Bards

O black and unknown bards of long ago,
How came your lips to touch the sacred fire?
How, in your darkness, did you come to know
The power and beauty of the minstrel's lyre?
Who first from midst his bonds lifted his eyes?
Who first from out the still watch, lone and long,
Feeling the ancient faith of prophets rise
Within his dark-kept soul, burst into song?

Heart of what slave poured out such melody
As "Steal away to Jesus"? On its strains
His spirit must have nightly floated free,
Though still about his hands he felt his chains.
Who heard great "Jordan roll"? Whose starward eye
Saw chariot "swing low"? And who was he
That breathed that comforting, melodic sigh,
"Nobody knows de trouble I see"?

What merely living clod, what captive thing,
Could up toward God through all its darkness grope,
And find within its deadened heart to sing
These songs of sorrow, love, and faith, and hope?
How did it catch that subtle undertone,
That note in music heard not with the ears?
How sound the elusive reed so seldom blown,
Which stirs the soul or melts the heart to tears.

Not that great German master in his dream
Of harmonies that thundered amongst the stars

At the creation, ever heard a theme
Nobler than "Go down, Moses." Mark its bars,
How like a mighty trumpet-call they stir
The blood. Such are the notes that men have sung
Going to valorous deeds; such tones there were
That helped make history when Time was young.

There is a wide, wide wonder in it all,
That from degraded rest and servile toil
The fiery spirit of the seer should call
These simple children of the sun and soil.
O black slave singers, gone, forgot, unfamed,
You—you alone, of all the long, long line
Of those who've sung untaught, unknown, unnamed,
Have stretched out upward, seeking the divine.

You sang not deeds of heroes or of kings;
No chant of bloody war, no exulting pean
Of arms-won triumphs; but your humble strings
You touched in chord with music empyrean.

To America

How would you have us, as we are?
Or sinking 'neath the load we bear?
Our eyes fixed forward on a star?
Or gazing empty at despair?

Rising or falling? Men or things?
With dragging pace or footsteps fleet?
Strong, willing sinews in your wings?
Or tightening chains about your feet?

The White Witch

O, brothers mine, take care! Take care!
The great white witch rides out to-night,
Trust not your prowess nor your strength;
Your only safety lies in flight;
For in her glance there is a snare,
And in her smile there is a blight.

The great white witch you have not seen?
Then, younger brothers mine, forsooth,
Like nursery children you have looked
For ancient hag and snaggled tooth;
But no, not so; the witch appears
In all the glowing charms of youth.

Her lips are like carnations red,
Her face like new-born lilies fair,
Her eyes like ocean waters blue,
She moves with subtle grace and air,
And all about her head there floats
The golden glory of her hair.

But though she always thus appears
In form of youth and mood of mirth,
Unnumbered centuries are hers,
The infant planets saw her birth;
The child of throbbing Life is she,
Twin sister to the greedy earth.

And back behind those smiling lips,
And down within those laughing eyes,
And underneath the soft caress
Of hand and voice and purring sighs,
The shadow of the panther lurks,
The spirit of the vampire lies.

For I have seen the great white witch,
And she has led me to her lair,
And I have kissed her red, red lips

And cruel face so white and fair;
Around me she has twined her arms,
And bound me with her yellow hair.

I felt those red lips burn and sear
My body like a living coal;
Obeyed the power of those eyes
As the needle trembles to the pole;
And did not care although I felt
The strength go ebbing from my soul.

Oh! she has seen your strong young limbs,
And heard your laughter loud and gay,
And in your voices she has caught
The echo of a far-off day,
When man was closer to the earth;
And she has marked you for her prey.

She feels the old Antæan strength
In you, the great dynamic beat
Of primal passions, and she sees
In you the last besieged retreat
Of love relentless, lusty, fierce,
Love pain-ecstatic, cruel-sweet.

O, brothers mine, take care! Take care!
The great white witch rides out to-night.
O, younger brothers mine, beware!
Look not upon her beauty bright;
For in her glance there is a snare,
And in her smile there is a blight.

Sunset in the Tropics

A silver flash from the sinking sun,
Then a shot of crimson across the sky
That, bursting, lets a thousand colors fly
And riot among the clouds; they run,

Deepening in purple, flaming in gold,
Changing, and opening fold after fold,
Then fading through all of the tints of the rose into gray,
Till, taking quick fright at the coming night,
They rush out down the west,
In hurried quest
Of the fleeing day.

Now above where the tardiest color flares a moment yet,
One point of light, now two, now three are set
To form the starry stairs,—
And, in her fire-fly crown,
Queen Night, on velvet slippered feet, comes softly down.

Brer Rabbit, You's de Cutes' of 'Em All

Once der was a meetin' in de wilderness,
All de critters of creation dey was dar;
Brer Rabbit, Brer 'Possum, Brer Wolf, Brer Fox,
King Lion, Mister Terrapin, Mister B'ar.
De question fu' discussion was, "Who is de bigges' man?"
Dey 'pinted ole Jedge Owl to decide;
He polished up his spectacles an' put 'em on his nose,
An' to the question slowly he replied:

"Brer Wolf am mighty cunnin',
Brer Fox am mighty sly,
Brer Terrapin an' 'Possum—kinder small;
Brer Lion's mighty vicious,
Brer B'ar he's sorter 'spicious,
Brer Rabbit, you's de cutes' of 'em all."

Dis caused a great confusion 'mongst de animals,
Ev'y critter claimed dat he had won de prize;
Dey 'sputed an' dey arg'ed, dey growled an' dey roared,
Den putty soon de dus' begin to rise.
Brer Rabbit he jes' stood aside an' urged 'em on to fight.

Brer Lion he mos' tore Brer B'ar in two;
W'en dey was all so tiahd dat dey couldn't catch der bref
Brer Rabbit he jes' grabbed de prize an' flew.

Brer Wolf am mighty cunnin',
Brer Fox am mighty sly,
Brer Terrapin an' Possum—kinder small;
Brer Lion's mighty vicious,
Brer B'ar he's sorter 'spicious,
Brer Rabbit, you's de cutes' of 'em all.

The Creation

And God stepped out on space,
And he looked around and said:
I'm lonely—
I'll make me a world.

And far as the eye of God could see
Darkness covered everything,
Blacker than a hundred midnights
Down in a cypress swamp.

Then God smiled,
And the light broke,
And the darkness rolled up on one side,
And the light stood shining on the other,
And God said: That's good!

Then God reached out and took the light in his hands,
And God rolled the light around in his hands
Until he made the sun;
And he set that sun a-blazing in the heavens.
And the light that was left from making the sun
God gathered it up in a shining ball
And flung it against the darkness,
Spangling the night with the moon and stars.
Then down between

The darkness and the light
He hurled the world;
And God said: That's good!

Then God himself stepped down—
And the sun was on his right hand,
And the moon was on his left;
The stars were clustered about his head,
And the earth was under his feet.
And God walked, and where he trod
His footsteps hollowed the valleys out
And bulged the mountains up.

Then he stopped and looked and saw
That the earth was hot and barren.
So God stepped over to the edge of the world
And he spat out the seven seas—
He batted his eyes, and the lightnings flashed—
He clapped his hands, and the thunders rolled—
And the waters above the earth came down,
The cooling waters came down.

Then the green grass sprouted,
And the little red flowers blossomed,
The pine tree pointed his finger to the sky,
And the oak spread out his arms,
The lakes cuddled down in the hollows of the ground,
And the rivers ran down to the sea;
And God smiled again,
And the rainbow appeared,
And curled itself around his shoulder.

Then God raised his arm and he waved his hand
Over the sea and over the land,
And he said: Bring forth! Bring forth!
And quicker than God could drop his hand,
Fishes and fowls
And beasts and birds
Swam the rivers and the seas,
Roamed the forests and the woods,

And split the air with their wings.
And God said: That's good!

Then God walked around,
And God looked around
On all that he had made.
He looked at his sun,
And he looked at his moon,
And he looked at his little stars;
He looked on his world
With all its living things,
And God said: I'm lonely still.

Then God sat down—
On the side of a hill where he could think;
By a deep, wide river he sat down;
With his head in his hands,
God thought and thought,
Till he thought: I'll make me a man!

Up from the bed of the river
God scooped the clay;
And by the bank of the river
He kneeled him down;
And there the great God Almighty
Who lit the sun and fixed it in the sky,
Who flung the stars to the most far corner of the night,
Who rounded the earth in the middle of his hand;
This Great God,
Like a mammy bending over her baby,
Kneeled down in the dust
Toiling over a lump of clay
Till he shaped it in his own image;

Then into it he blew the breath of life,
And man became a living soul.
Amen. Amen.

The Judgment Day

In that great day,
People, in that great day,
God's a-going to rain down fire.
God's a-going to sit in the middle of the air
To judge the quick and the dead.

Early one of these mornings,
God's a-going to call for Gabriel,
That tall, bright angel, Gabriel;
And God's a-going to say to him: Gabriel,
Blow your silver trumpet,
And wake the living nations.

And Gabriel's going to ask him: Lord,
How loud must I blow it?
And God's a-going to tell him: Gabriel,
Blow it calm and easy.
Then putting one foot on the mountain top,
And the other in the middle of the sea,
Gabriel's going to stand and blow his horn,
To wake the living nations.

Then God's a-going to say to him: Gabriel,
Once more blow your silver trumpet,
And wake the nations underground.

And Gabriel's going to ask him: Lord
How loud must I blow it?
And God's a-going to tell him: Gabriel,
Like seven peals of thunder.
Then the tall, bright angel, Gabriel,
Will put one foot on the battlements of heaven
And the other on the steps of hell,
And blow that silver trumpet
Till he shakes old hell's foundations.

And I feel Old Earth a-shuddering—
And I see the graves a-bursting—
And I hear a sound,
A blood-chilling sound.
What sound is that I hear?
It's the clicking together of the dry bones,
Bone to bone—the dry bones.
And I see coming out of the bursting graves,
And marching up from the valley of death,
The army of the dead.

And the living and the dead in the twinkling of an eye
Are caught up in the middle of the air,
Before God's judgment bar.

Oh-o-oh, sinner,
Where will you stand,
In that great day when God's a-going to rain down fire?
Oh, you gambling man—where will you stand?
You whore-mongering man—where will you stand?
Liars and backsliders—where will you stand,
In that great day when God's a-going to rain down fire?

And God will divide the sheep from the goats,
The one on the right, the other on the left.
And to them on the right God's a-going to say:
Enter into my kingdom.
And those who've come through great tribulations,
And washed their robes in the blood of the Lamb,
They will enter in—
Clothed in spotless white,
With starry crowns upon their heads,
And silver slippers on their feet,
And harps within their hands;—

And two by two they'll walk
Up and down the golden street,
Feasting on the milk and honey
Singing new songs of Zion,

Chattering with the angels
All around the Great White Throne.

And to them on the left God's a-going to say:
Depart from me into everlasting darkness,
Down into the bottomless pit.
And the wicked like lumps of lead will start to fall,
Headlong for seven days and nights they'll fall,
Plumb into the big, black, red-hot mouth of hell,
Belching out fire and brimstone.
And their cries like howling, yelping dogs,
Will go up with the fire and smoke from hell,
But God will stop his ears.

Too late, sinner! Too late!
Good-bye, sinner! Good-bye!
In hell, sinner! In hell!
Beyond the reach of the love of God.

And I hear a voice, crying, crying:
Time shall be no more!
Time shall be no more!
Time shall be no more!
And the sun will go out like a candle in the wind,
The moon will turn to dripping blood,
The stars will fall like cinders,
And the sea will burn like tar;
And the earth shall melt away and be dissolved,
And the sky will roll up like a scroll.
With a wave of his hand God will blot out time,
And start the wheel of eternity.

Sinner, oh, sinner,
Where will you stand
In that great day when God's a-going to rain down fire?

EDWIN FORD PIPER

(1871–1939)

Big Swimming

Rain on the high prairies,
In dusk of autumnal hills;
Under the creaking saddle
My cheerless pony plods. . . .

Down where the obscure water
Lapping the lithe willows
Sunders the chilling plain—
Rusty-hearted and travel-worn—
We set our bodies
To the November flood.

The farther shore is a cloud
Beyond midnight. . . .

Big swimming.

Indian Counsel

Do not be always looking on the fire—
It will dry up your eyes and make you blind.

Look upon falling snow and running water,
On crinkleroot and brightening willow bark;
The dancing crane, the coyote, and the moon;
On laughing children.

    No, not on the fire—
You will go blind.

LEONORA SPEYER

(1872–1956)

Witch!

Ashes of me,
Whirl in the fires I may not name.
Lick, lovely flame!

Will the fagot not burn?
Throw on the tired broom
Stabled still in my room.

I have ridden wide and well.
Shall I say with whom?
(Stop the town bell!)

Listen now,
Listen now if you dare:
I have lain with hope
Under the dreadful bough,
I have suckled Judas' rope
As it swung on the air—

Go find the silver pieces in the moon.
I hid them there.

To a Song of Sappho Discovered in Egypt

And Sappho's flowers, so few,
But roses all.
          MELEAGER.

Jonah wept within the whale;
But you have sung these centuries
Under the brown banks of the Nile
Within a dead dried crocodile:
So fares the learned tale.

When they embalmed the sacred beast
The Sapphic scroll was white and strong
To wrap the spices that were needed,
Its song unheard, its word unheeded
By crocodile or priest.

The song you sang on Lesbos when
Atthis was kind, or Mica sad;
The startled whale spewed Jonah wide,
From out the monster mummified
Your roses sing again.

Your roses! from the seven strands
Of the small harp whereon they grew;
The holy beast has had his pleasure,
His bellyful of Attic measure
Under the desert sands.

Along strange winds your petals blew
In singing fragments, roses all;
The air is heavy on the Nile,
The drowsy gods drowse on the while
As gods are wont to do.

W. C. HANDY
(1873–1958)

St. Louis Blues

I hate to see de ev'nin' sun go down,
Hate to see de ev'nin' sun go down,
'Cause ma baby, he done lef dis town.

Feelin' tomorrow lak ah feel today,
Feel tomorrow lak ah feel today,
I'll pack my trunk, make ma gitaway.

St. Louis woman, wid her diamon' rings,
Pulls dat man roun' by her apron strings.
'Twant for powder an' for store-bought hair,
De man ah love would not gone nowhere, nowhere.

Got de St. Louis Blues jes as blue as ah can be,
Dat man got a heart lak a rock cast in the sea,
Or else he wouldn't have gone so far from me.

Been to de Gypsy to get ma fortune tole,
To de Gypsy done got ma fortune tole,
'Cause I'm most wile 'bout ma Jelly Roll.

Gypsy done tole me, "Don't you wear no black."
Yes she done tole me, "Don't you wear no black,
Go to St. Louis. You can win him back."

Help me to Cairo, make St. Louis by maself,
Git to Cairo, find ma ole friend Jeff.
Gwine to pin maself close to his side,
If ah flag his train, I sho' can ride.

I loves dat man lak a schoolboy loves his pie,
Lak a Kentucky Col'nel loves his mint an' rye,
I'll love ma baby till the day ah die.

You ought to see dat stovepipe brown of mine,
Lak he owns de Dimon Joseph line,
He'd make a cross-eyed 'oman go stone blin'.

Blacker than midnight, teeth lak flags of truce,
Blackest man in de whole St. Louis,
Blacker de berry, sweeter am de juice.

About a crap game, he knows a pow'ful lot,
But when work-time comes, he's on de dot.
Gwine to ask him for a cold ten-spot,
What it takes to git it, he's cert'nly got.

A black-headed gal makes a freight train jump the track,
Said a black-headed gal makes a freight train jump the track,
But a long tall gal makes a preacher ball the Jack.

Lawd, a blonde-headed woman makes a good man leave the
    town,
I said blonde-headed woman makes a good man leave the
    town,
But a red-headed woman makes a boy slap his papa down.

Oh ashes to ashes and dust to dust,
I said ashes to ashes and dust to dust,
If my blues don't get you my jazzing must.

Beale Street Blues

I've seen the lights of gay Broadway,
Old Market Street down by the Frisco Bay,
I've strolled the Prado, I've gambled on the Bourse
The seven wonders of the world I've seen
And many are the places I have been.

Take my advice folks and see Beale Street first.

You'll see pretty Browns in beautiful gowns,
You'll see tailor-mades and hand-me-downs
You'll meet honest men and pickpockets skilled,
You'll find that bus'ness never closes till somebody gets killed.

I'd rather be here than any place I know,
I'd rather be here than any place I know
It's goin' to take the Sargent
For to make me go,

Goin' to the river,
Maybe, bye and bye,
Goin' to the river, and there's a reason why,
Because the river's wet,
And Beale Street's done gone dry.

You'll see Hog-Nose rest'rants and Chitlin' Cafés,
You'll see Jugs that tell of by-gone days,
And places, once places, now just a sham,
You'll see Golden Balls enough to pave the New Jerusalem.

I'd rather be here than any place I know,
I'd rather be here than any place I know
It's goin' to take the Sargent
For to make me go,

Goin' to the river,
Maybe, bye and bye,
Goin' to the river, and there's a reason why,
Because the river's wet,
And Beale Street's done gone dry.

If Beale Street could talk,
If Beale Street could talk,
Married men would have to take their beds and walk,
Except one or two, who never drink booze,
And the blind man on the corner who sings the Beale Street
      Blues.

I'd rather be here than any place I know,
I'd rather be here than any place I know
It's goin' to take the Sargent
For to make me go,

Goin' to the river,
Maybe, bye and bye,
Goin' to the river, and there's a reason why,
Because the river's wet,
And Beale Street's done gone dry.

LOLA RIDGE

(1873–1941)

from
The Ghetto

I

Cool inaccessible air
Is floating in velvety blackness shot with steel-blue lights,
But no breath stirs the heat
Leaning its ponderous bulk upon the Ghetto
And most on Hester street . . .

The heat . . .
Nosing in the body's overflow,
Like a beast pressing its great steaming belly close,
Covering all avenues of air . . .

The heat in Hester street,
Heaped like a dray
With the garbage of the world.

Bodies dangle from the fire escapes
Or sprawl over the stoops . . .
Upturned faces glimmer pallidly—
Herring-yellow faces, spotted as with a mold,
And moist faces of girls
Like dank white lilies,
And infants' faces with open parched mouths that suck at the
      air as at empty teats.

Young women pass in groups,
Converging to the forums and meeting halls,
Surging indomitable, slow
Through the gross underbrush of heat.
Their heads are uncovered to the stars,

And they call to the young men and to one another
With a free camaraderie.
Only their eyes are ancient and alone . . .

The street crawls undulant,
Like a river addled
With its hot tide of flesh
That ever thickens.
Heavy surges of flesh
Break over the pavements,
Clavering like a surf—
Flesh of this abiding
Brood of those ancient mothers who saw the dawn break over
        Egypt . . .
And turned their cakes upon the dry hot stones
And went on
Till the gold of the Egyptians fell down off their arms . . .
Fasting and athirst . . .
And yet on. . . .

Did they vision—with those eyes darkly clear,
That looked the sun in the face and were not blinded—
Across the centuries
The march of their enduring flesh?
Did they hear—
Under the molten silence
Of the desert like a stopped wheel—
(And the scorpions tick-ticking on the sand . . .)
The infinite procession of those feet?

VI

In this dingy café
The old men sit muffled in woollens.
Everything is faded, shabby, colorless, old . . .
The chairs, loose-jointed,
Creaking like old bones—
The tables, the waiters, the walls,
Whose mottled plaster
Blends in one tone with the old flesh.

Young life and young thought are alike barred,
And no unheralded noises jolt old nerves,
And old wheezy breaths
Pass around old thoughts, dry as snuff,
And there is no divergence and no friction
Because life is flattened and ground as by many mills.

And it is here the Committee—
Sweet-breathed and smooth of skin
And supple of spine and knee,
With shining unpouched eyes
And the blood, high-powered,
Leaping in flexible arteries—
The insolent, young, enthusiastic, undiscriminating
    Committee,
Who would placard tombstones
And scatter leaflets even in graves,
Comes trampling with sacrilegious feet!

The old men turn stiffly,
Mumbling to each other.
They are gentle and torpid and busy with eating.
But one lifts a face of clayish pallor,
There is a dull fury in his eyes, like little rusty grates.
He rises slowly,
Trembling in his many swathings like an awakened mummy,
Ridiculous yet terrible.
—And the Committee flings him a waste glance,
Dropping a leaflet by his plate.

A lone fire flickers in the dusty eyes.
The lips chant inaudibly.
The warped shrunken body straightens like a tree.
And he curses . . .
With uplifted arms and perished fingers,
Claw-like, clutching. . . .

So centuries ago
The old men cursed Acosta,
When they, prophetic, heard upon their sepulchres
Those feet that may not halt nor turn aside for ancient things.

The Fifth-Floor Window

Walls . . . iridescent with eyes
that stare into the courtyard
at the still thing lying
in the turned-back snow . . .
stark precipice of walls
with a foam of white faces
lathering their stone lips . . .
faces of the shawled women
the walls pour forth without aim
under the vast pallor of the sky.

They point at the fifth-floor window
and whisper one to the other:
"It's hard on a man out of work
an' the mother gone out of his door
with a younger lover . . ."

The blanched morning stares
in like a face flattened against the pane
where the little girl used to cry all day
with a feeble and goading cry.
Her father, with his eyes at bay
before the vague question of the light,
says that she fell . . .
Between his twitching lips
a stump of cigarette
smoulders, like a burning root.

Only the wind was abroad
in high cold hours
of the icy and sightless night
with back to the stars—
night growing white and still as a pillar of salt
and the snow mushing without sound—
when something hurtled through the night
and drifted like a larger snow-flake
in the trek of the blind snow
that stumbled over it in heaps—

only white-furred wind
pawed at the fifth-floor window
and nosed cigarette-butts on the sill . . .
till the window closed down softly
on the silvery fleece of wind
that tore and left behind its flying fringes.

Now the wind
down the valley of the tenements
sweeps in weakened rushes
and meddles with the clothes-lines
where little white pinafores sway stiffly
like dead geese.
Over the back-yards
that are laid out smooth and handsome as a corpse
under the seamless snow,
the sky is a vast ash pit
where the buried sun
rankles in a livid spot.

Kerensky

Not for you would the winds
that tossed you like great paws
crouch and be still . . .
The winds asked a lustier mate
for their savage maulings . . .
one like green withes, unbreakable,
one pliant with the strength of rooted things
that bend unto their bases
and leap up resilient
with the deep urge of earth
shoving behind her own.

For such do the winds canter
and hold arching backs . . .

but not for you, Kerensky,
lover of the storm,
thing of frail daring
that the storm rejected . . .
flower the storm spewed white and broken
out of its red path.

ELSA VON FREYTAG-LORINGHOVEN

(1874–1927)

A Dozen Cocktails—Please

No spinsterlollypop for me—yes—we have
No bananas—I got lusting palate—I
Always eat them— — — — —
They have dandy celluloid tubes—all sizes—
Tinted diabolically as a baboon's hind-complexion.
A man's a—
Piffle! Will-o'-th'-wisp! What's the dread
Matter with the up-to-date-American-
Home-comforts? Bum insufficient for the
Should-be wellgroomed upsy!
That's the leading question.
There's the vibrator— — —
Coy flappertoy! I am adult citizen with
Vote—I demand my unstinted share
In roofeden—witchsabbath of our baby-
Lonian obelisk.
What's radio for—if you please?
"Eve's dart pricks snookums upon
Wirefence."
An apple a day— — —
It'll come— — — —
Ha! When? I'm no tongueswallowing yogi.
Progress is ravishing—
It doesn't *me*—
Nudge it—
Kick it—
Prod it—
Push it—
Broadcast— — — —
That's the lightning idea!
S.O.S. national shortage of— —
What?

How are we going to put it befitting
Lifted upsys?
Psh! Any sissy poet has sufficient freezing
Chemicals in his Freudian icechest to snuff all
Cockiness. We'll hire one.
Hell! Not that! That's the trouble— —
Cock *crow*—silly!
Oh fine!
They're in France—the air on the line—
The Poles— — — — — —
Have them send waves—like candy—
Valentines— — —
"Say it with— — —
Bolts!
Oh thunder!
Serpentine aircurrents— — —
Hhhhhphsssssssss! The very word penetrates
I feel whoozy!
I like that. I don't hanker after
Billyboys—but I am entitled
To be deeply shocked.
So are we—but you fill the hiatus.
Dear—I ain't queer—I need it straight— —
A dozen cocktails—please— — — —

Klink—Hratzvenga

(Deathwail)

Narin—Tzarissamanili

(He is dead!)

Ildrich mitzdonja—astatootch
Ninj—iffe kniek—
Ninj—iffe kniek!
Arr—karr—
Arrkarr—barr
Karrarr—barr—

Arr—
Arrkarr—
Mardar
Mar—dóórde—dar—

Mardoodaar! ! !

Mardoodd—va—hist—kniek— —
Hist—kniek?
Goorde mee—niss— — —
Goorde mee! ! !
Narin—tzarissamanilj—
Narin—tzarissamanilj! ! !
Hee—hassee?
O—voorrr!

Kardirdesporvorde—hadoorde—klossnux
Kalsinjevasnije—alquille—masré
Alquille masréje paquille—paquille
Ojombe—ojoombe—ojé— — — —
Narin—tzarissamanilj—
Narin—tzarissamanilj ! ! !
Vé—O—voorrr—!
Vévoorrr—
Vrmbbbjjj—sh—
Sh—sh— —
Ooh ! ! !
Vrmbbbjjj—sh—sh—
Sh—sh—
Vrmm.

Café du Dome

For the love of Mike!
Look at that—
Marcelled—
Be-whiskered—
Be-spatted—
Pathetic—
Lymphatic—
Aesthetic—
Pigpink
Quaint—
Natty—
Saintkyk!

Garçon

Un pneumatic cross avec suctiondiscs topped avec thistle-tire
   . . . s'il vous plaît.

ROBERT FROST

(1874–1963)

The Pasture

I'm going out to clean the pasture spring;
I'll only stop to rake the leaves away
(And wait to watch the water clear, I may):
I sha'n't be gone long.—You come too.

I'm going out to fetch the little calf
That's standing by the mother. It's so young,
It totters when she licks it with her tongue.
I sha'n't be gone long.—You come too.

Storm Fear

When the wind works against us in the dark,
And pelts with snow
The lower chamber window on the east,
And whispers with a sort of stifled bark,
The beast,
'Come out! Come out!'—
It costs no inward struggle not to go,
Ah, no!
I count our strength,
Two and a child,
Those of us not asleep subdued to mark
How the cold creeps as the fire dies at length,—
How drifts are piled,
Dooryard and road ungraded,
Till even the comforting barn grows far away,
And my heart owns a doubt
Whether 'tis in us to arise with day
And save ourselves unaided.

Mowing

There was never a sound beside the wood but one,
And that was my long scythe whispering to the ground.
What was it it whispered? I knew not well myself;
Perhaps it was something about the heat of the sun,
Something, perhaps, about the lack of sound—
And that was why it whispered and did not speak.
It was no dream of the gift of idle hours,
Or easy gold at the hand of fay or elf:
Anything more than the truth would have seemed too weak
To the earnest love that laid the swale in rows,
Not without feeble-pointed spikes of flowers
(Pale orchises), and scared a bright green snake.
The fact is the sweetest dream that labor knows.
My long scythe whispered and left the hay to make.

The Tuft of Flowers

I went to turn the grass once after one
Who mowed it in the dew before the sun.

The dew was gone that made his blade so keen
Before I came to view the leveled scene.

I looked for him behind an isle of trees;
I listened for his whetstone on the breeze.

But he had gone his way, the grass all mown,
And I must be, as he had been,—alone,

'As all must be,' I said within my heart,
'Whether they work together or apart.'

But as I said it, swift there passed me by
On noiseless wing a bewildered butterfly,

Seeking with memories grown dim o'er night
Some resting flower of yesterday's delight.

And once I marked his flight go round and round,
As where some flower lay withering on the ground.

And then he flew as far as eye could see,
And then on tremulous wing came back to me.

I thought of questions that have no reply,
And would have turned to toss the grass to dry;

But he turned first, and led my eye to look
At a tall tuft of flowers beside a brook,

A leaping tongue of bloom the scythe had spared
Beside a reedy brook the scythe had bared.

The mower in the dew had loved them thus,
By leaving them to flourish, not for us,

Nor yet to draw one thought of ours to him,
But from sheer morning gladness at the brim.

The butterfly and I had lit upon,
Nevertheless, a message from the dawn,

That made me hear the wakening birds around,
And hear his long scythe whispering to the ground,

And feel a spirit kindred to my own;
So that henceforth I worked no more alone;

But glad with him, I worked as with his aid,
And weary, sought at noon with him the shade;

And dreaming, as it were, held brotherly speech
With one whose thought I had not hoped to reach.

'Men work together,' I told him from the heart,
'Whether they work together or apart.'

Mending Wall

Something there is that doesn't love a wall,
That sends the frozen-ground-swell under it,
And spills the upper boulders in the sun;
And makes gaps even two can pass abreast.
The work of hunters is another thing:
I have come after them and made repair
Where they have left not one stone on a stone,
But they would have the rabbit out of hiding,
To please the yelping dogs. The gaps I mean,
No one has seen them made or heard them made,
But at spring mending-time we find them there.
I let my neighbor know beyond the hill;
And on a day we meet to walk the line
And set the wall between us once again.
We keep the wall between us as we go.
To each the boulders that have fallen to each.
And some are loaves and some so nearly balls
We have to use a spell to make them balance:
'Stay where you are until our backs are turned!'
We wear our fingers rough with handling them.
Oh, just another kind of outdoor game,
One on a side. It comes to little more:
There where it is we do not need the wall:
He is all pine and I am apple orchard.
My apple trees will never get across
And eat the cones under his pines, I tell him.
He only says, 'Good fences make good neighbors.'
Spring is the mischief in me, and I wonder
If I could put a notion in his head:
'*Why* do they make good neighbors? Isn't it
Where there are cows? But here there are no cows.
Before I built a wall I'd ask to know
What I was walling in or walling out,
And to whom I was like to give offense.
Something there is that doesn't love a wall,
That wants it down.' I could say 'Elves' to him,
But it's not elves exactly, and I'd rather
He said it for himself. I see him there

Bringing a stone grasped firmly by the top
In each hand, like an old-stone savage armed.
He moves in darkness as it seems to me,
Not of woods only and the shade of trees.
He will not go behind his father's saying,
And he likes having thought of it so well
He says again, 'Good fences make good neighbors.'

The Death of the Hired Man

Mary sat musing on the lamp-flame at the table
Waiting for Warren. When she heard his step,
She ran on tip-toe down the darkened passage
To meet him in the doorway with the news
And put him on his guard. 'Silas is back.'
She pushed him outward with her through the door
And shut it after her. 'Be kind,' she said.
She took the market things from Warren's arms
And set them on the porch, then drew him down
To sit beside her on the wooden steps.

'When was I ever anything but kind to him?
But I'll not have the fellow back,' he said.
'I told him so last haying, didn't I?
If he left then, I said, that ended it.
What good is he? Who else will harbor him
At his age for the little he can do?
What help he is there's no depending on.
Off he goes always when I need him most.
He thinks he ought to earn a little pay,
Enough at least to buy tobacco with,
So he won't have to beg and be beholden.
"All right," I say, "I can't afford to pay
Any fixed wages, though I wish I could."
"Someone else can." "Then someone else will have to."
I shouldn't mind his bettering himself
If that was what it was. You can be certain,
When he begins like that, there's someone at him

Trying to coax him off with pocket-money,—
In haying time, when any help is scarce.
In winter he comes back to us. I'm done.'

'Sh! not so loud: he'll hear you,' Mary said.

'I want him to: he'll have to soon or late.'

'He's worn out. He's asleep beside the stove.
When I came up from Rowe's I found him here,
Huddled against the barn-door fast asleep,
A miserable sight, and frightening, too—
You needn't smile—I didn't recognize him—
I wasn't looking for him—and he's changed.
Wait till you see.'

                    'Where did you say he'd been?'

'He didn't say. I dragged him to the house,
And gave him tea and tried to make him smoke.
I tried to make him talk about his travels.
Nothing would do: he just kept nodding off.'

'What did he say? Did he say anything?'

'But little.'

            'Anything? Mary, confess
He said he'd come to ditch the meadow for me.'

'Warren!'

            'But did he? I just want to know.'

'Of course he did. What would you have him say?
Surely you wouldn't grudge the poor old man
Some humble way to save his self-respect.
He added, if you really care to know,
He meant to clear the upper pasture, too.
That sounds like something you have heard before?
Warren, I wish you could have heard the way

He jumbled everything. I stopped to look
Two or three times—he made me feel so queer—
To see if he was talking in his sleep.
He ran on Harold Wilson—you remember—
The boy you had in haying four years since.
He's finished school, and teaching in his college.
Silas declares you'll have to get him back.
He says they two will make a team for work:
Between them they will lay this farm as smooth!
The way he mixed that in with other things.
He thinks young Wilson a likely lad, though daft
On education—you know how they fought
All through July under the blazing sun,
Silas up on the cart to build the load,
Harold along beside to pitch it on.'

'Yes, I took care to keep well out of earshot.'

'Well, those days trouble Silas like a dream.
You wouldn't think they would. How some things linger!
Harold's young college boy's assurance piqued him.
After so many years he still keeps finding
Good arguments he sees he might have used.
I sympathize. I know just how it feels
To think of the right thing to say too late.
Harold's associated in his mind with Latin.
He asked me what I thought of Harold's saying
He studied Latin like the violin
Because he liked it—that an argument!
He said he couldn't make the boy believe
He could find water with a hazel prong—
Which showed how much good school had ever done him.
He wanted to go over that. But most of all
He thinks if he could have another chance
To teach him how to build a load of hay—'

'I know, that's Silas' one accomplishment.
He bundles every forkful in its place,
And tags and numbers it for future reference,
So he can find and easily dislodge it
In the unloading. Silas does that well.

He takes it out in bunches like big birds' nests.
You never see him standing on the hay
He's trying to lift, straining to lift himself.'

'He thinks if he could teach him that, he'd be
Some good perhaps to someone in the world.
He hates to see a boy the fool of books.
Poor Silas, so concerned for other folk,
And nothing to look backward to with pride,
And nothing to look forward to with hope,
So now and never any different.'

Part of a moon was falling down the west,
Dragging the whole sky with it to the hills.
Its light poured softly in her lap. She saw it
And spread her apron to it. She put out her hand
Among the harp-like morning-glory strings,
Taut with the dew from garden bed to eaves,
As if she played unheard some tenderness
That wrought on him beside her in the night.
'Warren,' she said, 'he has come home to die:
You needn't be afraid he'll leave you this time.'

'Home,' he mocked gently.

                    'Yes, what else but home?
It all depends on what you mean by home.
Of course he's nothing to us, any more
Than was the hound that came a stranger to us
Out of the woods, worn out upon the trail.'

'Home is the place where, when you have to go there,
They have to take you in.'

                    'I should have called it
Something you somehow haven't to deserve.'

Warren leaned out and took a step or two,
Picked up a little stick, and brought it back
And broke it in his hand and tossed it by.

'Silas has better claim on us you think
Than on his brother? Thirteen little miles
As the road winds would bring him to his door.
Silas has walked that far no doubt today.
Why doesn't he go there? His brother's rich,
A somebody—director in the bank.'

'He never told us that.'

                       'We know it though.'

'I think his brother ought to help, of course.
I'll see to that if there is need. He ought of right
To take him in, and might be willing to—
He may be better than appearances.
But have some pity on Silas. Do you think
If he had any pride in claiming kin
Or anything he looked for from his brother,
He'd keep so still about him all this time?'

'I wonder what's between them.'

                            'I can tell you.
Silas is what he is—we wouldn't mind him—
But just the kind that kinsfolk can't abide.
He never did a thing so very bad.
He don't know why he isn't quite as good
As anybody. Worthless though he is,
He won't be made ashamed to please his brother.'

'*I* can't think Si ever hurt anyone.'

'No, but he hurt my heart the way he lay
And rolled his old head on that sharp-edged chair-back.
He wouldn't let me put him on the lounge.
You must go in and see what you can do.
I made the bed up for him there tonight.
You'll be surprised at him—how much he's broken.
His working days are done; I'm sure of it.'

'I'd not be in a hurry to say that.'

'I haven't been. Go, look, see for yourself.
But, Warren, please remember how it is:
He's come to help you ditch the meadow.
He has a plan. You mustn't laugh at him.
He may not speak of it, and then he may.
I'll sit and see if that small sailing cloud
Will hit or miss the moon.'

                         It hit the moon.
Then there were three there, making a dim row,
The moon, the little silver cloud, and she.
Warren returned—too soon, it seemed to her,
Slipped to her side, caught up her hand and waited.

'Warren?' she questioned.

                         'Dead,' was all he answered.

Home Burial

He saw her from the bottom of the stairs
Before she saw him. She was starting down,
Looking back over her shoulder at some fear.
She took a doubtful step and then undid it
To raise herself and look again. He spoke
Advancing toward her: 'What is it you see
From up there always—for I want to know.'
She turned and sank upon her skirts at that,
And her face changed from terrified to dull.
He said to gain time: 'What is it you see,'
Mounting until she cowered under him.
'I will find out now—you must tell me, dear.'
She, in her place, refused him any help
With the least stiffening of her neck and silence.
She let him look, sure that he wouldn't see,
Blind creature; and awhile he didn't see.
But at last he murmured, 'Oh,' and again, 'Oh.'

'What is it—what?' she said.

                    'Just that I see.'

'You don't,' she challenged. 'Tell me what it is.'

'The wonder is I didn't see at once.
I never noticed it from here before.
I must be wonted to it—that's the reason.
The little graveyard where my people are!
So small the window frames the whole of it.
Not so much larger than a bedroom, is it?
There are three stones of slate and one of marble,
Broad-shouldered little slabs there in the sunlight
On the sidehill. We haven't to mind *those*.
But I understand: it is not the stones,
But the child's mound—'

                    'Don't, don't, don't, don't,' she cried.

She withdrew shrinking from beneath his arm
That rested on the bannister, and slid downstairs;
And turned on him with such a daunting look,
He said twice over before he knew himself:
'Can't a man speak of his own child he's lost?'

'Not you! Oh, where's my hat? Oh, I don't need it!
I must get out of here. I must get air.
I don't know rightly whether any man can.'

'Amy! Don't go to someone else this time.
Listen to me. I won't come down the stairs.'
He sat and fixed his chin between his fists.
'There's something I should like to ask you, dear.'

'You don't know how to ask it.'

                    'Help me, then.'

Her fingers moved the latch for all reply.

'My words are nearly always an offense.
I don't know how to speak of anything
So as to please you. But I might be taught
I should suppose. I can't say I see how.
A man must partly give up being a man
With women-folk. We could have some arrangement
By which I'd bind myself to keep hands off
Anything special you're a-mind to name.
Though I don't like such things 'twixt those that love.
Two that don't love can't live together without them.
But two that do can't live together with them.'
She moved the latch a little. 'Don't—don't go.
Don't carry it to someone else this time.
Tell me about it if it's something human.
Let me into your grief. I'm not so much
Unlike other folks as your standing there
Apart would make me out. Give me my chance.
I do think, though, you overdo it a little.
What was it brought you up to think it the thing
To take your mother-loss of a first child
So inconsolably—in the face of love.
You'd think his memory might be satisfied—'

'There you go sneering now!'

                              'I'm not, I'm not!
You make me angry. I'll come down to you.
God, what a woman! And it's come to this,
A man can't speak of his own child that's dead.'

'You can't because you don't know how to speak.
If you had any feelings, you that dug
With your own hand—how could you?—his little grave;
I saw you from that very window there,
Making the gravel leap and leap in air,
Leap up, like that, like that, and land so lightly
And roll back down the mound beside the hole.
I thought, Who is that man? I didn't know you.
And I crept down the stairs and up the stairs
To look again, and still your spade kept lifting.

Then you came in. I heard your rumbling voice
Out in the kitchen, and I don't know why,
But I went near to see with my own eyes.
You could sit there with the stains on your shoes
Of the fresh earth from your own baby's grave
And talk about your everyday concerns.
You had stood the spade up against the wall
Outside there in the entry, for I saw it.'

'I shall laugh the worst laugh I ever laughed.
I'm cursed. God, if I don't believe I'm cursed.'

'I can repeat the very words you were saying.
"Three foggy mornings and one rainy day
Will rot the best birch fence a man can build."
Think of it, talk like that at such a time!
What had how long it takes a birch to rot
To do with what was in the darkened parlor.
You *couldn't* care! The nearest friends can go
With anyone to death, comes so far short
They might as well not try to go at all.
No, from the time when one is sick to death,
One is alone, and he dies more alone.
Friends make pretense of following to the grave,
But before one is in it, their minds are turned
And making the best of their way back to life
And living people, and things they understand.
But the world's evil. I won't have grief so
If I can change it. Oh, I won't, I won't!'

'There, you have said it all and you feel better.
You won't go now. You're crying. Close the door.
The heart's gone out of it: why keep it up.
Amy! There's someone coming down the road!'

'*You*—oh, you think the talk is all. I must go—
Somewhere out of this house. How can I make you—'

'If—you—do!' She was opening the door wider.
'Where do you mean to go? First tell me that.
I'll follow and bring you back by force. I *will!*—'

After Apple-Picking

My long two-pointed ladder's sticking through a tree
Toward heaven still,
And there's a barrel that I didn't fill
Beside it, and there may be two or three
Apples I didn't pick upon some bough.
But I am done with apple-picking now.
Essence of winter sleep is on the night,
The scent of apples: I am drowsing off.
I cannot rub the strangeness from my sight
I got from looking through a pane of glass
I skimmed this morning from the drinking trough
And held against the world of hoary grass.
It melted, and I let it fall and break.
But I was well
Upon my way to sleep before it fell,
And I could tell
What form my dreaming was about to take.
Magnified apples appear and disappear,
Stem end and blossom end,
And every fleck of russet showing clear.
My instep arch not only keeps the ache,
It keeps the pressure of a ladder-round.
I feel the ladder sway as the boughs bend.
And I keep hearing from the cellar bin
The rumbling sound
Of load on load of apples coming in.
For I have had too much
Of apple-picking: I am overtired
Of the great harvest I myself desired.
There were ten thousand thousand fruit to touch,
Cherish in hand, lift down, and not let fall.
For all
That struck the earth,
No matter if not bruised or spiked with stubble,
Went surely to the cider-apple heap
As of no worth.
One can see what will trouble
This sleep of mine, whatever sleep it is.

Were he not gone,
The woodchuck could say whether it's like his
Long sleep, as I describe its coming on,
Or just some human sleep.

The Wood-Pile

Out walking in the frozen swamp one gray day,
I paused and said, 'I will turn back from here.
No, I will go on farther—and we shall see.'
The hard snow held me, save where now and then
One foot went through. The view was all in lines
Straight up and down of tall slim trees
Too much alike to mark or name a place by
So as to say for certain I was here
Or somewhere else: I was just far from home.
A small bird flew before me. He was careful
To put a tree between us when he lighted,
And say no word to tell me who he was
Who was so foolish as to think what *he* thought.
He thought that I was after him for a feather—
The white one in his tail; like one who takes
Everything said as personal to himself.
One flight out sideways would have undeceived him.
And then there was a pile of wood for which
I forgot him and let his little fear
Carry him off the way I might have gone,
Without so much as wishing him good-night.
He went behind it to make his last stand.
It was a cord of maple, cut and split
And piled—and measured, four by four by eight.
And not another like it could I see.
No runner tracks in this year's snow looped near it.
And it was older sure than this year's cutting,
Or even last year's or the year's before.
The wood was gray and the bark warping off it
And the pile somewhat sunken. Clematis
Had wound strings round and round it like a bundle.

What held it though on one side was a tree
Still growing, and on one a stake and prop,
These latter about to fall. I thought that only
Someone who lived in turning to fresh tasks
Could so forget his handiwork on which
He spent himself, the labor of his ax,
And leave it there far from a useful fireplace
To warm the frozen swamp as best it could
With the slow smokeless burning of decay.

The Road Not Taken

Two roads diverged in a yellow wood,
And sorry I could not travel both
And be one traveler, long I stood
And looked down one as far as I could
To where it bent in the undergrowth;

Then took the other, as just as fair,
And having perhaps the better claim,
Because it was grassy and wanted wear;
Though as for that the passing there
Had worn them really about the same,

And both that morning equally lay
In leaves no step had trodden black.
Oh, I kept the first for another day!
Yet knowing how way leads on to way,
I doubted if I should ever come back.

I shall be telling this with a sigh
Somewhere ages and ages hence:
Two roads diverged in a wood, and I—
I took the one less traveled by,
And that has made all the difference.

An Old Man's Winter Night

All out-of-doors looked darkly in at him
Through the thin frost, almost in separate stars,
That gathers on the pane in empty rooms.
What kept his eyes from giving back the gaze
Was the lamp tilted near them in his hand.
What kept him from remembering what it was
That brought him to that creaking room was age.
He stood with barrels round him—at a loss.
And having scared the cellar under him
In clomping here, he scared it once again
In clomping off;—and scared the outer night,
Which has its sounds, familiar, like the roar
Of trees and crack of branches, common things,
But nothing so like beating on a box.
A light he was to no one but himself
Where now he sat, concerned with he knew what,
A quiet light, and then not even that.
He consigned to the moon, such as she was,
So late-arising, to the broken moon
As better than the sun in any case
For such a charge, his snow upon the roof,
His icicles along the wall to keep;
And slept. The log that shifted with a jolt
Once in the stove, disturbed him and he shifted,
And eased his heavy breathing, but still slept.
One aged man—one man—can't keep a house,
A farm, a countryside, or if he can,
It's thus he does it of a winter night.

Hyla Brook

By June our brook's run out of song and speed.
Sought for much after that, it will be found
Either to have gone groping underground
(And taken with it all the Hyla breed
That shouted in the mist a month ago,

Like ghost of sleigh-bells in a ghost of snow)—
Or flourished and come up in jewel-weed,
Weak foliage that is blown upon and bent
Even against the way its waters went.
Its bed is left a faded paper sheet
Of dead leaves stuck together by the heat—
A brook to none but who remember long.
This as it will be seen is other far
Than with brooks taken otherwhere in song.
We love the things we love for what they are.

The Oven Bird

There is a singer everyone has heard,
Loud, a mid-summer and a mid-wood bird,
Who makes the solid tree trunks sound again.
He says that leaves are old and that for flowers
Mid-summer is to spring as one to ten.
He says the early petal-fall is past
When pear and cherry bloom went down in showers
On sunny days a moment overcast;
And comes that other fall we name the fall.
He says the highway dust is over all.
The bird would cease and be as other birds
But that he knows in singing not to sing.
The question that he frames in all but words
Is what to make of a diminished thing.

Bond and Free

Love has earth to which she clings
With hills and circling arms about—
Wall within wall to shut fear out.
But Thought has need of no such things,
For Thought has a pair of dauntless wings.

On snow and sand and turf, I see
Where Love has left a printed trace
With straining in the world's embrace.

And such is Love and glad to be.
But Thought has shaken his ankles free.

Thought cleaves the interstellar gloom
And sits in Sirius' disc all night,
Till day makes him retrace his flight,
With smell of burning on every plume,
Back past the sun to an earthly room.

His gains in heaven are what they are.
Yet some say Love by being thrall
And simply staying possesses all
In several beauty that Thought fares far
To find fused in another star.

Birches

When I see birches bend to left and right
Across the lines of straighter darker trees,
I like to think some boy's been swinging them.
But swinging doesn't bend them down to stay
As ice-storms do. Often you must have seen them
Loaded with ice a sunny winter morning
After a rain. They click upon themselves
As the breeze rises, and turn many-colored
As the stir cracks and crazes their enamel.
Soon the sun's warmth makes them shed crystal shells
Shattering and avalanching on the snow-crust—
Such heaps of broken glass to sweep away
You'd think the inner dome of heaven had fallen.
They are dragged to the withered bracken by the load,
And they seem not to break; though once they are bowed
So low for long, they never right themselves:

You may see their trunks arching in the woods
Years afterwards, trailing their leaves on the ground
Like girls on hands and knees that throw their hair
Before them over their heads to dry in the sun.
But I was going to say when Truth broke in
With all her matter-of-fact about the ice-storm
I should prefer to have some boy bend them
As he went out and in to fetch the cows—
Some boy too far from town to learn baseball,
Whose only play was what he found himself,
Summer or winter, and could play alone.
One by one he subdued his father's trees
By riding them down over and over again
Until he took the stiffness out of them,
And not one but hung limp, not one was left
For him to conquer. He learned all there was
To learn about not launching out too soon
And so not carrying the tree away
Clear to the ground. He always kept his poise
To the top branches, climbing carefully
With the same pains you use to fill a cup
Up to the brim, and even above the brim.
Then he flung outward, feet first, with a swish,
Kicking his way down through the air to the ground.
So was I once myself a swinger of birches.
And so I dream of going back to be.
It's when I'm weary of considerations,
And life is too much like a pathless wood
Where your face burns and tickles with the cobwebs
Broken across it, and one eye is weeping
From a twig's having lashed across it open.
I'd like to get away from earth awhile
And then come back to it and begin over.
May no fate willfully misunderstand me
And half grant what I wish and snatch me away
Not to return. Earth's the right place for love:
I don't know where it's likely to go better.
I'd like to go by climbing a birch tree,
And climb black branches up a snow-white trunk
Toward heaven, till the tree could bear no more,

But dipped its top and set me down again.
That would be good both going and coming back.
One could do worse than be a swinger of birches.

Putting in the Seed

You come to fetch me from my work tonight
When supper's on the table, and we'll see
If I can leave off burying the white
Soft petals fallen from the apple tree
(Soft petals, yes, but not so barren quite,
Mingled with these, smooth bean and wrinkled pea;)
And go along with you ere you lose sight
Of what you came for and become like me,
Slave to a springtime passion for the earth.
How Love burns through the Putting in the Seed
On through the watching for that early birth
When, just as the soil tarnishes with weed,
The sturdy seedling with arched body comes
Shouldering its way and shedding the earth crumbs.

The Sound of Trees

I wonder about the trees.
Why do we wish to bear
Forever the noise of these
More than another noise
So close to our dwelling place?
We suffer them by the day
Till we lose all measure of pace,
And fixity in our joys,
And acquire a listening air.
They are that that talks of going
But never gets away;
And that talks no less for knowing,
As it grows wiser and older,

That now it means to stay.
My feet tug at the floor
And my head sways to my shoulder
Sometimes when I watch trees sway,
From the window or the door.
I shall set forth for somewhere,
I shall make the reckless choice
Some day when they are in voice
And tossing so as to scare
The white clouds over them on.
I shall have less to say,
But I shall be gone.

'Out, Out—'

The buzz saw snarled and rattled in the yard
And made dust and dropped stove-length sticks of wood,
Sweet-scented stuff when the breeze drew across it.
And from there those that lifted eyes could count
Five mountain ranges one behind the other
Under the sunset far into Vermont.
And the saw snarled and rattled, snarled and rattled,
As it ran light, or had to bear a load.
And nothing happened: day was all but done.
Call it a day, I wish they might have said
To please the boy by giving him the half hour
That a boy counts so much when saved from work.
His sister stood beside them in her apron
To tell them 'Supper.' At the word, the saw,
As if to prove saws knew what supper meant,
Leaped out at the boy's hand, or seemed to leap—
He must have given the hand. However it was,
Neither refused the meeting. But the hand!
The boy's first outcry was a rueful laugh,
As he swung toward them holding up the hand
Half in appeal, but half as if to keep
The life from spilling. Then the boy saw all—
Since he was old enough to know, big boy

Doing a man's work, though a child at heart—
He saw all spoiled. 'Don't let him cut my hand off—
The doctor, when he comes. Don't let him, sister!'
So. But the hand was gone already.
The doctor put him in the dark of ether.
He lay and puffed his lips out with his breath.
And then—the watcher at his pulse took fright.
No one believed. They listened at his heart.
Little—less—nothing!—and that ended it.
No more to build on there. And they, since they
Were not the one dead, turned to their affairs.

A Star in a Stone-Boat

For Lincoln MacVeagh

Never tell me that not one star of all
That slip from heaven at night and softly fall
Has been picked up with stones to build a wall.

Some laborer found one faded and stone cold,
And saving that its weight suggested gold,
And tugged it from his first too certain hold,

He noticed nothing in it to remark.
He was not used to handling stars thrown dark
And lifeless from an interrupted arc.

He did not recognize in that smooth coal
The one thing palpable besides the soul
To penetrate the air in which we roll.

He did not see how like a flying thing
It brooded ant-eggs, and had one large wing,
One not so large for flying in a ring,

And a long Bird of Paradise's tail,
(Though these when not in use to fly and trail
It drew back in its body like a snail);

Nor know that he might move it from the spot,
The harm was done; from having been star-shot
The very nature of the soil was hot

And burning to yield flowers instead of grain,
Flowers fanned and not put out by all the rain
Poured on them by his prayers prayed in vain.

He moved it roughly with an iron bar,
He loaded an old stone-boat with the star
And not, as you might think, a flying car,

Such as even poets would admit perforce
More practical than Pegasus the horse
If it could put a star back in its course.

He dragged it through the plowed ground at a pace
But faintly reminiscent of the race
Of jostling rock in interstellar space.

It went for building stone, and I, as though
Commanded in a dream, forever go
To right the wrong that this should have been so.

Yet ask where else it could have gone as well,
I do not know—I cannot stop to tell:
He might have left it lying where it fell.

From following walls I never lift my eye
Except at night to places in the sky
Where showers of charted meteors let fly.

Some may know what they seek in school and church,
And why they seek it there; for what I search
I must go measuring stone walls, perch on perch;

Sure that though not a star of death and birth,
So not to be compared, perhaps, in worth
To such resorts of life as Mars and Earth,

Though not, I say, a star of death and sin,
It yet has poles, and only needs a spin
To show its worldly nature and begin

To chafe and shuffle in my calloused palm
And run off in strange tangents with my arm
As fish do with the line in first alarm.

Such as it is, it promises the prize
Of the one world complete in any size
That I am like to compass, fool or wise.

The Witch of Coös

I stayed the night for shelter at a farm
Behind the mountain, with a mother and son,
Two old-believers. They did all the talking.

MOTHER. Folks think a witch who has familiar spirits
She could call up to pass a winter evening,
But won't, should be burned at the stake or something.
Summoning spirits isn't 'Button, button,
Who's got the button,' I would have them know.

SON. Mother can make a common table rear
And kick with two legs like an army mule.

MOTHER. And when I've done it, what good have I done?
Rather than tip a table for you, let me
Tell you what Ralle the Sioux Control once told me.
He said the dead had souls, but when I asked him
How could that be—I thought the dead were souls,
He broke my trance. Don't that make you suspicious
That there's something the dead are keeping back?
Yes, there's something the dead are keeping back.

SON. You wouldn't want to tell him what we have
Up attic, mother?

MOTHER. Bones—a skeleton.

SON. But the headboard of mother's bed is pushed
Against the attic door: the door is nailed.
It's harmless. Mother hears it in the night
Halting perplexed behind the barrier
Of door and headboard. Where it wants to get
Is back into the cellar where it came from.

MOTHER. We'll never let them, will we, son! We'll never!

SON. It left the cellar forty years ago
And carried itself like a pile of dishes
Up one flight from the cellar to the kitchen,
Another from the kitchen to the bedroom,
Another from the bedroom to the attic,
Right past both father and mother, and neither stopped it.
Father had gone upstairs; mother was downstairs.
I was a baby: I don't know where I was.

MOTHER. The only fault my husband found with me—
I went to sleep before I went to bed,
Especially in winter when the bed
Might just as well be ice and the clothes snow.
The night the bones came up the cellar-stairs
Toffile had gone to bed alone and left me,
But left an open door to cool the room off
So as to sort of turn me out of it.
I was just coming to myself enough
To wonder where the cold was coming from,
When I heard Toffile upstairs in the bedroom
And thought I heard him downstairs in the cellar.
The board we had laid down to walk dry-shod on
When there was water in the cellar in spring
Struck the hard cellar bottom. And then someone
Began the stairs, two footsteps for each step,
The way a man with one leg and a crutch,
Or a little child, comes up. It wasn't Toffile:
It wasn't anyone who could be there.
The bulkhead double-doors were double-locked

And swollen tight and buried under snow.
The cellar windows were banked up with sawdust
And swollen tight and buried under snow.
It was the bones. I knew them—and good reason.
My first impulse was to get to the knob
And hold the door. But the bones didn't try
The door; they halted helpless on the landing,
Waiting for things to happen in their favor.
The faintest restless rustling ran all through them.
I never could have done the thing I did
If the wish hadn't been too strong in me
To see how they were mounted for this walk.
I had a vision of them put together
Not like a man, but like a chandelier.
So suddenly I flung the door wide on him.
A moment he stood balancing with emotion,
And all but lost himself. (A tongue of fire
Flashed out and licked along his upper teeth.
Smoke rolled inside the sockets of his eyes.)
Then he came at me with one hand outstretched,
The way he did in life once; but this time
I struck the hand off brittle on the floor,
And fell back from him on the floor myself.
The finger-pieces slid in all directions.
(Where did I see one of those pieces lately?
Hand me my button-box—it must be there.)
I sat up on the floor and shouted, 'Toffile,
It's coming up to you.' It had its choice
Of the door to the cellar or the hall.
It took the hall door for the novelty,
And set off briskly for so slow a thing,
Still going every which way in the joints, though,
So that it looked like lightning or a scribble,
From the slap I had just now given its hand.
I listened till it almost climbed the stairs
From the hall to the only finished bedroom,
Before I got up to do anything;
Then ran and shouted, 'Shut the bedroom door,
Toffile, for my sake!' 'Company?' he said,
'Don't make me get up; I'm too warm in bed.'

So lying forward weakly on the handrail
I pushed myself upstairs, and in the light
(The kitchen had been dark) I had to own
I could see nothing. 'Toffile, I don't see it.
It's with us in the room though. It's the bones.'
'What bones?' 'The cellar bones—out of the grave.'
That made him throw his bare legs out of bed
And sit up by me and take hold of me.
I wanted to put out the light and see
If I could see it, or else mow the room,
With our arms at the level of our knees,
And bring the chalk-pile down. 'I'll tell you what—
It's looking for another door to try.
The uncommonly deep snow has made him think
Of his old song, *The Wild Colonial Boy*,
He always used to sing along the tote road.
He's after an open door to get outdoors.
Let's trap him with an open door up attic.'
Toffile agreed to that, and sure enough,
Almost the moment he was given an opening,
The steps began to climb the attic stairs.
I heard them. Toffile didn't seem to hear them.
'Quick!' I slammed to the door and held the knob.
'Toffile, get nails.' I made him nail the door shut
And push the headboard of the bed against it.
Then we asked was there anything
Up attic that we'd ever want again.
The attic was less to us than the cellar.
If the bones liked the attic, let them have it.
Let them stay in the attic. When they sometimes
Come down the stairs at night and stand perplexed
Behind the door and headboard of the bed,
Brushing their chalky skull with chalky fingers,
With sounds like the dry rattling of a shutter,
That's what I sit up in the dark to say—
To no one any more since Toffile died.
Let them stay in the attic since they went there.
I promised Toffile to be cruel to them
For helping them be cruel once to him.

SON. We think they had a grave down in the cellar.

MOTHER. We know they had a grave down in the cellar.

SON. We never could find out whose bones they were.

MOTHER. Yes, we could too, son. Tell the truth for once.
They were a man's his father killed for me.
I mean a man he killed instead of me.
The least I could do was to help dig their grave.
We were about it one night in the cellar.
Son knows the story: but 'twas not for him
To tell the truth, suppose the time had come.
Son looks surprised to see me end a lie
We'd kept all these years between ourselves
So as to have it ready for outsiders.
But tonight I don't care enough to lie—
I don't remember why I ever cared.
Toffile, if he were here, I don't believe
Could tell you why he ever cared himself. . . .

She hadn't found the finger-bone she wanted
Among the buttons poured out in her lap.
I verified the name next morning: Toffile.
The rural letter box said Toffile Lajway.

Nothing Gold Can Stay

Nature's first green is gold,
Her hardest hue to hold.
Her early leaf's a flower;
But only so an hour.
Then leaf subsides to leaf.
So Eden sank to grief,
So dawn goes down to day.
Nothing gold can stay.

Fire and Ice

Some say the world will end in fire,
Some say in ice.
From what I've tasted of desire
I hold with those who favor fire.
But if it had to perish twice,
I think I know enough of hate
To say that for destruction ice
Is also great
And would suffice.

Dust of Snow

The way a crow
Shook down on me
The dust of snow
From a hemlock tree

Has given my heart
A change of mood
And saved some part
Of a day I had rued.

Stopping by Woods on a Snowy Evening

Whose woods these are I think I know.
His house is in the village though;
He will not see me stopping here
To watch his woods fill up with snow.

My little horse must think it queer
To stop without a farmhouse near
Between the woods and frozen lake
The darkest evening of the year.

He gives his harness bells a shake
To ask if there is some mistake.
The only other sound's the sweep
Of easy wind and downy flake.

The woods are lovely, dark and deep,
But I have promises to keep,
And miles to go before I sleep,
And miles to go before I sleep.

For Once, Then, Something

Others taunt me with having knelt at well-curbs
Always wrong to the light, so never seeing
Deeper down in the well than where the water
Gives me back in a shining surface picture
Me myself in the summer heaven godlike
Looking out of a wreath of fern and cloud puffs.
Once, when trying with chin against a well-curb,
I discerned, as I thought, beyond the picture,
Through the picture, a something white, uncertain,
Something more of the depths—and then I lost it.
Water came to rebuke the too clear water.
One drop fell from a fern, and lo, a ripple
Shook whatever it was lay there at bottom,
Blurred it, blotted it out. What was that whiteness?
Truth? A pebble of quartz? For once, then, something.

The Onset

Always the same, when on a fated night
At last the gathered snow lets down as white
As may be in dark woods, and with a song
It shall not make again all winter long
Of hissing on the yet uncovered ground,
I almost stumble looking up and round,

As one who overtaken by the end
Gives up his errand, and lets death descend
Upon him where he is, with nothing done
To evil, no important triumph won,
More than if life had never been begun.

Yet all the precedent is on my side:
I know that winter death has never tried
The earth but it has failed: the snow may heap
In long storms an undrifted four feet deep
As measured against maple, birch, and oak,
It cannot check the peeper's silver croak;
And I shall see the snow all go down hill
In water of a slender April rill
That flashes tail through last year's withered brake
And dead weeds, like a disappearing snake.
Nothing will be left white but here a birch,
And there a clump of houses with a church.

To Earthward

Love at the lips was touch
As sweet as I could bear;
And once that seemed too much;
I lived on air

That crossed me from sweet things
The flow of—was it musk
From hidden grapevine springs
Down hill at dusk?

I had the swirl and ache
From sprays of honeysuckle
That when they're gathered shake
Dew on the knuckle.

I craved strong sweets, but those
Seemed strong when I was young;
The petal of the rose
It was that stung.

Now no joy but lacks salt
That is not dashed with pain
And weariness and fault;
I crave the stain

Of tears, the aftermark
Of almost too much love,
The sweet of bitter bark
And burning clove.

When stiff and sore and scarred
I take away my hand
From leaning on it hard
In grass and sand,

The hurt is not enough:
I long for weight and strength
To feel the earth as rough
To all my length.

The Need of Being Versed in Country Things

The house had gone to bring again
To the midnight sky a sunset glow.
Now the chimney was all of the house that stood,
Like a pistil after the petals go.

The barn opposed across the way,
That would have joined the house in flame
Had it been the will of the wind, was left
To bear forsaken the place's name.

No more it opened with all one end
For teams that came by the stony road
To drum on the floor with scurrying hoofs
And brush the mow with the summer load.

The birds that came to it through the air
At broken windows flew out and in,
Their murmur more like the sigh we sigh
From too much dwelling on what has been.

Yet for them the lilac renewed its leaf,
And the aged elm, though touched with fire;
And the dry pump flung up an awkward arm;
And the fence post carried a strand of wire.

For them there was really nothing sad.
But though they rejoiced in the nest they kept,
One had to be versed in country things
Not to believe the phoebes wept.

Spring Pools

These pools that, though in forests, still reflect
The total sky almost without defect,
And like the flowers beside them, chill and shiver,
Will like the flowers beside them soon be gone,
And yet not out by any brook or river,
But up by roots to bring dark foliage on.

The trees that have it in their pent-up buds
To darken nature and be summer woods—
Let them think twice before they use their powers
To blot out and drink up and sweep away
These flowery waters and these watery flowers
From snow that melted only yesterday.

The Freedom of the Moon

I've tried the new moon tilted in the air
Above a hazy tree-and-farmhouse cluster
As you might try a jewel in your hair.
I've tried it fine with little breadth of luster,
Alone, or in one ornament combining
With one first-water star almost as shining.

I put it shining anywhere I please.
By walking slowly on some evening later,
I've pulled it from a crate of crooked trees,
And brought it over glossy water, greater,
And dropped it in, and seen the image wallow,
The color run, all sorts of wonder follow.

Once by the Pacific

The shattered water made a misty din.
Great waves looked over others coming in,
And thought of doing something to the shore
That water never did to land before.
The clouds were low and hairy in the skies,
Like locks blown forward in the gleam of eyes.
You could not tell, and yet it looked as if
The shore was lucky in being backed by cliff,
The cliff in being backed by continent;
It looked as if a night of dark intent
Was coming, and not only a night, an age.
Someone had better be prepared for rage.
There would be more than ocean-water broken
Before God's last *Put out the Light* was spoken.

A Minor Bird

I have wished a bird would fly away,
And not sing by my house all day;

Have clapped my hands at him from the door
When it seemed as if I could bear no more.

The fault must partly have been in me.
The bird was not to blame for his key.

And of course there must be something wrong
In wanting to silence any song.

Bereft

Where had I heard this wind before
Change like this to a deeper roar?
What would it take my standing there for,
Holding open a restive door,
Looking down hill to a frothy shore?
Summer was past and day was past.
Somber clouds in the west were massed.
Out in the porch's sagging floor,
Leaves got up in a coil and hissed,
Blindly struck at my knee and missed.
Something sinister in the tone
Told me my secret must be known:
Word I was in the house alone
Somehow must have gotten abroad,
Word I was in my life alone,
Word I had no one left but God.

Tree at My Window

Tree at my window, window tree,
My sash is lowered when night comes on;
But let there never be curtain drawn
Between you and me.

Vague dream-head lifted out of the ground,
And thing next most diffuse to cloud,
Not all your light tongues talking aloud
Could be profound.

But, tree, I have seen you taken and tossed,
And if you have seen me when I slept,
You have seen me when I was taken and swept
And all but lost.

That day she put our heads together,
Fate had her imagination about her,
Your head so much concerned with outer,
Mine with inner, weather.

Acquainted with the Night

I have been one acquainted with the night.
I have walked out in rain—and back in rain.
I have outwalked the furthest city light.

I have looked down the saddest city lane.
I have passed by the watchman on his beat
And dropped my eyes, unwilling to explain.

I have stood still and stopped the sound of feet
When far away an interrupted cry
Came over houses from another street,

But not to call me back or say good-by;
And further still at an unearthly height,
One luminary clock against the sky

Proclaimed the time was neither wrong nor right.
I have been one acquainted with the night.

West-Running Brook

'Fred, where is north?'

                'North? North is there, my love.
The brook runs west.'

               'West-running Brook then call it.'
(West-running Brook men call it to this day.)
'What does it think it's doing running west
When all the other country brooks flow east
To reach the ocean? It must be the brook
Can trust itself to go by contraries
The way I can with you—and you with me—
Because we're—we're—I don't know what we are.
What are we?'

          'Young or new?'

               'We must be something.
We've said we two. Let's change that to we three.
As you and I are married to each other,
We'll both be married to the brook. We'll build
Our bridge across it, and the bridge shall be
Our arm thrown over it asleep beside it.
Look, look, it's waving to us with a wave
To let us know it hears me.'

             'Why, my dear,
That wave's been standing off this jut of shore—'

(The black stream, catching on a sunken rock,
Flung backward on itself in one white wave,
And the white water rode the black forever,
Not gaining but not losing, like a bird
White feathers from the struggle of whose breast
Flecked the dark stream and flecked the darker pool
Below the point, and were at last driven wrinkled
In a white scarf against the far shore alders.)
'That wave's been standing off this jut of shore
Ever since rivers, I was going to say,
Were made in heaven. It wasn't waved to us.'

'It wasn't, yet it was. If not to you
It was to me—in an annunciation.'

'Oh, if you take it off to lady-land,
As't were the country of the Amazons
We men must see you to the confines of
And leave you there, ourselves forbid to enter,—
It is your brook! I have no more to say.'

'Yes, you have, too. Go on. You thought of something.'

'Speaking of contraries, see how the brook
In that white wave runs counter to itself.
It is from that in water we were from
Long, long before we were from any creature.
Here we, in our impatience of the steps,
Get back to the beginning of beginnings,
The stream of everything that runs away.
Some say existence like a Pirouot
And Pirouette, forever in one place,
Stands still and dances, but it runs away,
It seriously, sadly, runs away
To fill the abyss' void with emptiness.
It flows beside us in this water brook,
But it flows over us. It flows between us
To separate us for a panic moment.
It flows between us, over us, and *with* us.
And it is time, strength, tone, light, life, and love—

And even substance lapsing unsubstantial;
The universal cataract of death
That spends to nothingness—and unresisted,
Save by some strange resistance in itself,
Not just a swerving, but a throwing back,
As if regret were in it and were sacred.
It has this throwing backward on itself
So that the fall of most of it is always
Raising a little, sending up a little.
Our life runs down in sending up the clock.
The brook runs down in sending up our life.
The sun runs down in sending up the brook.
And there is something sending up the sun.
It is this backward motion toward the source,
Against the stream, that most we see ourselves in,
The tribute of the current to the source.
It is from this in nature we are from.
It is most us.'

          'Today will be the day
You said so.'

          'No, today will be the day
You said the brook was called West-running Brook.'

'Today will be the day of what we both said.'

The Investment

Over back where they speak of life as staying
('You couldn't call it living, for it ain't'),
There was an old, old house renewed with paint,
And in it a piano loudly playing.

Out in the plowed ground in the cold a digger,
Among unearthed potatoes standing still,
Was counting winter dinners, one a hill,
With half an ear to the piano's vigor.

All that piano and new paint back there,
Was it some money suddenly come into?
Or some extravagance young love had been to?
Or old love on an impulse not to care—

Not to sink under being man and wife,
But get some color and music out of life?

Two Tramps in Mud Time

Out of the mud two strangers came
And caught me splitting wood in the yard.
And one of them put me off my aim
By hailing cheerily 'Hit them hard!'
I knew pretty well why he dropped behind
And let the other go on a way.
I knew pretty well what he had in mind:
He wanted to take my job for pay.

Good blocks of oak it was I split,
As large around as the chopping block;
And every piece I squarely hit
Fell splinterless as a cloven rock.
The blows that a life of self-control
Spares to strike for the common good
That day, giving a loose to my soul,
I spent on the unimportant wood.

The sun was warm but the wind was chill.
You know how it is with an April day
When the sun is out and the wind is still,
You're one month on in the middle of May.
But if you so much as dare to speak,
A cloud comes over the sunlit arch,
A wind comes off a frozen peak,
And you're two months back in the middle of March.

A bluebird comes tenderly up to alight
And turns to the wind to unruffle a plume
His song so pitched as not to excite
A single flower as yet to bloom.
It is snowing a flake: and he half knew
Winter was only playing possum.
Except in color he isn't blue,
But he wouldn't advise a thing to blossom.

The water for which we may have to look
In summertime with a witching-wand,
In every wheelrut's now a brook,
In every print of a hoof a pond.
Be glad of water, but don't forget
The lurking frost in the earth beneath
That will steal forth after the sun is set
And show on the water its crystal teeth.

The time when most I loved my task
These two must make me love it more
By coming with what they came to ask.
You'd think I never had felt before
The weight of an ax-head poised aloft,
The grip on earth of outspread feet,
The life of muscles rocking soft
And smooth and moist in vernal heat.

Out of the woods two hulking tramps
(From sleeping God knows where last night,
But not long since in the lumber camps).
They thought all chopping was theirs of right.
Men of the woods and lumberjacks,
They judged me by their appropriate tool.
Except as a fellow handled an ax,
They had no way of knowing a fool.

Nothing on either side was said.
They knew they had but to stay their stay
And all their logic would fill my head:
As that I had no right to play

With what was another man's work for gain.
My right might be love but theirs was need.
And where the two exist in twain
Theirs was the better right—agreed.

But yield who will to their separation,
My object in living is to unite
My avocation and my vocation
As my two eyes make one in sight.
Only where love and need are one,
And the work is play for mortal stakes,
Is the deed ever really done
For Heaven and the future's sakes.

A Drumlin Woodchuck

One thing has a shelving bank,
Another a rotting plank,
To give it cozier skies
And make up for its lack of size.

My own strategic retreat
Is where two rocks almost meet,
And still more secure and snug,
A two-door burrow I dug.

With those in mind at my back
I can sit forth exposed to attack
As one who shrewdly pretends
That he and the world are friends.

All we who prefer to live
Have a little whistle we give,
And flash, at the least alarm
We dive down under the farm.

We allow some time for guile
And don't come out for a while
Either to eat or drink.
We take occasion to think.

And if after the hunt goes past
And the double-barreled blast
(Like war and pestilence
And the loss of common sense),

If I can with confidence say
That still for another day,
Or even another year,
I will be there for you, my dear,

It will be because, though small
As measured against the All,
I have been so instinctively thorough
About my crevice and burrow.

Desert Places

Snow falling and night falling fast, oh, fast
In a field I looked into going past,
And the ground almost covered smooth in snow,
But a few weeds and stubble showing last.

The woods around it have it—it is theirs.
All animals are smothered in their lairs.
I am too absent-spirited to count;
The loneliness includes me unawares.

And lonely as it is that loneliness
Will be more lonely ere it will be less—
A blanker whiteness of benighted snow
With no expression, nothing to express.

They cannot scare me with their empty spaces
Between stars—on stars where no human race is.
I have it in me so much nearer home
To scare myself with my own desert places.

The Strong Are Saying Nothing

The soil now gets a rumpling soft and damp,
And small regard to the future of any weed.
The final flat of the hoe's approval stamp
Is reserved for the bed of a few selected seed.

There is seldom more than a man to a harrowed piece.
Men work alone, their lots plowed far apart,
One stringing a chain of seed in an open crease,
And another stumbling after a halting cart.

To the fresh and black of the squares of early mold
The leafless bloom of a plum is fresh and white;
Though there's more than a doubt if the weather is not
    too cold
For the bees to come and serve its beauty aright.

Wind goes from farm to farm in wave on wave,
But carries no cry of what is hoped to be.
There may be little or much beyond the grave,
But the strong are saying nothing until they see.

Neither Out Far Nor In Deep

The people along the sand
All turn and look one way.
They turn their back on the land.
They look at the sea all day.

As long as it takes to pass
A ship keeps raising its hull;
The wetter ground like glass
Reflects a standing gull.

The land may vary more;
But wherever the truth may be—
The water comes ashore,
And the people look at the sea.

They cannot look out far.
They cannot look in deep.
But when was that ever a bar
To any watch they keep?

Design

I found a dimpled spider, fat and white,
On a white heal-all, holding up a moth
Like a white piece of rigid satin cloth—
Assorted characters of death and blight
Mixed ready to begin the morning right,
Like the ingredients of a witches' broth—
A snow-drop spider, a flower like a froth,
And dead wings carried like a paper kite.

What had that flower to do with being white,
The wayside blue and innocent heal-all?
What brought the kindred spider to that height,
Then steered the white moth thither in the night?
What but design of darkness to appall?—
If design govern in a thing so small.

Unharvested

A scent of ripeness from over a wall.
And come to leave the routine road
And look for what had made me stall,
There sure enough was an apple tree
That had eased itself of its summer load,
And of all but its trivial foliage free,
Now breathed as light as a lady's fan.
For there there had been an apple fall
As complete as the apple had given man.
The ground was one circle of solid red.

May something go always unharvested!
May much stay out of our stated plan,
Apples or something forgotten and left,
So smelling their sweetness would be no theft.

Provide, Provide

The witch that came (the withered hag)
To wash the steps with pail and rag,
Was once the beauty Abishag,

The picture pride of Hollywood.
Too many fall from great and good
For you to doubt the likelihood.

Die early and avoid the fate.
Or if predestined to die late,
Make up your mind to die in state.

Make the whole stock exchange your own!
If need be occupy a throne,
Where nobody can call *you* crone.

Some have relied on what they knew;
Others on being simply true.
What worked for them might work for you.

No memory of having starred
Atones for later disregard,
Or keeps the end from being hard.

Better to go down dignified
With boughten friendship at your side
Than none at all. Provide, provide!

On a Bird Singing in Its Sleep

A bird half wakened in the lunar noon
Sang halfway through its little inborn tune.
Partly because it sang but once all night
And that from no especial bush's height;
Partly because it sang ventriloquist
And had the inspiration to desist
Almost before the prick of hostile ears,
It ventured less in peril than appears.
It could not have come down to us so far
Through the interstices of things ajar
On the long bead chain of repeated birth
To be a bird while we are men on earth
If singing out of sleep and dream that way
Had made it much more easily a prey.

The Silken Tent

She is as in a field a silken tent
At midday when a sunny summer breeze
Has dried the dew and all its ropes relent,
So that in guys it gently sways at ease,
And its supporting central cedar pole,

That is its pinnacle to heavenward
And signifies the sureness of the soul,
Seems to owe naught to any single cord,
But strictly held by none, is loosely bound
By countless silken ties of love and thought
To everything on earth the compass round,
And only by one's going slightly taut
In the capriciousness of summer air
Is of the slightest bondage made aware.

All Revelation

A head thrusts in as for the view,
But where it is it thrusts in from
Or what it is it thrusts into
By that Cyb'laean avenue,
And what can of its coming come,

And whither it will be withdrawn,
And what take hence or leave behind,
These things the mind has pondered on
A moment and still asking gone.
Strange apparition of the mind!

But the impervious geode
Was entered, and its inner crust
Of crystals with a ray cathode
At every point and facet glowed
In answer to the mental thrust.

Come In

As I came to the edge of the woods,
Thrush music—hark!
Now if it was dusk outside,
Inside it was dark.

Too dark in the woods for a bird
By sleight of wing
To better its perch for the night,
Though it still could sing.

The last of the light of the sun
That had died in the west
Still lived for one song more
In a thrush's breast.

Far in the pillared dark
Thrush music went—
Almost like a call to come in
To the dark and lament.

But no, I was out for stars:
I would not come in.
I meant not even if asked,
And I hadn't been.

The Most of It

He thought he kept the universe alone;
For all the voice in answer he could wake
Was but the mocking echo of his own
From some tree-hidden cliff across the lake.
Some morning from the boulder-broken beach
He would cry out on life, that what it wants
Is not its own love back in copy speech,
But counter-love, original response.
And nothing ever came of what he cried
Unless it was the embodiment that crashed
In the cliff's talus on the other side,
And then in the far distant water splashed,

But after a time allowed for it to swim,
Instead of proving human when it neared
And someone else additional to him,
As a great buck it powerfully appeared,
Pushing the crumpled water up ahead,
And landed pouring like a waterfall,
And stumbled through the rocks with horny tread,
And forced the underbrush—and that was all.

Never Again Would Birds' Song Be the Same

He would declare and could himself believe
That the birds there in all the garden round
From having heard the daylong voice of Eve
Had added to their own an oversound,
Her tone of meaning but without the words.
Admittedly an eloquence so soft
Could only have had an influence on birds
When call or laughter carried it aloft.
Be that as may be, she was in their song.
Moreover her voice upon their voices crossed
Had now persisted in the woods so long
That probably it never would be lost.
Never again would birds' song be the same.
And to do that to birds was why she came.

The Subverted Flower

She drew back; he was calm:
'It is this that had the power.'
And he lashed his open palm
With the tender-headed flower.
He smiled for her to smile,
But she was either blind
Or willfully unkind.
He eyed her for a while

For a woman and a puzzle.
He flicked and flung the flower,
And another sort of smile
Caught up like finger tips
The corners of his lips
And cracked his ragged muzzle.
She was standing to the waist
In goldenrod and brake,
Her shining hair displaced.
He stretched her either arm
As if she made it ache
To clasp her—not to harm;
As if he could not spare
To touch her neck and hair.
'If this has come to us
And not to me alone—'
So she thought she heard him say;
Though with every word he spoke
His lips were sucked and blown
And the effort made him choke
Like a tiger at a bone.
She had to lean away.
She dared not stir a foot,
Lest movement should provoke
The demon of pursuit
That slumbers in a brute.
It was then her mother's call
From inside the garden wall
Made her steal a look of fear
To see if he could hear
And would pounce to end it all
Before her mother came.
She looked and saw the shame:
A hand hung like a paw,
An arm worked like a saw
As if to be persuasive,
An ingratiating laugh
That cut the snout in half,
An eye become evasive.
A girl could only see

That a flower had marred a man,
But what she could not see
Was that the flower might be
Other than base and fetid:
That the flower had done but part,
And what the flower began
Her own too meager heart
Had terribly completed.
She looked and saw the worst.
And the dog or what it was,
Obeying bestial laws,
A coward save at night,
Turned from the place and ran.
She heard him stumble first
And use his hands in flight.
She heard him bark outright.
And oh, for one so young
The bitter words she spit
Like some tenacious bit
That will not leave the tongue.
She plucked her lips for it,
And still the horror clung.
Her mother wiped the foam
From her chin, picked up her comb
And drew her backward home.

Directive

Back out of all this now too much for us,
Back in a time made simple by the loss
Of detail, burned, dissolved, and broken off
Like graveyard marble sculpture in the weather,
There is a house that is no more a house
Upon a farm that is no more a farm
And in a town that is no more a town.
The road there, if you'll let a guide direct you
Who only has at heart your getting lost,
May seem as if it should have been a quarry—
Great monolithic knees the former town

Long since gave up pretense of keeping covered.
And there's a story in a book about it:
Besides the wear of iron wagon wheels
The ledges show lines ruled southeast northwest,
The chisel work of an enormous Glacier
That braced his feet against the Arctic Pole.
You must not mind a certain coolness from him
Still said to haunt this side of Panther Mountain.
Nor need you mind the serial ordeal
Of being watched from forty cellar holes
As if by eye pairs out of forty firkins.
As for the woods' excitement over you
That sends light rustle rushes to their leaves,
Charge that to upstart inexperience.
Where were they all not twenty years ago?
They think too much of having shaded out
A few old pecker-fretted apple trees.
Make yourself up a cheering song of how
Someone's road home from work this once was,
Who may be just ahead of you on foot
Or creaking with a buggy load of grain.
The height of the adventure is the height
Of country where two village cultures faded
Into each other. Both of them are lost.
And if you're lost enough to find yourself
By now, pull in your ladder road behind you
And put a sign up CLOSED to all but me.
Then make yourself at home. The only field
Now left's no bigger than a harness gall.
First there's the children's house of make believe,
Some shattered dishes underneath a pine,
The playthings in the playhouse of the children.
Weep for what little things could make them glad.
Then for the house that is no more a house,
But only a belilaced cellar hole,
Now slowly closing like a dent in dough.
This was no playhouse but a house in earnest.
Your destination and your destiny's
A brook that was the water of the house,
Cold as a spring as yet so near its source,

Too lofty and original to rage.
(We know the valley streams that when aroused
Will leave their tatters hung on barb and thorn.)
I have kept hidden in the instep arch
Of an old cedar at the waterside
A broken drinking goblet like the Grail
Under a spell so the wrong ones can't find it,
So can't get saved, as Saint Mark says they mustn't.
(I stole the goblet from the children's playhouse.)
Here are your waters and your watering place.
Drink and be whole again beyond confusion.

A Cliff Dwelling

There sandy seems the golden sky
And golden seems the sandy plain.
No habitation meets the eye
Unless in the horizon rim,
Some halfway up the limestone wall,
That spot of black is not a stain
Or shadow, but a cavern hole,
Where someone used to climb and crawl
To rest from his besetting fears.
I see the callus on his sole
The disappearing last of him
And of his race starvation slim,
Oh, years ago—ten thousand years.

Choose Something Like a Star

O Star (the fairest one in sight),
We grant your loftiness the right
To some obscurity of cloud—
It will not do to say of night,
Since dark is what brings out your light.
Some mystery becomes the proud.

But to be wholly taciturn
In your reserve is not allowed.
Say something to us we can learn
By heart and when alone repeat.
Say something! And it says, 'I burn.'
But say with what degree of heat.
Talk Fahrenheit, talk Centigrade.
Use language we can comprehend.
Tell us what elements you blend.
It gives us strangely little aid,
But does tell something in the end.
And steadfast as Keats' Eremite,
Not even stooping from its sphere,
It asks a little of us here.
It asks of us a certain height,
So when at times the mob is swayed
To carry praise or blame too far,
We may choose something like a star
To stay our minds on and be staid.

A Cabin in the Clearing

for Alfred Edwards

MIST

I don't believe the sleepers in this house
Know where they are.

SMOKE

     They've been here long enough
To push the woods back from around the house
And part them in the middle with a path.

MIST

And still I doubt if they know where they are.
And I begin to fear they never will.
All they maintain the path for is the comfort
Of visiting with the equally bewildered.
Nearer in plight their neighbors are than distance.

SMOKE

I am the guardian wraith of starlit smoke
That leans out this and that way from their chimney.
I will not have their happiness despaired of.

MIST

No one—not I—would give them up for lost
Simply because they don't know where they are.
I am the damper counterpart of smoke
That gives off from a garden ground at night
But lifts no higher than a garden grows.
I cotton to their landscape. That's who I am.
I am no further from their fate than you are.

SMOKE

They must by now have learned the native tongue.
Why don't they ask the Red Man where they are?

MIST

They often do, and none the wiser for it.
So do they also ask philosophers
Who come to look in on them from the pulpit.
They will ask anyone there is to ask—
In the fond faith accumulated fact
Will of itself take fire and light the world up.
Learning has been a part of their religion.

SMOKE

If the day ever comes when they know who
They are, they may know better where they are.
But who they are is too much to believe—
Either for them or the onlooking world.
They are too sudden to be credible.

MIST

Listen, they murmur talking in the dark
On what should be their daylong theme continued.
Putting the lamp out has not put their thought out.
Let us pretend the dewdrops from the eaves
Are you and I eavesdropping on their unrest—

A mist and smoke eavesdropping on a haze—
And see if we can tell the bass from the soprano.

Than smoke and mist who better could appraise
The kindred spirit of an inner haze.

One More Brevity

I opened the door so my last look
Should be taken outside a house and book.
Before I gave up seeing and slept
I said I would see how Sirius kept
His watch-dog eye on what remained
To be gone into if not explained.
But scarcely was my door ajar,
When past the leg I thrust for bar
Slipped in to be my problem guest,
Not a heavenly dog made manifest,
But an earthly dog of the carriage breed;
Who, having failed of the modern speed,
Now asked asylum—and I was stirred
To be the one so dog-preferred.
He dumped himself like a bag of bones,
He sighed himself a couple of groans,
And head to tail then firmly curled
Like swearing off on the traffic world.
I set him water, I set him food.
He rolled an eye with gratitude
(Or merely manners it may have been),
But never so much as lifted chin.
His hard tail loudly smacked the floor
As if beseeching me, "Please, no more,
I can't explain—tonight at least."
His brow was perceptibly trouble-creased.
So I spoke in terms of adoption thus:
"Gustie, old boy, Dalmatian Gus,
You're right, there's nothing to discuss.
Don't try to tell me what's on your mind,
The sorrow of having been left behind,

Or the sorrow of having run away.
All that can wait for the light of day.
Meanwhile feel obligation-free.
Nobody has to confide in me."
'Twas too one-sided a dialogue,
And I wasn't sure I was talking dog.
I broke off baffled. But all the same
In fancy, I ratified his name,
Gustie, Dalmatian Gus, that is,
And started shaping my life to his,
Finding him in his right supplies
And sharing his miles of exercise.

Next morning the minute I was about
He was at the door to be let out
With an air that said, "I have paid my call.
You mustn't feel hurt if now I'm all
For getting back somewhere or further on."
I opened the door and he was gone.
I was to taste in little the grief
That comes of dogs' lives being so brief,
Only a fraction of ours at most.
He might have been the dream of a ghost
In spite of the way his tail had smacked
My floor so hard and matter-of-fact.
And things have been going so strangely since
I wouldn't be too hard to convince,
I might even claim, he was Sirius
(Think of presuming to call him Gus)
The star itself, Heaven's greatest star,
Not a meteorite, but an avatar,
Who had made an overnight descent
To show by deeds he didn't resent
My having depended on him so long,
And yet done nothing about it in song.
A symbol was all he could hope to convey,
An intimation, a shot of ray,
A meaning I was supposed to seek,
And finding, wasn't disposed to speak.

The Draft Horse

With a lantern that wouldn't burn
In too frail a buggy we drove
Behind too heavy a horse
Through a pitch-dark limitless grove.

And a man came out of the trees
And took our horse by the head
And reaching back to his ribs
Deliberately stabbed him dead.

The ponderous beast went down
With a crack of a broken shaft.
And the night drew through the trees
In one long invidious draft.

The most unquestioning pair
That ever accepted fate
And the least disposed to ascribe
Any more than we had to to hate,

We assumed that the man himself
Or someone he had to obey
Wanted us to get down
And walk the rest of the way.

Questioning Faces

The winter owl banked just in time to pass
And save herself from breaking window glass.
And her wings straining suddenly aspread
Caught color from the last of evening red
In a display of underdown and quill
To glassed-in children at the window sill.

AMY LOWELL

(1874–1925)

The Pike

In the brown water,
Thick and silver-sheened in the sunshine,
Liquid and cool in the shade of the reeds,
A pike dozed.
Lost among the shadows of stems
He lay unnoticed.
Suddenly he flicked his tail,
And a green-and-copper brightness
Ran under the water.

Out from under the reeds
Came the olive-green light,
And orange flashed up
Through the sun-thickened water.
So the fish passed across the pool,
Green and copper,
A darkness and a gleam,
And the blurred reflections of the willows on the
      opposite bank
Received it.

Patterns

I walk down the garden paths,
And all the daffodils
Are blowing, and the bright blue squills.
I walk down the patterned garden-paths
In my stiff, brocaded gown.
With my powdered hair and jewelled fan,
I too am a rare
Pattern. As I wander down
The garden paths.

My dress is richly figured,
And the train
Makes a pink and silver stain
On the gravel, and the thrift
Of the borders.
Just a plate of current fashion,
Tripping by in high-heeled, ribboned shoes.
Not a softness anywhere about me,
Only whalebone and brocade.
And I sink on a seat in the shade
Of a lime tree. For my passion
Wars against the stiff brocade.
The daffodils and squills
Flutter in the breeze
As they please.
And I weep;
For the lime-tree is in blossom
And one small flower has dropped upon my bosom.

And the plashing of waterdrops
In the marble fountain
Comes down the garden-paths.
The dripping never stops.
Underneath my stiffened gown
Is the softness of a woman bathing in a marble basin,
A basin in the midst of hedges grown
So thick, she cannot see her lover hiding,
But she guesses he is near,
And the sliding of the water
Seems the stroking of a dear
Hand upon her.
What is Summer in a fine brocaded gown!
I should like to see it lying in a heap upon the ground.
All the pink and silver crumpled up on the ground.

I would be the pink and silver as I ran along the paths,
And he would stumble after,
Bewildered by my laughter.
I should see the sun flashing from his sword-hilt and the
     buckles on his shoes.

I would choose
To lead him in a maze along the patterned paths,
A bright and laughing maze for my heavy-booted lover.
Till he caught me in the shade,
And the buttons of his waistcoat bruised my body as he
    clasped me,
Aching, melting, unafraid.
With the shadows of the leaves and the sundrops,
And the plopping of the waterdrops,
All about us in the open afternoon—
I am very like to swoon
With the weight of this brocade,
For the sun sifts through the shade.

Underneath the fallen blossom
In my bosom,
Is a letter I have hid.
It was brought to me this morning by a rider from the Duke.
"Madam, we regret to inform you that Lord Hartwell
Died in action Thursday se'nnight."
As I read it in the white, morning sunlight,
The letters squirmed like snakes.
"Any answer, Madam," said my footman.
"No," I told him.
"See that the messenger takes some refreshment.
No, no answer."
And I walked into the garden,
Up and down the patterned paths,
In my stiff, correct brocade.
The blue and yellow flowers stood up proudly in the sun,
Each one.
I stood upright too,
Held rigid to the pattern
By the stiffness of my gown.
Up and down I walked,
Up and down.

In a month he would have been my husband.
In a month, here, underneath this lime,
We would have broke the pattern;

He for me, and I for him,
He as Colonel, I as Lady,
On this shady seat.
He had a whim
That sunlight carried blessing.
And I answered, "It shall be as you have said."
Now he is dead.

In Summer and in Winter I shall walk
Up and down
The patterned garden-paths
In my stiff, brocaded gown.
The squills and daffodils
Will give place to pillared roses, and to asters, and to snow.
I shall go
Up and down,
In my gown.
Gorgeously arrayed,
Boned and stayed,
And the softness of my body will be guarded from embrace
By each button, hook, and lace.
For the man who should loose me is dead,
Fighting with the Duke in Flanders,
In a pattern called a war.
Christ! What are patterns for?

Thompson's Lunch Room—
Grand Central Station

Study in Whites

Wax-white—
Floor, ceiling, walls.
Ivory shadows
Over the pavement
Polished to cream surfaces
By constant sweeping.
The big room is coloured like the petals
Of a great magnolia,

And has a patina
Of flower bloom
Which makes it shine dimly
Under the electric lamps.
Chairs are ranged in rows
Like sepia seeds
Waiting fulfilment.
The chalk-white spot of a cook's cap
Moves unglossily against the vaguely bright wall—
Dull chalk-white striking the retina like a blow
Through the wavering uncertainty of steam.
Vitreous-white of glasses with green reflections,
Ice-green carboys, shifting—greener, bluer—with the jar of
    moving water.
Jagged green-white bowls of pressed glass
Rearing snow-peaks of chipped sugar
Above the lighthouse-shaped castors
Of grey pepper and grey-white salt.
Grey-white placards: "Oyster Stew, Cornbeef Hash,
    Frankfurters":
Marble slabs veined with words in meandering lines.
Dropping on the white counter like horn notes
Through a web of violins,
The flat yellow lights of oranges,
The cube-red splashes of apples,
In high plated *épergnes*.
The electric clock jerks every half-minute:
"Coming!—Past!"
"Three beef-steaks and a chicken-pie,"
Bawled through a slide while the clock jerks heavily.
A man carries a china mug of coffee to a distant chair.
Two rice puddings and a salmon salad
Are pushed over the counter;
The unfulfilled chairs open to receive them.
A spoon falls upon the floor with the impact of metal striking
    stone,
And the sound throws across the room
Sharp, invisible zigzags
Of silver.

Spring Longing

The South wind blows open the folds of my dress,
My feet leave wet tracks in the earth of my garden,
The willows along the canal sing
                    with new leaves turned upon the wind.

    I walk along the tow-path
    Gazing at the level water.
    Should I see a ribbed edge
    Running upon its clearness,
    I should know that this was caused
    By the prow of the boat
    In which you are to return.

Vernal Equinox

The scent of hyacinths, like a pale mist, lies between me and
        my book;
And the South Wind, washing through the room,
Makes the candles quiver.
My nerves sting at a spatter of rain on the shutter,
And I am uneasy with the thrusting of green shoots
Outside, in the night.

Why are you not here to overpower me with your tense and
        urgent love?

Venus Transiens

        Tell me,
        Was Venus more beautiful
        Than you are,
        When she topped
        The crinkled waves,
        Drifting shoreward

On her plaited shell?
Was Botticelli's vision
Fairer than mine;
And were the painted rosebuds
He tossed his lady,
Of better worth
Than the words I blow about you
To cover your too great loveliness
As with a gauze
Of misted silver?
For me,
You stand poised
In the blue and buoyant air,
Cinctured by bright winds,
Treading the sunlight.
And the waves which precede you
Ripple and stir
The sands at my feet.

Bright Sunlight

The wind has blown a corner of your shawl
Into the fountain,
Where it floats and drifts
Among the lily-pads
Like a tissue of sapphires.
But you do not heed it,
Your fingers pick at the lichens
On the stone edge of the basin,
And your eyes follow the tall clouds
As they sail over the ilex-trees.

The Weather-Cock Points South

I put your leaves aside,
One by one:
The stiff, broad outer leaves;
The smaller ones,
Pleasant to touch, veined with purple;
The glazed inner leaves.
One by one
I parted you from your leaves,
Until you stood up like a white flower
Swaying slightly in the evening wind.

White flower,
Flower of wax, of jade, of unstreaked agate;
Flower with surfaces of ice,
With shadows faintly crimson.
Where in all the garden is there such a flower?
The stars crowd through the lilac leaves
To look at you.
The low moon brightens you with silver.

The bud is more than the calyx.
There is nothing to equal a white bud,
Of no colour, and of all,
Burnished by moonlight,
Thrust upon by a softly-swinging wind.

Shore Grass

The moon is cold over the sand-dunes,
And the clumps of sea-grasses flow and glitter;
The thin chime of my watch tells the quarter after midnight;
And still I hear nothing
But the windy beating of the sea.

Lilacs

Lilacs,
False blue,
White,
Purple,
Colour of lilac,
Your great puffs of flowers
Are everywhere in this my New England.
Among your heart-shaped leaves
Orange orioles hop like music-box birds and sing
Their little weak soft songs;
In the crooks of your branches
The bright eyes of song sparrows sitting on spotted eggs
Peer restlessly through the light and shadow
Of all Springs.
Lilacs in dooryards
Holding quiet conversations with an early moon;
Lilacs watching a deserted house
Settling sideways into the grass of an old road;
Lilacs, wind-beaten, staggering under a lopsided shock of
     bloom
Above a cellar dug into a hill.
You are everywhere.
You were everywhere.
You tapped the window when the preacher preached his
     sermon,
And ran along the road beside the boy going to school.
You stood by pasture-bars to give the cows good milking,
You persuaded the housewife that her dish pan was of silver
And her husband an image of pure gold.
You flaunted the fragrance of your blossoms
Through the wide doors of Custom Houses—
You, and sandal-wood, and tea,
Charging the noses of quill-driving clerks
When a ship was in from China.
You called to them: "Goose-quill men, goose-quill men,
May is a month for flitting,"
Until they writhed on their high stools

And wrote poetry on their letter-sheets behind the propped-
    up ledgers.
Paradoxical New England clerks,
Writing inventories in ledgers, reading the "Song of
    Solomon" at night,
So many verses before bed-time,
Because it was the Bible.
The dead fed you
Amid the slant stones of graveyards.
Pale ghosts who planted you
Came in the night-time
And let their thin hair blow through your clustered stems.
You are of the green sea,
And of the stone hills which reach a long distance.
You are of elm-shaded streets with little shops where they sell
    kites and marbles,
You are of great parks where everyone walks and nobody is at
    home.
You cover the blind sides of greenhouses
And lean over the top to say a hurry-word through the glass
To your friends, the grapes, inside.

Lilacs,
False blue,
White,
Purple,
Colour of lilac,
You have forgotten your Eastern origin,
The veiled women with eyes like panthers,
The swollen, aggressive turbans of jewelled Pashas.
Now you are a very decent flower,
A reticent flower,
A curiously clear-cut, candid flower,
Standing beside clean doorways,
Friendly to a house-cat and a pair of spectacles,
Making poetry out of a bit of moonlight
And a hundred or two sharp blossoms.

Maine knows you,
Has for years and years;
New Hampshire knows you,
And Massachusetts
And Vermont.
Cape Cod starts you along the beaches to Rhode Island;
Connecticut takes you from a river to the sea.
You are brighter than apples,
Sweeter than tulips,
You are the great flood of our souls
Bursting above the leaf-shapes of our hearts,
You are the smell of all Summers,
The love of wives and children,
The recollection of the gardens of little children,
You are State Houses and Charters
And the familiar treading of the foot to and fro on a road it
      knows.
May is lilac here in New England,
May is a thrush singing "Sun up!" on a tip-top ash-tree,
May is white clouds behind pine-trees
Puffed out and marching upon a blue sky.
May is a green as no other,
May is much sun through small leaves,
May is soft earth,
And apple-blossoms,
And windows open to a South wind.
May is a full light wind of lilac
From Canada to Narragansett Bay.

Lilacs,
False blue,
White,
Purple,
Colour of lilac.
Heart-leaves of lilac all over New England,
Roots of lilac under all the soil of New England,
Lilac in me because I am New England,
Because my roots are in it,
Because my leaves are of it,
Because my flowers are for it,

Because it is my country
And I speak to it of itself
And sing of it with my own voice
Since certainly it is mine.

Meeting-House Hill

I must be mad, or very tired,
When the curve of a blue bay beyond a railroad track
Is shrill and sweet to me like the sudden springing of a tune,
And the sight of a white church above thin trees in a city
     square
Amazes my eyes as though it were the Parthenon.
Clear, reticent, superbly final,
With the pillars of its portico refined to a cautious elegance,
It dominates the weak trees,
And the shot of its spire
Is cool, and candid,
Rising into an unresisting sky.
Strange meeting-house
Pausing a moment upon a squalid hill-top.
I watch the spire sweeping the sky,
I am dizzy with the movement of the sky,
I might be watching a mast
With its royals set full
Straining before a two-reef breeze.
I might be sighting a tea-clipper,
Tacking into the blue bay,
Just back from Canton
With her hold full of green and blue porcelain,
And a Chinese coolie leaning over the rail
Gazing at the white spire
With dull, sea-spent eyes.

Katydids

Shore of Lake Michigan

Katydids scraped in the dim trees,
And I thought they were little white skeletons
Playing the fiddle with a pair of finger-bones.

How long is it since Indians walked here,
Stealing along the sands with smooth feet?
How long is it since Indians died here
And the creeping sands scraped them bone from bone?
Dead Indians under the sands, playing their bones against
       strings of wampum.
The roots of new, young trees have torn their graves asunder,
But in the branches sit little white skeletons
Rasping a bitter death-dirge through the August night.

New Heavens for Old

I am useless.
What I do is nothing,
What I think has no savour.
There is an almanac between the windows:
It is of the year when I was born.

My fellows call to me to join them,
They shout for me,
Passing the house in a great wind of vermilion banners.
They are fresh and fulminant,
They are indecent and strut with the thought of it,
They laugh, and curse, and brawl,
And cheer a holocaust of "Who comes firsts!" at the iron
       fronts of the houses at the two edges of the street.
Young men with naked hearts jeering between iron house-
       fronts,
Young men with naked bodies beneath their clothes
Passionately conscious of them,
Ready to strip off their clothes,

Ready to strip off their customs, their usual routine,
Clamouring for the rawness of life,
In love with appetite,
Proclaiming it as a creed,
Worshipping youth,
Worshipping themselves.
They call for women and the women come,
They bare the whiteness of their lusts to the dead gaze of the
    old house-fronts,
They roar down the street like flame,
They explode upon the dead houses like new, sharp fire.

But I—
I arrange three roses in a Chinese vase:
A pink one,
A red one,
A yellow one.
I fuss over their arrangement.
Then I sit in a South window
And sip pale wine with a touch of hemlock in it,
And think of Winter nights,
And field-mice crossing and re-crossing
The spot which will be my grave.

Dissonance

From my window I can see the moonlight stroking the
    smooth surface of the river.
The trees are silent, there is no wind.
Admirable pre-Raphaelite landscape,
Lightly touched with ebony and silver.
I alone am out of keeping:
An angry red gash
Proclaiming the restlessness
Of an incongruous century.

GERTRUDE STEIN

(1874–1946)

from
Tender Buttons

Objects

A carafe, that is a blind glass.

A kind in glass and a cousin, a spectacle and nothing strange a single hurt color and an arrangement in a system to pointing. All this and not ordinary, not unordered in not resembling. The difference is spreading.

Glazed Glitter.

Nickel, what is nickel, it is originally rid of a cover.

The change in that is that red weakens an hour. The change has come. There is no search. But there is, there is that hope and that interpretation and sometime, surely any is unwelcome, sometime there is breath and there will be a sinecure and charming very charming is that clean and cleansing. Certainly glittering is handsome and convincing.

There is no gratitude in mercy and in medicine. There can be breakages in Japanese. That is no programme. That is no color chosen. It was chosen yesterday, that showed spitting and perhaps washing and polishing. It certainly showed no obligation and perhaps if borrowing is not natural there is some use in giving.

A substance in a cushion.

The change of color is likely and a difference a very little difference is prepared. Sugar is not a vegetable.

Callous is something that hardening leaves behind what will be soft if there is a genuine interest in there being present as many girls as men. Does this change. It shows that dirt is clean when there is a volume.

A cushion has that cover. Supposing you do not like to change, supposing it is very clear that there is no change in appearance, supposing that there is regularity and a costume is that any the worse than an oyster and an exchange. Come to season that is there any extreme use in feather and cotton. Is there not much more joy in a table and more chairs and very likely roundness and a place to put them.

A circle of fine card board and a chance to see a tassel.

What is the use of a violent kind of delightfulness if there is no pleasure in not getting tired of it. The question does not come before there is a quotation. In any kind of place there is a top to covering and it is a pleasure at any rate there is some venturing in refusing to believe nonsense. It shows what use there is in a whole piece if one uses it and it is extreme and very likely the little things could be dearer but in any case there is a bargain and if there is the best thing to do is to take it away and wear it and then be reckless be reckless and re-solved on returning gratitude.

Light blue and the same red with purple makes a change. It shows that there is no mistake. Any pink shows that and very likely it is reasonable. Very likely there should not be a finer fancy present. Some increase means a calamity and this is the best preparation for three and more being together. A little calm is so ordinary and in any case there is sweetness and some of that.

A seal and matches and a swan and ivy and a suit.

A closet, a closet does not connect under the bed. The band if it is white and black, the band has a green string. A sight a whole sight and a little groan grinding makes a trim-ming such a sweet singing trimming and a red thing not a round thing but a white thing, a red thing and a white thing.

The disgrace is not in carelessness nor even in sewing it comes out out of the way.

What is the sash like. The sash is not like anything mustard it is not like a same thing that has stripes, it is not even more hurt than that, it has a little top.

A box.

Out of kindness comes redness and out of rudeness comes rapid same question, out of an eye comes research, out of selection comes painful cattle. So then the order is that a white way of being round is something suggesting a pin and is it disappointing, it is not, it is so rudimentary to be analysed and see a fine substance strangely, it is so earnest to have a green point not to red but to point again.

A piece of coffee.

More of double.

A place in no new table.

A single image is not splendor. Dirty is yellow. A sign of more in not mentioned. A piece of coffee is not a detainer. The resemblance to yellow is dirtier and distincter. The clean mixture is whiter and not coal color, never more coal color than altogether.

The sight of a reason, the same sight slighter, the sight of a simpler negative answer, the same sore sounder, the intention to wishing, the same splendor, the same furniture.

The time to show a message is when too late and later there is no hanging in a blight.

A not torn rose-wood color. If it is not dangerous then a pleasure and more than any other if it is cheap is not cheaper. The amusing side is that the sooner there are no fewer the more certain is the necessity dwindled. Supposing that the case contained rose-wood and a color. Supposing that there was no reason for a distress and more likely for a number, supposing that there was no astonishment, is it not necessary to mingle astonishment.

The settling of stationing cleaning is one way not to shatter scatter and scattering. The one way to use custom is to use soap and silk for cleaning. The one way to see cotton is to have a design concentrating the illusion and the illustration. The perfect way is to accustom the thing to have a lining and the shape of a ribbon and to be solid, quite solid in standing and to use heaviness in morning. It is light enough in that. It has that shape nicely. Very nicely may not be exaggerating. Very strongly may be sincerely fainting. May be strangely flattering. May not be strange in everything. May not be strange to.

Dirt and not copper.

Dirt and not copper makes a color darker. It makes the shape so heavy and makes no melody harder. It makes mercy and relaxation and even a strength to spread a table fuller. There are more places not empty. They see cover.

Nothing elegant.

A charm a single charm is doubtful. If the red is rose and there is a gate surrounding it, if inside is let in and there places change then certainly something is upright. It is earnest.

Mildred's umbrella.

A cause and no curve, a cause and loud enough, a cause and extra a loud clash and an extra wagon, a sign of extra, a sac a small sac and an established color and cunning, a slender grey and no ribbon, this means a loss a great loss a restitution.

A method of a cloak.

A single climb to a line, a straight exchange to a cane, a desperate adventure and courage and a clock, all this which is a system, which has feeling, which has resignation and success, all makes an attractive black silver.

A red stamp.

If lilies are lily white if they exhaust noise and distance and even dust, if they dusty will dirt a surface that has no extreme grace, if they do this and it is not necessary it is not at all necessary if they do this they need a catalogue.

A box.

A large box is handily made of what is necessary to replace any substance. Suppose an example is necessary, the plainer it is made the more reason there is for some outward recognition that there is a result.

A box is made sometimes and them to see to see to it neatly and to have the holes stopped up makes it necessary to use paper.

A custom which is necessary when a box is used and taken is that a large part of the time there are three which have different connections. The one is on the table. The two are on the table. The three are on the table. The one, one is the same length as is shown by the cover being longer. The other is different there is more cover that shows it. The other is different and that makes the corners have the same shade the eight are in singular arrangement to make four necessary.

Lax, to have corners, to be lighter than some weight, to indicate a wedding journey, to last brown and not curious, to be wealthy, cigarettes are established by length and by doubling.

Left open, to be left pounded, to be left closed, to be circulating in summer and winter, and sick color that is grey that is not dusty and red shows, to be sure cigarettes do measure an empty length sooner than a choice in color.

Winged, to be winged means that white is yellow and pieces pieces that are brown are dust color if dust is washed off, then it is choice that is to say it is fitting cigarettes sooner than paper.

An increase why is an increase idle, why is silver cloister, why is the spark brighter, if it is brighter is there any result, hardly more than ever.

A plate.

An occasion for a plate, an occasional resource is in buying and how soon does washing enable a selection of the same thing neater. If the party is small a clever song is in order.

Plates and a dinner set of colored china. Pack together a string and enough with it to protect the center, cause a considerable haste and gather more as it is cooling, collect more trembling and not any even trembling, cause a whole thing to be a church.

A sad size a size that is not sad is blue as every bit of blue is precocious. A kind of green a game in green and nothing flat nothing quite flat and more round, nothing a particular color strangely, nothing breaking the losing of no little piece.

A splendid address a really splendid address is not shown by giving a flower freely, it is not shown by a mark or by wetting.

Cut cut in white, cut in white so lately. Cut more than any other and show it. Show it in the stem and in starting and in evening coming complication.

A lamp is not the only sign of glass. The lamp and the cake are not the only sign of stone. The lamp and the cake and the cover are not the only necessity altogether.

A plan a hearty plan, a compressed disease and no coffee, not even a card or a change to incline each way, a plan that has that excess and that break is the one that shows filling.

A seltzer bottle.

Any neglect of many particles to a cracking, any neglect of this makes around it what is lead in color and certainly discolor in silver. The use of this is manifold. Supposing a certain time selected is assured, suppose it is even necessary, suppose no other extract is permitted and no more handling is needed, suppose the rest of the message is mixed with a very long slender needle and even if it could be any black border, supposing all this altogether made a dress and suppose it was actual, suppose the mean way to state it was occasional, if you suppose this in August and even more melodiously, if you suppose this even in the necessary incident of there certainly being no middle in summer and winter, suppose this and an elegant settlement a very elegant settlement is more than of consequence, it is not final and sufficient and substituted. This which was so kindly a present was constant.

A long dress.

What is the current that makes machinery, that makes it crackle, what is the current that presents a long line and a necessary waist. What is this current.

What is the wind, what is it.

Where is the serene length, it is there and a dark place is not a dark place, only a white and red are black, only a yellow and green are blue, a pink is scarlet, a bow is every color. A line distinguishes it. A line just distinguishes it.

A red hat.

A dark grey, a very dark grey, a quite dark grey is monstrous ordinarily, it is so monstrous because there is no red in it. If red is in everything it is not necessary. Is that not an argument for any use of it and even so is there any place that is better, is there any place that has so much stretched out.

A blue coat.

A blue coat is guided guided away, guided and guided away, that is the particular color that is used for that length and not any width not even more than a shadow.

A piano.

If the speed is open, if the color is careless, if the event is overtaken, if the selection of a strong scent is not awkward, if the button holder is held by all the waving color and there is no color, not any color. If there is no dirt in a pin and there can be none scarcely, if there is not then the place is the same as up standing.

This is no dark custom and it even is not acted in any such a way that a restraint is not spread. That is spread, it shuts and it lifts and awkwardly not awkwardly the center is in standing.

A chair.

A widow in a wise veil and more garments shows that shadows are even. It addresses no more, it shadows the stage and learning. A regular arrangement, the severest and the most preserved is that which has the arrangement not more than always authorised.

A suitable establishment, well housed, practical, patient and staring, a suitable bedding, very suitable and not more particularly than complaining, anything suitable is so necessary.

A fact is that when the direction is just like that, no more, longer, sudden and at the same time not any sofa, the main action is that without a blaming there is no custody.

Practice measurement, practice the sign that means that really means a necessary betrayal, in showing that there is wearing.

Hope, what is a spectacle, a spectacle is the resemblance be-
tween the circular side place and nothing else, nothing else.

To choose it is ended, it is actual and more than that it has
it certainly has the same treat, and a seat all that is practiced
and more easily much more easily ordinarily.

Pick a barn, a whole barn, and bend more slender accents
than have ever been necessary, shine in the darkness necessarily.

Actually not aching, actually not aching, a stubborn bloom
is so artificial and even more than that, it is a spectacle, it is a
binding accident, it is animosity and accentuation.

If the chance to dirty diminishing is necessary, if it is why is
there no complexion, why is there no rubbing, why is there
no special protection.

A frightful release.

A bag which was left and not only taken but turned away
was not found. The place was shown to be very like the last
time. A piece was not exchanged, not a bit of it, a piece was
left over. The rest was mismanaged.

A purse.

A purse was not green, it was not straw color, it was hardly
seen and it has a use a long use and the chain, the chain was
never missing, it was not misplaced, it showed that it was
open, that is all that it showed.

A mounted umbrella.

What was the use of not leaving it there where it would
hang what was the use if there was no chance of ever seeing
it come there and show that it was handsome and right in the
way it showed it. The lesson is to learn that it does show it,
that it shows it and that nothing, that there is nothing, that
there is no more to do about it and just so much more is
there plenty of reason for making an exchange.

A cloth.

Enough cloth is plenty and more, more is almost enough
for that and besides if there is no more spreading is there
plenty of room for it. Any occasion shows the best way.

More.

An elegant use of foliage and grace and a little piece of white cloth and oil.

Wondering so winningly in several kinds of oceans is the reason that makes red so regular and enthusiastic. The reason that there is more snips are the same shining very colored rid of no round color.

A new cup and saucer.

Enthusiastically hurting a clouded yellow bud and saucer, enthusiastically so is the bite in the ribbon.

Objects.

Within, within the cut and slender joint alone, with sudden equals and no more than three, two in the center make two one side.

If the elbow is long and it is filled so then the best example is all together.

The kind of show is made by squeezing.

Eye glasses.

A color in shaving, a saloon is well placed in the center of an alley.

A cutlet.

A blind agitation is manly and uttermost.

Careless water.

No cup is broken in more places and mended, that is to say a plate is broken and mending does do that it shows that culture is japanese. It shows the whole element of angels and orders. It does more to choosing and it does more to that ministering counting. It does, it does change in more water.

Supposing a single piece is a hair supposing more of them are orderly, does that show that strength, does that show that joint, does that show that balloon famously. Does it.

A paper.

A courteous occasion makes a paper show no such occasion and this makes readiness and eyesight and likeness and a stool.

A drawing.

The meaning of this is entirely and best to say the mark, best to say it best to show sudden places, best to make bitter, best to make the length tall and nothing broader, anything between the half.

Water raining.

Water astonishing and difficult altogether makes a meadow and a stroke.

Cold climate.

A season in yellow sold extra strings makes lying places.

Malachite.

The sudden spoon is the same in no size. The sudden spoon is the wound in the decision.

An umbrella.

Coloring high means that the strange reason is in front not more in front behind. Not more in front in peace of the dot.

A petticoat.

A light white, a disgrace, an ink spot, a rosy charm.

A waist.

A star glide, a single frantic sullenness, a single financial grass greediness.

Object that is in wood. Hold the pine, hold the dark, hold in the rush, make the bottom.

A piece of crystal. A change, in a change that is remarkable there is no reason to say that there was a time.

A woolen object gilded. A country climb is the best disgrace, a couple of practices any of them in order is so left.

A time to eat.

A pleasant simple habitual and tyrannical and authorised and educated and resumed and articulate separation. This is not tardy.

A little bit of a tumbler.

A shining indication of yellow consists in there having been more of the same color than could have been expected when all four were bought. This was the hope which made the six and seven have no use for any more places and this necessarily spread into nothing. Spread into nothing.

A fire.

What was the use of a whole time to send and not send if there was to be the kind of thing that made that come in. A letter was nicely sent.

A handkerchief.

A winning of all the blessings, a sample not a sample because there is no worry.

Red roses.

A cool red rose and a pink cut pink, a collapse and a sold hole, a little less hot.

In between.

In between a place and candy is a narrow foot path that shows more mounting than anything, so much really that a calling meaning a bolster measured a whole thing with that. A virgin a whole virgin is judged made and so between curves and outlines and real seasons and more out glasses and a perfectly unprecedented arrangement between old ladies and mild colds there is no satin wood shining.

Colored Hats.

Colored hats are necessary to show that curls are worn by an addition of blank spaces, this makes the difference between single lines and broad stomachs, the least thing is lightening, the least thing means a little flower and a big delay a big delay that makes more nurses than little women really little women. So clean is a light that nearly all of it shows pearls and little ways. A large hat is tall and me and all custard whole.

A feather.

A feather is trimmed, it is trimmed by the light and the bug and the post, it is trimmed by little leaning and by all sorts of mounted reserves and loud volumes. It is surely cohesive.

A brown.

A brown which is not liquid not more so is relaxed and yet there is a change, a news is pressing.

A little called Pauline.

A little called anything shows shudders.

Come and say what prints all day. A whole few watermelon. There is no pope.

No cut in pennies and little dressing and choose wide soles and little spats really little spices.

A little lace makes boils. This is not true.

Gracious of gracious and a stamp a blue green white bow a blue green lean, lean on the top.

If it is absurd then it is leadish and nearly set in where there is a tight head.

A peaceful life to arise her, noon and moon and moon. A letter a cold sleeve a blanket a shaving house and nearly the best and regular window.

Nearer in fairy sea, nearer and farther, show white has lime in sight, show a stitch of ten. Count, count more so that thicker and thicker is leaning.

I hope she has her cow. Bidding a wedding, widening received treading, little leading, mention nothing.

Cough out cough out in the leather and really feather it is not for.

Please could, please could, jam it not plus more sit in when.

A sound.

Elephant beaten with candy and little pops and chews all bolts and reckless reckless rats, this is this.

A table.

A table means does it not my dear it means a whole steadiness. Is it likely that a change.

A table means more than a glass even a looking glass is tall. A table means necessary places and a revision a revision of a little thing it means it does mean that there has been a stand, a stand where it did shake.

Shoes.

To be a wall with a damper a stream of pounding way and nearly enough choice makes a steady midnight. It is pus.

A shallow hole rose on red, a shallow hole in and in this makes ale less. It shows shine.

A dog.

A little monkey goes like a donkey that means to say that means to say that more sighs last goes. Leave with it. A little monkey goes like a donkey.

A white hunter.

A white hunter is nearly crazy.

A leave.

In the middle of a tiny spot and nearly bare there is a nice thing to say that wrist is leading. Wrist is leading.

Suppose an eyes.

Suppose it is within a gate which open is open at the hour of closing summer that is to say it is so.

All the seats are needing blackening. A white dress is in sign. A soldier a real soldier has a worn lace a worn lace of different sizes that is to say if he can read, if he can read he is a size to show shutting up twenty-four.

Go red go red, laugh white.

Suppose a collapse in rubbed purr, in rubbed purr get.

Little sales ladies little sales ladies little saddles of mutton.

Little sales of leather and such beautiful beautiful, beautiful beautiful.

A shawl.

A shawl is a hat and hurt and a red ballon and an under coat and a sizer a sizer of talks.

A shawl is a wedding, a piece of wax a little build. A shawl.

Pick a ticket, pick it in strange steps and with hollows. There is hollow hollow belt, a belt is a shawl.

A plate that has a little bobble, all of them, any so.

Please a round it is ticket.

It was a mistake to state that a laugh and a lip and a laid climb and a depot and a cultivator and little choosing is a point it.

Book.

Book was there, it was there. Book was there. Stop it, stop it, it was a cleaner, a wet cleaner and it was not where it was wet, it was not high, it was directly placed back, not back again, back, it was returned, it was needless, it put a bank, a bank when, a bank care.

Suppose a man a realistic expression of resolute reliability suggests pleasing itself white all white and no head does that mean soap. It does not so. It means kind wavers and little chance to beside beside rest. A plain.

Suppose ear rings, that is one way to breed, breed that. Oh chance to say, oh nice old pole. Next best and nearest a pillar. Chest not valuable, be papered.

Cover up cover up the two with a little piece of string and hope rose and green, green.

Please a plate, put a match to the seam and really then really then, really then it is a remark that joins many many lead games. It is a sister and sister and a flower and a flower and a dog and a colored sky a sky colored grey and nearly that nearly that let.

Peeled pencil, choke.

Rub her coke.

It was black, black took.

Black ink best wheel bale brown.

Excellent not a hull house, not a pea soup, no bill no care, no precise no past pearl pearl goat.

This is this dress, aider.

Aider, why aider why whow, whow stop touch, aider whow, aider stop the muncher, muncher munchers.

A jack in kill her, a jack in, makes a meadowed king, makes a to let.

Susie Asado

Sweet sweet sweet sweet sweet tea.
      Susie Asado.
Sweet sweet sweet sweet sweet tea.
      Susie Asado.
Susie Asado which is a told tray sure.
A lean on the shoe this means slips slips hers.
When the ancient light grey is clean it is yellow, it is a silver seller.
This is a please this is a please there are the saids to jelly. These are the wets these say the sets to leave a crown to Incy.
Incy is short for incubus.
A pot. A pot is a beginning of a rare bit of trees. Trees tremble, the old vats are in bobbles, bobbles which shade and shove and render clean, render clean must.
      Drink pups.
Drink pups drink pups lease a sash hold, see it shine and a bobolink has pins. It shows a nail.
What is a nail. A nail is unison.
Sweet sweet sweet sweet sweet tea.

from
Lifting Belly

Lifting Belly Is So Kind

Kiss my lips. She did.
Kiss my lips again she did.
Kiss my lips over and over and over again she did.

I have feathers.

Gentle fishes.

Do you think about apricots. We find them very beautiful. It is not alone their color it is their seeds that charm us. We find it a change.

Lifting belly is so strange.

I came to speak about it.

Selected raisins well then grapes grapes are good.

Change your name.

Question and garden.

It's raining. Don't speak about it.

My baby is a dumpling I want to tell her something.

Wax candles. We have bought a great many wax candles. Some are decorated. They have not been lighted.

I do not mention roses.

Exactly.

Actually.

Question and butter.

I find the butter very good.

Lifting belly is so kind.

Lifting belly fattily.

Doesn't that astonish you.

You did want me.

Say it again.

Strawberry.

Lifting beside belly.

Lifting kindly belly.

Sing to me I say.

Some are wives not heroes.

Lifting belly merely.

Sing to me I say.

Lifting belly. A reflection.

Lifting belly adjoins more prizes.

Fit to be.

I have fit on a hat.

Have you.

What did you say to excuse me. Difficult paper and scattered.

Lifting belly is so kind.

What shall you say about that. Lifting belly is so kind.

What is a veteran.

A veteran is one who has fought.

Who is the best.

The king and the queen and the mistress.

Nobody has a mistress.

Lifting belly is so kind.

To-day we decided to forgive Nellie.

Anybody can describe dresses.

How do you do what is the news.

Lifting belly is so kind.

Lifting belly exactly.

The king and the prince of Montenegro.

Lifting belly is so kind.

Lifting belly to please me.

Excited.

Excited are you.

I can whistle, the train can whistle we can hear the whistle, the boat whistle. The train is not running to-day. Mary whistle whistle for the whim.

Didn't you say you'd write it better.

Mrs. Vettie. It is necessary to have a Ford.

Yes sir.

Dear Mrs. Vettie. Smile to me.

I am.

Dear Mrs. Vettie never better.

Yes indeed so.

Lifting belly is most kind.

What did I say, that I was a great poet like the English only sweeter.

When I think of this afternoon and the garden I see what you mean.

You are not thinking of the pleasure.

Lifting belly again.

What did I mention when I drew a pansy that pansy and petunia both begin with p.

Lifting belly splendidly.

We have wishes.

Let us say we know it.

Did I say anything about it. I know the title. We know the title.

Lifting belly is so kind.
We have made no mistake.
The Montenegrin family.
A condition to a wide admiration.
Lifting belly before all.
You don't mean disobedience.
Lifting belly all around.
Eat the little girl I say.
Listen to me. Did you expect it to go back. Why do you do
to stop.
What do you do to stop.
What do you do to go on.
I do the same.
Yes wishes. Oh yes wishes.
What do you do to turn a corner.
What do you do to sing.
We don't mention singing.
What do you do to be reformed.
You know.
Yes wishes.
What do you do to measure.
I do it in such a way.
I hope to see them come.
Lifting belly go around.
I was sorry to be blistered.
We were such company.
Did she say jelly.
Jelly my jelly.
Lifting belly is so round.
Big Caesars.
Two Caesars.
Little seize her.
Too.
Did I do my duty.
Did I wet my knife.
No I don't mean whet.
Exactly four teeth.
Little belly is so kind.
What did you say about accepting.
Yes.

Lifting belly another lifting belly.
I question the weather.
It is not necessary.
Lifting belly oh lifting belly in time.
Yes indeed.
Be to me.
Did you say this was this.
Mr. Louis.
Do not mention Mr. Louis.
Little axes.
Yes indeed little axes and rubbers.
This is a description of an automobile.
I understand all about them.
Lifting belly is so kind.
So is whistling.
A great many whistles are shrill.
Lifting belly connects.
Lifting belly again.
Sympathetic blessing.
Not curls.
Plenty of wishes.
All of them fulfilled.
Lifting belly you don't say so.
Climb trees.
Lifting belly has sparks.
Sparks of anger and money.
Lifting belly naturally celebrates.
We naturally celebrate.
Connect me in places.
Lifting belly.
No no don't say that.
Lifting belly oh yes.
Tax this.
Running behind a mountain.
I fly to thee.
Lifting belly.
Shall I chat.
I mean pugilists.
Oh yes trainer.
Oh yes yes.

Say it again to study.
It has been perfectly fed.
Oh yes I do.
Belly alright.
Lifting belly very well.
Lifting belly this.
So sweet.
To me.
Say anything a pudding made of Caesars.
Lobster. Baby is so good to baby.
I correct blushes. You mean wishes.
I collect pearls. Yes and colors.
All colors are dogs. Oh yes Beddlington.
Now I collect songs.
Lifting belly is so nice.
I wrote about it to him.
I wrote about it to her.
Not likely not very likely that they will seize rubber. Not
very likely that they will seize rubber.
Lifting belly yesterday.
And to-day.
And to-morrow.
A train to-morrow.
Lifting belly is so exacting.
Lifting belly asks any more.
Lifting belly captures.
Seating.
Have a swim.
Lifting belly excuses.
Can you swim.
Lifting belly for me.
When this you see remember me.
Oh yes.
Yes.
Researches and a cab.
A cab right.
Lifting belly phlegmatically.
Bathing bathing in bliss.
I am very well satisfied with meat.
Kindness to my wife.

Lifting belly to a throne.
Search it for me.
Yes wishes.
I say it again I am perfection in behavior and circumstance.
Oh yes alright.
Levelheaded fattuski.
I do not wish to be Polish.
Quite right in singing.
Lifting belly is so recherché.
Lifting belly.
Up.
Correct me.
I believe he makes together of pieces.
Lifting belly.
Not that.
Think of me.
Oh yes.
Lifting belly for me.
Right there.
Not that yesterday.
Fetch missions.
Lifting belly or Dora.
Lifting belly.
Yes Misses.
Lifting belly separately all day.
I say lifting belly.
An example.
A good example.
Cut me a slice.
You see what I wish.
I wish a seat and Caesar.
Caesar is plural.
I can think.
And so can I.
And argue.
Oh yes you see.
What I see.
You see me.
Yes stretches.
Stretches and stretches of happiness.

Should you have put it away.
Yes you should have put it away.
Do not think so much.
I do not.
Have you a new title.
Lifting belly articulately.
It is not a problem.
Kissing and singing.
We have the habit when we wash.
In singing we say how do you do how do you like the war.
Little dumps of it.
Did you hear that man. What did he say close it.
Lifting belly lifting pleasure.
What can we say about wings.
Wings and refinement.
Come to me.
Sleepy.
Sleepily we think.
Wings after lunch.
I don't think.
No don't I regret a silver sugar.
And I platinum knitting needles.
And I sherry glasses.
I do not care for sherry I used to use it for castor-oil.
You mean licorice.
He is so fond of coffee.
Let me tell you about kissing. We saw a piece of mistletoe.
We exchanged a pillow. We murmured training and we were
asleep.
This is what happened Saturday.
Another day we said sour grass it grows in fields. So do
daisies and green flowers.
I have never noticed green flowers.
Lifting belly is my joy.
What did I tell Caesars.
That I recognised them.
It is the custom to answer swimming.
Catch a call.
Does the moonlight make any difference to you.
Lifting belly yes Miss.

I can lean upon a pencil.
Lifting belly yes address me.
I address you.
Lifting belly magnetically.
Did you make a mistake.
Wave to me.
Lifting belly permanently.
What did the Caesars.
What did they all say.
They said that they were not deceived.
Lifting belly such a good example. And is so readily watch-
ful.
What do you think of watches.
Collect lobsters.
And sweetbreads.
And a melon.
And salad.
Do not have a term.
You mean what do you call it.
Yes sir.
Sing to me.
Lifting belly is neglected.
The Caesar.
Oh yes the Caesar.
Oh yes the Caesar.
Lifting belly pencils to me.
And pens.
Lifting belly and the intention.
I particularly like what I know.
Lifting belly sublimely.
We made a fire this evening.
Cooking is cheap.
I do not care for Ethel.
That's a very good one. I say that's a very good one.
Yes and we think.
A rhyme, I understand nectarine. I also understand egg.
A special case you are.
Lifting belly and Caesar.
Did I explain it.
Have I explained it to you.

Have I explained it to you in season. Have I perplexed you. You have not perplexed me nor mixed me. You have addressed me as Caesar. This is the answer that I expected. When I said do not mention any words I meant no indifference. I meant do your duty and do not forget that I establish myself.

You establish yourself.

When this you see believe me.

Lifting belly etcetera.

Lifting belly and a hand. A hand is black and not by toil. I do not like fat resemblances. There are none such.

Lifting belly and kind.

This is the pencil for me.

Lifting belly squeezes.

Remember what I said about a rhyme.

Don't call it again.

Say white spots.

Do not mention disappointment in cups.

Oh you are so sweet.

Lifting belly believe me.

Believe it is for pleasure that I do it.

Not foreign pleasure.

Oh no.

My pleasure in Susie.

Lifting belly so kind.

So kindly.

Lifting belly gratuitously.

Lifting belly increase.

Do this to me.

Lifting belly famously.

When did I say I thought it.

When you heard it.

Oh yes.

Bright eyes I make you ties.

No mockings.

This is to say I knit woolen stockings for you. And I understand it and I am very grateful.

Making a spectacle.

Drinking prepared water.

Laughing together.

Asking lifting belly to be particular.
Lifting belly is so kind.
She was like that.
Star spangled banner, story of Savannah.
She left because she was going to have the child with her.
Lifting belly don't think of it.
Believe me in truth and marriage.
Believe that I use the best paper that I can get.
Do you believe me.
Lifting belly is not an invitation.
Call me semblances.
I call you a cab sir.
That's the way she tells it.
Lifting belly is so accurate.
I congratulate you in being respectable and respectably married.
Call me Helen.
Not at all.
You may call me Helen.
That's what we said.
Lifting belly with firmness and pride.
Lifting belly with industry beside.
Heated heated with cold.
Some people are heated with linen.
Lifting belly comes extra.
This is a picture of lifting belly having a cow.
Oh yes you can say it of me.
When this you see remember me.
Lifting belly says pardon.
Pardon for what.
For having made a mistake.
Can you imagine what I say.
I say impossible.
Lifting belly is recognised.
Lifting belly presumably.
Do we run together.
I say do we run together.
I do not like stubbornness.
Come and sing.
Lifting belly.

I sing lifting belly.

I say lifting belly and then I say lifting belly and Caesars. I say lifting belly gently and Caesars gently. I say lifting belly again and Caesars again. I say lifting belly and I say Caesars and I say lifting belly Caesars and cow come out. I say lifting belly and Caesars and cow come out.

Can you read my print.

Lifting belly say can you see the Caesars. I can see what I kiss.

Of course you can.

Lifting belly high.

That is what I adore always more and more.

Come out cow.

Little connections.

Yes oh yes cow come out.

Lifting belly unerringly.

A wonderful book.

Baby my baby I backhand for thee.

She is a sweet baby and well baby and me.

This is the way I see it.

Lifting belly can you say it.

Lifting belly persuade me.

Lifting belly persuade me.

You'll find it very easy to sing to me.

What can you say.

Lifting belly set.

I can not pass a door.

You mean odor.

I smell sweetly.

So do you.

Lifting belly plainly.

Can you sing.

Can you sing for me.

Lifting belly settled.

Can you excuse money.

Lifting belly has a dress.

Lifting belly in a mess.

Lifting belly in order.

Complain I don't complain.

She is my sweetheart.

Why doesn't she resemble an other.
This I cannot say here.
Full of love and echoes. Lifting belly is full of love.
Can you.
Can you can you.
Can you buy a Ford.
Did you expect that.
Lifting belly hungrily.
Not lonesomely.
But enthusiastically.
Lifting belly altogether.
Were you wise.
Were you wise to do so.
Can you say winking.
Can you say Francis Ferdinand has gone to the West.
Can you neglect me.
Can you establish the clock.
Yes I can when I am good.
Lifting belly precariously.
Lifting belly is noted.
Are you noted with me.
Come to sing and sit.
This is not the time for discussion.
A splendid table little table.
A splendid little table.
Can you be fortunate.
Yes sir.
What is a man.
What is a woman.
What is a bird.
Lifting belly must please me.
Yes can you think so.
Lifting belly cherished and flattered.
Lifting belly naturally.
Can you extract.
Can you be through so quickly.
No I cannot get through so quickly.
Are you afraid of negro sculpture.
I have my feelings.
Lifting belly is so exact.

Lifting belly is favored by me.
Lifting belly cautiously.
I lift it in place of the music.
You mean it is the same.
I mean everything.
Can you not whistle.
Call me for that.
And sing.
I sing too.
Lifting belly counts.
My idea is.
Yes I know what your idea is.
Lifting belly knows all about the wind.
Yes indeed Miss.
Yes indeed.
Can you suspect me.
We are glad that we do not deceive.
Lifting belly or regular.
Lifted belly behind.
Candidly.
Can you say that there is a mistake.
In the wash.
No in respect to the woman.
Can you say we meant to send her away.
Lifting belly is so orderly.
She makes no mistake.
She does not indeed.
Lifting belly heroically.
Can you think of that.
Can you guess what I mean.
Yes I can.
Lovely sweet.
Calville cow.
And that is it.
Lifting belly resignedly.
Now you laugh.
Lifting belly for me.
When this you see remember me.
Can you be sweet.
You are.

We are so likely.
We are so likely to be sweet.
Lifting belly handy.
Can you mention lifting belly. I can.
Yes indeed I know what I say.
Do you.
Lifting belly is so much.
Lifting belly grandly.
You can be sweet.
We see it.
We are tall.
We are wellbred.
We can say we do like what we have.
Lifting belly is mine.
I am more than ever inclined to how do you do. That's the way to wish it.
Lifting belly is so good.
That is natural.
Lifting belly exactly.
Calville cow is all to me.
Don't excite me.
Lifting belly exactly.
That's respectable.
Lifting belly is all to me.
Pretty Caesars yes they do.
Can you spell mixing.
I hear you.
How do you do.
Can you tell me about imposing.
When are you careful to speak.
Lifting belly categorically.
Think of it.
Lifting belly in the mind.
The Honorable Graham Murray.
My honorable Graham Murray.
What can you say.
I can say that I find it most useful and very warm, yet light.
Lifting belly astonishingly.
Can you mention her brother.
Yes.

Her father.
Yes.
A married couple.
Yes.
Lifting belly names it.
Look at that.
Yes that's what I said.
I put down something on lifting belly.
Humph.
Lifting belly bells.
Can you think of singing. In the little while in which I say
stop it you are not spoiled.
Can you be spoiled. I do not think so.
I think not.
I think everything of you.
Lifting belly is rich.
Chickens are rich.
I cannot disguise nice.
Don't you need to.
I think not.
Lifting belly exactly.
Why can lifting belly please me.
Lifting belly can please me because it is an occupation I
enjoy.
Rose is a rose is a rose is a rose.
In print on top.
What can you do.
I can answer my question.
Very well answer this.
Who is Mr. Mc Bride.
In the way of laughing.
Lifting belly is an intention.
You are sure you know the meaning of any word.
Leave me to see.
Pink.
My pink.
Hear me to-day.
It is after noon.
I mean that literally.
It is after noon.

Little lifting belly is a quotation.
Frankly what do you say to me.
I say that I need protection.
You shall have it.
After that what do you wish.
I want you to mean a great deal to me.
Exactly.
And then.
And then blandishment.
We can see that very clearly.
Lifting belly is perfect.
Do you stretch farther.
Come eat it.
What did I say.
To whom.
Calville or a cow.
We were in a fashion deceived in Calville but not in a cow.
I understand when they say they mean something by it.
Lifting belly grandly.
Lifting belly sufficiently.
Come and be awake.
Certainly this morning.
Lifting belly very much.
I do not feel that I will be deceived.
Lifting belly fairly.
You mean follow.
I mean I follow.
Need you wish me to say lifting belly is recognised. No it is
not necessary lifting belly is not peculiar. It is recognised. Can
you recognise it. In a flash.
Thank you for me.
Can you excuse any one for loving its dearest. I said from.
That is eaten.
Can you excuse any one from loving its dearest.
No I cannot.
A special fabric.
Can you begin a new thing.
Can I begin.
We have a dress.
You have a dress.

A dress by him.
Feel me.
I feel you.
Then it is fair to me.
Let me sing.
Certainly.
And you too Miss Polly.
What can you say.
I can say that there is no need of regretting a ball.
Mount Fatty.
That is a tremendous way.
Leave me to sing about it to-day.
And then there was a cake. Please give it to me. She did.
When can there be glasses. We are so pleased with it.
Go on to-morrow.
He cannot understand women. I can.
Believe me in this way.
I can understand the woman.
Lifting belly carelessly. I do not lift baby carelessly.
Lifting belly because there is no mistake. I planned to flour-
ish. Of course you did.
Lifting belly is exacting. You mean exact. I mean exacting.
Lifting belly is exacting.
Can you say see me.
Lifting belly is exciting.
Can you explain a mistake.
There is no mistake.
You have mentioned the flour.
Lifting belly is full of charm.
They are very nice candles.
Lifting belly is resourceful.
What can lifting belly say.
Oh yes I was not mistaken. Were not you indeed.
Lifting belly lifting belly lifting belly on then lifting belly.
Can you make an expression. Thanks for the cigarette.
How pretty.
How fast. What. How fast the cow comes out.
Lifting belly a permanent caress.
Lifting belly bored.

You don't say so.
Lifting belly now.
Cow.
Lifting belly exactly.
I have often been pleased with this thing.
Lifting belly is necessarily venturesome.
You mean by that that you are collected. I hope I am.
What is an evening dress. What is a cape. What is a suit. What is a fur collar.
Lifting belly needs to speak.
Land Rising next time.
Lifting belly has no choice.
Lifting belly seems to me to be remarkably kind.
Can you hear me witness that I was wolfish. I can. And that I do not interfere with you. No I cannot countenance you here. Countenance what do you mean by that. I mean that it is a pleasure to prepare you. Thank you my dear.
Lifting belly is so kind.
Can you recollect this for me.
Lifting belly naturally.
Can you believe the truth.
Fredericka or Frederica.
Can you give me permission.
The Loves.
I never forget the Caesars.
Or the dears.
Lifting belly casually.
Where the head gets thin.
Lifting belly never mind.
You do please me.
Lifting belly restless.
Not at all.
Lifting belly there.
Expand my chest endlessly.
You did not do so.
Lifting belly is loved.
You know I am always ready to please you.
Lifting belly in a breath.
Lifting belly.

You do speak kindly.
We speak very kindly.
Lifting belly is so bold.

Idem the Same

A Valentine to Sherwood Anderson

I knew too that through them I knew too that he was through, I knew too that he threw them. I knew too that they were through, I knew too I knew too, I knew I knew them.

I knew to them.

If they tear a hunter through, if they tear through a hunter, if they tear through a hunt and a hunter, if they tear through the different sizes of the six, the different sizes of the six which are these, a woman with a white package under one arm and a black package under the other arm and dressed in brown with a white blouse, the second Saint Joseph the third a hunter in a blue coat and black garters and a plaid cap, a fourth a knife grinder who is full faced and a very little woman with black hair and a yellow hat and an excellently smiling appropriate soldier. All these as you please.

In the meantime examples of the same lily. In this way please have you rung.

WHAT DO I SEE.

A very little snail.
A medium sized turkey.
A small band of sheep.
A fair orange tree.
All nice wives are like that.
Listen to them from here.
Oh.
You did not have an answer.
Here.
Yes.

A VERY VALENTINE.

Very fine is my valentine.
Very fine and very mine.
Very fine is my valentine very mine and very fine.
Very fine is my valentine and mine, very fine very mine and mine is my valentine.

WHY DO YOU FEEL DIFFERENTLY.

Why do you feel differently about a very little snail and a big one.

Why do you feel differently about a medium sized turkey and a very large one.

Why do you feel differently about a small band of sheep and several sheep that are riding.

Why do you feel differently about a fair orange tree and one that has blossoms as well.

Oh very well.

All nice wives are like that.

To Be.
No Please.
To Be
They can please
Not to be
Do they please.
Not to be
Do they not please
Yes please.
Do they please
No please.
Do they not please
No please.
Do they please.
Please.
If you please.
And if you please.
And if they please.
And they please.

To be pleased
Not to be pleased.
Not to be displeased.
To be pleased and to please.

KNEELING.

One two three four five six seven eight nine and ten.

The tenth is a little one kneeling and giving away a rooster with this feeling.

I have mentioned one, four five seven eight and nine.

Two is also giving away an animal.

Three is changed as to disposition.

Six is in question if we mean mother and daughter, black and black caught her, and she offers to be three she offers it to me.

That is very right and should come out below and just so.

BUNDLES FOR THEM.
A History of Giving Bundles.

We were able to notice that each one in a way carried a bundle, they were not a trouble to them nor were they all bundles as some of them were chickens some of them pheasants some of them sheep and some of them bundles, they were not a trouble to them and then indeed we learned that it was the principal recreation and they were so arranged that they were not given away, and to-day they were given away.

I will not look at them again.

They will not look for them again.

They have not seen them here again.

They are in there and we hear them again.

In which way are stars brighter than they are. When we have come to this decision. We mention many thousands of buds. And when I close my eyes I see them.

If you hear her snore
It is not before you love her
You love her so that to be her beau is very lovely
She is sweetly there and her curly hair is very lovely

She is sweetly here and I am very near and that is very lovely.

She is my tender sweet and her little feet are stretched out well which is a treat and very lovely

Her little tender nose is between her little eyes which close and are very lovely.

She is very lovely and mine which is very lovely.

ON HER WAY.

If you can see why she feels that she kneels if you can see why he knows that he shows what he bestows, if you can see why they share what they share, need we question that there is no doubt that by this time if they had intended to come they would have sent some notice of such intention. She and they and indeed the decision itself is not early dissatisfaction.

IN THIS WAY.

Keys please, it is useless to alarm any one it is useless to alarm some one it is useless to be alarming and to get fertility in gardens in salads in heliotrope and in dishes. Dishes and wishes are mentioned and dishes and wishes are not capable of darkness. We like sheep. And so does he.

LET US DESCRIBE.

Let us describe how they went. It was a very windy night and the road although in excellent condition and extremely well graded has many turnings and although the curves are not sharp the rise is considerable. It was a very windy night and some of the larger vehicles found it more prudent not to venture. In consequence some of those who had planned to go were unable to do so. Many others did go and there was a sacrifice, of what shall we, a sheep, a hen, a cock, a village, a ruin, and all that and then that having been blessed let us bless it.

from
Stanzas in Meditation

STANZA X

I have tried earnestly to express
Just what I guess will not distress
Nor even oppress or yet caress
Beside which tried which well beside
They will not only will not be tried.
It is not trying not to know what they mean
By which they come to be welcome as they heard
I have been interrupted by myself by this.
This may be which is not an occasion
To compel this to feel that that is so
I do not dearly love to liven it as much
As when they meant to either change it or not
I do not change it either or not.
This is how they like to do what they like to do.
I have thought often of how however our change
That is to say the sun is warm to-day because
Yesterday it was also warm
And the day before it was not warm
The sun as it shone was not warm
And so moreover as when the sun shone it was not warm
So yesterday as well as to-day
The sun when it shone was warm
And so they do not include our a cloud
Not at all it had nothing to do with a cloud
It had not to do with the wind
It had not to do with the sun
Nor had it to do with the pleasure of the weather either.
It had to do with that this is what there had been.
It is very pleasant that it is this that it should have been
And now that it is not only that it is warmer
Now very well there is often that they will
Have what they look when they look there or there
To make a mistake and change to make a mistake and change
To have not changed a mistake and to make a mistake and
    change.

Change the prophecy to the weather
Change the care to their whether they will
Nothing now to allow
It is very strange that very often
The beginning makes it truly be
That they will rather have it be
So that to return to be will they be
There will they be there with them
I should often know that it makes a difference not to look
    about
Because if to do they that is is it
Not which it makes any difference or
But just what with containing
They need or made so surrounded
In spite of in a delay of delayed
It is often very changed to churn
Now no one churns butter any more.
That is why that is where they are here.
I wish I had not mentioned it either.
This whole stanza is to be about how it does not make any
    difference.
I have meant this.
Might it be yes yes will it
Might it not be as much as once having it
Might it not only be allowed
And if not does not it bring back
Or bring back what is it
If they bring it back not for me
And if it brings it back for me
Or if it brings it back for me
So and so further than if.
It is easy to be often told and moved
Moved may be made of sun and sun of rain
Or if not not at all.
Just when they should be thought of so forth.
What they say and what they do
One is one and two is two
Or if not two who.

from
The World Is Round

I am Rose my eyes are blue
I am Rose and who are you
I am Rose and when I sing
I am Rose like anything.

ANNA HEMPSTEAD BRANCH

(1875–1937)

The Monk in the Kitchen

I

Order is a lovely thing;
On disarray it lays its wing,
Teaching simplicity to sing.
It has a meek and lowly grace,
Quiet as a nun's face.
Lo—I will have thee in this place!
Tranquil well of deep delight,
Transparent as the water, bright—
All things that shine through thee appear
As stones through water, sweetly clear,
Thou clarity,
That with angelic charity
Revealest beauty where thou art,
Spread thyself like a clean pool.
Then all the things that in thee are
Shall seem more spiritual and fair,
Reflections from serener air—
Sunken shapes of many a star
In the high heavens set afar.

II

Ye stolid, homely, visible things,
Above you all brood glorious wings
Of your deep entities, set high,
Like slow moons in a hidden sky.
But you, their likenesses, are spent
Upon another element.
Truly ye are but seemings—
The shadowy cast-off gleamings
Of bright solidities. Ye seem
Soft as water, vague as dream;
Image, cast in a shifting stream.

217

III

What are ye?
I know not.
Brazen pan and iron pot,
Yellow brick and gray flag-stone
That my feet have trod upon—
Ye seem to me
Vessels of bright mystery.
For ye do bear a shape, and so
Though ye were made by man, I know
An inner Spirit also made
And ye his breathings have obeyed.

IV

Shape, the strong and awful Spirit,
Laid his ancient hand on you.
He waste chaos doth inherit;
He can alter and subdue.
Verily, he doth lift up
Matter, like a sacred cup.
Into deep substance he reached, and lo
Where ye were not, ye were; and so
Out of useless nothing, ye
Groaned and laughed and came to be.
And I use you, as I can,
Wonderful uses, made for man,
Iron pot and brazen pan.

V

What are ye?
I know not;
Nor what I really do
When I move and govern you.
There is no small work unto God.
He requires of us greatness;
Of his least creature
A high angelic nature,
Stature superb and bright completeness.

He sets to us no humble duty.
Each act that he would have us do
Is haloed round with strangest beauty.
Terrific deeds and cosmic tasks
Of his plainest child he asks.
When I polish the brazen pan
I hear a creature laugh afar
In the gardens of a star,
And from his burning presence run
Flaming wheels of many a sun.
Whoever makes a thing more bright,
He is an angel of all light.
When I cleanse this earthen floor
My spirit leaps to see
Bright garments trailing over it.
Wonderful lustres cover it,
A cleanness made by me.
Purger of all men's thoughts and ways,
With labor do I sound Thy praise,
My work is done for Thee.
Whoever makes a thing more bright,
He is an angel of all light.
Therefore let me spread abroad
The beautiful cleanness of my God.

VI

One time in the cool of dawn
Angels came and worked with me.
The air was soft with many a wing.
They laughed amid my solitude
And cast bright looks on everything.
Sweetly of me did they ask
That they might do my common task.
And all were beautiful—but one
With garments whiter than the sun
Had such a face
Of deep, remembered grace,
That when I saw I cried—"Thou art
The great Blood-Brother of my heart.

Where have I seen thee?"—And he said,
"When we are dancing 'round God's throne,
How often thou art there.
Beauties from thy hands have flown
Like white doves wheeling in mid air.
Nay—thy soul remembers not?
Work on, and cleanse thy iron pot."

VII

What are we? I know not.

In the Beginning Was the Word

It took me ten days
To read the Bible through.
Then I saw what I saw,
And I knew what I knew.

I would rise before the dawn,
When the stars were in the sky;
I would go and read the Book,
Till the sun rode high.

In the silence of the noon,
I would read with a will.
I was one who had climbed
To an high, burning hill.

At dusk I fell asleep
With my head on the page.
Then I woke—then I read—
Till it seemed like an age.

For a great wind blows
Through Ezekiel and John,
They are all one flesh
That the Spirit blows upon.

And suddenly the words
Seemed to quicken and to shine;
They glowed like the bread,
They purpled like the wine.

Like bread that had been wheat
In a thousand ample plains,
Sown and harvested by men
From the suns—from the rains.

Like wine that had been grapes
In a thousand vineyards strong—
That was trampled by men's feet
With a shout, with a song.

Like the Bread, like the Wine,
That we eat with one accord—
The body and the blood
Of the supper of the Lord.

And the wine may be old
And the wine may be new—
But it all is the Lord's—
And I knew what I knew.

For a great wind blows
Through Ezekiel and John,
They are all one flesh
That the Spirit blows upon.

And a letter is a power,
And a name is a rune—
And an alphabet, my friends,
Is a strange and ancient tune.

And each letter is a throne
From which fearful splendors stream—
I could see them flash like fire
With an arch-angelic gleam.

And within each word a city
Shone more far than eye could reach—
Where the people shone like stars
With a great new speech.

And each city was an angel,
And they sang with one accord—
Crying, 'Holy, holy, holy,'
In the presence of the Lord.

The Book felt like flesh,
It would breathe—it would sing—
It would throb beneath my hand
Like a breast, like a wing.

It would cry, it would groan,
It would shout and complain—
It would seem to climb a hill
With its solemn stress of pain.

It would grapple with fierce powers,
With a deep interior strife.
It would seem to heave and lift
With a terrible, glad life.

And my flesh was in the Book,
And its blood was in me;
I could feel it throb within,
As plain as it could be

I was filled with its powers,
And I cried all alone,
'The Lord is in the tomb,
And my body is the stone.'

I was anguished, I was dumb,
When the powers began to move,
That shall stir the aching ground,
That shall shake the earth with love.

Then my flesh, which was the stone,
Felt the hills begin to lift.
The seas shook and heaved,
And the stars began to shift.

And the words rushed on
And each letter was a throne.
They swept through my flesh,
Through my brain, through my bone,

With a great, fearful rush,
I felt it clean through.
Oh, I saw what I saw,
And I knew what I knew.

And I swung one side
When the ghostly power began.
Then the Book stood up—
And I saw it was a Man.

For a great wind blows
Through Ezekiel and John.
They are all one flesh
That the Spirit blows upon.

It took me ten days
To read the Bible through—
Then I saw what I saw,
And I knew what I knew.

from
Sonnets from a Lockbox

XIV

What witchlike spell weaves here its deep design,
And sells its pattern to the ignorant buyer.
Oh lacelike cruelty with stitches fine—
Which stings the flesh with its sharp mesh of fire.
God of the Thief and Patron of the Liar,
I think that it is best not to inquire
Upon whose wheel was spun this mortal thread;
What dyed this curious robe so rich a red;
With shivering hues it is embroiderèd.
With changing colors like unsteady eyes.
I think the filigree is Medea's wreath.
Oh, treacherous splendor! In this lustrous prize
Of gold and silver weaving, madness lies.
Who purchases this garment—Sire—buys death.

XXII

I used to think . . . Number was fixed and still,
Rigid as marble, like an altar cast
In rocklike splendor. Now I perceive at last
Its changing modes of supernatural will.
Now I perceive wild garments floating free.
I hear the planetary music crashing.
Great chorals sway with Bacchic energy.
The churchly cycles move, their mild eyes flashing.

So number within number shines and sings
And with interior energy doth beget
The godlike shapes of many an alphabet,
Bodied in air, with their deep patternings.
Their magnetisms create my flesh anew.
Great Festivals like goddesses advancing—
I know full well if I abide in you
I shall feast well and shall be saved by dancing.

XXVI

Around this rod my writing self might twist—
And fold the splendor of its poisoned mesh,
Its spangled scales of gold and amethyst,
The brilliant convolutions of the flesh.
Not yet my sinuous coil from the ground
Can lift its lust—save by this one escape.
This fearful straightness I may wreathe around
As close as binds the skin upon the grape.
Now upward springs the fierce determined power,
And its sharp brightness shoots my sensuous nerves.
With godlike speed in this unearthly hour
I break in splendor all my glittering curves.
Now by this straightness, I lay hold on God
Who in His Town set up His Holy Rod.

XXXI

I say that words are men and when we spell
In alphabets we deal with living things;
With feet and thighs and breasts, fierce heads, strong wings;
Maternal Powers, great Bridals, Heaven and Hell.
There is a menace in the tales we tell.
From out the throne from which all language springs
Voices proceed and fires and thunderings.
Oh when we speak, Great God, let us speak well.
Beware of shapes, beware of letterings,
For in them lies such magic as alters dream,
Shakes cities down and moves the inward scheme.
Beware the magic of the coin that sings.
These coins are graved with supernatural powers
And magic wills that are more strong than ours.

SHERWOOD ANDERSON

(1876–1941)

American Spring Song

In the spring, when winds blew and farmers were plowing
    fields,
It came into my mind to be glad because of my brutality.

Along a street I went and over a bridge.

I went through many streets in my city and over many
    bridges.

Men and women I struck with my fists and my hands began
    to bleed.

Under a bridge I crawled and stood trembling with joy
At the river's edge.

Because it was spring and soft sunlight came through the
    cracks of the bridge
I tried to understand myself.

Out of the mud at the river's edge I moulded myself a god,
A grotesque little god with a twisted face,
A god for myself and my men.

You see now, brother, how it was.

I was a man with clothes made by a Jewish tailor,
Cunningly wrought clothes, made for a nameless one.

I wore a white collar and some one had given me a jeweled
    pin
To wear at my throat.
That amused and hurt me too.

No one knew that I knelt in the mud beneath the bridge
In the city of Chicago.

You see I am whispering my secret to you.

I want you to believe in my insanity and to understand that I
    love God—

That's what I want.

And then, you see, it was spring
And soft sunlight came through the cracks of the bridge.

I had been long alone in a strange place where no gods came.

Creep, men, and kiss the twisted face of my mud god.

I'll not hit you with my bleeding fists.

I'm a twisted god myself.

It is spring and love has come to me—
Love has come to me and to my men.

SARAH N. CLEGHORN

(1876–1959)

Comrade Jesus

Thanks to Saint Matthew, who had been
At mass-meetings in Palestine,
We know whose side was spoken for
When Comrade Jesus had the floor.

"Where sore they toil and hard they lie,
Among the great unwashed, dwell I.
The tramp, the convict, I am he:
Cold-shoulder him, cold-shoulder me."

By Dives' door, with thoughtful eye,
He did tomorrow prophesy:—
"The Kingdom's gate is low and small:
The rich can scarce wedge through at all."

"A dangerous man," said Caiaphas,
"An ignorant demagogue, alas.
Friend of low women, it is he
Slanders the upright Pharisee."

For law and order, it was plain,
For Holy Church, he must be slain.
The troops were there to awe the crowd:
Mob violence was not allowed.

Their clumsy force with force to foil,
His strong, clean hands he would not soil.
He saw their childishness quite plain
Between the lightnings of his pain.

Between the twilights of his end
He made his fellow-felon friend.
With swollen tongue and blinded eyes
Invited him to Paradise.

Ah, let no Local him refuse!
Comrade Jesus hath paid his dues.
Whatever other be debarred,
Comrade Jesus hath his red card.

The Golf Links Lie So Near the Mill

The golf links lie so near the mill
    That almost every day
The laboring children can look out
    And see the men at play.

WILLIAM ELLERY LEONARD

(1876–1944)

from
Two Lives

XXV

That once the gentle mind of my dead wife
Did love that fiery Roman (dead like her)—
Lucretius and his vast hexameter—
I number with the ironies of life.
That I, who turned his Latian verse to mine
For her, the while she typed each page for me,
Should, in my English, just have reached that line
Fourth from the end of the Book of Death (Book Three),
When Death rode out for her—was that design?—
If so, of God or Devil?—the line which saith,
"*O Mors aeterna*—O eternal Death"—
The last, last letters she fingered key by key! . . .
But when, long after, I had wrought the rest,
I said these verses, walking down the west:

XXVI
INDIAN SUMMER

(O Earth-and-Autumn of the Setting Sun,
She is not by, to know my task is done!)

In the brown grasses slanting with the wind,
Lone as a lad whose dog's no longer near,
Lone as a mother whose only child has sinned,
Lone on the loved hill . . . and below me here
The thistle-down in tremulous atmosphere
Along red clusters of the sumach streams;
The shriveled stalks of goldenrod are sere,
And crisp and white their flashing old racemes.
(. . . forever . . . forever . . . forever . . .)
This is the lonely season of the year,
This is the season of our lonely dreams.

(O Earth-and-Autumn of the setting Sun,
She is not by, to know my task is done!)

The corn-shocks westward on the stubble plain
Show like an Indian village of dead days;
The long smoke trails behind the crawling train,
And floats atop the distant woods ablaze
With orange, crimson, purple. The low haze
Dims the scarped bluffs above the inland sea,
Whose wide and slaty waters in cold glaze
Await yon full-moon of the night-to-be.
(. . . far . . . and far . . . and far . . .)
These are the solemn horizons of man's ways,
These the horizons of solemn thought to me.

(O Earth-and-Autumn of the Setting Sun,
She is not by to know my task is done!)

And this the hill she visited, as friend;
And this the hill she lingered on, as bride—
Down in the yellow valley is the end:
They laid her . . . in no evening Autumn tide. . . .
Under fresh flowers of that May morn, beside
The queens and cave-women of ancient earth. . . .

This is the hill . . . and over my city's towers,
Across the world from sunset, yonder in air,
Shines, through its scaffoldings, a civic dome
Of pilèd masonry, which shall be ours
To give, completed, to our children there. . . .
And yonder far roof of my abandoned home
Shall house new laughter. . . . Yet I tried. . . . I tried. . . .
And, ever wistful of the doom to come,
I built her many a fire for love . . . for mirth. . . .
(When snows were falling on our oaks outside,
Dear, many a winter fire upon the hearth) . . .
(. . . farewell . . . farewell . . . farewell . . .)
We dare not think too long on those who died,
While still so many yet must come to birth.

MARSDEN HARTLEY

(1877–1943)

Fishmonger

I have taken scales from off
The cheeks of the moon.
I have made fins from bluejays' wings,
I have made eyes from damsons in the shadow.
I have taken flushes from the peachlips in the sun.
From all these I have made a fish of heaven for you,
Set it swimming on a young October sky.
I sit on the bank of the stream and watch
The grasses in amazement
As they turn to ashy gold.
Are the fishes from the rainbow
Still beautiful to you,
For whom they are made,
For whom I have set them,
Swimming?

————————

Lapping of waters
thick, upon razorblade
selvages of sand,
pipers running on them,
wetting their shins
in the wave,
leaving little, lost signatures
of outmoded love,
patched, frayed, uncalled-for
love,
bauble bursting love,
dear inviolable thing—
for whom was right,
for whom was wrong,
devil-throng.

Wingaersheek Beach

Shell,
sitting still,
whitely, ghastly, immovable
unless wind whip it other way
on white sand whiter in a sandway
than itself
holding, folding, moulding
last curve, ancestral swirl
bleached whiter
lying lighter
for the whiter way, jeopardy
of lying, by wind, sun, mist, rain, bent and torn
sandpeep's breast in flawless emulation
lip in death like it
when death strike it
white
or speechlessness of one
gone white with ashy blight
fear to lose a tithe of it
thing held, from fright of it.

What Have We All—A Soliloquy of Essences

What have we all, we
who have nothing left but longing to be free
of our lashed satiety.
The world has shapes we never
saw before.
The angles once familiar
broken
split into alien integers
forsaken
bit by bit, the once endearing touch
we saw
like bright veins upon wet leaf
showing now curves of our grief

now chaff blown from the sheaf,
suffering the explicit torture of being awake
for imagination's sake
in order not to feel
press of grinding wheel—
what love
costs more to prove
than heart being torn
from the vision?

These beautiful wild untamable
creatures
dying to keep their features
to keep hearts from shivering to death
and bone from its sickened breath
and white decision.

West Pitch at the Falls

For years, so long, I had imagined
the slopes thickly strewn with pines—
could it have been the rising spray from the
falls from the tumbling waters of spring
freshets veiling the scene, making it seem
more heavily wooded than it now is?
We of the place have often seen the river
swell, rise to the bridge, almost carry it
away, as it in times past already has done,
between Lewiston
and lovely Auburn.

Contrasting the scene when as a boy the river
froze and we skated on the edges of the river
above the falls, while the men featured horse racing
in the center up stream; here and there on the
sides, men cutting cakes of ice eighteen inches thick.
I can see when I want to the images of the two
sisters who threw themselves into the tossing

foam, ending the dismal struggle; all of this
before my time, the story of it from the elders
frightening young minds, at the height of the light
brown foam, avoiding carefully the descent to the
tall Niagara.
In and out of the spring freshet foam
appear the long streams of visions to the
height of the iron bridge above—
the faces of those not now there, and yet still visible.
Now—
gulls gather on thin strips of earth near the
falls, as if talking of old times.

This Crusty Fragment

This crusty fragment
of windbeat island
for only silence and
wild winds meant,
in my hand—
dark as an eagle's shoulder
or the look of something
terrible and rare
come up for whiffs of air—
battling once with
volcanic insurrection—
lying still,
warming my palm
with late-fallen flares of sun
upon
its mold-hued face.
I like it near me;
I do not fear me
to kiss its jagged cheek
because I am meek
with love of home place.

I have kissed hard lip
of continent;
I have taken it in arm.
But now, where is its charm
when fainting hope
is but blurred gleam of
periscope?

There will be party soon,
chiefly for the young.
They will be dancing at the party,
dancing with their foolish blood
for it is strong. Youth at the flood—
how can it know—
it is so young, so cold,
so old.

There will be bits
of islands broken
as this one in my hand,
unthinkable token
of desperate demand.

Indian Point

When the surf licks with its tongues
these volcanic personal shapes, which we,
defining for ourselves as rocks, accept
them as such, at its feverish incoming—
isn't it too, in its way, something like
the plain image of life?
Those restless entities disturbing solid
substances with a curious, irrelevant,
common fret—
and, like so many simple looking elements, when
they seem the most playful, it is then that
they are most dangerous.
The bright woman looking out to sea

through the crisp telescope of her advancing
years,
there is no doubt but that she discovers the
same image as the child, who remarks the
radiant glint of his marbles on the top spray
of the wave he once played with,
or as the fringed lace on the dress of a
Titan's wife—
the inwash cooling at least the eye with
a something exceptional white or green or
blue, too pale almost to mention, if
frightening to the marrow,
for many have been sent to their death trusting
too much, while regarding it affectionately,
the sea.

As the Buck Lay Dead

As the buck lay dead, tied to the fender
of a car
coming down from Matagamon way,
I saw the dried blood on his tongue of
a thousand summer dreams and winter
cogitations—
the scratches on his hooves were signatures
of the many pungent sticks and branches.
The torn place in his chest was made
by a man
letting out visceral debris to save weight-giving
morsels to many a greedy fox or other wild
thing—
over the glaze of his half-shut eye
hung miseries of superlative moments
struck dumb.

WALTER CONRAD ARENSBERG

(1878–1954)

Voyage à l'Infini

The swan existing
Is like a song with an accompaniment
Imaginary.

Across the glassy lake,
Across the lake to the shadow of the willows,
It is accompanied by an image,
—As by Debussy's
"Reflets dans l'eau."

The swan that is
Reflects
Upon the solitary water—breast to breast
With the duplicity:
"The other one!"

And breast to breast it is confused.
O visionary wedding! O stateliness of the procession!
It is accompanied by the image of itself
Alone.

At night
The lake is a wide silence,
Without imagination.

Ing

Ing? Is it possible to mean ing?
Suppose
     for the termination in *g*
              a disoriented
              series
     of the simple fractures
              in sleep.
               Soporific
     has accordingly a value for soap
                so present to
                sew pieces.
                And *p* says: Peace is.
And suppose the *i*
              to be big in ing
              as Beginning.
                Then Ing is to ing
as aloud
     accompanied by times
and the meaning is a possibility
                of ralsis.

Arithmetical Progression of the Verb "To Be"

On a sheet of paper
     dropped with the intention of demolishing
     space
     by the simple subtraction of a necessary plane
draw a line that leaves the present
     in addition
     carrying forward to the uncounted columns
           of the spatial ruin
           now considered as complete
     the remainder of the past.

The act of disappearing
      which in the three-dimensional
      is the fate of the convergent
          vista
is thus
      under the form of the immediate
arrested in a perfect parallel
      of being
      in part.

Axiom

From a determinable horizon
      absent
      spectacularly from a midnight
      which has yet to make public
         a midnight
      in the first place incompatibly copied
the other
      in observance of the necessary end
              guarantees
the simultaneous insularity
         of a structure
         self-contained
a little longer
      than the general direction
         of goods opposed
         tangentically.

Theorem

For purposes of illusion
      the actual ascent of two waves
         transparent to a basis
         which has a disappearance of its own
is timed
      at the angle of incidence
               to the swing of a suspended lens
from which the waves wash
           the protective coloration.
Through the resultant exposure
              to a temporal process
an emotion
      ideally distant
         assumes on the uneven surface
               descending
      as the identity to be demonstrated
the three dimensions
         with which it is incommensurate.

ADELAIDE CRAPSEY

(1878–1914)

November Night

Listen. .
With faint dry sound,
Like steps of passing ghosts,
The leaves, frost-crisp'd, break from the trees
And fall.

Release

With swift
Great sweep of her
Magnificent arm my pain
Clanged back the doors that shut my soul
From life.

Triad

These be
Three silent things:
The falling snow. . the hour
Before the dawn. . the mouth of one
Just dead.

Snow

Look up. .
From bleakening hills
Blows down the light, first breath
Of wintry wind. . . look up, and scent
The snow!

Anguish

Keep thou
Thy tearless watch
All night but when blue-dawn
Breathes on the silver moon, then weep!
Then weep!

Trapped

Well and
If day on day
Follows, and weary year
On year. . and ever days and years. .
Well?

Moon-Shadows

Still as
On windless nights
The moon-cast shadows are,
So still will be my heart when I
Am dead.

Susanna and the Elders

"Why do
You thus devise
Evil against her?" "For that
She is beautiful, delicate;
Therefore."

The Guarded Wound

If it
Were lighter touch
Than petal of flower resting
On grass, oh still too heavy it were,
Too heavy!

Night Winds

The old
Old winds that blew
When chaos was, what do
They tell the clattered trees that I
Should weep?

Arbutus

Not Spring's
Thou art, but her's,
Most cool, most virginal,
Winter's, with thy faint breath, thy snows
Rose-tinged.

Amaze

I know
Not these my hands
And yet I think there was
A woman like me once had hands
Like these.

The Warning

Just now,
Out of the strange
Still dusk. . as strange, as still. .
A white moth flew. Why am I grown
So cold?

Niagara

Seen on a Night in November

How frail
Above the bulk
Of crashing water hangs,
Autumnal, evanescent, wan,
The moon.

On Seeing Weather-Beaten Trees

Is it as plainly in our living shown,
By slant and twist, which way the wind hath blown?

The Sun-Dial

Every day,
Every day,
Tell the hours
By their shadows,
By their shadows.

Song

I make my shroud but no one knows,
So shimmering fine it is and fair,
With stitches set in even rows.
I make my shroud but no one knows.

In door-way where the lilac blows,
Humming a little wandering air,
I make my shroud and no one knows,
So shimmering fine it is and fair.

The Witch

When I was girl by Nilus stream
    I watched the desert stars arise;
My lover, he who dreamed the Sphinx,
    Learned all his dreaming from my eyes.

I bore in Greece a burning name,
    And I have been in Italy
Madonna to a painter-lad,
    And mistress to a Medici.

And have you heard (and I have heard)
    Of puzzled men with decorous mien,
Who judged—The wench knows far too much—
    And burnt her on the Salem green?

The Lonely Death

In the cold I will rise, I will bathe
In waters of ice; myself
Will shiver, and shrive myself,
Alone in the dawn, and anoint
Forehead and feet and hands;
I will shutter the windows from light,
I will place in their sockets the four
Tall candles and set them a-flame
In the grey of the dawn; and myself
Will lay myself straight in my bed,
And draw the sheet under my chin.

Fragment

Nor moon,—
Nor stars . . . the dark and in
The dark the grey
Ghost glimmer of the olive trees
The black straight rows
Of cypress

To a Hermit Thrush

Art thou
Not kin to him
Who loved Mark's wife and both
Died for it? O, thou harper in
Green woods?

DON MARQUIS
(1878–1937)

from
the coming of archy

expression is the need of my soul
i was once a vers libre bard
but i died and my soul went into the body of a cockroach
it has given me a new outlook upon life

i see things from the under side now
thank you for the apple peelings in the wastepaper basket
but your paste is getting so stale i cant eat it
there is a cat here called mehitabel i wish you would have
removed she nearly ate me the other night why dont she
catch rats that is what she is supposed to be for
there is a rat here she should get without delay

most of these rats here are just rats
but this rat is like me he has a human soul in him
he used to be a poet himself
night after night i have written poetry for you
on your typewriter
and this big brute of a rat who used to be a poet
comes out of his hole when it is done
and reads it and sniffs at it
he is jealous of my poetry
he used to make fun of it when we were both human
he was a punk poet himself
and after he has read it he sneers
and then he eats it

i wish you would have mehitabel kill that rat
or get a cat that is onto her job
and i will write you a series of poems showing how things
        look
to a cockroach

that rats name is freddy
the next time freddy dies i hope he wont be a rat
but something smaller i hope i will be a rat
in the next transmigration and freddy a cockroach
i will teach him to sneer at my poetry then

dont you ever eat any sandwiches in your office
i havent had a crumb of bread for i dont know how long
or a piece of ham or anything but apple parings
and paste leave a piece of paper in your machine
every night you can call me archy

the song of mehitabel

this is the song of mehitabel
of mehitabel the alley cat
as i wrote you before boss
mehitabel is a believer
in the pythagorean
theory of the transmigration
of the soul and she claims
that formerly her spirit
was incarnated in the body
of cleopatra
that was a long time ago
and one must not be
surprised if mehitabel
has forgotten some of her
more regal manners

i have had my ups and downs
but wotthehell wotthehell
yesterday sceptres and crowns
fried oysters and velvet gowns
and today i herd with bums
but wotthehell wotthehell

i wake the world from sleep
as i caper and sing and leap
when i sing my wild free tune
wotthehell wotthehell
under the blear eyed moon
i am pelted with cast off shoon
but wotthehell wotthehell

do you think that i would change
my present freedom to range
for a castle or moated grange
wotthehell wotthehell
cage me and i d go frantic
my life is so romantic
capricious and corybantic
and i m toujours gai toujours gai

i know that i am bound
for a journey down the sound
in the midst of a refuse mound
but wotthehell wotthehell
oh i should worry and fret
death and i will coquette
there s a dance in the old dame yet
toujours gai toujours gai

i once was an innocent kit
wotthehell wotthehell
with a ribbon my neck to fit
and bells tied onto it
o wotthehell wotthehell
but a maltese cat came by
with a come hither look in his eye
and a song that soared to the sky
and wotthehell wotthehell
and i followed adown the street
the pad of his rhythmical feet
o permit me again to repeat
wotthehell wotthehell

my youth i shall never forget
but there s nothing i really regret
wotthehell wotthehell
there s a dance in the old dame yet
toujours gai toujours gai

the things that i had not ought to
i do because i ve gotto
wotthehell wotthehell
and i end with my favorite motto
toujours gai toujours gai

boss sometimes i think
that our friend mehitabel
is a trifle too gay
                              archy

aesop revised by archy

a wolf met a spring
lamb drinking
at a stream
and said to her
you are the lamb
that muddied this stream
all last year
so that i could not get
a clean fresh drink
i am resolved that
this outrage
shall not be enacted again
this season
i am going to kill you
just a moment
said the lamb
i was not born last
year so it could not
have been i

the wolf then pulled
a number of other
arguments as to why the lamb
should die
but in each case the lamb
pretty innocent that she was
easily proved
herself guiltless
well well said the wolf
enough of argument
you are right and i am wrong
but i am going to eat
you anyhow
because i am hungry
stop exclamation point
cried a human voice
and a man came over
the slope of the ravine
vile lupine marauder
you shall not kill that
beautiful and innocent
lamb for i shall save her
exit the wolf
left upper entrance
snarling
poor little lamb
continued our human hero
sweet tender little thing
it is well that i appeared
just when i did
it makes my blood boil
to think of the fright
to which you have been
subjected in another
moment i would have been
too late come home with me
and the lamb frolicked
about her new found friend
gamboling as to the sound
of a wordsworthian tabor

and leaping for joy
as if propelled by a stanza
from william blake
these vile and bloody wolves
went on our hero
in honest indignation
they must be cleared out
of the country
the meads must be made safe
for sheepocracy
and so jollying her along
with the usual human hokum
he led her to his home
and the son of a gun
did not even blush when
they passed the mint bed
gently he cut her throat
all the while inveighing
against the inhuman wolf
and tenderly he cooked her
and lovingly he sauced her
and meltingly he ate her
and piously he said a grace
thanking his gods
for their bountiful gifts to him
and after dinner
he sat with his pipe
before the fire meditating
on the brutality of wolves
and the injustice of
the universe
which allows them to harry
poor innocent lambs
and wondering if he
had not better
write to the papers
for as he said
for god s sake can t
something be done about it
                                    archy

archy confesses

coarse
jocosity
catches the crowd
shakespeare
and i
are often
low browed

the fish wife
curse
and the laugh
of the horse
shakespeare
and i
are frequently
coarse

aesthetic
excuses
in bill s behalf
are adduced
to refine
big bill s
coarse laugh

but bill
he would chuckle
to hear such guff
he pulled
rough stuff
and he liked
rough stuff

hoping you
are the same
         archy

CARL SANDBURG

(1878–1967)

Chicago

Hog Butcher for the World,
Tool Maker, Stacker of Wheat,
Player with Railroads and the Nation's Freight
    Handler;
Stormy, husky, brawling,
City of the Big Shoulders:

They tell me you are wicked and I believe them, for I have
    seen your painted women under the gas lamps luring the
    farm boys.
And they tell me you are crooked and I answer: Yes, it is true
    I have seen the gunman kill and go free to kill again.
And they tell me you are brutal and my reply is: On the faces
    of women and children I have seen the marks of wanton
    hunger.
And having answered so I turn once more to those who sneer
    at this my city, and I give them back the sneer and say to
    them:
Come and show me another city with lifted head singing so
    proud to be alive and coarse and strong and cunning.
Flinging magnetic curses amid the toil of piling job on job,
    here is a tall bold slugger set vivid against the little soft
    cities;
Fierce as a dog with tongue lapping for action, cunning as a
    savage pitted against the wilderness,
        Bareheaded,
        Shoveling,
        Wrecking,
        Planning,
        Building, breaking, rebuilding,
Under the smoke, dust all over his mouth, laughing with
    white teeth,

Under the terrible burden of destiny laughing as a young man
    laughs,
Laughing even as an ignorant fighter laughs who has never
    lost a battle,
Bragging and laughing that under his wrist is the pulse, and
    under his ribs the heart of the people,
               Laughing!
Laughing the stormy, husky, brawling laughter of Youth, half-
    naked, sweating, proud to be Hog Butcher, Tool Maker,
    Stacker of Wheat, Player with Railroads and Freight
    Handler to the Nation.

The Harbor

Passing through huddled and ugly walls
By doorways where women
Looked from their hunger-deep eyes,
Haunted with shadows of hunger-hands,
Out from the huddled and ugly walls,
I came sudden, at the city's edge,
On a blue burst of lake,
Long lake waves breaking under the sun
On a spray-flung curve of shore;
And a fluttering storm of gulls,
Masses of great gray wings
And flying white bellies
Veering and wheeling free in the open.

Mag

I wish to God I never saw you, Mag.
I wish you never quit your job and came along with me.
I wish we never bought a license and a white dress
For you to get married in the day we ran off to a minister
And told him we would love each other and take care of each
    other

Always and always long as the sun and the rain lasts
    anywhere.
Yes, I'm wishing now you lived somewhere away from here
And I was a bum on the bumpers a thousand miles away dead
    broke.
        I wish the kids had never come
        And rent and coal and clothes to pay for
        And a grocery man calling for cash,
        Every day cash for beans and prunes.
        I wish to God I never saw you, Mag.
        I wish to God the kids had never come.

Mamie

Mamie beat her head against the bars of a little Indiana town
    and dreamed of romance and big things off somewhere
    the way the railroad trains all ran.
She could see the smoke of the engines get lost down where
    the streaks of steel flashed in the sun and when the news-
    papers came in on the morning mail she knew there was
    a big Chicago far off, where all the trains ran.
She got tired of the barber shop boys and the post office chat-
    ter and the church gossip and the old pieces the band
    played on the Fourth of July and Decoration Day
And sobbed at her fate and beat her head against the bars and
    was going to kill herself
When the thought came to her that if she was going to die
    she might as well die struggling for a clutch of romance
    among the streets of Chicago.
She has a job now at six dollars a week in the basement of the
    Boston Store
And even now she beats her head against the bars in the same
    old way and wonders if there is a bigger place the rail-
    roads run to from Chicago where maybe there is
                romance
                and big things
                and real dreams
                that never go smash.

Fog

The fog comes
on little cat feet.

It sits looking
over harbor and city
on silent haunches
and then moves on.

Under a Hat Rim

While the hum and the hurry
Of passing footfalls
Beat in my ear like the restless surf
Of a wind-blown sea,
A soul came to me
Out of the look on a face.

Eyes like a lake
Where a storm-wind roams
Caught me from under
The rim of a hat.
I thought of a midsea wreck
and bruised fingers clinging
to a broken state-room door.

Nocturne in a Deserted Brickyard

Stuff of the moon
Runs on the lapping sand
Out to the longest shadows.
Under the curving willows,
And round the creep of the wave line,
Fluxions of yellow and dusk on the waters
Make a wide dreaming pansy of an old pond in the night.

Window

Night from a railroad car window
Is a great, dark, soft thing
Broken across with slashes of light.

Harrison Street Court

I heard a woman's lips
Speaking to a companion
Say these words:

"A woman what hustles
Never keeps nothin'
For all her hustlin'.
Somebody always gets
What she goes on the street for.
If it ain't a pimp
It's a bull what gets it.
I been hustlin' now
Till I ain't much good any more.
I got nothin' to show for it.
Some man got it all,
Every night's hustlin' I ever did."

Languages

There are no handles upon a language
Whereby men take hold of it
And mark it with signs for its remembrance.
It is a river, this language,
Once in a thousand years
Breaking a new course
Changing its way to the ocean.
It is mountain effluvia
Moving to valleys
And from nation to nation
Crossing borders and mixing.

Languages die like rivers.
Words wrapped round your tongue today
And broken to shape of thought
Between your teeth and lips speaking
Now and today
Shall be faded hieroglyphics
Ten thousand years from now.
Sing—and singing—remember
Your song dies and changes
And is not here to-morrow
Any more than the wind
Blowing ten thousand years ago.

Sunset from Omaha Hotel Window

Into the blue river hills
The red sun runners go
And the long sand changes
And to-day is a goner
And to-day is not worth haggling over.

    Here in Omaha
    The gloaming is bitter
    As in Chicago
    Or Kenosha.

The long sand changes.
To-day is a goner.
Time knocks in another brass nail.
Another yellow plunger shoots the dark.

    Constellations
    Wheeling over Omaha
    As in Chicago
    Or Kenosha.

The long sand is gone
        and all the talk is stars.
They circle in a dome over Nebraska.

Adelaide Crapsey

Among the bumble-bees in red-top hay, a freckled field of
    brown-eyed Susans dripping yellow leaves in July,
        I read your heart in a book.

And your mouth of blue pansy—I know somewhere I have
    seen it rain-shattered.

And I have seen a woman with her head flung between her
    naked knees, and her head held there listening to the sea,
    the great naked sea shouldering a load of salt.

And the blue pansy mouth sang to the sea:
        Mother of God, I'm so little a thing,
        Let me sing longer,
        Only a little longer.

And the sea shouldered its salt in long gray combers hauling
    new shapes on the beach sand.

Bilbea

(From tablet writing, Babylonian excavations of 4th millennium B.C.)

Bilbea, I was in Babylon on Saturday night.
I saw nothing of you anywhere.
I was at the old place and the other girls were there, but no
    Bilbea.

Have you gone to another house? or city?
Why don't you write?
I was sorry. I walked home half-sick.

Tell me how it goes.
Send me some kind of a letter.
And take care of yourself.

Portrait of a Motor Car

It's a lean car . . . a long-legged dog of a car . . . a gray-
   ghost eagle car.
The feet of it eat the dirt of a road . . . the wings of it eat the
   hills.
Danny the driver dreams of it when he sees women in red
   skirts and red sox in his sleep.
It is in Danny's life and runs in the blood of him . . . a lean
   gray-ghost car.

Cool Tombs

When Abraham Lincoln was shoveled into the tombs, he for-
   got the copperheads and the assassin . . . in the dust, in
   the cool tombs.

And Ulysses Grant lost all thought of con men and Wall
   Street, cash and collateral turned ashes . . . in the dust,
   in the cool tombs.

Pocahontas' body, lovely as a poplar, sweet as a red haw in
   November or a pawpaw in May, did she wonder? does
   she remember? . . . in the dust, in the cool tombs?

Take any streetful of people buying clothes and groceries,
   cheering a hero or throwing confetti and blowing tin
   horns . . . tell me if the lovers are losers . . . tell me if
   any get more than the lovers . . . in the dust . . . in the
   cool tombs.

Galoots

Galoots, you hairy, hankering,
Snousle on the bones you eat, chew at the gristle and lick the
   last of it.

Grab off the bones in the paws of other galoots—hook your
    claws in their sleazy mouths—snap and run.
If long-necks sit on their rumps and sing wild cries to the
    winter moon, chasing their tails to the flickers of foolish
    stars . . . let 'em howl.
Galoots fat with too much, galoots lean with too little, ga-
    loot millions and millions, snousle and snicker on, plug
    your exhausts, hunt your snacks of fat and lean, grab off
    yours.

Manual System

Mary has a thingamajig clamped on her ears
And sits all day taking plugs out and sticking plugs in.
Flashes and flashes—voices and voices
                  calling for ears to pour words in
Faces at the ends of wires asking for other faces
                at the ends of other wires:
All day taking plugs out and sticking plugs in,
Mary has a thingamajig clamped on her ears.

Cahoots

Play it across the table.
What if we steal this city blind?
If they want any thing let 'em nail it down.

Harness bulls, dicks, front office men,
And the high goats up on the bench,
Ain't they all in cahoots?
Ain't it fifty-fifty all down the line,
Petemen, dips, boosters, stick-ups and guns—
        what's to hinder?

Go fifty-fifty.
If they nail you call in a mouthpiece.
Fix it, you gazump, you slant-head, fix it.
          Feed 'em. . . .

Nothin' ever sticks to my fingers, nah, nah,
          nothin' like that,
But there ain't no law we got to wear mittens—
          huh—is there?
Mittens, that's a good one—mittens!
There oughta be a law everybody wear mittens.

from
The People, Yes

4

The people know what the land knows
the numbers odd and even of the land
the slow hot wind of summer and its withering
or again the crimp of the driving white blizzard
and neither of them to be stopped
neither saying anything else than:
          "I'm not arguing. I'm telling you."

The old-timer on the desert was gray
and grizzled with ever seeing the sun:
          "For myself I don't care whether it rains.
          I've seen it rain.
          But I'd like to have it rain
          pretty soon sometime.
          Then my son could see it.
          He's never seen it rain."

"Out here on the desert,"
          said the first woman who said it,
                    "the first year you don't believe
                    what others tell you

and the second year you don't
believe what you tell yourself."

"I weave thee, I weave thee,"
sang the weaving Sonora woman.
"I weave thee,
thou art for a Sonora fool."

And the fool spoke of her,
over wine mentioned her:
"She can teach a pair of stilts to dance."

"What is the east? Have you been in the east?"
the New Jersey woman asked the little girl
the wee child growing up in Arizona who said:
"Yes, I've been in the east,
the east is where trees come
between you and the sky."

Another baby in Cleveland, Ohio,
in Cuyahoga County, Ohio—
why did she ask:
"Papa,
what is the moon
supposed to advertise?"

And the boy in Winnetka, Illinois who wanted to know:
"Is there a train so long you can't count the cars?
Is there a blackboard so long it will hold all the numbers?"

What of the Athenian last year on whose bosom
a committee hung a medal to say to the world
here is a champion heavyweight poet?
He stood on a two-masted schooner
and flung his medal far out on the sea bosom.
"And why not?
Has anybody ever given the ocean a medal?
Who of the poets equals the music of the sea?
And where is a symbol of the people
unless it is the sea?"

"Is it far to the next town?"
  asked the Arkansas traveller
  who was given the comfort:
     "It seems farther than it is
      but you'll find it ain't."

Six feet six was Davy Tipton
and he had the proportions
as kingpin Mississippi River pilot
nearly filling the pilothouse
as he took the wheel with a laugh:
"Big rivers ought to have big men."

On the homestretch of a racetrack
in the heart of the bluegrass country
in Lexington, Kentucky
they strewed the ashes of a man
who had so ordered in his will.
     He loved horses
     and wanted his dust
in the flying hoofs of the homestretch.

19

     The people, yes, the people,
Everyone who got a letter today
And those the mail-carrier missed,
The women at the cookstoves preparing meals, in a sewing
     corner mending, in a basement laundering, woman the
     homemaker,
The women at the factory tending a stitching machine, some
     of them the mainstay of the jobless man at home
     cooking, laundering,
Streetwalking jobhunters, walkers alive and keen, sleepwalkers
     drifting along, the stupefied and hopeless down-and-
     outs, the game fighters who will die fighting,
Walkers reading signs and stopping to study windows, the
     signs and windows aimed straight at their eyes, their
     wants,

Women in and out of doors to look and feel, to try on, to buy
    and take away, to order and have it charged and
    delivered, to pass by on account of price and conditions,
The shopping crowds, the newspaper circulation, the
    bystanders who witness parades, who meet the boat, the
    train, who throng in wavelines to a fire, an explosion, an
    accident—
The people, yes—
Their shoe soles wearing holes in stone steps, their hands and
    gloves wearing soft niches in banisters of granite, two
    worn foot-tracks at the general-delivery window,
Driving their cars, stop and go, red light, green light, and the
    law of the traffic cop's fingers, on their way, loans and
    mortgages, margins to cover,
Payments on the car, the bungalow, the radio, the electric
    icebox, accumulated interest on loans for past payments,
    the writhing point of where the money will come from,
Crime thrown in their eyes from every angle, crimes against
    property and person, crime in the prints and films, crime
    as a lurking shadow ready to spring into reality, crime as
    a method and a technic,
Comedy as an offset to crime, the laughmakers, the odd
    numbers in the news and the movies, original clowns and
    imitators, and in the best you never know what's coming
    next even when it's hokum,
And sports, how a muff in the seventh lost yesterday's game
    and now they are learning to hit Dazzy's fadeaway ball
    and did you hear how Foozly plowed through that line
    for a touchdown this afternoon?
And daily the death toll of the speed wagons; a cripple a
    minute in fenders, wheels, steel and glass splinters; a
    stammering witness before a coroner's jury, "It
    happened so sudden I don't know what happened."
And in the air a decree: life is a gamble; take a chance; you
    pick a number and see what you get: anything can
    happen in this sweepstakes: around the corner may be
    prosperity or the worst depression yet: who knows?
    nobody: you pick a number, you draw a card, you shoot
    the bones.

In the poolrooms the young hear, "Ashes to ashes, dust to
dust, If the women don't get you then the whiskey
must," and in the churches, "We walk by faith and not
by sight,"

Often among themselves in their sessions of candor the
young saying, "Everything's a racket, only the gyp artists
get by."

And over and beyond the latest crime or comedy always that
relentless meal ticket saying dont-lose-me, hold your job,
glue your mind on that job or when your last nickel is
gone you live on your folks or sign for relief,

And the terror of these unknowns is a circle of black ghosts
holding men and women in toil and danger, and
sometimes shame, beyond the dreams of their blossom
days, the days before they set out on their own.

What is this "occupational disease" we hear about? It's a
sickness that breaks your health on account of the work
you're in. That's all. Another kind of work and you'd
have been as good as any of them. You'd have been your
old self.

And what is this "hazardous occupation"? Why that's where
you're liable to break your neck or get smashed on the
job so you're no good on that job any more and that's
why you can't get any regular life insurance so long as
you're on that job.

These are heroes then—among the plain people—Heroes, did
you say? And why not? They give all they've got and ask
no questions and take what comes and what more do
you want?

On the street you can see them any time, some with jobs,
some nothing doing, here a down-and-out, there a game
fighter who will die fighting.

On a Flimmering Floom You Shall Ride

Summary and footnote of and on the testimony of the poet MacLeish under appointment as Assistant Secretary of State, under oath before a Congressional examining committee pressing him to divulge the portents and meanings of his poems.

Nobody noogers the shaff of a sloo.
Nobody slimbers a wench with a winch
Nor higgles armed each with a niggle
    and each the flimdrat of a smee,
    each the inbiddy hum of a smoo.

Then slong me dorst with the flagdarsh.
Then creep me deep with the crawbright.
Let idle winds ploodaddle the dorshes.
And you in the gold of the gloaming
You shall be sloam with the hoolriffs.

On a flimmering floom you shall ride.
They shall tell you bedish and desist.
On a flimmering floom you shall ride.

JOE HILL

(1879–1915)

The Preacher and the Slave

(Tune: "Sweet Bye and Bye")

Long-haired preachers come out every night,
Try to tell you what's wrong and what's right;
But when asked how 'bout something to eat
They will answer with voices so sweet:

Chorus:

You will eat, bye and bye,
  In that glorious land above the sky;
Work and pray, live on hay,
You'll get pie in the sky when you die.

The starvation army they play,
They sing and they clap and they pray.
Till they get all your coin on the drum,
Then they tell you when you are on the bum:

Chorus:

You will eat, bye and bye,
In that glorious land above the sky;
Work and pray, live on hay,
You'll get pie in the sky when you die.

Holy Rollers and jumpers come out,
They holler, they jump and they shout.
Give your money to Jesus they say,
He will cure all diseases today.

If you fight hard for children and wife—
Try to get something good in this life—
You're a sinner and bad man, they tell,
When you die you will sure go to hell.

Workingmen of all countries unite,
Side by side we for freedom will fight:
When the world and its wealth we have gained
To the grafters we'll sing this refrain:

Last Chorus:

You will eat, bye and bye.
When you've learned how to cook and to fry;
Chop some wood, 'twill do you good,
And you'll eat in the sweet bye and bye.

VACHEL LINDSAY

(1879–1931)

General William Booth Enters Into Heaven

(To be sung to the tune of The Blood of the Lamb
with indicated instrument)

I

[*Bass drum beaten loudly.*]
Booth led boldly with his big bass drum—
(Are you washed in the blood of the Lamb?)
The Saints smiled gravely and they said: "He's come."
(Are you washed in the blood of the Lamb?)
Walking lepers followed, rank on rank,
Lurching bravoes from the ditches dank,
Drabs from the alleyways and drug fiends pale—
Minds still passion-ridden, soul-powers frail:—
Vermin-eaten saints with mouldy breath,
Unwashed legions with the ways of Death—
(Are you washed in the blood of the Lamb?)

[*Banjos.*]
Every slum had sent its half-a-score
The round world over. (Booth had groaned for more.)
Every banner that the wide world flies
Bloomed with glory and transcendent dyes.
Big-voiced lasses made their banjos bang,
Tranced, fanatical they shrieked and sang:—
"Are you washed in the blood of the Lamb?"
Hallelujah! It was queer to see
Bull-necked convicts with that land make free.
Loons with trumpets blowed a blare, blare, blare
On, on upward thro' the golden air!
(Are you washed in the blood of the Lamb?)

II

[*Bass drum slower and softer.*]
Booth died blind and still by Faith he trod,
Eyes still dazzled by the ways of God.
Booth led boldly, and he looked the chief
Eagle countenance in sharp relief,
Beard a-flying, air of high command
Unabated in that holy land.

[*Sweet flute music.*]
Jesus came from out the court-house door,
Stretched his hands above the passing poor.
Booth saw not, but led his queer ones there
Round and round the mighty court-house square.
Yet in an instant all that blear review
Marched on spotless, clad in raiment new.
The lame were straightened, withered limbs uncurled
And blind eyes opened on a new, sweet world.

[*Bass drum louder.*]
Drabs and vixens in a flash made whole!
Gone was the weasel-head, the snout, the jowl!
Sages and sibyls now, and athletes clean,
Rulers of empires, and of forests green!

[*Grand chorus of all instruments. Tambourines to the
    foreground.*]
The hosts were sandalled, and their wings were fire!
(Are you washed in the blood of the Lamb?)
But their noise played havoc with the angel-choir.
(Are you washed in the blood of the Lamb?)
O, shout Salvation! It was good to see
Kings and Princes by the Lamb set free.
The banjos rattled and the tambourines
Jing-jing-jingled in the hands of Queens.

[*Reverently sung, no instruments.*]
And when Booth halted by the curb for prayer
He saw his Master thro' the flag-filled air.
Christ came gently with a robe and crown
For Booth the soldier, while the throng knelt down.
He saw King Jesus. They were face to face,
And he knelt a-weeping in that holy place.
Are you washed in the blood of the Lamb?

The Eagle That Is Forgotten

[*John P. Altgeld. Born Dec. 30, 1847; died March 12, 1902*]

Sleep softly * * * eagle forgotten * * * under the stone.
Time has its way with you there, and the clay has its own.

"We have buried him now," thought your foes, and in secret
    rejoiced.
They made a brave show of their mourning, their hatred
    unvoiced.
They had snarled at you, barked at you, foamed at you day
    after day,
Now you were ended. They praised you, * * * and laid you
    away.

The others that mourned you in silence and terror and truth,
The widow bereft of her crust, and the boy without youth,
The mocked and the scorned and the wounded, the lame and
    the poor
That should have remembered forever, * * * remember no
    more.

Where are those lovers of yours, on what name do they call
The lost, that in armies wept over your funeral pall?
They call on the names of a hundred high-valiant ones,
A hundred white eagles have risen the sons of your sons,
The zeal in their wings is a zeal that your dreaming began
The valor that wore out your soul in the service of man.

Sleep softly, * * * eagle forgotten, * * * under the stone,
Time has its way with you there and the clay has its own.
Sleep on, O brave hearted, O wise man, that kindled the
　　　flame—
To live in mankind is far more than to live in a name,
To live in mankind, far, far more * * * than to live in a name.

The Congo

A Study of the Negro Race

I. THEIR BASIC SAVAGERY

Fat black bucks in a wine-barrel room,
Barrel-house kings, with feet unstable,
Sagged and reeled and pounded on the table,
Pounded on the table,

A deep rolling bass.

Beat an empty barrel with the handle of a
　　　broom,
Hard as they were able,
Boom, boom, Boom,
With a silk umbrella and the handle of a broom,
Boomlay, boomlay, boomlay, Boom.
Then I had religion, Then I had a vision.
I could not turn from their revel in derision.
Then I saw the Congo, creeping
　　　through the black,
Cutting through the forest with a
　　　golden track.

More deliberate. Solemnly chanted.

Then along that riverbank
A thousand miles
Tattooed cannibals danced in files;
Then I heard the boom of the blood-lust song
And a thigh-bone beating on a tin-pan gong.
And "Blood" screamed the whistles and the
　　　fifes of the warriors,
"Blood" screamed the skull-faced, lean
　　　witch-doctors,

A rapidly piling climax of speed and racket.

"Whirl ye the deadly voo-doo rattle,
Harry the uplands,
Steal all the cattle,
Rattle-rattle, rattle-rattle,
Bing.
Boomlay, boomlay, boomlay, Boom,"
A roaring, epic, rag-time tune   *With a philoso-*
From the mouth of the Congo   *phic pause.*
To the Mountains of the Moon.
Death is an Elephant,
Torch-eyed and horrible,   *Shrilly and*
Foam-flanked and terrible.   *with a heavily*
Boom, steal the pygmies,   *accented metre.*
Boom, kill the Arabs,
Boom, kill the white men,
Hoo, Hoo, Hoo.   *Like the wind*
Listen to the yell of Leopold's ghost   *in the chimney.*
Burning in Hell for his hand-maimed host.
Hear how the demons chuckle and yell
Cutting his hands off, down in Hell.
Listen to the creepy proclamation,
Blown through the lairs of the forest-nation,
Blown past the white-ants' hill of clay,
Blown past the marsh where the butterflies
  play:—
"Be careful what you do,
Or Mumbo-Jumbo, God of the Congo,   *All the o sounds*
And all of the other   *very golden.*
Gods of the Congo,   *Heavy accents*
Mumbo-Jumbo will hoo-doo you,   *very heavy.*
Mumbo-Jumbo will hoo-doo you,   *Light accents*
Mumbo-Jumbo will hoo-doo you."   *very light. Last*
   line whispered.

II. THEIR IRREPRESSIBLE HIGH SPIRITS

Wild crap-shooters with a whoop and a call   *Rather shrill*
Danced the juba in their gambling-hall   *and high.*
And laughed fit to kill, and shook the town,
And guyed the policemen and laughed them down
With a boomlay, boomlay, boomlay, Boom.

THEN I SAW THE CONGO, CREEPING THROUGH
    THE BLACK,

Read exactly as in first section.

CUTTING THROUGH THE FOREST WITH A
    GOLDEN TRACK.

A negro fairyland swung into view,
A minstrel river
Where dreams come true.
The ebony palace soared on high
Through the blossoming trees to the evening
    sky.
The inlaid porches and casements shone
With gold and ivory and elephant-bone.
And the black crowd laughed till their sides
    were sore
At the baboon butler in the agate door,
And the well-known tunes of the parrot band
That trilled on the bushes of that magic land.

Lay emphasis on the delicate ideas. Keep as light-footed as possible.

A troupe of skull-faced witch-men came
Through the agate doorway in suits of flame,
Yea, long-tailed coats with a gold-leaf crust
And hats that were covered with diamond-dust.
And the crowd in the court gave a whoop and
    a call
And danced the juba from wall to wall.
But the witch-men suddenly stilled the throng
With a stern cold glare, and a stern old
    song:—
"Mumbo-jumbo will hoo-doo you." . . .
Just then from the doorway, as fat as shotes,
Came the cake-walk princes in their long
    red coats,
Canes with a brilliant lacquer shine,
And tall silk hats that were red as wine.
And they pranced with their butterfly partners
    there,
Coal-black maidens with pearls in their hair,
Knee-skirts trimmed with the jassamine sweet,
And bells on their ankles and little black-feet.

With pomposity.

With a great deliberation and ghostliness.

With overwhelming assurance, good cheer, and pomp.

With growing speed and sharply marked dance-rhythm.

And the couples railed at the chant and the
    frown
Of the witch-men lean, and laughed them down.
(O rare was the revel, and well worth while
That made those glowering witch-men smile.)

The cake-walk royalty then began
To walk for a cake that was tall as a man
To the tune of "Boomlay, boomlay, Boom,"
While the witch-men laughed, with a
    sinister air,

With a touch of negro dialect, and as rapidly as possible toward the end.

And sang with the scalawags prancing there:—
"Walk with care, walk with care,
Or Mumbo-Jumbo, God of the Congo,
And all of the other
Gods of the Congo,
Mumbo-Jumbo will hoo-doo you.
Beware, beware, walk with care,
Boomlay, boomlay, boomlay, boom.
Boomlay, boomlay, boomlay, boom,
Boomlay, boomlay, boomlay, boom,
Boomlay, boomlay, boomlay,
Boom."
Oh rare was the revel, and well worth while
That made those glowering witch-men smile.

Slow philo-sophic calm.

III. The Hope of their Religion

A good old negro in the slums of the town
Preached at a sister for her velvet gown.
Howled at a brother for his low-down ways,
His prowling, guzzling, sneak-thief days.
Beat on the Bible till he wore it out
Starting the jubilee revival shout.
And some had visions, as they stood on chairs,
And sang of Jacob, and the golden stairs,
And they all repented, a thousand strong
From their stupor and savagery and sin and
    wrong

Heavy bass. With a literal imitation of camp-meeting racket, and trance.

And slammed with their hymn books till they
    shook the room
With "glory, glory, glory,"
And "Boom, boom, Boom,"
THEN I SAW THE CONGO, CREEPING THROUGH
    THE BLACK
CUTTING THROUGH THE JUNGLE WITH A
    GOLDEN TRACK.

Exactly as in the first section. Begin with terror and power, end with joy.

And the gray sky opened like a new-rent veil
And showed the apostles with their coats of
    mail.
In bright white steele they were seated round
And their fire-eyes watched where the Congo
    wound.
And the twelve Apostles, from their thrones on
    high
Thrilled all the forest with their heavenly cry:—
"Mumbo-Jumbo will die in the jungle;
Never again will he hoo-doo you,
Never again will he hoo-doo you."

Sung to the tune of "Hark, ten thousand harps and voices."

Then along that river, a thousand miles
The vine-snared trees fell down in files.
Pioneer angels cleared the way
For a Congo paradise, for babes at play,
For sacred capitals, for temples clean.
Gone were the skull-faced witch-men lean.

With growing deliberation and joy.

There, where the wild ghost-gods had wailed
A million boats of the angels sailed
With oars of silver, and prows of blue
And silken pennants that the sun shone through.
'Twas a land transfigured, 'twas a new creation.
Oh, a singing wind swept the negro nation
And on through the backwoods clearing flew:—
"Mumbo-Jumbo is dead in the jungle.
Never again will he hoo-doo you.
Never again will he hoo-doo you."

In a rather high key—as delicately as possible.

To the tune of "Hark, ten thousand harps and voices."

Redeemed were the forests, the beasts and the
    men,
And only the vulture dared again
By the far, lone mountains of the moon
To cry, in the silence, the Congo tune:—
"Mumbo-Jumbo will hoo-doo you,
Mumbo-Jumbo will hoo-doo you.
Mumbo . . . Jumbo . . . will . . . hoo-doo . . .
    you."

Dying down into a pene- trating, terrified whisper.

Factory Windows Are Always Broken

Factory windows are always broken.
Somebody's always throwing bricks,
Somebody's always heaving cinders,
Playing ugly Yahoo tricks.

Factory windows are always broken.
Other windows are let alone.
No one throws through the chapel-window
The bitter, snarling, derisive stone.

Factory windows are always broken.
Something or other is going wrong.
Something is rotten—I think, in Denmark.
End of the factory-window song.

Abraham Lincoln Walks at Midnight

(In Springfield, Illinois)

It is portentous, and a thing of state
That here at midnight, in our little town
A mourning figure walks, and will not rest,
Near the old court-house pacing up and down,

Or by his homestead, or in shadowed yards
He lingers where his children used to play,
Or through the market, on the well-worn stones
He stalks until the dawn-stars burn away.

A bronzed, lank man! His suit of ancient black,
A famous high top-hat and plain worn shawl
Make him the quaint great figure that men love,
The prairie-lawyer, master of us all.

He cannot sleep upon his hillside now.
He is among us:—as in times before!
And we who toss and lie awake for long
Breathe deep, and start, to see him pass the door.

His head is bowed. He thinks on men and kings.
Yea, when the sick world cries, how can he sleep?
Too many peasants fight, they know not why,
Too many homesteads in black terror weep.

The sins of all the war-lords burn his heart.
He sees the dreadnaughts scouring every main.
He carries on his shawl-wrapped shoulders now
The bitterness, the folly and the pain.

He cannot rest until a spirit-dawn
Shall come;—the shining hope of Europe free:
The league of sober folk, the Workers' Earth,
Bringing long peace to Cornland, Alp and Sea.

It breaks his heart that kings must murder still,
That all his hours of travail here for men
Seem yet in vain. And who will bring white peace
That he may sleep upon his hill again?

Mae Marsh, Motion Picture Actress

In "Man's Genesis," "The Wild Girl of the Sierras,"
"The Wharf Rat," "A Girl of the Paris Streets," etc.

I

The arts are old, old as the stones
From which man carved the sphinx austere.
Deep are the days the old arts bring:
Ten thousand years of yesteryear.

II

She is madonna in an art
As wild and young as her sweet eyes:
A frail dew flower from this hot lamp
That is today's divine surprise.

Despite raw lights and gloating mobs
She is not seared: a picture still:
Rare silk the fine director's hand
May weave for magic if he will.

When ancient films have crumbled like
Papyrus rolls of Egypt's day,
Let the dust speak: "Her pride was high,
All but the artist hid away:

"Kin to the myriad artist clan
Since time began, whose work is dear."
The deep new ages come with her,
Tomorrow's years of yesteryear.

Bryan, Bryan, Bryan, Bryan

The Campaign of Eighteen Ninety-six, as Viewed at
the Time by a Sixteen Year Old, etc.

I

In a nation of one hundred fine, mob-hearted, lynching,
    relenting, repenting millions,
There are plenty of sweeping, swinging, stinging, gorgeous
    things to shout about,
And knock your old blue devils out.

I brag and chant of Bryan, Bryan, Bryan,
Candidate for president who sketched a silver Zion,
The one American Poet who could sing out doors.
He brought in tides of wonder, of unprecedented splendor,
Wild roses from the plains, that made hearts tender,
All the funny circus silks
Of politics unfurled,
Bartlett pears of romance that were honey at the cores,
And torchlights down the street, to the end of the world.

There were truths eternal in the gab and tittle-tattle.
There were real heads broken in the fustian and the rattle.
There were real lines drawn:
Not the silver and the gold,
But Nebraska's cry went eastward against the dour and old,
The mean and cold.

It was eighteen ninety-six, and I was just sixteen
And Altgeld ruled in Springfield, Illinois,
When there came from the sunset Nebraska's shout of joy:—
In a coat like a deacon, in a black Stetson hat
He scourged the elephant plutocrats
With barbed wire from the Platte.
The scales dropped from their mighty eyes.
They saw that summer's noon
A tribe of wonders coming
To a marching tune.

Oh the long horns from Texas,
The jay hawks from Kansas,
The plop-eyed bungaroo and giant giassicus,
The varmint, chipmunk, bugaboo,
The horned-toad, prairie-dog and ballyhoo,
From all the new-born states arow,
Bidding the eagles of the west fly on,
Bidding the eagles of the west fly on.
The fawn, prodactyl and thing-a-ma-jig,
The rakaboor, the hellangone,
The whangdoodle, batfowl and pig,
The coyote, wild-cat and grizzly in a glow,
In a miracle of health and speed, the whole breed abreast,
They leaped the Mississippi, blue border of the West,
From the Gulf to Canada, two thousand miles long:—
Against the towns of Tubal Cain,
Ah,—sharp was their song.
Against the ways of Tubal Cain, too cunning for the young,
The long-horn calf, the buffalo and wampus gave tongue.

These creatures were defending things Mark Hanna never
        dreamed:
The moods of airy childhood that in desert dews gleamed,
The gossamers and whimsies,
The monkeyshines and didoes
Rank and strange
Of the canyons and the range,
The ultimate fantastics
Of the far western slope,
And of prairie schooner children
Born beneath the stars,
Beneath falling snows,
Of the babies born at midnight
In the sod huts of lost hope,
With no physician there,
Except a Kansas prayer,
With the Indian raid a howling through the air.

And all these in their helpless days
By the dour East oppressed,
Mean paternalism
Making their mistakes for them,
Crucifying half the West,
Till the whole Atlantic coast
Seemed a giant spiders' nest.

And these children and their sons
At last rode through the cactus,
A cliff of mighty cowboys
On the lope,
With gun and rope.
And all the way to frightened Maine the old East heard them
    call,
And saw our Bryan by a mile lead the wall
Of men and whirling flowers and beasts,
The bard and the prophet of them all.
Prairie avenger, mountain lion,
Bryan, Bryan, Bryan, Bryan,
Gigantic troubadour, speaking like a siege gun,
Smashing Plymouth Rock with his boulders from the West,
And just a hundred miles behind, tornadoes piled across the
    sky,
Blotting out sun and moon,
A sign on high.

Headlong, dazed and blinking in the weird green light,
The scalawags made moan,
Afraid to fight.

II

When Bryan came to Springfield, and Altgeld gave him
    greeting,
Rochester was deserted, Divernon was deserted,
Mechanicsburg, Riverton, Chickenbristle, Cotton Hill,
Empty: for all Sangamon drove to the meeting—
In silver-decked racing cart,
Buggy, buckboard, carryall,
Carriage, phaeton, whatever would haul,

And silver-decked farm-wagons gritted, banged and rolled,
With the new tale of Bryan by the iron tires told.

The State House loomed afar,
A speck, a hive, a football,
A captive balloon!
And the town was all one spreading wing of bunting, plumes,
    and sunshine,
Every rag and flag, and Bryan picture sold,
When the rigs in many a dusty line
Jammed our streets at noon,
And joined the wild parade against the power of gold.

We roamed, we boys from High School
With mankind,
While Springfield gleamed,
Silk-lined.
Oh Tom Dines, and Art Fitzgerald,
And the gangs that they could get!
I can hear them yelling yet.
Helping the incantation,
Defying aristocracy,
With every bridle gone,
Ridding the world of the low down mean,
Bidding the eagles of the West fly on,
Bidding the eagles of the West fly on,
We were bully, wild and wooly,
Never yet curried below the knees.
We saw flowers in the air,
Fair as the Pleiades, bright as Orion,
—Hopes of all mankind,
Made rare, resistless, thrice refined.
Oh we bucks from every Springfield ward!
Colts of democracy—
Yet time-winds out of Chaos from the star-fields of the Lord.

The long parade rolled on. I stood by my best girl.
She was a cool young citizen, with wise and laughing eyes.
With my necktie by my ear, I was stepping on my dear,
But she kept like a pattern, without a shaken curl.

She wore in her hair a brave prairie rose.
Her gold chums cut her, for that was not the pose.
No Gibson Girl would wear it in that fresh way.
But we were fairy Democrats, and this was our day.

The earth rocked like the ocean, the sidewalk was a deck.
The houses for the moment were lost in the wide wreck.
And the bands played strange and stranger music as they
    trailed along.
Against the ways of Tubal Cain,
Ah, sharp was their song!
The demons in the bricks, the demons in the grass,
The demons in the bank-vaults peered out to see us pass,
And the angels in the trees, the angels in the grass,
The angels in the flags, peered out to see us pass.
And the sidewalk was our chariot, and the flowers bloomed
    higher,
And the street turned to silver and the grass turned to fire,
And then it was but grass, and the town was there again,
A place for women and men.

III

Then we stood where we could see
Every band,
And the speaker's stand.
And Bryan took the platform.
And he was introduced.
And he lifted his hand
And cast a new spell.
Progressive silence fell
In Springfield,
In Illinois,
Around the world.
Then we heard these glacial boulders across the prairie rolled:
"The people have a right to make their own mistakes. . . .
You shall not crucify mankind
Upon a cross of gold."

And everybody heard him—
In the streets and State House yard.
And everybody heard him
In Springfield,
In Illinois,
Around and around and around the world,
That danced upon its axis
And like a darling broncho whirled.

IV

July, August, suspense.
Wall Street lost to sense.
August, September, October,
More suspense,
And the whole East down like a wind-smashed fence.

Then Hanna to the rescue,
Hanna of Ohio,
Rallying the roller-tops,
Rallying the bucket-shops,
Threatening drouth and death,
Promising manna,
Rallying the trusts against the bawling flannelmouth;
Invading misers' cellars,
Tin-cans, socks,
Melting down the rocks,
Pouring out the long green to a million workers,
Spondulix by the mountain-load, to stop each new tornado,
And best the cheapskate, blatherskite,
Populistic, anarchistic,
Deacon—desperado.

V

Election night at midnight:
Boy Bryan's defeat.
Defeat of western silver.
Defeat of the wheat.
Victory of letterfiles
And plutocrats in miles

With dollar signs upon their coats,
Diamond watchchains on their vests
And spats on their feet.
Victory of custodians,
Plymouth Rock,
And all that inbred landlord stock.
Victory of the neat.
Defeat of the aspen groves of Colorado valleys,
The blue bells of the Rockies,
And blue bonnets of old Texas,
By the Pittsburg alleys.
Defeat of alfalfa and the Mariposa lily.
Defeat of the Pacific and the long Mississippi.
Defeat of the young by the old and silly.
Defeat of tornadoes by the poison vats supreme.
Defeat of my boyhood, defeat of my dream.

VI

Where is McKinley, that respectable McKinley,
The man without an angle or a tangle,
Who soothed down the city man and soothed down the
        farmer,
The German, the Irish, the Southerner, the Northerner,
Who climbed every greasy pole, and slipped through every
        crack;
Who soothed down the gambling hall, the bar-room, the
        church,
The devil vote, the angel vote, the neutral vote,
The desperately wicked, and their victims on the rack,
The gold vote, the silver vote, the brass vote, the lead vote,
Every vote. . . .

Where is McKinley, Mark Hanna's McKinley,
His slave, his echo, his suit of clothes?
Gone to join the shadows, with the pomps of that time,
And the flame of that summer's prairie rose.

Where is Cleveland whom the Democratic platform
Read from the party in a glorious hour?
Gone to join the shadows with pitchfork Tillman,
And sledge-hammer Altgeld who wrecked his power.

Where is Hanna, bull dog Hanna,
Low browed Hanna, who said: "Stand pat"?
Gone to his place with old Pierpont Morgan.
Gone somewhere . . . with lean rat Platt.

Where is Roosevelt, the young dude cowboy,
Who hated Bryan, then aped his way?
Gone to join the shadows with mighty Cromwell
And tall King Saul, till the Judgment day.

Where is Altgeld, brave as the truth,
Whose name the few still say with tears?
Gone to join the ironies with Old John Brown,
Whose fame rings loud for a thousand years.

Where is that boy, that Heaven-born Bryan,
That Homer Bryan, who sang from the West?
Gone to join the shadows with Altgeld the Eagle,
Where the kings and the slaves and the troubadours rest.

The Daniel Jazz

*Let the leader train the audience to roar like lions, and to
join in the refrain "Go chain the lions down," before
he begins to lead them in this jazz.*

Darius the Mede was a king and a wonder.   *Beginning*
His eye was proud, and his voice was thunder.   *with a strain*
He kept bad lions in a monstrous den.   *of "Dixie."*
He fed up the lions on Christian men.

Daniel was the chief hired man of the land.
He stirred up the jazz in the palace band.
He whitewashed the cellar. He shovelled in
    the coal.
And Daniel kept a-praying:—"Lord save my
    soul."
Daniel kept a-praying "Lord save my soul."
Daniel kept a-praying "Lord save my soul."

With a touch of "Alexan- der's Ragtime Band."

Daniel was the butler, swagger and swell.
He ran up stairs. He answered the bell.
And *he* would let in whoever came a-calling:—
Saints so holy, scamps so appalling.
"Old man Ahab leaves his card.
Elisha and the bears are a-waiting in the yard.
Here comes Pharaoh and his snakes a-calling.
Here comes Cain and his wife a-calling.
Shadrach, Meshach and Abednego for tea.
Here comes Jonah and the whale,
And the *Sea!*
Here comes St. Peter and his fishing pole.
Here comes Judas and his silver a-calling.
Here comes old Beelzebub a-calling."
And Daniel kept a-praying:—"Lord save my soul."
Daniel kept a-praying:—"Lord save my soul."
Daniel kept a-praying:—"Lord save my soul."

His sweetheart and his mother were Christian and meek.
They washed and ironed for Darius every week.
One Thursday he met them at the door:—
Paid them as usual, but acted sore.

He said:—"Your Daniel is a dead little pigeon.
He's a good hard worker, but he talks religion."
And he showed them Daniel in the lion's cage.
Daniel standing quietly, the lions in a rage.
His good old mother cried:—
"Lord save him."
And Daniel's tender sweetheart cried:—
"Lord save him."

And she was a golden lily in the dew.
And she was as sweet as an apple on the tree
And she was as fine as a melon in the corn-field,
Gliding and lovely as a ship on the sea,
Gliding and lovely as a ship on the sea.

And she prayed to the Lord:—
"*Send* Gabriel. *Send* Gabriel."

King Darius said to the lions:—
"Bite Daniel. Bite Daniel.
Bite him. Bite him. Bite him!"

Thus roared the lions:—
"We want Daniel, Daniel, Daniel,
We want Daniel, Daniel, Daniel,
Grrrrrrrrrrrrrrrrrrrrrrrrrrrrrrrrrrrrrrrrr
Grrrrrrrrrrrrrrrrrrrrrrrrrrrrrrrrrrrrrrrrr

*Here the
audience
roars with
the leader.*

And Daniel did not frown,
Daniel did not cry.
He kept on looking at the sky.
And the Lord said to Gabriel:—
"Go chain the lions down,
Go chain the lions down.
Go chain the lions down.
Go chain the lions down."

*The audience
sings this with
the leader, to
the old negro
tune.*

And *Gabriel* chained the lions,
And *Gabriel* chained the lions,
And *Gabriel* chained the lions,
And Daniel got out of the den,
And Daniel got out of the den,
And Daniel got out of the den.
And Darius said:—"You're a Christian child,"
Darius said:—"You're a Christian child,"
Darius said:—"You're a Christian child,"
And gave him his job again,
And gave him his job again,
And gave him his job again.

WALLACE STEVENS

(1879–1955)

Sunday Morning

I

Complacencies of the peignoir, and late
Coffee and oranges in a sunny chair,
And the green freedom of a cockatoo
Upon a rug mingle to dissipate
The holy hush of ancient sacrifice.
She dreams a little, and she feels the dark
Encroachment of that old catastrophe,
As a calm darkens among water-lights.
The pungent oranges and bright, green wings
Seem things in some procession of the dead,
Winding across wide water, without sound.
The day is like wide water, without sound,
Stilled for the passing of her dreaming feet
Over the seas, to silent Palestine,
Dominion of the blood and sepulchre.

II

Why should she give her bounty to the dead?
What is divinity if it can come
Only in silent shadows and in dreams?
Shall she not find in comforts of the sun,
In pungent fruit and bright, green wings, or else
In any balm or beauty of the earth,
Things to be cherished like the thought of heaven?
Divinity must live within herself:
Passions of rain, or moods in falling snow;
Grievings in loneliness, or unsubdued
Elations when the forest blooms; gusty
Emotions on wet roads on autumn nights;
All pleasures and all pains, remembering
The bough of summer and the winter branch.
These are the measures destined for her soul.

293

III

Jove in the clouds had his inhuman birth.
No mother suckled him, no sweet land gave
Large-mannered motions to his mythy mind.
He moved among us, as a muttering king,
Magnificent, would move among his hinds,
Until our blood, commingling, virginal,
With heaven, brought such requital to desire
The very hinds discerned it, in a star.
Shall our blood fail? Or shall it come to be
The blood of paradise? And shall the earth
Seem all of paradise that we shall know?
The sky will be much friendlier then than now,
A part of labor and a part of pain,
And next in glory to enduring love,
Not this dividing and indifferent blue.

IV

She says, "I am content when wakened birds,
Before they fly, test the reality
Of misty fields, by their sweet questionings;
But when the birds are gone, and their warm fields
Return no more, where, then, is paradise?"
There is not any haunt of prophesy,
Nor any old chimera of the grave,
Neither the golden underground, nor isle
Melodious, where spirits gat them home,
Nor visionary south, nor cloudy palm
Remote on heaven's hill, that has endured
As April's green endures; or will endure
Like her remembrance of awakened birds,
Or her desire for June and evening, tipped
By the consummation of the swallow's wings.

V

She says, "But in contentment I still feel
The need of some imperishable bliss."
Death is the mother of beauty; hence from her,

Alone, shall come fulfilment to our dreams
And our desires. Although she strews the leaves
Of sure obliteration on our paths,
The path sick sorrow took, the many paths
Where triumph rang its brassy phrase, or love
Whispered a little out of tenderness,
She makes the willow shiver in the sun
For maidens who were wont to sit and gaze
Upon the grass, relinquished to their feet.
She causes boys to pile new plums and pears
On disregarded plate. The maidens taste
And stray impassioned in the littering leaves.

VI

Is there no change of death in paradise?
Does ripe fruit never fall? Or do the boughs
Hang always heavy in that perfect sky,
Unchanging, yet so like our perishing earth,
With rivers like our own that seek for seas
They never find, the same receding shores
That never touch with inarticulate pang?
Why set the pear upon those river-banks
Or spice the shores with odors of the plum?
Alas, that they should wear our colors there,
The silken weavings of our afternoons,
And pick the strings of our insipid lutes!
Death is the mother of beauty, mystical,
Within whose burning bosom we devise
Our earthly mothers waiting, sleeplessly.

VII

Supple and turbulent, a ring of men
Shall chant in orgy on a summer morn
Their boisterous devotion to the sun,
Not as a god, but as a god might be,
Naked among them, like a savage source.
Their chant shall be a chant of paradise,
Out of their blood, returning to the sky;
And in their chant shall enter, voice by voice,

The windy lake wherein their lord delights,
The trees, like serafin, and echoing hills,
That choir among themselves long afterward.
They shall know well the heavenly fellowship
Of men that perish and of summer morn.
And whence they came and whither they shall go
The dew upon their feet shall manifest.

VIII

She hears, upon that water without sound,
A voice that cries, "The tomb in Palestine
Is not the porch of spirits lingering.
It is the grave of Jesus, where he lay."
We live in an old chaos of the sun,
Or old dependency of day and night,
Or island solitude, unsponsored, free,
Of that wide water, inescapable.
Deer walk upon our mountains, and the quail
Whistle about us their spontaneous cries;
Sweet berries ripen in the wilderness;
And, in the isolation of the sky,
At evening, casual flocks of pigeons make
Ambiguous undulations as they sink,
Downward to darkness, on extended wings.

Peter Quince at the Clavier

I

Just as my fingers on these keys
Make music, so the self-same sounds
On my spirit make a music, too.

Music is feeling, then, not sound;
And thus it is that what I feel,
Here in this room, desiring you,

Thinking of your blue-shadowed silk,
Is music. It is like the strain
Waked in the elders by Susanna;

Of a green evening, clear and warm,
She bathed in her still garden, while
The red-eyed elders, watching, felt

The basses of their beings throb
In witching chords, and their thin blood
Pulse pizzicati of Hosanna.

II

In the green water, clear and warm,
Susanna lay.
She searched
The touch of springs,
And found
Concealed imaginings.
She sighed,
For so much melody.

Upon the bank, she stood
In the cool
Of spent emotions.
She felt, among the leaves,
The dew
Of old devotions.

She walked upon the grass,
Still quavering.
The winds were like her maids,
On timid feet,
Fetching her woven scarves,
Yet wavering.

A breath upon her hand
Muted the night.
She turned—

A cymbal crashed,
And roaring horns.

III

Soon, with a noise like tambourines,
Came her attendant Byzantines.

They wondered why Susanna cried
Against the elders by her side;

And as they whispered, the refrain
Was like a willow swept by rain.

Anon, their lamps' uplifted flame
Revealed Susanna and her shame.

And then, the simpering Byzantines
Fled, with a noise like tambourines.

IV

Beauty is momentary in the mind—
The fitful tracing of a portal;
But in the flesh it is immortal.

The body dies; the body's beauty lives.
So evenings die, in their green going,
A wave, interminably flowing.
So gardens die, their meek breath scenting
The cowl of winter, done repenting.
So maidens die, to the auroral
Celebration of a maiden's choral.

Susanna's music touched the bawdy strings
Of those white elders; but, escaping,
Left only Death's ironic scraping.
Now, in its immortality, it plays
On the clear viol of her memory,
And makes a constant sacrament of praise.

Thirteen Ways of Looking at a Blackbird

I

Among twenty snowy mountains,
The only moving thing
Was the eye of the black bird.

II

I was of three minds,
Like a tree
In which there are three blackbirds.

III

The blackbird whirled in the autumn winds.
It was a small part of the pantomime.

IV

A man and a woman
Are one.
A man and a woman and a blackbird
Are one.

V

I do not know which to prefer,
The beauty of inflections
Or the beauty of innuendoes,
The blackbird whistling
Or just after.

VI

Icicles filled the long window
With barbaric glass.
The shadow of the blackbird
Crossed it, to and fro.
The mood
Traced in the shadow
An indecipherable cause.

VII

O thin men of Haddam,
Why do you imagine golden birds?
Do you not see how the blackbird
Walks around the feet
Of the women about you?

VIII

I know noble accents
And lucid, inescapable rhythms;
But I know, too,
That the blackbird is involved
In what I know.

IX

When the blackbird flew out of sight,
It marked the edge
Of one of many circles.

X

At the sight of blackbirds
Flying in a green light,
Even the bawds of euphony
Would cry out sharply.

XI

He rode over Connecticut
In a glass coach.
Once, a fear pierced him,
In that he mistook
The shadow of his equipage
For blackbirds.

XII

The river is moving.
The blackbird must be flying.

XIII

It was evening all afternoon.
It was snowing
And it was going to snow.
The blackbird sat
In the cedar-limbs.

Nomad Exquisite

As the immense dew of Florida
Brings forth
The big-finned palm
And green vine angering for life,

As the immense dew of Florida
Brings forth hymn and hymn
From the beholder,
Beholding all these green sides
And gold sides of green sides,

And blessed mornings,
Meet for the eye of the young alligator,
And lightning colors
So, in me, come flinging
Forms, flames, and the flakes of flames.

Infanta Marina

Her terrace was the sand
And the palms and the twilight.

She made of the motions of her wrist
The grandiose gestures
Of her thought.

The rumpling of the plumes
Of this creature of the evening
Came to be sleights of sails
Over the sea.

And thus she roamed
In the roamings of her fan,

Partaking of the sea,
And of the evening,
As they flowed around
And uttered their subsiding sound.

Domination of Black

At night, by the fire,
The colors of the bushes
And of the fallen leaves,
Repeating themselves,
Turned in the room,
Like the leaves themselves
Turning in the wind.
Yes: but the color of the heavy hemlocks
Came striding.
And I remembered the cry of the peacocks.

The colors of their tails
Were like the leaves themselves
Turning in the wind,
In the twilight wind.
They swept over the room,
Just as they flew from the boughs of the hemlocks
Down to the ground.
I heard them cry—the peacocks.
Was it a cry against the twilight
Or against the leaves themselves
Turning in the wind,
Turning as the flames

Turned in the fire,
Turning as the tails of the peacocks
Turned in the loud fire,
Loud as the hemlocks
Full of the cry of the peacocks?
Or was it a cry against the hemlocks?

Out of the window,
I saw how the planets gathered
Like the leaves themselves
Turning in the wind.
I saw how the night came,
Came striding like the color of the heavy hemlocks.
I felt afraid.
And I remembered the cry of the peacocks.

The Snow Man

One must have a mind of winter
To regard the frost and the boughs
Of the pine-trees crusted with snow;

And have been cold a long time
To behold the junipers shagged with ice,
The spruces rough in the distant glitter

Of the January sun; and not to think
Of any misery in the sound of the wind,
In the sound of a few leaves,

Which is the sound of the land
Full of the same wind
That is blowing in the same bare place

For the listener, who listens in the snow,
And, nothing himself, beholds
Nothing that is not there and the nothing that is.

Tea at the Palaz of Hoon

Not less because in purple I descended
The western day through what you called
The loneliest air, not less was I myself.

What was the ointment sprinkled on my beard?
What were the hymns that buzzed beside my ears?
What was the sea whose tide swept through me there?

Out of my mind the golden ointment rained,
And my ears made the blowing hymns they heard.
I was myself the compass of that sea:

I was the world in which I walked, and what I saw
Or heard or felt came not but from myself;
And there I found myself more truly and more strange.

The Emperor of Ice-Cream

Call the roller of big cigars,
The muscular one, and bid him whip
In kitchen cups concupiscent curds.
Let the wenches dawdle in such dress
As they are used to wear, and let the boys
Bring flowers in last month's newspapers.
Let be be finale of seem.
The only emperor is the emperor of ice-cream.

Take from the dresser of deal,
Lacking the three glass knobs, that sheet
On which she embroidered fantails once
And spread it so as to cover her face.
If her horny feet protrude, they come
To show how cold she is, and dumb.
Let the lamp affix its beam.
The only emperor is the emperor of ice-cream.

Disillusionment of Ten O'Clock

The houses are haunted
By white night-gowns.
None are green,
Or purple with green rings,
Or green with yellow rings,
Or yellow with blue rings.
None of them are strange,
With socks of lace
And beaded ceintures.
People are not going
To dream of baboons and periwinkles.
Only, here and there, an old sailor,
Drunk and asleep in his boots,
Catches tigers
In red weather.

To the One of Fictive Music

Sister and mother and diviner love,
And of the sisterhood of the living dead
Most near, most clear, and of the clearest bloom,
And of the fragrant mothers the most dear
And queen, and of diviner love the day
And flame and summer and sweet fire, no thread
Of cloudy silver sprinkles in your gown
Its venom of renown, and on your head
No crown is simpler than the simple hair.

Now, of the music summoned by the birth
That separates us from the wind and sea,
Yet leaves us in them, until earth becomes,
By being so much of the things we are,
Gross effigy and simulacrum, none
Gives motion to perfection more serene
Than yours, out of our imperfections wrought,
Most rare, or ever of more kindred air
In the laborious weaving that you wear.

For so retentive of themselves are men
That music is intensest which proclaims
The near, the clear, and vaunts the clearest bloom,
And of all vigils musing the obscure,
That apprehends the most which sees and names,
As in your name, an image that is sure,
Among the arrant spices of the sun,
O bough and bush and scented vine, in whom
We give ourselves our likest issuance.

Yet not too like, yet not so like to be
Too near, too clear, saving a little to endow
Our feigning with the strange unlike, whence springs
The difference that heavenly pity brings.
For this, musician, in your girdle fixed
Bear other perfumes. On your pale head wear
A band entwining, set with fatal stones.
Unreal, give back to us what once you gave:
The imagination that we spurned and crave.

The Death of a Soldier

Life contracts and death is expected,
As in a season of autumn.
The soldier falls.

He does not become a three-days personage,
Imposing his separation,
Calling for pomp.

Death is absolute and without memorial,
As in a season of autumn,
When the wind stops,

When the wind stops and, over the heavens,
The clouds go, nevertheless,
In their direction.

Sea Surface Full of Clouds

I

In that November off Tehuantepec,
The slopping of the sea grew still one night
And in the morning summer hued the deck

And made one think of rosy chocolate
And gilt umbrellas. Paradisal green
Gave suavity to the perplexed machine

Of ocean, which like limpid water lay.
Who, then, in that ambrosial latitude
Out of the light evolved the moving blooms,

Who, then, evolved the sea-blooms from the clouds
Diffusing balm in that Pacific calm?
C'était mon enfant, mon bijou, mon âme.

The sea-clouds whitened far below the calm
And moved, as blooms move, in the swimming green
And in its watery radiance, while the hue

Of heaven in an antique reflection rolled
Round those flotillas. And sometimes the sea
Poured brilliant iris on the glistening blue.

II

In that November off Tehuantepec
The slopping of the sea grew still one night.
At breakfast jelly yellow streaked the deck

And made one think of chop-house chocolate
And sham umbrellas. And a sham-like green
Capped summer-seeming on the tense machine

Of ocean, which in sinister flatness lay.
Who, then, beheld the rising of the clouds
That strode submerged in that malevolent sheen,

Who saw the mortal massives of the blooms
Of water moving on the water-floor?
C'était mon frère du ciel, ma vie, mon or.

The gongs rang loudly as the windy booms
Hoo-hooed it in the darkened ocean-blooms.
The gongs grew still. And then blue heaven spread

Its crystalline pendentives on the sea
And the macabre of the water-glooms
In an enormous undulation fled.

III

In that November off Tehuantepec,
The slopping of the sea grew still one night
And a pale silver patterned on the deck

And made one think of porcelain chocolate
And pied umbrellas. An uncertain green,
Piano-polished, held the tranced machine

Of ocean, as a prelude holds and holds.
Who, seeing silver petals of white blooms
Unfolding in the water, feeling sure

Of the milk within the saltiest spurge, heard, then,
The sea unfolding in the sunken clouds?
Oh! C'était mon extase et mon amour.

So deeply sunken were they that the shrouds,
The shrouding shadows, made the petals black
Until the rolling heaven made them blue,

A blue beyond the rainy hyacinth,
And smiting the crevasses of the leaves
Deluged the ocean with a sapphire blue.

IV

In that November off Tehuantepec
The night-long slopping of the sea grew still.
A mallow morning dozed upon the deck

And made one think of musky chocolate
And frail umbrellas. A too-fluent green
Suggested malice in the dry machine

Of ocean, pondering dank stratagem.
Who then beheld the figures of the clouds
Like blooms secluded in the thick marine?

Like blooms? Like damasks that were shaken off
From the loosed girdles in the spangling must.
C'était ma foi, la nonchalance divine.

The nakedness would rise and suddenly turn
Salt masks of beard and mouths of bellowing,
Would—But more suddenly the heaven rolled

Its bluest sea-clouds in the thinking green,
And the nakedness became the broadest blooms,
Mile-mallows that a mallow sun cajoled.

V

In that November off Tehuantepec
Night stilled the slopping of the sea. The day
Came, bowing and voluble, upon the deck,

Good clown. . . . One thought of Chinese chocolate
And large umbrellas. And a motley green
Followed the drift of the obese machine

Of ocean, perfected in indolence.
What pistache one, ingenious and droll,
Beheld the sovereign clouds as jugglery

And the sea as turquoise-turbaned Sambo, neat
At tossing saucers—cloudy-conjuring sea?
C'était mon esprit bâtard, l'ignominie.

The sovereign clouds came clustering. The conch
Of loyal conjuration trumped. The wind
Of green blooms turning crisped the motley hue

To clearing opalescence. Then the sea
And heaven rolled as one and from the two
Came fresh transfigurings of freshest blue.

The Idea of Order at Key West

She sang beyond the genius of the sea.
The water never formed to mind or voice,
Like a body wholly body, fluttering
Its empty sleeves; and yet its mimic motion
Made constant cry, caused constantly a cry,
That was not ours although we understood,
Inhuman, of the veritable ocean.

The sea was not a mask. No more was she.
The song and water were not medleyed sound
Even if what she sang was what she heard,
Since what she sang was uttered word by word.
It may be that in all her phrases stirred
The grinding water and the gasping wind;
But it was she and not the sea we heard.

For she was the maker of the song she sang.
The ever-hooded, tragic-gestured sea
Was merely a place by which she walked to sing.
Whose spirit is this? we said, because we knew
It was the spirit that we sought and knew
That we should ask this often as she sang.

If it was only the dark voice of the sea
That rose, or even colored by many waves;
If it was only the outer voice of sky
And cloud, of the sunken coral water-walled,
However clear, it would have been deep air,
The heaving speech of air, a summer sound
Repeated in a summer without end
And sound alone. But it was more than that,
More even than her voice, and ours, among
The meaningless plungings of water and the wind,
Theatrical distances, bronze shadows heaped
On high horizons, mountainous atmospheres
Of sky and sea.
                    It was her voice that made
The sky acutest at its vanishing.
She measured to the hour its solitude.
She was the single artificer of the world
In which she sang. And when she sang, the sea,
Whatever self it had, became the self
That was her song, for she was the maker. Then we,
As we beheld her striding there alone,
Knew that there never was a world for her
Except the one she sang and, singing, made.

Ramon Fernandez, tell me, if you know,
Why, when the singing ended and we turned
Toward the town, tell why the glassy lights,
The lights in the fishing boats at anchor there,
As the night descended, tilting in the air,
Mastered the night and portioned out the sea,
Fixing emblazoned zones and fiery poles,
Arranging, deepening, enchanting night.

Oh! Blessed rage for order, pale Ramon,
The maker's rage to order words of the sea,
Words of the fragrant portals, dimly-starred,
And of ourselves and of our origins,
In ghostlier demarcations, keener sounds.

The Sun This March

The exceeding brightness of this early sun
Makes me conceive how dark I have become,

And re-illumines things that used to turn
To gold in broadest blue, and be a part

Of a turning spirit in an earlier self.
That, too, returns from out the winter's air,

Like an hallucination come to daze
The corner of the eye. Our element,

Cold is our element and winter's air
Brings voices as of lions coming down.

Oh! Rabbi, rabbi, fend my soul for me
And true savant of this dark nature be.

Meditation Celestial & Terrestrial

The wild warblers are warbling in the jungle
Of life and spring and of the lustrous inundations,
Flood on flood, of our returning sun.

Day after day, throughout the winter,
We hardened ourselves to live by bluest reason
In a world of wind and frost,

And by will, unshaken and florid
In mornings of angular ice,
That passed beyond us through the narrow sky.

But what are radiant reason and radiant will
To warblings early in the hilarious trees
Of summer, the drunken mother?

A Postcard from the Volcano

Children picking up our bones
Will never know that these were once
As quick as foxes on the hill;

And that in autumn, when the grapes
Made sharp air sharper by their smell
These had a being, breathing frost;

And least will guess that with out bones
We left much more, left what still is
The look of things, left what we felt

At what we saw. The spring clouds blow
Above the shuttered mansion-house,
Beyond our gate and the windy sky

Cries out a literate despair.
We knew for long the mansion's look
And what we said of it became

A part of what it is . . . Children,
Still weaving budded aureoles,
Will speak our speech and never know,

Will say of the mansion that it seems
As if he that lived there left behind
A spirit storming in blank walls,

A dirty house in a gutted world,
A tatter of shadows peaked to white,
Smeared with the gold of the opulent sun.

Autumn Refrain

The skreak and skritter of evening gone
And grackles gone and sorrows of the sun,
The sorrows of sun, too, gone . . . the moon and moon,
The yellow moon of words about the nightingale
In measureless measures, not a bird for me
But the name of a bird and the name of a nameless air
I have never—shall never hear. And yet beneath
The stillness of everything gone, and being still,
Being and sitting still, something resides,
Some skreaking and skrittering residuum,
And grates these evasions of the nightingale
Though I have never—shall never hear that bird.
And the stillness is in the key, all of it is,
The stillness is all in the key of that desolate sound.

Poetry Is a Destructive Force

That's what misery is,
Nothing to have at heart.
It is to have or nothing.

It is a thing to have,
A lion, an ox in his breast,
To feel it breathing there.

Corazon, stout dog,
Young ox, bow-legged bear,
He tastes its blood, not spit.

He is like a man
In the body of a violent beast.
Its muscles are his own . . .

The lion sleeps in the sun.
Its nose is on its paws.
It can kill a man.

The Poems of Our Climate

I

Clear water in a brilliant bowl,
Pink and white carnations. The light
In the room more like a snowy air,
Reflecting snow. A newly-fallen snow
At the end of winter when afternoons return.
Pink and white carnations—one desires
So much more than that. The day itself
Is simplified: a bowl of white,
Cold, a cold porcelain, low and round,
With nothing more than the carnations there.

II

Say even that this complete simplicity
Stripped one of all one's torments, concealed
The evilly compounded, vital I
And made it fresh in a world of white,
A world of clear water, brilliant-edged,
Still one would want more, one would need more,
More than a world of white and snowy scents.

III

There would still remain the never-resting mind,
So that one would want to escape, come back
To what had been so long composed.
The imperfect is our paradise.
Note that, in this bitterness, delight,
Since the imperfect is so hot in us,
Lies in flawed words and stubborn sounds.

Study of Two Pears

I

Opusculum paedagogum.
The pears are not viols,
Nudes or bottles.
They resemble nothing else.

II

They are yellow forms
Composed of curves
Bulging toward the base.
They are touched red.

III

They are not flat surfaces
Having curved outlines.
They are round
Tapering toward the top.

IV

In the way they are modelled
There are bits of blue.
A hard dry leaf hangs
From the stem.

V

The yellow glistens.
It glistens with various yellows,
Citrons, oranges and greens
Flowering over the skin.

VI

The shadows of the pears
Are blobs on the green cloth.
The pears are not seen
As the observer wills.

The Man on the Dump

Day creeps down. The moon is creeping up.
The sun is a corbeil of flowers the moon Blanche
Places there, a bouquet. Ho-ho . . . The dump is full
Of images. Days pass like papers from a press.
The bouquets come here in the papers. So the sun,
And so the moon, both come, and the janitor's poems
Of every day, the wrapper on the can of pears,
The cat in the paper-bag, the corset, the box
From Esthonia: the tiger chest, for tea.

The freshness of night has been fresh a long time.
The freshness of morning, the blowing of day, one says
That it puffs as Cornelius Nepos reads, it puffs
More than, less than or it puffs like this or that.
The green smacks in the eye, the dew in the green
Smacks like fresh water in a can, like the sea
On a cocoanut—how many men have copied dew
For buttons, how many women have covered themselves
With dew, dew dresses, stones and chains of dew, heads
Of the floweriest flowers dewed with the dewiest dew.
One grows to hate these things except on the dump.

Now, in the time of spring (azaleas, trilliums,
Myrtle, viburnums, daffodils, blue phlox),
Between that disgust and this, between the things
That are on the dump (azaleas and so on)
And those that will be (azaleas and so on),
One feels the purifying change. One rejects
The trash.

        That's the moment when the moon creeps up
To the bubbling of bassoons. That's the time
One looks at the elephant-colorings of tires.
Everything is shed; and the moon comes up as the moon
(All its images are in the dump) and you see
As a man (not like an image of a man),
You see the moon rise in the empty sky.

One sits and beats an old tin can, lard pail.
One beats and beats for that which one believes.
That's what one wants to get near. Could it after all
Be merely oneself, as superior as the ear
To a crow's voice? Did the nightingale torture the ear,
Pack the heart and scratch the mind? And does the ear
Solace itself in peevish birds? Is it peace,
Is it a philosopher's honeymoon, one finds
On the dump? Is it to sit among mattresses of the dead,
Bottles, pots, shoes and grass and murmur *aptest eve*:
Is it to hear the blatter of grackles and say
Invisible priest; is it to eject, to pull
The day to pieces and cry *stanza my stone?*
Where was it one first heard of the truth? The the.

Landscape with Boat

An anti-master-man, floribund ascetic.

He brushed away the thunder, then the clouds,
Then the colossal illusion of heaven. Yet still
The sky was blue. He wanted imperceptible air.
He wanted to see. He wanted the eye to see
And not be touched by blue. He wanted to know,
A naked man who regarded himself in the glass
Of air, who looked for the world beneath the blue,
Without blue, without any turquoise tint or phase,
Any azure under-side or after-color. Nabob
Of bones, he rejected, he denied, to arrive
At the neutral centre, the ominous element,
The single-colored, colorless, primitive.

It was not as if the truth lay where he thought,
Like a phantom, in an uncreated night.
It was easier to think it lay there. If
It was nowhere else, it was there and because
It was nowhere else, its place had to be supposed,
Itself had to be supposed, a thing supposed

In a place supposed, a thing that he reached
In a place that he reached, by rejecting what he saw
And denying what he heard. He would arrive.
He had only not to live, to walk in the dark,
To be projected by one void into
Another.

        It was his nature to suppose,
To receive what others had supposed, without
Accepting. He received what he denied.
But as truth to be accepted, he supposed
A truth beyond all truths.

               He never supposed
That he might be truth, himself, or part of it,
That the things that he rejected might be part
And the irregular turquoise, part, the perceptible blue
Grown denser, part, the eye so touched, so played
Upon by clouds, the ear so magnified
By thunder, parts, and all these things together,
Parts, and more things, parts. He never supposed divine
Things might not look divine, nor that if nothing
Was divine then all things were, the world itself,
And that if nothing was the truth, then all
Things were the truth, the world itself was the truth.

Had he been better able to suppose:
He might sit on a sofa on a balcony
Above the Mediterranean, emerald
Becoming emeralds. He might watch the palms
Flap green ears in the heat. He might observe
A yellow wine and follow a steamer's track
And say, "The thing I hum appears to be
The rhythm of this celestial pantomime."

Phosphor Reading by His Own Light

It is difficult to read. The page is dark.
Yet he knows what it is that he expects.

The page is blank or a frame without a glass
Or a glass that is empty when he looks.

The greenness of night lies on the page and goes
Down deeply in the empty glass . . .

Look, realist, not knowing what you expect.
The green falls on you as you look,

Falls on and makes and gives, even a speech.
And you think that that is what you expect,

That elemental parent, the green night,
Teaching a fusky alphabet.

Notes Toward a Supreme Fiction
To Henry Church

And for what, except for you, do I feel love?
Do I press the extremest book of the wisest man
Close to me, hidden in me day and night?
In the uncertain light of single, certain truth,
Equal in living changingness to the light
In which I meet you, in which we sit at rest,
For a moment in the central of our being,
The vivid transparence that you bring is peace.

It Must Be Abstract

I

Begin, ephebe, by perceiving the idea
Of this invention, this invented world,
The inconceivable idea of the sun.

You must become an ignorant man again
And see the sun again with an ignorant eye
And see it clearly in the idea of it.

Never suppose an inventing mind as source
Of this idea nor for that mind compose
A voluminous master folded in his fire.

How clean the sun when seen in its idea,
Washed in the remotest cleanliness of a heaven
That has expelled us and our images . . .

The death of one god is the death of all.
Let purple Phoebus lie in umber harvest,
Let Phoebus slumber and die in autumn umber,

Phoebus is dead, ephebe. But Phoebus was
A name for something that never could be named.
There was a project for the sun and is.

There is a project for the sun. The sun
Must bear no name, gold flourisher, but be
In the difficulty of what it is to be.

II

It is the celestial ennui of apartments
That sends us back to the first idea, the quick
Of this invention; and yet so poisonous

Are the ravishments of truth, so fatal to
The truth itself, the first idea becomes
The hermit in a poet's metaphors,

Who comes and goes and comes and goes all day.
May there be an ennui of the first idea?
What else, prodigious scholar, should there be?

The monastic man is an artist. The philosopher
Appoints man's place in music, say, today.
But the priest desires. The philosopher desires.

And not to have is the beginning of desire.
To have what is not is its ancient cycle.
It is desire at the end of winter, when

It observes the effortless weather turning blue
And sees the myosotis on its bush.
Being virile, it hears the calendar hymn.

It knows that what it has is what is not
And throws it away like a thing of another time,
As morning throws off stale moonlight and shabby sleep.

III

The poem refreshes life so that we share,
For a moment, the first idea . . . It satisfies
Belief in an immaculate beginning

And sends us, winged by an unconscious will,
To an immaculate end. We move between these points:
From that ever-early candor to its late plural

And the candor of them is the strong exhilaration
Of what we feel from what we think, of thought
Beating in the heart, as if blood newly came,

An elixir, an excitation, a pure power.
The poem, through candor, brings back a power again
That gives a candid kind to everything.

We say: At night an Arabian in my room,
With his damned hoobla-hoobla-hoobla-how,
Inscribes a primitive astronomy

Across the unscrawled fores the future casts
And throws his stars around the floor. By day
The wood-dove used to chant his hoobla-hoo

And still the grossest iridescence of ocean
Howls hoo and rises and howls hoo and falls.
Life's nonsense pierces us with strange relation.

IV

The first idea was not our own. Adam
In Eden was the father of Descartes
And Eve made air the mirror of herself,

Of her sons and of her daughters. They found themselves
In heaven as in a glass; a second earth;
And in the earth itself they found a green—

The inhabitants of a very varnished green.
But the first idea was not to shape the clouds
In imitation. The clouds preceded us.

There was a muddy centre before we breathed.
There was a myth before the myth began,
Venerable and articulate and complete.

From this the poem springs: that we live in a place
That is not our own and, much more, not ourselves
And hard it is in spite of blazoned days.

We are the mimics. Clouds are pedagogues.
The air is not a mirror but bare board,
Coulisse bright-dark, tragic chiaroscuro

And comic color of the rose, in which
Abysmal instruments make sounds like pips
Of the sweeping meanings that we add to them.

V

The lion roars at the enraging desert,
Reddens the sand with his red-colored noise,
Defies red emptiness to evolve his match,

Master by foot and jaws and by the mane,
Most supple challenger. The elephant
Breaches the darkness of Ceylon with blares,

The glitter-goes on surfaces of tanks,
Shattering velvetest far-away. The bear,
The ponderous cinnamon, snarls in his mountain

At summer thunder and sleeps through winter snow.
But you, ephebe, look from your attic window,
Your mansard with a rented piano. You lie

In silence upon your bed. You clutch the corner
Of the pillow in your hand. You writhe and press
A bitter utterance from your writhing, dumb,

Yet voluble of dumb violence. You look
Across the roofs as sigil and as ward
And in your centre mark them and are cowed . . .

These are the heroic children whom time breeds
Against the first idea—to lash the lion,
Caparison elephants, teach bears to juggle.

VI

Not to be realized because not to
Be seen, not to be loved nor hated because
Not to be realized. Weather by Franz Hals,

Brushed up by brushy winds in brushy clouds,
Wetted by blue, colder for white. Not to
Be spoken to, without a roof, without

First fruits, without the virginal of birds,
The dark-blown ceinture loosened, not relinquished.
Gay is, gay was, the gay forsythia

And yellow, yellow thins the Northern blue.
Without a name and nothing to be desired,
If only imagined but imagined well.

My house has changed a little in the sun.
The fragrance of the magnolias comes close,
False flick, false form, but falseness close to kin.

It must be visible or invisible,
Invisible or visible or both:
A seeing and unseeing in the eye.

The weather and the giant of the weather,
Say the weather, the mere weather, the mere air:
An abstraction blooded, as a man by thought.

VII

It feels good as it is without the giant,
A thinker of the first idea. Perhaps
The truth depends on a walk around a lake,

A composing as the body tires, a stop
To see hepatica, a stop to watch
A definition growing certain and

A wait within that certainty, a rest
In the swags of pine-trees bordering the lake.
Perhaps there are times of inherent excellence,

As when the cock crows on the left and all
Is well, incalculable balances,
At which a kind of Swiss perfection comes

And a familiar music of the machine
Sets up its Schwärmerei, not balances
That we achieve but balances that happen,

As a man and woman meet and love forthwith.
Perhaps there are moments of awakening,
Extreme, fortuitous, personal, in which

We more than awaken, sit on the edge of sleep,
As on an elevation, and behold
The academies like structures in a mist.

VIII

Can we compose a castle-fortress-home,
Even with the help of Viollet-le-Duc,
And set the MacCullough there as major man?

The first idea is an imagined thing.
The pensive giant prone in violet space
May be the MacCullough, an expedient,

Logos and logic, crystal hypothesis,
Incipit and a form to speak the word
And every latent double in the word,

Beau linguist. But the MacCullough is MacCullough.
It does not follow that major man is man.
If MacCullough himself lay lounging by the sea,

Drowned in its washes, reading in the sound,
About the thinker of the first idea,
He might take habit, whether from wave or phrase,

Or power of the wave, or deepened speech,
Or a leaner being, moving in on him,
Of greater aptitude and apprehension,

As if the waves at last were never broken,
As if the language suddenly, with ease,
Said things it had laboriously spoken.

IX

The romantic intoning, the declaimed clairvoyance
Are parts of apotheosis, appropriate
And of its nature, the idiom thereof.

They differ from reason's click-clack, its applied
Enflashings. But apotheosis is not
The origin of the major man. He comes,

Compact in invincible foils, from reason,
Lighted at midnight by the studious eye,
Swaddled in revery, the object of

The hum of thoughts evaded in the mind,
Hidden from other thoughts, he that reposes
On a breast forever precious for that touch,

For whom the good of April falls tenderly,
Falls down, the cock-birds calling at the time.
My dame, sing for this person accurate songs.

He is and may be but oh! he is, he is,
This foundling of the infected past, so bright,
So moving in the manner of his hand.

Yet look not at his colored eyes. Give him
No names. Dismiss him from your images.
The hot of him is purest in the heart.

X

The major abstraction is the idea of man
And major man is its exponent, abler
In the abstract than in his singular,

More fecund as principle than particle,
Happy fecundity, flor-abundant force,
In being more than an exception, part,

Though an heroic part, of the commonal.
The major abstraction is the commonal,
The inanimate, difficult visage. Who is it?

What rabbi, grown furious with human wish,
What chieftain, walking by himself, crying
Most miserable, most victorious,

Does not see these separate figures one by one,
And yet see only one, in his old coat,
His slouching pantaloons, beyond the town,

Looking for what was, where it used to be?
Cloudless the morning. It is he. The man
In that old coat, those sagging pantaloons,

It is of him, ephebe, to make, to confect
The final elegance, not to console
Nor sanctify, but plainly to propound.

It Must Change

I

The old seraph, parcel-gilded, among violets
Inhaled the appointed odor, while the doves
Rose up like phantoms from chronologies.

The Italian girls wore jonquils in their hair
And these the seraph saw, had seen long since,
In the bandeaux of the mothers, would see again.

The bees came booming as if they had never gone,
As if hyacinths had never gone. We say
This changes and that changes. Thus the constant

Violets, doves, girls, bees and hyacinths
Are inconstant objects of inconstant cause
In a universe of inconstancy. This means

Night-blue is an inconstant thing. The seraph
Is satyr in Saturn, according to his thoughts.
It means the distaste we feel for this withered scene

Is that it has not changed enough. It remains,
It is a repetition. The bees come booming
As if— The pigeons clatter in the air.

An erotic perfume, half of the body, half
Of an obvious acid is sure what it intends
And the booming is blunt, not broken in subtleties.

II

The President ordains the bee to be
Immortal. The President ordains. But does
The body lift its heavy wing, take up,

Again, an inexhaustible being, rise
Over the loftiest antagonist
To drone the green phrases of its juvenal?

Why should the bee recapture a lost blague,
Find a deep echo in a horn and buzz
The bottomless trophy, new hornsman after old?

The President has apples on the table
And barefoot servants round him, who adjust
The curtains to a metaphysical t

And the banners of the nation flutter, burst
On the flag-poles in a red-blue dazzle, whack
At the halyards. Why, then, when in golden fury

Spring vanishes the scraps of winter, why
Should there be a question of returning or
Of death in memory's dream? Is spring a sleep?

This warmth is for lovers at last accomplishing
Their love, this beginning, not resuming, this
Booming and booming of the new-come bee.

III

The great statue of the General Du Puy
Rested immobile, though neighboring catafalques
Bore off the residents of its noble Place.

The right, uplifted foreleg of the horse
Suggested that, at the final funeral,
The music halted and the horse stood still.

On Sundays, lawyers in their promenades
Approached this strongly-heightened effigy
To study the past, and doctors, having bathed

Themselves with care, sought out the nerveless frame
Of a suspension, a permanence, so rigid
That it made the General a bit absurd,

Changed his true flesh to an inhuman bronze.
There never had been, never could be, such
A man. The lawyers disbelieved, the doctors

Said that as keen, illustrious ornament,
As a setting for geraniums, the General,
The very Place Du Puy, in fact, belonged

Among our more vestigial states of mind.
Nothing had happened because nothing had changed.
Yet the General was rubbish in the end.

IV

Two things of opposite natures seem to depend
On one another, as a man depends
On a woman, day on night, the imagined

On the real. This is the origin of change.
Winter and spring, cold copulars, embrace
And forth the particulars of rapture come.

Music falls on the silence like a sense,
A passion that we feel, not understand.
Morning and afternoon are clasped together

And North and South are an intrinsic couple
And sun and rain a plural, like two lovers
That walk away as one in the greenest body.

In solitude the trumpets of solitude
Are not of another solitude resounding;
A little string speaks for a crowd of voices.

The partaker partakes of that which changes him.
The child that touches takes character from the thing,
The body, it touches. The captain and his men

Are one and the sailor and the sea are one.
Follow after, O my companion, my fellow, my self,
Sister and solace, brother and delight.

V

On a blue island in a sky-wide water
The wild orange trees continued to bloom and to bear,
Long after the planter's death. A few limes remained,

Where his house had fallen, three scraggy trees weighted
With garbled green. These were the planter's turquoise
And his orange blotches, these were his zero green,

A green baked greener in the greenest sun.
These were his beaches, his sea-myrtles in
White sand, his patter of the long sea-slushes.

There was an island beyond him on which rested,
An island to the South, on which rested like
A mountain, a pine-apple pungent as Cuban summer.

And là-bas, là-bas, the cool bananas grew,
Hung heavily on the great banana tree,
Which pierces clouds and bends on half the world.

He thought often of the land from which he came,
How that whole country was a melon, pink
If seen rightly and yet a possible red.

An unaffected man in a negative light
Could not have borne his labor nor have died
Sighing that he should leave the banjo's twang.

VI

Bethou me, said sparrow, to the crackled blade,
And you, and you, bethou me as you blow,
When in my coppice you behold me be.

Ah, ké! the bloody wren, the felon jay,
Ké-ké, the jug-throated robin pouring out,
Bethou, bethou, bethou me in my glade.

There was such idiot minstrelsy in rain,
So many clappers going without bells,
That these bethous compose a heavenly gong.

One voice repeating, one tireless chorister,
The phrases of a single phrase, ké-ké,
A single text, granite monotony,

One sole face, like a photograph of fate,
Glass-blower's destiny, bloodless episcopus,
Eye without lid, mind without any dream—

These are of minstrels lacking minstrelsy,
Of an earth in which the first leaf is the tale
Of leaves, in which the sparrow is a bird

Of stone, that never changes. Bethou him, you
And you, bethou him and bethou. It is
A sound like any other. It will end.

VII

After a lustre of the moon, we say
We have not the need of any paradise,
We have not the need of any seducing hymn.

It is true. Tonight the lilacs magnify
The easy passion, the ever-ready love
Of the lover that lies within us and we breathe

An odor evoking nothing, absolute.
We encounter in the dead middle of the night
The purple odor, the abundant bloom.

The lover sighs as for accessible bliss,
Which he can take within him on his breath,
Possess in his heart, conceal and nothing known.

For easy passion and ever-ready love
Are of our earthy birth and here and now
And where we live and everywhere we live,

As in the top-cloud of a May night-evening,
As in the courage of the ignorant man,
Who chants by book, in the heat of the scholar, who writes

The book, hot for another accessible bliss:
The fluctuations of certainty, the change
Of degrees of perception in the scholar's dark.

VIII

On her trip around the world, Nanzia Nunzio
Confronted Ozymandias. She went
Alone and like a vestal long-prepared.

I am the spouse. She took her necklace off
And laid it in the sand. As I am, I am
The spouse. She opened her stone-studded belt.

I am the spouse, divested of bright gold,
The spouse beyond emerald or amethyst,
Beyond the burning body that I bear.

I am the woman stripped more nakedly
Than nakedness, standing before an inflexible
Order, saying I am the contemplated spouse.

Speak to me that, which spoken, will array me
In its own only precious ornament.
Set on me the spirit's diamond coronal.

Clothe me entire in the final filament,
So that I tremble with such love so known
And myself am precious for your perfecting.

Then Ozymandias said the spouse, the bride
Is never naked. A fictive covering
Weaves always glistening from the heart and mind.

IX

The poem goes from the poet's gibberish to
The gibberish of the vulgate and back again.
Does it move to and fro or is it of both

At once? Is it a luminous flittering
Or the concentration of a cloudy day?
Is there a poem that never reaches words

And one that chaffers the time away?
Is the poem both peculiar and general?
There's a meditation there, in which there seems

To be an evasion, a thing not apprehended or
Not apprehended well. Does the poet
Evade us, as in a senseless element?

Evade, this hot, dependent orator,
The spokesman at our bluntest barriers,
Exponent by a form of speech, the speaker

Of a speech only a little of the tongue?
It is the gibberish of the vulgate that he seeks.
He tries by a peculiar speech to speak

The peculiar potency of the general,
To compound the imagination's Latin with
The lingua franca et jocundissima.

                          X

A bench was his catalepsy, Theatre
Of Trope. He sat in the park. The water of
The lake was full of artificial things,

Like a page of music, like an upper air,
Like a momentary color, in which swans
Were seraphs, were saints, were changing essences.

The west wind was the music, the motion, the force
To which the swans curveted, a will to change,
A will to make iris frettings on the blank.

There was a will to change, a necessitous
And present way, a presentation, a kind
Of volatile world, too constant to be denied,

The eye of a vagabond in metaphor
That catches our own. The casual is not
Enough. The freshness of transformation is

The freshness of a world. It is our own,
It is ourselves, the freshness of ourselves,
And that necessity and that presentation

Are rubbings of a glass in which we peer.
Of these beginnings, gay and green, propose
The suitable amours. Time will write them down.

It Must Give Pleasure

I

To sing jubilas at exact, accustomed times,
To be crested and wear the mane of a multitude
And so, as part, to exult with its great throat,

To speak of joy and to sing of it, borne on
The shoulders of joyous men, to feel the heart
That is the common, the bravest fundament,

This is a facile exercise. Jerome
Begat the tubas and the fire-wind strings,
The golden fingers picking dark-blue air:

For companies of voices moving there,
To find of sound the bleakest ancestor,
To find of light a music issuing

Whereon it falls in more than sensual mode.
But the difficultest rigor is forthwith,
On the image of what we see, to catch from that

Irrational moment its unreasoning,
As when the sun comes rising, when the sea
Clears deeply, when the moon hangs on the wall

Of heaven-haven. These are not things transformed.
Yet we are shaken by them as if they were.
We reason about them with a later reason.

II

The blue woman, linked and lacquered, at her window
Did not desire that feathery argentines
Should be cold silver, neither that frothy clouds

Should foam, be foamy waves, should move like them,
Nor that the sexual blossoms should repose
Without their fierce addictions, nor that the heat

Of summer, growing fragrant in the night,
Should strengthen her abortive dreams and take
In sleep its natural form. It was enough

For her that she remembered: the argentines
Of spring come to their places in the grape leaves
To cool their ruddy pulses; the frothy clouds

Are nothing but frothy clouds; the frothy blooms
Waste without puberty; and afterward,
When the harmonious heat of August pines

Enters the room, it drowses and is the night.
It was enough for her that she remembered.
The blue woman looked and from her window named

The corals of the dogwood, cold and clear,
Cold, coldly delineating, being real,
Clear and, except for the eye, without intrusion.

III

A lasting visage in a lasting bush,
A face of stone in an unending red,
Red-emerald, red-slitted-blue, a face of slate,

An ancient forehead hung with heavy hair,
The channel slots of rain, the red-rose-red
And weathered and the ruby-water-worn,

The vines around the throat, the shapeless lips,
The frown like serpents basking on the brow,
The spent feeling leaving nothing of itself,

Red-in-red repetitions never going
Away, a little rusty, a little rouged,
A little roughened and ruder, a crown

The eye could not escape, a red renown
Blowing itself upon the tedious ear.
An effulgence faded, dull cornelian

Too venerably used. That might have been.
It might and might have been. But as it was,
A dead shepherd brought tremendous chords from hell

And bade the sheep carouse. Or so they said.
Children in love with them brought early flowers
And scattered them about, no two alike.

IV

We reason of these things with later reason
And we make of what we see, what we see clearly
And have seen, a place dependent on ourselves.

There was a mystic marriage in Catawba,
At noon it was on the mid-day of the year
Between a great captain and the maiden Bawda.

This was their ceremonial hymn: Anon
We loved but would no marriage make. Anon
The one refused the other one to take,

Foreswore the sipping of the marriage wine.
Each must the other take not for his high,
His puissant front nor for her subtle sound,

The shoo-shoo-shoo of secret cymbals round.
Each must the other take as sign, short sign
To stop the whirlwind, balk the elements.

The great captain loved the ever-hill Catawba
And therefore married Bawda, whom he found there,
And Bawda loved the captain as she loved the sun.

They married well because the marriage-place
Was what they loved. It was neither heaven nor hell.
They were love's characters come face to face.

V

We drank Meursault, ate lobster Bombay with mango
Chutney. Then the Canon Aspirin declaimed
Of his sister, in what a sensible ecstasy

She lived in her house. She had two daughters, one
Of four, and one of seven, whom she dressed
The way a painter of pauvred color paints.

But still she painted them, appropriate to
Their poverty, a gray-blue yellowed out
With ribbon, a rigid statement of them, white,

With Sunday pearls, her widow's gayety.
She hid them under simple names. She held
Them closelier to her by rejecting dreams.

The words they spoke were voices that she heard.
She looked at them and saw them as they were
And what she felt fought off the barest phrase.

The Canon Aspirin, having said these things,
Reflected, humming an outline of a fugue
Of praise, a conjugation done by choirs.

Yet when her children slept, his sister herself
Demanded of sleep, in the excitements of silence
Only the unmuddled self of sleep, for them.

VI

When at long midnight the Canon came to sleep
And normal things had yawned themselves away,
The nothingness was a nakedness, a point,

Beyond which fact could not progress as fact.
Thereon the learning of the man conceived
Once more night's pale illuminations, gold

Beneath, far underneath, the surface of
His eye and audible in the mountain of
His ear, the very material of his mind.

So that he was the ascending wings he saw
And moved on them in orbits' outer stars
Descending to the children's bed, on which

They lay. Forth then with huge pathetic force
Straight to the utmost crown of night he flew.
The nothingness was a nakedness, a point

Beyond which thought could not progress as thought.
He had to choose. But it was not a choice
Between excluding things. It was not a choice

Between, but of. He chose to include the things
That in each other are included, the whole,
The complicate, the amassing harmony.

VII

He imposes orders as he thinks of them,
As the fox and snake do. It is a brave affair.
Next he builds capitols and in their corridors,

Whiter than wax, sonorous, fame as it is,
He establishes statues of reasonable men,
Who surpassed the most literate owl, the most erudite

Of elephants. But to impose is not
To discover. To discover an order as of
A season, to discover summer and know it,

To discover winter and know it well, to find,
Not to impose, not to have reasoned at all,
Out of nothing to have come on major weather,

It is possible, possible, possible. It must
Be possible. It must be that in time
The real will from its crude compoundings come,

Seeming, at first, a beast disgorged, unlike,
Warmed by a desperate milk. To find the real,
To be stripped of every fiction except one,

The fiction of an absolute— Angel,
Be silent in your luminous cloud and hear
The luminous melody of proper sound.

VIII

What am I to believe? If the angel in his cloud,
Serenely gazing at the violet abyss,
Plucks on his strings to pluck abysmal glory,

Leaps downward through evening's revelations, and
On his spredden wings, needs nothing but deep space,
Forgets the gold centre, the golden destiny,

Grows warm in the motionless motion of his flight,
Am I that imagine this angel less-satisfied?
Are the wings his, the lapis-haunted air?

Is it he or is it I that experience this?
Is it I then that keep saying there is an hour
Filled with expressible bliss, in which I have

No need, am happy, forget need's golden hand,
Am satisfied without solacing majesty,
And if there is an hour there is a day,

There is a month, a year, there is a time
In which majesty is a mirror of the self:
I have not but I am and as I am, I am.

These external regions, what do we fill them with
Except reflections, the escapades of death,
Cinderella fulfilling herself beneath the roof?

IX

Whistle aloud, too weedy wren. I can
Do all that angels can. I enjoy like them,
Like men besides, like men in light secluded,

Enjoying angels. Whistle, forced bugler,
That bugles for the mate, nearby the nest,
Cock bugler, whistle and bugle and stop just short,

Red robin, stop in your preludes, practicing
Mere repetitions. These things at least comprise
An occupation, an exercise, a work,

A thing final in itself and, therefore, good:
One of the vast repetitions final in
Themselves and, therefore, good, the going round

And round and round, the merely going round,
Until merely going round is a final good,
The way wine comes at a table in a wood.

And we enjoy like men, the way a leaf
Above the table spins its constant spin,
So that we look at it with pleasure, look

At it spinning its eccentric measure. Perhaps,
The man-hero is not the exceptional monster,
But he that of repetition is most master.

X

Fat girl, terrestrial, my summer, my night,
How is it I find you in difference, see you there
In a moving contour, a change not quite completed?

You are familiar yet an aberration.
Civil, madam, I am, but underneath
A tree, this unprovoked sensation requires

That I should name you flatly, waste no words,
Check your evasions, hold you to yourself.
Even so when I think of you as strong or tired,

Bent over work, anxious, content, alone,
You remain the more than natural figure. You
Become the soft-footed phantom, the irrational

Distortion, however fragrant, however dear.
That's it: the more than rational distortion,
The fiction that results from feeling. Yes, that.

They will get it straight one day at the Sorbonne.
We shall return at twilight from the lecture
Pleased that the irrational is rational,

Until flicked by feeling, in a gilderd street,
I call you by name, my green, my fluent mundo.
You will have stopped revolving except in crystal.

———

Soldier, there is a war between the mind
And sky, between thought and day and night. It is
For that the poet is always in the sun,

Patches the moon together in his room
To his Virgilian cadences, up down,
Up down. It is a war that never ends.

Yet it depends on yours. The two are one.
They are a plural, a right and left, a pair,
Two parallels that meet if only in

The meeting of their shadows or that meet
In a book in a barrack, a letter from Malay.
But your war ends. And after it you return

With six meats and twelve wines or else without
To walk another room . . . Monsieur and comrade,
The soldier is poor without the poet's lines,

His petty syllabi, the sounds that stick,
Inevitably modulating, in the blood.
And war for war, each has its gallant kind.

How simply the fictive hero becomes the real;
How gladly with proper words the soldier dies,
If he must, or lives on the bread of faithful speech.

God Is Good. It Is a Beautiful Night

Look round, brown moon, brown bird, as you rise to fly,
Look round at the head and zither
On the ground.

Look round you as you start to rise, brown moon,
At the book and shoe, the rotted rose
At the door.

This was the place to which you came last night,
Flew close to, flew to without rising away.
Now, again,

In your light, the head is speaking. It reads the book.
It becomes the scholar again, seeking celestial
Rendezvous,

Picking thin music on the rustiest string,
Squeezing the reddest fragrance from the stump
Of summer.

The venerable song falls from your fiery wings.
The song of the great space of your age pierces
The fresh night.

The Motive for Metaphor

You like it under the trees in autumn,
Because everything is half dead.
The wind moves like a cripple among the leaves
And repeats words without meaning.

In the same way, you were happy in spring,
With the half colors of quarter-things,
The slightly brighter sky, the melting clouds,
The single bird, the obscure moon—

The obscure moon lighting an obscure world
Of things that would never be quite expressed,
Where you yourself were never quite yourself
And did not want nor have to be,

Desiring the exhilarations of changes:
The motive for metaphor, shrinking from
The weight of primary noon,
The A B C of being,

The ruddy temper, the hammer
Of red and blue, the hard sound—
Steel against intimation—the sharp flash,
The vital, arrogant, fatal, dominant X.

Men Made Out of Words

What should we be without the sexual myth,
The human revery or poem of death?

Castratos of moon-mash—Life consists
Of propositions about life. The human

Revery is a solitude in which
We compose these propositions, torn by dreams,

By the terrible incantations of defeats
And by the fear that defeats and dreams are one.

The whole race is a poet that writes down
The eccentric propositions of its fate.

The Auroras of Autumn

I

This is where the serpent lives, the bodiless.
His head is air. Beneath his tip at night
Eyes open and fix on us in every sky.

Or is this another wriggling out of the egg,
Another image at the end of the cave,
Another bodiless for the body's slough?

This is where the serpent lives. This is his nest,
These fields, these hills, these tinted distances,
And the pines above and along and beside the sea.

This is form gulping after formlessness,
Skin flashing to wished-for disappearances
And the serpent body flashing without the skin.

This is the height emerging and its base
These lights may finally attain a pole
In the midmost midnight and find the serpent there,

In another nest, the master of the maze
Of body and air and forms and images,
Relentlessly in possession of happiness.

This is his poison: that we should disbelieve
Even that. His meditations in the ferns,
When he moved so slightly to make sure of sun,

Made us no less as sure. We saw in his head,
Black beaded on the rock, the flecked animal,
The moving grass, the Indian in his glade.

II

Farewell to an idea . . . A cabin stands,
Deserted, on a beach. It is white,
As by a custom or according to

An ancestral theme or as a consequence
Of an infinite course. The flowers against the wall
Are white, a little dried, a kind of mark

Reminding, trying to remind, of a white
That was different, something else, last year
Or before, not the white of an aging afternoon,

Whether fresher or duller, whether of winter cloud
Or of winter sky, from horizon to horizon.
The wind is blowing the sand across the floor.

Here, being visible is being white,
Is being of the solid of white, the accomplishment
Of an extremist in an exercise . . .

The season changes. A cold wind chills the beach.
The long lines of it grow longer, emptier,
A darkness gathers though it does not fall

And the whiteness grows less vivid on the wall.
The man who is walking turns blankly on the sand.
He observes how the north is always enlarging the change,

With its frigid brilliances, its blue-red sweeps
And gusts of great enkindlings, its polar green,
The color of ice and fire and solitude.

III

Farewell to an idea . . . The mother's face,
The purpose of the poem, fills the room.
They are together, here, and it is warm,

With none of the prescience of oncoming dreams.
It is evening. The house is evening, half dissolved.
Only the half they can never possess remains,

Still-starred. It is the mother they possess,
Who gives transparence to their present peace.
She makes that gentler that can gentle be.

And yet she too is dissolved, she is destroyed.
She gives transparence. But she has grown old.
The necklace is a carving not a kiss.

The soft hands are a motion not a touch.
The house will crumble and the books will burn.
They are at ease in a shelter of the mind

And the house is of the mind and they and time,
Together, all together. Boreal night
Will look like frost as it approaches them

And to the mother as she falls asleep
And as they say good-night, good-night. Upstairs
The windows will be lighted, not the rooms.

A wind will spread its windy grandeurs round
And knock like a rifle-butt against the door.
The wind will command them with invincible sound.

IV

Farewell to an idea . . . The cancellings,
The negations are never final. The father sits
In space, wherever he sits, of bleak regard,

As one that is strong in the bushes of his eyes.
He says no to no and yes to yes. He says yes
To no; and in saying yes he says farewell.

He measures the velocities of change.
He leaps from heaven to heaven more rapidly
Than bad angels leap from heaven to hell in flames.

But now he sits in quiet and green-a-day.
He assumes the great speeds of space and flutters them
From cloud to cloudless, cloudless to keen clear

In flights of eye and ear, the highest eye
And the lowest ear, the deep ear that discerns,
At evening, things that attend it until it hears

The supernatural preludes of its own,
At the moment when the angelic eye defines
Its actors approaching, in company, in their masks.

Master O master seated by the fire
And yet in space and motionless and yet
Of motion the ever-brightening origin,

Profound, and yet the king and yet the crown,
Look at this present throne. What company,
In masks, can choir it with the naked wind?

V

The mother invites humanity to her house
And table. The father fetches tellers of tales
And musicians who mute much, muse much, on the tales.

The father fetches negresses to dance,
Among the children, like curious ripenesses
Of pattern in the dance's ripening.

For these the musicians make insidious tones,
Clawing the sing-song of their instruments.
The children laugh and jangle a tinny time.

The father fetches pageants out of air,
Scenes of the theatre, vistas and blocks of woods
And curtains like a naive pretence of sleep.

Among these the musicians strike the instinctive poem.
The father fetches his unherded herds,
Of barbarous tongue, slavered and panting halves

Of breath, obedient to his trumpet's touch.
This then is Chatillon or as you please.
We stand in the tumult of a festival.

What festival? This loud, disordered mooch?
These hospitaliers? These brute-like guests?
These musicians dubbing at a tragedy,

A-dub, a-dub, which is made up of this:
That there are no lines to speak? There is no play.
Or, the persons act one merely by being here.

VI

It is a theatre floating through the clouds,
Itself a cloud, although of misted rock
And mountains running like water, wave on wave,

Through waves of light. It is of cloud transformed
To cloud transformed again, idly, the way
A season changes color to no end,

Except the lavishing of itself in change,
As light changes yellow into gold and gold
To its opal elements and fire's delight,

Splashed wide-wise because it likes magnificence
And the solemn pleasures of magnificent space.
The cloud drifts idly through half-thought-of forms.

The theatre is filled with flying birds,
Wild wedges, as of a volcano's smoke, palm-eyed
And vanishing, a web in a corridor

Or massive portico. A capitol,
It may be, is emerging or has just
Collapsed. The denouement has to be postponed . . .

This is nothing until in a single man contained,
Nothing until this named thing nameless is
And is destroyed. He opens the door of his house

On flames. The scholar of one candle sees
An Arctic effulgence flaring on the frame
Of everything he is. And he feels afraid.

VII

Is there an imagination that sits enthroned
As grim as it is benevolent, the just
And the unjust, which in the midst of summer stops

To imagine winter? When the leaves are dead,
Does it take its place in the north and enfold itself,
Goat-leaper, crystalled and luminous, sitting

In highest night? And do these heavens adorn
And proclaim it, the white creator of black, jetted
By extinguishings, even of planets as may be,

Even of earth, even of sight, in snow,
Except as needed by way of majesty,
In the sky, as crown and diamond cabala?

It leaps through us, through all our heavens leaps,
Extinguishing our planets, one by one,
Leaving, of where we were and looked, of where

We knew each other and of each other thought,
A shivering residue, chilled and foregone,
Except for that crown and mystical cabala.

But it dare not leap by chance in its own dark.
It must change from destiny to slight caprice.
And thus its jetted tragedy, its stele

And shape and mournful making move to find
What must unmake it and, at last, what can,
Say, a flippant communication under the moon.

VIII

There may be always a time of innocence.
There is never a place. Or if there is no time,
If it is not a thing of time, nor of place,

Existing in the idea of it, alone,
In the sense against calamity, it is not
Less real. For the oldest and coldest philosopher,

There is or may be a time of innocence
As pure principle. Its nature is its end,
That it should be, and yet not be, a thing

That pinches the pity of the pitiful man,
Like a book at evening beautiful but untrue,
Like a book on rising beautiful and true.

It is like a thing of ether that exists
Almost as predicate. But it exists,
It exists, it is visible, it is, it is.

So, then, these lights are not a spell of light,
A saying out of a cloud, but innocence.
An innocence of the earth and no false sign

Or symbol of malice. That we partake thereof,
Lie down like children in this holiness,
As if, awake, we lay in the quiet of sleep,

As if the innocent mother sang in the dark
Of the room and on an accordion, half-heard,
Created the time and place in which we breathed . . .

IX

And of each other thought—in the idiom
Of the work, in the idiom of an innocent earth,
Not of the enigma of the guilty dream.

We were as Danes in Denmark all day long
And knew each other well, hale-hearted landsmen,
For whom the outlandish was another day

Of the week, queerer than Sunday. We thought alike
And that made brothers of us in a home
In which we fed on being brothers, fed

And fattened as on a decorous honeycomb.
This drama that we live—We lay sticky with sleep.
This sense of the activity of fate—

The rendezvous, when she came alone,
By her coming became a freedom of the two,
An isolation which only the two could share.

Shall we be found hanging in the trees next spring?
Of what disaster in this the imminence:
Bare limbs, bare trees and a wind as sharp as salt?

The stars are putting on their glittering belts.
They throw around their shoulders cloaks that flash
Like a great shadow's last embellishment.

It may come tomorrow in the simplest word,
Almost as part of innocence, almost,
Almost as the tenderest and the truest part.

X

An unhappy people in a happy world—
Read, rabbi, the phases of this difference.
An unhappy people in an unhappy world—

Here are too many mirrors for misery.
A happy people in an unhappy world—
It cannot be. There's nothing there to roll

On the expressive tongue, the finding fang.
A happy people in a happy world—
Buffo! A ball, an opera, a bar.

Turn back to where we were when we began:
An unhappy people in a happy world.
Now, solemnize the secretive syllables.

Read to the congregation, for today
And for tomorrow, this extremity,
This contrivance of the spectre of the spheres,

Contriving balance to contrive a whole,
The vital, the never-failing genius,
Fulfilling his meditations, great and small.

In these unhappy he meditates a whole,
The full of fortune and the full of fate,
As if he lived all lives, that he might know,

In hall harridan, not hushful paradise,
To a haggling of wind and weather, by these lights
Like a blaze of summer straw, in winter's nick.

Large Red Man Reading

There were ghosts that returned to earth to hear his phrases,
As he sat there reading, aloud, the great blue tabulae.
They were those from the wilderness of stars that had
          expected more.

There were those that returned to hear him read from the
          poem of life,

Of the pans above the stove, the pots on the table, the tulips
    among them.
They were those that would have wept to step barefoot into
    reality,

That would have wept and been happy, have shivered in the
    frost
And cried out to feel it again, have run fingers over leaves
And against the most coiled thorn, have seized on what was
    ugly

And laughed, as he sat there reading, from out of the purple
    tabulae,
The outlines of being and its expressings, the syllables of its
    law:
Poesis, poesis, the literal characters, the vatic lines,

Which in those ears and in those thin, those spended hearts,
Took on color, took on shape and the size of things as they
    are
And spoke the feeling for them, which was what they had
    lacked.

To an Old Philosopher in Rome

On the threshold of heaven, the figures in the street
Become the figures of heaven, the majestic movement
Of men growing small in the distances of space,
Singing, with smaller and still smaller sound,
Unintelligible absolution and an end—

The threshold, Rome, and that more merciful Rome
Beyond, the two alike in the make of the mind.
It is as if in a human dignity
Two parallels become one, a perspective, of which
Men are part both in the inch and in the mile.

How easily the blown banners change to wings . . .
Things dark on the horizons of perception,
Become accompaniments of fortune, but
Of the fortune of the spirit, beyond the eye,
Not of its sphere, and yet not far beyond,

The human end in the spirit's greatest reach,
The extreme of the known in the presence of the extreme
Of the unknown. The newsboys' muttering
Becomes another murmuring; the smell
Of medicine, a fragrantness not to be spoiled . . .

The bed, the books, the chair, the moving nuns,
The candle as it evades the sight, these are
The sources of happiness in the shape of Rome,
A shape within the ancient circles of shapes,
And these beneath the shadow of a shape

In a confusion on bed and books, a portent
On the chair, a moving transparence on the nuns,
A light on the candle tearing against the wick
To join a hovering excellence, to escape
From fire and be part only of that of which

Fire is the symbol: the celestial possible.
Speak to your pillow as if it was yourself.
Be orator but with an accurate tongue
And without eloquence, O, half-asleep,
Of the pity that is the memorial of this room,

So that we feel, in this illumined large,
The veritable small, so that each of us
Beholds himself in you, and hears his voice
In yours, master and commiserable man,
Intent on your particles of nether-do,

Your dozing in the depths of wakefulness,
In the warmth of your bed, at the edge of your chair, alive
Yet living in two worlds, impenitent
As to one, and, as to one, most penitent,
Impatient for the grandeur that you need

In so much misery; and yet finding it
Only in misery, the afflatus of ruin,
Profound poetry of the poor and of the dead,
As in the last drop of the deepest blood,
As it falls from the heart and lies there to be seen,

Even as the blood of an empire, it might be,
For a citizen of heaven though still of Rome.
It is poverty's speech that seeks us out the most.
It is older than the oldest speech of Rome.
This is the tragic accent of the scene.

And you—it is you that speak it, without speech,
The loftiest syllables among loftiest things,
The one invulnerable man among
Crude captains, the naked majesty, if you like,
Of bird-nest arches and of rain-stained vaults.

The sounds drift in. The buildings are remembered.
The life of the city never lets go, nor do you
Ever want it to. It is part of the life in your room.
Its domes are the architecture of your bed.
The bells keep on repeating solemn names

In choruses and choirs of choruses,
Unwilling that mercy should be a mystery
Of silence, that any solitude of sense
Should give you more than their peculiar chords
And reverberations clinging to whisper still.

It is a kind of total grandeur at the end,
With every visible thing enlarged and yet
No more than a bed, a chair and moving nuns,
The immensest theatre, the pillared porch,
The book and candle in your ambered room,

Total grandeur of a total edifice,
Chosen by an inquisitor of structures
For himself. He stops upon this threshold,
As if the design of all his words takes form
And frame from thinking and is realized.

Final Soliloquy of the Interior Paramour

Light the first light of evening, as in a room
In which we rest and, for small reason, think
The world imagined is the ultimate good.

This is, therefore, the intensest rendezvous.
It is in that thought that we collect ourselves,
Out of all the indifferences, into one thing:

Within a single thing, a single shawl
Wrapped tightly round us, since we are poor, a warmth,
A light, a power, the miraculous influence.

Here, now, we forget each other and ourselves.
We feel the obscurity of an order, a whole,
A knowledge, that which arranged the rendezvous,

Within its vital boundary, in the mind.
We say God and the imagination are one . . .
How high that highest candle lights the dark.

Out of this same light, out of the central mind,
We make a dwelling in the evening air,
In which being there together is enough.

The Rock

I

Seventy Years Later

It is an illusion that we were ever alive,
Lived in the houses of mothers, arranged ourselves
By our own motions in a freedom of air.

Regard the freedom of seventy years ago.
It is no longer air. The houses still stand,
Though they are rigid in rigid emptiness.

Even our shadows, their shadows, no longer remain.
The lives these lived in the mind are at an end.
They never were . . . The sounds of the guitar

Were not and are not. Absurd. The words spoken
Were not and are not. It is not to be believed.
The meeting at noon at the edge of the field seems like

An invention, an embrace between one desperate clod
And another in a fantastic consciousness,
In a queer assertion of humanity:

A theorem proposed between the two—
Two figures in a nature of the sun,
In the sun's design of its own happiness,

As if nothingness contained a métier,
A vital assumption, an impermanence
In its permanent cold, an illusion so desired

That the green leaves came and covered the high rock,
That the lilacs came and bloomed, like a blindness cleaned,
Exclaiming bright sight, as it was satisfied,

In a birth of sight. The blooming and the musk
Were being alive, an incessant being alive,
A particular of being, that gross universe.

II

The Poem as Icon

It is not enough to cover the rock with leaves.
We must be cured of it by a cure of the ground
Or a cure of ourselves, that is equal to a cure

Of the ground, a cure beyond forgetfulness.
And yet the leaves, if they broke into bud,
If they broke into bloom, if they bore fruit,

And if we ate the incipient colorings
Of their fresh culls might be a cure of the ground.
The fiction of the leaves is the icon

Of the poem, the figuration of blessedness,
And the icon is the man. The pearled chaplet of spring,
The magnum wreath of summer, time's autumn snood,

Its copy of the sun, these cover the rock.
These leaves are the poem, the icon and the man.
These are a cure of the ground and of ourselves,

In the predicate that there is nothing else.
They bud and bloom and bear their fruit without change.
They are more than leaves that cover the barren rock.

They bud the whitest eye, the pallidest sprout,
New senses in the engenderings of sense,
The desire to be at the end of distances,

The body quickened and the mind in root.
They bloom as a man loves, as he lives in love.
They bear their fruit so that the year is known,

As if its understanding was brown skin,
The honey in its pulp, the final found,
The plenty of the year and of the world.

In this plenty, the poem makes meanings of the rock,
Of such mixed motion and such imagery
That its barrenness becomes a thousand things

And so exists no more. This is the cure
Of leaves and of the ground and of ourselves.
His words are both the icon and the man.

III

Forms of the Rock in a Night-Hymn

The rock is the gray particular of man's life,
The stone from which he rises, up—and—ho,
The step to the bleaker depths of his descents . . .

The rock is the stern particular of the air,
The mirror of the planets, one by one,
But through man's eye, their silent rhapsodist,

Turquoise the rock, at odious evening bright
With redness that sticks fast to evil dreams;
The difficult rightness of half-risen day.

The rock is the habitation of the whole,
Its strength and measure, that which is near, point A
In a perspective that begins again

At B: the origin of the mango's rind.
It is the rock where tranquil must adduce
Its tranquil self, the main of things, the mind,

The starting point of the human and the end,
That in which space itself is contained, the gate
To the enclosure, day, the things illumined

By day, night and that which night illumines,
Night and its midnight-minting fragrances,
Night's hymn of the rock, as in a vivid sleep.

A Discovery of Thought

At the antipodes of poetry, dark winter,
When the trees glitter with that which despoils them,
Daylight evaporates, like a sound one hears in sickness.

One is a child again. The gold beards of waterfalls
Are dissolved as in an infancy of blue snow.
It is an arbor against the wind, a pit in the mist,

A trinkling in the parentage of the north,
The cricket of summer forming itself out of ice.
And always at this antipodes, of leaden loaves

Held in the hands of blue men that are lead within,
One thinks that it could be that the first word spoken,
The desire for speech and meaning gallantly fulfilled,

The gathering of the imbecile against his motes
And the wry antipodes whirled round the world away—
One thinks, when the houses of New England catch the first
      sun,

The first word would be of the susceptible being arrived,
The immaculate disclosure of the secret, no more obscured.
The sprawling of winter might suddenly stand erect,

Pronouncing its new life and ours, not autumn's prodigal
      returned,
But an antipodal, far-fetched creature, worthy of birth,
The true tone of the metal of winter in what it says:

The accent of deviation in the living thing
That is its life preserved, the effort to be born
Surviving being born, the event of life.

The Course of a Particular

Today the leaves cry, hanging on branches swept by wind,
Yet the nothingness of winter becomes a little less.
It is still full of icy shades and shapen snow.

The leaves cry . . . One holds off and merely hears the cry.
It is a busy cry, concerning someone else.
And though one says that one is part of everything,

There is a conflict, there is a resistance involved;
And being part is an exertion that declines:
One feels the life of that which gives life as it is.

The leaves cry. It is not a cry of divine attention,
Nor the smoke-drift of puffed-out heroes, nor human cry.
It is the cry of leaves that do not transcend themselves,

In the absence of fantasia, without meaning more
Than they are in the final finding of the ear, in the thing
Itself, until, at last, the cry concerns no one at all.

The Plain Sense of Things

After the leaves have fallen, we return
To a plain sense of things. It is as if
We had come to an end of the imagination,
Inanimate in an inert savoir.

It is difficult even to choose the adjective
For this blank cold, this sadness without cause.
The great structure has become a minor house.
No turban walks across the lessened floors.

The greenhouse never so badly needed paint.
The chimney is fifty years old and slants to one side.
A fantastic effort has failed, a repetition
In a repetitiousness of men and flies.

Yet the absence of the imagination had
Itself to be imagined. The great pond,
The plain sense of it, without reflections, leaves,
Mud, water like dirty glass, expressing silence

Of a sort, silence of a rat come out to see,
The great pond and its waste of the lilies, all this
Had to be imagined as an inevitable knowledge,
Required, as a necessity requires.

The Planet on the Table

Ariel was glad he had written his poems.
They were of a remembered time
Or of something seen that he liked.

Other makings of the sun
Were waste and welter
And the ripe shrub writhed.

His self and the sun were one
And his poems, although makings of his self,
Were no less makings of the sun.

It was not important that they survive.
What mattered was that they should bear
Some lineament or character,

Some affluence, if only half-perceived,
In the poverty of their words,
Of the planet of which they were part.

The River of Rivers in Connecticut

There is a great river this side of Stygia,
Before one comes to the first black cataracts
And trees that lack the intelligence of trees.

In that river, far this side of Stygia,
The mere flowing of the water is a gayety,
Flashing and flashing in the sun. On its banks,

No shadow walks. The river is fateful,
Like the last one. But there is no ferryman.
He could not bend against its propelling force.

It is not to be seen beneath the appearances
That tell of it. The steeple at Farmington
Stands glistening and Haddam shines and sways.

It is the third commonness with light and air,
A curriculum, a vigor, a local abstraction . . .
Call it, once more, a river, an unnamed flowing,

Space-filled, reflecting the seasons, the folk-lore
Of each of the senses; call it, again and again,
The river that flows nowhere, like a sea.

Not Ideas About the Thing But the Thing Itself

At the earliest ending of winter,
In March, a scrawny cry from outside
Seemed like a sound in his mind.

He knew that he heard it,
A bird's cry, at daylight or before,
In the early March wind.

The sun was rising at six,
No longer a battered panache above snow . . .
It would have been outside.

It was not from the vast ventriloquism
Of sleep's faded papier-mâché . . .
The sun was coming from outside.

That scrawny cry—it was
A chorister whose c preceded the choir.
It was part of the colossal sun,

Surrounded by its choral rings,
Still far away. It was like
A new knowledge of reality.

Reality Is an Activity
of the Most August Imagination

Last Friday, in the big light of last Friday night,
We drove home from Cornwall to Hartford, late.

It was not a night blown at a glassworks in Vienna
Or Venice, motionless, gathering time and dust.

There was a crush of strength in a grinding going round,
Under the front of the westward evening star,

The vigor of glory, a glittering in the veins,
As things emerged and moved and were dissolved,

Either in distance, change or nothingness,
The visible transformations of summer night,

An argentine abstraction approaching form
And suddenly denying itself away.

There was an insolid billowing of the solid.
Night's moonlight lake was neither water nor air.

Of Mere Being

The palm at the end of the mind,
Beyond the last thought, rises
In the bronze decor,

A gold-feathered bird
Sings in the palm, without human meaning,
Without human feeling, a foreign song.

You know then that it is not the reason
That makes us happy or unhappy.
The bird sings. Its feathers shine.

The palm stands on the edge of space.
The wind moves slowly in the branches.
The bird's fire-fangled feathers dangle down.

ANGELINA WELD GRIMKÉ

(1880–1958)

Dawn

Grey trees, grey skies, and not a star;
    Grey mist, grey hush;
And then, frail, exquisite, afar,
    A hermit-thrush.

Dusk

Twin stars through my purpling pane,
    The shriveling husk
Of a yellowing moon on the wane,
    And the dusk.

Grass Fingers

Touch me, touch me,
Little cool grass fingers,
Elusive, delicate grass fingers.
With your shy brushings,
Touch my face—
My naked arms—
My thighs—
My feet.
Is there nothing that is kind?
You need not fear me.
Soon I shall be too far beneath you,
For you to reach me, even,
With your tiny, timorous toes.

Tenebris

There is a tree, by day,
That, at night,
Has a shadow,
A hand huge and black,
With fingers long and black.
　All through the dark,
Against the white man's house,
　In the little wind,
The black hand plucks and plucks
　At the bricks.
The bricks are the color of blood and very small.
　Is it a black hand,
　Or is it a shadow?

A Mona Lisa

I.

I should like to creep
Through the long brown grasses
　That are your lashes;
I should like to poise
　On the very brink
Of the leaf-brown pools
　That are your shadowed eyes;
I should like to cleave
　Without sound,
Their glimmering waters,
　Their unrippled waters,
I should like to sink down
　And down
　　And down . . . .
　　　And deeply drown.

2.

Would I be more than a bubble breaking?
　　Or an ever-widening circle
　　Ceasing at the marge?
Would my white bones
　　Be the only white bones
Wavering back and forth, back and forth
　　In their depths?

Epitaph on a Living Woman

There were tiny flames in her eyes,
Her mouth was a flame,
And her flesh. . . . .
　　Now she is ashes.

FRANKLIN P. ADAMS
(1881–1960)

If—

*If Miss Edna St. Vincent Millay had written Mr. Longfellow's
"The Rainy Day."*

> The day is dark and dreary;
> Denuded is the tree;
> The wind is never weary—
> But oh, you are of me!
>
> I ponder on the present;
> You muse upon the past.
> And love is only pleasant
> Because it cannot last.
>
> Still, heart! and cease your aching;
> The world is rich in rhymes,
> And hearts can stand a breaking
> About a billion times.

If Mr. H. W. Longfellow had written Miss Millay's

> "My candle burns at both ends,
> It will not last the night;
> But ah, my foes, and oh, my friends,
> It gives a lovely light."
>
> Between the dark and the daylight
> My bayberry candle burns;
> It shines from out my window
> For the traveler who returns.

It shines with a holy radiance,
    And a sacred light it sends;
It flames with a pure candescence,
    And it burns at both its ends.

Not with a blaze consuming;
    Not with a blistering flame;
Not with a flagrant passion
    Or a heat I dare not name.

But to blaze the path of friendship
    Its flame my candle lends,
For its light is the light eternal
    That burns at both its ends.

WITTER BYNNER
(1881–1968)

Opus 2

Hope
Is the antelope
Over the hills;
Fear
Is the wounded deer
Bleeding in rills;
Care
Is the heavy bear
Tearing at meat;
Fun
Is the mastodon
Vanished complete . . .

And I am the stag with the golden horn
Waiting till my day is born.

Emanuel Morgan

Opus 17

Man-thunder, woman-lightning,
    Rumble, gleam;
Refusal,
    Scream.

Needles and pins of pain
    All pointed the same way;
Parallel lines of pain
    When the lips are gray
    And know not what they say:
Rain,
Rain.

But after the whirl of fright
   And great shouts and flashes,
   The pounding clashes
   And deep slashes,
   After the scattered ashes
 Of the night,
 Heaven's height
   Abashes
   With a gleam through unknown lashes
 Of delicious points of light.

               Emanuel Morgan

The Wave

You come with the light on your face
Of the turn of a river from trees to the open sun,
You are the wandering spirit of the most beloved place—
And yet you are a joy not there begun
Nor anywhere, but always about to be,
The invisible succeeding crest
That follows from the open sea
And shall be loveliest.

I have no language, hardly any word
To name you with, I have no flight of hands
To swim your surface closer than a bird:
For endless changing countermands
Your face and blinds me blacker than a crest of sun,
O joy not yet begun
But only about to be,
O sweet invisible unceasing wave
Following me, following me
Through the sea-like grave!

The Wall

How is it,
That you, whom I can never know,
My beloved,
Are a wall between me and those I have known well—
So that my familiars vanish
Farther than the blue roofs of Nankow
And are lost among the desert hills?

Lightning

There is a solitude in seeing you,
Followed by your company when you are gone.
You are like heaven's veins of lightning.
I cannot see till afterward
How beautiful you are.
There is a blindness in seeing you,
Followed by the sight of you when you are gone.

Horses

Words are hoops
Through which to leap upon meanings,
Which are horses' backs,
Bare, moving.

A Sigh

Still must I tamely
Talk sense with these others?

How long
Before I shall be with you again,
Magnificently saying nothing!

The Moon

Red leaped
The moon,
From behind the black hill of night . . .
And soon it was silver forever
And there was no change . . .

Until its time came . . .

And its setting was as white as a corpse,
Among the flowers of dawn.

Tiles

Chinese magicians had conjured their chance,
And they hunted, with their hooded birds of glee,
The heat that rises from the summer-grass
And shakes against the sea.
And when they had caught a wide expanse
In nets of careful wizardry,
They colored it like molten glass
For roofs, imperially,
With blue from a cavern, green from a morass
And yellow from weeds in the heart of the sea,
And they laid long rows on the dwellings of romance
In perfect alchemy—
And before they ascended like a peal of brass,
They and their tiptoeing hawks of glee
Had topped all China with a roof that slants
And shakes against the sea.

Wistaria

Clouds dream and disappear;
Waters dream in a rainbow and are gone;
Fire-dreams change with the sun

Or when a poppy closes;
But now is the time of year
For the dark earth, one by one,
To dream quieter dreams. And nothing she has ever done
Has given more ease
To her perplexities
Than the dreaming of dreams like these:
Not irises,
Not any spear
Of lilies nor cup of roses,
But these pale, purple images,
As if, from willows or from pepper-trees,
Shadows were glimmering on the Buddha's knees.

Donald Evans

So I shall never hear from his own lips
That things had gone too ill with him awhile,
Nor ever see again, but in eclipse,
The brown precision of his smile.

It does not seem his way at all,
Shooting no firecrackers to a friend,
Making the usual interval
Unusual and finite and an end.

It is not hushed, like other deaths, nor grim,
Nor tragic nor heroic news,
But more as if we had not noticed him
Go by on lightly squeaking shoes

And down the coffins of the race
Tiptoe and stumble till he found his own,
Then clear his throat and decorate his face
With the consummate silence of a stone.

Driftwood

Come, warm your hands
From the cold wind of time.
I have built here, under the moon
A many-colored fire
With fragments of wood
That have been part of a tree
And part of a ship.

Were leaves more real,
Or driven nails,
Or fingers of builders,
Than these burning violets?
Come, warm your hands
From the cold wind of time.
There's a fire under the moon.

Drinking Alone with the Moon

From a pot of wine among the flowers
I drank alone. There was no one with me—
Till, raising my cup, I asked the bright moon
To bring me my shadow and make us three.
Alas, the moon was unable to drink
And my shadow tagged me vacantly;
But still for a while I had these friends
To cheer me through the end of spring. . . .
I sang. The moon encouraged me.
I danced. My shadow tumbled after.
As long as I knew, we were boon companions.
And then I was drunk, and we lost one another.
. . . . Shall goodwill ever be secure?
I watched the long road of the River of Stars.

LI PO

Lovers

From somewhere over the houses, through the silence,
Through the late night, come windy ripples of music.
There's a lighted cigarette-end in the black street,
Moving beside the music he has brought her.
Behind a shuttered window, there's a girl
Smiling into her pillow. And now by her hand
There's a candle lighted and put out again.
And the shadow of a bird leaves its perch for a smaller twig.

A Foreigner

Chapala still remembers the foreigner
Who came with a pale red beard and pale blue eyes
And a pale white skin that covered a dark soul;
They remember the night when he thought he saw a hand
Reach through a broken window and fumble at a lock;
They remember a tree on the beach where he used to sit
And ask the burros questions about peace;
They remember him walking, walking away from something.

Idols

I

They must have buried him away from the lake
Lest he be discontented with his grave
And forsaking the image at his ear, rise up
And sail. No edge of water was visible
From where he had lain so many hundred years
That every bone was fibrous like old wood,
And his moony skull came crumbling in my hand
When I removed the god that whispered there.

2

Within that skull hate had once eaten, and love
Had spun its intricate iridescent web,
And then the worms and the wet earth had worn
Both love and hate down to the marrow-bone.
Fingers that mingle now with yellow roots
And indeterminably feed the world
May once have baked the fingers of this god
That, still intact, grope after human clay.

3

What surer god have I ever seen than this
Which I deliver from an earthen womb,
This idol made of clay, made of man,
This fantasy, this mute insensate whim
Enduring still beside its maker's dust?
These are the open eyes, the lips that speak
Wonderful things, this is the living thought
That make the man alive and alive again.

4

Lie close to me, my poem, and comfort me,
Console me with substance lovelier than mine,
Breathe me alive a thousand years from now,
Whisper—beside that rim of an empty moon,
Under the earth, the moon I thought with once—
That once to have thought, once to have used the earth,
Is to have made a god more durable
Than flesh and bone. Lie close to me, my poem.

Defeat

On a train in Texas German prisoners eat
With white American soldiers, seat by seat,
While black American soldiers sit apart,
The white men eating meat, the black men heart.
Now, with that other war a century done,
Not the live North but the dead South has won,
Not yet a riven nation comes awake.
Whom are we fighting this time, for God's sake?
Mark well the token of the separate seat.
It is again ourselves whom we defeat.

The Titanic

A time comes when a majority of those you remember
Are not among the living but among the dead.
Some of them went down long ago on the *Titanic*.
Justus Miles Forman, for instance.
Who now besides me remembers him,
That tall suave presence with slim waist and pomaded words,
That dark edge of a jungle in exact clothes,
And Charles Frohman, that dumpling of finance with a heart
    nonetheless,
And who else vanished suddenly on the *Titanic*?
But was it the *Titanic* after all?
And is it not always as sudden?
Is it not a shadow springing at you round a corner of the
    street,
The immense imminence of nothing on something?
There is no answer save the vibrations of a voice which
    happens to be living
And might just as well happen to be dead.

from
New Poems 1960

All tempest
Has
Like a navel
A hole in its middle
Through which a gull may fly
In silence

———

Any other time would have done
But not now
Because now there is no time
And when there is no time
It only stands still on its own center
Waiting to be wound

Once upon a time somebody will unwind it
And then what a time
In no time at all

———

But for these apertures
Said the turtle
Man would not have lost
The address of the gods

He hid it in here
In my shell
And I have had no use for it
Yet

ABBIE HUSTON EVANS

(1881–1983)

Juniper

For some twisted reason I
Love what many men pass by,—
Lean-fingered and rock-clinging things,
Bitter-berried, far from springs
Of sweet water, wringing up
Moisture from the rock's own cup,
Or drinking in at every pore
Dew and sea mist, if no more;
All things harsh and slow of root,
Pungent, racy, sparse of fruit,
Heather, gorse, and upland fir,
Lichen, moss,—and juniper!

What are two lean years, or three,
Bantling of Necessity,
Who on stony-breasted earth
Long since learned to thrive on dearth?
Long as ledges, will endure
Your rock-fed green and roots obscure,—
Ay, will batten on the stone
After man is dust and bone.

The Old Yellow Shop

In farming country you are sure to find them,
Little gray wooden buildings boarded up,
Astride a stone wall, or lost in a thicket,
With what shut in?—Well, I think if you pried
A warped board free and climbed in through a window,
You might find much the same thing as I found
In the Yellow Shop on my grandfather's farm:

Darkness at first; pencils of steady sunlight
Alive with dust, that slanted in through chinks,
And such a smell of cedar you would know,
Before your eyes grew wide enough to see,
That the place was full of stacks of fragrant shingles.
Then, tattered paper hanging from the wall,
Crude blue, perhaps, and red—brick-red—and brown,
That chocolate-brown the old folks seemed to fancy.
That might be all.

           —Or might not be.

                        For after
I had stood there for a while, held by the quiet,
A sense of ended things grew up about me.
Someone had lived there once,—I think a cobbler;
It was a place where men had come and gone,
Men of my blood, whose names I did not know;
Whose feet had worn the hollow in the threshold
That let the light in underneath the door;
Whose lives had been blown out, one after one,
By the wind of Time, like candles in a row
Set up to be extinguished.—Yet this shell,
The haunt of dead men, still gave back the sun,
And stood up to the hail and sleet of winter.
—I gripped the nearest thing my hand could find,
A cleat someone had hammered to the wall
To help him clamber to the loft above,
And looked out through the window toward the wood-lot.

The shadow of the Shop ran dark across
The field, which but for that lay in the sun
Serene and smiling and inscrutable;
The air was sweet; blackberry and wild aster
Nodded outside the window in the shade,—
Perpetual things, that, springing year by year,
Are old, by repetition, like the sea;
There was a cricket busy in the stubble,
And a flutter of wings in bushes round the corner;
And in the place, the sense of something ended.
I nailed it up and left it there behind me.

And to this day I never pass the Shop,
Off in its corner, with its blinded eye,
With shingles curling loose and flecks of yellow
Still clinging to the silver of the gray,
But I grow insolent with glorying
In lovely life!—O dancing candle-flame,
Not yet blown out by the delaying wind!

Under Cover

Rain with the old sound, with the country sough
From fields and meadows overpast and trees
That strip it into whip-lash, I hear now
Beat on this hill and cut about its knees.
Now while the lithe wind turns and springs again
On the spent tree, and rain floods down the glass,
I hear the sounds earth knew before we men
Came on, and shall know after we shall pass.
While ancient rumor rising to a shriek
Comes in to tell of matters we forget,
I am one more of the beasts of the field in bleak
Ecstatic cover, huddled from the wet.
    So stands the ox, so crouches now the mole,
    So sits the dry woodpecker in his hole.

Fringed Gentians

In run-out ground in coveys
They startle; here and there
They put blue in italics
Where few stare.

On the bright edge of meadows
When orchises have dried,
Where cranberries streak carmine
They stand beside.

Tight-sheathed, fierce-single, wiry,
Going about to die
They undertake a color
To rock the sky.

"Why, stern, clip blue down foursquare,
Yet fringe it?"—Steady of eye,
New England answers nothing,
Finger-high.

Martian Landscape

I think of the Martian landscape late delivered
To the eye of man by digits of a code
Reporting shades of grayness, darker, lighter,
In dull procession; in the end disclosing
To the rapt eye the unimagined craters.

—And I see a poem, word by word assembled
In markings down a page flash into code,
And bring in sightings of another landscape
No eye has seen before.

JOHN G. NEIHARDT

(1881–1973)

from
The Song of the Messiah

In vain against the formless wolves of air
The holy men wrought magic. Songs that ran
Beyond the hoarded memories of man,
With might beyond the grip of words, they sang;
But still the hidden claw and secret fang
Were mightier, and would not go away.
Grotesqueries of terror shaped in clay
To simulate the foe, and named with names
Of dreadful sound, were given to the flames;
But it was hope that perished. Empty air
Was peopled for the haunted fever-stare;
And when some final horror loosed the jaw,
What shape could image what the dying saw
That none might ever see and live to tell?

By night when sleep made thin the hollow shell
Between what is forever and what seems,
Came voices, awful in a hush of dreams,
Upon the old; and in that dreams are wise
When hearing is but silence and the eyes
Are dark with sun and moon, the weird news spread.
"There is no hope for us," the old men said,
"For we have sold our Mother to the lust
Of strangers, and her breast is bitter dust,
Her thousand laps are empty! She was kind
Before the white men's seeing made us blind
And greedy for the shadows they pursue.
The fed-on-shadows shall be shadows too;
Their trails shall end in darkness. We have sinned;
And all our story is a midnight wind
That moans a little longer and is still.
There was a time when every gazing hill

Was holy with the wonder that it saw,
And every valley was a place of awe,
And what the grass knew never could be told.
It was the living Spirit that we sold—
And what can help us?"

                    Still the evil grew.
It fell upon the cattle, gaunt and few,
That pawed the crusted winter to the bone.
The weirdly wounded flesh of them was blown
To putrid bubbles. Diabolic fire
Burned out the vain last animal desire
In caving paunches, and their muzzles bled.
They staggered, staring. And the wolves were fed.

So Hunger throve. And many of the lean,
Who, having eyes for seeing, had not seen,
And, having ears for hearing, had not heard,
Fed hope a little with the wrathful word
And clamored 'round the agencies. "Our lands,"
They said, "we sold to you for empty hands
And empty bellies and a white man's lie!
Where is the food we bought? Our children die!
The clothing? For our people shiver. Look!
The money for the ponies that you took
Ten snows ago? The Great White Father's friends
Have stolen half the little that he sends.
The starving of our babies makes them fat.
We want to tell the Great White Father that.
We cannot live on promises and lies."

But there were weighty matters for the wise
In Washington, and bellies that were round;
And gold made music yonder, and the sound
Of mourning was a whisper.

ELIZABETH MADOX ROBERTS

(1881–1941)

Evening Song

I draw my sight in when I sleep.
I gather back my word and call.
I take my senses from the air
And wind them in a little ball.

I curl them in a lonely ball,
And wind them in a lonely mesh.
I fold it over with my dream,
And wind it round and round with flesh.

The Song of the Dove

The dove-cries on the tower stones
Roll softly down and call my name,
Lay a stone on my name.

They call with heavy weighted tones,
Fall softly down to still my name,
Lay a stone on my name.

An Old Love in Song

"Oh, my truelove," is part of it,
Or was it "My truelove and I?" . . .
It trembles on old memories
And walks on by.

I asked an old man and he said,
"That song? Why everybody knows . . ."
He said, but when he tried to sing,
"I can't remember how it goes."

He said, "My father used to sing
A verse of it," and then he said,
"It really came before my day
And those that used it all are dead."

It walks tiptoe on other thoughts.
It's hardly there for you to touch,
But once,—my hand was on the door,
It leaned against the latch.

"Oh, my truelove" is dead and lost,
And no one sings it now at all,
But once I saw it on a shelf;
It curved against an ancient bowl.

They used to sing it by the doors
On summer nights, and yet, and yet,
It wasn't anything to keep;
It was something to forget.

I saw it lying in the ground
In a deep hole that I had made. . . .
I dug beside an old rose bush—
I touched it with my spade.

Disconsolate Morning

The sparse season, the lean
Time before the cold spring.
The first of the dwarf rush,
Arrowhead and arrow-grass
And the cold glow on the willow bush.

The cold birds twit
Over the spent boughs.
The water in the mill leat
Runs silver-black, and the hills
Are green-cold with winter wheat.

The gaunt foxes are hid
In the river bluffs,
And the gaunt hounds skulk
On the kill's brow,
Or they lie beside the hearth and hulk

A phantom hare. A lean day.
The woods-path leads nowhere,
Or it leads to the stone shaft
Where the shell rocks are piled,
Where the sea has left its draft.

MINA LOY

(1882–1966)

Songs to Joannes

I

Spawn   of   Fantasies
Silting the appraisable
Pig Cupid   his rosy snout
Rooting erotic garbage
"Once upon a time"
Pulls a weed   white star-topped
Among wild oats   sown in mucous-membrane

I would   an   eye in a Bengal light
Eternity in a sky-rocket
Constellations in an ocean
Whose rivers run no fresher
Than a trickle of saliva

These   are suspect places

I must live in my lantern
Trimming subliminal flicker
Virginal   to the bellows
Of Experience
                         Coloured   glass

II

                         The skin-sack
In which a wanton duality
Packed
All the completion of my infructuous impulses
Something the shape of a man
To the casual vulgarity of the merely observant
More of a clock-work mechanism
Running down against time

To which I am not paced
    My finger-tips are numb from fretting your hair
A God's door-mat
        On the threshold of your mind

   III

We might have coupled
In the bed-ridden monopoly of a moment
Or broken flesh with one another
At the profane communion table
Where wine is spill'd on promiscuous lips

We might have given birth to a butterfly
With the daily news
Printed in blood on its wings

   IV

Once in a mezzanino
The starry ceiling
Vaulted an unimaginable family
Bird-like abortions
With human throats
And Wisdom's eyes
Who wore lamp-shade red dresses
And woolen hair

One bore a baby
In a padded porte-enfant
Tied with a sarsenet ribbon
To her goose's wings

But for the abominable shadows
I would have lived
Among their fearful furniture
To teach them to tell me their secrets
Before I guessed
—Sweeping the brood clean out

V

Midnight empties the street
Of all but us
Three
I am undecided which way back
⠀⠀⠀⠀⠀⠀To the left a boy
—One wing has been washed in the rain
⠀⠀The other will never be clean any more—
Pulling door-bells to remind
Those that are snug
⠀⠀⠀⠀⠀⠀⠀To the right a haloed ascetic
⠀⠀⠀⠀⠀⠀⠀Threading houses
Probes wounds for souls
—The poor can't wash in hot water—
And I don't know which turning to take
Since you got home to yourself—first

VI

I know the Wire-Puller intimately
And if it were not for the people
On whom you keep one eye
You could look straight at me
And Time would be set back

VII

My pair of feet
Smack the flag-stones
That are something left over from your walking
The wind stuffs the scum of the white street
Into my lungs and my nostrils
Exhilarated birds
Prolonging flight into the night
Never reaching— — — — — — —

VIII

I am the jealous store-house of the candle-ends
That lit your adolescent learning
— — — — — — — — —

Behind God's eyes
There might
Be other lights

IX

When we lifted
Our eye-lids on Love
A cosmos
Of coloured voices
And laughing honey

And spermatozoa
At the core of Nothing
In the milk of the Moon

X

Shuttle-cock and battle-door
A little pink-love
And feathers are strewn

XI

Dear one   at your mercy
Our Universe
Is only
A colorless onion
You derobe
Sheath by sheath
            Remaining
A disheartening odour
About your nervy hands

XII

Voices break on the confines of passion
Desire   Suspicion   Man   Woman
Solve in the humid carnage

Flesh from flesh
Draws the inseparable delight
Kissing at gasps   to catch it

Is it true
That I have set you apart
Inviolate in an utter crystallization
Of all   the jolting of the crowd
Taught me willingly to live to share

Or are you
Only the other half
Of an ego's necessity
Scourging pride with compassion
To the shallow sound of dissonance
And boom of escaping breath

XIII

Come to me   There is something
I have got to tell you   and I can't tell
Something taking shape
Something that has a new name
A new dimension
A new use
A new illusion

It is ambient   And it is in your eyes
Something shiny   Something only for you
                      Something that I must not see

It is in my ears   Something very resonant
Something that you must not hear
                       Something only for me

Let us be very jealous
Very suspicious
Very conservative
Very cruel
Or we might make an end of the jostling of aspirations
Disorb inviolate egos

Where two or three are welded together
They shall become god
— — — — — — —
Oh that's right
Keep away from me   Please give me a push
Don't let me understand you   Don't realise me
Or we might tumble together
Depersonalized
Identical
Into the terrific Nirvana
Me you — you — me

XIV

Today
Everlasting   passing   apparent   imperceptible
To you
I bring the nascent virginity of
—Myself   for the moment

No love   or the other thing
Only the impact of lighted bodies
Knocking sparks off each other
In chaos

XV

Seldom   Trying for Love
Fantasy dealt them out as gods
Two or three men   looked only human

But you alone
Superhuman   apparently
I had to be caught in the weak eddy
Of your drivelling humanity
            To love you most

XVI

We might have lived together
In the lights of the Arno
Or gone apple stealing under the sea
Or played
Hide and seek in love and cob-webs
And a lullaby on a tin-pan

And   talked till there were no more tongues
To talk with
And never have known any better

XVII

I don't care
Where the legs of the legs of the furniture are walking to
Or what is hidden in the shadows they stride
Or what would look at me
If the shutters were not shut

Red   a warm colour on the battle-field
Heavy on my knees as a counterpane
Count counter
I counted   the fringe of the towel
Till two tassels clinging together
Let the square room fall away
From a round vacuum
Dilating with my breath

XVIII

Out of the severing
Of hill from hill
The interim

Of star from star
The nascent
Static
Of night

   XIX

Nothing so conserving
As cool cleaving
Note of the Q H U
Clear carving
Breath-giving
Pollen smelling
Space

White telling
Of slaking
Drinkable
Through fingers
Running water
Grass haulms
Grow to

Leading astray
Of fireflies
Aerial quadrille
Bouncing
Off one another
Again conjoining
In recaptured pulses
Of light

You too
Had something
At that time
Of a green-lit glow-worm
— — — — — — —
Yet slowly drenched
To raylessness
In rain

XX

Let Joy go solace-winged
To flutter whom she may concern

XXI

I store up nights against you
Heavy with shut-flower's nightmares
— — — — — — — — —

Stack noons
Curled to the solitaire
Core of the
Sun

XXII

Green things grow
Salads
For the cerebral
Forager's revival
Upon bossed bellies
Of mountains
Rolling in the sun
And flowered flummery
Breaks
To my silly shoes

In ways without you
I go
Gracelessly
As things go

XXIII

Laughter in solution
Stars in a stare
Irredeemable pledges
Of pubescent consummations
Rot
To the recurrent moon

Bleach
To the pure white
Wickedness of pain

XXIV

The procreative truth of Me
Petered out
In pestilent
Tear drops
Little lusts and lucidities
And prayerful lies
Muddled with the heinous acerbity
Of your street-corner smile

XXV

Licking the Arno
The little rosy
Tongue of Dawn
Interferes with our eyelashes
— — — — — — —

We twiddle to it
Round and round
Faster
And turn into machines

Till the sun
Subsides in shining
Melts some of us
Into abysmal pigeon-holes
Passion has bored
In warmth

Some few of us
Grow to the level of cool plains
Cutting our foot-hold
With steel eyes

XXVI

Shedding our petty pruderies
From slit eyes

We sidle up
To Nature
— — — that irate pornographist

XXVII

Nucleus   Nothing
Inconceivable concept
Insentient repose
The hands of races
Drop off from
Immodifiable plastic

The contents
Of our ephemeral conjunction
In aloofness from Much
Flowed to approachment of — — — —
NOTHING
There was a man and a woman
In the way
While the Irresolvable
Rubbed with our daily deaths
Impossible eyes

XXVIII

The steps go up for ever
And they are white
And the first step   is the last white
Forever
Coloured   conclusions
Smelt   to synthetic
Whiteness
Of my
Emergence
And I am burnt quite white

In the climacteric
Withdrawal of your sun
And wills and words all white
Suffuse
Illimitable monotone

White   where there is nothing to see
But a white towel
Wipes the cymophanous sweat
—Mist rise of living—
From your
Etiolate body
And the white dawn
Of your   New Day
Shuts down on me

Unthinkable   that white over there
— — — Is smoke from your house

XXIX

Evolution   fall foul of
Sexual equality
Prettily miscalculate
Similitude

Unnatural selection
Breed such sons and daughters
As shall jibber at each other
Uninterpretable cryptonyms
Under the moon

Give them some way of braying brassily
For caressive calling
Or to homophonous hiccoughs
Transpose the laugh
Let them suppose that tears
Are snowdrops or molasses
Or anything
Than human insufficiencies
Begging dorsal vertebrae

Let meeting be the turning
To the antipodean
And Form   a blurr
Anything
Than seduce them
To the one
As simple satisfaction
For the other

Let them clash together
From their incognitoes
In seismic orgasm

For far further
Differentiation
Rather than watch
Own-self distortion
Wince in the alien ego

   XXX

In some
Prenatal plagiarism
Fœtal buffoons
Caught tricks
— — — — —

From archetypal pantomime
Stringing emotions
Looped aloft
— — — —

For the blind eyes
That Nature knows us with
And the most of Nature   is green
— — — — — — — — —

What guaranty
For the proto-form
We fumble
Our souvenir ethics to
— — — — — — —

XXXI

Crucifixion
Of a busy-body
Longing to interfere so
With the intimacies
Of your insolent isolation

Crucifixion
Of an illegal ego's
Eclosion
On your equilibrium
Caryatid   of an idea

Crucifixion
Wracked arms
Index extremities
In vacuum
To the unbroken fall

XXXII

The moon is cold
Joannes
Where the Mediterranean — — — — —

XXXIII

The prig of passion — — — —
To your professorial paucity

Proto-plasm was raving mad
Evolving us — — —

XXXIV

Love — — — the preeminent litterateur

Poe

a lyric elixir of death

    embalms
    the spindle spirits of your hour glass loves
                    on moon spun nights

sets
    icicled canopy
    for corpses of poesy
    with roses and northern lights

    Where frozen nightingales in ilix aisles

                    sing burial rites

Apology of Genius

Ostracized as we are with God—
    The watchers of the civilized wastes
    reverse their signals on our track

    Lepers of the moon
    all magically diseased
    we come among you
    innocent
    of our luminous sores

    unknowing
    how perturbing lights
    our spirit
    on the passion of Man
    until you turn on us your smooth fools' faces
    like buttocks bared in aboriginal mockeries

    We are the sacerdotal clowns
    who feed upon the wind and stars
    and pulverous pastures of poverty

Our wills are formed
by curious disciplines
beyond your laws

You may give birth to us
or marry us
the chances of your flesh
are not our destiny—

The cuirass of the soul
still shines—
And we are unaware
if you confuse
such brief
corrosion with possession

In the raw caverns of the Increate
we forge the dusk of Chaos
to that imperious jewellery of the Universe
        —the Beautiful—

While to your eyes
        A delicate crop
of criminal mystic immortelles
stands to the censor's scythe.

Lunar Baedeker

A silver Lucifer
serves
cocaine in cornucopia

To some somnambulists
of adolescent thighs
draped
in satirical draperies

Peris in livery
prepare
Lethe
for posthumous parvenues

Delirious Avenues
lit
with the chandelier souls
of infusoria
from Pharoah's tombstones

lead
to mercurial doomsdays
Odious oasis
in furrowed phosphorous— — —

the eye-white sky-light
white-light district
of lunar lusts

— — — Stellectric signs
"Wing shows on Starway"
"Zodiac carrousel"

Cyclones
of ecstatic dust
and ashes whirl
crusaders
from hallucinatory citadels
of shattered glass
into evacuate craters

A flock of dreams
browse on Necropolis

From the shores
of oval oceans
in the oxidized Orient

Onyx-eyed Odalisques
and ornithologists
observe
the flight
of Eros obsolete

And "Immortality"
mildews . . .
in the museums of the moon

"Nocturnal cyclops"
"Crystal concubine"
— — — — — — —
Pocked with personification
the fossil virgin of the skies
waxes and wanes— — — —

Der Blinde Junge

The dam Bellona
littered
her eyeless offspring
Kriegsopfer
upon the pavements of Vienna

Sparkling precipitate
the spectral day
involves
the visionless obstacle

this slow blind face
pushing
its virginal nonentity
against the light

Pure purposeless eremite
of centripetal sentience

Upon the carnose horologe of the ego
the vibrant tendon index moves not

since the black lightning desecrated
the retinal altar

Void and extinct
this planet of the soul
strains from the craving throat
in static flight upslanting

A downy youth's snout
nozzling the sun
drowned in dumbfounded instinct

Listen!
illuminati of the coloured earth
How this expressionless "thing"
blows out damnation and concussive dark

Upon a mouth-organ

Brancusi's Golden Bird

The toy
become the aesthetic archetype

As if
        some patient peasant God
        had rubbed and rubbed
        the Alpha and Omega
        of Form
        into a lump of metal

        A naked orientation
        unwinged   unplumed
          —the ultimate rhythm
        has lopped the extremities

of crest and claw
from
the nucleus of flight

The absolute act
of art
conformed
to continent sculpture
—bare as the brow of Osiris—
this breast of revelation

an incandescent curve
licked by chromatic flames
in labyrinths of reflections

This gong
of polished hyperaesthesia

shrills with brass
as the aggressive light
strikes
its significance

The immaculate
conception
of the inaudible bird
occurs
in gorgeous reticence . . .

Gertrude Stein

Curie
of the laboratory
of vocabulary
   she crushed
the tonnage
of consciousness
congealed to phrases
   to extract
a radium of the word

On Third Avenue

I

"You should have disappeared years ago"—

so disappear
on Third Avenue
to share the heedless incognito

of shuffling shadow-bodies
animate with frustration

whose silence'   only potence is
respiration
preceding the eroded bronze contours
of their other aromas

through the monstrous air
of this red-lit thoroughfare.

Here and there
saturnine
neon-signs
set afire
a feature
on their hueless overcast
of down-cast countenances.

For their ornateness
Time, the contortive tailor,
on and off,
clowned with sweat-sculptured cloth
to press

upon these irreparable dummies
an eerie undress
of mummies
half unwound.

2

Such are the compensations of poverty,
to see———

Like an electric fungus
sprung from its own effulgence
of intercircled jewellery
reflected on the pavement,

like a reliquary sedan-chair,
out of a legend, dumped there,

before a ten-cent Cinema,

a sugar-coated box-office
enjail a Goddess
aglitter, in her runt of a tower,
with ritual claustrophobia.

Such are compensations of poverty,
to see———

Transient in the dust,
the brilliancy
of a trolley
loaded with luminous busts;

lovely in anonymity
they vanish
with the mirage
of their passage.

ANNE SPENCER

(1882–1976)

At the Carnival

Gay little Girl-of-the-Diving-Tank,
I desire a name for you,
Nice, as a right glove fits;
For you—who amid the malodorous
Mechanics of this unlovely thing,
Are darling of spirit and form.
I know you—a glance, and what you are
Sits-by-the-fire in my heart.
My Limousine-Lady knows you, or
Why does the slant-envy of her eye mark
Your straight air and radiant inclusive smile?
Guilt pins a fig-leaf; Innocence is its own adorning.
The bull-necked man knows you—this first time
His itching flesh sees form divine and vibrant health,
And thinks not of his avocation.
I came incuriously—
Set on no diversion save that my mind
Might safely nurse its brood of misdeeds
In the presence of a blind crowd.
The color of life was gray.
Everywhere the setting seemed right
For my mood!
Here the sausage and garlic booth
Sent unholy incense skyward;
There a quivering female-thing
Gestured assignations, and lied
To call it dancing;
There, too, were games of chance
With chances for none;
But oh! Girl-of-the-Tank, at last!
Gleaming Girl, how intimately pure and free
The gaze you send the crowd,
As though you know the dearth of beauty

In its sordid life.
We need you—my Limousine-Lady,
The bull-necked man, and I.
Seeing you here brave and water-clean,
Leaven for the heavy ones of earth,
I am swift to feel that what makes
The plodder glad is good; and
Whatever is good is God.
The wonder is that you are here;
I have seen the queer in queer places,
But never before a heaven-fed
Naiad of the Carnival-Tank!
Little Diver, Destiny for you,
Like as for me, is shod in silence;
Years may seep into your soul
The bacilli of the usual and the expedient;
I implore Neptune to claim his child to-day!

Lines to a Nasturtium

(A lover muses)

Flame-flower, Day-torch, Mauna Loa,
I saw a daring bee, to-day, pause, and soar,
    Into your flaming heart;
Then did I hear crisp crinkled laughter
As the furies after tore him apart?
    A bird, next, small and humming,
Looked into your startled depths and fled. . . .
Surely, some dread sight, and dafter
    Than human eyes as mine can see,
Set the stricken air waves drumming
    In his flight.

    Day-torch, Flame-flower, cool-hot Beauty,
I cannot see, I cannot hear your flutey
Voice lure your loving swain,
But I know one other to whom you are in beauty
Born in vain:
Hair like the setting sun,
Her eyes a rising star,
Motions gracious as reeds by Babylon, bar
All your competing;
Hands like, how like, brown lilies sweet,
Cloth of gold were fair enough to touch her feet. . . .
Ah, how the senses flood at my repeating,
As once in her fire-lit heart I felt the furies
Beating, beating.

BADGER CLARK JR.

(1883–1957)

A Border Affair

Spanish is the lovin' tongue,
   Soft as music, light as spray.
'Twas a girl I learnt it from,
   Livin' down Sonora way.
I don't look much like a lover,
Yet I say her love words over
   Often when I'm all alone—
   "Mi amor, mi corazon."

Nights when she knew where I'd ride
   She would listen for my spurs,
Fling the big door open wide,
   Raise them laughin' eyes of her
And my heart would nigh stop beatin'
When I heard her tender greetin',
   Whispered soft for me alone
   "Mi amor! mi corazon!"

Moonlight in the patio,
   Old Señora noddin' near,
Me and Juana talkin' low
   So the Madre couldn't hear—
How those hours would go a-flyin'!
And too soon I'd hear her sighin'
   In her little sorry tone—
   "Adios, mi corazon!"

But one time I had to fly
   For a foolish gamblin' fight,
And we said a swift goodbye
   In that black, unlucky night.
When I'd loosed her arms from clingin'

416

With her words the hoofs kep' ringin'
   As I galloped north alone—
     "Adios, mi corazon!"

Never seen her since that night,
   I kain't cross the Line, you know.
She was Mex and I was white;
   Like as not it's better so.
Yet I've always sort of missed her
Since that last wild night I kissed her,
   Left her heart and lost my own—
     "Adios, mi corazon!"

MAX EASTMAN
(1883–1969)

To John Reed

Jack, you are quiet now among the dead.
The pulse of the young lion and the fire
In that bright engine of extreme desire
That never would be tired or quieted,
That could fight, laugh, give, love, and sing,
And understand, so carelessly—so strong
That you amazed us with your tender song—
It all is dead now, dead and mouldering.

They say you died for Communism—they
Who to some absent god must always give
The choicest even of the fruits of youth.
Your god was life. Because you chose to live,
Death found you in the torrent of the fray,
Exulting in the future and the truth.

To Genevieve Taggard Who Called
Me Traitor in a Poem

"When print on paper tells, in the time's affairs
How he betrays and clouds the precarious cause
He once led well, I feel a pang and tears.
The microscope of love's near-scrutiny
Saw this in small (trembling with less passive tears
—So much lay in him that was life to me,
And he with me so mingled). So was I—
And so ensued the heartbreak of the years.

Yet I never thought to such a ruinous end
And such complete corrosion to see him come,
Here, stamped on paper, false! O traitorous friend,
So long ago detected, here in sum."

So!
You've cast me for the traitor in your show!
You mount a box, rip out your breast, and cry:
"It's true! He *is* a traitor! I, I, I,
Who loved him with this bosom testify!"

TO THE SAME AFTER REFLECTION

You are, you know, a trifle histrionic.
I said so on the day—remember?—when we two,
Having compared our angers in Platonic
Retrospection, found them both untrue,
Found our pains mated, or exchanged them, chaffing
Each in the other his own fault, and laughing
As true friends better than true lovers do.
The woods were mossy and the trees close-stalked
Pushed us with leaves together, yet we walked
Hand only pressing hand in childhood fashion,
Knowing—at least I knew, for I was reasoning—
We held in the brief heaven of our hearts a thing
More pure, and that is pure indeed, than passion.

Not solely in reproach I cried so hoarsely
That you, although your words like star tides flow,
Are staging yourself nakedly and coarsely.
Still less in cruelty now I remind you
Of what, if you believed me once, you know,
That life's explicit shine does sometimes blind you—
It shone like sun-hot poppies on your youth—
To life's implicit and yet simple truth.

"When print on paper tells . . ." So (and for such a cause!)
Begins your drama of rescinded love,
Your weeping of strong tears in your strong verse.
Poor canceled love! And what to me is worse,
Friendship recanted, both the general laws
And recent leaf-fringed pledge thereof
Between us, broken. "Print on paper tells . . ."
So begins. And of like argument the end:
"Here, stamped on paper, false, O traitorous friend!"

What a great thing is paper! And what print!
How expertly your eyeless poem spells
The cause of blindness, the new instrument
That in the tyrant's fist exceeds the sword!
When justice, freedom, beauty, truth are slain,
How could your love survive which was half pain?

And yet . . . love can meet death with dignity.
No single word has passed from you to me
Since we our infant angers merged and lulled
In a cradle of sweet trust. No private word.
This public notice only: LOVE ANNULLED,
(Administrative Order 99)
In strict adherence to the party line.

ARTHUR DAVISON FICKE

(1883–1945)

Opus 118

If bathing were a virtue, not a lust,
I would be dirtiest.

To some, housecleaning is a holy rite.
For myself, houses would be empty
But for the golden motes dancing in sunbeams.

Tax-assessors frequently overlook valuables.
Today they noted my jade.
But my memory of you escaped them.

Anne Knish

Opus 131

I am weary of salmon dawns
And of cinnamon sunsets;
Silver-grey and iron-grey
Of winter dusk and morn
Torture me; and in the amethystine shadows
Of snow, and in the mauve of curving clouds
Some poison has dwelling.

Ivory on a fan of Venice,
Black-pearl of a bowl of Japan,
Prismatic lustres of Phœnician glass,
Fawn-tinged embroideries from looms of Bagdad,
The green of ancient bronze, cinereous tinge
Of iron gods,—
These, and the saffron of old cerements,

Violet wine,
Zebra-striped onyx,
Are to me like the narrow walls of home
To the land-locked sailor.

   I must have fire-brands!
I must have leaves!
I must have sea-deeps!

Anne Knish

ALFRED KREYMBORG

The Tree

I am four monkeys.
One hangs from a limb,
tail-wise,
chattering at the earth;
another is cramming his belly with cocoanut;
the third is up in the top branches,
quizzing the sky;
and the fourth—
he's chasing another monkey.
How many monkeys are you?

Ants

Who made the world, sir?
I don't know, son—
See the ants on that hill, with a fly.

Who made the world, sir?
Some say that God—
The fly is dead, son.
They're dragging him to their hole.

Who made God, sir?
I don't know—
Now he's gone, son.
The ants are an indefatigable race.

Who made God, sir?
Observe how they swarm all over the hill.
They're hunting another fly.

They're funny, sir.
They are.

Culture

There is only one.
Only one sun.
Only one moon.
And you too.
Be that.

Improvisation

Wind:
Why do you play
that long beautiful adagio,
that archaic air,
to-night?
Will it never end?
Or is it the beginning,
some prelude you seek?

Is it a tale you strum?
Yesterday, yesterday—
Have you no more for us?

Wind:
Play on.
There is nor hope
nor mutiny
in you.

Tiger Lily

To have reached
the ultimate top
of the stalk,
single and tall;
to hang like a bell
through sheer weight
of oneself;
to have six petals,
refusing the straight
for the curve,
dipping pin-pricks
around the horizon;
to have six tongues
which, however the mood
of the wind may blow,
refuse to clap into sound;
and to keep withal
one's finest marvel,
one's passionate specks
invisible:
Tiger lily,
if I bow,
it is not
in imitation;
it is
in recognition
of true being.

WILLIAM CARLOS WILLIAMS

(1883–1963)

The Young Housewife

At ten A.M. the young housewife
moves about in negligée behind
the wooden walls of her husband's house.
I pass solitary in my car.

Then again she comes to the curb
to call the ice-man, fish-man, and stands
shy, uncorseted, tucking in
stray ends of hair, and I compare her
to a fallen leaf.

The noiseless wheels of my car
rush with a crackling sound over
dried leaves as I bow and pass smiling.

Pastoral

When I was younger
it was plain to me
I must make something of myself.
Older now
I walk back streets
admiring the houses
of the very poor:
roof out of line with sides
the yards cluttered
with old chicken wire, ashes,
furniture gone wrong;
the fences and outhouses
built of barrel-staves
and parts of boxes, all,
if I am fortunate,

smeared a bluish green
that properly weathered
pleases me best
of all colors.

No one
will believe this
of vast import to the nation.

Chicory and Daisies

I

Lift your flowers
on bitter stems
chicory!
Lift them up
out of the scorched ground!
Bear no foliage
but give yourself
wholly to that!
Strain under them
you bitter stems
that no beast eats—
and scorn greyness!
Into the heat with them:
cool!
luxuriant! sky-blue!
The earth cracks and
is shriveled up;
the wind moans piteously;
the sky goes out
if you should fail.

II

I saw a child with daisies
for weaving into the hair
tear the stems
with her teeth!

Dawn

Ecstatic bird songs pound
the hollow vastness of the sky
with metallic clinkings—
beating color up into it
at a far edge,—beating it, beating it
with rising, triumphant ardor,—
stirring it into warmth,
quickening in it a spreading change,—
bursting wildly against it as
dividing the horizon, a heavy sun
lifts himself—is lifted—
bit by bit above the edge
of things,—runs free at last
out into the open—! lumbering
glorified in full release upward—

                              songs cease.

Spring Strains

In a tissue-thin monotone of blue-grey buds
crowded erect with desire against
the sky—
            tense blue-grey twigs
slenderly anchoring them down, drawing
them in—
            two blue-grey birds chasing
a third struggle in circles, angles,
swift convergings to a point that bursts
instantly!
            Vibrant bowing limbs
pull downward, sucking in the sky
that bulges from behind, plastering itself
against them in packed rifts, rock blue
and dirty orange!
                  But—
(Hold hard, rigid jointed trees!)

the blinding and red-edged sun-blur—
creeping energy, concentrated
counterforce—welds sky, buds, trees,
rivets them in one puckering hold!
Sticks through! Pulls the whole
counter-pulling mass upward, to the right,
locks even the opaque, not yet defined
ground in a terrific drag that is
loosening the very tap-roots!

On a tissue-thin monotone of blue-grey buds
two blue-grey birds, chasing a third,
at full cry! Now they are
flung outward and up—disappearing suddenly!

Sympathetic Portrait of a Child

The murderer's little daughter
who is barely ten years old
jerks her shoulders
right and left
so as to catch a glimpse of me
without turning round.

Her skinny little arms
wrap themselves
this way then that
reversely about her body!
Nervously
she crushes her straw hat
about her eyes
and tilts her head
to deepen the shadow—
smiling excitedly!

As best as she can
she hides herself
in the full sunlight

her cordy legs writhing
beneath the little flowered dress
that leaves them bare
from mid-thigh to ankle—

Why has she chosen me
for the knife
that darts along her smile?

January Morning

Suite:

I

I have discovered that most of
the beauties of travel are due to
the strange hours we keep to see them:

the domes of the Church of
the Paulist Fathers in Weehawken
against a smoky dawn—the heart stirred—
are beautiful as Saint Peters
approached after years of anticipation.

II

Though the operation was postponed
I saw the tall probationers
in their tan uniforms
                    hurrying to breakfast!

III

—and from basement entries
neatly coiffed, middle aged gentlemen
with orderly moustaches and
well-brushed coats

IV

—and the sun, dipping into the avenues
streaking the tops of
the irregular red houselets,
                         and
the gay shadows dropping and dropping.

V

—and a young horse with a green bed-quilt
on his withers shaking his head:
bared teeth and nozzle high in the air!

VI

—and a semicircle of dirt-colored men
about a fire bursting from an old
ash can,

VII

              —and the worn,
blue car rails (like the sky!)
gleaming among the cobbles!

VIII

—and the rickety ferry-boat "Arden"!
What an object to be called "Arden"
among the great piers,—on the
ever new river!
              "Put me a Touchstone
at the wheel, white gulls, and we'll
follow the ghost of the Half Moon
to the North West Passage—and through!
(at Albany!) for all that!"

IX

Exquisite brown waves—long
circlets of silver moving over you!
enough with crumbling ice crusts among you!

The sky has come down to you,
lighter than tiny bubbles, face to
face with you!
                    His spirit is
a white gull with delicate pink feet
and a snowy breast for you to
hold to your lips delicately!

                    X

The young doctor is dancing with happiness
in the sparkling wind, alone
at the prow of the ferry! He notices
the curdy barnacles and broken ice-crusts
left at the slip's base by the low tide
and thinks of summer and green
shell crusted ledges among
                    the emerald eel-grass!

                    XI

Who knows the Palisades as I do
knows the river breaks east from them
above the city—but they continue south
—under the sky—to bear a crest of
little peering houses that brighten
with dawn behind the moody
water-loving giants of Manhattan.

                    XII

Long yellow rushes bending
above the white snow patches;
purple and gold ribbon
of the distant wood:
                    what an angle
you make with each other as
you lie there in contemplation.

XIII

Work hard all your young days
and they'll find you too, some morning
staring up under
your chiffonier at its warped
bass-wood bottom and your soul—
out!
—among the little sparrows
behind the shutter.

XIV

—and the flapping flags are at
half mast for the dead admiral.

XV

All this—
          was for you, old woman.
I wanted to write a poem
that you would understand.
For what good is it to me
if you can't understand it?
                    But you got to try hard—
But—
     Well, you know how
the young girls run giggling
on Park Avenue after dark
when they ought to be home in bed?
Well,
that's the way it is with me somehow.

Romance Moderne

Tracks of rain and light linger in
the spongy greens of a nature whose
flickering mountain—bulging nearer,
ebbing back into the sun

hollowing itself away to hold a lake,—
or brown stream rising and falling
at the roadside, turning about,
churning itself white, drawing
green in over it,—plunging glassy funnels
fall—
    And—the other world—
the windshield a blunt barrier:
Talk to me. Sh! they would hear us.
—the backs of their heads facing us—
The stream continues its motion of
a hound running over rough ground.

Trees vanish—reappear—vanish:
detached dance of gnomes—as a talk
dodging remarks, glows and fades.
—The unseen power of words—
And now that a few of the moves
are clear the first desire is
to fling oneself out at the side into
the other dance, to other music.
Peer Gynt. Rip Van Winkle. Diana.

If I were young I would try a new alignment—
alight nimbly from the car, Good-bye!—
Childhood companions linked two and two
criss-cross: four, three, two, one.
Back into self, tentacles withdrawn.
Feel about in warm self-flesh.
Since childhood, since childhood!
Childhood is a toad in the garden, a
happy toad. All toads are happy
and belong in gardens. A toad to Diana!

Lean forward. Punch the steersman
behind the ear. Twirl the wheel!
Over the edge! Screams! Crash!
The end. I sit above my head—
a little removed—or
a thin wash of rain on the roadway

—I am never afraid when he is driving,—
interposes new direction,
rides us sideswise, unforeseen
into the ditch! All threads cut!
Death! Black. The end. The very end—

I would sit separate weighing a
small red handful: the dirt of these parts,
sliding mists sheeting the alders
against the touch of fingers creeping
to mine. All stuff of the blind emotions.
But—stirred, the eye seizes
for the first time—The eye awake!—
anything, a dirt bank with green stars
of scrawny weed flattened upon it under
a weight of air—For the first time!—
or a yawning depth: Big!
Swim around in it, through it—
all directions and find
vitreous seawater stuff—
God how I love you!—or, as I say,
a plunge into the ditch. The end. I sit
examining my red handful. Balancing
—this—in and out—agh.

Love you? It's
a fire in the blood, willy-nilly!
It's the sun coming up in the morning.
Ha, but it's the grey moon too, already up
in the morning. You are slow.
Men are not friends where it concerns
a woman? Fighters. Playfellows.
White round thighs! Youth! Sighs—!
It's the fillip of novelty. It's—

Mountains. Elephants humping along
against the sky—indifferent to
light withdrawing its tattered shreds,
worn out with embraces. It's
the fillip of novelty. It's a fire in the blood.

Oh get a flannel shirt, white flannel
or pongee. You'd look so well!
I married you because I liked your nose.
I wanted you! I wanted you
in spite of all they'd say—

Rain and light, mountain and rain,
rain and river. Will you love me always?
—A car overturned and two crushed bodies
under it.—Always! Always!
And the white moon already up.
White. Clean. All the colors.
A good head, backed by the eye—awake!
backed by the emotions—blind—
River and mountain, light and rain—or
rain, rock, light, trees—divided:
rain-light counter rocks-trees or
trees counter rain-light-rocks or—

Myriads of counter processions
crossing and recrossing, regaining
the advantage, buying here, selling there
—You are sold cheap everywhere in town!—
lingering, touching fingers, withdrawing
gathering forces into blares, hummocks,
peaks and rivers—river meeting rock
—I wish that you were lying there dead
and I sitting here beside you.—
It's the grey moon—over and over.
It's the clay of these parts.

The Desolate Field

Vast and grey, the sky
is a simulacrum
to all but him whose days
are vast and grey, and—
In the tall, dried grasses

a goat stirs
with nozzle searching the ground.
—my head is in the air
but who am I . . ?
And amazed my heart leaps
at the thought of love
vast and grey
yearning silently over me.

Thursday

I have had my dream—like others—
and it has come to nothing, so that
I remain now carelessly
with feet planted on the ground
and look up at the sky—
feeling my clothes about me,
the weight of my body in my shoes,
the rim of my hat, air passing in and out
at my nose—and decide to dream no more.

Queen-Anne's-Lace

Her body is not so white as
anemone petals nor so smooth—nor
so remote a thing. It is a field
of the wild carrot taking
the field by force; the grass
does not raise above it.
Here is no question of whiteness,
white as can be, with a purple mole
at the center of each flower.
Each flower is a hand's span
of her whiteness. Wherever
his hand has lain there is
a tiny purple blemish. Each part

is a blossom under his touch
to which the fibres of her being
stem one by one, each to its end,
until the whole field is a
white desire, empty, a single stem,
a cluster, flower by flower,
a pious wish to whiteness gone over—
or nothing.

The Widow's Lament in Springtime

Sorrow is my own yard
where the new grass
flames as it has flamed
often before but not
with the cold fire
that closes round me this year.
Thirtyfive years
I lived with my husband.
The plumtree is white today
with masses of flowers.
Masses of flowers
load the cherry branches
and color some bushes
yellow and some red
but the grief in my heart
is stronger than they
for though they were my joy
formerly, today I notice them
and turn away forgetting.
Today my son told me
that in the meadows,
at the edge of the heavy woods
in the distance, he saw
trees of white flowers.
I feel that I would like
to go there
and fall into those flowers
and sink into the marsh near them.

The Lonely Street

School is over. It is too hot
to walk at ease. At ease
in light frocks they walk the streets
to while the time away.
They have grown tall. They hold
pink flames in their right hands.
In white from head to foot,
with sidelong, idle look—
in yellow, floating stuff,
black sash and stockings—
touching their avid mouths
with pink sugar on a stick—
like a carnation each holds in her hand—
they mount the lonely street.

from
Spring and All

By the road to the contagious hospital
under the surge of the blue
mottled clouds driven from the
northeast—a cold wind. Beyond, the
waste of broad, muddy fields
brown with dried weeds, standing and fallen

patches of standing water
the scattering of tall trees

All along the road the reddish
purplish, forked, upstanding, twiggy
stuff of bushes and small trees
with dead, brown leaves under them
leafless vines—

Lifeless in appearance, sluggish
dazed spring approaches—

They enter the new world naked,
cold, uncertain of all
save that they enter. All about them
the cold, familiar wind—

Now the grass, tomorrow
the stiff curl of wildcarrot leaf

One by one objects are defined—
It quickens: clarity, outline of leaf

But now the stark dignity of
entrance—Still, the profound change
has come upon them: rooted, they
grip down and begin to awaken

———————

Pink confused with white
flowers and flowers reversed
take and spill the shaded flame
darting it back
into the lamp's horn

petals aslant darkened with mauve

red where in whorls
petal lays its glow upon petal
round flamegreen throats

petals radiant with transpiercing light
contending
                         above

the leaves
reaching up their modest green
from the pot's rim

and there, wholly dark, the pot
gay with rough moss.

———————

The Easter stars are shining
above lights that are flashing—
coronal of the black—

                         Nobody
to say it—
                Nobody to say: pinholes

Thither I would carry her
among the lights—
Burst it asunder
break through to the fifty words
necessary—

                    a crown for her head with
castles upon it, skyscrapers
filled with nut-chocolates—

                         dovetame winds—
stars of tinsel
from the great end of a cornucopia
of glass

———————

Black winds from the north
enter black hearts. Barred from
seclusion in lilies they strike
to destroy—

Beastly humanity
where the wind breaks it—

                         strident voices, heat
quickened, built of waves

Drunk with goats or pavements

Hate is of the night and the day
of flowers and rocks. Nothing
is gained by saying the night breeds
murder—It is the classical mistake

The day

All that enters in another person
all grass, all blackbirds flying
all azalea trees in flower
salt winds—

Sold to them men knock blindly together
splitting their heads open

That is why boxing matches and
Chinese poems are the same—That is why
Hartley praises Miss Wirt

There is nothing in the twist
of the wind but—dashes of cold rain

It is one with submarine vistas
purple and black fish turning
among undulant seaweed—

Black wind, I have poured my heart out
to you until I am sick of it—

Now I run my hand over you feeling
the play of your body—the quiver
of its strength—

The grief of the bowmen of Shu
moves nearer—There is
an approach with difficulty from
the dead—the winter casing of grief

How easy to slip
into the old mode, how hard to
cling firmly to the advance—

The rose is obsolete
but each petal ends in
an edge, the double facet
cementing the grooved
columns of air—The edge
cuts without cutting

meets—nothing—renews
itself in metal or porcelain—

whither? It ends—

But if it ends
the start is begun
so that to engage roses
becomes a geometry—

Sharper, neater, more cutting
figured in majolica—
the broken plate
glazed with a rose

Somewhere the sense
makes copper roses
steel roses—

The rose carried weight of love
but love is at an end—of roses

It is at the edge of the
petal that love waits

Crisp, worked to defeat
laboredness—fragile
plucked, moist, half-raised
cold, precise, touching

What

The place between the petal's
edge and the

From the petal's edge a line starts
that being of steel
infinitely fine, infinitely
rigid penetrates
the Milky Way
without contact—lifting
from it—neither hanging
nor pushing—

The fragility of the flower
unbruised
penetrates space

———————

The sunlight in a
yellow plaque upon the
varnished floor

is full of a song
inflated to
fifty pounds pressure

at the faucet of
June that rings
the triangle of the air

pulling at the
anemones in
Persephone's cow pasture—

When from among
the steel rocks leaps
J. P. M.

who enjoyed
extraordinary privileges
among virginity

to solve the core
of whirling flywheels
by cutting

the Gordian knot
with a Veronese or
perhaps a Rubens—

whose cars are about
the finest on
the market today—

And so it comes
to motor cars—
which is the son

leaving off the g
of sunlight and grass—
Impossible

to say, impossible
to underestimate—
wind, earthquakes in

Manchuria, a
partridge
from dry leaves

———

What about all this writing?

O "Kiki"
O Miss Margaret Jarvis
The backhandspring

I: clean
     clean
     clean: yes . . New-York

Wrigley's, appendicitis, John Marin:
skyscraper soup—

Either that or a bullet!

Once
anything might have happened
You lay relaxed on my knees—
the starry night
spread out warm and blind
above the hospital—

Pah!

It is unclean
which is not straight to the mark—

In my life the furniture eats me

the chairs, the floor
the walls
which heard your sobs
drank up my emotion—
they which alone know everything

and snitched on us in the morning—

What to want?

Drunk we go forward surely
Not I

beds, beds, beds
elevators, fruit, night-tables
breasts to see, white and blue—
to hold in the hand, to nozzle

It is not onion soup
Your sobs soaked through the walls
breaking the hospital to pieces

Everything
—windows, chairs
obscenely drunk, spinning—
white, blue, orange
—hot with our passion

wild tears, desperate rejoinders
my legs, turning slowly
end over end in the air!

But what would you have?

All I said was:
there, you see, it is broken

stockings, shoes, hairpins
your bed, I wrapped myself round you—

I watched.

You sobbed, you beat your pillow
you tore your hair
you dug your nails into your sides

I was your nightgown
                          I   watched!

Clean is he alone
after whom stream
the broken pieces of the city—
flying apart at his approaches

but I merely
caress you curiously

fifteen years ago and you still
go about the city, they say
patching up sick school children

———————

In passing with my mind
on nothing in the world

but the right of way
I enjoy on the road by

virtue of the law—
I saw

an elderly man who
smiled and looked away

to the north past a house—
a woman in blue

who was laughing and
leaning forward to look up

into the man's half
averted face

and a boy of eight who was
looking at the middle of

the man's belly
at a watchchain—

The supreme importance
of this nameless spectacle

sped me by them
without a word—

Why bother where I went?
for I went spinning on the

four wheels of my car
along the wet road until

I saw a girl with one leg
over the rail of a balcony

————

O tongue
licking
the sore on
her netherlip

O toppled belly

O passionate cotton
stuck with
matted hair

elysian slobber
from her mouth
upon
the folded handkerchief

I can't die

—moaned the old
jaundiced woman
rolling her
saffron eyeballs

I can't die
I can't die

————

Our orchestra
is the cat's nuts—

Banjo jazz
with a nickelplated

amplifier to
soothe

the savage beast—
Get the rhythm

That sheet stuff
's a lot a cheese.

Man
gimme the key

and lemme loose—
I make 'em crazy

with my harmonies—
Shoot it Jimmy

Nobody
Nobody else

but me—
They can't copy it

———————

The pure products of America
go crazy—
mountain folk from Kentucky

or the ribbed north end of
Jersey
with its isolate lakes and

valleys, its deaf-mutes, thieves
old names
and promiscuity between

devil-may-care men who have taken
to railroading
out of sheer lust of adventure—

and young slatterns, bathed
in filth
from Monday to Saturday

to be tricked out that night
with gauds
from imaginations which have no

peasant traditions to give them
character
but flutter and flaunt

sheer rags—succumbing without
emotion
save numbed terror

under some hedge of choke-cherry
or viburnum—
which they cannot express—

Unless it be that marriage
perhaps
with a dash of Indian blood

will throw up a girl so desolate
so hemmed round
with disease or murder

that she'll be rescued by an
agent—
reared by the state and

sent out at fifteen to work in
some hard pressed
house in the suburbs—

some doctor's family, some Elsie—
voluptuous water
expressing with broken

brain the truth about us—
her great
ungainly hips and flopping breasts

addressed to cheap
jewelry
and rich young men with fine eyes

as if the earth under our feet
were
an excrement of some sky

and we degraded prisoners
destined
to hunger until we eat filth

while the imagination strains
after deer
going by fields of goldenrod in

the stifling heat of September
Somehow
it seems to destroy us

It is only in isolate flecks that
something
is given off

No one
to witness
and adjust, no one to drive the car

---

so much depends
upon

a red wheel
barrow

glazed with rain
water

beside the white
chickens

The veritable night
of wires and stars

the moon is in
the oak tree's crotch

and sleepers in
the windows cough

athwart the round
and pointed leaves

and insects sting
while on the grass

the whitish moonlight
tearfully

assumes the attitudes
of afternoon—

But it is real
where peaches hang

recalling death's
long-promised symphony

whose tuneful wood
and stringish undergrowth

are ghosts existing
without being

save to come with juice
and pulp to assuage

the hungers which
the night reveals

so that now at last
the truth's aglow

with devilish peace
forestalling day

which dawns tomorrow
with dreadful reds

the heart to predicate
with mists that loved

the ocean and the fields—
Thus moonlight

is the perfect
human touch

———

Somebody dies every four minutes
in New York State—

To hell with you and your poetry—
You will rot and be blown
through the next solar system
with the rest of the gases—

What the hell do you know about it?

AXIOMS

Don't get killed

Careful Crossing Campaign
Cross Crossings Cautiously

THE HORSES	black
	&
PRANCED	white

What's the use of sweating over
this sort of thing, Carl; here
it is all set up—

Outings in New York City

Ho for the open country

Don't stay shut up in hot rooms
Go to one of the Great Parks
Pelham Bay for example

It's on Long Island Sound
with bathing, boating
tennis, baseball, golf, etc.

Acres and acres of green grass
wonderful shade trees, rippling brooks

      Take the Pelham Bay Park Branch
      of the Lexington Ave. (East Side)
      Line and you are there in a few
      minutes

Interborough Rapid Transit Co.

Young Sycamore

I must tell you
this young tree
whose round and firm trunk
between the wet

pavement and the gutter
(where water
is trickling) rises
bodily

into the air with
one undulant
thrust half its height—
and then

dividing and waning
sending out
young branches on
all sides—

hung with cocoons—
it thins
till nothing is left of it
but two

eccentric knotted
twigs
bending forward
hornlike at the top

Hemmed-in Males

The saloon is gone up the creek
with the black sand round its
mouth, it went floating like

a backhouse on the Mississippi in
flood time but it went up
the creek into Limbo from whence

only empty bottles ever return
and that's where George is
He's gone upstream to ask 'em

to let him in at the hole
in the wall where the W.C.T.U.
sits knitting elastic stockings

for varicose veins. Poor George
he's got a job now as janitor
in Lincoln School but the saloon

is gone forever with pictures
of Sullivan and Kilrain on
the walls and Pop Anson holding

a bat. Poor George, they've cut
out his pituitary gland and his
vas deferens is in the spittoon—

You can laugh at him without his
organs but that's the way with
a river when it wants to

drown you, it sucks you in and
you feel the old saloon sinking
under you and you say good-by

just as George did, good-by poetry
the black sand's got me, the old
days are over, there's no place

any more for me to go now
except home—

On Gay Wallpaper

The green-blue ground
is ruled with silver lines
to say the sun is shining

And on this moral sea
of grass or dreams lie flowers
or baskets of desires

Heaven knows what they are
between cerulean shapes
laid regularly round

Mat roses and tridentate
leaves of gold
threes, threes and threes

Three roses and three stems
the basket floating
standing in the horns of blue

Repeated to the ceiling
to the windows
where the day

Blows in
the scalloped curtains to
the sound of rain

————————

There are no perfect waves—
Your writings are a sea
full of misspellings and
faulty sentences. Level. Troubled.

A center distant from the land
touched by the wings
of nearly silent birds
that never seem to rest—

This is the sadness of the sea—
waves like words, all broken—
a sameness of lifting and falling mood.

I lean watching the detail
of brittle crest, the delicate
imperfect foam, yellow weed
one piece like another—

There is no hope—if not a coral
island slowly forming
to wait for birds to drop
the seeds will make it habitable

———————

The moon, the dried weeds
and the Pleiades—

Seven feet tall
the dark, dried weedstalks
make a part of the night
a red lace
on the blue milky sky

Write—
by a small lamp

the Pleiades are almost
nameless
and the moon is tilted
and halfgone

And in runningpants and
with ecstatic, æsthetic faces
on the illumined
signboard are leaping
over printed hurdles and
"¼ of their energy comes from bread"

two
gigantic highschool boys
ten feet tall

This Is Just To Say

I have eaten
the plums
that were in
the icebox

and which
you were probably
saving
for breakfast

Forgive me
they were delicious
so sweet
and so cold

Flowers by the Sea

When over the flowery, sharp pasture's
edge, unseen, the salt ocean

lifts its form—chickory and daisies
tied, released seem hardly flowers alone

but color and the movement—or the shape
perhaps—of restlessness, whereas

the sea is circled and sways
peacefully upon its plantlike stem

The Yachts

contend in a sea which the land partly encloses
shielding them from the too heavy blows
of an ungoverned ocean which when it chooses

tortures the biggest hulls, the best man knows
to pit against its beatings, and sinks them pitilessly.
Mothlike in mists, scintillant in the minute

brilliance of cloudless days, with broad bellying sails
they glide to the wind tossing green water
from their sharp prows while over them the crew crawls

ant-like, solicitously grooming them, releasing,
making fast as they turn, lean far over and having
caught the wind again, side by side, head for the mark.

In a well guarded arena of open water surrounded by
lesser and greater craft which, sycophant, lumbering
and flittering follow them, they appear youthful, rare

as the light of a happy eye, live with the grace
of all that in the mind is fleckless, free and
naturally to be desired. Now the sea which holds them

is moody, lapping their glossy sides, as if feeling
for some slightest flaw but fails completely.
Today no race. Then the wind comes again. The yachts

move, jockeying for a start, the signal is set and they
are off. Now the waves strike at them but they are too
well made, they slip through, though they take in canvas.

Arms with hands grasping seek to clutch at the prows.
Bodies thrown recklessly in the way are cut aside.
It is a sea of faces about them in agony, in despair

until the horror of the race dawns staggering the mind,
the whole sea become an entanglement of watery bodies
lost to the world bearing what they cannot hold. Broken,

beaten, desolate, reaching from the dead to be taken up
they cry out, failing, failing! their cries rising
in waves still as the skillful yachts pass over.

Perpetuum Mobile: The City

               —a dream
          we dreamed
                    each
          separately
                    we two

          of love
                    and of
          desire—

          that fused
          in the night—

          in the distance
                    over
          the meadows

                    by day
          impossible—
                    The city
          disappeared
                    when
          we arrived—

                    A dream
          a little false
          toward which
                    now

we stand
          and stare
transfixed—

All at once
          in the east
rising!

          All white!

          small
as a flower—

a locust cluster
a shad bush
          blossoming

Over the swamps
          a wild
magnolia bud—
          greenish
white
a northern
          flower—

And so
          we live
          looking—

At night
          it wakes
On the black
          sky—

a dream
          toward which
we love—
at night
          more
than a little
          false—

We have bred
we have dug
we have figured up
our costs
we have bought
an old rug—

We batter at our
unsatisfactory
            brilliance—

There is no end
        to desire—

Let us break
            through
and go there—

in
            vain!

—delectable
        amusement:

Milling about—

Money! in
armored trucks—
Two men
            walking
at two paces from
            each other
their right hands
            at the hip—

on the butt of
an automatic—

till they themselves
hold up the bank
and themselves
      drive off
for themselves
      the money
in an armored car—

      For love!

Carefully
      carefully tying
carefully

      selected
whisps of long
dark hair
      whisp
by whisp
upon the stubs
of his kinky wool—

For two hours
three hours
      they worked—
      until
he coiled
      the thick
knot upon
that whorish
      head—

Dragged
      insensible
upon his face
by the lines—

—a running horse

      For love!

Their eyes
          blown out—

—for love, for love!

Neither the rain
Nor the storm—

can keep them

          for love!

from the daily
accomplishment
          of their
appointed rounds—

Guzzling
the creamy foods
          while
out of sight
          in
the sub-cellar—
the waste fat
the old vegetables
          chucked down
a chute
          the foulest
sink in the world—

And go
on the out-tide
ten thousand
          cots
floating to sea
          like weed
that held back
the pristine ships—
And fattened there
          an eel
in the water pipe—

No end—

There!
          There!
There!

          —a dream
of lights
          hiding

the iron reason
          and stone
a settled
          cloud—

City

          whose stars
of matchless
          splendor—
          and
in bright-edged
          clouds
the moon—

          bring

silence

          breathlessly—

Tearful city
          on a summer's day
the hard grey
          dwindling
in a wall of
          rain—

          farewell!

Paterson: Episode 17

Beat hell out of it
  Beautiful Thing
    spotless cap
and crossed white straps
over the dark rippled cloth—
  Lift the stick
above that easy head
where you sit by the ivied
church, one arm
  buttressing you
long fingers spread out
among the clear grass prongs—
  and drive it down
  Beautiful Thing
that your caressing body kiss
  and kiss again
that holy lawn—

And again: obliquely—
legs curled under you as a
  deer's leaping—
pose of supreme indifference
  sacrament
to a summer's day
  Beautiful Thing
in the unearned suburbs
  then pause
  the arm fallen—
what memories
of what forgotten face
brooding upon that lily stem?

  The incredible
nose straight from the brow
  the empurpled lips
and dazzled half sleepy eyes
  Beautiful Thing
of some trusting animal

makes a temple
of its place of savage slaughter
      revealing
the damaged will incites still
      to violence
consummately beautiful thing
and falls about your resting
      shoulders—

Gently! Gently!
as in all things an opposite
      that awakes
the fury, conceiving
      knowledge
by way of despair that has
      no place
to lay its glossy head—
Save only—Not alone!
      Never, if possible
alone! to escape the accepted
      chopping block
and a square hat!—

And as reverie gains and
      your joints loosen
      the trick's done!
Day is covered and we see you—
      but not alone!
drunk and bedraggled to release
the strictness of beauty
under a sky full of stars
      Beautiful Thing
and a slow moon—
                           The car
      had stopped long since
      when the others
came and dragged those out
      who had you there
      indifferent
to whatever the anesthetic

Beautiful Thing
might slum away the bars—

Reek of it!
    What does it matter?
    could set free
only the one thing—
But you!
—in your white lace dress
    "the dying swan"
and high heeled slippers—tall
as you already were—
    till your head
through fruitful exaggeration
was reaching the sky and the
prickles of its ecstasy
    Beautiful Thing!

And the guys from Paterson
    beat up
the guys from Newark and told
them to stay the hell out
of their territory and then
socked you one
    across the nose
    Beautiful Thing
for good luck and emphasis
    cracking it
till I must believe that all
desired women have had each
    in the end
    a busted nose
and live afterward marked up
    Beautiful Thing
    for memory's sake
to be credible in their deeds

Then back to the party!
   and they maled
and femaled you jealously
   Beautiful Thing
as if to discover when and
   by what miracle
there should escape what?
still to be possessed
out of what part
   Beautiful Thing
should it look?
   or be extinguished—
Three days in the same dress
   up and down—
   It would take
a Dominie to be patient
   Beautiful Thing
with you—

The stroke begins again—
   regularly
automatic
   contrapuntal to
the flogging
like the beat of famous lines
in the few excellent poems
   woven to make you
   gracious
and on frequent occasions
   foul drunk
   Beautiful Thing
pulse of release
   to the attentive
and obedient mind.

These

are the desolate, dark weeks
when nature in its barrenness
equals the stupidity of man.

The year plunges into night
and the heart plunges
lower than night

to an empty, windswept place
without sun, stars or moon
but a peculiar light as of thought

that spins a dark fire—
whirling upon itself until,
in the cold, it kindles

to make a man aware of nothing
that he knows, not loneliness
itself—Not a ghost but

would be embraced—emptiness,
despair—(They
whine and whistle) among

the flashes and booms of war;
houses of whose rooms
the cold is greater than can be thought,

the people gone that we loved,
the beds lying empty, the couches
damp, the chairs unused—

Hide it away somewhere
out of the mind, let it get roots
and grow, unrelated to jealous

ears and eyes—for itself.
In this mine they come to dig—all.
Is this the counterfoil to sweetest

music? The source of poetry that
seeing the clock stopped, says,
The clock has stopped

that ticked yesterday so well?
and hears the sound of lakewater
splashing—that is now stone.

Between Walls

the back wings
of the

hospital where
nothing

will grow lie
cinders

in which shine
the broken

pieces of a green
bottle

The Last Words of My English Grandmother

There were some dirty plates
and a glass of milk
beside her on a small table
near the rank, disheveled bed—

Wrinkled and nearly blind
she lay and snored
rousing with anger in her tones
to cry for food,

Gimme something to eat—
They're starving me—
I'm all right I won't go
to the hospital. No, no, no

Give me something to eat
Let me take you
to the hospital, I said
and after you are well

you can do as you please.
She smiled, Yes
you do what you please first
then I can do what I please—

Oh, oh, oh! she cried
as the ambulance men lifted
her to the stretcher—
Is this what you call

making me comfortable?
By now her mind was clear—
Oh you think you're smart
you young people,

she said, but I'll tell you
you don't know anything.
Then we started.
On the way

we passed a long row
of elms. She looked at them
awhile out of
the ambulance window and said,

What are all those
fuzzy-looking things out there?
Trees? Well, I'm tired
of them and rolled her head away.

The Predicter of Famine

White day, black river
corrugated and swift—

as the stone of the sky
on the prongy ring
of the tarnished city
is smooth and without motion:

A gull flies low
upstream, his beak tilted
sharply, his eye
alert to the providing water.

A Sort of a Song

Let the snake wait under
his weed
and the writing
be of words, slow and quick, sharp
to strike, quiet to wait,
sleepless.

—through metaphor to reconcile
the people and the stones.
Compose. (No ideas
but in things) Invent!
Saxifrage is my flower that splits
the rocks.

Paterson: The Falls

What common language to unravel?
The Falls, combed into straight lines
from that rafter of a rock's
lip. Strike in! the middle of

some trenchant phrase, some
well packed clause. Then . .
This is my plan. 4 sections: First,
the archaic persons of the drama.

An eternity of bird and bush,
resolved. An unraveling:
the confused streams aligned, side
by side, speaking! Sound

married to strength, a strength
of falling—from a height! The wild
voice of the shirt-sleeved
Evangelist rivaling, Hear

me! I am the Resurrection
and the Life! echoing
among the bass and pickerel, slim
eels from Barbados, Sargasso

Sea, working up the coast to that
bounty, ponds and wild streams—
Third, the old town: Alexander Hamilton
working up from St. Croix,

from that sea! and a deeper, whence
he came! stopped cold
by that unmoving roar, fastened
there: the rocks silent

but the water, married to the stone,
voluble, though frozen; the water
even when and though frozen
still whispers and moans—

And in the brittle air
a factory bell clangs, at dawn, and
snow whines under their feet. Fourth,
the modern town, a

disembodied roar! the cataract and
its clamor broken apart—and from
all learning, the empty
ear struck from within, roaring . .

The Dance

In Breughel's great picture, The Kermess,
the dancers go round, they go round and
around, the squeal and the blare and the
tweedle of bagpipes, a bugle and fiddles
tipping their bellies (round as the thick-
sided glasses whose wash they impound)
their hips and their bellies off balance
to turn them. Kicking and rolling about
the Fair Grounds, swinging their butts, those
shanks must be sound to bear up under such
rollicking measures, prance as they dance
in Breughel's great picture, The Kermess.

Burning the Christmas Greens

Their time past, pulled down
cracked and flung to the fire
—go up in a roar

All recognition lost, burnt clean
clean in the flame, the green
dispersed, a living red,
flame red, red as blood wakes
on the ash—

and ebbs to a steady burning
the rekindled bed become
a landscape of flame

At the winter's midnight
we went to the trees, the coarse
holly, the balsam and
the hemlock for their green

At the thick of the dark
the moment of the cold's
deepest plunge we brought branches
cut from the green trees

to fill our need, and over
doorways, about paper Christmas
bells covered with tinfoil
and fastened by red ribbons

we stuck the green prongs
in the windows hung
woven wreaths and above pictures
the living green. On the

mantle we built a green forest
and among those hemlock
sprays put a herd of small
white deer as if they

were walking there. All this!
and it seemed gentle and good
to us. Their time past,
relief! The room bare. We

stuffed the dead grate
with them upon the half burntout
log's smoldering eye, opening
red and closing under them

and we stood there looking down.
Green is a solace

a promise of peace, a fort
against the cold (though we

did not say so) a challenge
above the snow's
hard shell. Green (we might
have said) that, where

small birds hide and dodge
and lift their plaintive
rallying cries, blocks for them
and knocks down

the unseeing bullets of
the storm. Green spruce boughs
pulled down by a weight of
snow—Transformed!

Violence leaped and appeared.
Recreant! roared to life
as the flame rose through and
our eyes recoiled from it.

In the jagged flames green
to red, instant and alive. Green!
those sure abutments . . . Gone!
lost to mind

and quick in the contracting
tunnel of the grate
appeared a world! Black
mountains, black and red—as

yet uncolored—and ash white,
an infant landscape of shimmering
ash and flame and we, in
that instant, lost,

breathless to be witnesses,
as if we stood
ourselves refreshed among
the shining fauna of that fire.

The Descent

The descent beckons
        as the ascent beckoned.
                Memory is a kind
of accomplishment,
        a sort of renewal
              even
an initiation, since the spaces it opens are new places
        inhabited by hordes
              heretofore unrealized,
of new kinds—
        since their movements
              are towards new objectives
(even though formerly they were abandoned).

No defeat is made up entirely of defeat—since
the world it opens is always a place
        formerly
              unsuspected. A
world lost,
        a world unsuspected,
              beckons to new places
and no whiteness (lost) is so white as the memory
of whiteness   .

With evening, love wakens
        though its shadows
              which are alive by reason
of the sun shining—
        grow sleepy now and drop away
              from desire   .

Love without shadows stirs now
        beginning to awaken
              as night
advances.

The descent
　　　　made up of despairs
　　　　　　　and without accomplishment
realizes a new awakening:
　　　　　　which is a reversal
of despair.
　　　　　　For what we cannot accomplish, what
is denied to love,
　　　　　　what we have lost in the anticipation—
　　　　　　　　a descent follows,
endless and indestructible　　　.

To Daphne and Virginia

The smell of the heat is boxwood
　　　　when rousing us
　　　　　　a movement of the air
stirs our thoughts
　　　　that had no life in them
　　　　　　to a life, a life in which
two women agonize:
　　　　to live and to breathe is no less.
　　　　　　Two young women.
The box odor
　　　is the odor of that of which
　　　　　partaking separately,
each to herself
　　　I partake also
　　　　　　.　　.　　separately.

Be patient that I address you in a poem,
　　　　there is no other
　　　　　　fit medium.
The mind
　　　lives there. It is uncertain,
　　　　　can trick us and leave us
agonized. But for resources
　　　what can equal it?

There is nothing. We
should be lost
without its wings to
fly off upon.

The mind is the cause of our distresses
but of it we can build anew.
Oh something more than
it flies off to:
a woman's world,
of crossed sticks, stopping
thought. A new world
is only a new mind.
And the mind and the poem
are all apiece.
Two young women
to be snared,
odor of box,
to bind and hold them
for the mind's labors.

All women are fated similarly
facing men
and there is always
another, such as I,
who loves them,
loves all women, but
finds himself, touching them,
like other men,
often confused.

I have two sons,
the husbands of these women,
who live also
in a world of love,
apart.

                    Shall this odor of box in the heat
not also touch them
          fronting a world of women
                    from which they are
debarred
          by the very scents which draw them on
                    against easy access?

In our family we stammer unless,
          half mad,
                    we come to speech at last   .

And I am not
          a young man.
                    My love encumbers me,
It is a love
          less than
                    a young man's love but,
like this box odor
          more penetrant, infinitely
                    more penetrant,
in that sense not to be resisted.

There is, in the hard
          give and take
                    of a man's life with a woman
a thing which is not the stress itself
          but beyond
                    and above
that,
          something that wants to rise
                    and shake itself
free. We are not chickadees
          on a bare limb
                    with a worm in the mouth.

The worm is in our brains
         and concerns them
                  and not food for our
offspring, wants to disrupt
         our thought
                  and throw it
to the newspapers
         or anywhere.
                  There is, in short,
a counter stress,
         born of the sexual shock,
                  which survives it
consonant with the moon,
         to keep its own mind.
                  There is, of course,
more.
         Women
                  are not alone
in that. At least
         while this healing odor is abroad
                  one can write a poem.

Staying here in the country
         on an old farm
                  we eat our breakfasts
on a balcony under an elm.
         The shrubs below us
                  are neglected. And
there, penned in,
         or he would eat the garden,
                  lives a pet goose who
tilts his head
         sidewise
                  and looks up at us,
a very quiet old fellow
         who writes no poems.
                  Fine mornings we sit there
while birds
         come and go.
                  A pair of robins

is building a nest   .
          for the second time
                    this season. Men
against their reason
          speak of love, sometimes,
                    when they are old. It is
all they can do   .
          or watch a heavy goose
                    who waddles, slopping noisily in the mud
                              of his pool.

To a Man Dying on His Feet

—not that we are not all
          "dying on our feet"
                    but the look you give me
and to which I bow,
          is more immediate.
                    It is keenly alert,
suspicious of me—
          as of all that are living—and
                    apologetic.
Your jaw
          wears the stubble
                    of a haggard beard,
a dirty beard,
          which resembles
                    the snow through which
your long legs
          are conducting you.
                    Whither? Where are you going?
This would be a fine day
          to go on a journey.
                    Say to Florida
where at this season
          all go
                    now-a-days.

There grows the hibiscus,
  the star jasmine
    and more than I can tell
but the odors
  from what I know
    must be alluring.
Come with me there!
  you look like a good guy,
    come this evening.
The plane leaves at 6:30
  or have you another appointment?

The World Contracted to a Recognizable Image

  at the small end of an illness
  there was a picture
  probably Japanese
  which filled my eye

  an idiotic picture
  except it was all I recognized
  the wall lived for me in that picture
  I clung to it as a fly

DONALD EVANS

(1884–1921)

En Monocle

Born with a monocle he stares at life,
And sends his soul on pensive promenades;
He pays a high price for discarded gods,
And then regilds them to renew their strife.
His calm moustache points to the ironies,
And a fawn-coloured laugh sucks in the night,
Full of the riant mists that turn to white
In brief lost battles with banalities.

Masters are makeshifts and a path to tread
For blue pumps that are ardent for the air;
Features are fixtures when the face is fled,
And we are left the husks of tarnished hair;
But he is one who lusts uncomforted
To kiss the naked phrase quite unaware.

In the Vices

Gay and audacious crime glints in his eyes,
And his mad talk, raping the commonplace,
Gleefully runs a devil-praising race,
And none can ever follow where he flies.
He streaks himself with vices tenderly;
He cradles sin, and with a figleaf fan
Taps his green cat, watching a bored sun span
The wasted minutes to eternity.

Once I took up his trail along the dark,
Wishful to track him to the witches' flame,
To see the bubbling of the sneer and snare.
The way led through a fragrant starlit park,
And soon upon a harlot's house I came—
Within I found him playing at solitaire!

ARTURO GIOVANNITTI

(1884–1959)

The Walker

I hear footsteps over my head all night.

They come and they go. Again they come and they go all
night.

They come one eternity in four paces and they go one
eternity in four paces, and between the coming and the
going there is Silence and the Night and the Infinite.

For infinite are the nine feet of a prison cell, and endless is the
march of him who walks between the yellow brick wall and
the red iron gate, thinking things that cannot be chained
and cannot be locked, but that wander far away in the
sunlit world, each in a wild pilgrimage after a destined goal.

Throughout the restless night I hear the footsteps over my
head.

Who walks? I know not. It is the phantom of the jail, the
sleepless brain, a man, the man, the Walker.

One-two-three-four: four paces and the wall.

One-two-three-four: four paces and the iron gate.

He has measured his space, he has measured it accurately,
scrupulously, minutely, as the hangman measures the rope
and the grave-digger the coffin—so many feet, so many
inches, so many fractions of an inch for each of the four
paces.

One-two-three-four. Each step sounds heavy and hollow over
my head, and the echo of each step sounds hollow within
my head as I count them in suspense and in dread that
once, perhaps, in the endless walk, there may be five steps
instead of four between the yellow brick wall and the red
iron gate.

But he has measured the space so accurately, so scrupulously,
so minutely that nothing breaks the grave rhythm of the
slow, fantastic march.

When all are asleep (and who knows but I when all sleep?)
   three things are still awake in the night: the Walker, my
   heart and the old clock which has the soul of a fiend—for
   never, since a coarse hand with red hair on its fingers
   swung for the first time the pendulum in the jail, has the
   old clock tick-tocked a full hour of joy.
Yet the old clock which marks everything, and records
   everything, and to everything tolls the death knell, the wise
   old clock that knows everything, does not know the
   number of the footsteps of the Walker, nor the throbs of
   my heart.
For not for the Walker, nor for my heart is there a second, a
   minute, an hour or anything that is in the old clock—there
   is nothing but the night, the sleepless night, the watchful,
   wistful night, and footsteps that go, and footsteps that
   come and the wild, tumultuous beatings that trail after
   them forever.

All the sounds of the living beings and inanimate things, and
   all the voices and all the noises of the night I have heard in
   my wistful vigil.
I have heard the moans of him who bewails a thing that is
   dead and the sighs of him who tries to smother a thing that
   will not die;
I have heard the stifled sobs of the one who weeps with his
   head under the coarse blanket, and the whisperings of the
   one who prays with his forehead on the hard, cold stone of
   the floor;
I have heard him who laughs the shrill, sinister laugh of folly
   at the horror rampant on the yellow wall and at the red
   eyes of the nightmare glaring through the iron bars;
I have heard in the sudden icy silence him who coughs a dry,
   ringing cough, and wished madly that his throat would not
   rattle so and that he would not spit on the floor, for no
   sound was more atrocious than that of his sputum upon
   the floor;
I have heard him who swears fearsome oaths which I listen to
   in reverence and awe, for they are holier than the virgin's
   prayer;

And I have heard, most terrible of all, the silence of two
    hundred brains all possessed by one single, relentless,
    unforgiving, desperate thought.
All this have I heard in the watchful night,
And the murmur of the wind beyond the walls,
And the tolls of a distant bell,
And the woeful dirge of the rain,
And the remotest echoes of the sorrowful city
And the terrible beatings, wild beatings, mad beatings of the
    One Heart which is nearest to my heart.
All this have I heard in the still night;
But nothing is louder, harder, drearier, mightier, more awful
    than the footsteps I hear over my head all night.

Yet fearsome and terrible are all the footsteps of men upon
    the earth, for they either descend or climb.
They descend from little mounds and high peaks and lofty
    altitudes, through wide roads and narrow paths, down
    noble marble stairs and creaky stairs of wood—and some
    go down to the cellar, and some to the grave, and some
    down to the pits of shame and infamy, and still some to the
    glory of an unfathomable abyss where there is nothing but
    the staring white, stony eyeballs of Destiny.
And again other footsteps climb. They climb to life and to
    love, to fame, to power, to vanity, to truth, to glory and to
    the scaffold—to everything but Freedom and the Ideal.
And they all climb the same roads and the same stairs others
    go down; for never, since man began to think how to
    overcome and overpass man, have other roads and other
    stairs been found.
They descend and they climb, the fearful footsteps of men,
    and some limp, some drag, some speed, some trot, some
    run—they are quiet, slow, noisy, brisk, quick, feverish, mad,
    and most awful is their cadence to the ears of the one who
    stands still.
But of all the footsteps of men that either descend or climb,
    no footsteps are so fearsome and terrible as those that go
    straight on the dead level of a prison floor, from a yellow
    stone wall to a red iron gate.

All through the night he walks and he thinks. Is it more
frightful because he walks and his footsteps sound hollow
over my head, or because he thinks and speaks not his
thoughts?

But does he think? Why should he think? Do I think? I only
hear the footsteps and count them. Four steps and the wall.
Four steps and the gate. But beyond? Beyond? Where goes
he beyond the gate and the wall?

He goes not beyond. His thought breaks there on the iron
gate. Perhaps it breaks like a wave of rage, perhaps like a
sudden flow of hope, but it always returns to beat the wall
like a billow of helplessness and despair.

He walks to and fro within the narrow whirlpit of this ever
storming and furious thought. Only one thought—
constant, fixed, immovable, sinister, without power and
without voice.

A thought of madness, frenzy, agony and despair, a hell-
brewed thought, for it is a natural thought. All things
natural are things impossible while there are jails in the
world—bread, work, happiness, peace, love.

But he thinks not of this. As he walks he thinks of the most
superhuman, the most unattainable, the most impossible
thing in the world:

He thinks of a small brass key that turns just half around and
throws open the red iron gate.

That is all the Walker thinks, as he walks throughout the
night.

And that is what two hundred minds drowned in the darkness
and the silence of the night think, and that is also what I
think.

Wonderful is the supreme wisdom of the jail that makes all
think the same thought. Marvelous is the providence of the
law that equalizes all, even in mind and sentiment. Fallen is
the last barrier of privilege, the aristocracy of the intellect.
The democracy of reason has leveled all the two hundred
minds to the common surface of the same thought.

I, who have never killed, think like the murderer;

I, who have never stolen, reason like the thief;

I think, reason, wish, hope, doubt, wait like the hired assassin, the embezzler, the forger, the counterfeiter, the incestuous, the raper, the drunkard, the prostitute, the pimp, I, I who used to think of love and life and flowers and song and beauty and the ideal.

A little key, a little key as little as my little finger, a little key of shining brass.

All my ideas, my thoughts, my dreams are congealed in a little key of shiny brass.

All my brain, all my soul, all the suddenly surging latent powers of my deepest life are in the pocket of a white-haired man dressed in blue.

He is great, powerful, formidable, the man with the white hair, for he has in his pocket the mighty talisman which makes one man cry, and one man pray, and one laugh, and one cough, and one walk, and all keep awake and listen and think the same maddening thought.

Greater than all men is the man with the white hair and the small brass key, for no other man in the world could compel two hundred men to think for so long the same thought. Surely when the light breaks I will write a hymn unto him which shall hail him greater than Mohammed and Arbues and Torquemada and Mesmer, and all the other masters of other men's thoughts. I shall call him Almighty, for he holds everything of all and of me in a little brass key in his pocket.

Everything of me he holds but the branding iron of contempt and the claymore of hatred for the monstrous cabala that can make the apostle and the murderer, the poet and the procurer, think of the same gate, the same key and the same exit on the different sunlit highways of life.

My brother, do not walk any more.

It is wrong to walk on a grave. It is a sacrilege to walk four steps from the headstone to the foot and four steps from the foot to the headstone.

If you stop walking, my brother, no longer will this be a
  grave, for you will give me back my mind that is chained to
  your feet and the right to think my own thoughts.
I implore you, my brother, for I am weary of the long vigil,
  weary of counting your steps, and heavy with sleep.
Stop, rest, sleep, my brother, for the dawn is well nigh and it
  is not the key alone that can throw open the gate.

WILBERT SNOW
(1884–1977)

Advice to a Clam-Digger

(An American Georgic)

Go when the friendly moon permits the tides
To drop far out at early morn or eve;
When eel-grass lies in windrows on the flats,
And rockweed lays its khaki counterpanes
On barnacles that cling to sunken ledges;
Seek out a place where mud-enameled sand
Looks like a colander whose holes emit
Little salt-water geysers when you step;
Then, facing shoreward, dig till you become
A lame and muddy partner of the cove.

Marvels undreamed of suddenly unfold
The secrets they have kept concealed so long;
The rancid mud-clams whose white shells betray
A worthlessness within, like beggar's gold,
Or empty conkles farther up the beach;
The iridescent clam-worms blue and green
With escalading red and yellow fringes,
Like Chinese dragons whose soft tentacles
Expand, contract, and writhe in oozy slime;
Long-buried whore's eggs; razor-fish with shells
Brown as old ivory and smooth as glass;
Or soggy timbers from a derelict
Who left her oaken bones upon a ledge
In some northeaster forty years ago.

You soon discover that the big returns
Lie nestled near the rocks that dot the cove;
Dig slowly there, lest you should break their shells,
For at a single forkful three or four
Will lay white buttocks bare before your eyes.
Protruding heads that keep a passage clear,

494

Aware of you, will scramble for their homes,
Spraying your eyes and face with stinging brine,
Engendering illusion that the shells
Are burrowing a fathom deep in mud.
Their flight is aided by the tousling in
Of saucy waters playing hide-and-seek
In every drain and crevice of the flats,
Laughing at your attempts to keep them out,
And salvaging dominion for the sea.

Your roller full, haul up your rubber boots
And wade into the green and golden cove
Where little flounders flit beneath your feet.
Pull bits of rockweed from vermilion cobbles
And wash the thick-accumulated mud
From off your hoe handle; then souse your hod
And watch the shades of blue intensify:
The sparkling freshness on the dripping shells
Which disappears as suddenly as dew
From violets or daisies in the sun,
Will teach you why the Indian long ago
Used these fair shells for ornaments and wampum,
And piled them in the self-same spot for years,
Until his heaped-up mounds were monuments
Where all spring wanderers might come and camp.

Fail not before you go to glance around
And view the low-tide pageant of the shore:
The apprehensive manner of a gull
Who sits with white breast bulging to the breeze,
And flashes right and left his sulphur bill;
The slower movements of the pearl-gray crane
Who stands in eel-grass on a single leg,
Surveys the fishing prospects, then moves on,
To light again, survey, and move once more,
Till he has sounded out the channel's length;
The yellow bubbles on the flood tide making
A creamy dressing for the green sea-lettuce;
The dignity of rusty-iron rocks
Studded with bands of sharp white barnacles;

The breakers, if the wind blows hard off shore,
That chase each other on the sunken reefs,
And spout like white whales on an Arctic sea;
Or, if the earth be hushed to twilight calm,
The violet, dark-wine, and purple tints
That crown the flowing surface of the tide.

SARA TEASDALE

(1884–1933)

The Shrine

There is no lord within my heart,
　Left silent as an empty shrine
　Where rose and myrtle intertwine,
Within a place apart.

No god is there of carven stone
　To watch with still approving eyes
　My thoughts like steady incense rise;
I dream and weep alone.

But if I keep my altar fair,
　Some morning I shall lift my head
　From roses deftly garlanded
To find the god is there.

The Look

Strephon kissed me in the spring,
　Robin in the fall,
But Colin only looked at me
　And never kissed at all.

Strephon's kiss was lost in jest,
　Robin's lost in play,
But the kiss in Colin's eyes
　Haunts me night and day.

At Night

We are apart; the city grows quiet between us,
  She hushes herself, for midnight makes heavy her eyes,
The tangle of traffic is ended, the cars are empty,
  Five streets divide us, and on them the moonlight lies.

Oh are you asleep, or lying awake, my lover?
  Open your dreams to my love and your heart to my words,
I send you my thoughts—the air between us is laden,
  My thoughts fly in at your window, a flock of wild birds.

Moods

I am the still rain falling,
  Too tired for singing mirth—
Oh, be the green fields calling,
  Oh, be for me the earth!

I am the brown bird pining
  To leave the nest and fly—
Oh, be the fresh cloud shining,
  Oh, be for me the sky!

I Shall Not Care

When I am dead and over me bright April
  Shakes out her rain-drenched hair,
Tho' you should lean above me broken-hearted,
  I shall not care.

I shall have peace, as leafy trees are peaceful
  When rain bends down the bough,
And I shall be more silent and cold-hearted
  Than you are now.

Enough

It is enough for me by day
   To walk the same bright earth with him;
Enough that over us by night
   The same great roof of stars is dim.

I have no care to bind the wind
   Or set a fetter on the sea—
It is enough to feel his love
   Blow by like music over me.

Summer Night, Riverside

In the wild soft summer darkness
How many and many a night we two together
Sat in the park and watched the Hudson
Wearing her lights like golden spangles
Glinting on black satin.
The rail along the curving pathway
Was low in a happy place to let us cross,
And down the hill a tree that dripped with bloom
Sheltered us
While your kisses and the flowers,
Falling, falling,
Tangled my hair. . . .

The frail white stars moved slowly over the sky.

And now, far off
In the fragrant darkness
The tree is tremulous again with bloom
For June comes back.

To-night what girl
When she goes home,
Dreamily before her mirror shakes from her hair
This year's blossoms, clinging in its coils?

After Love

There is no magic when we meet,
    We speak as other people do,
You work no miracle for me
    Nor I for you.

You were the wind and I the sea—
    There is no splendor any more,
I have grown listless as the pool
    Beside the shore.

But tho' the pool is safe from storm
    And from the tide has found surcease,
It grows more bitter than the sea,
    For all its peace.

Night Song at Amalfi

I asked the heaven of stars
    What I should give my love—
It answered me with silence,
    Silence above.

I asked the darkened sea
    Down where the fishers go—
It answered me with silence,
    Silence below.

Oh, I could give him weeping,
    Or I could give him song—
But how can I give silence
    My whole life long?

Jewels

If I should see your eyes again,
   I know how far their look would go—
Back to a morning in the park
   With sapphire shadows on the snow.

Or back to oak trees in the spring
   When you unloosed my hair and kissed
The head that lay against your knees
   In the leaf shadow's amethyst.

And still another shining place
   We would remember—how the dun
Wild mountain held us on its crest
   One diamond morning white with sun.

But I will turn my eyes from you
   As women turn to put away
The jewels they have worn at night
   And cannot wear in sober day.

Wood Song

I heard a wood thrush in the dusk
   Twirl three notes and make a star—
My heart that walked with bitterness
   Came back from very far.

Three shining notes were all he had,
   And yet they made a starry call—
I caught life back against my breast
   And kissed it, scars and all.

The Broken Field

My soul is a dark ploughed field
  In the cold rain;
My soul is a broken field
  Ploughed by pain.

Where grass and bending flowers
  Were growing,
The field lies broken now
  For another sowing.

Great Sower when you tread
  My field again,
Scatter the furrows there
  With better grain.

"A Little While"

A little while when I am gone
  My life will live in music after me,
As spun foam lifted and borne on
  After the wave is lost in the full sea.

A while these nights and days will burn
  In song with the bright frailty of foam,
Living in light before they turn
  Back to the nothingness that is their home.

"There Will Come Soft Rains"

(War Time)

There will come soft rains and the smell of the ground,
And swallows circling with their shimmering sound;

And frogs in the pools singing at night,
And wild plum-trees in tremulous white;

Robins will wear their feathery fire
Whistling their whims on a low fence-wire;

And not one will know of the war, not one
Will care at last when it is done.

Not one would mind, neither bird nor tree
If mankind perished utterly;

And Spring herself, when she woke at dawn,
Would scarcely know that we were gone.

The Unchanging

Sun-swept beaches with a light wind blowing
    From the immense blue circle of the sea,
And the soft thunder where long waves whiten—
    These were the same for Sappho as for me.

Two thousand years—much has gone by forever,
    Change takes the gods and ships and speech of men—
But here on the beaches that time passes over
    The heart aches now as then.

The Sanctuary

If I could keep my innermost Me
Fearless, aloof and free
Of the least breath of love or hate,
And not disconsolate
At the sick load of sorrow laid on men;
If I could keep a sanctuary there
Free even of prayer,
If I could do this, then,
With quiet candor as I grew more wise
I could look even at God with grave forgiving eyes.

"I Shall Live To Be Old"

I shall live to be old, who feared I should die young,
    I shall live to be old,
I shall cling to life as the leaves to the creaking oak
    In the rustle of falling snow and the cold.

The other trees let loose their leaves on the air
    In their russet and red,
I have lived long enough to wonder which is the best,
    And to envy sometimes the way of the early dead.

Moon's Ending

Moon, worn thin to the width of a quill,
    In the dawn clouds flying,
How good to go, light into light, and still
    Giving light, dying.

Lines

These are the ultimate highlands,
Like chord on chord of music
Climbing to rest
On the highest peak and the bluest
Large on the luminous heavens
Deep in the west.

EZRA POUND

(1885–1972)

De Aegypto

I, even I, am he who knoweth the roads
Through the sky, and the wind thereof is my body.

I have beheld the Lady of Life,
I, even I, who fly with the swallows.

Green and grey is her raiment,
Trailing along the wind.

I, even I, am he who knoweth the roads
Through the sky, and the wind thereof is my body.

Manus animam pinxit,
My pen is in my hand

To write the acceptable word . . .
My mouth to chant the pure singing!

Who hath the mouth to receive it,
The song of the Lotus of Kumi?

I, even I, am he who knoweth the roads
Through the sky, and the wind thereof is my body.

I am flame that riseth in the sun,
I, even I, who fly with the swallows.

The moon is upon my forehead,
The winds are under my lips.

The moon is a great pearl in the waters of sapphire,
Cool to my fingers the flowing waters.

I, even I, am he who knoweth the roads
Through the sky, and the wind thereof is my body.

I will return unto the halls of the flowing,
Of the truth of the children of Ashu.

I, even I, am he who knoweth the roads
Of the sky, and the wind thereof is my body.

Sestina: Altaforte

Loquitur: *En* Bertrans de Born.
    Dante Alighieri put this man in hell for that he was
       a stirrer-up of strife.
    Eccovi!
    Judge ye!
    Have I dug him up again?
The scene is at his castle, Altaforte. "Papiols" is his
       jongleur.
"The Leopard," the *device* of Richard (Cœur de Lion).

I

Damn it all! all this our South stinks peace.
You whoreson dog, Papiols, come! Let's to music!
I have no life save when the swords clash.
But ah! when I see the standards gold, vair, purple, opposing
And the broad fields beneath them turn crimson,
Then howl I my heart nigh mad with rejoicing.

II

In hot summer have I great rejoicing
When the tempests kill the earth's foul peace,
And the light'nings from black heav'n flash crimson,
And the fierce thunders roar me their music
And the winds shriek through the clouds mad, opposing,
And through all the riven skies God's swords clash.

III

Hell grant soon we hear again the swords clash!
And the shrill neighs of destriers in battle rejoicing,
Spiked breast to spiked breast opposing!
Better one hour's stour than a year's peace
With fat boards, bawds, wine and frail music!
Bah! there's no wine like the blood's crimson!

IV

And I love to see the sun rise blood-crimson.
And I watch his spears through the dark clash
And it fills all my heart with rejoicing
And pries wide my mouth with fast music
When I see him so scorn and defy peace,
His lone might 'gainst all darkness opposing.

V

The man who fears war and squats opposing
My words for stour, hath no blood of crimson
But is fit only to rot in womanish peace
Far from where worth's won and the swords clash
For the death of such sluts I go rejoicing;
Yea, I fill all the air with my music.

VI

Papiols, Papiols, to the music!
There's no sound like to swords swords opposing,
No cry like the battle's rejoicing
When our elbows and swords drip the crimson
And our charges 'gainst "The Leopard's" rush clash.
May God damn for ever all who cry "Peace!"

VII

And let the music of the swords make them crimson!
Hell grant soon we hear again the swords clash!
Hell blot black for alway the thought "Peace"!

Planh for the Young English King

That is, Prince Henry Plantagenet, elder brother to Richard "Cœur de Lion."
From the Provençal of Bertrans de Born "Si tuit li dol elh plor elh marrimen."

If all the grief and woe and bitterness,
All dolour, ill and every evil chance
That ever came upon this grieving world
Were set together they would seem but light
Against the death of the young English King.
Worth lieth riven and Youth dolorous,
The world o'ershadowed, soiled and overcast,
Void of all joy and full of ire and sadness.

Grieving and sad and full of bitterness
Are left in teen the liegemen courteous,
The joglars supple and the troubadours.
O'er much hath ta'en Sir Death that deadly warrior
In taking from them the young English King,
Who made the freest hand seem covetous.
'Las! Never was nor will be in this world
The balance for this loss in ire and sadness!

O skilful Death and full of bitterness,
Well mayst thou boast that thou the best chevalier
That any folk e'er had, hast from us taken;
Sith nothing is that unto worth pertaineth
But had its life in the young English King,
And better were it, should God grant his pleasure
That he should live than many a living dastard
That doth but wound the good with ire and sadness.

From this faint world, how full of bitterness
Love takes his way and holds his joy deceitful,
Sith no thing is but turneth unto anguish
And each to-day 'vails less than yestere'en,
Let each man visage this young English King
That was most valiant mid all worthiest men!

Gone is his body fine and amorous,
Whence have we grief, discord and deepest sadness.

Him, whom it pleased for our great bitterness
To come to earth to draw us from misventure,
Who drank of death for our salvacioun,
Him do we pray as to a Lord most righteous
And humble eke, that the young English King
He please to pardon, as true pardon is,
And bid go in with honouréd companions
There where there is no grief, nor shall be sadness.

The Seafarer

(From the early Anglo-Saxon text)

May I for my own self song's truth reckon,
Journey's jargon, how I in harsh days
Hardship endured oft.
Bitter breast-cares have I abided,
Known on my keel many a care's hold,
And dire sea-surge, and there I oft spent
Narrow nightwatch nigh the ship's head
While she tossed close to cliffs. Coldly afflicted,
My feet were by frost benumbed.
Chill its chains are; chafing sighs
Hew my heart round and hunger begot
Mere-weary mood. Lest man know not
That he on dry land loveliest liveth,
List how I, care-wretched, on ice-cold sea,
Weathered the winter, wretched outcast
Deprived of my kinsmen;
Hung with hard ice-flakes, where hail-scur flew,
There I heard naught save the harsh sea
And ice-cold wave, at whiles the swan cries,
Did for my games the gannet's clamour,
Sea-fowls' loudness was for me laughter,
The mews' singing all my mead-drink.
Storms, on the stone-cliffs beaten, fell on the stern

In icy feathers; full oft the eagle screamed
With spray on his pinion.
                              Not any protector
May make merry man faring needy.
This he little believes, who aye in winsome life
Abides 'mid burghers some heavy business,
Wealthy and wine-flushed, how I weary oft
Must bide above brine.
Neareth nightshade, snoweth from north,
Frost froze the land, hail fell on earth then
Corn of the coldest. Nathless there knocketh now
The heart's thought that I on high streams
The salt-wavy tumult traverse alone.
Moaneth alway my mind's lust
That I fare forth, that I afar hence
Seek out a foreign fastness.
For this there's no mood-lofty man over earth's midst,
Not though he be given his good, but will have in his youth
        greed;
Nor his deed to the daring, nor his king to the faithful
But shall have his sorrow for sea-fare
Whatever his lord will.
He hath not heart for harping, nor in ring-having
Nor winsomeness to wife, nor world's delight
Nor any whit else save the wave's slash,
Yet longing comes upon him to fare forth on the water.
Bosque taketh blossom, cometh beauty of berries,
Fields to fairness, land fares brisker,
All this admonisheth man eager of mood,
The heart turns to travel so that he then thinks
On flood-ways to be far departing.
Cuckoo calleth with gloomy crying,
He singeth summerward, bodeth sorrow,
The bitter heart's blood. Burgher knows not—
He the prosperous man—what some perform
Where wandering them widest draweth.
So that but now my heart burst from my breast-lock,
My mood 'mid the mere-flood,
Over the whale's acre, would wander wide.
On earth's shelter cometh oft to me,

Eager and ready, the crying lone-flyer,
Whets for the whale-path the heart irresistibly,
O'er tracks of ocean; seeing that anyhow
My lord deems to me this dead life
On loan and on land, I believe not
That any earth-weal eternal standeth
Save there be somewhat calamitous
That, ere a man's tide go, turn it to twain.
Disease or oldness or sword-hate
Beats out the breath from doom-gripped body.
And for this, every earl whatever, for those speaking after—
Laud of the living, boasteth some last word,
That he will work ere he pass onward,
Frame on the fair earth 'gainst foes his malice,
Daring ado, . . .
So that all men shall honour him after
And his laud beyond them remain 'mid the English,
Aye, for ever, a lasting life's-blast,
Delight mid the doughty.
                              Days little durable,
And all arrogance of earthen riches,
There come now no kings nor Cæsars
Nor gold-giving lords like those gone.
Howe'er in mirth most magnified,
Whoe'er lived in life most lordliest,
Drear all this excellence, delights undurable!
Waneth the watch, but the world holdeth.
Tomb hideth trouble. The blade is layed low.
Earthly glory ageth and seareth.
No man at all going the earth's gait,
But age fares against him, his face paleth,
Grey-haired he groaneth, knows gone companions,
Lordly men are to earth o'ergiven,
Nor may he then the flesh-cover, whose life ceaseth,
Nor eat the sweet nor feel the sorry,
Nor stir hand nor think in mid heart,
And though he strew the grave with gold,
His born brothers, their buried bodies
Be an unlikely treasure hoard.

The Return

See, they return; ah, see the tentative
    Movements, and the slow feet,
    The trouble in the pace and the uncertain
Wavering!

See, they return, one, and by one,
With fear, as half-awakened;
As if the snow should hesitate
And murmur in the wind,
           and half turn back;
These were the "Wing'd-with-Awe,"
        Inviolable.

Gods of the wingèd shoe!
With them the silver hounds,
        sniffing the trace of air!

Haie! Haie!
    These were the swift to harry;
    These the keen-scented;
    These were the souls of blood.

    Slow on the leash,
           pallid the leash-men!

Portrait d'une Femme

Your mind and you are our Sargasso Sea,
London has swept about you this score years
And bright ships left you this or that in fee:
Ideas, old gossip, oddments of all things,
Strange spars of knowledge and dimmed wares of price.
Great minds have sought you—lacking someone else.
You have been second always. Tragical?
No. You preferred it to the usual thing:
One dull man, dulling and uxorious,

One average mind—with one thought less, each year.
Oh, you are patient, I have seen you sit
Hours, where something might have floated up.
And now you pay one. Yes, you richly pay.
You are a person of some interest, one comes to you
And takes strange gain away:
Trophies fished up; some curious suggestion;
Fact that leads nowhere; and a tale for two,
Pregnant with mandrakes, or with something else
That might prove useful and yet never proves,
That never fits a corner or shows use,
Or finds its hour upon the loom of days:
The tarnished, gaudy, wonderful old work;
Idols and ambergris and rare inlays,
These are your riches, your great store; and yet
For all this sea-hoard of deciduous things,
Strange woods half sodden, and new brighter stuff:
In the slow float of differing light and deep,
No! there is nothing! In the whole and all,
Nothing that's quite your own.
                    Yet this is you.

Of Jacopo del Sellaio

This man knew out the secret ways of love,
No man could paint such things who did not know.

And now she's gone, who was his Cyprian,
And you are here, who are "The Isles" to me.

And here's the thing that lasts the whole thing out:
The eyes of this dead lady speak to me.

The Garden

En robe de parade.
—Samain.

Like a skein of loose silk blown against a wall
She walks by the railing of a path in Kensington Gardens,
And she is dying piece-meal
        of a sort of emotional anæmia.

And round about there is a rabble
Of the filthy, sturdy, unkillable infants of the very poor.
They shall inherit the earth.

In her is the end of breeding.
Her boredom is exquisite and excessive.
She would like some one to speak to her,
And is almost afraid that I
        will commit that indiscretion.

A Pact

I make a pact with you, Walt Whitman—
I have detested you long enough.
I come to you as a grown child
Who has had a pig-headed father;
I am old enough now to make friends.
It was you that broke the new wood,
Now is a time for carving.
We have one sap and one root—
Let there be commerce between us.

In a Station of the Metro

The apparition of these faces in the crowd;
Petals on a wet, black bough.

Les Millwin

The little Millwins attend the Russian Ballet.
The mauve and greenish souls of the little Millwins
Were seen lying along the upper seats
Like so many unused boas.

The turbulent and undisciplined host of art students—
The rigorous deputation from "Slade"—
Was before them.

With arms exalted, with fore-arms
Crossed in great futuristic X's, the art students
Exulted, they beheld the splendours of *Cleopatra*.

And the little Millwins beheld these things;
With their large and anæmic eyes they looked out upon this
      configuration.

Let us therefore mention the fact,
For it seems to us worthy of record.

A Song of the Degrees

I

Rest me with Chinese colours,
For I think the glass is evil.

II

The wind moves above the wheat—
With a silver crashing,
A thin war of metal.

I have known the golden disc,
I have seen it melting above me.
I have known the stone-bright place,
      The hall of clear colours.

III

O glass subtly evil, O confusion of colours!
O light bound and bent in, O soul of the captive,
Why am I warned? Why am I sent away?
Why is your glitter full of curious mistrust?
O glass subtle and cunning, O powdery gold!
O filaments of amber, two-faced iridescence!

Tame Cat

"It rests me to be among beautiful women.
   Why should one always lie about such matters?

I repeat:
It rests me to converse with beautiful women
Even though we talk nothing but nonsense,

The purring of the invisible antennæ
Is both stimulating and delightful."

Liu Ch'e

The rustling of the silk is discontinued,
Dust drifts over the court-yard,
There is no sound of foot-fall, and the leaves
Scurry into heaps and lie still,
And she the rejoicer of the heart is beneath them:

A wet leaf that clings to the threshold.

Fan-Piece, For Her Imperial Lord

O fan of white silk,
      clear as frost on the grass-blade,
You also are laid aside.

The Study in Æsthetics

The very small children in patched clothing,
Being smitten with an unusual wisdom,
Stopped in their play as she passed them
And cried up from their cobbles:
>   *Guarda! Ahi, guarda! ch' è be'a!**

But three years after this
I heard the young Dante, whose last name I do not know—
For there are, in Sirmione, twenty-eight young Dantes and
    thirty-four Catulli;
And there had been a great catch of sardines,
And his elders
Were packing them in the great wooden boxes
For the market in Brescia, and he
Leapt about, snatching at the bright fish
And getting in both of their ways;
And in vain they commanded him to *sta fermo!*
And when they would not let him arrange
The fish in the boxes
He stroked those which were already arranged,
Murmuring for his own satisfaction
This identical phrase:
>   *Ch' è be'a.*

And at this I was mildly abashed.

   * *Bella.*

Exile's Letter

To So-Kin of Rakuyo, ancient friend, Chancellor of Gen.
Now I remember that you built me a special tavern
By the south side of the bridge at Ten-Shin.
With yellow gold and white jewels, we paid for songs and
    laughter
And we were drunk for month on month, forgetting the
    kings and princes.

Intelligent men came drifting in from the sea and from the
    west border,
And with them, and with you especially
There was nothing at cross purpose,
And they made nothing of sea-crossing or of mountain
    crossing,
If only they could be of that fellowship,
And we all spoke out our hearts and minds, and without
    regret.

And then I was sent off to South Wei,
        smothered in laurel groves,
And you to the north of Raku-hoku,
Till we had nothing but thoughts and memories in common.

And then, when separation had come to its worst,
We met, and travelled into Sen-Go,
Through all the thirty-six folds of the turning and twisting
    waters,
Into a valley of the thousand bright flowers,
That was the first valley;
And into ten thousand valleys full of voices and pine-winds.
And with silver harness and reins of gold,
Out came the East of Kan foreman and his company.
And there came also the "True man" of Shi-yo to meet me,
Playing on a jewelled mouth-organ.
In the storied houses of San-Ko they gave us more Sennin
    music,
Many instruments, like the sound of young phœnix broods.
The foreman of Kan Chu, drunk, danced
        because his long sleeves wouldn't keep still
With that music-playing,
And I, wrapped in brocade, went to sleep with my head on
    his lap,
And my spirit so high it was all over the heavens,
And before the end of the day we were scattered like stars, or
    rain.
I had to be off to So, far away over the waters,
You back to your river-bridge.

And your father, who was brave as a leopard,
Was governor in Hei Shu, and put down the barbarian rabble.
And one May he had you send for me,
                despite the long distance.
And what with broken wheels and so on, I won't say it wasn't
        hard going,
Over roads twisted like sheeps' guts.
And I was still going, late in the year,
                in the cutting wind from the North,
And thinking how little you cared for the cost,
                and you caring enough to pay it.
And what a reception:
Red jade cups, food well set on a blue jewelled table,
And I was drunk, and had no thought of returning.
And you would walk out with me to the western corner of
        the castle,
To the dynastic temple, with water about it clear as blue jade,
With boats floating, and the sound of mouth-organs and
        drums,
With ripples like dragon-scales, going grass green on the
        water,
Pleasure lasting, with courtezans, going and coming without
        hindrance,
With the willow flakes falling like snow,
And the vermilioned girls getting drunk about sunset,
And the water a hundred feet deep reflecting green eyebrows
—Eyebrows painted green are a fine sight in young
        moonlight,
Gracefully painted—
And the girls singing back at each other,
Dancing in transparent brocade,
And the wind lifting the song, and interrupting it,
Tossing it up under the clouds.
                And all this comes to an end.
                And is not again to be met with.
I went up to the court for examination,
Tried Layu's luck, offered the Choyo song,
And got no promotion,
                and went back to the East Mountains white-headed.
And once again, later, we met at the South bridge-head.

And then the crowd broke up, you went north to San palace,
And if you ask how I regret that parting:
It is like the flowers falling at Spring's end
        Confused, whirled in a tangle.
What is the use of talking, and there is no end of talking,
There is no end of things in the heart.

I call in the boy,
Have him sit on his knees here
      To seal this,
And send it a thousand miles, thinking.

                   By Rihaku

The River-Merchant's Wife: A Letter

While my hair was still cut straight across my forehead
I played about the front gate, pulling flowers.
You came by on bamboo stilts, playing horse,
You walked about my seat, playing with blue plums.
And we went on living in the village of Chokan:
Two small people, without dislike or suspicion.

At fourteen I married My Lord you.
I never laughed, being bashful.
Lowering my head, I looked at the wall.
Called to, a thousand times, I never looked back.

At fifteen I stopped scowling,
I desired my dust to be mingled with yours
Forever and forever, and forever.
Why should I climb the look out?

At sixteen you departed,
You went into far Ku-to-Yen, by the river of swirling eddies,
And you have been gone five months.
The monkeys make sorrowful noise overhead.
You dragged your feet when you went out.

By the gate now, the moss is grown, the different mosses,
Too deep to clear them away!
The leaves fall early this autumn, in wind.
The paired butterflies are already yellow with August
Over the grass in the West garden,
They hurt me.
I grow older,
If you are coming down through the narrows of the river
    Kiang,
Please let me know beforehand,
And I will come out to meet you,
                As far as Cho-fu-Sa.

BY RIHAKU

Lament of the Frontier Guard

By the North Gate, the wind blows full of sand,
Lonely from the beginning of time until now!
Trees fall, the grass goes yellow with autumn.
I climb the towers and towers
              to watch out the barbarous land:
Desolate castle, the sky, the wide desert.
There is no wall left to this village.
Bones white with a thousand frosts,
High heaps, covered with trees and grass;
Who brought this to pass?
Who has brought the flaming imperial anger?
Who has brought the army with drums and with kettle-
    drums?
Barbarous kings.
A gracious spring, turned to blood-ravenous autumn,
A turmoil of wars-men, spread over the middle kingdom,
Three hundred and sixty thousand,
And sorrow, sorrow like rain.
Sorrow to go, and sorrow, sorrow returning,
Desolate, desolate fields,

And no children of warfare upon them,
        No longer the men for offence and defence.
Ah, how shall you know the dreary sorrow at the North Gate,
With Riboku's name forgotten,
And we guardsmen fed to the tigers.

BY RIHAKU

Papyrus

Spring . . .
Too long . . .
Gongula . . .

Near Perigord

A Perigord, pres del muralh
Tan que i puosch' om gitar ab malh.

You'd have men's hearts up from the dust
And tell their secrets, Messire Cino,
Right enough? Then read between the lines of Uc St. Circ,
Solve me the riddle, for you know the tale.

Bertrans, En Bertrans, left a fine canzone:
"Maent, I love you, you have turned me out.
The voice at Montfort, Lady Agnes' hair,
Bel Miral's stature, the viscountess' throat,
Set all together, are not worthy of you . . ."
And all the while you sing out that canzone,
Think you that Maent lived at Montaignac
One at Chalais, another at Malemort
Hard over Brive—for every lady a castle,
Each place strong.

        Oh, *is* it easy enough?
Tairiran held hall in Montaignac,

His brother-in-law was all there was of power
In Perigord, and this good union
Gobbled all the land, and held it later for some hundred
    years.
And our En Bertrans was in Altafort,
Hub of the wheel, the stirrer-up of strife,
As caught by Dante in the last wallow of hell—
The headless trunk "that made its head a lamp."
For separation wrought out separation,
And he who set the strife between brother and brother
And had his way with the old English king,
Viced in such torture for the "counterpass."

    How would you live, with neighbours set about you—
Poictiers and Brive, untaken Rochecouart,
Spread like the finger-tips of one frail hand;
And you on that great mountain of a palm—
Not a neat ledge, not Foix between its streams,
But one huge back half-covered up with pine,
Worked for and snatched from the string-purse of Born—
The four round towers, four brothers—mostly fools:
What could he do but play the desperate chess,
And stir old grudges?
        "Pawn your castles, lords!
Let the Jews pay."
        And the great scene—
(That, maybe, never happened!)
        Beaten at last,
Before the hard old king:
        "Your son, ah, since he died
My wit and worth are cobwebs brushed aside
In the full flare of grief. Do what you will."

    Take the whole man, and ravel out the story.
He loved this lady in castle Montaignac?
The castle flanked him—he had need of it.
You read to-day, how long the overlords of Perigord,
The Talleyrands, have held the place, it was no transient
    fiction.
And Maent failed him? Or saw through the scheme?

And all his net-like thought of new alliance?
Chalais is high, a-level with the poplars.
Its lowest stones just meet the valley tips
Where the low Dronne is filled with water-lilies.
And Rochecouart can match it, stronger yet,
The very spur's end, built on sheerest cliff,
And Malemort keeps its close hold on Brive,
While Born, his own close purse, his rabbit warren,
His subterranean chamber with a dozen doors,
A-bristle with antennæ to feel roads,
To sniff the traffic into Perigord.
And that hard phalanx, that unbroken line,
The ten good miles from there to Maent's castle,
All of his flank—how could he do without her?
And all the road to Cahors, to Toulouse?
What would he do without her?

               "Papiol,
Go forthright singing—Anhes, Cembelins.
There is a throat; ah, there are two white hands;
There is a trellis full of early roses,
And all my heart is bound about with love.
Where am I come with compound flatteries—
What doors are open to fine compliment?"
And every one half jealous of Maent?
He wrote the catch to pit their jealousies
Against her; give her pride in them?

Take his own speech, make what you will of it—
And still the knot, the first knot, of Maent?

   Is it a love poem? Did he sing of war?
Is it an intrigue to run subtly out,
Born of a jongleur's tongue, freely to pass
Up and about and in and out the land,
Mark him a craftsman and a strategist?
(St. Leider had done as much at Polhonac,
Singing a different stave, as closely hidden.)
Oh, there is precedent, legal tradition,
To sing one thing when your song means another,

"Et albirar ab lor bordon—"
Foix' count knew that. What is Sir Bertrans' singing?

Maent, Maent, and yet again Maent,
Or war and broken heaumes and politics?

II

    End fact. Try fiction. Let us say we see
En Bertrans, a tower-room at Hautefort,
Sunset, the ribbon-like road lies, in red cross-light,
South toward Montaignac, and he bends at a table
Scribbling, swearing between his teeth, by his left hand
Lie little strips of parchment covered over,
Scratched and erased with *al* and *ochaisos.*
Testing his list of rhymes, a lean man? Bilious?
With a red straggling beard?
And the green cat's-eye lifts toward Montaignac.

    Or take his "magnet" singer setting out,
Dodging his way past Aubeterre, singing at Chalais
    In the vaulted hall,
Or, by a lichened tree at Rochecouart
Aimlessly watching a hawk above the valleys,
Waiting his turn in the mid-summer evening,
Thinking of Aelis, whom he loved heart and soul . . .
To find her half alone, Montfort away,
And a brown, placid, hated woman visiting her,
Spoiling his visit, with a year before the next one.
Little enough?
Or carry him forward. "Go through all the courts,
My Magnet," Bertrans had said.

    We came to Ventadour
In the mid love court, he sings out the canzon,
No one hears save Arrimon Luc D'Esparo—
No one hears aught save the gracious sound of compliments.
Sir Arrimon counts on his fingers, Montfort,
Rochecouart, Chalais, the rest, the tactic,
Malemort, guesses beneath, sends word to Cœur de Lion:

The compact, de Born smoked out, trees felled
About his castle, cattle driven out!
Or no one sees it, and En Bertrans prospered?

And ten years after, or twenty, as you will,
Arnaut and Richard lodge beneath Chalus:
The dull round towers encroaching on the field,
The tents tight drawn, horses at tether
Further and out of reach, the purple night,
The crackling of small fires, the bannerets,
The lazy leopards on the largest banner,
Stray gleams on hanging mail, an armourer's torch-flare
Melting on steel.

And in the quietest space
They probe old scandals, say de Born is dead;
And we've the gossip (skipped six hundred years).
Richard shall die to-morrow—leave him there
Talking of *trobar clus* with Daniel.
And the "best craftsman" sings out his friend's song,
Envies its vigour . . . and deplores the technique,
Dispraises his own skill?—That's as you will.
And they discuss the dead man,
Plantagenet puts the riddle: "Did he love her?"
And Arnaut parries: "Did he love your sister?
True, he has praised her, but in some opinion
He wrote that praise only to show he had
The favour of your party; had been well received."

"You knew the man."
              "*You* knew the man.
I am an artist, you have tried both métiers."
"You were born near him."
              "Do we know our friends?"
"Say that he saw the castles, say that he loved Maent!"
"Say that he loved her, does it solve the riddle?"
    End the discussion, Richard goes out next day
And gets a quarrel-bolt shot through his vizard,
Pardons the bowman, dies,

Ends our discussion. Arnaut ends
"In sacred odour"—(that's apocryphal!)
And we can leave the talk till Dante writes:
Surely I saw, and still before my eyes
Goes on that headless trunk, that bears for light
Its own head swinging, gripped by the dead hair,
And like a swinging lamp that says, "Ah me!
I severed men, my head and heart
Ye see here severed, my life's counterpart."

Or take En Bertrans?

III

Ed eran due in uno, ed uno in due.
Inferno, XXVIII, 125.

"Bewildering spring, and by the Auvezere
Poppies and day's-eyes in the green émail
Rose over us; and we knew all that stream,
And our two horses had traced out the valleys;
Knew the low flooded lands squared out with poplars,
In the young days when the deep sky befriended.
        And great wings beat above us in the twilight,
And the great wheels in heaven
Bore us together . . . surging . . . and apart . . .
Believing we should meet with lips and hands.

   High, high and sure . . . and then the counter-thrust:
'Why do you love me? Will you always love me?
But I am like the grass, I can not love you.'
Or, 'Love, and I love and love you,
And hate your mind, not *you*, your soul, your hands.'

        So to this last estrangement, Tairiran!

        There shut up in his castle, Tairiran's,
She who had nor ears nor tongue save in her hands,
Gone—ah, gone—untouched, unreachable!
She who could never live save through one person,
She who could never speak save to one person,
And all the rest of her a shifting change,
A broken bundle of mirrors . . . !"

Alba

When the nightingale to his mate
  Sings day-long and night late
  My love and I keep state
    In bower,
    In flower,
    'Till the watchman on the tower
  Cry:
      "Up! Thou rascal, Rise,
      I see the white
          Light
          And the night
                Flies."

from
Homage to Sextus Propertius

I

Shades of Callimachus, Coan ghosts of Philetas
It is in your grove I would walk,
I who come first from the clear font
Bringing the Grecian orgies into Italy,
                and the dance into Italy.
Who hath taught you so subtle a measure,
                in what hall have you heard it;
What foot beat out your time-bar,
          what water has mellowed your whistles?

Out-weariers of Apollo will, as we know, continue their
      Martian generalities,
    We have kept our erasers in order.
A new-fangled chariot follows the flower-hung horses;
A young Muse with young loves clustered about her
                ascends with me into the æther, . . .
And there is no high-road to the Muses.

Annalists will continue to record Roman reputations,
Celebrities from the Trans-Caucasus will belaud Roman
    celebrities
And expound the distentions of Empire,
But for something to read in normal circumstances?
For a few pages brought down from the forked hill unsullied?
I ask a wreath which will not crush my head.
               And there is no hurry about it;
I shall have, doubtless, a boom after my funeral,
Seeing that long standing increases all things
                     regardless of quality.
And who would have known the towers
             pulled down by a deal-wood horse;
Or of Achilles withstaying waters by Simois
Or of Hector spattering wheel-rims,
Or of Polydmantus, by Scamander, or Helenus and
    Deiphoibos?
Their door-yards would scarcely know them, or Paris.
Small talk O Ilion, and O Troad
              twice taken by Oetian gods,
If Homer had not stated your case!

And I also among the later nephews of this city
            shall have my dog's day,
With no stone upon my contemptible sepulchre;
My vote coming from the temple of Phoebus in Lycia, at
    Patara,
And in the meantime my songs will travel,
And the devirginated young ladies will enjoy them
        when they have got over the strangeness,
For Orpheus tamed the wild beasts—
          and held up the Threician river;
And Cithaeron shook up the rocks by Thebes
    and danced them into a bulwark at his pleasure,
And you, O Polyphemus? Did harsh Galatea almost
Turn to your dripping horses, because of a tune, under
    Aetna?
We must look into the matter.
Bacchus and Apollo in favour of it,

There will be a crowd of young women doing homage to my
    palaver,
Though my house is not propped up by Taenarian columns
    from Laconia (associated with Neptune and Cerberus),
Though it is not stretched upon gilded beams:
My orchards do not lie level and wide
                  as the forests of Phaeacia,
                  the luxurious and Ionian,
Nor are my caverns stuffed stiff with a Marcian vintage,
My cellar does not date from Numa Pompilius,
Nor bristle with wine jars,
Nor is it equipped with a frigidaire patent;
Yet the companions of the Muses
           will keep their collective nose in my books,
And weary with historical data, they will turn to my dance
    tune.

Happy who are mentioned in my pamphlets,
        the songs shall be a fine tomb-stone over their beauty.
           But against this?
Neither expensive pyramids scraping the stars in their route,
Nor houses modelled upon that of Jove in East Elis,
Nor the monumental effigies of Mausolus,
           are a complete elucidation of death.

Flame burns, rain sinks into the cracks
And they all go to rack ruin beneath the thud of the years.
Stands genius a deathless adornment,
        a name not to be worn out with the years.

VI

When, when, and whenever death closes our eyelids,
Moving naked over Acheron
Upon the one raft, victor and conquered together,
Marius and Jugurtha together,
              one tangle of shadows.

Caesar plots against India,
Tigris and Euphrates shall, from now on, flow at his bidding,
Tibet shall be full of Roman policemen,
The Parthians shall get used to our statuary
                    and acquire a Roman religion;
One raft on the veiled flood of Acheron,
          Marius and Jugurtha together.

Nor at my funeral either will there be any long trail,
                    bearing ancestral lares and images;
No trumpets filled with my emptiness,
Nor shall it be on an Attalic bed;
          The perfumed cloths shall be absent.
A small plebeian procession.
          Enough, enough and in plenty
There will be three books at my obsequies
Which I take, my not unworthy gift, to Persephone.

You will follow the bare scarified breast
Nor will you be weary of calling my name, nor too weary
          To place the last kiss on my lips
When the Syrian onyx is broken.

          "He who is now vacant dust
          Was once the slave of one passion:"
Give that much inscription
          "Death why tardily come?"

You, sometimes, will lament a lost friend,
          For it is a custom:
This care for past men,

Since Adonis was gored in Idalia, and the Cytherean
Ran crying with out-spread hair,
          In vain, you call back the shade,
In vain, Cynthia. Vain call to unanswering shadow,
          Small talk comes from small bones.

Hugh Selwyn Mauberley

(Life and Contacts)

"Vocat æstus in umbram"
Nemesianus Ec. IV.

Ode Pour L'Election De Son Sepulchre

I

For three years, out of key with his time,
He strove to resuscitate the dead art
Of poetry; to maintain "the sublime"
In the old sense. Wrong from the start—

No, hardly but, seeing he had been born
In a half savage country, out of date;
Bent resolutely on wringing lilies from the acorn;
Capaneus; trout for factitious bait;

Ἴδμεν γάρ τοι πάνθ', ὅσ' ἐνὶ Τροίη
Caught in the unstopped ear;
Giving the rocks small lee-way
The chopped seas held him, therefore, that year.

His true Penelope was Flaubert,
He fished by obstinate isles;
Observed the elegance of Circe's hair
Rather than the mottoes on sun-dials.

Unaffected by "the march of events,"
He passed from men's memory in *l'an trentiesme*
De son eage; the case presents
No adjunct to the Muses' diadem.

II

The age demanded an image
Of its accelerated grimace,
Something for the modern stage,
Not, at any rate, an Attic grace;

Not, not certainly, the obscure reveries
Of the inward gaze;
Better mendacities
Than the classics in paraphrase!

The "age demanded" chiefly a mould in plaster,
Made with no loss of time,
A prose kinema, not, not assuredly, alabaster
Or the "sculpture" of rhyme.

III

The tea-rose tea-gown, etc.
Supplants the mousseline of Cos,
The pianola "replaces"
Sappho's barbitos.

Christ follows Dionysus,
Phallic and ambrosial
Made way for macerations;
Caliban casts out Ariel.

All things are a flowing,
Sage Heracleitus says;
But a tawdry cheapness
Shall outlast our days.

Even the Christian beauty
Defects—after Samothrace;
We see τὸ καλόν
Decreed in the market place.

Faun's flesh is not to us,
Nor the saint's vision.
We have the press for wafer;
Franchise for circumcision.

All men, in law, are equals.
Free of Peisistratus,
We choose a knave or an eunuch
To rule over us.

O bright Apollo,
τίν' ἄνδρα, τίν' ἥρωα, τίνα θεόν,
What god, man, or hero
Shall I place a tin wreath upon!

IV

These fought in any case,
and some believing, pro domo, in any case . .

Some quick to arm,
some for adventure,
some from fear of weakness,
some from fear of censure,
some for love of slaughter, in imagination,
learning later . . .

some in fear, learning love of slaughter;
Died some pro patria, non dulce non et decor . .
walked eye-deep in hell
believing in old men's lies, then unbelieving
came home, home to a lie,
home to many deceits,
home to old lies and new infamy;
usury age-old and age-thick
and liars in public places.

Daring as never before, wastage as never before.
Young blood and high blood,
Fair cheeks, and fine bodies;

fortitude as never before

frankness as never before,
disillusions as never told in the old days,
hysterias, trench confessions,
laughter out of dead bellies.

V

There died a myriad,
And of the best, among them,
For an old bitch gone in the teeth,
For a botched civilization,

Charm, smiling at the good mouth,
Quick eyes gone under earth's lid,

For two gross of broken statues,
For a few thousand battered books.

Yeux Glauques

Gladstone was still respected,
When John Ruskin produced
"Kings' Treasuries"; Swinburne
And Rossetti still abused.

Fœtid Buchanan lifted up his voice
When that faun's head of hers
Became a pastime for
Painters and adulterers.

The Burne-Jones cartons
Have preserved her eyes;
Still, at the Tate, they teach
Cophetua to rhapsodize;

Thin like brook-water,
With a vacant gaze.
The English Rubaiyat was still-born
In those days.

The thin, clear gaze, the same
Still darts out faun-like from the half-ruin'd face,
Questing and passive. . . .
"Ah, poor Jenny's case" . . .

Bewildered that a world
Shows no surprise
At her last maquero's
Adulteries.

"Siena Mi Fe'; Disfecemi Maremma"

Among the pickled fœtuses and bottled bones,
Engaged in perfecting the catalogue,
I found the last scion of the
Senatorial families of Strasbourg, Monsieur Verog.

For two hours he talked of Gallifet;
Of Dowson; of the Rhymers' Club;
Told me how Johnson (Lionel) died
By falling from a high stool in a pub . . .

But showed no trace of alcohol
At the autopsy, privately performed—
Tissue preserved—the pure mind
Arose toward Newman as the whiskey warmed.

Dowson found harlots cheaper than hotels;
Headlam for uplift; Image impartially imbued
With raptures for Bacchus, Terpsichore and the Church.
So spoke the author of "The Dorian Mood,"

M. Verog, out of step with the decade,
Detached from his contemporaries,
Neglected by the young,
Because of these reveries.

Brennbaum

The sky-like limpid eyes,
The circular infant's face,
The stiffness from spats to collar
Never relaxing into grace;
The heavy memories of Horeb, Sinai and the forty years,

Showed only when the daylight fell
Level across the face
Of Brennbaum "The Impeccable."

Mr. Nixon

In the cream gilded cabin of his steam yacht
Mr. Nixon advised me kindly, to advance with fewer
Dangers of delay. "Consider
　　　　"Carefully the reviewer.

"I was as poor as you are;
"When I began I got, of course,
"Advance on royalties, fifty at first," said Mr. Nixon,
"Follow me, and take a column,
"Even if you have to work free.

"Butter reviewers. From fifty to three hundred
"I rose in eighteen months;
"The hardest nut I had to crack
"Was Dr. Dundas.

"I never mentioned a man but with the view
"Of selling my own works.
"The tip's a good one, as for literature
"It gives no man a sinecure.

"And no one knows, at sight a masterpiece.
"And give up verse, my boy,
"There's nothing in it."
　.　　.　　.　　.　　.　　.　　.

Likewise a friend of Bloughram's once advised me:
Don't kick against the pricks,
Accept opinion. The "Nineties" tried your game
And died, there's nothing in it.

X

Beneath the sagging roof
The stylist has taken shelter,
Unpaid, uncelebrated,
At last from the world's welter

Nature receives him,
With a placid and uneducated mistress
He exercises his talents
And the soil meets his distress.

The haven from sophistications and contentions
Leaks through its thatch;
He offers succulent cooking;
The door has a creaking latch.

XI

"Conservatrix of Milésien"
Habits of mind and feeling,
Possibly. But in Ealing
With the most bank-clerkly of Englishmen?

No, "Milésian" is an exaggeration.
No instinct has survived in her
Older than those her grandmother
Told her would fit her station.

XII

"Daphne with her thighs in bark
Stretches toward me her leafy hands,"—
Subjectively. In the stuffed-satin drawing-room
I await The Lady Valentine's commands,

Knowing my coat has never been
Of precisely the fashion
To stimulate, in her,
A durable passion;

Doubtful, somewhat, of the value
Of well-gowned approbation
Of literary effort,
But never of The Lady Valentine's vocation:

Poetry, her border of ideas,
The edge, uncertain, but a means of blending
With other strata
Where the lower and higher have ending;

A hook to catch the Lady Jane's attention,
A modulation toward the theatre,
Also, in the case of revolution,
A possible friend and comforter.

Conduct, on the other hand, the soul
"Which the highest cultures have nourished"
To Fleet St. where
Dr. Johnson flourished;

Beside this thoroughfare
The sale of half-hose has
Long since superseded the cultivation
Of Pierian roses.

Envoi (1919)

Go, dumb-born book,
Tell her that sang me once that song of Lawes;
Hadst thou but song
As thou hast subjects known,
Then were there cause in thee that should condone
Even my faults that heavy upon me lie
And build her glories their longevity.

Tell her that sheds
Such treasure in the air,
Recking naught else but that her graces give
Life to the moment,

I would bid them live
As roses might, in magic amber laid,
Red overwrought with orange and all made
One substance and one colour
Braving time.

Tell her that goes
With song upon her lips
But sings not out the song, nor knows
The maker of it, some other mouth,
May be as fair as hers,
Might, in new ages, gain her worshippers,
When our two dusts with Waller's shall be laid,
Siftings on siftings in oblivion,
Till change hath broken down
All things save Beauty alone.

1920 (Mauberley)

I

Turned from the "eau-forte
Par Jaquemart"
To the strait head
Of Messalina:

"His true Penelope
Was Flaubert,"
And his tool
The engraver's.

Firmness,
Not the full smile,
His art, but an art
In profile;

Colourless
Pier Francesca,
Pisanello lacking the skill
To forge Achaia.

II

"Qu'est ce qu'ils savent de l'amour, et qu'est ce qu'ils peuvent comprendre?

S'ils ne comprennent pas la poésie, s'ils ne sentent pas la musique, qu'est ce qu'ils peuvent comprendre de cette passion en comparaison avec laquelle la rose est grossière et le parfum des violettes un tonnerre?" CAID ALI

For three years, diabolus in the scale,
He drank ambrosia,
All passes, ANANGKE prevails,
Came end, at last, to that Arcadia.

He had moved amid her phantasmagoria,
Amid her galaxies,
NUKTOS AGALMA

.   .   .   .

Drifted .   .   .   . drifted precipitate,
Asking time to be rid of .   .   .   .
Of his bewilderment; to designate
His new found orchid.   .   .   .

To be certain .   .   .   . certain .   .   .   .
(Amid ærial flowers) .   . time for arrangements—
Drifted on
To the final estrangement;

Unable in the supervening blankness
To sift TO AGATHON from the chaff
Until he found his sieve .   .   .   .
Ultimately, his seismograph:

—Given that is his "fundamental passion"
This urge to convey the relation
Of eye-lid and cheek-bone
By verbal manifestations;

To present the series
Of curious heads in medallion—

He had passed, inconscient, full gaze,
The wise-banded irises
And botticellian sprays implied
In their diastasis;

Which anæsthesis, noted a year late,
And weighed, revealed his great affect,
(Orchid), mandate
Of Eros, a retrospect.

      .   .   .

Mouths biting empty air,
The still stone dogs,
Caught in metamorphosis, were
Left him as epilogues.

"The Age Demanded"

Vide Poem II. Page 532

For this agility chance found
Him of all men, unfit
As the red-beaked steeds of
The Cytheræan for a chain bit.

The glow of porcelain
Brought no reforming sense
To his perception
Of the social inconsequence.

Thus, if her colour
Came against his gaze,
Tempered as if
It were through a perfect glaze

He made no immediate application
Of this to relation of the state
To the individual, the month was more temperate
Because this beauty had been.

. . . . .

The coral isle, the lion-coloured sand
Burst in upon the porcelain revery:
Impetuous troubling
Of his imagery.

. . . . . .

Mildness, amid the neo-Nietzschean clatter,
His sense of graduations,
Quite out of place amid
Resistance to current exacerbations,

Invitation, mere invitation to perceptivity
Gradually led him to the isolation
Which these presents place
Under a more tolerant, perhaps, examination.

By constant elimination
The manifest universe
Yielded an armour
Against utter consternation,

A Minoan undulation,
Seen, we admit, amid ambrosial circumstances
Strengthened him against
The discouraging doctrine of chances,

And his desire for survival,
Faint in the most strenuous moods,
Became an Olympian *apathein*
In the presence of selected perceptions.

A pale gold, in the aforesaid pattern,
The unexpected palms
Destroying, certainly, the artist's urge,
Left him delighted with the imaginary
Audition of the phantasmal sea-surge,

Incapable of the least utterance or composition,
Emendation, conservation of the "better tradition"
Refinement of medium, elimination of superfluities,
August attraction or concentration.

Nothing, in brief, but maudlin confession
Irresponse to human aggression,
Amid the precipitation, down-float
Of insubstantial manna,
Lifting the faint susurrus
Of his subjective hosannah.

Ultimate affronts to human redundancies;

Non-esteem of self-styled "his betters"
Leading, as he well knew,
To his final
Exclusion from the world of letters.

IV

Scattered Moluccas
Not knowing, day to day,
The first day's end, in the next noon;
The placid water
Unbroken by the Simoon;

Thick foliage
Placid beneath warm suns,
Tawn fore-shores
Washed in the cobalt of oblivions;

Or through dawn-mist
The grey and rose
Of the juridical
Flamingoes;

A consciousness disjunct,
Being but this overblotted
Series
Of intermittences;

Coracle of Pacific voyages,
The unforecasted beach:
Then on an oar
Read this:

"I was
And I no more exist;
Here drifted
An hedonist."

Medallion

Luini in porcelain!
The grand piano
Utters a profane
Protest with her clear soprano.

The sleek head emerges
From the gold-yellow frock
As Anadyomene in the opening
Pages of Reinach.

Honey-red, closing the face-oval,
A basket-work of braids which seem as if they were
Spun in King Minos' hall
From metal, or intractable amber;

The face-oval beneath the glaze,
Bright in its suave bounding-line, as,
Beneath half-watt rays,
The eyes turn topaz.

Canto II

Hang it all, Robert Browning,
there can be but the one "Sordello."
But Sordello, and my Sordello?
Lo Sordels si fo di Mantovana.
So-shu churned in the sea.
Seal sports in the spray-whited circles of cliff-wash,
Sleek head, daughter of Lir,
         eyes of Picasso
Under black fur-hood, lithe daughter of Ocean;
And the wave runs in the beach-groove:
"Eleanor, ἑλέναυς and ἑλέπτολις!"
         And poor old Homer blind, blind, as a bat,
Ear, ear for the sea-surge, murmur of old men's voices:
"Let her go back to the ships,
Back among Grecian faces, lest evil come on our own,
Evil and further evil, and a curse cursed on our children,
Moves, yes she moves like a goddess
And has the face of a god
         and the voice of Schoeney's daughters,
And doom goes with her in walking,
Let her go back to the ships,
         back among Grecian voices."
And by the beach-run, Tyro,
         Twisted arms of the sea-god,
Lithe sinews of water, gripping her, cross-hold,
And the blue-gray glass of the wave tents them,
Glare azure of water, cold-welter, close cover.
Quiet sun-tawny sand-stretch,
The gulls broad out their wings,
         nipping between the splay feathers;
Snipe come for their bath,
         bend out their wing-joints,
Spread wet wings to the sun-film,
And by Scios,
         to left of the Naxos passage,
Naviform rock overgrown,
         algæ cling to its edge,

There is a wine-red glow in the shallows,
       a tin flash in the sun-dazzle.

The ship landed in Scios,
       men wanting spring-water,
And by the rock-pool a young boy loggy with vine-must,
       "To Naxos? Yes, we'll take you to Naxos,
Cum' along lad." "Not that way!"
"Aye, that way is Naxos."
       And I said: "It's a straight ship."
And an ex-convict out of Italy
       knocked me into the fore-stays,
(He was wanted for manslaughter in Tuscany)
       And the whole twenty against me,
Mad for a little slave money.
       And they took her out of Scios
And off her course . . .
       And the boy came to, again, with the racket,
And looked out over the bows,
       and to eastward, and to the Naxos passage.
God-sleight then, god-sleight:
       Ship stock fast in sea-swirl,
Ivy upon the oars, King Pentheus,
       grapes with no seed but sea-foam,
Ivy in scupper-hole.
Aye, I, Acœtes, stood there,
       and the god stood by me,
Water cutting under the keel,
Sea-break from stern forrards,
       wake running off from the bow,
And where was gunwale, there now was vine-trunk,
And tenthril where cordage had been,
       grape-leaves on the rowlocks,
Heavy vine on the oarshafts,
And, out of nothing, a breathing,
       hot breath on my ankles,
Beasts like shadows in glass,
       a furred tail upon nothingness.
Lynx-purr, and heathery smell of beasts,
       where tar smell had been,

Sniff and pad-foot of beasts,
        eye-glitter out of black air.
The sky overshot, dry, with no tempest,
Sniff and pad-foot of beasts,
        fur brushing my knee-skin,
Rustle of airy sheaths,
        dry forms in the *æther.*
And the ship like a keel in ship-yard,
        slung like an ox in smith's sling,
Ribs stuck fast in the ways,
        grape-cluster over pin-rack,
        void air taking pelt.
Lifeless air become sinewed,
        feline leisure of panthers,
Leopards sniffing the grape shoots by scupper-hole,
Crouched panthers by fore-hatch,
And the sea blue-deep about us,
        green-ruddy in shadows,
And Lyæus: "From now, Acœtes, my altars,
Fearing no bondage,
        fearing no cat of the wood,
Safe with my lynxes,
        feeding grapes to my leopards,
Olibanum is my incense,
        the vines grow in my homage."

The back-swell now smooth in the rudder-chains,
Black snout of a porpoise
        where Lycabs had been,
Fish-scales on the oarsmen.
        And I worship.
I have seen what I have seen.
        When they brought the boy I said:
"He has a god in him,
        though I do not know which god."
And they kicked me into the fore-stays.
I have seen what I have seen:
        Medon's face like the face of a dory,
Arms shrunk into fins. And you, Pentheus,
Had as well listen to Tiresias, and to Cadmus,

or your luck will go out of you.
Fish-scales over groin muscles,
        lynx-purr amid sea . . .
And of a later year,
        pale in the wine-red algæ,
If you will lean over the rock,
        the coral face under wave-tinge,
Rose-paleness under water-shift,
        Ileuthyeria, fair Dafne of sea-bords,
The swimmer's arms turned to branches,
Who will say in what year,
        fleeing what band of tritons,
The smooth brows, seen, and half seen,
        now ivory stillness.

And So-shu churned in the sea, So-shu also,
        using the long moon for a churn-stick . . .
Lithe turning of water,
        sinews of Poseidon,
Black azure and hyaline,
        glass wave over Tyro,
Close cover, unstillness,
        bright welter of wave-cords,
Then quiet water,
        quiet in the buff sands,
Sea-fowl stretching wing-joints,
        splashing in rock-hollows and sand-hollows
In the wave-runs by the half-dune;
Glass-glint of wave in the tide-rips against sunlight,
        pallor of Hesperus,
Grey peak of the wave,
        wave, colour of grape's pulp,

Olive grey in the near,
        far, smoke grey of the rock-slide,
Salmon-pink wings of the fish-hawk
        cast grey shadows in water,
The tower like a one-eyed great goose
        cranes up out of the olive-grove,

And we have heard the fauns chiding Proteus
      in the smell of hay under the olive-trees,
And the frogs singing against the fauns
      in the half-light.
And . . .

Canto IV

Palace in smoky light,
Troy but a heap of smouldering boundary stones,
ANAXIFORMINGES! Aurunculeia!
Hear me. Cadmus of Golden Prows!
The silver mirrors catch the bright stones and flare,
Dawn, to our waking, drifts in the green cool light;
Dew-haze blurs, in the grass, pale ankles moving.
Beat, beat, whirr, thud, in the soft turf
      under the apple trees,
Choros nympharum, goat-foot, with the pale foot alternate;
Crescent of blue-shot waters, green-gold in the shallows,
A black cock crows in the sea-foam;

And by the curved, carved foot of the couch,
      claw-foot and lion head, an old man seated
Speaking in the low drone . . . :
         Ityn!
Et ter flebiliter, Ityn, Ityn!
And she went toward the window and cast her down,
      "All the while, the while, swallows crying:
Ityn!
      "It is Cabestan's heart in the dish."
      "It is Cabestan's heart in the dish?
      "No other taste shall change this."
And she went toward the window,
      the slim white stone bar
Making a double arch;
Firm even fingers held to the firm pale stone;

Swung for a moment,
   and the wind out of Rhodez
Caught in the full of her sleeve.
   . . . the swallows crying:
'Tis. 'Tis. Ytis!
   Actæon . . .
    and a valley,
The valley is thick with leaves, with leaves, the trees,
The sunlight glitters, glitters a-top,
Like a fish-scale roof,
   Like the church roof in Poictiers
If it were gold.
   Beneath it, beneath it
Not a ray, not a slivver, not a spare disc of sunlight
Flaking the black, soft water;
Bathing the body of nymphs, of nymphs, and Diana,
Nymphs, white-gathered about her, and the air, air,
Shaking, air alight with the goddess,
   fanning their hair in the dark,
Lifting, lifting and waffing:
Ivory dipping in silver,
   Shadow'd, o'ershadow'd
Ivory dipping in silver,
Not a splotch, not a lost shatter of sunlight.
Then Actæon: Vidal,
Vidal. It is old Vidal speaking,
   stumbling along in the wood,
Not a patch, not a lost shimmer of sunlight,
   the pale hair of the goddess.

The dogs leap on Actæon,
   "Hither, hither, Actæon,"
Spotted stag of the wood;
Gold, gold, a sheaf of hair,
   Thick like a wheat swath,
Blaze, blaze in the sun,
   The dogs leap on Actæon.

Stumbling, stumbling along in the wood,
Muttering, muttering Ovid:
            "Pergusa . . . pool . . . pool . . . Gargaphia,
"Pool . . . pool of Salmacis."
            The empty armour shakes as the cygnet moves.

Thus the light rains, thus pours, *e lo soleils plovil*
The liquid and rushing crystal
            beneath the knees of the gods.
Ply over ply, thin glitter of water;
Brook film bearing white petals.
The pines at Takasago
            grow with the pines of Isé!
The water whirls up the bright pale sand in the spring's
   mouth
"Behold the Tree of the Visages!"
Forked branch-tips, flaming as if with lotus.
            Ply over ply
The shallow eddying fluid,
            beneath the knees of the gods.

Torches melt in the glare
            set flame of the corner cook-stall,
Blue agate casing the sky (as at Gourdon that time)
            the sputter of resin,
Saffron sandal so petals the narrow foot: Hymenæus Io!
            Hymen, Io Hymenæe! Aurunculeia!
A scarlet flower is cast on the blanch-white stone.

            And So-Gioku, saying:
"This wind, sire, is the king's wind,
            This wind is wind of the palace,
Shaking imperial water-jets."
            And Ran-ti, opening his collar:
"This wind roars in the earth's bag,
            it lays the water with rushes;
No wind is the king's wind.
            Let every cow keep her calf."
"This wind is held in gauze curtains . . ."
            "No wind is the king's . . ."

The camel drivers sit in the turn of the stairs,
   Look down on Ecbatan of plotted streets,
"Danaë! Danaë!
   What wind is the king's?"
Smoke hangs on the stream,
The peach-trees shed bright leaves in the water,
Sound drifts in the evening haze,
   The bark scrapes at the ford,
Gilt rafters above black water,
   Three steps in an open field,
Gray stone-posts leading . . .

Père Henri Jacques would speak with the Sennin, on Rokku,
Mount Rokku between the rock and the cedars,
Polhonac,
As Gyges on Thracian platter set the feast,
Cabestan, Tereus,
   It is Cabestan's heart in the dish,
Vidal, or Ecbatan, upon the gilded tower in Ecbatan
Lay the god's bride, lay ever, waiting the golden rain.
By Garonne. "Saave!"
The Garonne is thick like paint,
Procession,—"Et sa'ave, sa'ave, sa'ave Regina!"—
Moves like a worm, in the crowd.
Adige, thin film of images,
Across the Adige, by Stefano, Madonna in hortulo,
As Cavalcanti had seen her.
   The Centaur's heel plants in the earth loam.
And we sit here . . .
   there in the arena . . .

Canto XIII

Kung walked
   by the dynastic temple
and into the cedar grove,
   and then out by the lower river,

And with him Khieu Tchi
          and Tian the low speaking
And "we are unknown," said Kung,
"You will take up charioteering?
          Then you will become known,
"Or perhaps I should take up charioteering, or archery?
"Or the practice of public speaking?"
And Tseu-lou said, "I would put the defences in order,"
And Khieu said, "If I were lord of a province
I would put it in better order than this is."
And Tchi said, "I would prefer a small mountain temple,
"With order in the observances,
          with a suitable performance of the ritual,"
And Tian said, with his hand on the strings of his lute
The low sounds continuing
          after his hand left the strings,
And the sound went up like smoke, under the leaves,
And he looked after the sound:
          "The old swimming hole,
"And the boys flopping off the planks,
"Or sitting in the underbrush playing mandolins."
          And Kung smiled upon all of them equally.
And Thseng-sie desired to know:
          "Which had answered correctly?"
And Kung said, "They have all answered correctly,
"That is to say, each in his nature."
And Kung raised his cane against Yuan Jang,
          Yuan Jang being his elder,
For Yuan Jang sat by the roadside pretending to
          be receiving wisdom.
And Kung said
          "You old fool, come out of it,
Get up and do something useful."
          And Kung said
"Respect a child's faculties
"From the moment it inhales the clear air,
"But a man of fifty who knows nothing
          Is worthy of no respect."
And "When the prince has gathered about him
"All the savants and artists, his riches will be fully employed."

And Kung said, and wrote on the bo leaves:
      If a man have not order within him
He can not spread order about him;
And if a man have not order within him
His family will not act with due order;
      And if the prince have not order within him
He can not put order in his dominions.
And Kung gave the words "order"
and "brotherly deference"
And said nothing of the "life after death."
And he said
      "Anyone can run to excesses,
It is easy to shoot past the mark,
It is hard to stand firm in the middle."

And they said: If a man commit murder
      Should his father protect him, and hide him?
And Kung said:
      He should hide him.

And Kung gave his daughter to Kong-Tchang
      Although Kong-Tchang was in prison.
And he gave his niece to Nan-Young
      although Nan-Young was out of office.
And Kung said "Wang ruled with moderation,
      In his day the State was well kept,
And even I can remember
A day when the historians left blanks in their writings,
I mean for things they didn't know,
But that time seems to be passing."
A day when the historians left blanks in their writings,
But that time seems to be passing."
And Kung said, "Without character you will
      be unable to play on that instrument
Or to execute the music fit for the Odes.
The blossoms of the apricot
      blow from the east to the west,
And I have tried to keep them from falling."

Canto XVII

So that the vines burst from my fingers
And the bees weighted with pollen
Move heavily in the vine-shoots:
        chirr—chirr—chir-rikk—a purring sound,
And the birds sleepily in the branches.
        ZAGREUS! IO ZAGREUS!
With the first pale-clear of the heaven
And the cities set in their hills,
And the goddess of the fair knees
Moving there, with the oak-woods behind her,
The green slope, with white hounds
        leaping about her;
And thence down to the creek's mouth, until evening,
Flat water before me,
        and the trees growing in water,
Marble trunks out of stillness,
On past the palazzi,
        in the stillness,
The light now, not of the sun.
        Chrysophrase,
And the water green clear, and blue clear;
On, to the great cliffs of amber.
        Between them,
Cave of Nerea,
    she like a great shell curved,
And the boat drawn without sound,
Without odour of ship-work,
Nor bird-cry, nor any noise of wave moving,
Nor splash of porpoise, nor any noise of wave moving,
Within her cave, Nerea,
        she like a great shell curved
In the suavity of the rock,
        cliff green-gray in the far,
In the near, the gate-cliffs of amber,
And the wave
        green clear, and blue clear,

And the cave salt-white, and glare-purple,
   cool, porphyry smooth,
    the rock sea-worn.
No gull-cry, no sound of porpoise,
Sand as of malachite, and no cold there,
   the light not of the sun.

Zagreus, feeding his panthers,
   the turf clear as on hills under light.
And under the almond-trees, gods,
   with them, *choros nympharum*. Gods,
Hermes and Athene,
    As shaft of compass,
Between them, trembled—
To the left is the place of fauns,
   sylva nympharum;
The low wood, moor-scrub,
   the doe, the young spotted deer,
   leap up through the broom-plants,
    as dry leaf amid yellow.
And by one cut of the hills,
   the great alley of Memnons.
Beyond, sea, crests seen over dune
Night sea churning shingle,
To the left, the alley of cypress.
     A boat came,
One man holding her sail,
Guiding her with oar caught over gunwale, saying:
"   There, in the forest of marble,
"   the stone trees—out of water—
"   the arbours of stone—
"   marble leaf, over leaf,
"   silver, steel over steel,
"   silver beaks rising and crossing,
"   prow set against prow,
"   stone, ply over ply,
"   the gilt beams flare of an evening"
Borso, Carmagnola, the men of craft, *i vitrei*,
Thither, at one time, time after time,
And the waters richer than glass,

Bronze gold, the blaze over the silver,
Dye-pots in the torch-light,
The flash of wave under prows,
And the silver beaks rising and crossing.
      Stone trees, white and rose-white in the darkness,
Cypress there by the towers,
       Drift under hulls in the night.

        "In the gloom the gold
Gathers the light about it." . . .

Now supine in burrow, half over-arched bramble,
One eye for the sea, through that peek-hole,
Gray light, with Athene.
Zothar and her elephants, the gold loin-cloth,
The sistrum, shaken, shaken,
       the cohorts of her dancers.
And Aletha, by bend of the shore,
      with her eyes seaward,
      and in her hands sea-wrack
Salt-bright with the foam.
Koré through the bright meadow,
      with green-gray dust in the grass:
"For this hour, brother of Circe."
Arm laid over my shoulder,
Saw the sun for three days, the sun fulvid,
As a lion lift over sand-plain;
        and that day,
And for three days, and none after,
Splendour, as the splendour of Hermes,
And shipped thence
      to the stone place,
Pale white, over water,
      known water,
And the white forest of marble, bent bough over bough,
The pleached arbour of stone,
Thither Borso, when they shot the barbed arrow at him,
And Carmagnola, between the two columns,
Sigismundo, after that wreck in Dalmatia.
     Sunset like the grasshopper flying.

Canto XXXVI

A lady asks me
         I speak in season
She seeks reason for an affect, wild often
That is so proud he hath Love for a name
Who denys it can hear the truth now
Wherefore I speak to the present knowers
Having no hope that low-hearted
         Can bring sight to such reason
Be there not natural demonstration
         I have no will to try proof-bringing
Or say where it hath birth
What is its virtu and power
Its being and every moving
Or delight whereby 'tis called "to love"
Or if man can show it to sight.

Where memory liveth,
         it takes its state
Formed like a diafan from light on shade
Which shadow cometh of Mars and remaineth
Created, having a name sensate,
Custom of the soul,
         will from the heart;
Cometh from a seen form which being understood
Taketh locus and remaining in the intellect possible
Wherein hath he neither weight nor still-standing,
Descendeth not by quality but shineth out
Himself his own effect unendingly
Not in delight but in the being aware
Nor can he leave his true likeness otherwhere.

He is not vertu but cometh of that perfection
Which is so postulate not by the reason
But 'tis felt, I say.
Beyond salvation, holdeth his judging force
Deeming intention to be reason's peer and mate,
Poor in discernment, being thus weakness' friend

Often his power cometh on death in the end,
Be it withstayed
        and so swinging counterweight.
Not that it were natural opposite, but only
Wry'd a bit from the perfect,
Let no man say love cometh from chance
Or hath not established lordship
Holding his power even though
        Memory hath him no more.

Cometh he to be
        when the will
From overplus
Twisteth out of natural measure,
Never adorned with rest Moveth he changing colour
Either to laugh or weep
Contorting the face with fear
        resteth but a little
Yet shall ye see of him That he is most often
With folk who deserve him
And his strange quality sets sighs to move
Willing man look into that forméd trace in his mind
And with such uneasiness as rouseth the flame.
Unskilled can not form his image,
He himself moveth not, drawing all to his stillness,
Neither turneth about to seek his delight
Nor yet to seek out proving
Be it so great or so small.

He draweth likeness and hue from like nature
So making pleasure more certain in seeming
Nor can stand hid in such nearness,
Beautys be darts tho' not savage
Skilled from such fear a man follows
Deserving spirit, that pierceth.
Nor is he known from his face
But taken in the white light that is allness
Toucheth his aim

Who heareth, seeth not form
But is led by its emanation.
Being divided, set out from colour,
Disjunct in mid darkness
Grazeth the light, one moving by other,
Being divided, divided from all falsity
Worthy of trust
From him alone mercy proceedeth.

Go, song, surely thou mayest
Whither it please thee
For so art thou ornate that thy reasons
Shall be praised from thy understanders,
With others hast thou no will to make company.

"Called thrones, balascio or topaze"
Eriugina was not understood in his time
"which explains, perhaps, the delay in condemning him"
And they went looking for Manicheans
And found, so far as I can make out, no Manicheans
So they dug for, and damned Scotus Eriugina
"Authority comes from right reason,
            never the other way on"
Hence the delay in condemning him
Aquinas head down in a vacuum,
            Aristotle which way in a vacuum?

Sacrum, sacrum, inluminatio coitu.
Lo Sordels si fo di Mantovana
            of a castle named Goito.
"Five castles!
"Five castles!"
            (king giv' him five castles)
"And what the hell do I know about dye-works?!"
His Holiness has written a letter:
            "CHARLES the Mangy of Anjou. . . .
. . way you treat your men is a scandal. . . ."
Dilectis miles familiaris . . . castra Montis Odorisii
Montis Sancti Silvestri pallete et pile . . .

In partibus Thetis. . . . vineland
                              land tilled
                              the land incult
                              pratis nemoribus pascuis
                              with legal jurisdiction
his heirs of both sexes,
   . . . sold the damn lot six weeks later,
Sordellus de Godio.
                    Quan ben m'albir e mon ric pensamen.

Canto XLV

With *Usura*

With usura hath no man a house of good stone
each block cut smooth and well fitting
that design might cover their face,
with usura
hath no man a painted paradise on his church wall
harpes et luthes
or where virgin receiveth message
and halo projects from incision,
with usura
seeth no man Gonzaga his heirs and his concubines
no picture is made to endure nor to live with
but it is made to sell and sell quickly
with usura, sin against nature,
is they bread ever more of stale rags
is they bread dry as paper,
with no mountain wheat, no strong flour
with usura the line grows thick
with usura is no clear demarcation
and no man can find site for his dwelling.
Stone cutter is kept from his stone
weaver is kept from his loom
WITH USURA
wool comes not to market
sheep bringeth no gain with usura

Usura is a murrain, usura
blunteth the needle in the maid's hand
and stoppeth the spinner's cunning. Pietro Lombardo
came not by usura
Duccio came not by usura
nor Pier della Francesca; Zuan Bellin' not by usura
nor was 'La Calunnia' painted.
Came not by usura Angelico; came not Ambrogio Praedis,
Came no church of cut stone signed: *Adamo me fecit.*
Not by usura St Trophime
Not by usura Saint Hilaire,
Usura rusteth the chisel
It rusteth the craft and the craftsman
It gnaweth the thread in the loom
None learneth to weave gold in her pattern;
Azure hath a canker by usura; cramoisi is unbroidered
Emerald findeth no Memling
Usura slayeth the child in the womb
It stayeth the young man's courting
It hath brought palsey to bed, lyeth
between the young bride and her bridegroom
    CONTRA NATURAM
They have brought whores for Eleusis
Corpses are set to banquet
at behest of usura.

Canto XLVII

Who even dead, yet hath his mind entire!
This sound came in the dark
First must thou go the road
    to hell
And to the bower of Ceres' daughter Proserpine,
Through overhanging dark, to see Tiresias,
Eyeless that was, a shade, that is in hell
So full of knowing that the beefy men know less than he,
Ere thou come to thy road's end.

          Knowledge the shade of a shade,
Yet must thou sail after knowledge
Knowing less than drugged beasts. *phtheggometha*
thasson
φθεγγώμεθα θᾶσσον
          The small lamps drift in the bay
And the sea's claw gathers them.
Neptunus drinks after neap-tide.
Tamuz! Tamuz!!
The red flame going seaward.
          By this gate art thou measured.
From the long boats they have set lights in the water,
The sea's claw gathers them outward.
Scilla's dogs snarl at the cliff's base,
The white teeth gnaw in under the crag,
But in the pale night the small lamps float seaward
                              Τυ Διώνα
                              TU DIONA

Καὶ Μοῖραι' ῎Αδονιν
Kai MOIRAI' ADONIN
The sea is streaked red with Adonis,
The lights flicker red in small jars.
Wheat shoots rise new by the altar,
          flower from the swift seed.
Two span, two span to a woman,
Beyond that she believes not. Nothing is of any importance.
To that is she bent, her intention
To that art thou called ever turning intention,
Whether by night the owl-call, whether by sap in shoot,
Never idle, by no means by no wiles intermittent
Moth is called over mountain
The bull runs blind on the sword, *naturans*
To the cave art thou called, Odysseus,
By Molü hast thou respite for a little,
By Molü art thou freed from the one bed
          that thou may'st return to another
The stars are not in her counting,
          To her they are but wandering holes.
Begin thy plowing
When the Pleiades go down to their rest,

Begin thy plowing
40 days are they under seabord,
Thus do in fields by seabord
And in valleys winding down toward the sea.
When the cranes fly high
        think of plowing.
By this gate art thou measured
Thy day is between a door and a door
Two oxen are yoked for plowing
Or six in the hill field
White bulk under olives, a score for drawing down stone,
Here the mules are gabled with slate on the hill road.
Thus was it in time.
And the small stars now fall from the olive branch,
Forked shadow falls dark on the terrace
More black than the floating martin
        that has no care for your presence,
His wing-print is black on the roof tiles
And the print is gone with his cry.
So light is thy weight on Tellus
Thy notch no deeper indented
Thy weight less than the shadow
Yet hast thou gnawed through the mountain,
        Scylla's white teeth less sharp.
Hast thou found a nest softer than cunnus
Or hast thou found better rest
Hast'ou a deeper planting, doth thy death year
Bring swifter shoot?
Hast thou entered more deeply the mountain?

The light has entered the cave. Io! Io!
The light has gone down into the cave,
Splendour on splendour!
By prong have I entered these hills:
That the grass grow from my body,
That I hear the roots speaking together,
The air is new on my leaf,
The forked boughs shake with the wind.
Is Zephyrus more light on the bough, Apeliota
more light on the almond branch?

By this door have I entered the hill.
Falleth,
Adonis falleth.
Fruit cometh after. The small lights drift out with the tide,
sea's claw has gathered them outward,
Four banners to every flower
The sea's claw draws the lamps outward.
Think thus of thy plowing
When the seven stars go down to their rest
Forty days for their rest, by seabord
And in valleys that wind down toward the sea
    Καὶ Μοῖραι' Ἄδονιν
    KAI MOIRAI' ADONIN
When the almond bough puts forth its flame,
When the new shoots are brought to the altar,
    Τυ Διώνα, Καὶ Μοῖραι
    TU DIONA, KAI MOIRAI
Καὶ Μοῖραι' Ἄδονιν
KAI MOIRAI' ADONIN
    that hath the gift of healing,
that hath the power over wild beasts.

Canto XLIX

For the seven lakes, and by no man these verses:
Rain; empty river; a voyage,
Fire from frozen cloud, heavy rain in the twilight
Under the cabin roof was one lantern.
The reeds are heavy; bent;
and the bamboos speak as if weeping.

Autumn moon; hills rise about lakes
against sunset
Evening is like a curtain of cloud,
a blurr above ripples; and through it
sharp long spikes of the cinnamon,
a cold tune amid reeds.
Behind hill the monk's bell

borne on the wind.
Sail passed here in April; may return in October
Boat fades in silver; slowly;
Sun blaze alone on the river.

Where wine flag catches the sunset
Sparse chimneys smoke in the cross light

Comes then snow scur on the river
And a world is covered with jade
Small boat floats like a lanthorn,
The flowing water clots as with cold. And at San Yin
they are a people of leisure.
Wild geese swoop to the sand-bar,
Clouds gather about the hole of the window
Broad water; geese line out with the autumn
Rooks clatter over the fishermen's lanthorns,
A light moves on the north sky line;
where the young boys prod stones for shrimp.
In seventeen hundred came Tsing to these hill lakes.
A light moves on the south sky line.

State by creating riches shd. thereby get into debt?
This is infamy; this is Geryon.
This canal goes still to TenShi
though the old king built it for pleasure

K E I   M E N   R A N   K E I
K I U   M A N   M A N   K E I
JITSU   GETSU   K O   KWA
T A N   FUKU   T A N   K A I

Sun up; work
sundown; to rest
dig well and drink of the water
dig field; eat of the grain
Imperial power is? and to us what is it?

The fourth; the dimension of stillness.
And the power over wild beasts.

Canto LXXXI

Zeus lies in Ceres' bosom
Taishan is attended of loves
   under Cythera, before sunrise
and he said: Hay aquí mucho catolicismo—(sounded
 catoli*th*ismo)
   y muy poco reliHion"
and he said: Yo creo que los reyes desparecen"
That was Padre José Elizondo
    in 1906 and in 1917
or about 1917
   and Dolores said: Come pan, niño," eat bread, me
   lad
Sargent had painted her
    before he descended
(i.e. if he descended
   but in those days he did thumb sketches,
impressions of the Velázquez in the Museo del Prado
and books cost a peseta,
    brass candlesticks in proportion,
hot wind came from the marshes
  and death-chill from the mountains.
And later Bowers wrote: "but such hatred,
 I had never conceived such"
and the London reds wouldn't show up, his friends
   (i.e. friends of Franco
working in London) and in Alcázar
forty years gone, they said: go back to the station to eat
you can sleep here for a peseta"
   goat bells tinkled all night
   and the hostess grinned: Eso es luto, *haw!*
mi marido es muerto
   (it is mourning, my husband is dead)
when she gave me paper to write on
with a black border half an inch or more deep,
  say 5/8ths, of the locanda
"We call *all* foreigners frenchies"
and the egg broke in Cabranez' pocket,
   thus making history. Basil says

they beat drums for three days
till all the drumheads were busted
      (simple village fiesta)
and as for his life in the Canaries . . .
Possum observed that the local   folk dance
was danced by the same dancers in divers localities
      in political welcome . . .
the technique of demonstration
      Cole studied that (not G.D.H., Horace)
"You will find" said old André Spire,
that every man on that board (Crédit Agricole)
has a brother-in-law
      "You the one, I the few"
      said John Adams
speaking of fears in the abstract
    to his volatile friend Mr Jefferson
(to break the pentameter, that was the first heave)
or as Jo Bard says: they never speak to each other,
if it is baker and concierge visibly
      it is La Rouchefoucauld and de Maintenon audibly.
"Te cavero le budella"
        "La corata a te"
In less than a geological epoch
      said Henry Mencken
"Some cook, some do not cook
    some things cannot be altered"
Ἰυγξ. . . . . ’εμὸν ποτί δῶμα τὸν ἄνδρα
What counts is the cultural level,
    thank Benin for this table ex packing box
      "doan yu tell no one I made it"
      from a mask fine as any in Frankfurt
"It'll get you offn th' groun"
      Light as the branch of Kuanon
And at first disappointed with shoddy
the bare ram-shackle quais, but then saw the
high buggy wheels
      and was reconciled,
George Santayana arriving in the port of Boston
and kept to the end of his life that faint *thethear*
of the Spaniard

as a grace quasi imperceptible
as did Muss the *v* for *u* of Romagna
and said the grief was a full act
      repeated for each new condoleress
working up to a climax.
and George Horace said he wd/ "get Beveridge" (Senator)
Beveridge wouldn't talk and he wouldn't write for the papers
but George got him by campin' in his hotel
and assailin' him at lunch breakfast an' dinner
      three articles
and my ole man went on hoein' corn
    while George was a-tellin' him,
come across a vacant lot
      where you'd occasionally see a wild rabbit
or mebbe only a loose one
    AOI!
    a leaf in the current
                at my grates no Althea

Libretto

Yet
Ere the season died a-cold
Borne upon a zephyr's shoulder
I rose through the aureate sky
        Lawes and Jenkyns guard thy rest
        Dolmetsch ever be thy guest,
Has he tempered the viol's wood
To enforce   both the grave   and the acute?
Has he curved us the bowl of the lute?
        Lawes and Jenkyns guard thy rest
        Dolmetsch ever be thy guest
Hast 'ou fashioned so airy a mood
    To draw up leaf from the root?
Hast 'ou found   a cloud   so light
    As seemed neither mist nor shade?

        Then resolve me, tell me aright
        If Waller sang or Dowland played.

Your eyen two wol sleye me sodenly
I may the beauté of hem nat susteyne

And for 180 years almost nothing.

Ed ascoltando al leggier mormorio
     there came new subtlety of eyes into my tent,
whether of spirit or hypostasis,
     but what the blindfold hides
or at carneval
                              nor any pair showed anger
     Saw but the eyes and stance between the eyes,
colour, diastasis,
     careless or unaware it had not the
   whole tent's room
nor was place for the full Εἰδώς
interpass, penetrate
     casting but shade beyond the other lights
          sky's clear
          night's sea
          green of the mountain pool
          shone from the unmasked eyes in half-mask's space.
What thou lovest well remains,
                         the rest is dross
What thou lov'st well shall not be reft from thee
What thou lov'st well is thy true heritage
Whose world, or mine or theirs
                         or is it of none?
First came the seen, then thus the palpable
     Elysium, though it were in the halls of hell,
What thou lovest well is thy true heritage

The ant's a centaur in his dragon world.
Pull down thy vanity, it is not man
Made courage, or made order, or made grace,
     Pull down thy vanity, I say pull down.
Learn of the green world what can be thy place
In scaled invention or true artistry,

Pull down thy vanity,
              Paquin pull down!
The green casque has outdone your elegance.

"Master thyself, then others shall thee beare"
     Pull down thy vanity
Thou art a beaten dog beneath the hail,
A swollen magpie in a fitful sun,
Half black half white
Nor knowst'ou wing from tail
Pull down thy vanity
          How mean thy hates
Fostered in falsity,
          Pull down thy vanity,
Rathe to destroy, niggard in charity,
Pull down thy vanity,
        I say pull down.

But to have done instead of not doing
        this is not vanity
To have, with decency, knocked
That a Blunt should open
      To have gathered from the air a live tradition
or from a fine old eye the unconquered flame
This is not vanity.
    Here error is all in the not done,
all in the diffidence that faltered,

Canto XC

Animus humanus amor non est,
sed ab ipso amor procedit, et
ideo seipso non diligit, sed amore
        qui seipso procedit.

"From the colour the nature
     & by the nature the sign!"
Beatific spirits welding together
     as in one ash-tree in Ygdrasail.

Baucis, Philemon.
Castalia is the name of that fount in the hill's fold,
the sea below,
narrow beach.
Templum aedificans, not yet marble,
"Amphion!"

And from the San Ku

孤

to the room in Poitiers where one can stand
casting no shadow,
That is Sagetrieb,
that is tradition.
Builders had kept the proportion,
did Jacques de Molay
know these proportions?
and was Erigena ours?
Moon's barge over milk-blue water
Kuthera δεινά
Kuthera sempiterna
Ubi amor, ibi oculus.
Vae qui cogitatis inutile.
quam in nobis similitudine divinae
reperetur imago.
"Mother Earth in thy lap"
said Randolph
ἠγάπησεν πολύ
liberavit masnatos.
Castalia like the moonlight
and the waves rise and fall,
Evita, beer-halls, semina motuum,
to parched grass, now is rain
not arrogant from habit,
but furious from perception,
Sibylla,
from under the rubble heap

m'elevasti

from the dulled edge beyond pain,

m'elevasti

out of Erebus, the deep-lying

from the wind under the earth,

m'elevasti

from the dulled air and the dust,

m'elevasti

by the great flight,

m'elevasti,

Isis Kuanon

from the cusp of the moon,

m'elevasti

the viper stirs in the dust,

the blue serpent

glides from the rock pool

And they take lights now down to the water

the lamps float from the rowers

the sea's claw drawing them outward.

"De fondo" said Juan Ramon,

like a mermaid, upward,

but the light perpendicular, upward

and to Castalia,

water jets from the rock

and in the flat pool as Arethusa's

a hush in papyri.

Grove hath its altar

under elms, in that temple, in silence

a lone nymph by the pool.

Wei and Han rushing together

two rivers together

bright fish and flotsam

torn bough in the flood

and the waters clear with the flowing

Out of heaviness where no mind moves at all

"birds for the mind" said Richardus,

"beasts as to body, for know-how"

Gaio! Gaio!

To Zeus with the six seraphs before him

The architect from the painter,

                the stone under elm
Taking form now,
            the rilievi,
        the curled stone at the marge
Faunus, sirenes,
        the stone taking form in the air
        ac ferae,
                    cervi,
                        the great cats approaching.
Pardus, leopardi, Bagheera
        drawn hither from woodland,
woodland ἐπὶ χθονί
            the trees rise
        and there is a wide sward between them
οἱ χθόνιοι myrrh and olibanum on the altar stone
giving perfume,
                and where was nothing
now is furry assemblage
            and in the boughs now are voices
grey wing, black wing, black wing shot with crimson
and the umbrella pines
                    as in Palatine,
as in pineta. χελιδών, χελιδών
For the procession of Corpus
            come now banners
comes flute tone
                οἱ χθόνιοι
    to new forest,
            thick smoke, purple, rising
bright flame now on the altar
            the crystal funnel of air
out of Erebus, the delivered,
            Tyro, Alcmene, free now, ascending
e i cavalieri,
            ascending,
no shades more,
                lights among them, enkindled,
and the dark shade of courage
                    ʾΗλέκτρα
        bowed still with the wrongs of Aegisthus.

Trees die & the dream remains
   Not love but that love flows from it
   ex animo
   & cannot ergo delight in itself
   but only in the love flowing from it.
UBI AMOR IBI OCULUS EST.

Canto CXVI

Came Neptunus
   his mind leaping
    like dolphins,
These concepts the human mind has attained.
To make Cosmos—
To achieve the possible—
Muss., wrecked for an error,
But the record
   the palimpsest—
a little light
   in great darkness—
cuniculi—
An old "crank" dead in Virginia.
Unprepared young burdened with records,
The vision of the Madonna
   above the cigar butts
    and over the portal.
"Have made a mass of laws"
   (mucchio di leggi)
Litterae nihil sanantes
   Justinian's,
a tangle of works unfinished.
I have brought the great ball of crystal;
   who can lift it?
Can you enter the great acorn of light?
   But the beauty is not the madness
Tho' my errors and wrecks lie about me.
And I am not a demigod,
I cannot make it cohere.

If love be not in the house there is nothing.
The voice of famine unheard.
How came beauty against this blackness,
Twice beauty under the elms—
        To be saved by squirrels and bluejays?
          "plus j'aime le chien"
Ariadne.
     Disney against the metaphysicals,
and Laforgue more than they thought in him,
Spire thanked me in proposito
And I have learned more from Jules
              (Jules Laforgue) since then
deeps in him,
     and Linnaeus.
           chi crescerà i nostri—
but about that terzo
     third heaven,
        that Venere,
again is all "paradiso"
   a nice quiet paradise
        over the shambles,
and some climbing
        before the take-off,
to "see again,"
the verb is "see," not "walk on"
i.e. it coheres all right
        even if my notes do not cohere.
Many errors,
     a little rightness,
to excuse his hell
        and my paradiso.
And as to why they go wrong,
       thinking of rightness
And as to who will copy this palimpsest?
     al poco giorno
          ed al gran cerchio d'ombra
But to affirm the gold thread in the pattern
           (Torcello)
al Vicolo d'oro
     (Tigullio).

To confess wrong without losing rightness:
Charity I have had sometimes,
      I cannot make it flow thru.
A little light, like a rushlight
        to lead back to splendour.

from
Notes for Canto CXVII et seq.

For the blue flash and the moments
          benedetta
the young for the old
       that is tragedy
And for one beautiful day there was peace.
     Brancusi's bird
         in the hollow of pine trunks
or when the snow was like sea foam
     Twilit sky leaded with elm boughs.
Under the Rupe Tarpeia
     weep out your jealousies—
To make a church
     or an altar to Zagreus   Ζαγρεύς
Son of Semele   Σεμέλη
Without jealousy
     like the double arch of a window
Or some great colonnade.

from
The Classic Anthology as Defined by Confucius

She:

> Curl-grass, curl-grass,
> to pick it, to pluck it
> to put in a bucket
> never a basket load
Here on Chou road, but a man in my mind!
> Put it down here by the road.

He:

> Pass, pass
> up over the pass,
a horse on a mountain road!
A winded horse on a high road,
give me a drink to lighten the load.
As the cup is gilt, love is spilt.
> Pain lasteth long.

Black horses, yellow with sweat,
are not come to the ridge-top yet.
> Drink deep of the rhino horn
But leave not love too long forlorn.

Tho' driver stumble and horses drop,
we come not yet to the stony top.
Let the foundered team keep on,
How should I leave my love alone!

———————

Pine boat a-shift
on drift of tide,
for flame in the ear, sleep riven,
driven; rift of the heart in dark
no wine will clear,
nor have I will to playe.

Mind that 's no mirror to gulp down all 's seen,
brothers I have, on whom I dare not lean,
angered to hear a fact, ready to scold.

My heart no turning-stone, mat to be rolled,
right being right, not whim nor matter of count,
true as a tree on mount.

Mob's hate, chance evils many, gone through,
aimed barbs not few;
at bite of the jest in heart
start up as to beat my breast.

O'ersoaring sun, moon malleable
alternately
lifting a-sky to wane;
sorrow about the heart like an unwashed shirt, I
clutch here at words,
having no force to fly.

Alba

Creeper grows over thorn,
bracken wilds over waste, he is gone,
Gone, I am alone.

Creeper overgrows thorn,
bracken spreads over the grave, he is gone,
Gone, I am alone.

The horn pillow is white like rice,
the silk shroud gleams as if with tatters of fire.
In the sunrise I am alone.

A summer's day,
winter's night, a hundred years
and we come to one house together.

Winter's day, summer's night,
each night as winter night,
each day long as of summer,
　　　　　　　　but at last to the one same house.

"Long wind, the dawn wind"

Falcon gone to the gloom
and the long wind of the forest
Forgetting the children I bore you,
                    North, North?

Thick oak on mount, six grafted pears in the low,
                    Whither, whither
                    North, north
                    forgetful so?

Plum trees of the mountain,
Peach blossoms of the plain
                    Whither, whither?
I am drunk with the pain.

———————

Vitex in swamp ground,
branched loveliness,
would I could share that shrub's unconsciousness.

Vitex negundo, casting thy flowers in air,
thy joy to be, and have no family care.

Vitex in low marsh ground,
thy small fruit grows
in tenderness,
having no heavy house.

Choruses from
Women of Trakis

Str. 1
(accom-
paniment
strings,
mainly
cellos):

PHOEBUS, Phoebus, ere thou slay
and lay flaked Night upon her blazing pyre,
Say, ere the last star-shimmer is run:
Where lies Alkmene's son, apart from me?
Aye, thou art keen, as is the lightning blaze,
Land way, sea ways,
   in these some slit hath he
found to escape thy scrutiny?

Ant. 1

DAYSAIR is left alone,
    so sorry a bird,
For whom, afore, so many suitors tried.
And shall I ask what thing is heart's desire,
Or how love fall to sleep with tearless eye,
So worn by fear away, of dangerous road,
A manless bride to mourn in vacant room,
Expecting ever the worse,
    of dooms to come?

Str. 2

NORTH WIND or South, so bloweth tireless
wave over wave to flood.
Cretan of Cadmus' blood, Orcus' shafts err not.
What home hast 'ou now,
    an some God stir not?

Ant. 2

PARDON if I reprove thee, Lady,
To save thee false hopes delayed.
Thinkst thou that man who dies,
Shall from King Chronos take
    unvaried happiness?
Nor yet's all pain.

(drums,
quietly
added
to music)

The shifty Night delays not,
Nor fates of men, nor yet rich goods and spoil.
Be swift to enjoy, what thou art swift to lose.

Let not the Queen choose despair.
Hath Zeus no eye (who saith it?)
    watching his progeny?

———————

(de-
claimed):
Str. 1:
    TORN between griefs, which grief shall I lament,
which first? Which last, in heavy argument?
One wretchedness to me in double load.

Ant. 1
    DEATH'S in the house,
      and death comes by the road.

(sung)
Str. 2
    THAT WIND might bear away my grief and me,
Sprung from the hearth-stone, let it bear me away.
God's Son is dead,
    that was so brave and strong,
And I am craven to behold such death
    Swift on the eye,
Pain hard to uproot,
    and this so vast
A splendour of ruin.

Ant. 2
    THAT NOW is here.
As Progne shrill upon the weeping air,
'tis no great sound.
    These strangers lift him home,
with shuffling feet, and love that keeps them still.
The great weight silent
    for no man can say
If sleep but feign
    or Death reign instantly.

ELINOR WYLIE

(1885–1928)

Beauty

Say not of Beauty she is good,
Or aught but beautiful,
Or sleek to doves' wings of the wood
Her wild wings of a gull.

Call her not wicked; that word's touch
Consumes her like a curse;
But love her not too much, too much,
For that is even worse.

O, she is neither good nor bad,
But innocent and wild!
Enshrine her and she dies, who had
The hard heart of a child.

Wild Peaches

I

When the world turns completely upside down
You say we'll emigrate to the Eastern Shore
Aboard a river-boat from Baltimore;
We'll live among wild peach trees, miles from town.
You'll wear a coonskin cap, and I a gown
Homespun, dyed butternut's dark gold color.
Lost, like your lotus-eating ancestor,
We'll swim in milk and honey till we drown.

The winter will be short, the summer long,
The autumn amber-hued, sunny and hot,
Tasting of cider and of scuppernong;

All seasons sweet, but autumn best of all.
The squirrels in their silver fur will fall
Like falling leaves, like fruit, before your shot.

2

The autumn frosts will lie upon the grass
Like bloom on grapes of purple-brown and gold.
The misted early mornings will be cold;
The little puddles will be roofed with glass.
The sun, which burns from copper into brass,
Melts these at noon, and makes the boys unfold
Their knitted mufflers; full as they can hold,
Fat pockets dribble chestnuts as they pass.

Peaches grow wild, and pigs can live in clover;
A barrel of salted herrings lasts a year;
The spring begins before the winter's over.
By February you may find the skins
Of garter snakes and water moccasins
Dwindled and harsh, dead-white and cloudy-clear.

3

When April pours the colors of a shell
Upon the hills, when every little creek
Is shot with silver from the Chesapeake
In shoals new-minted by the ocean swell,
When strawberries go begging, and the sleek
Blue plums lie open to the blackbird's beak,
We shall live well—we shall live very well.

The months between the cherries and the peaches
Are brimming cornucopias which spill
Fruits red and purple, somber-bloomed and black;
Then, down rich fields and frosty river beaches
We'll trample bright persimmons, while we kill
Bronze partridge, speckled quail, and canvasback.

4

Down to the Puritan marrow of my bones
There's something in this richness that I hate.
I love the look, austere, immaculate,
Of landscapes drawn in pearly monotones.
There's something in my very blood that owns
Bare hills, cold silver on a sky of slate,
A thread of water, churned to milky spate
Streaming through slanted pastures fenced with stones.

I love those skies, thin blue or snowy gray,
Those fields sparse-planted, rendering meager sheaves;
That spring, briefer than apple-blossom's breath,
Summer, so much too beautiful to stay,
Swift autumn, like a bonfire of leaves,
And sleepy winter, like the sleep of death.

August

Why should this Negro insolently stride
Down the red noonday on such noiseless feet?
Piled in his barrow, tawnier than wheat,
Lie heaps of smoldering daisies, somber-eyed,
Their copper petals shriveled up with pride,
Hot with a superfluity of heat,
Like a great brazier borne along the street
By captive leopards, black and burning pied.

Are there no water-lilies, smooth as cream,
With long stems dripping crystal? Are there none
Like those white lilies, luminous and cool,
Plucked from some hemlock-darkened northern stream
By fair-haired swimmers, diving where the sun
Scarce warms the surface of the deepest pool?

Village Mystery

The woman in the pointed hood
And cloak blue-gray like a pigeon's wing,
Whose orchard climbs to the balsam-wood,
Has done a cruel thing.

To her back door-step came a ghost,
A girl who had been ten years dead,
She stood by the granite hitching-post
And begged for a piece of bread.

Now why should I, who walk alone,
Who am ironical and proud,
Turn, when a woman casts a stone
At a beggar in a shroud?

I saw the dead girl cringe and whine,
And cower in the weeping air—
But, oh, she was no kin of mine,
And so I did not care!

Incantation

A white well
In a black cave;
A bright shell
In a dark wave.

A white rose
Black brambles hood;
Smooth bright snows
In a dark wood.

A flung white glove
In a dark fight;
A white dove
On a wild black night.

A white door
In a dark lane;
A bright core
To bitter black pain.

A white hand
Waved from dark walls;
In a burnt black land
Bright waterfalls.

A bright spark
Where black ashes are;
In the smothering dark
One white star.

Sonnet

You are the faintest freckles on the hide
Of fawns; the hoofprint stamped into the slope
Of slithering glaciers by the antelope;
The silk upon the mushroom's under side
Constricts you, and your eyelashes are wide
In pools uptilted on the hills; you grope
For swings of water twisted to a rope
Over a ledge where amber pebbles glide.
Shelley perceived you on the Caucasus;
Blake prisoned you in glassy grains of sand
And Keats in goblin jars from Samarcand;
Poor Coleridge found you in a poppy-seed;
But you escape the clutching most of us,
Shaped like a ghost, and imminent with speed.

Let No Charitable Hope

Now let no charitable hope
Confuse my mind with images
Of eagle and of antelope:
I am in nature none of these.

I was, being human, born alone;
I am, being woman, hard beset;
I live by squeezing from a stone
The little nourishment I get.

In masks outrageous and austere
The years go by in single file;
But none has merited my fear,
And none has quite escaped my smile.

Preference

These to me are beautiful people;
Thick hair sliding in a ripple;
A tall throat, round as a column;
A mournful mouth, small and solemn,
Having to confound the mourner
Irony in either corner;
The limbs fine, narrow and strong;
Like the wind they walk along,
Like the whirlwind, bad to follow;
The cheekbones high, the cheeks hollow,
The eyes large and wide apart.
They carry a dagger in the heart
So keen and clean it never rankles. . . .
They wear small bones in wrists and ankles.

Self-Portrait

A lens of crystal whose transparence calms
Queer stars to clarity, and disentangles
Fox-fires to form austere refracted angles:
A texture polished on the horny palms
Of vast equivocal creatures, beast or human:
A flint, a substance finer-grained than snow,
Graved with the Graces in intaglio
To set sarcastic sigil on the woman.

This for the mind, and for the little rest
A hollow scooped to blackness in the breast,
The simulacrum of a cloud, a feather:
Instead of stone, instead of sculptured strength,
This soul, this vanity, blown hither and thither
By trivial breath, over the whole world's length.

Now That Your Eyes Are Shut

Now that your eyes are shut
Not even a dusty butterfly may brush them;
My flickering knife has cut
Life from sonorous lion throats to hush them.

If pigeons croon too loud
Or lambs bleat proudly, they must come to slaughter,
And I command each cloud
To be precise in spilling silent water.

Let light forbear those lids;
I have forbidden the feathery ash to smutch them;
The spider thread that thrids
The gray-plumed grass has not my leave to touch them.

My casual ghost may slip,
Issuing tiptoe, from the pure inhuman;
The tissues of my lip
Will bruise your eyelids, while I am a woman.

Confession of Faith

I lack the braver mind
That dares to find
The lover friend, and kind.

I fear him to the bone;
I lie alone
By the beloved one,

And, breathless for suspense,
Erect defense
Against love's violence

Whose silences portend
A bloody end
For lover never friend.

But, in default of faith,
In futile breath,
I dream no ill of Death.

Parting Gift

I cannot give you the Metropolitan Tower;
I cannot give you heaven;
Nor the nine Visigoth crowns in the Cluny Museum;
Nor happiness, even.
But I can give you a very small purse
Made out of field-mouse skin,
With a painted picture of the universe
And seven blue tears therein.

I cannot give you the island of Capri;
I cannot give you beauty;
Nor bake you marvelous crusty cherry pies
With love and duty.
But I can give you a very little locket
Made out of wildcat hide:
Put it into your left-hand pocket
And never look inside.

Green Hair

I know you wonder why I wear
The hat which I have called Green Hair
And why I cover up my own
Which has a tawny chestnut tone
Warm, when all its lights are lit,
As a swarm of bees with the sun on it.
You say bronze hair is prettier
Than this strange green of feathery fur;
But there's a charm in this strange green
Which is so nearly blue; I've seen
A comb of coral set with pearls
Drawn through lengths of such green curls
In the green gloom of a chilly cave
Down, far down in a hollow wave;
And under ancient forest trees
Long green tresses such as these
Shadow like a falling veil
Shy secret faces, dusky pale;
And I have seen green locks like those
Deep in a glacier, under snows.
I have seen such green hair tossed
From the brows of a creature wandering lost
On the other side of a waning moon,
And in the golden sun at noon
I have seen young April plait
Flowers in showery hair like that,
And wring the rain from it in drops,
And spread it to dry on green hill-tops.
Now do you wonder that I wear
The hat which I have called Green Hair?
Thus with witchcraft I am crowned
And wrapped in marvels round and round;
There's sorcery in it, and surprise;
Believe your own dark-amber eyes
When mine of hazel look at you
Turned to incredible turquoise blue.

Ejaculation

In this short interval to tear
The living words from dying air,
To pull them to me, quick and brave
As swordfish from a silver wave,
To drag them dripping, cold and salt
To suffocation in this vault
The which a lid of vapour shuts,
To shake them down like hazel-nuts
Or golden acorns from an oak
Whose twigs are flame above the smoke,
To snatch them suddenly from dust
Like apples flavoured with the frost
Of mountain valleys marble-cupped,
To leap to them and interrupt
Their flight that cleaves the atmosphere
As white and arrowy troops of deer
Divide the forest,—make my words
Like feathers torn from living birds!

H.D.

(1886–1961)

Orchard

I saw the first pear
as it fell—
the honey-seeking, golden-banded,
the yellow swarm
was not more fleet than I,
(spare us from loveliness)
and I fell prostrate
crying:
you have flayed us
with your blossoms,
spare us the beauty
of fruit-trees.

The honey-seeking
paused not,
the air thundered their song,
and I alone was prostrate.

O rough-hewn
god of the orchard,
I bring you an offering—
do you, alone unbeautiful,
son of the god,
spare us from loveliness:

these fallen hazel-nuts,
stripped late of their green sheaths,
grapes, red-purple,
their berries
dripping with wine,
pomegranates already broken,
and shrunken figs
and quinces untouched,
I bring you as offering.

Oread

Whirl up, sea—
whirl your pointed pines,
splash your great pines
on our rocks,
hurl your green over us,
cover us with your pools of fir.

Sea Rose

Rose, harsh rose,
marred and with stint of petals,
meagre flower, thin,
sparse of leaf,

more precious
than a wet rose
single on a stem—
you are caught in the drift.

Stunted, with small leaf,
you are flung on the sand,
you are lifted
in the crisp sand
that drives in the wind.

Can the spice-rose
drip such acrid fragrance
hardened in a leaf?

Mid-Day

The light beats upon me.
I am startled—
a split leaf crackles on the paved floor—
I am anguished—defeated.

A slight wind shakes the seed-pods—
my thoughts are spent
as the black seeds.
My thoughts tear me,
I dread their fever.
I am scattered in its whirl.
I am scattered like
the hot shrivelled seeds.

The shrivelled seeds
are spilt on the path—
the grass bends with dust,
the grape slips
under its crackled leaf:
yet far beyond the spent seed-pods,
and the blackened stalks of mint,
the poplar is bright on the hill,
the poplar spreads out,
deep-rooted among trees.

O poplar, you are great
among the hill-stones,
while I perish on the path
among the crevices of the rocks.

Evening

The light passes
from ridge to ridge,
from flower to flower—
the hypaticas, wide-spread
under the light
grow faint—
the petals reach inward,
the blue tips bend
toward the bluer heart
and the flowers are lost.

The cornel-buds are still white,
but shadows dart
from the cornel-roots—
black creeps from root to root,
each leaf
cuts another leaf on the grass,
shadow seeks shadow,
then both leaf
and leaf-shadow are lost.

Garden

I

You are clear
O rose, cut in rock,
hard as the descent of hail.

I could scrape the colour
from the petals
like spilt dye from a rock.

If I could break you
I could break a tree.

If I could stir
I could break a tree—
I could break you.

II

O wind, rend open the heat,
cut apart the heat,
rend it to tatters.

Fruit cannot drop
through this thick air—
fruit cannot fall into heat

that presses up and blunts
the points of pears
and rounds the grapes.

Cut the heat—
plough through it,
turning it on either side
of your path.

Sea Violet

The white violet
is scented on its stalk,
the sea-violet
fragile as agate,
lies fronting all the wind
among the torn shells
on the sand-bank.

The greater blue violets
flutter on the hill,
but who would change for these
who would change for these
one root of the white sort?

Violet
your grasp is frail
on the edge of the sand-hill,
but you catch the light—
frost, a star edges with its fire.

Sea Poppies

Amber husk
fluted with gold,
fruit on the sand
marked with a rich grain,

treasure
spilled near the shrub-pines
to bleach on the boulders:

your stalk has caught root
among wet pebbles
and drift flung by the sea
and grated shells
and split conch-shells.

Beautiful, wide-spread,
fire upon leaf,
what meadow yields
so fragrant a leaf
as your bright leaf?

Storm

You crash over the trees,
you crack the live branch—
the branch is white,
the green crushed,
each leaf is rent like split wood.

You burden the trees
with black drops,
you swirl and crash—
you have broken off a weighted leaf
in the wind,
it is hurled out,
whirls up and sinks,
a green stone.

Sea Iris

I

Weed, moss-weed,
root tangled in sand,
sea-iris, brittle flower,
one petal like a shell
is broken,
and you print a shadow
like a thin twig.

Fortunate one,
scented and stinging,
rigid myrrh-bud,
camphor-flower,
sweet and salt—you are wind
in our nostrils.

II

Do the murex-fishers
drench you as they pass?
Do your roots drag up colour
from the sand?
Have they slipped gold under you—
rivets of gold?

Band of iris-flowers
above the waves,
you are painted blue,
painted like a fresh prow
stained among the salt weeds.

The Pool

Are you alive?
I touch you.
You quiver like a sea-fish.
I cover you with my net.
What are you—banded one?

Hippolytus Temporizes

I worship the greatest first—
(it were sweet, the couch,
the brighter ripple of cloth
over the dipped fleece;
the thought: her bones
under the flesh are white
as sand which along a beach
covers but keeps the print
of the crescent shapes beneath:
I thought:
between cloth and fleece,
so her body lies.)

I worship first, the great—
(ah, sweet, your eyes—
what God, invoked in Crete,
gave them the gift to part
as the Sidonian myrtle-flower
suddenly, wide and swart,
then swiftly,
the eye-lids having provoked our hearts—
as suddenly beat and close.)

I worship the feet, flawless,
that haunt the hills—
(ah, sweet, dare I think,
beneath fetter of golden clasp,
of the rhythm, the fall and rise

of yours, carven, slight
beneath straps of gold that keep
their slender beauty caught,
like wings and bodies
of trapped birds.)

I worship the greatest first—
(suddenly into my brain—
the flash of sun on the snow,
the fringe of light and the drift,
the crest and the hill-shadow—
ah, surely now I forget,
ah splendour, my goddess turns:
or was it the sudden heat,
beneath quivering of molten flesh,
of veins, purple as violets?)

Fragment 113

"Neither honey nor bee for me."
—SAPPHO.

Not honey,
not the plunder of the bee
from meadow or sand-flower
or mountain bush;
from winter-flower or shoot
born of the later heat:
not honey, not the sweet
stain on the lips and teeth:
not honey, not the deep
plunge of soft belly
and the clinging of the gold-edged
pollen-dusted feet;

though rapture blind my eyes,
and hunger crisp
dark and inert my mouth,
not honey, not the south,

not the tall stalk
of red twin-lilies,
nor light branch of fruit tree
caught in flexible light branch;

not honey, not the south;
ah flower of purple iris,
flower of white,
or of the iris, withering the grass—
for fleck of the sun's fire,
gathers such heat and power,
that shadow-print is light,
cast through the petals
of the yellow iris flower;

not iris—old desire—old passion—
old forgetfulness—old pain—
not this, nor any flower,
but if you turn again,
seek strength of arm and throat,
touch as the god;
neglect the lyre-note;
knowing that you shall feel,
about the frame,
no trembling of the string
but heat, more passionate
of bone and the white shell
and fiery tempered steel.

At Baia

I should have thought
in a dream you would have brought
some lovely, perilous thing,
orchids piled in a great sheath,
as who would say (in a dream)
I send you this,
who left the blue veins
of your throat unkissed.

Why was it that your hands
(that never took mine)
your hands that I could see
drift over the orchid heads
so carefully,
your hands, so fragile, sure to lift
so gently, the fragile flower stuff—
ah, ah, how was it

You never sent (in a dream)
the very form, the very scent,
not heavy, not sensuous,
but perilous—perilous—
of orchids, piled in a great sheath,
and folded underneath on a bright scroll
some word:

Flower sent to flower;
for white hands, the lesser white,
less lovely of flower leaf,

or

Lover to lover, no kiss,
no touch, but forever and ever this.

Song

You are as gold
as the half-ripe grain
that merges to gold again,
as white as the white rain
that beats through
the half-opened flowers
of the great flower tufts
thick on the black limbs
of an Illyrian apple bough.

Can honey distill such fragrance
as your bright hair—
for your face is as fair as rain,
yet as rain that lies clear
on white honey-comb,
lends radiance to the white wax,
so your hair on your brow
casts light for a shadow.

The Whole White World

The whole white world is ours,
and the world, purple with rose-bays,
bays, bush on bush,
group, thicket, hedge and tree,
dark islands in a sea
of grey-green olive or wild white-olive,
cut with the sudden cypress shafts,
in clusters, two or three,
or with one slender, single cypress-tree.

Slid from the hill,
as crumbling snow-peaks slide,
citron on citron fill
the valley, and delight
waits till our spirits tire
of forest, grove and bush
and purple flower of the laurel-tree.

Yet not one wearies,
joined is each to each
in happiness complete
with bush and flower:
ours is the wind-breath
at the hot noon-hour,
ours is the bee's soft belly
and the blush of the rose-petal,
lifted, of the flower.

Egypt

(To E. A. Poe)

Egypt had cheated us,
for Egypt took
through guile and craft
our treasure and our hope,
Egypt had maimed us,
offered dream for life,
an opiate for a kiss,
and death for both.

White poison flower we loved
and the black spike
of an ungarnered bush—
(a spice—or without taste—
we wondered—then we asked
others to take and sip
and watched their death)
Egypt we loved, though hate
should have withheld our touch.

Egypt had given us knowledge,
and we took, blindly,
through want of heart,
what Egypt brought;
knowing all poison,
what was that or this,
more or less perilous,
than this or that.

We pray you, Egypt,
by what perverse fate,
has poison brought with knowledge,
given us this—
not days of trance,
shadow, fore-doom of death,
but passionate grave thought,
belief enhanced,
ritual returned and magic;

Even in the uttermost black pit
of the forbidden knowledge,
wisdom's glance,
the grey eyes following
in the mid-most desert—
great shaft of rose,
fire shed across our path,
upon the face grown grey, a light,
Hellas re-born from death.

Helen

All Greece hates
the still eyes in the white face,
the lustre as of olives
where she stands,
and the white hands.

All Greece reviles
the wan face when she smiles,
hating it deeper still
when it grows wan and white,
remembering past enchantments
and past ills.

Greece sees unmoved,
God's daughter, born of love,
the beauty of cool feet
and slenderest knees,
could love indeed the maid,
only if she were laid,
white ash amid funereal cypresses.

Lethe

Nor skin nor hide nor fleece
    Shall cover you,
Nor curtain of crimson nor fine
Shelter of cedar-wood be over you,
    Nor the fir-tree
    Nor the pine.

Nor sight of whin nor gorse
    Nor river-yew,
Nor fragrance of flowering bush,
Nor wailing of reed-bird to waken you,
    Nor of linnet,
    Nor of thrush.

Nor word nor touch nor sight
    Of lover, you
Shall long through the night but for this:
The roll of the full tide to cover you
    Without question,
    Without kiss.

Trance

The floor
of the temple
is bright
with the rain,
the porch and lintel,
each pillar,
plain
in its sheet of metal;
silver,
silver flows
from the laughing Griffins;
the snows of Pentelicus
show dross beside

the King of Enydicus
and his bride,
Lycidoë,
outlined in the torch's flare;
beware, I say,
the loverless,
the sad,
the lost,
the comfortless;
I care
only for happier things,
the bare, bare open court,
(geometric,
with circumspect wing)
the naked plinth,
the statue's rare,
intolerant grace;
I am each of these,
I stare
till my eyes are a statue's eyes,
set in,
my eye-balls are glass,
my limbs marble,
my face fixed
in its marble mask;
only the wind
now fresh from the sea,
flutters a fold,
then lets fall a fold
on my knee.

Birds in Snow

See,
how they trace
across the very-marble
of this place,
bright sevens and printed fours,
elevens and careful eights,
abracadabra
of a mystic's lore
or symbol
outlined
on a wizard's gate;

like plaques of ancient writ
our garden flags now name
the great and very-great;
our garden flags acclaim
in carven hieroglyph,
here king and kinglet lie,
here prince and lady rest,
mystical queens sleep here
and heroes that are slain

in holy righteous war;
hieratic, slim and fair,
the tracery written here,
proclaims what's left unsaid
in Egypt of her dead.

from
Songs from Cyprus

Where is the nightingale,
in what myrrh-wood and dim?
ah, let the night come black,
for we would conjure back
all that enchanted him,
all that enchanted him.

Where is the bird of fire?
in what packed hedge or rose?
in what roofed ledge of flower?
no other creature knows
what magic lurks within,
what magic lurks within.

Bird, bird, bird, bird, we cry,
hear, pity us in pain:
hearts break in the sunlight,
hearts break in daylight rain,
only night heals again,
only night heals again.

from
Let Zeus Record

Stars wheel in purple, yours is not so rare
as Hesperus, nor yet so great a star
as bright Aldebaran or Sirius,
nor yet the stained and brilliant one of War;

stars turn in purple, glorious to the sight;
yours is not gracious as the Pleiads' are
nor as Orion's sapphires, luminous;

yet disenchanted, cold, imperious face,
when all the others, blighted, reel and fall,
your star, steel-set, keeps lone and frigid tryst
to freighted ships, baffled in wind and blast.

Epitaph

So I may say,
"I died of living,
having lived one hour";

so they may say,
"she died soliciting
illicit fervour";

so you may say,
"Greek flower; Greek ecstasy
reclaims for ever

one who died
following
intricate songs' lost measure."

The Mysteries

Renaissance Choros

Dark
days are past
and darker days draw near;
darkness on this side,
darkness over there
threatens the spirit
like massed hosts
a sheer
handful
of thrice-doomed spearsmen;
enemy this side,
enemy a part
of hill
and mountain-crest
and under-hill;
nothing before of mystery,
nothing past,

only the emptiness,
pitfall of death,
terror,
the flood,
the earthquake,
stormy ill;
then voice within the turmoil,
that slight breath
that tells as one flower may
of winter past
(that kills
with Pythian bow
the Delphic pest;)
one flower,
slight voice,
reveals
all holiness
with
"peace
be still."

II

A sceptre
and a flower-shaft
and a spear,
one flower may kill the winter,
so this rare
enchanter
and magician
and arch-mage;
one flower may slay the winter
and meet death,
so this
goes and returns
and dies
and comes to bless
again,
again;
a sceptre and a flower

and a near
protector
to the lost and impotent;
yea,
I am lost,
behold what star is near;
yea,
I am weak,
see
what enchanted armour
clothes the intrepid mind
that sheds the gear
of blighting thought;
behold what wit is here
what subtlety,
what humour
and what light;
see,
I am done,
no lover and none dear,
a voice within the fever,
that slight breath
belies our terror
and our hopelessness
"lo,
I am here."

III

"Not to destroy,
nay, but to sanctify
the flower
that springs
Adonis
from the dead;
behold,
behold
the lilies
how they grow,
behold how fair,

behold how pure a red,
(so love has died)
behold the lilies
bled
for love;
not emperor nor ruler,
none may claim
such splendour;
king may never boast
so beautiful a garment
as the host
of field
and mountain lilies."

IV

"Not to destroy,
nay, but to sanctify
each flame
that springs
upon the brow of Love;
not to destroy
but to re-invoke
and name
afresh each flower,
serpent
and bee
and bird;
behold,
behold
the spotted snake
how wise;
behold the dove,
the sparrow,
not one dies
without your father;
man sets the trap
and bids the arrow fly,
man snares the mother-bird
while passing by

the shivering fledglings,
leaving them to lie
starving;
no man,
no man,
no man
may ever fear
that this one,
winnowing the lovely air,
is overtaken by a bird of prey,
that this is stricken
in its wild-wood plight,
that this dies broken
in the wild-wood snare,
I
and my father
care."

v

"Not to destroy,
nay, but to sanctify
the fervour
of all ancient mysteries;
behold the dead are lost,
the grass has lain
trampled
and stained
and sodden;
behold,
behold,
behold
the grass disdains
the rivulet
of snow and mud and rain;
the grass,
the grass
rises
with flower-bud;
the grain

lifts its bright spear-head
to the sun again;
behold,
behold
the dead
are no more dead,
the grain is gold,
blade,
stalk
and seed within;
the mysteries
are in the grass
and rain."

VI

"The mysteries remain,
I keep the same
cycle of seed-time
and of sun and rain;
Demeter in the grass
I multiply,
renew and bless
Iacchus in the vine;
I hold the law,
I keep the mysteries true,
the first of these
to name the living, dead;
I am red wine and bread.

I keep the law,
I hold the mysteries true,
I am the vine,
the branches, you
and you."

from
Sigil

If you take the moon in your hands
and turn it round
(heavy, slightly tarnished platter)
you're there;

if you pull dry sea-weed from the sand
and turn it round
and wonder at the underside's bright amber,
your eyes

look out as they did here,
(you don't remember)
when my soul turned round,

perceiving the other-side of everything,
mullein-leaf, dogwood-leaf, moth-wing
and dandelion-seed under the ground.

————

Are these ashes in my hand
or a wand
to conjure a butterfly

out of a nest,
a dragon-fly
out of a leaf,

a moon-flower
from a flower husk,

or fire-flies
from a thicket?

Now let the cycle sweep us here and there,
we will not struggle;
somewhere,
under a forest-ledge,
a wild white-pear
will blossom;

somewhere,
under an edge of rock,
a sea will open;
slice of the tide-shelf
will show in coral, yourself,
in conch-shell,
myself;

somewhere,
over a field-hedge,
a wild bird
will lift up wild, wild throat,
and that song, heard,
will stifle out this note.

from
The Walls Do Not Fall

I

An incident here and there,
and rails gone (for guns)
from your (and my) old town square:

mist and mist-grey, no colour,
still the Luxor bee, chick and hare
pursue unalterable purpose

in green, rose-red, lapis;
they continue to prophesy
from the stone papyrus:

there, as here, ruin opens
the tomb, the temple; enter,
there as here, there are no doors:

the shrine lies open to the sky,
the rain falls, here, there
sand drifts; eternity endures:

ruin everywhere, yet as the fallen roof
leaves the sealed room
open to the air,

so, through our desolation,
thoughts stir, inspiration stalks us
through gloom:

unaware, Spirit announces the Presence;
shivering overtakes us,
as of old, Samuel:

trembling at a known street-corner,
we know not nor are known;
the Pythian pronounces—we pass on

to another cellar, to another sliced wall
where poor utensils show
like rare objects in a museum;

Pompeii has nothing to teach us,
we know crack of volcanic fissure,
slow flow of terrible lava,

pressure on heart, lungs, the brain
about to burst its brittle case
(what the skull can endure!):

over us, Apocryphal fire,
under us, the earth sway, dip of a floor,
slope of a pavement

where men roll, drunk
with a new bewilderment,
sorcery, bedevilment:

the bone-frame was made for
no such shock knit within terror,
yet the skeleton stood up to it:

the flesh? it was melted away,
the heart burnt out, dead ember,
tendons, muscles shattered, outer husk dismembered,

yet the frame held:
we passed the flame: we wonder
what saved us? what for?

IV

There is a spell, for instance,
in every sea-shell:

continuous, the sea-thrust
is powerless against coral,

bone, stone, marble
hewn from within by that craftsman,

the shell-fish:
oyster, clam, mollusc

is master-mason planning
the stone marvel:

yet that flabby, amorphous hermit
within, like the planet

senses the finite,
it limits its orbit

of being, its house,
temple, fane, shrine:

it unlocks the portals
at stated intervals:

prompted by hunger,
it opens to the tide-flow:

but infinity? no,
of nothing-too-much:

I sense my own limit,
my shell-jaws snap shut

at invasion of the limitless,
ocean-weight; infinite water

can not crack me, egg in egg-shell;
closed in, complete, immortal

full-circle, I know the pull
of the tide, the lull

as well as the moon;
the octopus-darkness

is powerless against
her cold immortality;

so I in my own way know
that the whale

can not digest me:
be firm in your own small, static, limited

orbit and the shark-jaws
of outer circumstance

will spit you forth:
be indigestible, hard, ungiving,

so that, living within,
you beget, self-out-of-self,

selfless,
that pearl-of-great-price.

V

When in the company of the gods,
I loved and was loved,

never was my mind stirred
to such rapture,

my heart moved
to such pleasure,

as now, to discover
over Love, a new Master:

His, the track in the sand
from a plum-tree in flower

to a half-open hut-door,
(or track would have been

but wind blows sand-prints from the sand,
whether seen or unseen):

His, the Genius in the jar
which the Fisherman finds,

He is Mage,
bringing myrrh.

VI

In me (the worm) clearly
is no righteousness, but this—

persistence; I escaped spider-snare,
bird-claw, scavenger bird-beak,

clung to grass-blade,
the back of a leaf

when storm-wind
tore it from its stem;

I escaped, I explored
rose-thorn forest,

was rain-swept
down the valley of a leaf;

was deposited on grass,
where mast by jewelled mast

bore separate ravellings
of encrusted gem-stuff

of the mist
from each banner-staff:

unintimidated by multiplicity
of magnified beauty,

such as your gorgon-great
dull eye can not focus

nor compass, I profit
by every calamity;

I eat my way out of it;
gorged on vine-leaf and mulberry,

parasite, I find nourishment:
when you cry in disgust,

a worm on the leaf,
a worm in the dust,

a worm on the ear-of-wheat,
I am yet unrepentant,

for I know how the Lord God
is about to manifest, when I,

the industrious worm,
spin my own shroud.

XIII

The Presence was spectrum-blue,
ultimate blue ray,

rare as radium, as healing;
my old self, wrapped round me,

was shroud (I speak of myself individually
but I was surrounded by companions

in this mystery);
do you wonder we are proud,

aloof,
indifferent to your good and evil?

peril, strangely encountered, strangely endured,
marks us;

we know each other
by secret symbols,

though, remote, speechless,
we pass each other on the pavement,

at the turn of the stair;
though no word pass between us,

there is subtle appraisement;
even if we snarl a brief greeting

or do not speak at all,
we know our Name,

we nameless initiates,
born of one mother,

companions
of the flame.

XIV

Yet we, the latter-day twice-born,
have our bad moments when

dragging the forlorn
husk of self after us,

we are forced to confess to
malaise and embarrassment;

we pull at this dead shell,
struggle but we must wait

till the new Sun dries off
the old-body humours;

awkwardly, we drag this stale
old will, old volition, old habit

about with us;
we are these people,

wistful, ironical, wilful,
who have no part in

new-world reconstruction,
in the confederacy of labour,

the practical issues of art
and the cataloguing of utilities:

O, do not look up
into the air,

you who are occupied
in the bewildering

sand-heap maze
of present-day endeavour;

you will be, not so much frightened
as paralysed with inaction,

and anyhow,
we have not crawled so very far

up our individual grass-blade
toward our individual star.

XXII

Now my right hand,
now my left hand

clutch your curled fleece;
take me home, take me home,

my voice wails from the ground;
take me home, Father:

pale as the worm in the grass,
yet I am a spark

struck by your hoof from a rock:
Amen, you are so warm,

hide me in your fleece,
crop me up with the new-grass;

let your teeth devour me,
let me be warm in your belly,

the sun-disk,
the re-born Sun.

XXIII

Take me home
where canals

flow
between iris-banks:

where the heron
has her nest:

where the mantis
prays on the river-reed:

where the grasshopper says
Amen, Amen, Amen.

XXVIII

O heart, small urn
of porphyry, agate or cornelian,

how imperceptibly the grain fell
between a heart-beat of pleasure

and a heart-beat of pain;
I do not know how it came

nor how long it had lain there,
nor can I say

how it escaped tempest
of passion and malice,

nor why it was not washed away
in flood of sorrow,

or dried up in the bleak drought
of bitter thought.

from
Tribute to the Angels

X

In the field-furrow
the rain-water

showed splintered edge
as of a broken mirror,

and in the glass
as in a polished spear,

glowed the star Hesperus,
white, far and luminous,

incandescent and near,
Venus, Aphrodite, Astarte,

star of the east,
star of the west,

Phosphorus at sun-rise,
Hesperus at sun-set.

XX

Invisible, indivisible Spirit,
how is it you come so near,

how is it that we dare
approach the high-altar?

we crossed the charred portico,
passed through a frame—doorless—

entered a shrine; like a ghost,
we entered a house through a wall;

then still not knowing
whether (like the wall)

we were there or not-there,
we saw the tree flowering;

it was an ordinary tree
in an old garden-square.

XXI

This is no rune nor riddle,
it is happening everywhere;

what I mean is—it is so simple
yet no trick of the pen or brush

could capture that impression;
music could do nothing with it,

nothing whatever; what I mean is—
but you have seen for yourself

that burnt-out wood crumbling . . .
you have seen for yourself.

XXII

A new sensation
is not granted to everyone,

not to everyone everywhere,
but to us here, a new sensation

strikes paralysing,
strikes dumb,

strikes the senses numb,
sets the nerves quivering;

I am sure you see
what I mean;

it was an old tree
such as we see everywhere,

anywhere here—and some barrel staves
and some bricks

and an edge of the wall
uncovered and the naked ugliness

and then . . . music? O, what I meant
by music when I said music, was—

music sets up ladders,
it makes us invisible,

it sets us apart,
it lets us escape;

but from the visible
there is no escape;

there is no escape from the spear
that pierces the heart.

XXIX

We have seen her
the world over,

Our Lady of the Goldfinch,
Our Lady of the Candelabra,

Our Lady of the Pomegranate,
Our Lady of the Chair;

we have seen her, an empress,
magnificent in pomp and grace,

and we have seen her
with a single flower

or a cluster of garden-pinks
in a glass beside her;

we have seen her snood
drawn over her hair,

or her face set in profile
with the blue hood and stars;

we have seen her head bowed down
with the weight of a domed crown,

or we have seen her, a wisp of a girl
trapped in a golden halo;

we have seen her with arrow, with doves
and a heart like a valentine;

we have seen her in fine silks imported
from all over the Levant,

and hung with pearls brought
from the city of Constantine;

we have seen her sleeve
of every imaginable shade

of damask and figured brocade;
it is true,

the painters did very well by her;
it is true, they missed never a line

of the suave turn of the head
or subtle shade of lowered eye-lid

or eye-lids half-raised; you find
her everywhere (or did find),

in cathedral, museum, cloister,
at the turn of the palace stair.

XXX

We see her hand in her lap,
smoothing the apple-green

or the apple-russet silk;
we see her hand at her throat,

fingering a talisman
brought by a crusader from Jerusalem;

we see her hand unknot a Syrian veil
or lay down a Venetian shawl

on a polished table that reflects
half a miniature broken column;

we see her stare past a mirror
through an open window,

where boat follows slow boat on the lagoon;
there are white flowers on the water.

XLIII

And the point in the spectrum
where all lights become one,

is white and white is not no-colour,
as we were told as children,

but all-colour;
where the flames mingle

and the wings meet, when we gain
the arc of perfection,

we are satisfied, we are happy,
we begin again;

I John saw. I testify
to rainbow feathers, to the span of heaven

and walls of colour,
the colonnades of jasper;

but when the jewel
melts in the crucible,

we find not ashes, not ash-of-rose,
not a tall vase and a staff of lilies,

not *vas spirituale*,
not *rosa mystica* even,

but a cluster of garden-pinks
or a face like a Christmas-rose.

from
The Flowering of the Rod

II

I go where I love and where I am loved,
into the snow;

I go to the things I love
with no thought of duty or pity;

I go where I belong, inexorably,
as the rain that has lain long

in the furrow; I have given
or would have given

life to the grain;
but if it will not grow or ripen

with the rain of beauty,
the rain will return to the cloud;

the harvester sharpens his steel on the stone;
but this is not our field,

we have not sown this;
pitiless, pitiless, let us leave

The-place-of-a-skull
to those who have fashioned it.

III

In resurrection, there is confusion
if we start to argue; if we stand and stare,

we do not know where to go;
in resurrection, there is simple affirmation

but do not delay to round up the others,
up and down the street; your going

in a moment like this, is the best proof
that you know the way;

does the first wild-goose stop to explain
to the others? no—he is off;

they follow or not,
that is their affair;

does the first wild-goose care
whether the others follow or not?

I don't think so—he is so happy to be off—
he knows where he is going;

so we must be drawn or we must fly,
like the snow-geese of the Arctic circle,

to the Carolinas or to Florida,
or like those migratory flocks

who still (they say) hover
over the lost island, Atlantis;

seeking what we once knew,
we know ultimately we will find

happiness; *to-day shalt thou be
with me in Paradise.*

IV

Blue-geese, white-geese, you may say,
yes, I know this duality, this double nostalgia;

I know the insatiable longing
in winter, for palm-shadow

and sand and burnt sea-drift;
but in the summer, as I watch

the wave till its edge of foam
touches the hot sand and instantly

vanishes like snow on the equator,
I would cry out, stay, stay;

then I remember delicate enduring frost
and its mid-winter dawn-pattern;

in the hot noon-sun, I think of the grey
opalescent winter-dawn; as the wave

burns on the shingle, I think,
you are less beautiful than frost;

but it is also true that I pray,
O, give me burning blue

and brittle burnt sea-weed
above the tide-line,

as I stand, still unsatisfied,
under the long shadow-on-snow of the pine.

V

Satisfied, unsatisfied,
satiated or numb with hunger,

this is the eternal urge,
this is the despair, the desire to equilibrate

the eternal variant;
you understand that insistent calling,

that demand of a given moment,
the will to enjoy, the will to live,

not merely the will to endure,
the will to flight, the will to achievement,

the will to rest after long flight;
but who knows the desperate urge

of those others—actual or perhaps now
mythical birds—who seek but find no rest

till they drop from the highest point of the spiral
or fall from the innermost centre of the ever-narrowing circle?

for they remember, they remember, as they sway and hover,
what once was—they remember, they remember—

they will not swerve—they have known bliss,
the fruit that satisfies—they have come back—

what if the islands are lost? what if the waters
cover the Hesperides? they would rather remember—

remember the golden apple-trees;
O, do not pity them, as you watch them drop one by one,

for they fall exhausted, numb, blind
but in certain ecstasy,

for theirs is the hunger
for Paradise.

VI

So I would rather drown, remembering—
than bask on tropic atolls

in the coral-seas; I would rather drown,
remembering—than rest on pine or fir-branch

where great stars pour down
their generating strength, Arcturus

or the sapphires of the Northern Crown;
I would rather beat in the wind, crying to these others:

yours is the more foolish circling,
yours is the senseless wheeling

round and round—yours has no reason—
I am seeking heaven;

yours has no vision,
I see what is beneath me, what is above me,

what men say is-not—I remember,
I remember, I remember—you have forgot:

you think, even before it is half-over,
that your cycle is at an end,

but you repeat your foolish circling—again, again, again;
again, the steel sharpened on the stone;

again, the pyramid of skulls;
I gave pity to the dead,

O blasphemy, pity is a stone for bread,
only love is holy and love's ecstasy

that turns and turns and turns about one centre,
reckless, regardless, blind to reality,

that knows the Islands of the Blest are there,
for *many waters can not quench love's fire.*

VII

Yet resurrection is a sense of direction,
resurrection is a bee-line,

straight to the horde and plunder,
the treasure, the store-room,

the honeycomb;
resurrection is remuneration,

food, shelter, fragrance
of myrrh and balm.

JOHN GOULD FLETCHER

(1886–1950)

Blue Symphony

I

The darkness rolls upward.
The thick darkness carries with it
Rain and a ravel of cloud.
The sun comes forth upon earth.

Palely the dawn
Leaves me facing timidly
Old gardens sunken:
And in the gardens is water.

Sombre wreck—autumnal leaves;
Shadowy roofs
In the blue mist,
And a willow-branch that is broken.

Oh, old pagodas of my soul, how you glittered across green
    trees!

Blue and cool:
Blue, tremulously,
Blow faint puffs of smoke
Across sombre pools.
The damp green smell of rotted wood;
And a heron that cries from out the water.

II

Through the upland meadows
I go alone.
For I dreamed of someone last night
Who is waiting for me.

Flower and blossom, tell me, do you know of her?

Have the rocks hidden her voice?
They are very blue and still.

Long upward road that is leading me,
Light hearted I quit you,
For the long loose ripples of the meadow grass
Invite me to dance upon them.

Quivering grass
Daintily poised
For her foot's tripping.

Oh, blown clouds, could I only race up like you,
Oh, the last slopes that are sun-drenched and steep!

Look, the sky!
Across black valleys
Rise blue-white aloft
Jagged unwrinkled mountains, ranges of death.

Solitude. Silence.

III

One chuckles by the brook for me:
One rages under the stone.
One makes a spout of his mouth
One whispers—one is gone.

One over there on the water
Spreads cold ripples
For me
Enticingly.

The vast dark trees
Flow like blue veils
Of tears
Into the water.

Sour sprites,
Moaning and chuckling,
What have you hidden from me?

"In the palace of the blue stone she lies forever
Bound hand and foot."

Was it the wind
That rattled the reeds together?

Dry reeds,
A faint shiver in the grasses.

IV

On the left hand there is a temple:
And a palace on the right-hand side.
Foot passengers in scarlet
Pass over the glittering tide.

Under the bridge
The old river flows
Low and monotonous
Day after day.

I have heard and have seen
All the news that has been:
Autumn's gold and Spring's green!

Now in my palace
I see foot passengers
Crossing the river:
Pilgrims of autumn
In the afternoons.

Lotus pools:
Petals in the water.
These are my dreams.

For me silks are outspread.
I take my ease, unthinking.

V

And now the lowest pine-branch
Is drawn across the disk of the sun.
Old friends who will forget me soon,
I must go on,
Towards those blue death-mountains
I have forgot so long.

In the marsh grasses
There lies forever
My last treasure,
With the hopes of my heart.

The ice is glazing over,
Torn lanterns flutter,
On the leaves is snow.

In the frosty evening
Toll the old bell for me
Once, in the sleepy temple.

Perhaps my soul will hear.

Afterglow:
Before the stars peep
I shall creep out into darkness.

HAZEL HALL

(1886–1924)

Seams

I was sewing a seam one day—
Just this way—
Flashing four silver stitches there
With thread, like this, fine as a hair,
And then four here, and there again,
When
The seam I sewed dropped out of sight . . .
I saw the sea come rustling in,
Big and grey, windy and bright . . .
Then my thread that was as thin
As hair, tangled up like smoke
And broke.
I threaded up my needle, then—
Four here, four there, and here again.

The Listening Macaws

Many sewing days ago
I cross-stitched on a black satin bag
Two listening macaws.

They were perched on a stiff branch
With every stitch of their green tails,
Their blue wings, yellow breasts and sharply turned heads,
Alert and listening.

Now sometimes on the edge of relaxation
My thought is caught back,
Like gathers along a gathering thread,
To the listening macaws;
And I am amazed at the futile energy
That has kept them,
Alert to the last stitch,
Listening into their black satin night.

Light Sleep

Women who sing themselves to sleep
Lie with their hands at rest,
Locked over them night-long as though to keep
Music against their breast.

They who have feared the night and lain
Mumbling themselves to peace
Sleep a light sleep lest they forget the strain
That brings them their release.

They dream, who hold beneath the hand
A crumpled shape of song,
Of trembling sound they do not understand,
Yet love the whole night long.

Women who sing themselves to sleep
Must lie in fear till day,
Clasping an amulet of words to keep
The leaning dark away.

Woman Death

Wash over her, wet light
Of this dissolving room.
Dusk smelling of night,
Lay on her placid gloom.
Wash over her; as waves push back the sands
Fold down her hands.

Many another rain
Of dusk has filled such walls;
Many a woman has lain
Submerged where the damp light falls,
Wanting her hands held down,
Finding it strange that they
Alone refuse to drown.

The mind after its day
Fills like an iron cup
With waters of the night.
The eyes wisely give up
The little they held of light.
Move over her, subdue her, Dark, until
Her hands are still.

Out of the east comes night;
From west, from north, from south,
Gathers the blackened light
To move against her mouth.
Many another has known
These four pressures of space,

Feeling her lips grow stone
And hollows curving her face,
And cared so little to feel.
Her light had never given
More than her dark might steal;
Then for this she had striven:
To feel the quiet moving on her hands
Like thin sea over sands.

Time gathers to break
In arrested thunder, gloom
Comes with thickness to make
Deep ocean of a room,
Comes to soothe and shape
The breathed-out breath.

Some who die escape
The rhythm of their death,
Some may die and know
Death as a broken song,
But a woman dies not so, not so;
A woman's death is long.

ROY HELTON

(b. 1886)

Lonesome Water

Drank lonesome water:
Weren't but a tad then
Up in a laurel thick
Digging for sang;
Came on a place where
The stones was holler;
Something below them
Tinkled and rang.

Dug where I heard it
Drippling below me:
Should a knowed better,
Should a been wise;
Leant down and drank it,
Clutching and gripping
The overhung cliv
With the ferns in my eyes.

Tweren't no tame water
I knowed in a minute;
Must a been laying there
Projecting round
Since winter went home;
Must a laid like a cushion,
Where the feet of the blossoms
Was tucked in the ground.

Tasted of heart leaf,
And that smells the sweetest,
Paw paw and spice bush
And wild briar rose;
Must a been counting
The heels of the spruce pines,

And neighboring round
Where angelica grows.

I'd drunk lonesome water,
I knowed in a minute:
Never larnt nothing
From then till today;
Nothing worth larning,
Nothing worth knowing.
I'm bound to the hills
And I can't get away.

Mean sort of dried up old
Groundhoggy feller,
Laying out cold here
Watching the sky;
Pore as a hipporwill,
Bent like a grass blade;
Counting up stars
Till they count too high.

I know where the grey foxes
Uses up yander,
Know what'll cure ye
Of ptisic or chills,
But I never been way from here,
Never got going:
I've drunk lonesome water.
I'm bound to the hills.

GEORGIA DOUGLAS JOHNSON

(1886–1966)

I Want To Die While You Love Me

I want to die while you love me,
   While yet you hold me fair,
While laughter lies upon my lips
   And lights are in my hair.

I want to die while you love me
   And bear to that still bed
Your kisses—turbulent, unspent,
   To warm me when I'm dead.

I want to die while you love me
   Oh, who would care to live,
'Til love has nothing more to ask
   And nothing more to give.

JOYCE KILMER

(1886–1918)

Trees

(For Mrs. Henry Mills Alden)

I think that I shall never see
A poem lovely as a tree.

A tree whose hungry mouth is prest
Against the earth's sweet flowing breast;

A tree that looks at God all day,
And lifts her leafy arms to pray;

A tree that may in Summer wear
A nest of robins in her hair;

Upon whose bosom snow has lain;
Who intimately lives with rain.

Poems are made by fools like me,
But only God can make a tree.

MA RAINEY

(1886–1939)

Southern Blues

House catch on fire
           and ain't no water 'round
If your house catch on fire
             ain't no water 'round
Throw your trunk out the window
               building burn on down

I went to the Gypsy
         to have my fortune told
I went to the Gypsy
         to have my fortune told
He said, Doggone you, girlie
            doggone your bad luck soul

I turned around
        went to the Gypsy next door
I turned around
        went to the Gypsy next door
He said, You'll get a man
          any where you go

Let me be your rag-doll
            until your chiny come
Let me be your rag-doll
          till your chiny come
If he beats me ragged
          he's got to rag it some

JOHN HALL WHEELOCK

(1886–1978)

The Fish-Hawk

On the large highway of the awful air that flows
   Unbounded between sea and heaven, while twilight
     screened
The sorrowful distances, he moved and had repose;
   On the huge wind of the Immensity he leaned
His steady body in long lapse of flight—and rose

Gradual, through broad gyres of ever-climbing rest,
   Up the clear stair of the eternal sky, and stood
Throned on the summit! Slowly, with his widening breast,
   Widened around him the enormous Solitude,
From the gray rim of ocean to the glowing west.

Headlands and capes forlorn of the far coast, the land
   Rolling her barrens toward the south, he, from his throne
Upon the gigantic wind, beheld: he hung—he fanned
   The abyss for mighty joy, to feel beneath him strown
Pale pastures of the sea, with heaven on either hand—

The world with all her winds and waters, earth and air,
   Fields, folds, and moving clouds. The awful and adored
Arches and endless aisles of vacancy, the fair
   Void of sheer heights and hollows hailed him as her lord
And lover in the highest, to whom all heaven lay bare!

Till from that tower of ecstasy, that baffled height,
   Stooping, he sank; and slowly on the world's wide way
Walked, with great wing on wing, the merciless, proud
     Might,
   Hunting the huddled and lone reaches for his prey
Down the dim shore—and faded in the crumbling light.

Slowly the dusk covered the land. Like a great hymn
  The sound of moving winds and waters was; the sea
Whispered a benediction, and the west grew dim
  Where evening lifted her clear candles quietly . . .
Heaven, crowded with stars, trembled from rim to rim.

Afternoon: Amagansett Beach

           The broad beach,
Sea-wind and the sea's irregular rhythm,
Great dunes with their pale grass, and on the beach
Driftwood, tangle of bones, an occasional shell,
Now coarse, now carven and delicate—whorls of time
Stranded in space, deaf ears listening
To lost time, old oceanic secrets.
Along the water's edge, in pattern casual
As the pattern of the stars, the pin-point air-holes,
Left by the sand-flea under the receding spume,
Wink and blink out again. A gull drifts over,
Wide wings crucified against the sky—
His shadow travels the shore, upon its margins
You will find his signature: one long line,
Two shorter lines curving out from it, a nearly
Perfect graph of the bird himself in flight.
His footprint is his image fallen from heaven.

Earth, Take Me Back

I have been dying a long time
In this cool valley-land, this green bowl ringed by hills—
The cup of a giant flower whose petals are
These forests round about, still wet
From the fresh April rains.
Night draws on. It is growing dark.
The trees are silent. The hills are dark and silent.
All things fall silent, or look the other way,
When you are dying.
There is a delicate haze over everything.
Soft clouds are floating like water-lily pads
On the dark pool of the sky. Between them
Stars come out . . .

SKIPWITH CANNELL

(1887–1957)

The King

Seven full-paunched eunuchs came to me
Bearing before them upon a silver shield
The secrets of my enemy.

As they crossed my threshold to stand,
With stately and hypocritical gesture
In a row before me,
One stumbled.
The dull incurious eyes of the others
Blazed into no laughter,
Only a haggard malice
At the discomfiture
Of their companion.

Why should such THINGS have a power
Not spoken for in the rules of men?

I would not receive them.
Covering my head, I motioned them
To go forth from my presence.

Where shall I find an enemy
Worthy of me as him they defaced?

As they left me,
Bearing with them
Lewd shield and scarlet crown,
One paused upon the threshold,
Insolent,
To sniff a flower.

Even him I permitted to go forth,
Safely, into the sunlight.

.   .   .   .

Therefore, I have renounced my kingdom;
In a little black boat I have set sail
Out
Upon the sea.

There is no land and the sea
Is black like cypresses waiting at midnight
In a place of tombs,
Is black like the pool of ink
In the palm of a sooth-sayer.

My boat
Fears the white-lipped waves that snatch at it,
Hungrily,
Furtively,
As they steal past like cats
Into the night:
Beneath me, in their hidden places,
The great fishes talk of me
In a tongue I have forgotten.

ROBINSON JEFFERS

(1887–1962)

Salmon Fishing

The days shorten, the south blows wide for showers now,
The south wind shouts to the rivers,
The rivers open their mouths and the salt salmon
Race up into the freshet.
In Christmas month against the smoulder and menace
Of a long angry sundown,
Red ash of the dark solstice, you see the anglers,
Pitiful, cruel, primeval,
Like the priests of the people that built Stonehenge,
Dark silent forms, performing
Remote solemnities in the red shallows
Of the river's mouth at the year's turn,
Drawing landward their live bullion, the bloody mouths
And scales full of the sunset
Twitch on the rocks, no more to wander at will
The wild Pacific pasture nor wanton and spawning
Race up into fresh water.

Shine, Perishing Republic

While this America settles in the mould of its vulgarity,
        heavily thickening to empire,
And protest, only a bubble in the molten mass, pops and
        sighs out, and the mass hardens,

I sadly smiling remember that the flower fades to make fruit,
        the fruit rots to make earth.
Out of the mother; and through the spring exultances,
        ripeness and decadence; and home to the mother.

You making haste haste on decay: not blameworthy; life is
 good, be it stubbornly long or suddenly
A mortal splendor: meteors are not needed less than
 mountains: shine, perishing republic.

But for my children, I would have them keep their distance
 from the thickening center; corruption
Never has been compulsory, when the cities lie at the
 monster's feet there are left the mountains.

And boys, be in nothing so moderate as in love of man, a
 clever servant, insufferable master.
There is the trap that catches noblest spirits, that caught—
 they say—God, when he walked on earth.

Granite and Cypress

White-maned, wide-throated, the heavy-shouldered children
 of the wind leap at the sea-cliff.
The invisible falcon
Brooded on water and bred them in wide waste places, in a
 bride-chamber wide to the stars' eyes
In the center of the ocean,
Where no prows pass nor island is lifted . . . the sea beyond
 Lobos is whitened with the falcon's
Passage, he is here now,
The sky is one cloud, his wing-feathers hiss in the white grass,
 my sapling cypresses writhing
In the fury of his passage
Dare not dream of their centuries of future endurance of
 tempest. (I have granite and cypress,
Both long-lasting,
Planted in the earth; but the granite sea-bowlders are prey to
 no hawk's wing, they have taken worse pounding,
Like me they remember
Old wars and are quiet; for we think that the future is one
 piece with the past, we wonder why tree-tops
And people are so shaken.)

Birds

The fierce musical cries of a couple of sparrowhawks hunting
    on the headland,
Hovering and darting, their heads northwestward,
Prick like silver arrows shot through a curtain the noise of the
    ocean
Trampling its granite; their red backs gleam
Under my window around the stone corners; nothing
    gracefuller, nothing
Nimbler in the wind. Westward the wave-gleaners,
The old gray sea-going gulls are gathered together, the
    northwest wind wakening
Their wings to the wild spirals of the wind-dance.
Fresh as the air, salt as the foam, play birds in the bright wind,
    fly falcons
Forgetting the oak and the pinewood, come gulls
From the Carmel sands and the sands at the river-mouth,
    from Lobos and out of the limitless
Power of the mass of the sea, for a poem
Needs multitude, multitudes of thoughts, all fierce, all flesh-
    eaters, musically clamorous
Bright hawks that hover and dart headlong, and ungainly
Gray hungers fledged with desire of transgression, salt slimed
    beaks, from the sharp
Rock-shores of the world and the secret waters.

Haunted Country

Here the human past is dim and feeble and alien to us
Our ghosts draw from the crowded future.
Fixed as the past how could it fail to drop weird shadows
And make strange murmurs about twilight?
In the dawn twilight metal falcons flew over the mountain,
Multitudes, and faded in the air; at moonrise
The farmer's girl by the still river is afraid of phantoms,
Hearing the pulse of a great city

Move on the water-meadow and stream off south; the
    country's
Children for all their innocent minds
Hide dry and bitter lights in the eye, they dream without
    knowing it
The inhuman years to be accomplished,
The inhuman powers, the servile cunning under pressure
In a land grown old, heavy and crowded.
There are happy places that fate skips; here is not one of
    them;
The tides of the brute womb, the excess
And weight of life spilled out like water, the last migration
Gathering against this holier valley-mouth
That knows its fate beforehand, the flow of the womb,
    banked back
By the older flood of the ocean, to swallow it.

Apology for Bad Dreams

I

In the purple light, heavy with redwood, the slopes drop
    seaward,
Headlong convexities of forest, drawn in together to the
    steep ravine. Below, on the sea-cliff,
A lonely clearing; a little field of corn by the streamside; a
    roof under spared trees. Then the ocean
Like a great stone someone has cut to a sharp edge and
    polished to shining. Beyond it, the fountain
And furnace of incredible light flowing up from the sunk sun.
    In the little clearing a woman
Is punishing a horse; she had tied the halter to a sapling at the
    edge of the wood, but when the great whip
Clung to the flanks the creature kicked so hard she feared he
    would snap the halter; she called from the house
The young man her son; who fetched a chain tie-rope, they
    working together

Noosed the small rusty links round the horse's tongue
And tied him by the swollen tongue to the tree.
Seen from this height they are shrunk to insect size,
Out of all human relation. You cannot distinguish
The blood dripping from where the chain is fastened,
The beast shuddering; but the thrust neck and the legs
Far apart. You can see the whip fall on the flanks . . .
The gesture of the arm. You cannot see the face of the
　　woman.
The enormous light beats up out of the west across the
　　cloud-bars of the trade-wind. The ocean
Darkens, the high clouds brighten, the hills darken together.
　　Unbridled and unbelievable beauty
Covers the evening world . . . not covers, grows apparent
　　out of it, as Venus down there grows out
From the lit sky. What said the prophet? "I create good: and I
　　create evil: I am the Lord."

II

This coast crying out for tragedy like all beautiful places,
(The quiet ones ask for quieter suffering: but here the granite
　　cliff the gaunt cypresses crown
Demands what victim? The dykes of red lava and black what
　　Titan? The hills like pointed flames
Beyond Soberanes, the terrible peaks of the bare hills under
　　the sun, what immolation?)
This coast crying out for tragedy like all beautiful places: and
　　like the passionate spirit of humanity
Pain for its bread: God's, many victims', the painful deaths,
　　the horrible transfigurements: I said in my heart,
"Better invent than suffer: imagine victims
Lest your own flesh be chosen the agonist, or you
Martyr some creature to the beauty of the place." And I said,
"Burn sacrifices once a year to magic
Horror away from the house, this little house here
You have built over the ocean with your own hands
Beside the standing boulders: for what are we,
The beast that walks upright, with speaking lips
And little hair, to think we should always be fed,

Sheltered, intact, and self-controlled? We sooner more liable
Than the other animals. Pain and terror, the insanities of
    desire; not accidents but essential,
And crowd up from the core": I imagined victims for those
    wolves, I made them phantoms to follow,
They have hunted the phantoms and missed the house. It is
    not good to forget over what gulfs the spirit
Of the beauty of humanity, the petal of a lost flower blown
    seaward by the night-wind, floats to its quietness.

III

Boulders blunted like an old bear's teeth break up from the
    headland; below them
All the soil is thick with shells, the tide-rock feasts of a dead
    people.
Here the granite flanks are scarred with ancient fire, the
    ghosts of the tribe
Crouch in the nights beside the ghost of a fire, they try to
    remember the sunlight,
Light has died out of their skies. These have paid something
    for the future
Luck of the country, while we living keep old griefs in
    memory: though God's
Envy is not a likely fountain of ruin, to forget evils calls down
Sudden reminders from the cloud: remembered deaths be our
    redeemers;
Imagined victims our salvation: white as the half moon at
    midnight
Someone flamelike passed me, saying, "I am Tamar
    Cauldwell, I have my desire,"
Then the voice of the sea returned, when she had gone by,
    the stars to their towers.
. . . Beautiful country burn again, Point Pinos down to the
    Sur Rivers
Burn as before with bitter wonders, land and ocean and the
    Carmel water.

IV

He brays humanity in a mortar to bring the savor
From the bruised root: a man having bad dreams, who
　　invents victims, is only the ape of that God.
He washes it out with tears and many waters, calcines it with
　　fire in the red crucible,
Deforms it, makes it horrible to itself: the spirit flies out and
　　stands naked, he sees the spirit,
He takes it in the naked ecstasy; it breaks in his hand, the
　　atom is broken, the power that massed it
Cries to the power that moves the stars, "I have come home
　　to myself, behold me.
I bruised myself in the flint mortar and burnt me
In the red shell, I tortured myself, I flew forth,
Stood naked of myself and broke me in fragments,
And here am I moving the stars that are me."
I have seen these ways of God: I know of no reason
For fire and change and torture and the old returnings.
He being sufficient might be still. I think they admit no
　　reason; they are the ways of my love.
Unmeasured power, incredible passion, enormous craft: no
　　thought apparent but burns darkly
Smothered with its own smoke in the human brain-vault: no
　　thought outside: a certain measure in phenomena:
The fountains of the boiling stars, the flowers on the
　　foreland, the ever-returning roses of dawn.

Hurt Hawks

I

The broken pillar of the wing jags from the clotted shoulder,
The wing trails like a banner in defeat,
No more to use the sky forever but live with famine
And pain a few days: cat nor coyote
Will shorten the week of waiting for death, there is game
　　without talons.

He stands under the oak-bush and waits
The lame feet of salvation; at night he remembers freedom
And flies in a dream, the dawns ruin it.
He is strong and pain is worse to the strong, incapacity is
    worse.
The curs of the day come and torment him
At distance, no one but death the redeemer will humble that
    head,
The intrepid readiness, the terrible eyes.
The wild God of the world is sometimes merciful to those
That ask mercy, not often to the arrogant.
You do not know him, you communal people, or you have
    forgotten him;
Intemperate and savage, the hawk remembers him;
Beautiful and wild, the hawks, and men that are dying,
    remember him.

II

I'd sooner, except the penalties, kill a man than a hawk; but
    the great redtail
Had nothing left but unable misery
From the bones too shattered for mending, the wing that
    trailed under his talons when he moved.
We had fed him six weeks, I gave him freedom,
He wandered over the foreland hill and returned in the
    evening, asking for death,
Not like a beggar, still eyed with the old
Implacable arrogance. I gave him the lead gift in the twilight.
    What fell was relaxed,
Owl-downy, soft feminine feathers; but what
Soared: the fierce rush: the night-herons by the flooded river
    cried fear at its rising
Before it was quite unsheathed from reality.

Tor House

If you should look for this place after a handful of lifetimes:
Perhaps of my planted forest a few
May stand yet, dark-leaved Australians or the coast cypress,
    haggard
With storm-drift; but fire and the axe are devils.
Look for foundations of sea-worn granite, my fingers had the
    art
To make stone love stone, you will find some remnant.
But if you should look in your idleness after ten thousand
    years:
It is the granite knoll on the granite
And lava tongue in the midst of the bay, by the mouth of the
    Carmel
River-valley, these four will remain
In the change of names. You will know it by the wild sea-
    fragrance of wind
Though the ocean may have climbed or retired a little;
You will know it by the valley inland that our sun and our
    moon were born from
Before the poles changed; and Orion in December
Evenings was strung in the throat of the valley like a lamp-
    lighted bridge.
Come in the morning you will see white gulls
Weaving a dance over blue water, the wane of the moon
Their dance-companion, a ghost walking
By daylight, but wider and whiter than any bird in the world.
My ghost you needn't look for; it is probably
Here, but a dark one, deep in the granite, not dancing on
    wind
With the mad wings and the day moon.

The Bed by the Window

I chose the bed down-stairs by the sea-window for a good
    death-bed
When we built the house; it is ready waiting,

Unused unless by some guest in a twelvemonth, who hardly
    suspects
Its latter purpose. I often regard it,
With neither dislike nor desire: rather with both, so equalled
That they kill each other and a crystalline interest
Remains alone. We are safe to finish what we have to finish;
And then it will sound rather like music
When the patient daemon behind the screen of sea-rock and
    sky
Thumps with his staff, and calls thrice: "Come, Jeffers."

The Place for No Story

The coast hills at Sovranes Creek;
No trees, but dark scant pasture drawn thin
Over rock shaped like flame;
The old ocean at the land's foot, the vast
Gray extension beyond the long white violence;
A herd of cows and the bull
Far distant, hardly apparent up the dark slope;
And the gray air haunted with hawks:
This place is the noblest thing I have ever seen. No
    imaginable
Human presence here could do anything
But dilute the lonely self-watchful passion.

Love the Wild Swan

"I hate my verses, every line, every word.
Oh pale and brittle pencils ever to try
One grass-blade's curve, or the throat of one bird
That clings to twig, ruffled against white sky.
Oh cracked and twilight mirrors ever to catch
One color, one glinting flash, of the splendor of things.
Unlucky hunter, Oh bullets of wax,
The lion beauty, the wild-swan wings, the storm of the
    wings."

—This wild swan of a world is no hunter's game.
Better bullets than yours would miss the white breast,
Better mirrors than yours would crack in the flame.
Does it matter whether you hate your . . . self? At least
Love your eyes that can see, your mind that can
Hear the music, the thunder of the wings. Love the wild
    swan.

Rock and Hawk

Here is a symbol in which
Many high tragic thoughts
Watch their own eyes.

This gray rock, standing tall
On the headland, where the sea-wind
Lets no tree grow,

Earthquake-proved, and signatured
By ages of storms: on its peak
A falcon has perched.

I think, here is your emblem
To hang in the future sky;
Not the cross, not the hive,

But this; bright power, dark peace;
Fierce consciousness joined with final
Disinterestedness;

Life with calm death; the falcon's
Realist eyes and act
Married to the massive

Mysticism of stone,
Which failure cannot cast down
Nor success make proud.

Prescription of Painful Ends

Lucretius felt the change of the world in his time, the great
    republic riding to the height
Whence every road leads downward; Plato in his time
    watched Athens
Dance the down path. The future is a misted landscape, no
    man sees clearly, but at cyclic turns
There is a change felt in the rhythm of events, as when an
    exhausted horse
Falters and recovers, then the rhythm of the running hoof-
    beats is changed: he will run miles yet,
But he must fall: we have felt it again in our own life-time,
    slip, shift and speed-up
In the gallop of the world; and now perceive that, come peace
    or war, the progress of Europe and America
Becomes a long process of deterioration—starred with
    famous Byzantiums and Alexandrias,
Surely,—but downward. One desires at such times
To gather the insights of the age summit against future loss,
    against the narrowing mind and the tyrants,
The pedants, the mystagogues, the barbarians: one builds
    poems for treasuries, time-conscious poems: Lucretius
Sings his great theory of natural origins and of wise conduct;
    Plato smiling carves dreams, bright cells
Of incorruptible wax to hive the Greek honey.

                        Our own time, much
    greater and far less fortunate,
Has acids for honey, and for fine dreams
The immense vulgarities of misapplied science and decaying
    Christianity: therefore one christens each poem, in
    dutiful
Hope of burning off at least the top layer of the time's
    uncleanness, from the acid-bottles.

For Una

I

I built her a tower when I was young—
Sometime she will die—
I built it with my hands, I hung
Stones in the sky.

Old but still strong I climb the stone—
Sometime she will die—
Climb the steep rough steps alone,
And weep in the sky.

Never weep, never weep.

II

Never be astonished, dear.
Expect change,
Nothing is strange.

We have seen the human race
Capture all its dreams,
All except peace.

We have watched mankind like Christ
Toil up and up,
To be hanged at the top.

No longer envying the birds,
That ancient prayer for
Wings granted: therefore

The heavy sky over London
Stallion-hoofed
Falls on the roofs.

These are the falling years,
They will go deep,
Never weep, never weep.

With clear eyes explore the pit.
Watch the great fall
With religious awe.

III

It is not Europe alone that is falling
Into blood and fire.
Decline and fall have been dancing in all men's souls
For a long while.

Sometime at the last gasp comes peace
To every soul.
Never to mine until I find out and speak
The things that I know.

IV

To-morrow I will take up that heavy poem again
About Ferguson, deceived and jealous man
Who bawled for the truth, the truth, and failed to endure
Its first least gleam. That poem bores me, and I hope will
　　bore
Any sweet soul that reads it, being some ways
My very self but mostly my antipodes;
But having waved the heavy artillery to fire
I must hammer on to an end.

　　　　　　　To-night, dear,
Let's forget all that, that and the war,
And enisle ourselves a little beyond time,
You with this Irish whiskey, I with red wine
While the stars go over the sleepless ocean,
And sometime after midnight I'll pluck you a wreath
Of chosen ones; we'll talk about love and death,
Rock-solid themes, old and deep as the sea,
Admit nothing more timely, nothing less real
While the stars go over the timeless ocean,
And when they vanish we'll have spent the night well.

Advice to Pilgrims

That our senses lie and our minds trick us is true, but in
general
They are honest rustics; trust them a little;
The senses more than the mind, and your own mind more
than another man's.
As to the mind's pilot, intuition,—
Catch him clean and stark naked he is first of truth-tellers;
dream-clothed, or dirty
With fears and wishes, he is prince of liars.
The first fear is of death: trust no immortalist. The first desire
Is to be loved: trust no mother's son.
Finally I say, let demogogues and world-redeemers babble
their emptiness
To empty ears; twice duped is too much.
Walk on gaunt shores and avoid the people; rock and wave
are good prophets;
Wise are the wings of the gull, pleasant her song.

Cassandra

The mad girl with the staring eyes and long white fingers
Hooked in the stones of the wall,
The storm-wrack hair and the screeching mouth: does it
matter, Cassandra,
Whether the people believe
Your bitter fountain? Truly men hate the truth; they'd liefer
Meet a tiger on the road.
Therefore the poets honey their truth with lying; but
religion-
Venders and political men
Pour from the barrel, new lies on the old, and are praised for
kindly
Wisdom. Poor bitch, be wise.
No: you'll still mumble in a corner a crust of truth, to men
And gods disgusting.—You and I, Cassandra.

Animals

At dawn a knot of sea-lions lies off the shore
In the slow swell between the rock and the cliff,
Sharp flippers lifted, or great-eyed heads, as they roll in the sea,
Bigger than draft-horses, and barking like dogs
Their all-night song. It makes me wonder a little
That life near kin to human, intelligent, hot-blooded, idle and
    singing, can float at ease
In the ice-cold midwinter water. Then, yellow dawn
Colors the south, I think about the rapid and furious lives in
    the sun:
They have little to do with ours; they have nothing to do with
    oxygen and salted water; they would look monstrous
If we could see them: the beautiful passionate bodies of living
    flame, batlike flapping and screaming,
Tortured with burning lust and acute awareness, that ride the
    storm-tides
Of the great fire-globe. They are animals, as we are. There are
    many other chemistries of animal life
Besides the slow oxidation of carbohydrates and amino-acids.

The Beauty of Things

To feel and speak the astonishing beauty of things—earth,
    stone and water,
Beast, man and woman, sun, moon and stars—
The blood-shot beauty of human nature, its thoughts,
    frenzies and passions,
And unhuman nature its towering reality—
For man's half dream; man, you might say, is nature
    dreaming, but rock
And water and sky are constant—to feel
Greatly, and understand greatly, and express greatly, the
    natural
Beauty, is the sole business of poetry.
The rest's diversion: those holy or noble sentiments, the
    intricate ideas,
The love, lust, longing: reasons, but not the reason.

Carmel Point

The extraordinary patience of things!
This beautiful place defaced with a crop of suburban houses—
How beautiful when we first beheld it,
Unbroken field of poppy and lupin walled with clean cliffs;
No intrusion but two or three horses pasturing,
Or a few milch cows rubbing their flanks on the outcrop
    rock-heads—
Now the spoiler has come: does it care?
Not faintly. It has all time. It knows the people are a tide
That swells and in time will ebb, and all
Their works dissolve. Meanwhile the image of the pristine
    beauty
Lives in the very grain of the granite,
Safe as the endless ocean that climbs our cliff.—As for us:
We must uncenter our minds from ourselves;
We must unhumanize our views a little, and become
    confident
As the rock and ocean that we were made from.

The Deer Lay Down Their Bones

I followed the narrow cliffside trail half way up the mountain
Above the deep river-canyon. There was a little cataract
    crossed the path, flinging itself
Over tree roots and rocks, shaking the jewelled fern-fronds,
    bright bubbling water
Pure from the mountain, but a bad smell came up.
    Wondering at it I clambered down the steep stream
Some forty feet, and found in the midst of bush-oak and
    laurel,
Hung like a bird's nest on the precipice brink a small hidden
    clearing,
Grass and a shallow pool. But all about there were bones
    lying in the grass, clean bones and stinking bones,
Antlers and bones: I understood that the place was a refuge
    for wounded deer; there are so many

Hurt ones escape the hunters and limp away to lie hidden;
  here they have water for the awful thirst
And peace to die in; dense green laurel and grim cliff
Make sanctuary, and a sweet wind blows upward from the
  deep gorge.—I wish my bones were with theirs.
But that's a foolish thing to confess, and a little cowardly. We
  know that life
Is on the whole quite equally good and bad, mostly gray
  neutral, and can be endured
To the dim end, no matter what magic of grass, water and
  precipice, and pain of wounds,
Makes death look dear. We have been given life and have used
  it—not a great gift perhaps—but in honesty
Should use it all. Mine's empty since my love died—Empty?
  The flame-haired grandchild with great blue eyes
That look like hers?—What can I do for the child? I gaze at
  her and wonder what sort of man
In the fall of the world . . . I am growing old, that is the
  trouble. My children and little grandchildren
Will find their way, and why should I wait ten years yet,
  having lived sixty-seven, ten years more or less,
Before I crawl out on a ledge of rock and die snapping, like a
  wolf
Who has lost his mate?—I am bound by my own thirty-year-
  old decision: who drinks the wine
Should take the dregs; even in the bitter lees and sediment
New discovery may lie. The deer in that beautiful place lay
  down their bones: I must wear mine.

Vulture

I had walked since dawn and lay down to rest on a bare
  hillside
Above the ocean. I saw through half-shut eyelids a vulture
  wheeling high up in heaven,
And presently it passed again, but lower and nearer, its orbit
  narrowing, I understood then

That I was under inspection. I lay death-still and heard the
     flight-feathers
Whistle above me and make their circle and come nearer. I
     could see the naked red head between the great wings
Beak downward staring. I said "My dear bird we are wasting
     time here.
These old bones will still work; they are not for you." But
     how beautiful he'd looked, gliding down
On those great sails; how beautiful he looked, veering away in
     the sea-light over the precipice. I tell you solemnly
That I was sorry to have disappointed him. To be eaten by
     that beak and become part of him, to share those wings
     and those eyes—
What a sublime end of one's body, what an enskyment; what
     a life after death.

————————

I have been warned. It is more than thirty years since I
     wrote—
Thinking of the narrative poems I made, which always
Ended in blood and pain, though beautiful enough—my
     pain, my blood,
They were my creatures—I understood, and wrote to myself:
"Make sacrifices once a year to magic
Horror away from the house"—for that hangs imminent
Over all men and all houses—"This little house here
You have built over the ocean with your own hands
Beside the standing sea-boulders . . ." So I listened
To my Demon warning me that evil would come
If my work ceased, if I did not make sacrifice
Of storied and imagined lives, Tamar and Cawdor
And Thurso's wife—"imagined victims be our redeemers"—
At that time I was sure of my fates and felt
My poems guarding the house, well-made watchdogs
Ready to bite.

               But time sucks out the juice,
A man grows old and indolent.

ORRICK JOHNS

(1887–1946)

Salon des Vers

The little verses seek their meal . . .
O chef appointed, glut these aches!
and from the noon of wine and cakes,
lo, fed to fullness, let them steal
into the dusk to violate
in verbal corybantic daze
each one his slim and guarded phrase
or line most dimply celibate.

Invitation

Idonean lemur, sport with me
beneath the amber cyprilune,
where roll in onomotope
the rumbles of maroon.

O Clovic shaft, these lobes await
the splitting glaive, inappetent . . .
O shadow-eyes aculeate,
return, relume, resent!

Wild Plum

They are unholy who are born
   To love wild plum at night,
Who once have passed it on a road
   Glimmering and white.

It is as though the darkness had
   Speech of silver words,
Or as though a cloud of stars
   Perched like ghostly birds.

They are unpitied from their birth
   And homeless in men's sight
Who love better than the earth
   Wild plum at night.

MARIANNE MOORE

(1887–1972)

To an Intra-Mural Rat

You make me think of many men
Once met to be forgot again
   Or merely resurrected
In a parenthesis of wit
That found them hastening through it
   Too brisk to be inspected.

To a Steam Roller

The illustration
is nothing to you without the application.
   You lack half wit. You crush all the particles down
     into close conformity, and then walk back and forth on
       them.

Sparkling chips of rock
are crushed down to the level of the parent block.
   Were not "impersonal judgment in æsthetic
     matters, a metaphysical impossibility," you

might fairly achieve
it. As for butterflies, I can hardly conceive
   of one's attending upon you, but to question
     the congruence of the complement is vain, if it exists.

Is Your Town Nineveh?

Why so desolate?
   in phantasmagoria about fishes,
     what disgusts you? Could
       not all personal upheaval in
         the name of freedom, be tabooed?

Is it Nineveh
   and are you Jonah
     in the sweltering east wind of your wishes?
       I myself, have stood
         there by the aquarium, looking
           at the Statue of Liberty.

The Past Is the Present

If external action is effete
   and rhyme is outmoded,
     I shall revert to you,
   Habakkuk, as on a recent occasion I was goaded
       into doing by XY, who was speaking of unrhymed
         verse.
This man said—I think that I repeat
   his identical words:
     'Hebrew poetry is
prose with a sort of heightened consciousness.' Ecstasy
       affords
         the occasion and expediency determines the form.

"He Wrote the History Book"

There! You shed a ray
   of whimsicality on a mask of profundity so
      terrific, that I have been dumbfounded by
it oftener than I care to say.
        The book? Titles are chaff.

Authentically
   brief and full of energy, you contribute to your father's
      legibility and are sufficiently
synthetic. Thank you for showing me
      your father's autograph.

Critics and Connoisseurs

There is a great amount of poetry in unconscious
   fastidiousness. Certain Ming
      products, imperial floor-coverings of coach
wheel yellow, are well enough in their way but I have seen
        something
     that I like better—a
       mere childish attempt to make an imperfectly
       ballasted animal stand up,
     similar determination to make a pup
       eat his meat on the plate.

I remember a swan under the willows in Oxford
   with flamingo colored, maple-
      leaflike feet. It reconnoitered like a battle
ship. Disbelief and conscious fastidiousness were the staple
     ingredients in its
       disinclination to move. Finally its hardihood
        was not proof against its
      proclivity to more fully appraise such bits
       of food as the stream

bore counter to it; it made away with what I gave it
   to eat. I have seen this swan and
      I have seen you; I have seen ambition without
   understanding in a variety of forms. Happening to stand
         by an ant hill, I have
            seen a fastidious ant carrying a stick, north,
               south, east, west, till it turned on
            itself, struck out from the flower bed into the
               lawn,
            and returned to the point

from which it had started. Then abandoning the stick as
   useless and overtaxing its
      jaws with a particle of whitewash pill-like but
heavy, it again went through the same course of pro-
            cedure. What is
         there in being able
            to say that one has dominated the stream in an
               attitude of self-defense;
            in proving that one has had the experience
               of carrying a stick?

                              .

                    To a Chameleon

Hid by the august foliage and fruit of the grape vine,
Twine
   Your anatomy
      Round the pruned and polished stem,
         Chameleon.
         Fire laid upon
      An emerald as long as
   The Dark King's massy
One,
Could not snap the spectrum up for food as you have done.

Like a Bulrush

or the spike
of a channel marker or the
moon, he superintended the demolition of his image in
the water by the wind; he did not strike

them at the
time as being different from
any other inhabitant of the water; it was as if he
were a seal in the combined livery

of bird plus
snake; it was as if he knew that
the penguins were not fish and as if in their bat blindness,
          they did not
realize that he was amphibious.

The Monkeys

winked too much and were afraid of snakes. The zebras,
        supreme in
their abnormality; the elephants with their fog-coloured skin
  and strictly practical appendages
      were there, the small cats; and the parrakeet—
        trivial and humdrum on examination, destroying
      bark and portions of the food it could not eat.

I recall their magnificence, now not more magnificent
than it is dim. It is difficult to recall the ornament,
    speech, and precise manner of what one might
      call the minor acquaintances twenty
        years back; but I shall not forget him—that Gilgamesh
           among
      the hairy carnivora—that cat with the

wedge-shaped, slate-gray marks on its forelegs and the
          resolute tail,
astringently remarking, 'They have imposed on us with their
          pale
   half-fledged protestations, trembling about
      in inarticulate frenzy, saying
         it is not for us to understand art; finding it
        all so difficult, examining the thing

as if it were inconceivably arcanic, as symmet-
rically frigid as if it had been carved out of chrysoprase
   or marble—strict with tension, malignant
      in its power over us and deeper
         than the sea when it proffers flattery in exchange for
          hemp,
        rye, flax, horses, platinum, timber, and fur.'

Those Various Scalpels

Those
various sounds consistently indistinct, like intermingled
          echoes
   struck from thin glasses successively at random—the
   inflection disguised: your hair, the tails of two
        fighting-cocks head to head in stone—like sculptured
        scimitars re-
      peating the curve of your ears in reverse order: your
          eyes,
      flowers of ice

and
snow sown by tearing winds on the cordage of disabled
        ships: your raised hand
     an ambiguous signature: your cheeks, those rosettes
     of blood on the stone floors of French châteaux, with
        regard to which the guides are so affirmative:
        your other hand

a
bundle of lances all alike, partly hid by emeralds from
    Persia
  and the fractional magnificence of Florentine
  goldwork—a collection of half a dozen little objects
    made fine
    with enamel in gray, yellow, and dragon-fly blue; a
      lemon, a

pear
and three bunches of grapes, tied with silver: your dress, a
    magnificent square
  cathedral tower of uniform
  and at the same time diverse appearance—a species of
    vertical vineyard rustling in the storm
    of conventional opinion. Are they weapons or scalpels?
    Whetted

to
brilliance by the hard majesty of that sophistication which
    is su-
  perior to opportunity, these things are rich
  instruments with which to experiment but surgery is
    not tentative. Why dissect destiny with instruments
    which
    are more highly specialized than the tissues of destiny
    itself?

The Fish

wade
through black jade.
   Of the crow-blue mussel-shells, one keeps
   adjusting the ash-heaps;
      opening and shutting itself like

an
injured fan.
   The barnacles which encrust the side
   of the wave, cannot hide
      there for the submerged shafts of the

sun,
split like spun
   glass, move themselves with spotlight swiftness
   into the crevices—
      in and out, illuminating

the
turquoise sea
   of bodies. The water drives a wedge
   of iron through the iron edge
      of the cliff; whereupon the stars,

pink
rice-grains, ink-
   bespattered jelly-fish, crabs like green
   lilies, and submarine
      toadstools, slide each on the other.

All
external
   marks of abuse are present on this
   defiant edifice—
      all the physical features of

ac-
cident—lack
    of cornice, dynamite grooves, burns, and
    hatchet strokes, these things stand
        out on it; the chasm-side is

dead.
Repeated
    evidence has proved that it can live
    on what can not revive
        its youth. The sea grows old in it.

Black Earth

Openly, yes,
with the naturalness
    of the hippopotamus or the alligator
    when it climbs out on the bank to experience the

sun, I do these
things which I do, which please
    no one but myself. Now I breathe and now I am sub-
    merged; the blemishes stand up and shout when the object

in view was a
renaissance; shall I say
    the contrary? The sediment of the river which
    encrusts my joints, makes me very gray but I am used

to it, it may
remain there; do away
    with it and I am myself done away with, for the
    patina of circumstance can but enrich what was

there to begin
with. This elephant-skin
    which I inhabit, fibred over like the shell of
    the cocoanut, this piece of black glass through which no
                light

can filter—cut
into checkers by rut
　　upon rut of unpreventable experience—
　　it is a manual for the peanut-tongued and the

hairy-toed. Black
but beautiful, my back
　　is full of the history of power. Of power? What
　　is powerful and what is not? My soul shall never

be cut into
by a wooden spear; through-
　　out childhood to the present time, the unity of
　　life and death has been expressed by the circumference

described by my
trunk; nevertheless I
　　perceive feats of strength to be inexplicable after
　　all; and I am on my guard; external poise, it

has its centre
well nurtured—we know
　　where—in pride; but spiritual poise, it has its centre where?
　　My ears are sensitized to more than the sound of

the wind. I see
and I hear, unlike the
　　wandlike body of which one hears so much, which was
　　　　　　　made
　　to see and not to see; to hear and not to hear;

that tree-trunk without
roots, accustomed to shout
　　its own thoughts to itself like a shell, maintained intact
　　by who knows what strange pressure of the atmosphere;
　　　　　　　that

spiritual
brother to the coral-
　　plant, absorbed into which, the equable sapphire light
　　becomes a nebulous green. The I of each is to

the I of each
a kind of fretful speech
    which sets a limit on itself; the elephant is
    black earth preceded by a tendril? Compared with those

phenomena
which vacillate like a
    translucence of the atmosphere, the elephant is
    that on which darts cannot strike decisively the first

time, a substance
needful as an instance
    of the indestructibility of matter; it
    has looked at the electricity and at the earth-

quake and is still
here; the name means thick. Will
    depth be depth, thick skin be thick, to one who can see no
    beautiful element of unreason under it?

Peter

Strong and slippery, built for the midnight grass-party
                confronted by four cats,
    he sleeps his time away—the detached first claw on his
            foreleg which corresponds
  to the thumb, retracted to its tip; the small tuft of fronds
    or katydid legs above each eye, still numbering the units
          in each group;
        the shadbones regularly set about the mouth, to
        droop or rise

in unison like the porcupine's quills—motionless. He lets
                himself be flat-
    tened out by gravity, as it were a piece of seaweed tamed
           and weakened by
    exposure to the sun; compelled when extended, to lie

stationary. Sleep is the result of his delusion that one
     must do as
    well as one can for oneself; sleep—epitome of
    what is to

him as to the average person, the end of life. Demonstrate
     on him how
  the lady caught the dangerous southern snake, placing a
     forked stick on either
  side of its innocuous neck; one need not try to stir
    him up; his prune shaped head and alligator eyes are
     not a party to the
      joke. Lifted and handled, he may be dangled like an
      eel or set

up on the forearm like a mouse; his eyes bisected by pupils
     of a pin's
  width, are flickeringly exhibited, then covered up. May
     be? I should say
  might have been; when he has been got the better of in a
    dream—as in a fight with nature or with cats—we all
     know it. Profound sleep is
      not with him, a fixed illusion. Springing about with
      froglike ac-

curacy, emitting jerky cries when taken in the hand, he is
     himself
  again; to sit caged by the rungs of a domestic chair would
     be unprofit-
  able—human. What is the good of hypocrisy? It
    is permissible to choose one's employment, to abandon
     the wire nail, the
      roly-poly, when it shows signs of being no longer a
      pleas-

ure, to score the adjacent magazine with a double line of
     strokes. He can
  talk, but insolently says nothing. What of it? When one is
     frank, one's very
  presence is a compliment. It is clear that he can see

the virtue of naturalness, that he is one of those who
        do not regard
    the published fact as a surrender. As for the disposition

invariably to affront, an animal with claws wants to have
        to use
    them; that eel-like extension of trunk into tail is not an
        accident. To
    leap, to lengthen out, divide the air—to purloin, to pursue.
        To tell the hen: fly over the fence, go in the wrong way
            —in your perturba-
            tion—this is life; to do less would be nothing but
            dishonesty.

When I Buy Pictures

Or what is closer to the truth,
when I look at that of which I may regard myself as the
        imaginary possessor,
I fix upon what would give me pleasure in my average
        moments:
the satire upon curiosity in which no more is discernible than
the intensity of the mood;
or quite the opposite—the old thing, the mediæval decorated
        hat-box,
in which there are hounds with waists diminishing like the
        waist of the hourglass
and deer and birds and seated people;
it may be no more than a square of parquetry; the literal
        biography perhaps,
in letters standing well apart upon a parchment-like expanse;
an artichoke in six varieties of blue; the snipe-legged
        hieroglyphic in three parts;
the silver fence protecting Adam's grave, or Michael taking
        Adam by the wrist.
Too stern an intellectual emphasis upon this quality or that,
        detracts from one's enjoyment;

it must not wish to disarm anything; nor may the approved
    triumph easily be honored—
that which is great because something else is small.
It comes to this: of whatever sort it is,
it must be "lit with piercing glances into the life of things";
it must acknowledge the spiritual forces which have made it.

Poetry

I, too, dislike it: there are things that are important beyond
        all this fiddle.
   Reading it, however, with a perfect contempt for it, one
        discovers in
    it after all, a place for the genuine.
     Hands that can grasp, eyes
      that can dilate, hair that can rise
        if it must, these things are important not because a

high-sounding interpretation can be put upon them but
        because they are
   useful. When they become so derivative as to become
        unintelligible,
    the same thing may be said for all of us, that we
     do not admire what
     we cannot understand: the bat
       holding on upside down or in quest of something to

eat, elephants pushing, a wild horse taking a roll, a tireless
        wolf under
   a tree, the immovable critic twitching his skin like a horse
        that feels a flea, the base-
   ball fan, the statistician—
     nor is it valid
       to discriminate against 'business documents and

school-books'; all these phenomena are important. One must
        make a distinction

however: when dragged into prominence by half poets, the
result is not poetry,
nor till the poets among us can be
'literalists of
the imagination'—above
insolence and triviality and can present

for inspection, 'imaginary gardens with real toads in them',
shall we have
it. In the meantime, if you demand on the one hand,
the raw material of poetry in
all its rawness and
that which is on the other hand
genuine, you are interested in poetry.

A Grave

Man looking into the sea,
taking the view from those who have as much right to it as
you have to it yourself,
it is human nature to stand in the middle of a thing
but you cannot stand in the middle of this:
the sea has nothing to give but a well excavated grave.
The firs stand in a procession, each with an emerald turkey-
foot at the top,
reserved as their contours, saying nothing;
repression, however, is not the most obvious characteristic of
the sea;
the sea is a collector, quick to return a rapacious look.
There are others besides you who have worn that look—
whose expression is no longer a protest; the fish no longer
investigate them
for their bones have not lasted:
men lower nets, unconscious of the fact that they are
desecrating a grave,
and row quickly away—the blades of the oars
moving together like the feet of water-spiders as if there were
no such thing as death.

The wrinkles progress upon themselves in a phalanx—
    beautiful under networks of foam,
and fade breathlessly while the sea rustles in and out of the
    seaweed;
the birds swim through the air at top speed, emitting cat-calls
    as heretofore—
the tortoise-shell scourges about the feet of the cliffs, in
    motion beneath them
and the ocean, under the pulsation of lighthouse and noise
    of bell-buoys,
advances as usual, looking as if it were not that ocean in
    which dropped things are bound to sink—
in which if they turn and twist, it is neither with volition nor
    consciousness.

Marriage

This institution,
perhaps one should say enterprise
out of respect for which
one says one need not change one's mind
about a thing one has believed in,
requiring public promises
of one's intention
to fulfil a private obligation:
I wonder what Adam and Eve
think of it by this time,
this fire-gilt steel
alive with goldenness;
how bright it shows—
"of circular traditions and impostures,
committing many spoils,"
requiring all one's criminal ingenuity
to avoid!
Psychology which explains everything
explains nothing,
and we are still in doubt.
Eve: beautiful woman—
I have seen her
when she was so handsome
she gave me a start,
able to write simultaneously
in three languages—
English, German and French—
and talk in the meantime;
equally positive in demanding a commotion
and in stipulating quiet:
"*I* should like to be alone";
to which the visitor replies,
"I should like to be alone;
why not be alone together?"
Below the incandescent stars
below the incandescent fruit,
the strange experience of beauty;
its existence is too much;

it tears one to pieces
and each fresh wave of consciousness
is poison.
"See her, see her in this common world,"
the central flaw
in that first crystal-fine experiment,
this amalgamation which can never be more
than an interesting impossibility,
describing it
as "that strange paradise
unlike flesh, stones,
gold or stately buildings,
the choicest piece of my life:
the heart rising
in its estate of peace
as a boat rises
with the rising of the water";
constrained in speaking of the serpent—
shed snakeskin in the history of politeness
not to be returned to again—
that invaluable accident
exonerating Adam.
And he has beauty also;
it's distressing—the O thou
to whom from whom,
without whom nothing—Adam;
"something feline,
something colubrine"—how true!
a crouching mythological monster
in that Persian miniature of emerald mines,
raw silk—ivory white, snow white,
oyster white and six others—
that paddock full of leopards and giraffes—
long lemon-yellow bodies
sown with trapezoids of blue.
Alive with words,
vibrating like a cymbal
touched before it has been struck,
he has prophesied correctly—
the industrious waterfall,

"the speedy stream
which violently bears all before it,
at one time silent as the air
and now as powerful as the wind."
"Treading chasms
on the uncertain footing of a spear,"
forgetting that there is in woman
a quality of mind
which as an instinctive manifestation
is unsafe,
he goes on speaking
in a formal customary strain,
of "past states, the present state,
seals, promises,
the evil one suffered,
the good one enjoys,
hell, heaven,
everything convenient
to promote one's joy."
In him a state of mind
perceives what it was not
intended that he should;
"he experiences a solemn joy
in seeing that he has become an idol."
Plagued by the nightingale
in the new leaves,
with its silence—
not its silence but its silences,
he says of it:
"It clothes me with a shirt of fire."
"He dares not clap his hands
to make it go on
lest it should fly off;
if he does nothing, it will sleep;
if he cries out, it will not understand."
Unnerved by the nightingale
and dazzled by the apple,
impelled by "the illusion of a fire
effectual to extinguish fire,"
compared with which

the shining of the earth
is but deformity—a fire
"as high as deep
as bright as broad
as long as life itself,"
he stumbles over marriage,
"a very trivial object indeed"
to have destroyed the attitude
in which he stood—
the ease of the philosopher
unfathered by a woman.
Unhelpful Hymen!
a kind of overgrown cupid
reduced to insignificance
by the mechanical advertising
parading as involuntary comment,
by that experiment of Adam's
with ways out but no way in—
the ritual of marriage,
augmenting all its lavishness;
its fiddle-head ferns,
lotus flowers, opuntias, white dromedaries,
its hippopotamus—
nose and mouth combined
in one magnificent hopper—
its snake and the potent apple.
He tells us
that "for love that will
gaze an eagle blind,
that is with Hercules
climbing the trees
in the garden of the Hesperides,
from forty-five to seventy
is the best age,"
commending it
as a fine art, as an experiment,
a duty or as merely recreation.
One must not call him ruffian
nor friction a calamity—
the fight to be affectionate:

"no truth can be fully known
until it has been tried
by the tooth of disputation."
The blue panther with black eyes,
the basalt panther with blue eyes,
entirely graceful—
one must give them the path—
the black obsidian Diana
who "darkeneth her countenance
as a bear doth,"
the spiked hand
that has an affection for one
and proves it to the bone,
impatient to assure you
that impatience is the mark of independence,
not of bondage.
"Married people often look that way"—
"seldom and cold, up and down,
mixed and malarial
with a good day and a bad."
We Occidentals are so unemotional,
self lost, the irony preserved
in "the Ahasuerus *tête-à-tête* banquet"
with its small orchids like snakes' tongues,
with its "good monster, lead the way,"
with little laughter
and munificence of humor
in that quixotic atmosphere of frankness
in which "four o'clock does not exist,
but at five o'clock
the ladies in their imperious humility
are ready to receive you";
in which experience attests
that men have power
and sometimes one is made to feel it.
He says, "What monarch would not blush
to have a wife
with hair like a shaving-brush?"
The fact of woman
is "not the sound of the flute

but very poison."
She says, "Men are monopolists
of 'stars, garters, buttons
and other shining baubles'—
unfit to be the guardians
of another person's happiness."
He says, "These mummies
must be handled carefully—
'the crumbs from a lion's meal,
a couple of shins and the bit of an ear';
turn to the letter M
and you will find
that 'a wife is a coffin,'
that severe object
with the pleasing geometry
stipulating space not people,
refusing to be buried
and uniquely disappointing,
revengefully wrought in the attitude
of an adoring child
to a distinguished parent."
She says, "This butterfly,
this waterfly, this nomad
that has 'proposed
to settle on my hand for life'—
What can one do with it?
There must have been more time
in Shakespeare's day
to sit and watch a play.
You know so many artists who are fools."
He says, "You know so many fools
who are not artists."
The fact forgot
that "some have merely rights
while some have obligations,"
he loves himself so much,
he can permit himself
no rival in that love.
She loves herself so much,
she cannot see herself enough—

a statuette of ivory on ivory,
the logical last touch
to an expansive splendor
earned as wages for work done:
one is not rich but poor
when one can always seem so right.
What can one do for them—
these savages
condemned to disaffect
all those who are not visionaries
alert to undertake the silly task
of making people noble?
This model of petrine fidelity
who "leaves her peaceful husband
only because she has seen enough of him"—
that orator reminding you,
"I am yours to command."
"Everything to do with love is mystery;
it is more than a day's work
to investigate this science."
One sees that it is rare—
that striking grasp of opposites
opposed each to the other, not to unity,
which in cycloid inclusiveness
has dwarfed the demonstration
of Columbus with the egg—
a triumph of simplicity—
that charitive Euroclydon
of frightening disinterestedness
which the world hates,
admitting:

    "I am such a cow,
    if I had a sorrow
    I should feel it a long time;
    I am not one of those
    who have a great sorrow
    in the morning
    and a great joy at noon";

which says: "I have encountered it
among those unpretentious
   protégés of wisdom,
where seeming to parade
as the debater and the Roman,
the statesmanship
of an archaic Daniel Webster
persists to their simplicity of temper
as the essence of the matter:

   'Liberty and union
   now and forever';

the Book on the writing-table;
the hand in the breast-pocket."

An Egyptian Pulled Glass Bottle
in the Shape of a Fish

Here we have thirst
And patience from the first,
   And art, as in a wave held up for us to see
   In its essential perpendicularity;

Not brittle but
Intense—the spectrum, that
   Spectacular and nimble animal the fish,
   Whose scales turn aside the sun's sword with their polish.

Silence

My father used to say,
"Superior people never make long visits,
have to be shown Longfellow's grave
nor the glass flowers at Harvard.
Self reliant like the cat—
that takes its prey to privacy,
the mouse's limp tail hanging like a shoelace from its mouth—
they sometimes enjoy solitude,
and can be robbed of speech
by speech which has delighted them.
The deepest feeling always shows itself in silence;
not in silence, but restraint."
Nor was he insincere in saying, " 'Make my house your inn'."
Inns are not residences.

To a Snail

If "compression is the first grace of style,"
you have it. Contractility is a virtue
as modesty is a virtue.
It is not the acquisition of any one thing
that is able to adorn,
or the incidental quality that occurs
as a concomitant of something well said,
that we value in style,
but the principle that is hid:
in the absence of feet, "a method of conclusions";
"a knowledge of principles,"
in the curious phenomenon of your occipital horn.

Bowls

On the green
with lignum vitae balls and ivory markers,
the pins planted in wild duck formation,
and quickly dispersed:
by this survival of ancient punctilio
in the manner of Chinese lacquer carving,
layer after layer exposed by certainty of touch and unhurried
    incision
so that only so much color shall be revealed as is necessary
    to the picture
I learn that we are precisians—
not citizens of Pompeii arrested in action
as a cross section of one's correspondence would seem to
    imply.
Renouncing a policy of boorish indifference
to everything that has been said since the days of Matilda,
I shall purchase an Etymological Dictionary of Modern English
that I may understand what is written
and like the ant and the spider
returning from time to time to headquarters,
shall answer the question
as to "why I like winter better than I like summer"
and acknowledge that it does not make me sick
to look modern playwrights and poets and novelists straight
    in the face—
that I feel just the same;
and I shall write to the publisher of the magazine
which will "appear the first day of the month
and disappear before one has had time to buy it
unless one takes proper precaution,"
and make an effort to please—
since he who gives quickly gives twice
in nothing so much as in a letter.

The Steeple-Jack

Dürer would have seen a reason for living
    in a town like this, with eight stranded whales
to look at; with the sweet sea air coming into your house
on a fine day, from water etched
    with waves as formal as the scales
on a fish.

One by one in two's and three's, the seagulls keep
    flying back and forth over the town clock,
or sailing around the lighthouse without moving their
        wings—
rising steadily with a slight
    quiver of the body—or flock
mewing where

a sea the purple of the peacock's neck is
    paled to greenish azure as Dürer changed
the pine green of the Tyrol to peacock blue and guinea
gray. You can see a twenty-five-
    pound lobster; and fish nets arranged
to dry. The

whirlwind fife-and-drum of the storm bends the salt
    marsh grass, disturbs stars in the sky and the
star on the steeple; it is a privilege to see so
much confusion. Disguised by what
    might seem the opposite, the sea-
side flowers and

trees are favored by the fog so that you have
    the tropics at first hand: the trumpet-vine,
fox-glove, giant snap-dragon, a salpiglossis that has
spots and stripes; morning-glories, gourds,
    or moon-vines trained on fishing-twine
at the back door;

cat-tails, flags, blueberries and spiderwort,
      striped grass, lichens, sunflowers, asters, daisies—
yellow and crab-claw ragged sailors with green bracts—
            toad-plant,
petunias, ferns; pink lilies, blue
      ones, tigers; poppies; black sweet-peas.
The climate

is not right for the banyan, frangipani, or
      jack-fruit trees; or for exotic serpent
life. Ring lizard and snake-skin for the foot, if you see fit;
but here they've cats, not cobras, to
      keep down the rats. The diffident
little newt

with white pin-dots on black horizontal spaced-
      out bands lives here; yet there is nothing that
ambition can buy or take away. The college student
named Ambrose sits on the hillside
      with his not-native books and hat
and sees boats

at sea progress white and rigid as if in
      a groove. Liking an elegance of which
the source is not bravado, he knows by heart the antique
sugar-bowl shaped summer-house of
      interlacing slats, and the pitch
of the church

spire, not true, from which a man in scarlet lets
      down a rope as a spider spins a thread;
he might be part of a novel, but on the sidewalk a
sign says C. J. Poole, Steeple-Jack,
      in black and white; and one in red
and white says

Danger. The church portico has four fluted
      columns, each a single piece of stone, made
modester by white-wash. This would be a fit haven for

waifs, children, animals, prisoners,
    and presidents who have repaid
sin-driven

senators by not thinking about them. The
    place has a school-house, a post-office in a
store, fish-houses, hen-houses, a three-masted
      schooner on
the stocks. The hero, the student,
    the steeple-jack, each in his way,
is at home.

It could not be dangerous to be living
    in a town like this, of simple people,
who have a steeple-jack placing danger-signs by the church
while he is gilding the solid-
      pointed star, which on a steeple
stands for hope.

Smooth Gnarled Crape Myrtle

    A brass-green bird with grass-
      green throat smooth as a nut springs from
        twig to twig askew, copying the
    Chinese flower piece—businesslike atom
      in the stiff-leafed tree's blue-
      pink dregs-of-wine pyramids
      of mathematic
      circularity; one of a
      pair. A redbird with a hatchet
      crest lights straight, on a twig
      between the two, bending the
        peculiar
        bouquet down; and there are

    moths and lady-bugs,
a boot-jack firefly with black wings

and a pink head. "The legendary white-
eared black bulbul that sings
   only in pure Sanskrit" should
   be here—"tame clever
true nightingale." The cardinal-
bird that is usually a
   pair, looks somewhat odd, like
   "the ambassadorial
     Inverness
    worn by one who dresses

in New York but dreams of
London." It was artifice saw,
   on a patch-box pigeon-egg, room for
fervent script, and wrote as with a bird's claw
   under the pair on the
   hyacinth-blue lid—"joined in
    friendship, crowned by love."
An aspect may deceive; as the
elephant's columbine-tubed trunk
   held waveringly out—
   an at will heavy thing—is
    delicate.
    Art is unfortunate.

One may be a blameless
bachelor, and it is but a step
   to Congreve. A Rosalindless
redbird comes where people are, knowing they
   have not made a point of
   being where he is—this bird
which says not sings, "without
   loneliness I should be more
   lonely, so I keep it"—half in
Japanese. And what of
   our clasped hands that swear, "By Peace
    Plenty; as
    by Wisdom Peace." Alas!

Bird-Witted

With innocent wide penguin eyes, three
   large fledgling mocking-birds below
the pussy-willow tree,
    stand in a row,
wings touching, feebly solemn,
till they see
      their no longer larger
      mother bringing
something which will partially
feed one of them.

Toward the high-keyed intermittent squeak
   of broken carriage-springs, made by
the three similar, meek-
    coated bird's-eye
freckled forms she comes; and when
from the beak
      of one, the still living
      beetle has dropped
out, she picks it up and puts
it in again.

Standing in the shade till they have dressed
   their thickly-filamented, pale
pussy-willow-surfaced
    coats, they spread tail
and wings, showing one by one,
the modest
      white stripe lengthwise on the
      tail and crosswise
underneath the wing, and the
accordion

is closed again. What delightful note
   with rapid unexpected flute-
sounds leaping from the throat
    of the astute
grown bird, comes back to one from

the remote
　　unenergetic sun-
　　lit air before.
the brood was here? How harsh
the bird's voice has become.

A piebald cat observing them,
　is slowly creeping toward the trim
trio on the tree-stem.
　　Unused to him
the three make room—uneasy
new problem.
　　　A dangling foot that missed
　　　its grasp, is raised
and finds the twig on which it
planned to perch. The

parent darting down, nerved by what chills
　the blood, and by hope rewarded—
of toil—since nothing fills
　squeaking unfed
mouths, wages deadly combat,
and half kills
　　　with bayonet beak and
　　　cruel wings, the
intellectual cautious-
ly c r e e p ing cat.

The Pangolin

Another armored animal—scale
    lapping scale with spruce-cone regularity until they
form the uninterrupted central
    tail-row! This near artichoke with head and legs and grit-
        equipped gizzard,
  the night miniature artist engineer is,
      yes, Leonardo da Vinci's replica—
        impressive animal and toiler of whom we seldom
          hear.
    Armor seems extra. But for him,
      the closing ear-ridge—
        or bare ear lacking even this small
        eminence and similarly safe

contracting nose and eye apertures
    impenetrably closable, are not;—a true ant-eater,
not cockroach-eater, who endures
  exhausting solitary trips through unfamiliar ground at
        night,
  returning before sunrise; stepping in the moonlight,
    on the moonlight peculiarly, that the outside
      edges of his hands may bear the weight and save the
        claws
    for digging. Serpentined about
      the tree, he draws
        away from danger unpugnacioulsy,
        with no sound but a harmless hiss; keeping

the fragile grace of the Thomas-
    of-Leighton Buzzard Westminster Abbey wrought-iron
        vine, or
rolls himself into a ball that has
  power to defy all effort to unroll it; strongly intailed,
        neat
  head for core, on neck not breaking off, with curled-in
        feet.
    Nevertheless he has sting-proof scales; and nest
      of rocks closed with earth from inside, which he
        can thus darken.

Sun and moon and day and night and man and beast
  each with a splendor
    which man in all his vileness cannot
    set aside; each with an excellence!

"Fearful yet to be feared," the armored
  ant-eater met by the driver-ant does not turn back, but
engulfs what he can, the flattened sword-
    edged leafpoints on the tail and artichoke set leg- and
                body-plates
  quivering violently when it retaliates
      and swarms on him. Compact like the furled fringed
                frill
        on the hat-brim of Gargallo's hollow iron head of a
        matador, he will drop and will
          then walk away
            unhurt, although if unintruded on,
            he cautiously works down the tree, helped

by his tail. The giant-pangolin-
    tail, graceful tool, as prop or hand or broom or ax,
                tipped like
an elephant's trunk with special skin,
    is not lost on this ant- and stone-swallowing uninjurable
    artichoke which simpletons thought a living fable
      whom the stones had nourished, whereas ants had
                done
        so. Pangolins are not aggressive animals; between
        dusk and day they have the not unchain-like machine-
                like
          form and frictionless creep of a thing
          made graceful by adversities, con-

versities. To explain grace requires
    a curious hand. If that which is at all were not forever,
why would those who graced the spires
    with animals and gathered there to rest, on cold luxurious
    low stone seats—a monk and monk and monk—between
                the thus
      ingenious roof-supports, have slaved to confuse

                    grace with a kindly manner, time in which to pay a
                        debt,
            the cure for sins, a graceful use
                of what are yet
                    approved stone mullions branching out across
                    the perpendiculars? A sailboat

was the first machine. Pangolins, made
        for moving quietly also, are models of exactness,
on four legs; on hind feet plantigrade,
        with certain postures of a man. Beneath sun and moon,
                    man slaving
        to make his life more sweet, leaves half the flowers worth
                    having,
            needing to choose wisely how to use his strength;
                a paper-maker like the wasp; a tractor of foodstuffs,
            like the ant; spidering a length
                of web from bluffs
                    above a stream; in fighting, mechanicked
                    like the pangolin; capsizing in

disheartenment. Bedizened or stark
        naked, man, the self, the being we call human, writing-
master to this world, griffons a dark
        "Like does not like like that is obnoxious"; and writes error
                    with four
r's. Among animals, *one* has a sense of humor.
            Humor saves a few steps, it saves years. Unignorant,
                modest and unemotional, and all emotion,
            he has everlasting vigor,
                power to grow,
                    though there are few creatures who can make
                        one
                    breathe faster and make one erecter.

Not afraid of anything is he,
            and then goes cowering forth, tread paced to meet an
                    obstacle

at every step. Consistent with the
   formula—warm blood, no gills, two pairs of hands and a
               few hairs—that
is a mammal; there he sits in his own habitat,
     serge-clad, strong-shod. The prey of fear, he, always
       curtailed, extinguished, thwarted by the dusk, work
           partly done,
   says to the alternating blaze,
     "Again the sun!
       anew each day; and new and new and new,
       that comes into and steadies my soul."

He "Digesteth Harde Yron"

   Although the aepyronis
     or roc that lived in Madagascar, and
the moa are extinct,
the camel-sparrow, linked
     with them in size—the large sparrow
Xenophon saw walking by a stream—was and is
a symbol of justice.

   This bird watches his chicks with
     a maternal concentration—and he's
been mothering the eggs
at night six weeks—his legs
     their only weapon of defense.
He is swifter than a horse; he has a foot hard
as a hoof; the leopard

   is not more suspicious. How
     could he, prized for plumes and eggs and young,
used even as a riding-beast, respect men
     hiding actor-like in ostrich skins, with the right hand
making the neck move as if alive
and from a bag the left hand strewing grain, that ostriches

might be decoyed and killed! Yes, this is he
whose plume was anciently
the plume of justice; he
    whose comic duckling head on its
great neck revolves with compass-needle nervousness
when he stands guard,

    in S-like foragings as he is
    preening the down on his leaden-skinned back.
The egg piously shown
as Leda's very own
    from which Castor and Pollux hatched,
was an ostrich-egg. And what could have been more fit
for the Chinese lawn it

    grazed on as a gift to an
    emperor who admired strange birds, than this
one, who builds his mud-made
nest in dust yet will wade
    in lake or sea till only the head shows.
                .   .   .   .   .   .

    Six hundred ostrich-brains served
    at one banquet, the ostrich-plume-tipped tent
and desert spear, jewel-
gorgeous ugly egg-shell
    goblets, eight pairs of ostriches
in harness, dramatize a meaning
always missed by the externalist.

    The power of the visible
    is the invisible; as even where
no tree of freedom grows,
so-called brute courage knows.
    Heroism is exhausting, yet
it contradicts a greed that did not wisely spare
the harmless solitaire

or great auk in its grandeur;
   unsolicitude having swallowed up
all giant birds but an alert gargantuan
   little-winged, magnificently speedy running-bird.
This one remaining rebel
is the sparrow-camel.

In Distrust of Merits

Strengthened to live, strengthened to die for
   medals and positioned victories?
They're fighting, fighting, fighting the blind
   man who thinks he sees,—
who cannot see that the enslaver is
enslaved; the hater, harmed. O shining O
     firm star, O tumultuous
       ocean lashed till small things go
   as they will, the mountainous
     wave makes us who look, know

depth. Lost at sea before they fought! O
   star of David, star of Bethlehem,
O black imperial lion
   of the Lord—emblem
of a risen world—be joined at last, be
joined. There is hate's crown beneath which all is
     death; there's love's without which none
       is king; the blessed deeds bless
     the halo. As contagion
       of sickness makes sickness,

contagion of trust can make trust. They're
     fighting in deserts and caves, one by
one, in battalions and squadrons;

they're fighting that I
may yet recover from the disease, My
Self; some have it lightly; some will die. "Man's
     wolf to man" and we devour
          ourselves. The enemy could not
          have made a greater breach in our
          defenses. One pilot-

ing a blind man can escape him, but
     Job disheartened by false comfort knew
that nothing can be so defeating
     as a blind man who
can see. O alive who are dead, who are
proud not to see, O small dust of the earth
          that walks so arrogantly,
               trust begets power and faith is
          an affectionate thing. We
               vow, we make this promise

to the fighting—it's a promise—"We'll
     never hate black, white, red, yellow, Jew,
Gentile, Untouchable." We are
     not competent to
make our vows. With set jaw they are fighting,
fighting, fighting,—some we love whom we know,
          some we love but know not—that
               hearts may feel and not be numb.
          It cures me; or am I what
               I can't believe in? Some

in snow, some on crags, some in quicksands,
     little by little, much by much, they
are fighting fighting fighting that where
     there was death there may
be life. "When a man is prey to anger,
he is moved by outside things; when he holds

his ground in patience patience
    patience, that is action or
beauty," the soldier's defense
    and hardest armor for

the fight. The world's an orphans' home. Shall
    we never have peace without sorrow?
without pleas of the dying for
    help that won't come? O
quiet form upon the dust, I cannot
look and yet I must. If these great patient
    dyings—all these agonies
        and wound bearings and bloodshed—
    can teach us how to live, these
        dyings were not wasted.

Hate-hardened heart, O heart of iron,
    iron is iron till it is rust.
There never was a war that was
    not inward; I must
fight till I have conquered in myself what
causes war, but I would not believe it.
    I inwardly did nothing.
        O Iscariot-like crime!
    Beauty is everlasting
        and dust is for a time.

The Mind Is an Enchanting Thing

is an enchanted thing
    like the glaze on a
katydid-wing
        subdivided by sun
        till the nettings are legion.
Like Gieseking playing Scarlatti;

like the apteryx-awl
    as a beak, or the

kiwi's rain-shawl
  of haired feathers, the mind
  feeling its way as though blind,
walks along with its eyes on the ground.

It has memory's ear
  that can hear without
having to hear.
    Like the gyroscope's fall,
    truly unequivocal
because trued by regnant certainty,

it is a power of
  strong enchantment. It
is like the dove-
    neck animated by
    sun; it is memory's eye;
it's conscientious inconsistency.

It tears off the veil; tears
  the temptation, the
mist the heart wears,
    from its eyes,—if the heart
    has a face; it takes apart
dejection. It's fire in the dove-neck's

iridescence; in the
  inconsistencies
of Scarlatti.
    Unconfusion submits
    its confusion to proof; it's
not a Herod's oath that cannot change.

Tom Fool at Jamaica

Look at Jonah embarking from Joppa, deterred by
the whale; hard going for a statesman whom nothing could
         detain,
  although one who would not rather die than repent.
    Be infallible at your peril, for your system will fail,
and select as a model the schoolboy in Spain
    who at the age of six, portrayed a mule and jockey
      who had pulled up for a snail.

    "There is submerged magnificence, as Victor Hugo
said." *Sentir avec ardeur*; that's it; magnetized by feeling.
    Tom Fool "makes an effort and makes it oftener
      than the rest"—out on April first, a day of some
        significance
in the ambiguous sense—the smiling
    Master Atkinson's choice, with that mark of a champion,
      the extra
      spur when needed. Yes, yes. "Chance

is a regrettable impurity"; like Tom Fool's
left white hind foot—an unconformity; though judging by
    results, a kind of cottontail to give him confidence.
      Up in the cupola comparing speeds, Fred Capossela
        keeps his head.
"It's tough," he said; "but I get 'em; and why shouldn't I?
I'm relaxed, I'm confident, and I *don't bet*." Sensational.
      He does not
    bet on his animated

valentines—his pink and black-striped, sashed or dotted
    silks.
Tom Fool is "a handy horse," with a chiseled foot. You've the
      beat
  of a dancer to a measure or harmonious rush
    of a porpoise at the prow where the racers all win
      easily—

like centaurs' legs in tune, as when kettledrums compete;
  nose rigid and suede nostrils spread, a light left hand on the
      rein, till
    well—this is a rhapsody.

Of course, speaking of champions, there was Fats Waller
with the feather touch, giraffe eyes, and that hand alighting in
Ain't Misbehavin'! Ozzie Smith and Eubie Blake
  ennoble the atmosphere; you recall the Lippizzaner;
the time Ted Atkinson charged by on Tiger Skin—
  no pursuers in sight—cat-loping along. And you may have
      seen a monkey
    on a greyhound. "But Tom Fool . . .

O To Be a Dragon

      If I, like Solomon, . . .
      could have my wish—

      my wish . . . O to be a dragon,
    a symbol of the power of Heaven—of silkworm
    size or immense; at times invisible.
      Felicitous phenomenon!

CHARLIE PATTON

(1887–1934)

High Water Everywhere

I

The back water done rose around Sumner, now,
        Drove me down the line
Back water done rose at Sumner, drove
        Poor Charlie down the line
And I tell the world the water
        Done struck through this town

Lord, the whole round country, lord
        River is overflowed
Lord, the whole round country
        Man it's overflowed
                (You know I can't stay here:
                I'm bound to go where it's
                high, boy)
I would go to the hilly country
        But they got me barred

Now look-a-here now, Leland
        River's rising high
Look-a-here now boys, around Leland, tell me
        River's raging high
                (Boy it's rising over there;
                yeah)
I'm gonna move over to Greenville
        'Fore I bid good-bye

Look-a-here, water done, now lordy, done broke
        Rose most every where
The water at Greenville and Leland
        Lord it done rose everywhere
                (Boy you can't never stay
                here)

I would go down to Rosedale, but they
        Tell me there's water there

Now the water, now mama
        Done struck *Charlie's* town
Well they tell me the water
        Done struck *Charlie's* town
            (Boy I'm going to
            Vicksburg)
Well I'm going to Vicksburg
        On the high of mine

I am going on dry water
        Where land don't never flow
Well I'm going over the hill where water
        Oh, don't never flow
            (Boy, *hit Sharkey County*
            and everything was down in
            Stover)
But *the whole county were leaving*
        Over in Tallahatchie sure
            (Boy I went to Tallahatchie:
            they got it over there)

Lord the water done wrecked all of
        That old Jackson road
Lord the water done ragëd
        Over the Jackson road
            (Boy it got my car)
I'm going back to the hilly country
        Won't be worried no more

2

        Back water at Blytheville
        Backed up all around
        Back water at Blytheville
        Done took Joiner town
        It was fifty families and children
        Come to sink and drown

The water was rising
Up in my friend's door
The water was rising
Up in my friend's door
The man said to his women folk
Lord, we'd better go

The water was rising
Got up in my bed
Lord, the water's rolling
Got up in my bed
I thought I would take a trip, lord
Out on the big *ice sled*

Awwwwww I hear, lord lord,
Water upon my door
          (You know what I mean)
          (Look-a-here)
I hear the ice lord
Lord, we're sinking down
I couldn't get no boat there
Marion City gone down

Ohhhhhh-ah the water rising
Families sinking down
Say now, the water was rising
At places all around
          (Boy, they's all around)
It was fifty men and children
Come to sink and drown

Ohhhhhh-oh lordy
Women and grown men down
Ohhhhhh-oh
Women and children sinking down
          (Lord have mercy)
I couldn't see no body home and
Wasn't no one to be found

JOHN REED

(1887–1920)

from
America in 1918

I have watched the summer day come up from the top of a
    pier of the Williamsburgh Bridge,
I have slept in a basket of squid at the Fulton Street Market,
Talked about God with the old cockney woman who sells
    hot-dogs under the Elevated at South Ferry,
Listen to tales of dago dips in the family parlor of the Hell-
    hole,
And from the top gallery of the Metropolitan heard Didur
    sing "Boris Godounov" . . .
I have shot craps with gangsters in the Gas House district,
And seen what happens to a green bull on San Juan Hill. . .
I can tell you where to hire a gunman to croak a squealor,
And where young girls are bought and sold, and how to get
    coke on 125th Street
And what men talk about behind Steve Brodie's, or in the
    private rooms of the Lafayette Baths. . .

Dear and familiar and ever-new to me is the city
As the body of my lover. . .
All sounds—harsh clatter of the Elevated, rumble of the
    subway,
Tapping of policemen's clubs on midnight pavements,
Hand-organs plaintive and monotonous, squawking motor-
    horns,
Gatling crepitation of airy riveters,
Muffled detonations deep down underground,
Flat bawling of newsboys, quick-clamoring ambulance gongs,
Deep nervous tooting from the evening harbor,
And the profound shuffling thunder of myriad feet. . .

All smells—smell of sample shoes, second-hand clothing,
Dutch bakeries, Sunday delicatessen, kosher cooking,
Smell of damp tons of newspapers along Park Row,

The Subway, smelling like the tomb of Rameses the Great,
The tired odor of infinite human dust-drug-stores,
And the sour slum stench of mean streets. . .

People—rock-eyed brokers gambling with Empires,
Swarthy insolent boot-blacks, cringing push-cart peddlers,
The white-capped wop flipping wheat-cakes in the window of
    Childs',
Sallow garment-workers coughing on a park-bench in the
    thin spring sun,
Dully watching the leaping fountain as they eat a handful of
    peanuts for lunch. . .
The steeple-jack swaying infinitesimal at the top of the
    Woolworth flag-pole,
Charity workers driving hard bargains for the degradation of
    the poor,
Worn-out snarling street-car conductors, sentimental prize
    fighters,
White wings scouring the roaring traffic-ways, foul-mouthed
    truck-drivers,
Spanish longshoremen heaving up freight-mountains, hollow-
    eyed silk workers,
Structural steel workers catching hot rivets on high-up
    spidery girders,
Sand-hogs in hissing air-locks under the North River,
    sweating subway muckers, hard-rock men blasting
    beneath Broadway,
Ward-leaders with uptilted cigars, planning mysterious
    underground battles for power,
Raucous soap-boxers in Union Square, preaching the
    everlasting crusade,
Pale half-fed cash-girls in department stores, gaunt children
    making paper-flowers in dim garrets,
Princess stenographers, and manicurists chewing gum with a
    queenly air,
Macs, whore-house madams, street-walkers, touts, bouncers,
    stool-pigeons. . .
All professions, races, temperaments, philosophies,
All history, all possibilities, all romance,
America . . . the world. . . !

IRVING BERLIN

(1888–1989)

Slumming on Park Avenue

Put on your slumming clothes and get your car,
Let's go sightseeing where the high-toned people are.
Come on, there's lots of fun in store for you,
See how the other half lives on Park Avenue.

Let's go slumming,
Take me slumming.
Let's go slumming on Park Avenue.

Let us hide behind a pair of fancy glasses,
And make faces when a member of the classes passes.

Let's go smelling,
Where they're dwelling,
Sniffing ev'rything the way they do.

Let us go to it, they do it,
Why can't we do it too.
Let's go slumming, nose thumbing,
On Park Avenue.

Let's go slumming,
Take me slumming.
Let's go slumming on Park Avenue.

Where the social hearts for Broadway lights are throbbing,
And they spend their nights in smart cafés hobknobbing,
    snobbing.

Come let's eye them,
Pass right by them
Looking down our noses as they do.

Let us go to it, they do it,
Why can't we do it too.
Let's go slumming, crumb bumming,
On Park Avenue.

T. S. ELIOT
(1888–1965)

The Love Song of J. Alfred Prufrock

S'io credesse che mia risposta fosse
A persona che mai tornasse al mondo,
Questa fiamma staria senza piu scosse.
Ma perciocche giammai di questo fondo
Non torno vivo alcun, s'i'odo il vero,
Senza tema d'infamia ti rispondo.

Let us go then, you and I,
When the evening is spread out against the sky
Like a patient etherized upon a table;
Let us go, through certain half-deserted streets,
The muttering retreats
Of restless nights in one-night cheap hotels
And sawdust restaurants with oyster-shells:
Streets that follow like a tedious argument
Of insidious intent
To lead you to an overwhelming question.
Oh, do not ask, "What is it?"
Let us go and make our visit.

In the room the women come and go
Talking of Michelangelo.

The yellow fog that rubs its back upon the window-panes,
The yellow smoke that rubs its muzzle on the window-panes,
Licked its tongue into the corners of the evening,
Lingered upon the pools that stand in drains,
Let fall upon its back the soot that falls from chimneys,
Slipped by the terrace, made a sudden leap,
And seeing that it was a soft October night,
Curled once about the house, and fell asleep.

And indeed there will be time
For the yellow smoke that slides along the street,
Rubbing its back upon the window-panes;
There will be time, there will be time
To prepare a face to meet the faces that you meet;
There will be time to murder and create,
And time for all the works and days of hands
That lift and drop a question on your plate;
Time for you and time for me,
And time yet for a hundred indecisions,
And for a hundred visions and revisions,
Before the taking of a toast and tea.

In the room the women come and go
Talking of Michelangelo.

And indeed there will be time
To wonder, "Do I dare?" and, "Do I dare?"
Time to turn back and descend the stair,
With a bald spot in the middle of my hair—
(They will say: "How his hair is growing thin!")
My morning coat, my collar mounting firmly to the chin,
My necktie rich and modest, but asserted by a simple pin—
(They will say: "But how his arms and legs are thin!")
Do I dare
Disturb the universe?
In a minute there is time
For decisions and revisions which a minute will reverse.

For I have known them all already, known them all:
Have known the evenings, mornings, afternoons,
I have measured out my life with coffee spoons;
I know the voices dying with a dying fall
Beneath the music from a farther room.
    So how should I presume?

And I have known the eyes already, known them all—
The eyes that fix you in a formulated phrase,
And when I am formulated, sprawling on a pin,
When I am pinned and wriggling on the wall,

Then how should I begin
To spit out all the butt-ends of my days and ways?
    And how should I presume?

And I have known the arms already, known them all—
Arms that are braceleted and white and bare
(But in the lamplight, downed with light brown hair!)
Is it perfume from a dress
That makes me so digress?
Arms that lie along a table, or wrap about a shawl.
    And should I then presume?
    And how should I begin?

                    *   *   *   *

Shall I say, I have gone at dusk through narrow streets
And watched the smoke that rises from the pipes
Of lonely men in shirt-sleeves, leaning out of windows? . . .

I should have been a pair of ragged claws
Scuttling across the floors of silent seas.

                    *   *   *   *

And the afternoon, the evening, sleeps so peacefully!
Smoothed by long fingers,
Asleep . . . tired . . . or it malingers,
Stretched on the floor, here beside you and me.
Should I, after tea and cakes and ices,
Have the strength to force the moment to its crisis?
But though I have wept and fasted, wept and prayed,
Though I have seen my head (grown slightly bald) brought
        in upon a platter,
I am no prophet—and here's no great matter;
I have seen the moment of my greatness flicker,
And I have seen the eternal Footman hold my coat, and
        snicker,
And in short, I was afraid.

And would it have been worth it, after all,
After the cups, the marmalade, the tea,
Among the porcelain, among some talk of you and me,
Would it have been worth while,
To have bitten off the matter with a smile,
To have squeezed the universe into a ball
To roll it toward some overwhelming question,
To say: "I am Lazarus, come from the dead,
Come back to tell you all, I shall tell you all"—
If one, settling a pillow by her head,
    Should say: "That is not what I meant at all;
    That is not it, at all."

And would it have been worth it, after all,
Would it have been worth while,
After the sunsets and the dooryards and the sprinkled streets,
After the novels, after the teacups, after the skirts that trail
    along the floor—
And this, and so much more?—
It is impossible to say just what I mean!
But as if a magic lantern threw the nerves in patterns on a
    screen:
Would it have been worth while
If one, settling a pillow or throwing off a shawl,
And turning toward the window, should say:
    "That is not it at all,
    That is not what I meant, at all."

*   *   *   *

No! I am not Prince Hamlet, nor was meant to be;
Am an attendant lord, one that will do
To swell a progress, start a scene or two,
Advise the prince; no doubt, an easy tool,
Deferential, glad to be of use,
Politic, cautious, and meticulous;
Full of high sentence, but a bit obtuse;
At times, indeed, almost ridiculous—
Almost, at times, the Fool.

I grow old . . . I grow old . . .
I shall wear the bottoms of my trousers rolled.

Shall I part my hair behind? Do I dare to eat a peach?
I shall wear white flannel trousers, and walk upon the beach.
I have heard the mermaids singing, each to each.

I do not think that they will sing to me.

I have seen them riding seaward on the waves
Combing the white hair of the waves blown back
When the wind blows the water white and black.

We have lingered in the chambers of the sea
By sea-girls wreathed with seaweed red and brown
Till human voices wake us, and we drown.

Portrait of a Lady

Thou hast committed—
Fornication: but that was in another country,
And besides, the wench is dead.
                              THE JEW OF MALTA

I

Among the smoke and fog of a December afternoon
You have the scene arrange itself—as it will seem to do—
With "I have saved this afternoon for you";
And four wax candles in the darkened room,
Four rings of light upon the ceiling overhead,
An atmosphere of Juliet's tomb
Prepared for all the things to be said, or left unsaid.
We have been, let us say, to hear the latest Pole
Transmit the Preludes, through his hair and fingertips.
"So intimate, this Chopin, that I think his soul
Should be resurrected only among friends
Some two or three, who will not touch the bloom
That is rubbed and questioned in the concert room."

—And so the conversation slips
Among velleities and carefully caught regrets
Through attenuated tones of violins
Mingled with remote cornets
And begins.

"You do not know how much they mean to me, my friends,
And how, how rare and strange it is, to find
In a life composed so much, so much of odds and ends,
(For indeed I do not love it . . . you knew? you are not
     blind!
How keen you are!)
To find a friend who has these qualities,
Who has, and gives
Those qualities upon which friendship lives.
How much it means that I say this to you—
Without these friendships—life, what *cauchemar*!"
Among the windings of the violins
And the ariettes
Of cracked cornets
Inside my brain a dull tom-tom begins
Absurdly hammering a prelude of its own,
Capricious monotone
That is at least one definite "false note."
—Let us take the air, in a tobacco trance,
Admire the monuments
Discuss the late events,
Correct our watches by the public clocks.
Then sit for half an hour and drink our bocks.

II

Now that lilacs are in bloom
She has a bowl of lilacs in her room
And twists one in her fingers while she talks.
"Ah, my friend, you do not know, you do not know
What life is, you who hold it in your hands";
(Slowly twisting the lilac stalks)
"You let it flow from you, you let it flow,
And youth is cruel, and has no remorse

And smiles at situations which it cannot see."
I smile, of course,
And go on drinking tea.
"Yet with these April sunsets, that somehow recall
My buried life, and Paris in the Spring,
I feel immeasurably at peace, and find the world
To be wonderful and youthful, after all."

The voice returns like the insistent out-of-tune
Of a broken violin on an August afternoon:
"I am always sure that you understand
My feelings, always sure that you feel,
Sure that across the gulf you reach your hand.

You are invulnerable, you have no Achilles' heel.
You will go on, and when you have prevailed
You can say: at this point many a one has failed.

But what have I, but what have I, my friend,
To give you, what can you receive from me?
Only the friendship and the sympathy
Of one about to reach her journey's end.

I shall sit here, serving tea to friends. . . ."

I take my hat: how can I make a cowardly amends
For what she has said to me?
You will see me any morning in the park
Reading the comics and the sporting page.
Particularly I remark
An English countess goes upon the stage.
A Greek was murdered at a Polish dance,
Another bank defaulter has confessed.
I keep my countenance,
I remain self-possessed
Except when a street piano, mechanical and tired
Reiterates some worn-out common song
With the smell of hyacinths across the garden
Recalling things that other people have desired.
Are these ideas right or wrong?

III

The October night comes down; returning as before
Except for a slight sensation of being ill at ease
I mount the stairs and turn the handle of the door
And feel as if I had mounted on my hands and knees.

"And so you are going abroad; and when do you return?
But that's a useless question.
You hardly know when you are coming back,
You will find so much to learn."
My smile falls heavily among the bric-à-brac.

"Perhaps you can write to me."
My self-possession flares up for a second;
This is as I had reckoned.
"I have been wondering frequently of late
(But our beginnings never know our ends!)
Why we have not developed into friends."
I feel like one who smiles, and turning shall remark
Suddenly, his expression in a glass.
My self-possession gutters; we are really in the dark.

"For everybody said so, all our friends,
They all were sure our feelings would relate
So closely! I myself can hardly understand.
We must leave it now to fate.
You will write, at any rate.
Perhaps it is not too late.
I shall sit here, serving tea to friends."

And I must borrow every changing shape
To find expression . . . dance, dance
Like a dancing bear,
Cry like a parrot, chatter like an ape.
Let us take the air, in a tobacco trance—

Well! and what if she should die some afternoon,
Afternoon grey and smoky, evening yellow and rose;
Should die and leave me sitting pen in hand

With the smoke coming down above the housetops;
Doubtful, for quite a while
Not knowing what to feel or if I understand
Or whether wise or foolish, tardy or too soon . . .
Would she not have the advantage, after all?
This music is successful with a "dying fall"
Now that we talk of dying—
And should I have the right to smile?

Preludes

I

The winter evening settles down
With smell of steaks in passageways.
Six o'clock.
The burnt-out ends of smoky days.
And now a gusty shower wraps
The grimy scraps
Of withered leaves about your feet
And newspapers from vacant lots;
The showers beat
On broken blinds and chimney-pots,
And at the corner of the street
A lonely cab-horse steams and stamps.
And then the lighting of the lamps.

II

The morning comes to consciousness
Of faint stale smells of beer
From the sawdust-trampled street
With all its muddy feet that press
To early coffee-stands.

With the other masquerades
That time resumes,
One thinks of all the hands
That are raising dingy shades
In a thousand furnished rooms.

III

You tossed a blanket from the bed,
You lay upon your back, and waited;
You dozed, and watched the night revealing
The thousand sordid images
Of which your soul was constituted;
They flickered against the ceiling.
And when all the world came back
And the light crept up between the shutters,
And you heard the sparrows in the gutters,
You had such a vision of the street
As the street hardly understands;
Sitting along the bed's edge, where
You curled the papers from your hair,
Or clasped the yellow soles of feet
In the palms of both soiled hands.

IV

His soul stretched tight across the skies
That fade behind a city block,
Or trampled by insistent feet
At four and five and six o'clock;
And short square fingers stuffing pipes,
And evening newspapers, and eyes
Assured of certain certainties,
The conscience of a blackened street
Impatient to assume the world.

I am moved by fancies that are curled
Around these images, and cling:
The notion of some infinitely gentle
Infinitely suffering thing.

Wipe your hand across your mouth, and laugh;
The worlds revolve like ancient women
Gathering fuel in vacant lots.

The Boston Evening Transcript

The readers of the *Boston Evening Transcript*
Sway in the wind like a field of ripe corn.

When evening quickens faintly in the street,
Wakening the appetites of life in some
And to others bringing the *Boston Evening Transcript*,
I mount the steps and ring the bell, turning
Wearily, as one would turn to nod good-bye to
    Rochefoucauld,
If the street were time and he at the end of the street,
And I say, "Cousin Harriet, here is the *Boston Evening
    Transcript*."

La Figlia Che Piange

Stand on the highest pavement of the stair—
Lean on a garden urn—
Weave, weave the sunlight in your hair—
Clasp your flowers to you with a pained surprise—
Fling them to the ground and turn
With a fugitive resentment in your eyes:
But weave, weave the sunlight in your hair.

So I would have had him leave,
So I would have had her stand and grieve,
So he would have left
As the soul leaves the body torn and bruised,
As the mind deserts the body it has used.
I should find
Some way incomparably light and deft,
Some way we both should understand,
Simple and faithless as a smile and shake of the hand.

She turned away, but with the autumn weather
Compelled my imagination many days,
Many days and many hours:

Her hair over her arms and her arms full of flowers.
And I wonder how they should have been together!
I should have lost a gesture and a pose.
Sometimes these cogitations still amaze
The troubled midnight and the noon's repose.

Sweeney Among the Nightingales

ὤμοι, πέπγηλμαι καιρίαν πγηλὴν ἔσω.

Why should I speak of the nightingale?
The nightingale sings of adulterate wrong.

Apeneck Sweeney spreads his knees
Letting his arms hang down to laugh,
The zebra stripes along his jaw
Swelling to maculate giraffe.

The circles of the stormy moon
Slide westward to the River Plate,
Death and the Raven drift above
And Sweeney guards the horned gate.

Gloomy Orion and the Dog
Are veiled; and hushed the shrunken seas;
The person in the Spanish cape
Tries to sit on Sweeney's knees

Slips and pulls the table cloth
Overturns a coffee cup,
Reorganized upon the floor
She yawns and draws a stocking up;

The silent man in mocha brown
Sprawls at the window sill and gapes;
The waiter brings in oranges
Bananas, figs and hot-house grapes;

The silent vertebrate exhales,
Contracts and concentrates, withdraws;
Rachel née Rabinovitch
Tears at the grapes with murderous paws;

She and the lady in the cape
Are suspect, thought to be in league;
Therefore the man with heavy eyes
Declines the gambit, shows fatigue,

Leaves the room and reappears
Outside the window, leaning in,
Branches of wistaria
Circumscribe a golden grin;

The host with someone indistinct
Converses at the door apart,
The nightingales are singing near
The Convent of the Sacred Heart,

And sang within the bloody wood
When Agamemnon cried aloud,
And let their liquid siftings fall
To stain the stiff dishonoured shroud.

Whispers of Immortality

Webster was much possessed by death
And saw the skull beneath the skin;
And breastless creatures under ground
Leaned backward with a lipless grin.

Daffodil bulbs instead of balls
Stared from the sockets of the eyes!
He knew that thought clings round dead limbs
Tightening its lusts and luxuries.

Donne, I suppose, was such another
Who found no substitute for sense,
To seize and clutch and penetrate;
Expert beyond experience,

He knew the anguish of the marrow
The ague of the skeleton;
No contact possible to flesh
Allayed the fever of the bone.
. . . . .

Grishkin is nice: her Russian eye
Is underlined for emphasis;
Uncorseted, her friendly bust
Gives promise of pneumatic bliss.

The couched Brazilian jaguar
Compels the scampering marmoset
With subtle effluence of cat;
Grishkin has a maisonnette;

The sleek Brazilian jaguar
Does not in its arboreal gloom
Distil so rank a feline smell
As Grishkin in a drawing-room.

And even the Abstract Entities
Circumambulate her charm;
But our lot crawls between dry ribs
To keep our metaphysics warm.

Gerontion

Thou hast nor youth nor age
But as it were an after dinner sleep
Dreaming of both.

Here I am, an old man in a dry month,
Being read to by a boy, waiting for rain.
I was neither at the hot gates

Nor fought in the warm rain
Nor knee deep in the salt marsh, heaving a cutlass,
Bitten by flies, fought.
My house is a decayed house,
And the jew squats on the window sill, the owner,
Spawned in some estaminet of Antwerp,
Blistered in Brussels, patched and peeled in London.
The goat coughs at night in the field overhead;
Rocks, moss, stonecrop, iron, merds.
The woman keeps the kitchen, makes tea,
Sneezes at evening, poking the peevish gutter.

                                    I an old man,
A dull head among windy spaces.

Signs are taken for wonders. "We would see a sign":
The word within a word, unable to speak a word,
Swaddled with darkness. In the juvescence of the year
Came Christ the tiger

In depraved May, dogwood and chestnut, flowering judas,
To be eaten, to be divided, to be drunk
Among whispers; by Mr. Silvero
With caressing hands, at Limoges
Who walked all night in the next room;
By Hakagawa, bowing among the Titians;
By Madame de Tornquist, in the dark room
Shifting the candles; Fräulein von Kulp
Who turned in the hall, one hand on the door. Vacant
     shuttles
Weave the wind. I have no ghosts,
An old man in a draughty house
Under a windy knob.

After such knowledge, what forgiveness? Think now
History has many cunning passages, contrived corridors
And issues, deceives with whispering ambitions,
Guides us by vanities. Think now
She gives when our attention is distracted
And what she gives, gives with such supple confusions

That the giving famishes the craving. Gives too late
What's not believed in, or if still believed,
In memory only, reconsidered passion. Gives too soon
Into weak hands, what's thought can be dispensed with
Till the refusal propagates a fear. Think
Neither fear nor courage saves us. Unnatural vices
Are fathered by our heroism. Virtues
Are forced upon us by our impudent crimes.
These tears are shaken from the wrath-bearing tree.

The tiger springs in the new year. Us he devours. Think at
    last
We have not reached conclusion, when I
Stiffen in a rented house. Think at last
I have not made this show purposelessly
And it is not by any concitation
Of the backward devils.
I would meet you upon this honestly.
I that was near your heart was removed therefrom
To lose beauty in terror, terror in inquisition.
I have lost my passion: why should I need to keep it
Since what is kept must be adulterated?
I have lost my sight, smell, hearing, taste and touch:
How should I use it for your closer contact?

These with a thousand small deliberations
Protract the profit of their chilled delirium,
Excite the membrane, when the sense has cooled,
With pungent sauces, multiply variety
In a wilderness of mirrors. What will the spider do,
Suspend its operations, will the weevil
Delay? De Bailhache, Fresca, Mrs. Cammel, whirled
Beyond the circuit of the shuddering Bear
In fractured atoms. Gull against the wind, in the windy straits
Of Belle Isle, or running on the Horn,
White feathers in the snow, the Gulf claims,
And an old man driven by the Trades
To a sleepy corner.

                Tenants of the house,
Thoughts of a dry brain in a dry season.

The Waste Land

Nam Sibyllam quidem Cumis ego ipse oculis meis
vidi in ampulla pendere, et cum illi pueri dicerent:
Σίβυλλα τί θέλεις; *respondebat illa:* ὰποθανεῖν θέλω.

I. The Burial of the Dead

April is the cruellest month, breeding
Lilacs out of the dead land, mixing
Memory and desire, stirring
Dull roots with spring rain.
Winter kept us warm, covering
Earth in forgetful snow, feeding
A little life with dried tubers.
Summer surprised us, coming over the Starnbergersee
With a shower of rain; we stopped in the colonnade,
And went on in sunlight, into the Hofgarten,
And drank coffee, and talked for an hour.
Bin gar keine Russin, stamm' aus Litauen, echt deutsch.
And when we were children, staying at the archduke's,
My cousin's, he took me out on a sled,
And I was frightened. He said, Marie,
Marie, hold on tight. And down we went.
In the mountains, there you feel free.
I read, much of the night, and go south in the winter.

What are the roots that clutch, what branches grow
Out of this stony rubbish? Son of man,
You cannot say, or guess, for you know only
A heap of broken images, where the sun beats,
And the dead tree gives no shelter, the cricket no relief,
And the dry stone no sound of water. Only
There is shadow under this red rock,
(Come in under the shadow of this red rock),
And I will show you something different from either
Your shadow at morning striding behind you
Or your shadow at evening rising to meet you;
I will show you fear in a handful of dust.

Frisch weht der Wind
Der Heimat zu.
Mein Irisch Kind,
Wo weilest du?

'You gave me hyacinths first a year ago;
'They called me the hyacinth girl.'
—Yet when we came back, late, from the Hyacinth garden,
Your arms full, and your hair wet, I could not
Speak, and my eyes failed, I was neither
Living nor dead, and I knew nothing,
Looking into the heart of light, the silence.
Oed' und leer das Meer.

Madame Sosostris, famous clairvoyante,
Had a bad cold, nevertheless
Is known to be the wisest woman in Europe,
With a wicked pack of cards. Here, said she,
Is your card, the drowned Phoenician Sailor,
(Those are pearls that were his eyes. Look!)
Here is Belladonna, the Lady of the Rocks,
The lady of situations.
Here is the man with three staves, and here the Wheel,
And here is the one-eyed merchant, and this card,
Which is blank, is something he carries on his back,
Which I am forbidden to see. I do not find
The Hanged Man. Fear death by water.
I see crowds of people, walking round in a ring.
Thank you. If you see dear Mrs. Equitone,
Tell her I bring the horoscope myself:
One must be so careful these days.

Unreal City,
Under the brown fog of a winter dawn,
A crowd flowed over London Bridge, so many,
I had not thought death had undone so many.
Sighs, short and infrequent, were exhaled,
And each man fixed his eyes before his feet.
Flowed up the hill and down King William Street,
To where Saint Mary Woolnoth kept the hours

With a dead sound on the final stroke of nine.
There I saw one I knew, and stopped him, crying 'Stetson!
'You who were with me in the ships at Mylae!
'That corpse you planted last year in your garden,
'Has it begun to sprout? Will it bloom this year?
'Or has the sudden frost disturbed its bed?
'Oh keep the Dog far hence, that's friend to men,
'Or with his nails he'll dig it up again!
'You! hypocrite lecteur!—mon semblable,—mon frère!'

II. A Game of Chess

The Chair she sat in, like a burnished throne,
Glowed on the marble, where the glass
Held up by standards wrought with fruited vines
From which a golden Cupidon peeped out
(Another hid his eyes behind his wing)
Doubled the flames of sevenbranched candelabra
Reflecting light upon the table as
The glitter of her jewels rose to meet it,
From satin cases poured in rich profusion;
In vials of ivory and coloured glass
Unstoppered, lurked her strange synthetic perfumes,
Unguent, powdered, or liquid—troubled, confused
And drowned the sense in odours; stirred by the air
That freshened from the window, these ascended
In fattening the prolonged candle-flames,
Flung their smoke into the laquearia,
Stirring the pattern on the coffered ceiling.
Huge sea-wood fed with copper
Burned green and orange, framed by the coloured stone,
In which sad light a carvèd dolphin swam.
Above the antique mantel was displayed
As though a window gave upon the sylvan scene
The change of Philomel, by the barbarous king
So rudely forced; yet there the nightingale
Filled all the desert with inviolable voice
And still she cried, and still the world pursues,
'Jug Jug' to dirty ears.

And other withered stumps of time
Were told upon the walls; staring forms
Leaned out, leaning, hushing the room enclosed.
Footsteps shuffled on the stair.
Under the firelight, under the brush, her hair
Spread out in fiery points
Glowed into words, then would be savagely still.

'My nerves are bad to-night. Yes, bad. Stay with me.
'Speak to me. Why do you never speak? Speak.
'What are you thinking of? What thinking? What?
'I never know what you are thinking. Think.'

I think we are in rats' alley
Where the dead men lost their bones.

'What is that noise?'
                         The wind under the door.
'What is that noise now? What is the wind doing?'
                         Nothing again nothing.
                                                'Do
'You know nothing? Do you see nothing? Do you remember
'Nothing?'
     I remember
Those are pearls that were his eyes.
'Are you alive, or not? Is there nothing in your head?'
                                                    But
O O O O that Shakespeherian Rag—
It's so elegant
So intelligent
'What shall I do now? What shall I do?'
'I shall rush out as I am, and walk the street
'With my hair down, so. What shall we do to-morrow?
'What shall we ever do?'
                         The hot water at ten.
And if it rains, a closed car at four.
And we shall play a game of chess,
Pressing lidless eyes and waiting for a knock upon the door.

When Lil's husband got demobbed, I said—
I didn't mince my words, I said to her myself,
Hurry up please it's time
Now Albert's coming back, make yourself a bit smart.
He'll want to know what you done with that money he gave
    you
To get yourself some teeth. He did, I was there.
You have them all out, Lil, and get a nice set,
He said, I swear, I can't bear to look at you.
And no more can't I, I said, and think of poor Albert,
He's been in the army four years, he wants a good time,
And if you don't give it him, there's others will, I said.
Oh is there, she said. Something o' that, I said.
Then I'll know who to thank, she said, and give me a straight
    look.
Hurry up please it's time
If you don't like it you can get on with it, I said.
Others can pick and choose if you can't.
But if Albert makes off, it won't be for lack of telling.
You ought to be ashamed, I said, to look so antique.
(And her only thirty-one.)
I can't help it, she said, pulling a long face,
It's them pills I took, to bring it off, she said.
(She's had five already, and nearly died of young George.)
The chemist said it would be alright, but I've never been the
    same.
You *are* a proper fool, I said.
Well, if Albert won't leave you alone, there it is, I said,
What you get married for if you don't want children?
Hurry up please it's time
Well, that Sunday Albert was home, they had a hot gammon,
And they asked me in to dinner, to get the beauty of it hot—
Hurry up please it's time
Hurry up please it's time
Goonight Bill. Goonight Lou. Goonight May. Goonight.
Ta ta. Goonight. Goonight.
Good night, ladies, good night, sweet ladies, good night,
    good night.

III. *The Fire Sermon*

The river's tent is broken: the last fingers of leaf
Clutch and sink into the wet bank. The wind
Crosses the brown land, unheard. The nymphs are departed.
Sweet Thames, run softly, till I end my song.
The river bears no empty bottles, sandwich papers,
Silk handkerchiefs, cardboard boxes, cigarette ends
Or other testimony of summer nights. The nymphs are
      departed.
And their friends, the loitering heirs of city directors;
Departed, have left no addresses.
By the waters of Leman I sat down and wept . . .
Sweet Thames, run softly till I end my song,
Sweet Thames, run softly, for I speak not loud or long.
But at my back in a cold blast I hear
The rattle of the bones, and chuckle spread from ear to ear.

A rat crept softly through the vegetation
Dragging its slimy belly on the bank
While I was fishing in the dull canal
On a winter evening round behind the gashouse
Musing upon the king my brother's wreck
And on the king my father's death before him.
White bodies naked on the low damp ground
And bones cast in a little low dry garret,
Rattled by the rat's foot only, year to year.
But at my back from time to time I hear
The sound of horns and motors, which shall bring
Sweeney to Mrs. Porter in the spring.
O the moon shone bright on Mrs. Porter
And on her daughter
They wash their feet in soda water
Et, O ces voix d'enfants, chantant dans la coupole!

Twit twit twit
Jug jug jug jug jug jug
So rudely forc'd.
Tereu

Unreal City
Under the brown fog of a winter noon
Mr. Eugenides, the Smyrna merchant
Unshaven, with a pocket full of currants
C.i.f. London: documents at sight,
Asked me in demotic French
To luncheon at the Cannon Street Hotel
Followed by a weekend at the Metropole.

At the violet hour, when the eyes and back
Turn upward from the desk, when the human engine waits
Like a taxi throbbing waiting,
I Tiresias, though blind, throbbing between two lives,
Old man with wrinkled female breasts, can see
At the violet hour, the evening hour that strives
Homeward, and brings the sailor home from sea,
The typist home at teatime, clears her breakfast, lights
Her stove, and lays out food in tins.
Out of the window perilously spread
Her drying combinations touched by the sun's last rays,
On the divan are piled (at night her bed)
Stockings, slippers, camisoles, and stays.
I Tiresias, old man with wrinkled dugs
Perceived the scene, and foretold the rest—
I too awaited the expected guest.
He, the young man carbuncular, arrives,
A small house agent's clerk, with one bold stare,
One of the low on whom assurance sits
As a silk hat on a Bradford millionaire.
The time is now propitious, as he guesses,
The meal is ended, she is bored and tired,
Endeavours to engage her in caresses
Which still are unreproved, if undesired.
Flushed and decided, he assaults at once;
Exploring hands encounter no defence;
His vanity requires no response,
And makes a welcome of indifference.
(And I Tiresias have foresuffered all
Enacted on this same divan or bed;
I who have sat by Thebes below the wall

And walked among the lowest of the dead.)
Bestows one final patronising kiss,
And gropes his way, finding the stairs unlit . . .

She turns and looks a moment in the glass,
Hardly aware of her departed lover;
Her brain allows one half-formed thought to pass:
'Well now that's done: and I'm glad it's over.'
When lovely woman stoops to folly and
Paces about her room again, alone,
She smoothes her hair with automatic hand,
And puts a record on the gramophone.

'This music crept by me upon the waters'
And along the Strand, up Queen Victoria Street.

O City city, I can sometimes hear
Beside a public bar in Lower Thames Street,
The pleasant whining of a mandoline
And a clatter and a chatter from within
Where fishmen lounge at noon: where the walls
Of Magnus Martyr hold
Inexplicable splendour of Ionian white and gold.

      The river sweats
      Oil and tar
      The barges drift
      With the turning tide
      Red sails
      Wide
      To leeward, swing on the heavy spar.
      The barges wash
      Drifting logs
      Down Greenwich reach
      Past the Isle of Dogs.
           Weialala leia
           Wallala leialala

      Elizabeth and Leicester
      Beating oars

The stern was formed
A gilded shell
Red and gold
The brisk swell
Rippled both shores
Southwest wind
Carried down stream
The peal of bells
White towers
　　　　Weialala leia
　　　　Wallala leialala

'Trams and dusty trees.
Highbury bore me. Richmond and Kew
Undid me. By Richmond I raised my knees
Supine on the floor of a narrow canoe.'

'My feet are at Moorgate, and my heart
Under my feet. After the event
He wept. He promised "a new start".
I made no comment. What should I resent?'
'On Margate Sands.
I can connect
Nothing with nothing.
The broken fingernails of dirty hands.
My people humble people who expect
Nothing.'

　　　la la

To Carthage then I came

Burning burning burning burning
O Lord Thou pluckest me out
O Lord Thou pluckest

burning

IV. Death by Water

Phlebas the Phoenician, a fortnight dead,
Forgot the cry of gulls, and the deep sea swell
And the profit and loss.
                  A current under sea
Picked his bones in whispers. As he rose and fell
He passed the stages of his age and youth
Entering the whirlpool.
                  Gentile or Jew
O you who turn the wheel and look to windward,
Consider Phlebas, who was once handsome and tall as you.

V. What the Thunder Said

After the torchlight red on sweaty faces
After the frosty silence in the gardens
After the agony in stony places
The shouting and the crying
Prison and place and reverberation
Of thunder of spring over distant mountains
He who was living is now dead
We who were living are now dying
With a little patience

Here is no water but only rock
Rock and no water and the sandy road
The road winding above among the mountains
Which are mountains of rock without water
If there were water we should stop and drink
Amongst the rock one cannot stop or think
Sweat is dry and feet are in the sand
If there were only water amongst the rock
Dead mountain mouth of carious teeth that cannot spit
Here one can neither stand nor lie nor sit
There is not even silence in the mountains
But dry sterile thunder without rain
There is not even solitude in the mountains
But red sullen faces sneer and snarl
From doors of mudcracked houses

                                    If there were water
And no rock
If there were rock
And also water
And water
A spring
A pool among the rock
If there were the sound of water only
Not the cicada
And dry grass singing
But sound of water over a rock
Where the hermit-thrush sings in the pine trees
Drip drop drip drop drop drop drop
But there is no water

Who is the third who walks always beside you?
When I count, there are only you and I together
But when I look ahead up the white road
There is always another one walking beside you
Gliding wrapt in a brown mantle, hooded
I do not know whether a man or a woman
—But who is that on the other side of you?

What is that sound high in the air
Murmur of maternal lamentation
Who are those hooded hordes swarming
Over endless plains, stumbling in cracked earth
Ringed by the flat horizon only
What is the city over the mountains
Cracks and reforms and bursts in the violet air
Falling towers
Jerusalem Athens Alexandria
Vienna London
Unreal

A woman drew her long black hair out tight
And fiddled whisper music on those strings
And bats with baby faces in the violet light
Whistled, and beat their wings
And crawled head downward down a blackened wall

And upside down in air were towers
Tolling reminiscent bells, that kept the hours
And voices singing out of empty cisterns and exhausted wells.

In this decayed hole among the mountains
In the faint moonlight, the grass is singing
Over the tumbled graves, about the chapel
There is the empty chapel, only the wind's home.
It has no windows, and the door swings,
Dry bones can harm no one.
Only a cock stood on the rooftree
Co co rico co co rico
In a flash of lightning. Then a damp gust
Bringing rain

Ganga was sunken, and the limp leaves
Waited for rain, while the black clouds
Gathered far distant, over Himavant.
The jungle crouched, humped in silence.
Then spoke the thunder
D A
Datta: what have we given?
My friend, blood shaking my heart
The awful daring of a moment's surrender
Which an age of prudence can never retract
By this, and this only, we have existed
Which is not to be found in our obituaries
Or in memories draped by the beneficent spider
Or under seals broken by the lean solicitor
In our empty rooms
D A
Dayadhvam: I have heard the key
Turn in the door once and turn once only
We think of the key, each in his prison
Thinking of the key, each confirms a prison
Only at nightfall, aetherial rumours
Revive for a moment a broken Coriolanus
D A
Damyata: The boat responded
Gaily, to the hand expert with sail and oar

The sea was calm, your heart would have responded
Gaily, when invited, beating obedient
To controlling hands

      I sat upon the shore
Fishing, with the arid plain behind me
Shall I at least set my lands in order?

London Bridge is falling down falling down falling down

Poi s'ascose nel foco che gli affina
Quando fiam ceu chelidon—O swallow swallow
Le Prince d'Aquitaine à la tour abolie
These fragments I have shored against my ruins
Why then Ile fit you. Hieronymo's mad againe.
Datta. Dayadhvam. Damyata.

    Shantih shantih shantih

NOTES

 Not only the title, but the plan and a good deal of the incidental symbolism of the poem were suggested by Miss Jessie L. Weston's book on the Grail legend: *From Ritual to Romance* (Cambridge). Indeed, so deeply am I indebted, Miss Weston's book will elucidate the difficulties of the poem much better than my notes can do; and I recommend it (apart from the great interest of the book itself) to any who think such elucidation of the poem worth the trouble. To another work of anthropology I am indebted in general, one which has influenced our generation profoundly; I mean *The Golden Bough*; I have used especially the two volumes *Atthis Adonis Osiris*. Anyone who is acquainted with these works will immediately recognise in the poem certain references to vegetation ceremonies.

I. THE BURIAL OF THE DEAD

 Line 20. Cf. Ezekiel II, i.
 23. Cf. Ecclesiastes XII, v.
 31. V. Tristan und Isolde, I, verses 5–8.
 42. Id. III, verse 24.
 46. I am not familiar with the exact constitution of the Tarot pack of cards, from which I have obviously departed to suit my own convenience. The Hanged Man, a member of the traditional pack, fits my purpose in two ways: because he is associated in my mind with the Hanged God of Frazer, and

because I associate him with the hooded figure in the passage of the disciples to Emmaus in Part V. The Phoenician Sailor and the Merchant appear later; also the "crowds of people," and Death by Water is executed in Part IV. The Man with Three Staves (an authentic member of the Tarot pack) I associate, quite arbitrarily, with the Fisher King himself.

60. Cf. Baudelaire:

> "Fourmillante cité, cité pleine de rêves,
> "Où le spectre en plein jour raccroche le passant."

63. Cf. Inferno III, 55–57:

> "si lunga tratta
> di gente, ch'io non avrei mai creduto
> che morte tanta n'avesse disfatta."

64. Cf. Inferno IV, 25–27:

> "Quivi, secondo che per ascoltare,
> "non avea pianto, ma' che di sospiri,
> "che l'aura eterna facevan tremare."

68. A phenomenon which I have often noticed.

74. Cf. the Dirge in Webster's *White Devil*.

76. V. Baudelaire, Preface to *Fleurs du Mal*.

II. A GAME OF CHESS

77. Cf. *Antony and Cleopatra*, II, ii, l. 190.

92. Laquearia. V. *Aeneid*, I, 726:

dependent lychni laquearibus aureis incensi, et noctem flammis funalia vincunt.

98. Sylvan scene. V. Milton, *Paradise Lost*, IV, 140.

99. V. Ovid, *Metamorphoses*, VI, Philomela.

100. Cf. Part III, l. 204.

115. Cf. Part III, l. 195.

118. Cf. Webster: "Is the wind in that door still?"

126. Cf. Part I, l. 37, 48.

138. Cf. the game of chess in Middleton's *Women beware Women*.

III. THE FIRE SERMON

176. V. Spenser, *Prothalamion*.

192. Cf. *The Tempest*, I, ii.

196. Cf. Day, *Parliament of Bees*:

> "When of the sudden, listening, you shall hear,
> "A noise of horns and hunting, which shall bring
> "Actaeon to Diana in the spring,
> "Where all shall see her naked skin . . ."

197. Cf. Marvell, *To His Coy Mistress*.

199. I do not know the origin of the ballad from which these lines are taken: it was reported to me from Sydney, Australia.

202. V. Verlaine, *Parsifal*.

210. The currants were quoted at a price "carriage and insurance free to London"; and the Bill of Lading etc. were to be handed to the buyer upon payment of the sight draft.

218. Tiresias, although a mere spectator and not indeed a "character," is yet the most important personage in the poem, uniting all the rest. Just as the one-eyed merchant, seller of currants, melts into the Phoenician Sailor, and the latter is not wholly distinct from Ferdinand Prince of Naples, so all the women are one woman, and the two sexes meet in Tiresias. What Tiresias *sees*, in fact, is the substance of the poem. The whole passage from Ovid is of great anthropological interest:

> . . . Cum Iunone iocos et maior vestra profecto est
> Quam, quae contingit maribus', dixisse, 'voluptas.'
> Illa negat; placuit quae sit sententia docti
> Quaerere Tiresiae: venus huic erat utraque nota.
> Nam duo magnorum viridi coeuntia silva
> Corpora serpentum baculi violaverat ictu
> Deque viro factus, mirabile, femina septem
> Egerat autumnos; octavo rursus eosdem
> Vidit et 'est vestrae si tanta potentia plagae,'
> Dixit 'ut auctoris sortem in contraria mutet,
> Nunc quoque vos feriam!' percussis anguibus isdem
> Forma prior rediit genetivaque venit imago.
> Arbiter hic igitur sumptus de lite iocosa
> Dicta Iovis firmat; gravius Saturnia iusto
> Nec pro materia fertur doluisse suique
> Iudicis aeterna damnavit lumina nocte,
> At pater omnipotens (neque enim licet inrita cuiquam
> Facta dei fecisse deo) pro lumine adempto
> Scire futura dedit poenamque levavit honore.

221. This may not appear as exact as Sappho's lines, but I had in mind the "longshore" or "dory" fisherman, who returns at nightfall.

253. V. Goldsmith, the song in *The Vicar of Wakefield*.

257. V. *The Tempest*, as above.

264. The interior of St. Magnus Martyr is to my mind one of the finest among Wren's interiors. See *The Proposed Demolition of Nineteen City Churches:* (P. S. King & Son, Ltd.).

266. The Song of the (three) Thames-daughters begins here. From line 292 to 306 inclusive they speak in turn. V. *Götterdämmerung*, III, i: the Rhine-daughters.

279. V. Froude, *Elizabeth* Vol. I, ch. iv, letter of De Quadra to Philip of Spain:

> "In the afternoon we were in a barge, watching the games on the river. (The queen) was alone with Lord Robert and myself on the poop, when they began to talk nonsense, and went so far that Lord Robert at last said, as I was on the spot there was no reason why they should not be married if the queen pleased."

293. Cf. *Purgatorio*, V, 133:

> "Ricorditi di me, che son la Pia;
> "Siena mi fe', disfecemi Maremma."

307. V. St. Augustine's *Confessions*: "to Carthage then I came, where a cauldron of unholy loves sang all about mine ears."

308. The complete text of the Buddha's Fire Sermon (which corresponds in importance to the Sermon on the Mount) from which these words are taken, will be found translated in the late Henry Clarke Warren's *Buddhism in Translation* (Harvard Oriental Series). Mr. Warren was one of the great pioneers of Buddhist studies in the Occident.

312. From St. Augustine's *Confessions* again. The collocation of these two representatives of eastern and western asceticism, as the culmination of this part of the poem, is not an accident.

V. WHAT THE THUNDER SAID

In the first part of Part V three themes are employed: the journey to Emmaus, the approach to the Chapel Perilous (see Miss Weston's book) and the present decay of eastern Europe.

357. This is *Turdus aonalaschkae pallasii*, the hermit-thrush which I have heard in Quebec County. Chapman says (*Handbook of Birds of Eastern North America*) "it is most at home in secluded woodland and thickety retreats. . . . Its notes are not remarkable for variety or volume, but in purity and sweetness of tone and exquisite modulation they are unequalled." Its "water-dripping song" is justly celebrated.

360. The following lines were stimulated by the account of one of the Antarctic expeditions (I forget which, but I think one of Shackleton's): it was related that the party of explorers, at the extremity of their strength, had the constant delusion that there was *one more member* than could actually be counted.

366–76. Cf. Hermann Hesse, *Blick ins Chaos*: "Schon ist halb Europa, schon ist zumindest der halbe Osten Europas auf dem Wege zum Chaos, fährt betrunken im heiligem Wahn am Abgrund entlang und singt dazu, singt betrunken und hymnisch wie Dmitri Karamasoff sang. Ueber diese Lieder lacht der Bürger beleidigt, der Heilige und Seher hört si mit Tränen."

401. "Datta, dayadhvam damyata" (Give, sympathise, control). The fable of the meaning of the Thunder is found in the *Brihadaranyaka—Upanishad*, 5, 1. A translation is found in Deussen's *Sechzig Upanishads des Veda*, p. 489.

407. Cf. Webster, *The White Devil*, V, vi:

> ". . . they'll remarry
> Ere the worm pierce your winding-sheet, ere the spider
> Make a thin curtain for your epitaphs."

411. Cf. *Inferno*, XXXIII, 46:

> "ed io sentii chiavar l'uscio di sotto
> all'orribile torre."

Also F. H. Bradley, *Appearance and Reality*, p. 346. "My external sensa-
tions are no less private to myself than are my thoughts or my feelings. In ei-
ther case my experience falls within my own circle, a circle closed on the
outside; and, with all its elements alike, every sphere is opaque to the others
which surround it. . . . In brief, regarded as an existence which appears in a
soul, the whole world for each is peculiar and private to that soul."

424. V. Weston: *From Ritual to Romance*; chapter on the Fisher King.

427. V. *Purgatorio*, XXVI, 148.
> " 'Ara vos prec, per aquella valor
>   'que vos guida al som de l'escalina,
>   'sovegna vos a temps de ma dolor.'
>   Poi s'ascose nel foco che gli affina."

428. V. *Pervigilium Veneris*. Cf. Philomela in Parts II and III.

429. V. Gerard de Nerval, Sonnet *El Desdichado*.

431. V. Kyd's *Spanish Tragedy*.

433. Shantih. Repeated as here, a formal ending to an Upanishad. "The
Peace which passeth understanding" is a feeble translation of the content of
this word.

The Hollow Men

A penny for the Old Guy

I

We are the hollow men
We are the stuffed men
Leaning together
Headpiece filled with straw. Alas!
Our dried voices, when
We whisper together
Are quiet and meaningless
As wind in dry grass
Or rats' feet over broken glass
In our dry cellar

Shape without form, shade without colour,
Paralysed force, gesture without motion;

Those who have crossed
With direct eyes, to death's other Kingdom
Remember us—if at all—not as lost
Violent souls, but only
As the hollow men
The stuffed men.

II

Eyes I dare not meet in dreams
In death's dream kingdom
These do not appear:
There, the eyes are
Sunlight on a broken column
There, is a tree swinging
And voices are
In the wind's singing
More distant and more solemn
Than a fading star.

Let me be no nearer
In death's dream kingdom
Let me also wear
Such deliberate disguises
Rat's coat, crowskin, crossed staves
In a field
Behaving as the wind behaves
No nearer—

Not that final meeting
In the twilight kingdom

III

This is the dead land
This is cactus land
Here the stone images
Are raised, here they receive
The supplication of a dead man's hand
Under the twinkle of a fading star.

Is it like this
In death's other kingdom
Waking alone
At the hour when we are
Trembling with tenderness
Lips that would kiss
Form prayers to broken stone.

IV

The eyes are not here
There are no eyes here
In this valley of dying stars
In this hollow valley
This broken jaw of our lost kingdoms

In this last of meeting places
We grope together
And avoid speech
Gathered on this beach of the tumid river

Sightless, unless
The eyes reappear
As the perpetual star
Multifoliate rose
Of death's twilight kingdom
The hope only
Of empty men.

V

Here we go round the prickly pear
Prickly pear prickly pear
Here we go round the prickly pear
At five o'clock in the morning.

Between the idea
And the reality
Between the motion
And the act
Falls the Shadow
                    For Thine is the Kingdom

Between the conception
And the creation
Between the emotion
And the response
Falls the Shadow
                    Life is very long

Between the desire
And the spasm
Between the potency
And the existence
Between the essence
And the descent
Falls the Shadow
                For Thine is the Kingdom

For Thine is
Life is
For Thine is the

This is the way the world ends
This is the way the world ends
This is the way the world ends
Not with a bang but a whimper.

Marina

Quis hic locus, quae regio, quae mundi plaga?

What seas what shores what grey rocks and what islands
What water lapping the bow
And scent of pine and the woodthrush singing through the
    fog
What images return
O my daughter.

Those who sharpen the tooth of the dog, meaning
Death
Those who glitter with the glory of the hummingbird,
    meaning
Death
Those who sit in the sty of contentment, meaning
Death
Those who suffer the ecstasy of the animals, meaning
Death

Are become unsubstantial, reduced by a wind,
A breath of pine, and the woodsong fog
By this grace dissolved in place

What is this face, less clear and clearer
The pulse in the arm, less strong and stronger—
Given or lent? more distant than stars and nearer than the eye

Whispers and small laughter between leaves and hurrying feet
Under sleep, where all the waters meet.

Bowsprit cracked with ice and paint cracked with heat.
I made this, I have forgotten
And remember.
The rigging weak and the canvas rotten
Between one June and another September.
Made this unknowing, half conscious, unknown, my own.
The garboard strake leaks, the seams need caulking.
This form, this face, this life
Living to live in a world of time beyond me; let me
Resign my life for this life, my speech for that unspoken,
The awakened, lips parted, the hope, the new ships.

What seas what shores what granite islands towards my
    timbers
And woodthrush calling through the fog
My daughter.

Ash-Wednesday

I

Because I do not hope to turn again
Because I do not hope
Because I do not hope to turn
Desiring this man's gift and that man's scope
I no longer strive to strive towards such things
(Why should the agèd eagle stretch its wings?)
Why should I mourn
The vanished power of the usual reign?

Because I do not hope to know again
The infirm glory of the positive hour
Because I do not think
Because I know I shall not know
The one veritable transitory power
Because I cannot drink
There, where trees flower, and springs flow, for there is
        nothing again

Because I know that time is always time
And place is always and only place
And what is actual is actual only for one time
And only for one place
I rejoice that things are as they are and
I renounce the blessèd face
And renounce the voice
Because I cannot hope to turn again
Consequently I rejoice, having to construct something
Upon which to rejoice

And pray to God to have mercy upon us
And I pray that I may forget
These matters that with myself I too much discuss
Too much explain
Because I do not hope to turn again

Let these words answer
For what is done, not to be done again
May the judgement not be too heavy upon us

Because these wings are no longer wings to fly
But merely vans to beat the air
The air which is now thoroughly small and dry
Smaller and dryer than the will
Teach us to care and not to care
Teach us to sit still.

Pray for us sinners now and at the hour of our death
Pray for us now and at the hour of our death.

II

Lady, three white leopards sat under a juniper-tree
In the cool of the day, having fed to satiety
On my legs my heart my liver and that which had been
    contained
In the hollow round of my skull. And God said
Shall these bones live? shall these
Bones live? And that which had been contained
In the bones (which were already dry) said chirping:
Because of the goodness of this Lady
And because of her loveliness, and because
She honours the Virgin in meditation,
We shine with brightness. And I who am here dissembled
Proffer my deeds to oblivion, and my love
To the posterity of the desert and the fruit of the gourd.
It is this which recovers
My guts the strings of my eyes and the indigestible portions
Which the leopards reject. The Lady is withdrawn
In a white gown, to contemplation, in a white gown.
Let the whiteness of bones atone to forgetfulness.
There is no life in them. As I am forgotten
And would be forgotten, so I would forget
Thus devoted, concentrated in purpose. And God said
Prophesy to the wind, to the wind only for only
The wind will listen. And the bones sang chirping
With the burden of the grasshopper, saying

Lady of silences
Calm and distressed
Torn and most whole
Rose of memory
Rose of forgetfulness
Exhausted and life-giving
Worried reposeful
The single Rose
Is now the Garden
Where all loves end
Terminate torment
Of love unsatisfied
The greater torment
Of love satisfied
End of the endless
Journey to no end
Conclusion of all that
Is inconclusible
Speech without word and
Word of no speech
Grace to the Mother
For the Garden
Where all love ends.

Under a juniper-tree the bones sang, scattered and shining
We are glad to be scattered, we did little good to each other,
Under a tree in the cool of the day, with the blessing of sand,
Forgetting themselves and each other, united
In the quiet of the desert. This is the land which ye
Shall divide by lot. And neither division nor unity
Matters. This is the land. We have our inheritance.

III

At the first turning of the second stair
I turned and saw below
The same shape twisted on the banister
Under the vapour in the fetid air
Struggling with the devil of the stairs who wears
The deceitful face of hope and of despair.

At the second turning of the second stair
I left them twisting, turning below;
There were no more faces and the stair was dark,
Damp, jaggèd, like an old man's mouth drivelling, beyond
    repair,
Or the toothed gullet of an agèd shark.

At the first turning of the third stair
Was a slotted window bellied like the fig's fruit
And beyond the hawthorn blossom and a pasture scene
The broadbacked figure drest in blue and green
Enchanted the maytime with an antique flute.
Blown hair is sweet, brown hair over the mouth blown,
Lilac and brown hair;
Distraction, music of the flute, stops and steps of the mind
    over the third stair,
Fading, fading; strength beyond hope and despair
Climbing the third stair.

Lord, I am not worthy
Lord, I am not worthy

                    but speak the word only.

IV

Who walked between the violet and the violet
Who walked between
The various ranks of varied green
Going in white and blue, in Mary's colour,
Talking of trivial things
In ignorance and in knowledge of eternal dolour
Who moved among the others as they walked,
Who then made strong the fountains and made fresh the
    springs

Made cool the dry rock and made firm the sand
In blue of larkspur, blue of Mary's colour,
Sovegna vos

Here are the years that walk between, bearing
Away the fiddles and the flutes, restoring
One who moves in the time between sleep and waking,
      wearing

White light folded, sheathed about her, folded.
The new years walk, restoring
Through a bright cloud of tears, the years, restoring
With a new verse the ancient rhyme. Redeem
The time. Redeem
The unread vision in the higher dream
While jewelled unicorns draw by the gilded hearse.

The silent sister veiled in white and blue
Between the yews, behind the garden god,
Whose flute is breathless, bent her head and signed but spoke
      no word

But the fountain sprang up and the bird sang down
Redeem the time, redeem the dream
The token of the word unheard, unspoken

Till the wind shake a thousand whispers from the yew

And after this our exile

V

If the lost word is lost, if the spent word is spent
If the unheard, unspoken
Word is unspoken, unheard;
Still is the unspoken word, the Word unheard,
The Word without a word, the Word within
The world and for the world;
And the light shone in darkness and
Against the Word the unstilled world still whirled
About the centre of the silent Word.

O my people, what have I done unto thee.

Where shall the word be found, where will the word
Resound? Not here, there is not enough silence
Not on the sea or on the islands, not
On the mainland, in the desert or the rain land,
For those who walk in darkness
Both in the day time and in the night time
The right time and the right place are not here
No place of grace for those who avoid the face
No time to rejoice for those who walk among noise and deny
    the voice

Will the veiled sister pray for
Those who walk in darkness, who chose thee and oppose
    thee,
Those who are torn on the horn between season and season,
    time and time, between
Hour and hour, word and word, power and power, those
    who wait
In darkness? Will the veiled sister pray
For children at the gate
Who will not go away and cannot pray:
Pray for those who chose and oppose

    O my people, what have I done unto thee.

Will the veiled sister between the slender
Yew trees pray for those who offend her
And are terrified and cannot surrender
And affirm before the world and deny between the rocks
In the last desert between the last blue rocks
The desert in the garden the garden in the desert
Of drouth, spitting from the mouth the withered apple-seed.

    O my people.

        VI

Although I do not hope to turn again
Although I do not hope
Although I do not hope to turn

Wavering between the profit and the loss
In this brief transit where the dreams cross
The dreamcrossed twilight between birth and dying
(Bless me father) though I do not wish to wish these things
From the wide window towards the granite shore
The white sails still fly seaward, seaward flying
Unbroken wings

And the lost heart stiffens and rejoices
In the lost lilac and the lost sea voices
And the weak spirit quickens to rebel
For the bent golden-rod and the lost sea smell
Quickens to recover
The cry of quail and the whirling plover
And the blind eye creates
The empty forms between the ivory gates
And smell renews the salt savour of the sandy earth

This is the time of tension between dying and birth
The place of solitude where three dreams cross
Between blue rocks
But when the voices shaken from the yew-tree drift away
Let the other yew be shaken and reply.

Blessèd sister, holy mother, spirit of the fountain, spirit of the
    garden,
Suffer us not to mock ourselves with falsehood
Teach us to care and not to care
Teach us to sit still
Even among these rocks,
Our peace in His will
And even among these rocks
Sister, mother
And spirit of the river, spirit of the sea,
Suffer me not to be separated

And let my cry come unto Thee.

Sweeney Agonistes

Fragments of an Aristophanic Melodrama

ORESTES: *You don't see them, you don't— but* I *see them: they are hunting me down, I must move on.*
—CHOEPHOROI.

Hence the soul cannot be possessed of the divine union, until it has divested itself of the love of created beings.
—ST. JOHN OF THE CROSS.

Fragment of a Prologue

DUSTY. DORIS.

DUSTY: How about Pereira?

DORIS: What about Pereira?
           I don't care.

DUSTY: You don't care!
           Who pays the rent?

DORIS: Yes he pays the rent

DUSTY: Well some men don't and some men do
           Some men don't and you know who

DORIS: You can have Pereira

DUSTY: What about Pereira?

DORIS: He's no gentleman, Pereira:
           You can't trust him!

DUSTY: Well that's true.
           He's no gentleman if you can't trust him
           And *if* you can't trust him—
           Then you never know what he's going to do.

DORIS: No it wouldn't do to be too nice to Pereira.

DUSTY: Now Sam's a gentleman through and through.

DORIS: I like Sam

DUSTY: *I* like Sam
           Yes and Sam's a nice boy too.
           He's a funny fellow

DORIS: He *is* a funny fellow
           He's like a fellow once I knew.
           He could make you laugh.

DUSTY: Sam can make you laugh:
           Sam's all right

DORIS: But Pereira won't do.
            We can't have Pereira
DUSTY: Well what you going to do?
TELEPHONE: Ting a ling ling
                    Ting a ling ling
DUSTY: That's Pereira
DORIS: Yes that's Pereira
DUSTY: Well what you going to do?
TELEPHONE: Ting a ling ling
                    Ting a ling ling
DUSTY: That's Pereira
DORIS: Well can't you stop that horrible noise?
            Pick up the receiver
DUSTY: What'll I say!
DORIS: Say what you like: say I'm ill,
            Say I broke my leg on the stairs
            Say we've had a fire
DUSTY: Hello Hello are you there?
            Yes this is Miss Dorrance's *flat*—
            Oh Mr. Pereira is that you? how do you do!
            Oh I'm *so* sorry. I *am* so sorry
            But Doris came home with a terrible chill
            No, just a chill
            Oh I *think* it's only a chill
            Yes indeed I hope so too—
            Well I *hope* we shan't have to call a doctor
            Doris just hates having a doctor
            She says will you ring up on Monday
            She hopes to be all right on Monday
            I say do you mind if I ring off now
            She's got her feet in mustard and water
            I said I'm giving her mustard and water
            All right, Monday you'll phone through.
            Yes I'll tell her. Good bye. Goooood bye.
            I'm sure, that's very kind of *you*.
                            Ah-h-h
DORIS: Now I'm going to cut the cards for to-night.
            Oh guess what the first is
DUSTY: First is. What is?

DORIS: The King of Clubs
DUSTY: That's Pereira
DORIS: It might be Sweeney
DUSTY: It's Pereira
DORIS: It might *just* as well be Sweeney
DUSTY: Well anyway it's very queer.
DORIS: Here's the four of diamonds, what's that mean?
DUSTY [*reading*]:   'A small sum of money, or a present
                        Of wearing apparel, or a party'.
                        That's queer too.
DORIS: Here's the three. What's that mean?
DUSTY: 'News of an absent friend'.—Pereira!
DORIS: The Queen of Hearts!—Mrs. Porter!
DUSTY: Or it might be you
DORIS: Or it might be you
          We're all hearts. You can't be sure.
          It just depends on what comes next.
          You've got to *think* when you read the cards,
          It's not a thing that anyone can do.
DUSTY: Yes I know you've a touch with the cards
          What comes next?
DORIS: What comes next. It's the six.
DUSTY: 'A quarrel. An estrangement. Separation of friends'.
DORIS: Here's the two of spades.
DUSTY: The *two* of *spades!*
          THAT'S THE COFFIN!!
DORIS: THAT'S THE COFFIN?
          Oh good heavens what'll I do?
          Just before a party too!
DUSTY: Well it needn't be yours, it may mean a friend.
DORIS: No it's mine. I'm sure it's mine.
          I dreamt of weddings all last night.
          Yes it's mine. I know it's mine.
          Oh good heavens what'll I do.
          Well I'm not going to draw any more,
          You cut for luck. You cut for luck.
          It might break the spell. You cut for luck.
DUSTY: The Knave of Spades.
DORIS: That'll be Snow

DUSTY: Or it might be Swarts
DORIS: Or it might be Snow
DUSTY: It's a funny thing how I draw court cards—
DORIS: There's a lot in the way you pick them up
DUSTY: There's an awful lot in the way you feel
DORIS: Sometimes they'll tell you nothing at all
DUSTY: You've got to know what you want to ask them
DORIS: You've got to know what you want to know
DUSTY: It's no use asking them too much
DORIS: It's no use asking more than once
DUSTY: Sometimes they're no use at all.
DORIS: I'd like to know about that coffin.
DUSTY: Well I never! What did I tell you?
            Wasn't I saying I always draw court cards?
            The Knave of Hearts!
                              [*Whistle outside of the window.*]
                    Well 1 *never!*
            What a co*in*cidence! Cards *are* queer!
                    [*Whistle again.*]
DORIS: Is that Sam?
DUSTY: Of course it's Sam!
DORIS: Of course, the Knave of Hearts *is* Sam!
DUSTY [*leaning out of the window*]:   Hello Sam!
WAUCHOPE: Hello dear!
            How many's up there?
DUSTY: Nobody's up here
            How many's down there?
WAUCHOPE: Four of us here.
            Wait till I put the car round the corner
            We'll be right up
DUSTY: All right, come up.
WAUCHOPE: We'll be right up.
DUSTY [*to* DORIS]:   Cards are queer.
DORIS: I'd like to know about that coffin.
            KNOCK KNOCK KNOCK
            KNOCK KNOCK KNOCK
            KNOCK
            KNOCK
            KNOCK

DORIS. DUSTY. WAUCHOPE. HORSFALL. KLIPSTEIN.
KRUMPACKER.

WAUCHOPE:	Hello Doris! Hello Dusty! How do you do! How come? how come? will you permit me— I think you girls both know Captain Horsfall— We want you to meet two friends of ours, American gentlemen here on business. Meet Mr. Klipstein. Meet Mr. Krumpacker.
KLIPSTEIN:	How do you do
KRUMPACKER:	How do you do
KLIPSTEIN:	I'm very pleased to make your acquaintance
KRUMPACKER:	Extremely pleased to become acquainted
KLIPSTEIN:	Sam—I should say Loot Sam Wauchope
KRUMPACKER:	Of the Canadian Expeditionary Force—
KLIPSTEIN:	The Loot has told us a lot about you.
KRUMPACKER:	We were all in the war together Klip and me and the Cap and Sam.
KLIPSTEIN:	Yes we did our bit, as you folks say, I'll tell the world we got the Hun on the run
KRUMPACKER:	What about that poker game? eh what Sam? What about that poker game in Bordeaux? Yes Miss Dorrance you get Sam To tell you about that poker game in Bordeaux.
DUSTY:	Do you know London well, Mr. Krumpacker?
KLIPSTEIN:	No we never been here before
KRUMPACKER:	We hit this town last night for the first time
KLIPSTEIN:	And I certainly hope it won't be the last time.
DORIS:	You like London, Mr. Klipstein?
KRUMPACKER:	Do we like London? do we like London! Do we like London!! Eh what Klip?
KLIPSTEIN:	Say, Miss—er—uh London's swell. We like London fine.
KRUMPACKER:	Perfectly slick.
DUSTY:	Why don't you come and live here then?

KLIPSTEIN: Well, no, Miss—er—you haven't quite got it
               (I'm afraid I didn't quite catch your name—
               But I'm very pleased to meet you all the
                   same)—
               London's a little too gay for us
               Yes I'll say a little too gay.
KRUMPACKER: Yes London's a little too gay for us
               Don't think I mean anything *coarse*—
               But I'm afraid we couldn't stand the pace.
               What about it Klip?
KLIPSTEIN: You said it, Krum.
               London's a slick place, London's a swell
                   place,
               London's a fine place to come on a visit—
KRUMPACKER: Specially when you got a real live Britisher
               A guy like Sam to show you around.
               Sam of course is at *home* in London,
               And he's promised to show us around.

Fragment of an Agon

SWEENEY. WAUCHOPE. HORSFALL. KLIPSTEIN.
KRUMPACKER. SWARTS. SNOW. DORIS. DUSTY.

SWEENEY: I'll carry you off
               To a cannibal isle.
DORIS: You'll be the cannibal!
SWEENEY: You'll be the missionary!
               You'll be my little seven stone missionary!
               I'll gobble you up. I'll be the cannibal.
DORIS: You'll carry me off? To a cannibal isle?
SWEENEY: I'll be the cannibal.
DORIS: I'll be the missionary.
               I'll convert you!
SWEENEY: I'll convert *you!*
               Into a stew.
               A nice little, white little, missionary stew.
DORIS: You wouldn't eat me!

SWEENEY: Yes I'd eat you!
In a nice little, white little, soft little, tender little,
Juicy little, right little, missionary stew.
You see this egg
You see this egg
Well that's life on a crocodile isle.
There's no telephones
There's no gramophones
There's no motor cars
No two-seaters, no six-seaters,
No Citroën, no Rolls-Royce.
Nothing to eat but the fruit as it grows.
Nothing to see but the palmtrees one way
And the sea the other way,
Nothing to hear but the sound of the surf.
Nothing at all but three things
DORIS: What things?
SWEENEY: Birth, and copulation, and death.
That's all, that's all, that's all, that's all,
Birth, and copulation, and death.
DORIS: I'd be bored.
SWEENEY: You'd be bored.
Birth, and copulation, and death.
DORIS: I'd be bored.
SWEENEY: You'd be bored.
Birth, and copulation, and death.
That's all the facts when you come to brass tacks:
Birth, and copulation, and death.
I've been born, and once is enough.
You dont remember, but I remember,
Once is enough.

SONG BY WAUCHOPE AND HORSFALL
SWARTS AS TAMBO. SNOW AS BONES
Under the bamboo
Bamboo bamboo
Under the bamboo tree
Two live as one
One live as two
Two live as three

Under the bam
Under the boo
Under the bamboo tree.

Where the breadfruit fall
And the penguin call
And the sound is the sound of the sea
Under the bam
Under the boo
Under the bamboo tree.

Where the Gauguin maids
In the banyan shades
Wear palmleaf drapery
Under the bam
Under the boo
Under the bamboo tree.

Tell me in what part of the wood
Do you want to flirt with me?
Under the breadfruit, banyan, palmleaf
Or under the bamboo tree?
Any old tree will do for me
Any old wood is just as good
Any old isle is just my style
Any fresh egg
Any fresh egg
And the sound of the coral sea.

DORIS: I dont like eggs; I never liked eggs;
          And I dont like life on your crocodile isle.

SONG BY KLIPSTEIN AND KRUMPACKER
    SNOW AND SWARTS AS BEFORE
    My little island girl
    My little island girl
    I'm going to stay with you
    And we wont worry what to do
    We wont have to catch any trains
    And we wont go home when it rains

We'll gather hibiscus flowers
For it wont be minutes but hours
For it wont be hours but years

diminuendo
> *And the morning*
> *And the evening*
> *And noontime*
> *And night*
> *Morning*
> *Evening*
> *Noontime*
> *Night*

DORIS: That's not life, that's no life
            Why I'd just as soon be dead.
SWEENEY: That's what life is. Just is
DORIS: What is?
            What's that life is?
SWEENEY: Life is death.
            I knew a man once did a girl in—
DORIS: Oh Mr. Sweeney, please dont talk,
            I cut the cards before you came
            And I drew the coffin
SWARTS: *You* drew the coffin?
DORIS: I drew the COFFIN very last card.
            I dont care for such conversation
            A woman runs a terrible risk.
SNOW: Let Mr. Sweeney continue his story.
            I assure you, Sir, we are very inter*e*sted.
SWEENEY: I knew a man once did a girl in
            Any man might do a girl in
            Any man has to, needs to, wants to
            Once in a lifetime, do a girl in.
            Well he kept her there in a bath
            With a gallon of lysol in a bath
SWARTS: These fellows always get pinched in the end.
SNOW: Excuse me, they dont all get pinched in the end.
            What about them bones on Epsom Heath?
            I seen that in the papers
            You seen it in the papers
            They *dont* all get pinched in the end.

DORIS: A woman runs a terrible risk.
SNOW: Let Mr. Sweeney continue his story.
SWEENEY: This one didn't get pinched in the end
             But that's another story too.
             This went on for a couple of months
             Nobody came
             And nobody went
             But he took in the milk and he paid the rent.
SWARTS: What did he do?
             All that time, what did he do?
SWEENEY: What did he do? what did he do?
             That dont apply.
             Talk to live men about what they do.
             He used to come and see me sometimes
             I'd give him a drink and cheer him up.
DORIS: Cheer him up?
DUSTY: Cheer him up?
SWEENEY: Well here again that dont apply
             But I've gotta use words when I talk to you.
             But here's what I was going to say.
             He didn't know if he was alive
                     and the girl was dead
             He didn't know if the girl was alive
                     and he was dead
             He didn't know if they both were alive
                     or both were dead
             If he was alive then the milkman wasn't
                     and the rent-collector wasn't
             And if they were alive then he was dead.
             There wasn't any joint
             There wasn't any joint
             For when you're alone
             When you're alone like he was alone
             You're either or neither
             I tell you again it dont apply
             Death or life or life or death
             Death is life and life is death
             I gotta use words when I talk to you
             But if you understand or if you dont
             That's nothing to me and nothing to you

We all gotta do what we gotta do
We're gona sit here and drink this booze
We're gona sit here and have a tune
We're gona stay and we're gona go
And somebody's gotta pay the rent
DORIS: I know who
SWEENEY: But that's nothing to me and nothing to you.

FULL CHORUS: WAUCHOPE, HORSFALL, KLIPSTEIN,
                    KRUMPACKER
When you're alone in the middle of the night and you
        wake in a sweat and a hell of a fright
When you're alone in the middle of the bed and you
        wake like someone hit you on the head
You've had a cream of a nightmare dream and you've got
        the hoo-ha's coming to you.
Hoo hoo hoo
You dreamt you waked up at seven o'clock and it's foggy
        and it's damp and it's dawn and it's dark
And you wait for a knock and the turning of a lock for
        you know the hangman's waiting for you.
And perhaps you're alive
And perhaps you're dead
Hoo ha ha
Hoo ha ha
Hoo
Hoo
Hoo
KNOCK KNOCK KNOCK
KNOCK KNOCK KNOCK
KNOCK
KNOCK
KNOCK

Burnt Norton

τοῦ λόγου δ'ἐόντος ξυνοῦ ζώουσιν
οἱ πολλοὶ ὡς ἰδίαν ἔχοντες φρόνησιν.
I. p. 77. Fr. 2.

ὁδὸς ἄνω κάτω μία καὶ ὡυτή.
I. p. 89. Fr. 60.

Diels: *Die Fragmente der Vorsokratiker*
(Herakleitos).

I

Time present and time past
Are both perhaps present in time future,
And time future contained in time past.
If all time is eternally present
All time is unredeemable.
What might have been is an abstraction
Remaining a perpetual possibility
Only in a world of speculation.
What might have been and what has been
Point to one end, which is always present.
Footfalls echo in the memory
Down the passage which we did not take
Towards the door we never opened
Into the rose-garden. My words echo
Thus, in your mind.
                          But to what purpose
Disturbing the dust on a bowl of rose-leaves
I do not know.
                          Other echoes
Inhabit the garden. Shall we follow?
Quick, said the bird, find them, find them,
Round the corner. Through the first gate,
Into our first world, shall we follow
The deception of the thrush? Into our first world.
There they were, dignified, invisible,
Moving without pressure, over the dead leaves,
In the autumn heat, through the vibrant air,

And the bird called, in response to
The unheard music hidden in the shrubbery,
And the unseen eyebeam crossed, for the roses
Had the look of flowers that are looked at.
There they were as our guests, accepted and accepting.
So we moved, and they, in a formal pattern,
Along the empty alley, into the box circle,
To look down into the drained pool.
Dry the pool, dry concrete, brown edged,
And the pool was filled with water out of sunlight,
And the lotos rose, quietly, quietly,
The surface glittered out of heart of light,
And they were behind us, reflected in the pool.
Then a cloud passed, and the pool was empty.
Go, said the bird, for the leaves were full of children,
Hidden excitedly, containing laughter.
Go, go, go, said the bird: human kind
Cannot bear very much reality.
Time past and time future
What might have been and what has been
Point to one end, which is always present.

II

Garlic and sapphires in the mud
Clot the bedded axle-tree.
The trilling wire in the blood
Sings below inveterate scars
And reconciles forgotten wars.
The dance along the artery
The circulation of the lymph
Are figured in the drift of stars
Ascend to summer in the tree
We move above the moving tree
In light upon the figured leaf
And hear upon the sodden floor
Below, the boarhound and the boar
Pursue their pattern as before
But reconciled among the stars.

At the still point of the turning world. Neither flesh nor
    fleshless;
Neither from nor towards; at the still point, there the dance
    is,
But neither arrest nor movement. And do not call it fixity,
Where past and future are gathered. Neither movement from
    nor towards,
Neither ascent nor decline. Except for the point, the still
    point,
There would be no dance, and there is only the dance.
I can only say, *there* we have been: but I cannot say where.
And I cannot say, how long, for that is to place it in time.

The inner freedom from the practical desire,
The release from action and suffering, release from the inner
And the outer compulsion, yet surrounded
By a grace of sense, a white light still and moving,
Erhebung without motion, concentration
Without elimination, both a new world
And the old made explicit, understood
In the completion of its partial ecstasy,
The resolution of its partial horror.
Yet the enchainment of past and future
Woven in the weakness of the changing body,
Protects mankind from heaven and damnation
Which flesh cannot endure.
                          Time past and time future
Allow but a little consciousness.
To be conscious is not to be in time
But only in time can the moment in the rose-garden,
The moment in the arbour where the rain beat,
The moment in the draughty church at smokefall
Be remembered; involved with past and future.
Only through time time is conquered.

                              III

Here is a place of disaffection
Time before and time after
In a dim light: neither daylight

Investing form with lucid stillness
Turning shadow into transient beauty
With slow rotation suggesting permanence
Nor darkness to purify the soul
Emptying the sensual with deprivation
Cleansing affection from the temporal.
Neither plenitude nor vacancy. Only a flicker
Over the strained time-ridden faces
Distracted from distraction by distraction
Filled with fancies and empty of meaning
Tumid apathy with no concentration
Men and bits of paper, whirled by the cold wind
That blows before and after time,
Wind in and out of unwholesome lungs
Time before and time after.
Eructation of unhealthy souls
Into the faded air, the torpid
Driven on the wind that sweeps the gloomy hills of London,
Hampstead and Clerkenwell, Campden and Putney,
Highgate, Primrose and Ludgate. Not here
Not here the darkness, in this twittering world.

Descend lower, descend only
Into the world of perpetual solitude,
World not world, but that which is not world,
Internal darkness, deprivation
And destitution of all property,
Desiccation of the world of sense,
Evacuation of the world of fancy,
Inoperancy of the world of spirit;
This is the one way, and the other
Is the same, not in movement
But abstention from movement; while the world moves
In appetency, on its metalled ways
Of time past and time future.

IV

Time and the bell have buried the day,
The black cloud carries the sun away.

Will the sunflower turn to us, will the clematis
Stray down, bend to us; tendril and spray
Clutch and cling?
Chill
Fingers of yew be curled
Down on us? After the kingfisher's wing
Has answered light to light, and is silent, the light is still
At the still point of the turning world.

V

Words move, music moves
Only in time; but that which is only living
Can only die. Words, after speech, reach
Into the silence. Only by the form, the pattern,
Can words or music reach
The stillness, as a Chinese jar still
Moves perpetually in its stillness.
Not the stillness of the violin, while the note lasts,
Not that only, but the co-existence,
Or say that the end precedes the beginning,
And the end and the beginning were always there
Before the beginning and after the end.
And all is always now. Words strain,
Crack and sometimes break, under the burden,
Under the tension, slip, slide, perish,
Decay with imprecision, will not stay in place,
Will not stay still. Shrieking voices
Scolding, mocking, or merely chattering,
Always assail them. The Word in the desert
Is most attacked by voices of temptation,
The crying shadow in the funeral dance,
The loud lament of the disconsolate chimera.

The detail of the pattern is movement,
As in the figure of the ten stairs.
Desire itself is movement
Not in itself desirable;
Love is itself unmoving,
Only the cause and end of movement,

Timeless, and undesiring
Except in the aspect of time
Caught in the form of limitation
Between un-being and being.
Sudden in a shaft of sunlight
Even while the dust moves
There rises the hidden laughter
Of children in the foliage
Quick now, here, now, always—
Ridiculous the waste sad time
Stretching before and after.

FENTON JOHNSON

(1888–1958)

Tired

I am tired of work; I am tired of building up somebody else's civilization.

Let us take a rest, M'Lissy Jane.

I will go down to the Last Chance Saloon, drink a gallon or two of gin, shoot a game or two of dice and sleep the rest of the night on one of Mike's barrels.

You will let the old shanty go to rot, the white people's clothes turn to dust, and the Calvary Baptist Church sink to the bottomless pit.

You will spend your days forgetting you married me and your nights hunting the warm gin Mike serves the ladies in the rear of the Last Chance Saloon.

Throw the children into the river; civilization has given us too many. It is better to die than it is to grow up and find out that you are colored.

Pluck the stars out of the heavens. The stars mark our destiny. The stars marked my destiny.

I am tired of civilization.

Aunt Hannah Jackson

Despite her sixty years Aunt Hannah Jackson rubs on other people's clothes.

Time has played havoc with her eyes and turned to gray her parched hair.

But her tongue is nimble as she talks to herself.

All day she talks to herself about her neighbors and her friends and the man she loved.

Yes, Aunt Hannah Jackson loved even as you and I and Wun Hop Sing.

"He was a good man," she says, "but a fool."

"So am I a fool and Mrs. Lee a fool and this Mrs. Goldstein that I work for a fool."

"All of us are fools."

For rubbing on other people's clothes Aunt Hannah Jackson gets a dollar and fifty cents a day and a worn out dress on Christmas.

For talking to herself Aunt Hannah Jackson gets a smile as we call her a good natured fool.

The Minister

I mastered pastoral theology, the Greek of the Apostles, and all the difficult subjects in a minister's curriculum.

I was as learned as any in this country when the Bishop ordained me.

And I went to preside over Mount Moriah, largest flock in the Conference.

I preached the Word as I felt it, I visited the sick and dying and comforted the afflicted in spirit.

I loved my work because I loved my God.

But I lost my charge to Sam Jenkins, who has not been to school four years in his life.

I lost my charge because I could not make my congregation shout.

And my dollar money was small, very small.

Sam Jenkins can tear a Bible to tatters and his congregation destroys the pews with their shouting and stamping.

Sam Jenkins leads in the gift of raising dollar money.

Such is religion.

HANIEL LONG

(1888–1956)

Daphnis and Chloe

You found it difficult to woo—
So do we who follow you.

Everyone would like to mate;
Everyone has had to wait.

So much beauty, so much burning!
But ages pass as we are learning.

Lightning

All evening I have watched the lightning:
it crests an unseen cloud with snow and foam,
veins it with fire, like a human hand, or a leaf,
flushes it sulphur and rose.
And through my own body
a vague trembling goes,
as though I too were vapor.

Cobweb

. . picks up a water snake
and licks its side; puts his tongue tip
to a granite ledge in the glen,
tasting the fused sand that way
                              or with his fingers
after the eye-taste, the eye-feel
. . lies on hot hillsides
among the fronds;
presses locust thorns into his side

791

till his blood responds
. . likes wild tangles
by field and stream;
likes flower-leaves that turn in,
honey and humming birds,
green pampas of scum
. . into all living wilderness
where nothing is numb
thrusting veins and antennae——
an earlier world in sure command
giving the orders

In the Dark World

The swaying, the trembling,
the branches interlocking——
these are but shadows, only you and I,
before we were born,
after we die.

Night brings back the stark——
hunger is our truth. Under the old planets
we shadows are hungry.

You who make music of everything you touch
in the dark room of my life
touch me.

Touch hunger, make it Apollo
in the dark world.

Day and Night

All the flowers by the lake
are for your shadow:
red hibiscus for your heart,
zuchil with golden centre and ivory petals
for your body,
and a flower I do not know
for the thought of you which haunts me.

Under the pepper trees
your shadow waits for me;
your shadow comes with me
down on the sand where waves beat.
There in the black night
I gather a memory in my arms,
murmur a song to nothing.

A New Music

This spring is going, too.
Clinging too long to nature,
He had hoped the tulip with the cup of flame
Might last forever; it drops its petals,
And the last iris fades into the dusk.

She gave him a drawing by Robert, called
                The Dance.
"You know well what I like," he said wryly,
And she, as in a dream, "Ruins,
With trees growing out of them,
People dancing and picnicking on them."

Fate distils us; she was right.
Suffering is a looking-glass
For reflections we might not see otherwise.
He hungers for people growing out of ruins,
That new life streaming forth, that deeper inward glowing

Of music and of tears—
What is so fecund as our ruins are?

Each spring crumples to petals in the pocket.
He is making a new music out of new feelings
For a June evening under the deep trees
Of an earth, of a life, that is all ruins,
That is all release
        —and most of it release
From what a man might fear
Destroyed him to part with.

For Tony, Embarking in Spring

Mrs. Davis' younger son was home
On furlough, but the boy who was on Bataan
She has not heard from. Nor has Max Ribera
Had any word from his boy on Bataan,
And Frank's boy was drowned
In the Indian ocean.
        Today at last it's spring.
The leaves of the pear tree follow the petals
So fast the tree is green and white. The ditches
Flash red with the peach petals they carry away
Singing. The flag went up on the new army hospital
Yesterday; today the major takes us out to see it.
We hear the war news generally at noon,
In your room, on your radio, and your mother sews your
    curtains.
We hear it, and then we go outdoors again
To get our bearings from the spring trees.
Goodbye, dear boy. Thought can be the life of God
In each man, and God is love.

Our Spring Needs Shoveling

Frogs and snakes and a dead cat or two
have fallen into the spring, the spring that is *our* spring;
dead leaves have come swirling down,
and the fence of saplings that kept intruders out
is all to pieces with hard rains, and adds painful debris.

    So dear friend:
let us go to our spring alone,
let us shovel out our decay, the snakes, the leaves,
the mud and boughs, and give the source of our youth
its old chance to be crystal.

The spring no longer flows—I know—and yet,
putting my ear close to the humid leaves
am I deceived, hearing the liquid murmur
of a god down in the earth?
But there's no point to these letters.
Letters allow us to continue an illusion.
It takes the actual living, the meeting in the village
to test friendship.

And if one feel deeply
what is the joy in a casual encounter
when the spring's clogged? And why waste time
talking Japan and China, or the agony
coming in Europe, or the unrest here?
Better far to do our private shovelling.

JOHN CROWE RANSOM

(1888–1974)

Spectral Lovers

By night they haunted a thicket of April mist,
As out of the rich ground strangely come to birth,
Else two immaculate angels fallen on earth.
Lovers they knew they were, but why unclasped, unkissed?
Why should two lovers go frozen asunder in fear?
And yet they were, they were.

Over the shredding of an April blossom
Her thrilling fingers touched him quick with care;
Of many delicate postures she cast a snare;
But for all the red heart beating in the pale bosom,
Her face as of cunningly tinctured ivory
Was hard with an agony.

Stormed by the little batteries of an April night,
Passionate being the essences of the field,
Should the penetrable walls of the crumbling prison yield
And open her treasure to the first clamorous knight?
"This is the mad moon, and must I surrender all?
If he but ask it, I shall."

And gesturing largely to the very moon of Easter,
Mincing his steps, and swishing the jubilant grass,
And beheading some field-flowers that had come to pass,
He had reduced his tributaries faster,
Had not considerations pinched his heart
Unfitly for his art.

"Am I reeling with the sap of April like a drunkard?
Blessed is he that taketh this richest of cities;
But it is so stainless, the sack were a thousand pities;
This is that marble fortress not to be conquered,
Lest its white peace in the black flame turn to tinder
And an unutterable cinder."

They passed me once in April, in the mist.
No other season is it, when one walks and discovers
Two clad in the shapes of angels, being spectral lovers,
Trailing a glory of moon-gold and amethyst,
Who touch their quick fingers fluttering like a bird
Whose songs shall never be heard.

Bells for John Whitesides' Daughter

There was such speed in her little body,
And such lightness in her footfall,
It is no wonder that her brown study
Astonishes us all.

Her wars were bruited in our high window.
We looked among orchard trees and beyond,
Where she took arms against her shadow,
Or harried unto the pond

The lazy geese, like a snow cloud
Dripping their snow on the green grass,
Tricking and stopping, sleepy and proud,
Who cried in goose, Alas,

For the tireless heart within the little
Lady with rod that made them rise
From their noon apple dreams, and scuttle
Goose-fashion under the skies!

But now go the bells, and we are ready;
In one house we are sternly stopped
To say we are vexed at her brown study,
Lying so primly propped.

Here Lies a Lady

Here lies a lady of beauty and high degree.
Of chills and fever she died, of fever and chills,
The delight of her husband, her aunts, an infant of three,
And of medicos marvelling sweetly on her ills.

For either she burned, and her confident eyes would blaze,
And her fingers fly in a manner to puzzle their heads—
What was she making? Why, nothing; she sat in a maze
Of old scraps of laces, snipped into curious shreds—

Or this would pass, and the light of her fire decline
Till she lay discouraged and cold as a thin stalk white and
      blown,
And would not open her eyes, to kisses, to wine;
The sixth of these states was her last; the cold settled down.

Sweet ladies, long may ye bloom, and toughly I hope ye may
      thole,
But was she not lucky? In flowers and lace and mourning,
In love and great honour we bade God rest her soul
After six little spaces of chill, and six of burning.

Judith of Bethulia

Beautiful as the flying legend of some leopard,
She had not yet chosen her great captain or prince
Depositary to her flesh, and our defence;
And a wandering beauty is a blade out of its scabbard.
You know how dangerous, gentlemen of threescore?
May you know it yet ten more.

Nor by process of veiling she grew the less fabulous.
Grey or blue veils, we were desperate to study
The invincible emanations of her white body,
And the winds at her ordered raiment were ominous.
Might she walk in the market, sit in the council of soldiers?
Only of the extreme elders.

But a rare chance was the girl's then, when the Invader
Trumpeted from the south, and rumbled from the north,
Beleaguered the city from four quarters of the earth,
Our soldiery too craven and sick to aid her—
Where were the arms could countervail his horde?
Her beauty was the sword.

She sat with the elders, and proved on their blear visage
How bright was the weapon unrusted in her keeping,
While he lay surfeiting on their harvest heaping,
Wasting the husbandry of their rarest vintage—
And dreaming of the broad-breasted dames for concubine?
These floated on his wine.

He was lapped with bay-leaves, and grass and fumiter weed,
And from under the wine-film encountered his mortal vision.
For even within his tent she accomplished his derision;
She loosed one veil and another, standing unafraid;
And he perished. Nor brushed her with even so much as a
    daisy?
She found his destruction easy.

The heathen are all perished. The victory was furnished,
We smote them hiding in our vineyards, barns, annexes,
And now their white bones clutter the holes of foxes,
And the chieftain's head, with grinning sockets, and
    varnished—
Is it hung on the sky with a hideous epitaphy?
No, the woman keeps the trophy.

May God send unto the virtuous lady her prince.
It is stated she went reluctant to that orgy,
Yet a madness fevers our young men, and not the clergy
Nor the elders have turned them unto modesty since.
Inflamed by the thought of her naked beauty with desire?
Yes, and chilled with fear and despair.

Nocturne

Where now is the young Adam, sultry in his Aiden?
And where is the goat-footed, pursuing his naked maiden?
Our man shall cut few capers in his dark seersucker coat,
His grave eye subduing the outrageous red tie at his throat,
Considering if he should carry his dutiful flesh to the ball,
Rather than open his book, which is flat, and metaphysical.

The centuries have blown hard, and dried his blood
Unto this dark quintessence of manhood;
Much water has passed the bridges, fretfully,
And borne his boats of passion to the sea;
There is no storm in this dusk, but a distant flash
Over the foamy sea where the great floods wash.

But still the plum-tree blooms, despite the rocks at its root,
Despite that everyone knows by now its wizened and little
    fruit,
And the white moon plunges wildly, it is a most ubiquitous
    ghost,
Always seeking her own old people that are a long time lost—
Till he is almost persuaded, and perhaps he would go to the
    ball,
If he had the heart, and the head, for a furious antique
    bacchanal.

Blackberry Winter

If the lady hath any loveliness, let it die.
For being drunken with the steam of Cuban cigars,
I find no pungence in the odour of stars,
And all my music goes out of me on a sigh.

But still would I sing to my maidenly apple-tree,
Before she has borne me a single apple of red;
The pictures of silver and apples of gold are dead;
But one more apple ripeneth yet maybe.

The garnished house of the Daughter of Heaven is cold.
I have seen her often, she stood all night on the hill,
Fiercely the pale youth clambered to her, till—
Hoarsely the rooster awakened him, footing the mould.

The breath of a girl is music—fall and swell—
The trumpets convolve in the warrior's chambered ear,
But I have listened, there is no one breathing here,
And all of the wars have dwindled since Troy fell.

But still I will haunt beneath my apple-tree,
Heedful again to star-looks and wind-words,
Anxious for the flash of whether eyes or swords,
And hoping a little, a little, that either may be.

Captain Carpenter

Captain Carpenter rose up in his prime
Put on his pistols and went riding out
But had got wellnigh nowhere at that time
Till he fell in with ladies in a rout.

It was a pretty lady and all her train
That played with him so sweetly but before
An hour she'd taken a sword with all her main
And twined him of his nose for evermore.

Captain Carpenter mounted up one day
And rode straightway into a stranger rogue
That looked unchristian but be that as may
The Captain did not wait upon prologue.

But drew upon him out of his great heart
The other swung against him with a club
And cracked his two legs at the shinny part
And let him roll and stick like any tub.

Captain Carpenter rode many a time
From male and female took he sundry harms
He met the wife of Satan crying "I'm
The she-wolf bids you shall bear no more arms."

Their strokes and counters whistled in the wind
I wish he had delivered half his blows
But where she should have made off like a hind
The bitch bit off his arms at the elbows.

And Captain Carpenter parted with his ears
To a black devil that used him in this wise
O Jesus ere his threescore and ten years
Another had plucked out his sweet blue eyes.

Captain Carpenter got up on his roan
And sallied from the gate in hell's despite
I heard him asking in the grimmest tone
If any enemy yet there was to fight?

"To any adversary it is fame
If he risk to be wounded by my tongue
Or burnt in two beneath my red heart's flame
Such are the perils he is cast among.

"But if he can he has a pretty choice
From an anatomy with little to lose
Whether he cut my tongue and take my voice
Or whether it be my round red heart he choose."

It was the neatest knave that ever was seen
Stepping in perfume from his lady's bower
Who at this word put in his merry mien
And fell on Captain Carpenter like a tower.

I would not knock old fellows in the dust
But there lay Captain Carpenter on his back
His weapons were the old heart in his bust
And a blade shook between rotten teeth alack.

The rogue in scarlet and grey soon knew his mind
He wished to get his trophy and depart
With gentle apology and touch refined
He pierced him and produced the Captain's heart.

God's mercy rest on Captain Carpenter now
I thought him Sirs an honest gentleman
Citizen husband soldier and scholar enow
Let jangling kites eat of him if they can.

But God's deep curses follow after those
That shore him of his goodly nose and ears
His legs and strong arms at the two elbows
And eyes that had not watered seventy years.

The curse of hell upon the sleek upstart
Who got the Captain finally on his back
And took the red red vitals of his heart
And made the kites to whet their beaks clack clack.

Philomela

Procne, Philomela, and Itylus,
Your names are liquid, your improbable tale
Is recited in the classic numbers of the nightingale.
Ah, but our numbers are not felicitous,
It goes not liquidly for us.

Perched on a Roman ilex, and duly apostrophized,
The nightingale descanted unto Ovid;
She has even appeared to the Teutons, the swilled and gravid;
At Fontainebleau it may be the bird was gallicized;
Never was she baptized.

To England came Philomela with her pain,
Fleeing the hawk her husband; querulous ghost,
She wanders when he sits heavy on his roost,
Utters herself in the original again,
The untranslatable refrain.

Not to these shores she came! this other Thrace,
Environ barbarous to the royal Attic;
How could her delicate dirge run democratic,
Delivered in a cloudless boundless public place
To an inordinate race?

I pernoctated with the Oxford students once,
And in the quadrangles, in the cloisters, on the Cher,
Precociously knocked at antique doors ajar,
Fatuously touched the hems of the hierophants,
Sick of my dissonance.

I went out to Bagley Wood, I climbed the hill;
Even the moon had slanted off in a twinkling,
I heard the sepulchral owl and a few bells tinkling,
There was no more villainous day to unfulfil,
The diuturnity was still.

Up from the darkest wood where Philomela sat,
Her fairy numbers issued. What then ailed me?
My ears are called capacious but they failed me,
Her classics registered a little flat!
I rose, and venomously spat.

Philomela, Philomela, lover of song,
I am in despair if we may make us worthy,
A bantering breed sophistical and swarthy;
Unto more beautiful, persistently more young
Thy fabulous provinces belong.

Janet Waking

Beautifully Janet slept
Till it was deeply morning. She woke then
And thought about her dainty-feathered hen,
To see how it had kept.

One kiss she gave her mother,
Only a small one gave she to her daddy
Who would have kissed each curl of his shining baby;
No kiss at all for her brother.

"Old Chucky, Old Chucky!" she cried,
Running on little pink feet upon the grass
To Chucky's house, and listening. But alas,
Her Chucky had died.

It was a transmogrifying bee
Came droning down on Chucky's old bald head
And sat and put the poison. It scarcely bled,
But how exceedingly

And purply did the knot
Swell with the venom and communicate
Its rigour! Now the poor comb stood up straight
But Chucky did not.

So there was Janet
Kneeling on the wet grass, crying her brown hen
(Translated far beyond the daughters of men)
To rise and walk upon it.

And weeping fast as she had breath
Janet implored us, "Wake her from her sleep!"
And would not be instructed in how deep
Was the forgetful kingdom of death.

Piazza Piece

—I am a gentleman in a dustcoat trying
To make you hear. Your ears are soft and small
And listen to an old man not at all,
They want the young men's whispering and sighing.
But see the roses on your trellis dying

And hear the spectral singing of the moon;
For I must have my lovely lady soon.
I am a gentleman in a dustcoat trying.

—I am a lady young in beauty waiting
Until my truelove comes, and then we kiss.
But what grey man among the vines is this
Whose words are dry and faint as in a dream?
Back from my trellis, sir, before I scream!
I am a lady young in beauty waiting.

The Equilibrists

Full of her long white arms and milky skin
He had a thousand times remembered sin.
Alone in the press of people travelled he,
Minding her jacinth and myrrh and ivory.

Mouth he remembered: the quaint orifice
From which came heat that flamed upon the kiss,
Till cold words came down spiral from the head,
Grey doves from the officious tower illsped.

Body: it was a white field ready for love.
On her body's field, with the gaunt tower above,
The lilies grew, beseeching him to take,
If he would pluck and wear them, bruise and break.

Eyes talking: Never mind the cruel words,
Embrace my flowers but not embrace the swords.
But what they said, the doves came straightway flying
And unsaid: Honor, Honor, they came crying.

Importunate her doves. Too pure, too wise,
Clambering on his shoulder, saying, Arise,
Leave me now, and never let us meet,
Eternal distance now command thy feet.

Predicament indeed, which thus discovers
Honor among thieves, Honor between lovers.
O such a little word is Honor, they feel!
But the grey word is between them cold as steel.

At length I saw these lovers fully were come
Into their torture of equilibrium:
Dreadfully had forsworn each other, and yet
They were bound each to each, and they did not forget.

And rigid as two painful stars, and twirled
About the clustered night their prison world,
They burned with fierce love always to come near,
But Honor beat them back and kept them clear.

Ah, the strict lovers, they are ruined now!
I cried in anger. But with puddled brow
Devising for those gibbeted and brave
Came I descanting: Man, what would you have?

For spin your period out, and draw your breath,
A kinder saeculum begins with Death.
Would you ascend to Heaven and bodiless dwell?
Or take your bodies honorless to Hell?

In Heaven you have heard no marriage is,
No white flesh tinder to your lecheries,
Your male and female tissue sweetly shaped
Sublimed away, and furious blood escaped.

Great lovers lie in Hell, the stubborn ones
Infatuate of the flesh upon the bones;
Stuprate, they rend each other when they kiss;
The pieces kiss again—no end to this.

But still I watched them spinning, orbited nice.
Their flames were not more radiant than their ice.
I dug in the quiet earth and wrought the tomb
And made these lines to memorize their doom:—

Equilibrists lie here; stranger, tread light;
Close, but untouching in each other's sight;
Mouldered the lips and ashy the tall skull,
Let them lie perilous and beautiful.

Blue Girls

Twirling your blue skirts, travelling the sward
Under the towers of your seminary,
Go listen to your teachers old and contrary
Without believing a word.

Tie the white fillets then about your lustrous hair
And think no more of what will come to pass
Than bluebirds that go walking on the grass
And chattering on the air.

Practise your beauty, blue girls, before it fail;
And I will cry with my loud lips and publish
Beauty which all our power shall never establish,
It is so frail.

For I could tell you a story which is true;
I know a lady with a terrible tongue,
Blear eyes fallen from blue,
All her perfections tarnished—and yet it is not long
Since she was lovelier than any of you.

Painted Head

By dark severance the apparition head
Smiles from the air a capital on no
Column or a Platonic perhaps head
On a canvas sky depending from nothing;

Stirs up an old illusion of grandeur
By tickling the instinct of heads to be
Absolute and to try decapitation
And to play truant from the body bush;

But too happy and beautiful for those sorts
Of head (homekeeping heads are happiest)
Discovers maybe thirty unwidowed years
Of not dishonoring the faithful stem;

Is nameless and has authored for the evil
Historian headhunters neither book
Nor state and is therefore distinct from tart
Heads with crowns and guilty gallery heads;

So that the extravagant device of art
Unhousing by abstraction this once head
Was capital irony by a loving hand
That knew the no treason of a head like this;

Makes repentance in an unlovely head
For having vinegarly traduced the flesh
Till, the hurt flesh recusing, the hard egg
Is shrunken to its own deathlike surface;

And an image thus. The body bears the head
(So hardly one they terribly are two)
Feeds and obeys and unto please what end?
Not to the glory of tyrant head but to

The increase of body. Beauty is of body.
The flesh contouring shallowly on a head
Is a rock-garden needing body's love
And best bodiness to colorify

The big blue birds sitting and sea-shell flats
And caves, and on the iron acropolis
To spread the hyacinthine hair and rear
The olive garden for the nightingales.

ALAN SEEGER

(1888–1916)

I Have a Rendezvous with Death . . .

I have a rendezvous with Death
At some disputed barricade,
When Spring comes back with rustling shade
And apple-blossoms fill the air—
I have a rendezvous with Death
When Spring brings back blue days and fair.

It may be he shall take my hand
And lead me into his dark land
And close my eyes and quench my breath—
It may be I shall pass him still.
I have a rendezvous with Death
On some scarred slope of battered hill,
When Spring comes round again this year
And the first meadow-flowers appear.

God knows 'twere better to be deep
Pillowed in silk and scented down,
Where Love throbs out in blissful sleep,
Pulse nigh to pulse, and breath to breath,
Where hushed awakenings are dear . . .
But I've a rendezvous with Death
At midnight in some flaming town,
When Spring trips north again this year,
And I to my pledged word am true,
I shall not fail that rendezvous.

CONRAD AIKEN

(1889–1973)

Morning Song of Senlin

It is morning, Senlin says, and in the morning
When the light drips through the shutters like the dew,
I arise, I face the sunrise,
And do the things my fathers learned to do.
Stars in the purple dusk above the rooftops
Pale in a saffron mist and seem to die,
And I myself on a swiftly tilting planet
Stand before a glass and tie my tie.

Vine leaves tap my window,
Dew-drops sing to the garden stones,
The robin chirps in the chinaberry tree
Repeating three clear tones.

It is morning. I stand by the mirror
And tie my tie once more.
While waves far off in a pale rose twilight
Crash on a white sand shore.
I stand by a mirror and comb my hair:
How small and white my face!—
The green earth tilts through a sphere of air
And bathes in a flame of space.

There are houses hanging above the stars
And stars hung under a sea . . .
And a sun far off in a shell of silence
Dapples my walls for me . . .

It is morning, Senlin says, and in the morning
Should I not pause in the light to remember god?
Upright and firm I stand on a star unstable,
He is immense and lonely as a cloud.
I will dedicate this moment before my mirror

To him alone, for him I will comb my hair.
Accept these humble offerings, cloud of silence!
I will think of you as I descend the stair.

Vine leaves tap my window,
The snail-track shines on the stones,
Dew-drops flash from the chinaberry tree
Repeating two clear tones.

It is morning, I awake from a bed of silence,
Shining I rise from the starless waters of sleep.
The walls are about me still as in the evening,
I am the same, and the same name still I keep.

The earth revolves with me, yet makes no motion,
The stars pale silently in a coral sky.
In a whistling void I stand before my mirror,
Unconcerned, and tie my tie.

There are horses neighing on far-off hills
Tossing their long white manes,
And mountains flash in the rose-white dusk,
Their shoulders black with rains . . .
It is morning. I stand by the mirror
And surprise my soul once more;
The blue air rushes above my ceiling,
There are suns beneath my floor . . .

. . . It is morning, Senlin says, I ascend from darkness
And depart on the winds of space for I know not where,
My watch is wound, a key is in my pocket,
And the sky is darkened as I descend the stair.
There are shadows across the windows, clouds in heaven,
And a god among the stars; and I will go
Thinking of him as I might think of daybreak
And humming a tune I know . . .

Vine-leaves tap at the window,
Dew-drops sing to the garden stones,
The robin chirps in the chinaberry tree
Repeating three clear tones.

Tetélestai

I

How shall we praise the magnificence of the dead,
The great man humbled, the haughty brought to dust?
Is there a horn we should not blow as proudly
For the meanest of us all, who creeps his days,
Guarding his heart from blows, to die obscurely?
I am no king, have laid no kingdoms waste,
Taken no princes captive, led no triumphs
Of weeping women through long walls of trumpets;
Say rather, I am no one, or an atom;
Say rather, two great gods, in a vault of starlight,
Play ponderingly at chess, and at the game's end
One of the pieces, shaken, falls to the floor
And runs to the darkest corner; and that piece
Forgotten there, left motionless, is I. . . .
Say that I have no name, no gifts, no power,
Am only one of millions, mostly silent;
One who came with eyes and hands and a heart,
Looked on beauty, and loved it, and then left it.
Say that the fates of time and space obscured me,
Led me a thousand ways to pain, bemused me,
Wrapped me in ugliness; and like great spiders
Dispatched me at their leisure. . . . Well, what then?
Should I not hear, as I lie down in dust,
The horns of glory blowing above my burial?

II

Morning and evening opened and closed above me:
Houses were built above me; trees let fall
Yellowing leaves upon me, hands of ghosts;

Rain has showered its arrows of silver upon me
Seeking my heart; winds have roared and tossed me;
Music in long blue waves of sound has borne me
A helpless weed to shores of unthought silence;
Time, above me, within me, crashed its gongs
Of terrible warning, sifting the dust of death;
And here I lie. Blow now your horns of glory
Harshly over my flesh, you trees, you waters!
You stars and suns, Canopus, Deneb, Rigel,
Let me, as I lie down, here in this dust,
Hear, far off, your whispered salutation!
Roar now above my decaying flesh, you winds,
Whirl out your earth-scents over this body, tell me
Of ferns and stagnant pools, wild roses, hillsides!
Anoint me, rain, let crash your silver arrows
On this hard flesh! I am the one who named you,
I lived in you, and now I die in you.
I your son, your daughter, treader of music,
Lie broken, conquered . . . Let me not fall in silence.

III

I, the restless one; the circler of circles;
Herdsman and roper of stars, who could not capture
The secret of self; I who was tyrant to weaklings,
Striker of children; destroyer of women; corrupter
Of innocent dreamers, and laugher at beauty; I,
Too easily brought to tears and weakness by music,
Baffled and broken by love, the helpless beholder
Of the war in my heart of desire with desire, the struggle
Of hatred with love, terror with hunger; I
Who laughed without knowing the cause of my laughter, who
    grew
Without wishing to grow, a servant to my own body;
Loved without reason the laughter and flesh of a woman,
Enduring such torments to find her! I who at last
Grow weaker, struggle more feebly, relent in my purpose,
Choose for my triumph an easier end, look backward
At earlier conquests; or, caught in the web, cry out
In a sudden and empty despair, 'Tetélestai!'

Pity me, now! I, who was arrogant, beg you!
Tell me, as I lie down, that I was courageous.
Blow horns of victory now, as I reel and am vanquished.
Shatter the sky with trumpets above my grave.

IV

. . . Look! this flesh how it crumbles to dust and is blown!
These bones, how they grind in the granite of frost and are
     nothing!
This skull, how it yawns for a flicker of time in the darkness,
Yet laughs not and sees not! It is crushed by a hammer of
     sunlight,
And the hands are destroyed. . . . Press down through the
     leaves of the jasmine,
Dig through the interlaced roots—nevermore will you find
     me;
I was no better than dust, yet you cannot replace me. . . .
Take the soft dust in your hand—does it stir: does it sing?
Has it lips and a heart? Does it open its eyes to the sun?
Does it run, does it dream, does it burn with a secret, or
     tremble
In terror of death? Or ache with tremendous decisions? . . .
Listen! . . . It says: 'I lean by the river. The willows
Are yellowed with bud. White clouds roar up from the south
And darken the ripples; but they cannot darken my heart,
Nor the face like a star in my heart! . . . Rain falls on the
     water
And pelts it, and rings it with silver. The willow trees glisten,
The sparrows chirp under the eaves; but the face in my heart
Is a secret of music. . . . I wait in the rain and am silent.'
Listen again! . . . It says: 'I have worked, I am tired,
The pencil dulls in my hand: I see through the window
Walls upon walls of windows with faces behind them,
Smoke floating up to the sky, an ascension of sea-gulls.
I am tired. I have struggled in vain, my decision was fruitless,
Why then do I wait? with darkness, so easy, at hand! . . .
But tomorrow, perhaps . . . I will wait and endure till
     tomorrow!' . . .
Or again: 'It is dark. The decision is made. I am vanquished

By terror of life. The walls mount slowly about me
In coldness. I had not the courage. I was forsaken.
I cried out, was answered by silence . . . Tetélestai! . . .'

v

Hear how it babbles!—Blow the dust out of your hand,
With its voices and visions, tread on it, forget it, turn
    homeward
With dreams in your brain. . . . This, then, is the humble,
    the nameless,—
The lover, the husband and father, the struggler with
    shadows,
The one who went down under shoutings of chaos, the
    weakling
Who cried his 'forsaken!' like Christ on the darkening
    hilltop! . . .
This, then, is the one who implores, as he dwindles to silence,
A fanfare of glory. . . . And which of us dares to deny him?

And in the Hanging Gardens

And in the hanging gardens there is rain
From midnight until one, striking the leaves
And bells of flowers, and stroking boles of planes,
And drawing slow arpeggios over pools,
And stretching strings of sound from eaves to ferns.
The princess reads. The knave of diamonds sleeps.
The king is drunk, and flings a golden goblet
Down from the turret window (curtained with rain)
Into the lilacs.

            And at one o'clock
The vulcan under the garden wakes and beats
The gong upon his anvil. Then the rain
Ceases, but gently ceases, dripping still,
And sound of falling water fills the dark
As leaves grow bold and upright, and as eaves

Part with water. The princess turns the page
Beside the candle, and between two braids
Of golden hair. And reads: "From there I went
Northward a journey of four days, and came
To a wild village in the hills, where none
Was living save the vulture and the rat,
And one old man, who laughed, but could not speak.
The roofs were fallen in; the well grown over
With weed; and it was there my father died.
Then eight days further, bearing slightly west,
The cold wind blowing sand against our faces,
The food tasting of sand. And as we stood
By the dry rock that marks the highest point
My brother said: 'Not too late is it yet
To turn, remembering home.' And we were silent
Thinking of home." The princess shuts her eyes
And feels the tears forming beneath her eyelids
And opens them, and tears fall on the page.
The knave of diamonds in the darkened room
Throws off his covers, sleeps, and snores again.
The king goes slowly down the turret stairs
To find the goblet.

         And at two o'clock
The vulcan in his smithy underground
Under the hanging gardens, where the drip
Of rain among the clematis and ivy
Still falls from sipping flower to purple flower,
Smites twice his anvil, and the murmur comes
Among the roots and vines. The princess reads:
"As I am sick, and cannot write you more,
Nor have not long to live, I give this letter
To him, my brother, who will bear it south
And tell you how I died. Ask how it was,
There in the northern desert, where the grass
Was withered, and the horses, all but one,
Perished" . . . The princess drops her golden head
Upon the page between her two white arms
And golden braids. The knave of diamonds wakes

And at his window in the darkened room
Watches the lilacs tossing, where the king
Seeks for the goblet.

                       And at three o'clock
The moon inflames the lilac heads, and thrice
The vulcan, in his root-bound smithy, clangs
His anvil; and the sounds creep softly up
Among the vines and walls. The moon is round,
Round as a shield above the turret top.
The princess blows her candle out, and weeps
In the pale room, where scent of lilac comes,
Weeping, with hands across her eyelids, thinking
Of withered grass, withered by sandy wind.
The knave of diamonds, in his darkened room,
Holds in his hands a key, and softly steps
Along the corridor, and slides the key
Into the door that guards her. Meanwhile, slowly,
The king, with raindrops on his beard and hands,
And dripping sleeves, climbs up the turret stairs,
Holding the goblet upright in one hand;
And pauses on the midmost step, to taste
One drop of wine, wherewith wild rain has mixed.

The Room

Through that window—all else being extinct
Except itself and me—I saw the struggle
Of darkness against darkness. Within the room
It turned and turned, dived downward. Then I saw
How order might—if chaos wished—become:
And saw the darkness crush upon itself,
Contracting powerfully; it was as if
It killed itself: slowly: and with much pain.
Pain. The scene was pain, and nothing but pain.
What else, when chaos draws all forces inward
To shape a single leaf? . . .

For the leaf came
Alone and shining in the empty room;
After a while the twig shot downward from it;
And from the twig a bough; and then the trunk,
Massive and coarse; and last the one black root.
The black root cracked the walls. Boughs burst the window:
The great tree took possession.

Tree of trees!
Remember (when time comes) how chaos died
To shape the shining leaf. Then turn, have courage,
Wrap arms and roots together, be convulsed
With grief, and bring back chaos out of shape.
I will be watching then as I watch now.
I will praise darkness now, but then the leaf.

Sea Holly

Begotten by the meeting of rock with rock,
The mating of rock and rock, rocks gnashing together;
Created so, and yet forgetful, walks
The seaward path, puts up her left hand, shades
Blue eyes, the eyes of rock, to see better
In slanting light the ancient sheep (which kneels
Biting the grass) the while her other hand,
Hooking the wicker handle, turns the basket
Of eggs. The sea is high to-day. The eggs
Are cheaper. The sea is blown from the southwest,
Confused, taking up sand and mud in waves,
The waves break, sluggish, in brown foam, the wind
Disperses (on the sheep and hawthorn) spray,—
And on her cheeks, the cheeks engendered of rock,
And eyes, the colour of rock. The left hand
Falls from the eyes, and undecided slides
Over the left breast on which muslin lightly
Rests, touching the nipple, and then down
The hollow side, virgin as rock, and bitterly
Caresses the blue hip.

It was for this,
This obtuse taking of the seaward path,
This stupid hearing of larks, this hooking
Of wicker, this absent observation of sheep
Kneeling in harsh sea-grass, the cool hand shading
The spray-stung eyes—it was for this the rock
Smote itself. The sea is higher today,
And eggs are cheaper. The eyes of rock take in
The seaward path that winds toward the sea,
The thistle-prodder, old woman under a bonnet,
Forking the thistles, her back against the sea,
Pausing, with hard hands on the handle, peering
With rock eyes from her bonnet.

It was for this,
This rock-lipped facing of brown waves, half sand
And half water, this tentative hand that slides
Over the breast of rock, and into the hollow
Soft side of muslin rock, and then fiercely
Almost as rock against the hip of rock—
It was for this in midnight the rocks met,
And dithered together, cracking and smoking.

It was for this
Barren beauty, barrenness of rock that aches
On the seaward path, seeing the fruitful sea,
Hearing the lark of rock that sings, smelling
The rock-flower of hawthorn, sweetness of rock—
It was for this, stone pain in the stony heart,
The rock loved and laboured; and all is lost.

from
Preludes for Memnon

I

Winter for a moment takes the mind; the snow
Falls past the arclight; icicles guard a wall;
The wind moans through a crack in the window;
A keen sparkle of frost is on the sill.
Only for a moment; as spring too might engage it,
With a single crocus in the loam, or a pair of birds;
Or summer with hot grass; or autumn with a yellow leaf.
Winter is there, outside, is here in me:
Drapes the planets with snow, deepens the ice on the moon,
Darkens the darkness that was already darkness.
The mind too has its snows, its slippery paths,
Walls bayonetted with ice, leaves ice-encased.
Here is the in-drawn room, to which you return
When the wind blows from Arcturus: here is the fire
At which you warm your hands and glaze your eyes;
The piano, on which you touch the cold treble;
Five notes like breaking icicles; and then silence.

The alarm-clock ticks, the pulse keeps time with it,
Night and the mind are full of sounds. I walk
From the fire-place, with its imaginary fire,
To the window, with its imaginary view.
Darkness, and snow ticking the window: silence,
And the knocking of chains on a motor-car, the tolling
Of a bronze bell, dedicated to Christ.
And then the uprush of angelic wings, the beating
Of wings demonic, from the abyss of the mind:
The darkness filled with a feathery whistling, wings
Numberless as the flakes of angelic snow,
The deep void swarming with wings and sound of wings,
The winnowing of chaos, the aliveness
Of depth and depth and depth dedicated to death.

Here are the bickerings of the inconsequential,
The chatterings of the ridiculous, the iterations
Of the meaningless. Memory, like a juggler,
Tosses its colored balls into the light, and again
Receives them into darkness. Here is the absurd,
Grinning like an idiot, and the omnivorous quotidian,
Which will have its day. A handful of coins,
Tickets, items from the news, a soiled handkerchief,
A letter to be answered, notice of a telephone call,
The petal of a flower in a volume of Shakspere,
The program of a concert. The photograph, too,
Propped on the mantel, and beneath it a dry rosebud;
The laundry bill, matches, an ash-tray, Utamaro's
Pearl-fishers. And the rug, on which are still the crumbs
Of yesterday's feast. These are the void, the night,
And the angelic wings that make it sound.

What is the flower? It is not a sigh of color,
Suspiration of purple, sibilation of saffron,
Nor aureate exhalation from the tomb.
Yet it is these because you think of these,
An emanation of emanations, fragile
As light, or glisten, or gleam, or coruscation,
Creature of brightness, and as brightness brief.
What is the frost? It is not the sparkle of death,
The flash of time's wing, seeds of eternity;
Yet it is these because you think of these.
And you, because you think of these, are both
Frost and flower, the bright ambiguous syllable
Of which the meaning is both no and yes.

Here is the tragic, the distorting mirror
In which your gesture becomes grandiose;
Tears form and fall from your magnificent eyes,
The brow is noble, and the mouth is God's.
Here is the God who seeks his mother, Chaos,—
Confusion seeking solution, and life seeking death.
Here is the rose that woos the icicle; the icicle
That woos the rose. Here is the silence of silences
Which dreams of becoming a sound, and the sound

Which will perfect itself in silence. And all
These things are only the uprush from the void,
The wings angelic and demonic, the sound of the abyss
Dedicated to death. And this is you.

II

Two coffees in the Español, the last
Bright drops of golden Barsac in a goblet,
Fig paste and candied nuts. . . . Hardy is dead,
And James and Conrad dead, and Shakspere dead,
And old Moore ripens for an obscene grave,
And Yeats for an arid one; and I, and you—
What winding sheet for us, what boards and bricks,
What mummeries, candles, prayers, and pious frauds?
You shall be lapped in Syrian scarlet, woman,
And wear your pearls, and your bright bracelets, too,
Your agate ring, and round your neck shall hang
Your dark blue lapis with its specks of gold.
And I, beside you—ah! but will that be?
For there are dark streams in this dark world, lady,
Gulf Streams and Arctic currents of the soul;
And I may be, before our consummation
Beds us together, cheek by jowl, in earth,
Swept to another shore, where my white bones
Will lie unhonored, or defiled by gulls.

What dignity can death bestow on us,
Who kiss beneath a streetlamp, or hold hands
Half hidden in a taxi, or replete
With coffee, figs and Barsac make our way
To a dark bedroom in a wormworn house?
The aspidistra guards the door; we enter,
Per aspidistra—then—*ad astra*—is it?—
And lock ourselves securely in our gloom
And loose ourselves from terror. . . . Here's my hand,
The white scar on my thumb, and here's my mouth
To stop your murmur; speechless let us lie,
And think of Hardy, Shakspere, Yeats and James;
Comfort our panic hearts with magic names;

Stare at the ceiling, where the taxi lamps
Make ghosts of light; and see, beyond this bed,
That other bed in which we will not move;
And, whether joined or separate, will not love.

H. P. LOVECRAFT

(1890–1937)

The Well

Farmer Seth Atwood was past eighty when
He tried to sink that deep well by his door,
With only Eb to help him bore and bore.
We laughed, and hoped he'd soon be sane again.
And yet, instead, young Eb went crazy, too,
So that they shipped him to the county farm.
Seth bricked the well-mouth up as tight as glue—
Then hacked an artery in his gnarled left arm.

After the funeral we felt bound to get
Out to that well and rip the bricks away,
But all we saw were iron hand-holds set
Down a black hole deeper than we could say.
And yet we put the bricks back—for we found
The hole too deep for any line to sound.

Alienation

His solid flesh had never been away,
For each dawn found him in his usual place,
But every night his spirit loved to race
Through gulfs and worlds remote from common day.
He had seen Yaddith, yet retained his mind,
And come back safely from the Ghooric zone,
When one still night across curved space was thrown
That beckoning piping from the voids behind.

He waked that morning as an older man,
And nothing since has looked the same to him.
Objects around float nebulous and dim—
False phantom trifles of some vaster plan.
His folk and friends are now an alien throng
To which he struggles vainly to belong.

CLAUDE McKAY

(1890–1948)

The Lynching

His spirit in smoke ascended to high heaven.
His father, by the cruellest way of pain,
Had bidden him to his bosom once again:
The awful sin remained still unforgiven.
All night a bright and solitary star
(Perchance the one that ever guided him,
Yet gave him up at last to Fate's wild whim)
Hung pitifully o'er the swinging char.
Day dawned, and soon the mixed crowds came to view
The ghastly body swaying in the sun:
The women thronged to look, but never a one
Showed sorrow in her eyes of steely blue;
And little lads, lynchers that were to be,
Danced round the dreadful thing in fiendish glee.

The Harlem Dancer

Applauding youths laughed with young prostitutes
And watched her perfect, half-clothed body sway;
Her voice was like the sound of blended flutes
Blown by black players upon a picnic day.
She sang and danced on gracefully and calm,
The light gauze hanging loose about her form;
To me she seemed a proudly-swaying palm
Grown lovelier for passing through a storm.
Upon her swarthy neck black, shiny curls
Profusely fell; and, tossing coins in praise,
The wine-flushed, bold-eyed boys, and even the girls,
Devoured her with eager, passionate gaze:
But, looking at her falsely-smiling face,
I knew her self was not in that strange place.

The Castaways

The vivid grass with visible delight
Springing triumphant from the pregnant earth;
And butterflies, and sparrows in brief flight
Chirping and dancing for the season's birth,
And dandelions and rare daffodils
That hold the deep-stirred heart with hands of gold
And thrushes sending forth their joyous trills;
Not these, not these did I at first behold:
But seated on the benches daubed with green,
The castaways of earth, some fast asleep,
With many a withered woman wedged between,
And over all life's shadows dark and deep:
Moaning I turned away, for misery
I have the strength to bear but not to see.

The Tropics in New York

Bananas ripe and green and ginger-root,
    Cocoa in pods and alligator pears,
And tangerines and mangoes and grape fruit,
    Fit for the highest prize at parish fairs,

Set in the window, bringing memories
    Of fruit trees laden by low-singing rills,
And dewy dawns and mystical blue skies
    In benediction over nun-like hills.

Mine eyes grew dim and I could no more gaze,
    A wave of longing through my body swept,
And, hungry for the old, familiar ways,
    I turned aside and bowed my head and wept.

Harlem Shadows

I hear the halting footsteps of a lass
    In Negro Harlem when the night lets fall
Its veil. I see the shapes of girls who pass
    Eager to heed desire's insistent call:
Ah, little dark girls, who in slippered feet
Go prowling through the night from street to street.

Through the long night until the silver break
    Of day the little gray feet know no rest,
Through the lone night until the last snow-flake
    Has dropped from heaven upon the earth's white breast,
The dusky, half-clad girls of tired feet
Are trudging, thinly shod, from street to street.

Ah, stern harsh world, that in the wretched way
    Of poverty, dishonour and disgrace,
Has pushed the timid little feet of clay.
    The sacred brown feet of my fallen race!
Ah, heart of me, the weary, weary feet
In Harlem wandering from street to street.

If We Must Die

If we must die, let it not be like hogs
Hunted and penned in an inglorious spot,
While round us bark the mad and hungry dogs,
Making their mock at our accursèd lot.
If we must die, O let us nobly die,
So that our precious blood may not be shed
In vain; then even the monsters we defy
Shall be constrained to honor us though dead!
O kinsmen! we must meet the common foe!
Though far outnumbered let us show us brave,
And for their thousand blows deal one death-blow!
What though before us lies the open grave?
Like men we'll face the murderous, cowardly pack,
Pressed to the wall, dying, but fighting back!

The White City

I will not toy with it nor bend an inch.
Deep in the secret chambers of my heart
I muse my life-long hate, and without flinch
I bear it nobly as I live my part.
My being would be a skeleton, a shell,
If this dark Passion that fills my every mood,
And makes my heaven in the white world's hell,
Did not forever feed me vital blood.
I see the mighty city through a mist—
The strident trains that speed the goaded mass,
The poles and spires and towers vapor-kissed,
The fortressed port through which the great ships pass,
The tides, the wharves, the dens I contemplate,
Are sweet like wanton loves because I hate.

Dawn in New York

The Dawn! The Dawn! The crimson-tinted, comes
Out of the low still skies, over the hills,
Manhattan's roofs and spires and cheerless domes!
The Dawn! My spirit to its spirit thrills.
Almost the mighty city is asleep,
No pushing crowd, no tramping, tramping feet.
But here and there a few cars groaning creep
Along, above, and underneath the street,
Bearing their strangely-ghostly burdens by,
The women and the men of garish nights,
Their eyes wine-weakened and their clothes awry,
Grotesques beneath the strong electric lights.
The shadows wane. The Dawn comes to New York.
And I go darkly-rebel to my work.

Africa

The sun sought thy dim bed and brought forth light,
The sciences were sucklings at thy breast;
When all the world was young in pregnant night
Thy slaves toiled at thy monumental best.
Thou ancient treasure-land, thou modern prize,
New peoples marvel at thy pyramids!
The years roll on, thy sphinx of riddle eyes
Watches the mad world with immobile lids.
The Hebrews humbled them at Pharaoh's name.
Cradle of Power! Yet all things were in vain!
Honor and Glory, Arrogance and Fame!
They went. The darkness swallowed thee again.
Thou art the harlot, now thy time is done,
Of all the mighty nations of the sun.

Outcast

For the dim regions whence my fathers came
My spirit, bondaged by the body, longs.
Words felt, but never heard, my lips would frame;
My soul would sing forgotten jungle songs.
I would go back to darkness and to peace,
But the great western world holds me in fee,
And I may never hope for full release
While to its alien gods I bend my knee.
Something in me is lost, forever lost,
Some vital thing has gone out of my heart,
And I must walk the way of life a ghost
Among the sons of earth, a thing apart;
For I was born, far from my native clime,
Under the white man's menace, out of time.

Birds of Prey

Their shadow dims the sunshine of our day,
As they go lumbering across the sky,
Squawking in joy of feeling safe on high,
Beating their heavy wings of owlish gray.
They scare the singing birds of earth away
As, greed-impelled, they circle threateningly,
Watching the toilers with malignant eye,
From their exclusive haven—birds of prey.
They swoop down for the spoil in certain might,
And fasten in our bleeding flesh their claws.
They beat us to surrender weak with fright,
And tugging and tearing without let or pause,
They flap their hideous wings in grim delight,
And stuff our gory hearts into their maws.

Subway Wind

Far down, down through the city's great, gaunt gut
    The gray train rushing bears the weary wind;
In the packed cars the fans the crowd's breath cut,
    Leaving the sick and heavy air behind.
And pale-cheeked children seek the upper door
    To give their summer jackets to the breeze;
Their laugh is swallowed in the deafening roar
    Of captive wind that moans for fields and seas;
Seas cooling warm where native schooners drift
    Through sleepy waters, while gulls wheel and sweep,
Waiting for windy waves the keels to lift
    Lightly among the islands of the deep;
Islands of lofty palm trees blooming white
    That lend their perfume to the tropic sea,
Where fields lie idle in the dew drenched night,
    And the Trades float above them fresh and free.

Jasmines

Your scent is in the room.
Swiftly it overwhelms and conquers me!
Jasmines, night jasmines, perfect of perfume,
Heavy with dew before the dawn of day!
Your face was in the mirror. I could see
You smile and vanish suddenly away,
Leaving behind the vestige of a tear.
Sad suffering face, from parting grown so dear!
Night jasmines cannot bloom in this cold place;
Without the street is wet and weird with snow;
The cold nude trees are tossing to and fro;
Too stormy is the night for your fond face;
For your low voice too loud the wind's mad roar.
But oh, your scent is here—jasmines that grow
Luxuriant, clustered round your cottage door!

Negro Spiritual

They've taken thee out of the simple soil,
Where the warm sun made mellowy thy tones
And voices plaintive from eternal toil,
Thy music spoke in liquid lyric moans;
They've stolen thee out of the brooding wood,
Where scenting bloodhounds caught thy whispered note,
And birds and flowers only understood
The sorrow sobbing from a choking throat;
And set thee in this garish marble hall
Of faces hard with conscience-worried pride,
Like convicts witnessing a carnival.
For whom an alien vandal mind has tried
To fashion thee for virtuoso wonders,
Drowning thy beauty in orchestral thunders.

COLE PORTER

(1891–1964)

I Get a Kick Out of You

Until the day
You came my way
I got no joy from being alive.
But now that you have given a kick to my life
I know that I'm slated to thrive.

I get no kick from champagne.
Mere alcohol doesn't thrill me at all,
So tell me why should it be true
That I get a kick out of you?
Some get a kick from cocaine.
I'm sure that if I took even one sniff
That would bore me terrific'ly too
Yet I get a kick out of you.
I get a kick ev'ry time I see
You're standing there before me.
I get a kick when you look at me
And whisper you adore me.
I get no kick in a plane.
I shouldn't care for those nights in the air
That the fair Mrs. Lindbergh goes through,
Yet I get a kick out of you.

Anything Goes

Times have changed
And we've often rewound the clock
Since the Puritans got a shock
When they landed on Plymouth Rock.
If today
Any shock they should try to stem,

'Stead of landing on Plymouth Rock,
Plymouth Rock would land on them.

In olden days, a glimpse of stocking
Was looked on as something shocking,
But now, God knows,
Anything goes.
Good authors too who once knew better words
Now only use four-letter words
Writing prose,
Anything goes.
If driving fast cars you like,
If low bars you like,
If old hymns you like,
If bare limbs you like,
If Mae West you like,
Or me undressed you like,
Why, nobody will oppose.
When ev'ry night, the set that's smart is in-
Truding in nudist parties in
Studios,
Anything goes.

When Missus Ned McLean (God bless her)
Can get Russian reds to "yes" her,
Then I suppose
Anything goes.
When Rockefeller still can hoard en-
Ough money to let Max Gordon
Produce his shows,
Anything goes.
The world has gone mad today
And good's bad today,
And black's white today,
And day's night today,
And that gent today
You gave a cent today
Once had several châteaux.
When folks who still can ride in jitneys
Find out Vanderbilts and Whitneys

Lack baby clo'es,
Anything goes.

If Sam Goldwyn can with great conviction
Instruct Anna Sten in diction,
Then Anna shows
Anything goes.
When you hear that Lady Mendl standing up
Now turns a handspring landing up-
On her toes,
Anything goes.
Just think of those shocks you've got
And those knocks you've got
And those blues you've got
From that news you've got
And those pains you've got
(If any brains you've got)
From those little radios.
So Missus R., with all her trimmin's,
Can broadcast a bed from Simmons
'Cause Franklin knows
Anything goes.

Just One of Those Things

As Dorothy Parker once said to her boy friend,
"Fare thee well,"
As Columbus announced when he knew he was bounced,
"It was swell, Isabelle, swell,"
As Abélard said to Héloïse,
"Don't forget to drop a line to me, please,"
As Juliet cried in her Romeo's ear,
"Romeo, why not face the fact, my dear?"

It was just one of those things,
Just one of those crazy flings,
One of those bells that now and then rings,
Just one of those things.

It was just one of those nights,
Just one of those fabulous flights,
A trip to the moon on gossamer wings,
Just one of those things.
If we'd thought a bit
Of the end of it,
When we started painting the town,
We'd have been aware
That our love affair
Was too hot not to cool down.
So goodbye, dear, and amen.
Here's hoping we meet now and then,
It was great fun,
But it was just one of those things.

DJUNA BARNES

(1892–1982)

Portrait of a Lady Walking

In the North birds feather a long wind.
She is beautiful.
The Fall lays ice on the lemon's rind.
Her slow ways are attendant on the dark mind.
The frost sets a brittle stillness on the pool.
Onto the cool short pile of the wet grass
Birds drop like a shower of glass.

The Walking-Mort

Call her walking-mort; say where she goes
She squalls her bush with blood. I slam a gate.
Report her axis bone it gigs the rose.
What say of mine? It turns a grinning grate.
Impugn her that she baits time with an awl.
What do my sessions then? They task a grave.
So, shall we stand, or shall we tread and wait
The mantled lumber of the buzzard's fall
(That maiden resurrection and the freight),
Or shall we freeze and wrangle by the wall?

JOHN PEALE BISHOP

(1892–1944)

Speaking of Poetry

The ceremony must be found
that will wed Desdemona to the huge Moor.

                    It is not enough—
to win the approval of the Senator
or to outwit his disapproval; honest Iago
can manage that: it is not enough. For then,
though she may pant again in his black arms
(his weight resilient as a Barbary stallion's)
she will be found
when the ambassadors of the Venetian state arrive
again smothered. These things have not been changed,
not in three hundred years.
                    (Tupping is still tupping
though that particular word is obsolete.
Naturally, the ritual would not be in Latin.)

For though Othello had his blood from kings
his ancestry was barbarous, his ways African,
his speech uncouth. It must be remembered
that though he valued an embroidery—
three mulberries proper on a silk like silver—
it was not for the subtlety of the stitches,
but for the magic in it. Whereas, Desdemona
once contrived to imitate in needlework
her father's shield, and plucked it out
three times, to begin again, each time
with diminished colors. This is a small point
but indicative.

Desdemona was small and fair,
delicate as a grasshopper
at the tag-end of summer: a Venetian
to her noble finger tips.

O, it is not enough
that they should meet, naked, at dead of night
in a small inn on a dark canal. Procurers
less expert than Iago can arrange as much.

The ceremony must be found

Traditional, with all its symbols
ancient as the metaphors in dreams;
strange, with never before heard music; continuous
until the torches deaden at the bedroom door.

In the Dordogne

We stood up before day
and shaved by metal mirrors
in the faint flame of a faulty candle.

And we hurried down the wide stone stairs
with a clirr of spur chains
on stone. And we thought
when the cocks crew
that the ghosts of a dead dawn
would rise and be off. But they stayed
under the window, crouched on the staircase,
the window now the color of morning.

The colonel slept in the bed of Sully
slept on: but we descended
and saw in a niche in the white wall
a Virgin and child, serene
who were stone: we saw sycamores:
three aged mages

scattering gifts of gold.
But when the wind blew, there were autumn odors
and the shadowed trees
had the dapplings of young fawns.

And each day one died or another
died: each week we sent out thousands
that returned by hundreds
wounded or gassed. And those that died
we buried close to the old wall
within a stone's throw of Perigord
under the tower of the troubadours.

And because we had courage
because there was courage and youth
ready to be wasted: because we endured
and were prepared for all endurance:
we thought something must come of it:
that the Virgin would raise her child and smile
the trees gather up their gold and go
that courage would avail something
and something we had never lost
be regained through wastage, by dying
by burying the others under the English tower.

The colonel slept on in the bed of Sully
under the ravelling curtains: the leaves fell
and were blown away: the young men rotted
under the shadow of the tower
in a land of small clear silent streams
where the coming on of evening is
the letting down of blue and azure veils
over the clear and silent streams
delicately bordered by poplars.

Young Men Dead

Bernard Peyton is dead
It is thirteen years:
Son of a decayed house
He might have made his roof
Less contumelious
Had there been time enough
Before they buried his bed;
Now it is thirteen years
At seventeen years old.
And Mooch of the bull-red
Hair who had so many dears
Enjoyed to the core
And Newlin who hadn't one
To answer his shy desire
Arc blanketed in the mould
Dead in the long war.
And I who have most reason
Remember them only when the sun
Is at his dullest season.

Metamorphoses of M

I

I have seen your feet gilded by morning
naked under your long gown. I have seen them
keep such state upon the unswept floor
I could have sworn Venetian artisans
had all night been awake, painting in gold,
to set your beauty on appropriate heels.
What wonder then that I insist on gilt
as covering for your feet, which might inlay
(if there were still such metamorphoses)
the morning and form a constellation
to take all eyes from Venus, though she stood
as from antiquity in naked light
till then unvying queen.

II

Your beauty is not used. Though you have lain
a thousand nights upon my bed, you rise
always so splendidly renewed that I have thought,
seeing the sweet continence of your breast,
mole-spotted, your small waist, and long slim thigh,
that even the unicorn that savage beast
if he should startle on you fresh from light
would be so marvelled by virginity
that he would come, trotting and mild,
to lay his head upon your fragrant lap
and be surprised.

The Return

After a phrase by Giorgio de Chirico

Night and we heard heavy and cadenced hoofbeats
Of troops departing: the last cohorts left
By the North Gate. That night some listened late
Leaning their eyelids toward Septentrion.

Morning flared and the young tore down the trophies
And warring ornaments: arches were strong
And in the sun but stone; no longer conquests
Circled our columns; all our state was down

In fragments. In the dust, old men with tufted
Eyebrows whiter than sunbaked faces gulped
As it fell. But they no more than we remembered
The old sea-fights, the soldiers' names and sculptors'.

We did not know the end was coming: nor why
It came; only that long before the end
Were many wanted to die. Then vultures starved
And sailed more slowly in the sky.

We still had taxes. Salt was high. The soldiers
Gone. Now there was much drinking and lewd
Houses all night loud with riot. But only
For a time. Soon the taverns had no roofs.

Strangely it was the young the almost boys
Who first abandoned hope; the old still lived
A little, at last a little lived in eyes.
It was the young whose child did not survive.

Some slept beneath the simulacra, until
The gods' faces froze. Then was fear.
Some had response in dreams, but morning restored
Interrogation. Then O then, O ruins!

Temples of Neptune invaded by the sea
And dolphins streaked like streams sportive
As sunlight rode and over the rushing floors
The sea unfurled and what was blue raced silver.

MAXWELL BODENHEIM

(1892–1954)

Death

I

A fan of smoke in the long, green-white revery of the sky,
Slowly curls apart.
So shall we rise and widen out in the silence of air.

II

An old man runs down a little yellow road
To an out-flung, white thicket uncovered by morning.
So shall I swing to the white sharpness of death.

Interlude

Sun-light recedes on the mountains, in long gold shafts,
Like the falling pillars of a temple.
Then singing silence almost too nimble for ears:
The mountain-tenors fling their broad voices
Into the blue hall of the sky,
And through a rigid column of these voices
Night dumbly walks.
Night, crushing sound between his fingers
Until it forms a lightly frozen couch
On which he dreams.

Rear Porches of an Apartment Building

A sky that has never known sun, moon, or stars,
A sky that is like a dead, kind face
Would have the color of your eyes,
O servant girl singing of pear-trees in the sun
And scraping the yellow fruit you once picked
When your lavender-white eyes were alive.
On the porch above you sit two women
With faces the color of dry brown earth;
They knit grey rosettes and nibble cakes.
And on the porch above them are three children
Gravely kissing each other's foreheads,
And an ample nurse with a huge red fan. . . .
The death of the afternoon to them
Is but the lengthening of blue-black shadows on brick walls.

ARCHIBALD MacLEISH

(1892–1982)

Ars Poetica

A poem should be palpable and mute
As a globed fruit

Dumb
As old medallions to the thumb

Silent as the sleeve-worn stone
Of casement ledges where the moss has grown—

A poem should be wordless
As the flight of birds

*   *   *

A poem should be motionless in time
As the moon climbs

Leaving, as the moon releases
Twig by twig the night entangled trees,

Leaving, as the moon behind the winter leaves,
Memory by memory the mind—

A poem should be motionless in time
As the moon climbs

*   *   *

A poem should be equal to:
Not true

For all the history of grief
An empty doorway and a maple leaf

For love
The leaning grasses and two lights above the sea—

A poem should not mean
But be

Cinema of a Man

The earth is bright through the boughs of the moon like a
    dead planet
It is silent it has no sound the sun is on it
It shines in the dark like a white stone in a deep meadow
It is round above it is flattened under with shadow

    * * * *
    * * * *

He sits in the rue St. Jacques at the iron table
It is dusk it is growing cold the roof stone glitters on the
    gable
The taxies turn in the rue du Pot de Fer
The gas jets brighten one by one behind the windows of the
    stair

    * * * *

This is his face the chin long the eyes looking

    * * * *

Now he sits on the porch of the Villa Serbelloni
He is eating white bread and brown honey
The sun is hot on the lake there are boats rowing
It is spring the rhododendrons are out the wind is blowing

    * * * *

Above Bordeaux by the canal
His shadow passes on the evening wall
His legs are crooked at the knee he has one shoulder
His arms are long he vanishes among the shadows of the
    alder

*   *   *   *

He wakes in the Grand Hotel Vierjahreszeiten
It is dawn the carts go by the curtains whiten
He sees her yellow hair she has neither father nor mother
Her name is Ann she has had him now and before another

*   *   *   *

This is his face in the light of the full moon
His skin is white and grey like the skin of a quadroon
His head is raised to the sky he stands staring
His mouth is still his face is still his eyes are staring

*   *   *   *

He walks with Ernest in the streets in Saragossa
They are drunk their mouths are hard they say *qué cosa*
They say the cruel words they hurt each other
Their elbows touch their shoulders touch their feet go on and
    on together

*   *   *   *

Now he is by the sea at St-Tropez
The pines roar in the wind it is hot it is noonday
He is naked he swims in the blue under the sea water
His limbs are drowned in the dapple of sun like the limbs of
    the sea's daughter

*   *   *   *

Now he is in Chicago he is sleeping
The footstep passes on the stone the roofs are dripping
The door is closed the walls are dark the shadows deepen
His head is motionless upon his arm his hand is open

*   *   *   *
*   *   *   *

Those are the cranes above the Karun River
They fly across the night their wings go over
They cross Orion and the south star of the Wain
A wave has broken in the sea beyond the coast of Spain

Return

When shall I behold again the cold limbed bare breasted
Daughters of the ocean I have not seen so long

Then it was always in sunshine
                              then they were running

There was this thunder of surf then to the left of us
Pines to the right
                    cicadas
                              We came alone
We left our people over the hill in the vineyard
There were sea birds here when we came. . . .

                              But I remember
Sand there where the stones are and isles to seaward

It may be this was all in another land

Or it may be I have forgotten now how the sea was

You, Andrew Marvell

And here face down beneath the sun
And here upon earth's noonward height
To feel the always coming on
The always rising of the night

To feel creep up the curving east
The earthy chill of dusk and slow
Upon those under lands the vast
And ever climbing shadow grow

And strange at Ecbatan the trees
Take leaf by leaf the evening strange
The flooding dark about their knees
The mountains over Persia change

And now at Kermanshah the gate
Dark empty and the withered grass
And through the twilight now the late
Few travellers in the westward pass

And Baghdad darken and the bridge
Across the silent river gone
And through Arabia the edge
Of evening widen and steal on

And deepen on Palmyra's street
The wheel rut in the ruined stone
And Lebanon fade out and Crete
High through the clouds and overblown

And over Sicily the air
Still flashing with the landward gulls
And loom and slowly disappear
The sails above the shadowy hulls

And Spain go under and the shore
Of Africa the gilded sand
And evening vanish and no more
The low pale light across that land

Nor now the long light on the sea

And here face downward in the sun
To feel how swift how secretly
The shadow of the night comes on. . . . .

Epistle To Be Left in the Earth

. . . . It is colder now
                     there are many stars
                               we are drifting
North by the Great Bear
                     the leaves are falling

The water is stone in the scooped rocks
                              to southward
Red sun grey air
              the crows are
Slow on their crooked wings
                              the jays have left us
Long since we passed the flares of Orion
Each man believes in his heart he will die
Many have written last thoughts and last letters
None know if our deaths are told or forever
None know if this wandering earth will be found

We lie down and the snow covers our garments
I pray you
              you (if any open this writing)
Make in your mouths the words that were our names

I will tell you all we have learned
                              I will tell you everything
The earth is round
                    there are springs under the orchards
The loam cuts with a blunt knife
                              beware of
Elms in thunder
                    the lights in the sky are stars
We think they do not see
                        we think also
The trees do not know nor the leaves of the grasses
                                        hear us
The birds too are ignorant
                        Do not listen
Do not stand at dark in the open windows
We before you have heard this
                        they are voices
They are not words at all but the wind rising
Also none among us has seen God
(. . . . . We have thought often
The flaws of sun in the late and driving weather
Pointed to one tree but it was not so)
As for the nights I warn you the nights are dangerous

The wind changes at night and the dreams come

It is very cold
               there are strange stars near Arcturus

Voices are crying an unknown name in the sky

Sentiments for a Dedication

Not to you
Unborn generations
Irrefutable judges of what must be true
Infallible reviewers of neglected reputations

('Posterity'
The same critics
Professor Philip in Doctor Phlap's goatee
The usual majority of female metics)

Not to you (though Christ
Is my sure witness
The fame I've got has not in all respects sufficed
And rediscovery would have its fitness)

Not to you these books
I choose the living
I'll take (I've taken) the blank brutal looks
You keep your sympathetic too late learned too generous
     forgiving

I speak to my own time
To no time after
I say Remember me Remember this one rhyme
When first the dead came round me with their whispering
     laughter

Those of one man's time
They shall be dead together
Dos that saw the tyrants in the lime
Ernest that saw the first snow in the fox's feather

Stephen that saw his wife
Cummings his quick fillies
Eliot the caul between the ribs of life
Pound—Pound cracking the eggs of a cock with the beautiful
    sword of Achilles

I speak to those of my own time
To none other
I say Remember me Remember this one rhyme
I say Remember me among you in that land my brothers

O living men Remember me Receive me among you.

Voyage West

There was a time for discoveries—
For the headlands looming above in the
First light and the surf and the
Crying of gulls: for the curve of the
Coast north into secrecy.

That time is past.
The last lands have been peopled.
The oceans are known now.

Señora: once the maps have all been made
A man were better dead than find new continents.

A man would better never have been born
Than find upon the open ocean flowers
Drifted from islands where there are no islands

Or midnight, out of sight of any land,
Smell on the altering air the odor of rosemary.

No fortune passes that misfortune—

To lift along the evening of the sky,
Certain as sun and sea, a new-found land
Steep from an ocean where no landfall can be.

EDNA ST. VINCENT MILLAY

(1892–1950)

Afternoon on a Hill

I will be the gladdest thing
    Under the sun!
I will touch a hundred flowers
    And not pick one.

I will look at cliffs and clouds
    With quiet eyes,
Watch the wind bow down the grass,
    And the grass rise.

And when lights begin to show
    Up from the town,
I will mark which must be mine,
    And then start down!

Sorrow

Sorrow like a ceaseless rain
    Beats upon my heart.
People twist and scream in pain,—
Dawn will find them still again;
This has neither wax nor wane,
    Neither stop nor start.

People dress and go to town;
    I sit in my chair.
All my thoughts are slow and brown:
Standing up or sitting down
Little matters, or what gown
    Or what shoes I wear.

Witch-Wife

She is neither pink nor pale,
　　And she never will be all mine;
She learned her hands in a fairy-tale,
　　And her mouth on a valentine.

She has more hair than she needs;
　　In the sun 'tis a woe to me!
And her voice is a string of colored beads,
　　Or steps leading into the sea.

She loves me all that she can,
　　And her ways to my ways resign;
But she was not made for any man,
　　And she never will be all mine.

———

If I should learn, in some quite casual way,
　　That you were gone, not to return again—
Read from the back-page of a paper, say,
　　Held by a neighbor in a subway train,
How at the corner of this avenue
　　And such a street (so are the papers filled)
A hurrying man—who happened to be you—
　　At noon to-day had happened to be killed,
I should not cry aloud—I could not cry
　　Aloud, or wring my hands in such a place—
I should but watch the station lights rush by
　　With a more careful interest on my face,
Or raise my eyes and read with greater care
Where to store furs and how to treat the hair.

Bluebeard

This door you might not open, and you did;
　　So enter now, and see for what slight thing
You are betrayed. . . . Here is no treasure hid,

No cauldron, no clear crystal mirroring
The sought-for truth, no heads of women slain
 For greed like yours, no writhings of distress,
But only what you see. . . . Look yet again—
 An empty room, cobwebbed and comfortless.
Yet this alone out of my life I kept
 Unto myself, lest any know me quite;
And you did so profane me when you crept
 Unto the threshold of this room to-night
That I must never more behold your face.
 This now is yours. I seek another place.

God's World

O world, I cannot hold thee close enough!
 Thy winds, thy wide grey skies!
 Thy mists, that roll and rise!
Thy woods, this autumn day, that ache and sag
And all but cry with colour! That gaunt crag
To crush! To lift the lean of that black bluff!
World, World, I cannot get thee close enough!

Long have I known a glory in it all,
  But never knew I this;
  Here such a passion is
As stretcheth me apart,—Lord, I do fear
Thou'st made the world too beautiful this year;
My soul is all but out of me,—let fall
No burning leaf; prithee, let no bird call.

First Fig

My candle burns at both ends;
 It will not last the night;
But ah, my foes, and oh, my friends—
 It gives a lovely light!

Second Fig

Safe upon the solid rock the ugly houses stand:
Come and see my shining palace built upon the sand!

Recuerdo

We were very tired, we were very merry—
We had gone back and forth all night on the ferry.
It was bare and bright, and smelled like a stable—
But we looked into a fire, we leaned across a table,
We lay on the hill-top underneath the moon;
And the whistles kept blowing, and the dawn came soon.

We were very tired, we were very merry—
We had gone back and forth all night on the ferry;
And you ate an apple, and I ate a pear,
From a dozen of each we had bought somewhere;
And the sky went wan, and the wind came cold,
And the sun rose dripping, a bucketful of gold.

We were very tired, we were very merry,
We had gone back and forth all night on the ferry.
We hailed, "Good morrow, mother!" to a shawl-covered head,
And bought a morning paper, which neither of us read;
And she wept, "God bless you!" for the apples and the pears,
And we gave her all our money but our subway fares.

I think I should have loved you presently,
And given in earnest words I flung in jest;
And lifted honest eyes for you to see,
And caught your hand against my cheek and breast;
And all my pretty follies flung aside
That won you to me, and beneath your gaze,
Naked of reticence and shorn of pride,

Spread like a chart my little wicked ways.
I, that had been to you, had you remained,
But one more waking from a recurrent dream,
Cherish no less the certain stakes I gained,
And walk your memory's halls, austere, supreme,
A ghost in marble of a girl you knew
Who would have loved you in a day or two.

———————

I shall forget you presently, my dear,
So make the most of this, your little day,
Your little month, your little half a year,
Ere I forget, or die, or move away,
And we are done forever; by and by
I shall forget you, as I said, but now,
If you entreat me with your loveliest lie
I will protest you with my favorite vow.
I would indeed that love were longer-lived,
And vows were not so brittle as they are,
But so it is, and nature has contrived
To struggle on without a break thus far,—
Whether or not we find what we are seeking
Is idle, biologically speaking.

Spring

To what purpose, April, do you return again?
Beauty is not enough.
You can no longer quiet me with the redness
Of little leaves opening stickily.
I know what I know.
The sun is hot on my neck as I observe
The spikes of the crocus.
The smell of the earth is good.
It is apparent that there is no death.
But what does that signify?

Not only under ground are the brains of men
Eaten by maggots.
Life in itself
Is nothing,
An empty cup, a flight of uncarpeted stairs.
It is not enough that yearly, down this hill,
April
Comes like an idiot, babbling and strewing flowers.

Eel-Grass

No matter what I say,
   All that I really love
Is the rain that flattens on the bay,
   And the eel-grass in the cove;
The jingle-shells that lie and bleach
   At the tide-line, and the trace
Of higher tides along the beach:
   Nothing in this place.

Passer Mortuus Est

Death devours all lovely things;
   Lesbia with her sparrow
Shares the darkness,—presently
   Every bed is narrow.

Unremembered as old rain
   Dries the sheer libation,
And the little petulant hand
   Is an annotation.

After all, my erstwhile dear,
   My no longer cherished,
Need we say it was not love,
   Now that love is perished?

Elegy

Let them bury your big eyes
In the secret earth securely,
Your thin fingers, and your fair,
Soft, indefinite-colored hair,—
All of these in some way, surely,
From the secret earth shall rise;
Not for these I sit and stare,
Broken and bereft completely;
Your young flesh that sat so neatly
On your little bones will sweetly
Blossom in the air.

But your voice,—never the rushing
Of a river underground,
Not the rising of the wind
In the trees before the rain,
Not the woodcock's watery call,
Not the note the white-throat utters,
Not the feet of children pushing
Yellow leaves along the gutters
In the blue and bitter fall,
Shall content my musing mind
For the beauty of that sound
That in no new way at all
Ever will be heard again.

Sweetly through the sappy stalk
Of the vigorous weed,
Holding all it held before,
Cherished by the faithful sun,
On and on eternally
Shall your altered fluid run,
Bud and bloom and go to seed;
But your singing days are done;
But the music of your talk
Never shall the chemistry
Of the secret earth restore.

All your lovely words are spoken.
Once the ivory box is broken,
Beats the golden bird no more.

———————

Euclid alone has looked on Beauty bare.
Let all who prate of Beauty hold their peace,
And lay them prone upon the earth and cease
To ponder on themselves, the while they stare
At nothing, intricately drawn nowhere
In shapes of shifting lineage; let geese
Gabble and hiss, but heroes seek release
From dusty bondage into luminous air.
O blinding hour, O holy, terrible day,
When first the shaft into his vision shone
Of light anatomized! Euclid alone
Has looked on Beauty bare. Fortunate they
Who, though once only and then but far away,
Have heard her massive sandal set on stone.

———————

What lips my lips have kissed, and where, and why,
I have forgotten, and what arms have lain
Under my head till morning; but the rain
Is full of ghosts to-night, that tap and sigh
Upon the glass and listen for reply,
And in my heart there stirs a quiet pain
For unremembered lads that not again
Will turn to me at midnight with a cry.
Thus in the winter stands the lonely tree,
Nor knows what birds have vanished one by one,
Yet knows its boughs more silent than before:
I cannot say what loves have come and gone,
I only know that summer sang in me
A little while, that in me sings no more.

The Wood Road

If I were to walk this way
   Hand in hand with Grief,
I should mark that maple-spray
   Coming into leaf.
I should note how the old burrs
   Rot upon the ground.
Yes, though Grief should know me hers
   While the world goes round,
It could not in truth be said
   This was lost on me:
A rock-maple showing red,
   Burrs beneath a tree.

Scrub

If I grow bitterly,
Like a gnarled and stunted tree,
Bearing harshly of my youth
Puckered fruit that sears the mouth;
If I make of my drawn boughs
An inhospitable house,
Out of which I never pry
Towards the water and the sky,
Under which I stand and hide
And hear the day go by outside;
It is that a wind too strong
Bent my back when I was young,
It is that I fear the rain
Lest it blister me again.

Never May the Fruit Be Plucked

Never, never may the fruit be plucked from the bough
And gathered into barrels.
He that would eat of love must eat it where it hangs.

Though the branches bend like reeds,
Though the ripe fruit splash in the grass or wrinkle on the
    tree,
He that would eat of love may bear away with him
Only what his belly can hold,
Nothing in the apron,
Nothing in the pockets.
Never, never may the fruit be gathered from the bough
And harvested in barrels.
The winter of love is a cellar of empty bins,
In an orchard soft with rot.

Siege

    This I do, being mad:
    Gather baubles about me,
    Sit in a circle of toys, and all the time
    Death beating the door in.

    White jade and an orange pitcher,
      Hindu idol, Chinese god,—
    Maybe next year, when I'm richer—
      Carved beads and a lotus pod. . . .

    And all this time
    Death beating the door in.

———————

I, being born a woman and distressed
By all the needs and notions of my kind,
Am urged by your propinquity to find
Your person fair, and feel a certain zest
To bear your body's weight upon my breast:
So subtly is the fume of life designed,
To clarify the pulse and cloud the mind,
And leave me once again undone, possessed.

Think not for this, however, the poor treason
Of my stout blood against my staggering brain,
I shall remember you with love, or season
My scorn with pity,—let me make it plain:
I find this frenzy insufficient reason
For conversation when we meet again.

———————

Gazing upon him now, severe and dead,
It seemed a curious thing that she had lain
Beside him many a night in that cold bed,
And that had been which would not be again.
From his desirous body the great heat
Was gone at last, it seemed, and the taut nerves
Loosened forever. Formally the sheet
Set forth for her to-day those heavy curves
And lengths familiar as the bedroom door.
She was as one that enters, sly, and proud,
To where her husband speaks before a crowd,
And sees a man she never saw before—
The man who eats his victuals at her side,
Small, and absurd, and hers: for once, not hers, unclassified.

Winter Night

Pile high the hickory and the light
Log of chestnut struck by the blight.
Welcome-in the winter night.

The day has gone in hewing and felling,
Sawing and drawing wood to the dwelling
For the night of talk and story-telling.

These are the hours that give the edge
To the blunted axe and the bent wedge,
Straighten the saw and lighten the sledge.

Here are question and reply,
And the fire reflected in the thinking eye.
So peace, and let the bob-cat cry.

Love is not all; it is not meat nor drink
Nor slumber nor a roof against the rain,
Nor yet a floating spar to men that sink
And rise and sink and rise and sink again;
Love can not fill the thickened lung with breath,
Nor clean the blood, nor set the fractured bone;
Yet many a man is making friends with death
Even as I speak, for lack of love alone.
It well may be that in a difficult hour,
Pinned down by pain and moaning for release,
Or nagged by want past resolution's power,
I might be driven to sell your love for peace,
Or trade the memory of this night for food.
It well may be. I do not think I would.

Rendezvous

Not for these lovely blooms that prank your chambers did I
    come. Indeed,
I could have loved you better in the dark;
That is to say, in rooms less bright with roses, rooms more
    casual, less aware
Of History in the wings about to enter with benevolent air
On ponderous tiptoe, at the cue "Proceed."
Not that I like the ash-trays over-crowded and the place in a
    mess,
Or the monastic cubicle too unctuously austere and stark,
But partly that these formal garlands for our Eighth Street
    Aphrodite are a bit too Greek,
And partly that to make the poor walls rich with our unaided
    loveliness
Would have been more *chic*.

Yet here I am, having told you of my quarrel with the taxi-
    driver over a line of Milton, and you laugh; and you are
    you, none other.
Your laughter pelts my skin with small delicious blows.
But I am perverse: I wish you had not scrubbed—with
    pumice, I suppose—
The tobacco stains from your beautiful fingers. And I wish I
    did not feel like your mother.

Menses

(He speaks, but to himself, being aware how it is with her)

Think not I have not heard.
Well-fanged the double word
And well-directed flew.

I felt it. Down my side
Innocent as oil I see the ugly venom slide:
Poison enough to stiffen us both, and all our friends;
But I am not pierced, so there the mischief ends.

There is more to be said; I see it coiling;
The impact will be pain.
Yet coil; yet strike again.
You cannot riddle the stout mail I wove
Long since, of wit and love.

As for my answer . . . stupid in the sun
He lies, his fangs drawn:
I will not war with you.

You know how wild you are. You are willing to be turned
To other matters; you would be grateful, even.
You watch me shyly. I (for I have learned
More things than one in our few years together)
Chafe at the churlish wind, the unseasonable weather.

"Unseasonable?" you cry, with harsher scorn
Than the theme warrants; "Every year it is the same!
'Unseasonable!' they whine, these stupid peasants!—and
    never since they were born
Have they known a spring less wintry! Lord, the shame,
The crying shame of seeing a man no wiser than the beasts he
    feeds—
His skull as empty as a shell!"

("Go to. You are unwell.")

Such is my thought, but such are not my words.

"What is the name," I ask, "of those big birds
With yellow breast and low and heavy flight,
That make such mournful whistling?"
                       "Meadowlarks,"
You answer primly, not a little cheered.
"Some people shoot them." Suddenly your eyes are wet
And your chin trembles. On my breast you lean,
And sob most pitifully for all the lovely things that are not
    and have been.

"How silly I am!—and I *know* how silly I am!"
You say; "You are very patient. You are very kind.
I shall be better soon. Just Heaven consign and damn
To tedious Hell this body with its muddy feet in my mind!"

Sonnet

I, too, beneath your moon, almighty Sex,
Go forth at nightfall crying like a cat,
Leaving the ivory tower I laboured at
For birds to foul and boys and girls to vex
With tittering chalk; and you, and the long necks
Of neighbours sitting where their mothers sat
Are well aware of shadowy this and that
In me, that's neither noble nor complex.

Such as I am, however, I have brought
To what it is, this tower; it is my own.
Though it was reared To Beauty, it was wrought
From what I had to build with: honest bone
Is there, and anguish; pride; and burning thought;
And lust is there, and nights not spent alone.

DONALD DAVIDSON

(1893–1968)

Sanctuary

You must remember this when I am gone,
And tell your sons—for you will have tall sons,
And times will come when answers will not wait.
Remember this: if ever defeat is black
Upon your eyelids, go to the wilderness
In the dread last of trouble, for your foe
Tangles there, more than you, and paths are strange
To him, that are your paths, in the wilderness,
And were your fathers' paths, and once were mine.

You must remember this, and mark it well
As I have told it—what my eyes have seen
And where my feet have walked beyond forgetting.
But tell it not often, tell it only at last
When your sons know what blood runs in their veins.
And when the danger comes, as come it will,
Go as your fathers went with woodsman's eyes
Uncursed, unflinching, studying only the path.

First, what you cannot carry, burn or hide.
Leave nothing here for *him* to take or eat.
Bury, perhaps, what you can surely find
If good chance ever bring you back again.
Level the crops. Take only what you need:
A little corn for an ash-cake, a little
Side-meat for your three days' wilderness ride.
Horses for your women and your children,
And one to lead, if you should have that many.
Then go. At once. Do not wait until
You see *his* great dust rising in the valley.
Then it will be too late.
Go when you hear that he has crossed Will's Ford.
Others will know and pass the word to you—
A tap on the blinds, a hoot-owl's cry at dusk.

Do not look back. You can see your roof afire
When you reach high ground. Yet do not look.
Do not turn. Do not look back.
Go further on. Go high. Go deep.

The line of this rail-fence east across the old-fields
Leads to the cane-bottoms. Back of that,
A white-oak tree beside a spring, the one
Chopped with three blazes on the hillward side.
There pick up the trail. I think it was
A buffalo path once or an Indian road.
You follow it three days along the ridge
Until you reach the spruce woods. Then a cliff
Breaks, where the trees are thickest, and you look
Into a cove, and right across, Chilhowee
Is suddenly there, and you are home at last.
Sweet springs of mountain water in that cove
Run always. Deer and wild turkey range.
Your kin, knowing the way, long there before you
Will have good fires and kettles on to boil,
Bough-shelters reared and thick beds of balsam.
There in tall timber you will be as free
As were your fathers once when Tryon raged
In Carolina hunting Regulators,
Or Tarleton rode to hang the old-time Whigs.
Some tell how in that valley young Sam Houston
Lived long ago with his brother, Oo-loo-te-ka,
Reading Homer among the Cherokee;
And others say a Spaniard may have found it
Far from De Soto's wandering turned aside,
And left his legend on a boulder there.
And some that this was a sacred place to all
Old Indian tribes before the Cherokee
Came to our eastern mountains. Men have found
Images carved in bird-shapes there and faces
Moulded into the great kind look of gods.
These old tales are like prayers. I only know
This is the secret refuge of our race
Told only from a father to his son,
A trust laid on your lips, as though a vow

To generations past and yet to come.
There, from the bluffs above, you may at last
Look back to all you left, and trace
His dust and flame, and plan your harrying
If you would gnaw his ravaging flank, or smite
Him in his glut among the smouldering ricks.

Or else, forgetting ruin, you may lie
On sweet grass by a mountain stream, to watch
The last wild eagle soar or the last raven
Cherish his brood within their rocky nest,
Or see, when mountain shadows first grow long,
The last enchanted white deer come to drink.

SAMUEL GREENBERG

(1893–1917)

The Glass Bubbles

The motion of gathering loops of water
Must either burst or remain in a moment.
The violet colors through the glass
Throw up little swellings that appear
And spatter as soon as another strikes
And is born; so pure are they of colored
Hues, that we feel the absent strength
Of its power. When they begin they gather
Like sand on the beach: each bubble
Contains a complete eye of water.

Secrecy

The apparent gale, vaned in winding storms,
Has filled the air with hail and mystic frost.
The peaceful alley through bowing elms revealed
Pregnant buds, where spring has failed the lewd heart.
Darkness over the ocean's deep was offering moonlight,
Movable, silver, vanishing waves that enrolled
The wild summer blossom that in sanguine
Peace bared the ray of gold; until bronze
Shades of autumn quietly lowered a
Humble veil upon the ground in preservation—
Thick clouds that separate over the
Spotless blue of glazing greys. A simple
Tint vanishes, as the storm of fusion
Displays the shocking flood that vapors have gathered.

Etching

The paper was pale,
But the untold phase
Hath told real its love
Of its mysterious graze.

Heavy tints, light scrawls,
Inner space left—
The yards, boats, rivers,
And castles of craft;

The portraits were thine
Of the phantom pound,
That the etching therein
Almost moved from its mound.

The heavens were paper
And clouds its grain,
As if its whiteness stirred
In the soul of an insane.

They were left on the walls,
Calling their eyes
That built them to crumble,
To nestle from ties.

God

I followed and breathed in silence.
What of its task is beheld?
My feeding thee has lent all
Which broke the current thread breeze
That kept the sprout of pregnant seas
Of weathered promising call.

The filing shades he only changes,
Tells the logos, its unearned dew
Not to feed, as if from cages,
His cloak that perfumes fragrant hew;
What of all the bulging mountains,
Sordid earth and rotting clays?
If then sense is suction fountains,
That same thought is but its ways.

African Desert

And we thought of wilderness
That bore the thousand angels,
That strew the dust
As fine as frost
Upon the fancied candles.

O, black as autumn night
Are fed the holy forests
That fertilized the grain,
That breathes the birth
Of chanted aurists.

The soaring swan of danger
That held the mighty plain—
The bitter seed of glittering age
Seems glad to mourn its twain.

To Dear Daniel

There is a loud noise of Death
Where I lay;
There is a loud noise of life
Far away.

From low and weary stride
Have I flown;
From low and weary pride
I have grown.

What does it matter now
To you or me?
What does it matter now
To whom it be?

Again the stain has come
To me;
Again the stain has come
For thee.

DOROTHY PARKER

(1893–1967)

Résumé

Razors pain you;
Rivers are damp;
Acids stain you;
And drugs cause cramp.
Guns aren't lawful;
Nooses give;
Gas smells awful;
You might as well live.

One Perfect Rose

A single flow'r he sent me, since we met.
    All tenderly his messenger he chose;
Deep-hearted, pure, with scented dew still wet—
    One perfect rose.

I knew the language of the floweret;
    "My fragile leaves," it said, "his heart enclose."
Love long has taken for his amulet
    One perfect rose.

Why is it no one ever sent me yet
    One perfect limousine, do you suppose?
Ah no, it's always just my luck to get
    One perfect rose.

Ballade at Thirty-Five

This, no song of an ingénue,
　　This, no ballad of innocence;
This, the rhyme of a lady who
　　Followed ever her natural bents.
　　This, a solo of sapience,
This, a chantey of sophistry,
　　This, the sum of experiments,—
I loved them until they loved me.

Decked in garments of sable hue,
　　Daubed with ashes of myriad Lents,
Wearing shower bouquets of rue,
　　Walk I ever in penitence.
　　Oft I roam, as my heart repents,
Through God's acre of memory,
　　Marking stones, in my reverence,
"I loved them until they loved me."

Pictures pass me in long review,—
　　Marching columns of dead events.
I was tender, and, often, true;
　　Ever a prey to coincidence.
　　Always knew I the consequence;
Always saw what the end would be.
　　We're as Nature has made us—hence
I loved them until they loved me.

L'ENVOI:

Princes, never I'd give offense,
　　Won't you think of me tenderly?
Here's my strength and my weakness, gents,—
　　I loved them until they loved me.

Men

They hail you as their morning star
Because you are the way you are.
If you return the sentiment,
They'll try to make you different;
And once they have you, safe and sound,
They want to change you all around.
Your moods and ways they put a curse on;
They'd make of you another person.
They cannot let you go your gait;
They influence and educate.
They'd alter all that they admired.
They make me sick, they make me tired.

News Item

Men seldom make passes
At girls who wear glasses.

Observation

If I don't drive around the park,
I'm pretty sure to make my mark.
If I'm in bed each night by ten,
I may get back my looks again,
If I abstain from fun and such,
I'll probably amount to much,
But I shall stay the way I am,
Because I do not give a damn.

Symptom Recital

I do not like my state of mind;
I'm bitter, querulous, unkind.
I hate my legs, I hate my hands,

I do not yearn for lovelier lands.
I dread the dawn's recurrent light;
I hate to go to bed at night.
I snoot at simple, earnest folk.
I cannot take the gentlest joke.
I find no peace in paint or type.
My world is but a lot of tripe.
I'm disillusioned, empty-breasted.
For what I think, I'd be arrested.
I am not sick, I am not well.
My quondam dreams are shot to hell.
My soul is crushed, my spirit sore;
I do not like me any more.
I cavil, quarrel, grumble, grouse.
I ponder on the narrow house.
I shudder at the thought of men. . . .
I'm due to fall in love again.

The Red Dress

I always saw, I always said
    If I were grown and free,
I'd have a gown of reddest red
    As fine as you could see,

To wear out walking, sleek and slow,
    Upon a Summer day,
And there'd be one to see me so,
    And flip the world away.

And he would be a gallant one,
    With stars behind his eyes,
And hair like metal in the sun,
    And lips too warm for lies.

I always saw us, gay and good,
    High honored in the town.
Now I am grown to womanhood. . . .
    I have the silly gown.

Bric-à-Brac

Little things that no one needs—
  Little things to joke about—
Little landscapes, done in beads,
  Little morals, woven out,
Little wreaths of gilded grass,
  Little brigs of whittled oak
Bottled painfully in glass;
  These are made by lonely folk.

Lonely folk have lines of days
  Long and faltering and thin;
Therefore—little wax bouquets,
  Prayers cut upon a pin,
Little maps of pinkish lands,
  Little charts of curly seas,
Little plats of linen strands,
  Little verses, such as these.

A Pig's-Eye View of Literature

*The Lives and Times of John Keats, Percy Bysshe Shelley,
and George Gordon Noel, Lord Byron*

Byron and Shelley and Keats
Were a trio of lyrical treats.
The forehead of Shelley was cluttered with curls,
And Keats never was a descendant of earls,
And Byron walked out with a number of girls,
  But it didn't impair the poetical feats
    Of Byron and Shelley,
    Of Byron and Shelley,
  Of Byron and Shelley and Keats.

Oscar Wilde

If, with the literate, I am
Impelled to try an epigram,
I never seek to take the credit;
We all assume that Oscar said it.

Harriet Beecher Stowe

The pure and worthy Mrs. Stowe
Is one we all are proud to know
As mother, wife, and authoress,—
Thank God I am content with less!

D. G. Rossetti

Dante Gabriel Rossetti
Buried all of his *libretti*,
Thought the matter over,—then
Went and dug them up again.

Thomas Carlyle

Carlyle combined the lit'ry life
With throwing teacups at his wife,
Remarking, rather testily,
"Oh, stop your dodging, Mrs. C.!"

Charles Dickens

Who call him spurious and shoddy
Shall do it o'er my lifeless body.
I heartily invite such birds
To come outside and say those words!

Alexandre Dumas and His Son

Although I work, and seldom cease,
At Dumas *père* and Dumas *fils*,
Alas, I cannot make me care
For Dumas *fils* and Dumas *père*.

Alfred Lord Tennyson

Should Heaven send me any son,
I hope he's not like Tennyson.
I'd rather have him play a fiddle
Than rise and bow and speak an idyll.

George Gissing

When I admit neglect of Gissing,
They say I don't know what I'm missing.
Until their arguments are subtler,
I think I'll stick to Samuel Butler.

Walter Savage Landor

Upon the work of Walter Landor
I am unfit to write with candor.
If you can read it, well and good;
But as for me, I never could.

George Sand

What time the gifted lady took
Away from paper, pen, and book,
She spent in amorous dalliance
(They do those things so well in France).

Bohemia

Authors and actors and artists and such
Never know nothing, and never know much.
Sculptors and singers and those of their kidney
Tell their affairs from Seattle to Sydney.
Playwrights and poets and such horses' necks
Start off from anywhere, end up at sex.
Diarists, critics, and similar roe
Never say nothing, and never say no.
People Who Do Things exceed my endurance;
God, for a man that solicits insurance!

Coda

There's little in taking or giving,
    There's little in water or wine;
This living, this living, this living
    Was never a project of mine.
Oh, hard is the struggle, and sparse is
    The gain of the one at the top,
For art is a form of catharsis,
    And love is a permanent flop,
And work is the province of cattle,
    And rest's for a clam in a shell,
So I'm thinking of throwing the battle—
    Would you kindly direct me to hell?

BIOGRAPHICAL NOTES

NOTE ON THE TEXTS

NOTES

INDEXES

Biographical Notes

Franklin P. Adams (November 15, 1881–March 23, 1960) b. Franklin Pierce Adams in Chicago, Illinois. Graduated from Armour Scientific Academy in 1899; attended University of Michigan for a year. Worked as insurance supply clerk in Chicago until 1901, when he began to write professionally for the *Chicago Journal.* Moved to New York, where he wrote humor columns for the *Evening Mail* (1904–13), *Tribune* (1914–22), *World* (1922–31), *Herald Tribune* (1931–37), and *Post* (1938–41); usually signed himself "F.P.A." From 1914, his column was called "The Conning Tower"; it often featured guest contributors, including Edna St. Vincent Millay, Sinclair Lewis, Groucho Marx, and James Thurber. Co-wrote musicals *Lo* (1911) with O. Henry and *The '49ers* (1922) with Ring Lardner and George S. Kaufman. Published many books, including *Tobogganing on Parnassus* (1911), *In Other Words* (1912), *By and Large* (1914), *Christopher Columbus* (1931), *The Diary of Our Own Samuel Pepys* (1935), and *The Melancholy Lute* (1936). Appeared regularly on the radio program "Information Please!" from 1938.

Henry Adams (February 16, 1838–March 27, 1918) b. Boston, Massachusetts. Grandson of John Quincy Adams, at whose home he was a frequent summer visitor; great-grandson of John Adams. Graduated Harvard 1858; studied law in Berlin and Dresden until 1860. Served as secretary to father, Charles Francis Adams, a congressman and later minister to Great Britain. Reported British reaction to Civil War as London correspondent of *The New York Times* (1861–62). Returned to Washington, D.C., in 1868 to work as journalist; attacked spoils system and campaigned for free trade and establishment of civil service. Appointed assistant professor of history at Harvard (1870–77); assumed editorship of *North American Review* (1870–76). Married Marion (Clover) Hooper in June 1872. Published biography *The Life of Albert Gallatin* (1879). With friends Clarence King and John and Clara Hay, the Adamses formed salon "The Five of Hearts." *Democracy*, fictional attack on Washington corruption, published anonymously in 1880, followed by biography *John Randolph* (1882) and another novel, *Esther* (1884). Wife committed suicide in December 1885. Adams made four-month tour of Japan with artist John La Farge in spring of 1886. *History of the United States during the Administrations of Thomas Jefferson and James Madison* published 1889–91. Traveled (1890–91) with La Farge in South Pacific; made other journeys to Cuba and Mexico. Lived mostly in Europe between 1897 and 1900. *Mont Saint Michel and Chartres* (1904) enjoyed wide success; *The Education of Henry Adams* (1907), published in private edition, was posthumously awarded Pulitzer Prize. Died in Washington.

Conrad Aiken (August 5, 1889–August 17, 1973) b. Conrad Potter Aiken in Savannah, Georgia, first of four children of William Ford Aiken, a doctor, and Anna Aiken Potter. In February 1901, father shot mother and then killed himself; Aiken discovered the bodies moments later. Adopted by an uncle in Cambridge, Massachusetts, while siblings were sent to live in Philadelphia. Entered Harvard in 1907. Formed close friendship with T. S. Eliot; elected to *Advocate* freshman year, named president junior year. Traveled to Europe, visiting Eliot in Paris; returned to Harvard in 1911 to earn degree. Married Jessie McDonald in 1912 and spent a year in Europe. First book of poetry, *Earth Triumphant* (1914), written during European stay, followed by *Turns and Movies* (1916) and *Nocturne of Remembered Spring* (1917). "Symphonies," a poetic series begun in 1915, comprised *The Jig of Forslin* (1916), *The Charnel Rose* (1918), *Senlin: A Biography* (1918), *The House of Dust* (1920), *The Pilgrimage of Festus* (1923), and *Changing Mind* (1925). Contributed literary criticism prolifically to newspapers and magazines. Moved to London with his family in 1921. Published *Priapus and the Pool* (1922) and the first of his novels, *Blue Voyage* (1927). Divorced wife in 1929 and married Clarissa Lorenz the following year. Met Malcolm Lowry, with whom he formed close friendship. Won Pulitzer Prize for his *Selected Poems* (1930). Published poetry collections *The Coming Forth By Day of Osiris Jones* (1931), *Preludes for Memnon* (1931), *Landscape West of Eden* (1934), and *Time in the Rock* (1936); also published novels including *Great Circle* (1933) and *King Coffin* (1935). Divorced second wife, and married Mary Hoover in 1937; moved to cottage on Cape Cod. Published *And in the Human Heart* (1940), *Brownstone Eclogues* (1942), *The Soldier* (1944), *The Kid* (1947), and *Skylight One* (1949); expanded the Symphonies as *The Divine Pilgrim* (1949). Named Fellow in American Letters of the Library of Congress in 1947, Poetry Consultant in 1950. Published autobiography, *Ushant*, in 1952, and won National Book Award two years later for *Collected Poems* (1953). Later books included *A Letter from Li Po* (1955), *The Flute Player* (1956), *Sheepfold Hill* (1958), *The Morning Song of Lord Zero* (1963), *A Seizure of Limericks* (1964), and *Thee* (1967). Moved back to Savannah with his wife in 1962. Received National Medal for Literature in 1969.

Sherwood Anderson (September 13, 1876–March 8, 1941) b. Camden, Ohio. Grew up in the nearby town of Clyde. Left high school to help support family; moved to Chicago after mother's death in 1895. Served in Cuba at end of Spanish-American War. Worked as advertising copywriter, and wrote essays and sketches for firm's newsletter. Married Cornelia Lane (first of four wives) in 1904; founded mail-order business in Elyria, Ohio. Published novels *Windy McPherson's Son* (1916) and *Marching Men* (1917). Stories of small-town life, published in *Masses, Seven Arts*, and other magazines, were collected in *Winesburg, Ohio* (1921); free-verse poetry collected in *Mid-American Chants* (1918) and *A New Testament* (1927); published novel *Poor White* (1920). Visited Paris and London in 1921; met Gertrude Stein and James Joyce. Published *The Triumph of the Egg* (1921), *Horses and Men* (1923), *Many Marriages* (1923), *Dark Laughter* (1925), *Sherwood Anderson's Notebook* (1926), and *Tar* (1926). Settled near Ripshin Creek, Virginia; bought two local newspapers, which he edited and wrote entirely; journalism collected in

Hello Towns! (1929). Later books included *Beyond Desire* (1932) and *Kit Brandon: A Portrait* (1936). Traveled widely during final years; died in Panama Canal Zone of peritonitis after swallowing part of a toothpick.

Walter Conrad Arensberg (April 4, 1878–January 29, 1954) b. Pittsburgh, Pennsylvania. Attended Harvard, where he met Wallace Stevens and Pitts Sanborn; earned A.B. in 1900. Spent a year in Italy. Pursued graduate study at Harvard (1903–4). Worked as a reporter for New York *Evening Post*; wrote occasional art reviews. Married Mary Louise Stevens in 1907; moved to Boston, devoting time to writing poetry and playing chess. In 1913, attended Armory Show in New York, then began collecting modern art. Early acquisitions included Jacques Villon's *Puteaux: Smoke and Trees in Bloom* and Marcel Duchamp's *Nude Descending a Staircase*. Became friends with a number of artists, musicians, and writers, including Charles Demuth, Francis Picabia, Man Ray, Alfred Stieglitz, Edgard Varèse, Carl Van Vechten, and Donald Evans. Published poems in *Poems* (1914) and *Idols* (1916). Funded Alfred Kreymborg's *Others* magazine. Acquired most of Duchamp's artwork; together they founded the magazines *Rongwrong* and *The Blind Man*. At his apartment, Arensberg held meetings that led to First Annual Exhibition of the Society of Independent Artists in 1917. Contributed manifesto to 1920 Dada issue of *Littérature*. Established Francis Bacon Foundation; attempted to prove, through cryptography, that Bacon wrote the works of Shakespeare. Published *The Cryptography of Dante* (1921) and *The Cryptography of Shakespeare* (1922). Moved to Hollywood in 1922. Acquired several Constantin Brancusi sculptures and an extensive collection of pre-Columbian Indian art. In 1950, donated major collections to Philadelphia Museum of Art, where a new wing was built to house the art.

Mary Austin (September 9, 1868–August 13, 1934) b. Mary Hunter in Carlinville, Illinois. Attended local Blackburn College, where she studied science and mathematics. After graduation, attempted to set up homestead with mother and brother near Fort Tejon, California. Worked as tutor in San Joaquin Valley. Married Wallace Austin in 1891; daughter Ruth born severely handicapped the following year. Began publishing short fiction in 1892 and taught for a year at the Normal School in Los Angeles (now UCLA) in 1899. Published *The Land of Little Rain*, a collection of sketches about the California desert, in 1903. Joined artists' colony in Carmel, California, and became acquainted with George Sterling, Jack London, and other writers; began writing novels, including *Isidro* (1905) and *Santa Lucia* (1908), and published *Lost Borders* (1909), another collection of sketches. Visited England in 1909 and formed friendships with George Bernard Shaw, H. G. Wells, Joseph Conrad, Herbert Hoover, and others. Divorced in 1914. Play *The Arrow Maker* (1911) produced in New York. Later novels included *A Woman of Genius* (1912), *The Lovely Lady* (1913), and *The Ford* (1917). Settled permanently in Santa Fe, New Mexico, where she built home Casa Querida. *The American Rhythm*, a study of Native American poetry, was published in 1923.

In the course of her career, corresponded with many writers and public fig-ures including Sinclair Lewis, Witter Bynner, Isadora Duncan, Robinson Jef-fers, Marianne Moore, Willa Cather, Diego Rivera, and Theodore Roosevelt. Her autobiography, *Earth Horizon*, appeared in 1932.

Djuna Barnes (June 12, 1892–June 18, 1982) b. Djuna Chappell Barnes in Cornwall-on-the-Hudson, New York. Mother, father, father's mistress, and their seven combined children lived in same house; educated by father and paternal grandmother. First published poems appeared in *Harper's Weekly* in 1911. Studied at Pratt Institute of Art in New York in 1912; contributed arti-cles and stories to newspapers and magazines. Supported mother, three brothers, and ailing grandmother. Lived in Greenwich Village. *The Book of Repulsive Women* published in 1915; several of her one-act plays were staged by the Provincetown Players, 1919–20. Sailed for Paris in 1920 on assignment for *McCall's* magazine. Moved briefly to Berlin in 1921, then returned to Paris the next year. Associates in Europe included James Joyce, Marsden Hartley, and Man Ray. Lived with Thelma Wood, an American artist, 1923–31. Pub-lished *A Book* (1923), collection of writings in various genres; *Ryder* (1928), a novel; *Ladies Almanack* (1928), satirical portrait of the literary salon of Natalie Barney, illustrated with drawings by Barnes; and *A Night Among the Horses* (1929), collection of stories and poems. Settled in England in 1932 with financial support from Peggy Guggenheim. Traveled to Tangier with poet Charles Henri Ford in 1933. Novel *Nightwood* published 1936; T. S. Eliot wrote introduction for American edition. Sold her Paris apartment in 1939 and moved to Greenwich Village. Suffered from alcoholism and had series of breakdowns. Published verse play *The Antiphon* (1958). Died in New York.

Irving Berlin (May 11, 1888–September 22, 1989) b. Israel Baline in Temun, Russia. Family settled on Lower East Side of New York in 1892. Appeared on stage in *The Show Girl* (1902); worked as song plugger and singing waiter. Wrote first published song, "Marie from Sunny Italy," in 1907; adopted pro-fessional name. Soon began enjoying success as songwriter, though he never learned to read or write music and could play piano only in key of F sharp major. Appeared as performer in *Up and Down Broadway* (1910). Enjoyed greatest success to date with "Alexander's Ragtime Band" (1911). Married Dorothy Goetz in February 1913; she died of typhoid the following July. Es-tablished his own music publishing company in 1919. Married Ellin Mackay in 1926. Steady succession of hit songs included "God Bless America" (1917), "A Pretty Girl Is Like a Melody" (1919), "What'll I Do?" (1924), "Always" (1925), "Blue Skies" (1927), "Puttin' on the Ritz" (1930), "Easter Parade" (1933), "Cheek to Cheek" (1935), "Let's Face the Music and Dance" (1936), "I've Got My Love To Keep Me Warm" (1937), and "White Christmas" (1945). His many musicals and revues included *Watch Your Step* (1914), *Yip Yip Yaphank* (1918), *As Thousands Cheer* (1935), *Louisiana Purchase* (1940), *Annie Get Your Gun* (1946), and *Call Me Madam* (1950).

John Peale Bishop (May 21, 1892–April 4, 1944) b. Charleston, West Virginia. After sporadic early education, interrupted by illness, attended Princeton, 1913–17. Formed close friendships with Edmund Wilson and F. Scott Fitzgerald (provided model for Thomas Parke D'Invilliers in Fitzgerald's *This Side of Paradise*); named class poet and editor of literary magazine. First poetry collection, *Green Fruit*, published 1917. Commissioned as infantry lieutenant after graduation; served with detachment guarding German prisoners; experience disinterring and reburying American soldiers became basis for story "Resurrection." Joined staff of *Vanity Fair* in New York; contributed many pieces to the magazine and became managing editor. Published *The Undertaker's Garland* (1922), collection of prose and poetry co-written with Edmund Wilson. Married Margaret Hutchins in 1922. Spent two years in Europe, mostly in Paris and Sorrento; came back to America for two years before returning in 1926 to France, where he lived in a hunting lodge northwest of Paris. Story collection *Many Thousands Gone* (1931) won Scribner's Prize; poetry collection *Now With His Love* published 1933. Returning to U.S., settled in South Chatham, Massachusetts. Published novel *Act of Darkness* (1935) and poetry collection *Minute Particulars* (1936); became poetry reviewer for *The Nation* in 1940. Supervised preparation of several anthologies of Latin American literature for Office of the Co-ordinator of Inter-American Affairs. *Collected Poems* published posthumously in 1948.

Maxwell Bodenheim (May 26, 1892–February 7, 1954) b. Maxwell Bodenheimer in Hermanville, Mississippi. Family moved to Chicago when he was nine. Received little formal education. Dropped out of high school; served in the army; traveled around the Southwest before returning to Chicago in 1912. Became part of literary circle associated with *Poetry*, including Harriet Monroe, Carl Sandburg, Edgar Lee Masters, and Sherwood Anderson. Published poems in *Poetry* and *The Little Review*. Corresponded with Alfred Kreymborg, editor of *Others*; moved to Greenwich Village in 1916. Met William Carlos Williams, Marianne Moore, Hart Crane, and edited some issues of *Others*. Published first book of poetry, *Minna and Myself* (dedicated to wife Minna Scheim), in 1918; the same year, co-wrote play *The Master-Poisoner* with Ben Hecht. Son Solbert born in 1920. Published many books, including poetry collections *Advice* (1920), *Introducing Irony* (1922), *Against This Age* (1923), *Returning to Emotion* (1927), *The King of Spain* (1928), and *Bringing Jazz!* (1930), and novels *Crazy Man* (1924), *Replenishing Jessica* (1925), and *Naked on Roller Skates* (1931). In Depression, found assistance through Federal Writers' Project, but was removed in 1940 because of suspected Communist associations. Won *Poetry*'s Oscar Blumenthal Award in 1939. Final book of new poetry, *Lights in the Valley*, appeared in 1942. Divorced Scheim in 1938, married Grace Finian in 1939. Suffering from alcoholism, hospitalized in Bellevue during the 1940's. *Selected Poems 1914–1944* (1946) was last book publication. Finian died in 1950. Married Ruth Fagan in 1952. Moved to rooming house near the Bowery in 1954, where he and his wife were murdered by a former mental patient who believed they were Communists.

Anna Hempstead Branch (March 18, 1875–September 8, 1937) b. New London, Connecticut. Graduated from Smith in 1897; later studied at American Academy of Dramatic Arts in New York. Worked as volunteer at Christadora, a Lower East Side settlement house, eventually serving on its board of directors. At Christadora, founded a Poets Guild that offered classes in drama and the arts; sponsored poetry readings by Edwin Arlington Robinson, Vachel Lindsay, Carl Sandburg, and others. Published poetry collections *Heart of the Road* (1901), *The Shoes That Danced* (1905), and *Rose of the Wind* (1910). Had close friendships with poets Edith Thomas, Josephine Preston Peabody, and Ridgely Torrence. Founded International Poetry Society. *Sonnets from a Lockbox* appeared in 1929, and *Last Poems*, edited by Torrence, was published posthumously in 1944.

Witter Bynner (August 10, 1881–June 1, 1968) b. Harold Witter Bynner in Brooklyn, New York. Moved with mother and brother Tim to live with relatives in Norwich, Connecticut; after father's death in 1891, family moved to Brookline, Massachusetts. Attended Harvard (1898–1902). Became active in woman suffrage movement. Moved to New York, where he worked as literary editor for *McClure's*, 1902–6. Published poetry collections *An Ode to Harvard* (1907) and *The New World* (1915); translated Euripides' *Iphigenia in Tauris* for a production by Isadora Duncan. Under pen names Emanuel Morgan and Anne Knish, Bynner and Harvard friend Arthur Davison Ficke invented mock poetic school known as Spectrism, writing parodies of modernist poetry collected in *Spectra: A Book of Poetic Experiments* (1916); they were taken seriously until Bynner revealed the hoax in 1918. Formed close friendship with Edna St. Vincent Millay. Traveled to China and Japan in 1917. In U.S., met Swiss painter Paul Thévenaz, who became close friend and lover. Taught poetry at Berkeley in 1918; his students included Genevieve Taggard, Hildegarde Flanner, and Ernest Walsh. In Berkeley met Chinese scholar Kiang Kang-hu, with whom he traveled in China, 1920–21. Published *Grenstone Poems* (1917), *The Beloved Stranger* (1919), *A Canticle of Pan* and *Pins for Wings* (1920), and *A Book of Plays* (1922). Moved to New Mexico in 1922, living in Santa Fe and then Taos, where he met D. H. Lawrence and his wife, Frieda (their trip together to Mexico provided basis for Lawrence's 1926 novel *The Plumed Serpent*). Published *Caravan* (1925), *Cake* (1926), *Indian Earth* (1929), *The Persistence of Poetry* (1929), and *The Jade Mountain* (1929), translation of a classical Chinese poetry anthology done in collaboration with Kiang. Began long-term relationship with Robert Nichols Hunt, who served as his assistant and secretary; established second home with Hunt in Chapala, Mexico, in 1940. Published *Against the Cold* (1940), translation *The Way of Life According to Laotzu* (1944), *Take Away the Darkness* (1947), *Journey with Genius* (1951), a memoir of his involvement with the Lawrences, *Book of Lyrics* (1955), and *New Poems, 1960*. Suffered severe stroke in 1965.

Skipwith Cannell (December 22, 1887–June 15, 1957) b. Humberston Skipwith Cannell Jr. in Philadelphia. Raised in Philadelphia: attended boarding school in Switzerland. Entered University of Virginia in 1906; majored in chemistry but did not earn a degree. Moved to France in 1912; lived in a barge on the Seine. Married Kathleen Eaton in 1913. Met John Gould Fletcher, who introduced Cannell to Ezra Pound; lived briefly in Kensington in the room below Pound's. Published poems in Pound's anthology *Des Imagistes* (1914). Moved to New York; published poems in *Poetry*, *Others*, and *Little Review*. Published last new poem in 1916. Volunteered for military service in 1917; sailed to France, separated from Kathleen, and married Juliette Del Grange. Attempted beekeeping on the Mediterranean coast, owned a candy store in Beaulieu, and operated a resort hotel in New Jersey. Moved in 1925 to Florida, where he worked as a night watchman, real estate salesman, and sewing machine salesman. Return to Philadelphia in 1932, and organized the Pennsylvania branch of the Bonus Expeditionary Force. Moved to Washington and worked as an economist and statistician at the Interstate Commerce Commission. Wrote long unpublished poem, "By the Rivers of Babylon," to which William Carlos Williams wrote an introduction. Wrote statistical study "A Method of Multiple Correlation," and co-authored two government studies, *Regional Shifts in the Postwar Traffic of Class I Railroads* and *Postwar Earnings of Class I Railroads* (both 1946).

Badger Clark Jr. (January 1, 1883–1957) b. Albia, Iowa. Family moved to Dakota Territory when Clark was three months old. Attended Dakota Wesleyan University for one year. Went to Cuba as part of an expedition to establish a farm community, soon abandoned for lack of funds; remained in Cuba until tried by local authorities for theft and carrying a gun. After acquittal, returned to South Dakota and worked briefly as a reporter; later spent time in Arizona because of lung problems. Worked at ranch near Tombstone; wrote verse letters to his family describing ranch life, one of which was published in *Pacific Monthly*. First poetry collection, *Sun and Saddle Leather*, appeared in 1915. His later books included *Grass Grown Trails* (1917), *Sky Lines and Wood Smoke* (1935), and the novel *Spike* (1923). He served as Poet Laureate of South Dakota, and his mountain home ("The Badger Hole") near Custer, South Dakota, became a museum after his death.

Sarah N. Cleghorn (February 4, 1876–April 4, 1959) b. Norfolk, Virginia. Spent early years in Wisconsin and Minnesota. Her mother died when she was nine, and she was raised by two aunts in Manchester, Vermont, where she lived for most of her life. Attended Radcliffe, 1895–96. A Quaker, she was active in many social and political causes, including pacifism, prison reform, abolition of child labor, and antivivisectionism; joined Socialist Party in 1913. Her poem "The Golf Links Lie So Near the Mill" achieved wide readership when it appeared in Franklin P. Adams' newspaper column "The Conning

Tower" in 1915. Taught at Brookwood Labor School in Katonah, New York, from 1920; taught drama and English at Manumit School in Pawling, New York, 1922–29. Her books included novels *A Turnpike Lady* (1907) and *The Spinster* (1916); an autobiography, *Threescore* (1936), for which her friend Robert Frost wrote the preface; and *The Seamless Robe* (1945), a collection of essays. Poetry was collected in *Portraits and Protests* (1917), *Ballad of Tuzu-lutlan* (1932), and *Poems of Peace and Freedom* (1945). With close friend Dorothy Canfield Fisher organized Poetry Society of Southern Vermont and collaborated on the books *Fellow Captains* (1916) and *Nothing Ever Happens and How It Does* (1940). Moved in 1943 to Philadelphia, where she died.

Adelaide Crapsey (September 9, 1878–October 8, 1914) b. Brooklyn Heights, New York. Father was appointed rector of St. Andrew's Church in Rochester, New York, in 1879; six younger children born in rectory. Sent in 1893 to Kemper Hall, boarding school in Kenosha, Wisconsin. Entered Vassar in 1897; named class poet. Graduated Phi Beta Kappa; taught at Kemper Hall. Studied at School of Archaeology in Rome, 1904–5. Father was tried for heresy and dismissed in 1906 from Episcopal Church for preaching "Social Christianity." Taught history and literature at high school in Connecticut, 1906–8. Chronic fatigue forced her to give up teaching. Attended Hague Peace Conference with father in 1907. Began long-term study of poetic meter in London. Returned to America in February 1911 to teach poetics at Smith. Diagnosed that year with tuberculin meningitis, but kept diagnosis secret from her family. Hospitalized after collapsing in her bath, then moved to private nursing home in Saranac, New York, as her health deteriorated. Invented Cinquain, five-line verse form with lines of 2, 4, 6, 8, and 2 syllables. Returned to Rochester in August 1914. Died of chronic pulmonary tuberculosis. *Verse* (1915) and unfinished treatise *A Study in English Metrics* (1918) published posthumously.

Donald Davidson (August 18, 1893–April 25, 1968) b. Donald Grady Davidson in Campbellsville, Tennessee. Entered Vanderbilt in 1909, but withdrew because of financial difficulties. Taught in small schools until 1914, when he had saved enough money to return to Vanderbilt, where he met John Crowe Ransom, member of intellectual circle associated with Sidney Mttron Hirsch. Awarded B.A. in absentia in 1917 while enrolled in Officers' Candidate School in Georgia. Married Theresa Sherrer in 1918. Saw combat on several French battlefields as first lieutenant in World War I. Served as head of English department at Kentucky Wesleyan College. Was a co-founder and editor of *The Fugitive*, magazine published (1922–25) by the Hirsch circle. Became book-page editor for *Nashville Tennessean* in 1924. Appointed professor of English at Vanderbilt in 1924. First poetry collection, *An Outland Piper*, published 1924, followed by *The Tall Men* (1927). Was one of 12 contributors to Southern Agrarian manifesto *I'll Take My Stand* (1930). Spent summers teaching at Bread Loaf Writers' Conference in Middlebury, Vermont, from 1931. His later books included *Lee in the Mountains* (1938), *The Attack on Leviathan:*

Regionalism and Nationalism in the United States (1938), *The Tennessee* (1946), and *Still Rebels, Still Yankees and Other Essays* (1957). *Poems: 1922–1961* appeared in 1966.

Frances Densmore (May 21, 1867–June 5, 1957) b. Frances Theresa Densmore in Red Wing, Minnesota. Studied music at Oberlin College Conservatory and later with private teachers in New York and Boston. Returned to Red Wing, where she taught music and played church organ. First heard American Indian music at the World's Columbian Exposition in 1893; interest further prompted by reading Alice C. Fletcher's *A Study of Omaha Music* (1893). Transcribed songs at Prairie Island Dakota reservation. Conducted first field study in 1905 at an Ojibwe village near Canadian border. With grant from Bureau of American Ethnology in 1907, purchased a cylinder recording device. Worked for B.A.E. among Dakota Sioux and Minnesota Ojibwe tribes, and visited other tribes in many parts of the United States and Canada. Secured permanent position at B.A.E. in 1925. In the course of her career she made over 2,500 cylinder recordings of American Indian music. Her many publications included *Chippewa Music* (1910, 1913), *Poems from Sioux and Chippewa Songs* (1917), *Teton Sioux Music* (1918), *Northern Ute Music* (1922), *Mandan and Hidatsa Music* (1923), *The American Indians and Their Music* (1926), *Papago Music* (1929), *Pawnee Music* (1929), *Menominee Music* (1932), *Yuman and Yaqui Music* (1932), *Cheyenne and Arapaho Music* (1936), *Music of Santo Domingo Pueblo, New Mexico* (1938), *Nootka and Quileute Music* (1939), *Choctaw Music* (1943), and *Music of the Indians of British Columbia* (1943).

H.D. (Hilda Doolittle) (September 10, 1886–September 27, 1961) b. Bethlehem, Pennsylvania; raised in Moravian community. Family moved to Upper Darby, Pennsylvania, in 1895, when father was named professor of astronomy at University of Pennsylvania. Attended Bryn Mawr College briefly in 1905; met Marianne Moore. Formed friendships with Ezra Pound and William Carlos Williams; she and Pound read each other's early poems, and were briefly engaged in 1907. Toured Europe in summer of 1911. Decided to settle in London, where Pound was living; through him, met literary circle including Ford Madox Ford, May Sinclair, W. B. Yeats, and Richard Aldington. Traveled with Aldington in France and Italy, 1911–12; they were married in 1913. Pound sent her poems (signed, at his suggestion, "H.D. Imagiste") to *Poetry*, and included her work in his anthology *Des Imagistes* (1914); she was subsequently included in Amy Lowell's anthology *Some Imagist Poets* (1915). First poetry collection, *Sea Garden*, published 1916. Estranged from Aldington, she had brief affair with D. H. Lawrence and conceived a child with composer Cecil Gray. Suffered near-fatal illness during pregnancy and was cared for by novelist Bryher (Annie Winnifred Ellerman), who became her intimate companion. Daughter Perdita born 1919. Visited Greece with Bryher and psychologist Havelock Ellis in 1920. Moved the following year with Bryher, Perdita, and her mother to Territet, Switzerland. Published poetry collections *Hymen* (1921), *Heliodora* (1924), *Hippolytus Temporizes* (1927), and *Red Roses* *for Bronze* (1931); wrote experimental prose works including *Palimpsest* (1926) and *Hedylus* (1928). Published film journal *Close Up* (1927–33), with Kenneth MacPherson, who directed three films which she acted in and edited: *Wing Beat* (1927), *Foothills* (1928), and *Borderline* (1930). Beginning in 1931, underwent psychoanalytic treatment with Mary Chadwick and then Hanns Sachs; in 1933 began daily sessions with Sigmund Freud. Her translation of Euripides' *Ion* was published in 1937. Experiences in London during the Blitz became the basis for *The Walls Do Not Fall* (1944), the first volume of a poetic trilogy completed by *Tribute to the Angels* (1945) and *The Flowering of the Rod* (1946). Formed friendship with Hugh Dowding, retired RAF air chief marshal, who shared her interest in spiritualism; attended weekly seances. In later years lived in Switzerland and Italy. Published prose works *By Avon River* (1949), a study of Shakespeare, *Tribute to Freud* (1956), and *Bid Me to Live* (1960), a novel. *Selected Poems* (1957) was edited by Norman Holmes Pearson, her close friend and literary adviser. The book-length poem *Helen in Egypt* was published a year after her death. Much of her writing was published posthumously, including the poems in *Hermetic Definition* (1971) and a good deal of previously unpublished work in *Collected Poems, 1912–1944* (1983), and the prose works *End to Torment*, a memoir of Pound (1979), *HERmione* (1981), and *The Gift* (1982).

W.E.B. Du Bois (February 23, 1868–August 29, 1963) b. William Edward Burghardt Du Bois in Great Barrington, Massachussetts. Entered Fisk University in 1885; edited the *Fisk Herald* and spent summers teaching in the South. Awarded A.B. from Fisk in 1888. Studied philosophy at Harvard, where his professors included William James and George Santayana. Awarded B.A. cum laude in 1890, and M.A. in history, 1891. Studied in Berlin for two years. Accepted chair in classics at Wilberforce University in 1894. Awarded Ph.D from Harvard in 1895; published dissertation, *The Suppression of the African Slave-Trade to the United States of America, 1638–1870* (1896). Married Nina Gomer in 1896. Organized prize-winning exhibition on black economic progress at the 1900 Paris Exposition; attended 1900 London Pan-African conference. *The Souls of Black Folk*, a collection of essays, published in 1903. Named general secretary of the Niagara Movement, dedicated to political and economic justice. Founded *Horizon*, monthly journal published 1907–10. Published biography *John Brown* (1909) and novel *The Quest of the Silver Fleece* (1911). Active in National Association for the Advancement of Colored People from its founding in 1909 through 1934, and from 1944 to 1948; edited and contributed prolifically to the NAACP's magazine *The Crisis*. Elected executive secretary to First Pan-African Congress in Paris, 1919. *Darkwater* (essays) published 1920. Visited West Africa in 1924 and spoke at Liberian presidential inauguration; traveled to Soviet Union in 1926. Published novel *Dark Princess* (1928). Resigned from NAACP in 1934. Published historical study *Black Reconstruction* (1935) and autobiography *Dusk of Dawn* (1940). Elected to National Institute of Arts and Letters, 1944. Served (1948–56) as vice-chairman of the Council of African Affairs, listed as subversive organization by the attorney general.

Founded Peace Information Center in 1950, which was soon disbanded due to pressure from Justice Department. Indicted under Foreign Agents Registration Act; charges later dismissed by the trial judge. Wife, Nina, died in 1950; married Shirley Graham the following year. Denied passport in 1952 by State Department; after passport was restored in 1958, settled in Ghana, obtaining citizenship shortly before his death in Accra. *Selected Poems* (1964) was published posthumously in Ghana.

Max Eastman (January 4, 1883–March 25, 1969) b. Max Forrester Eastman in Canandaigua, New York. Son of two Congregational ministers. Attended Mercersburg Academy and Williams College, where he earned a B.A. in 1905. Studied philosophy with John Dewey at Columbia University. Married Ida Rauh in 1911 (marriage ended in divorce). Published *Enjoyment of Poetry* (1913), a widely read survey; his own poetry was collected in *Child of the Amazons* (1913). Elected editor of *The Masses* in 1912; during his editorship contributors included Carl Sandburg, Randolph Bourne, Sherwood Anderson, Claude McKay, and managing editor Floyd Dell. The magazine's August 1917 issue, featuring anti-war material, was blocked by the post office under the Espionage Act; under pressure from government and financial strains, it ceased publication by the end of the year. Eastman was tried twice for sedition on grounds that *The Masses* had fomented draft resistance; charge was dismissed after both trials ended in hung juries. With his sister Crystal founded *The Liberator* in 1918. Visited Soviet Union in 1922 and formed close association with Leon Trotsky. Translated a number of Trotsky's writings, including the three-volume *History of the Russian Revolution* (1932). Married Soviet citizen Eliena Vassilyevna Krylenko. Published many books including *Since Lenin Died* (1925), *Marx, Lenin, and the Science of Revolution* (1926), *The Literary Mind: Its Place in an Age of Science* (1931), *Artists in Uniform: A Study of Literature and Bureaucratism* (1934), *The End of Socialism in Russia* (1937), *Marxism: Is It Science?* (1940), *Enjoyment of Living* (1948), and the memoir *Love and Revolution: My Journey Through an Epoch* (1964). He was a contributing editor of *Reader's Digest* from 1941 until his death. His poetry was collected in *Colors of Life* (1918), *Kinds of Love* (1931), and *Poems of Five Decades* (1954).

T. S. Eliot (September 26, 1888–January 4, 1965) b. Thomas Stearns Eliot in St. Louis, Missouri. Seventh child of Henry Ware and Charlotte Chauncy Stearns Eliot, a poet. Grew up in St. Louis, attending Smith Academy, founded by his grandfather. Studied at Milton Academy before entering Harvard in 1906. Studied Greek, Latin, German, French, and philosophy; teachers included George Santayana, Josiah Royce, and Bertrand Russell. Joined staff of the *Advocate*, which published his earliest poems. Remained at Harvard after earning A.B. in 1909; took Irving Babbitt's course in French literary criticism. Studied at the Sorbonne in Paris (1910–11); attended lectures of Henri Bergson. Composed "The Love Song of J. Alfred Prufrock" in 1911. Returned to Harvard in 1911 to pursue Ph.D. in philosophy; studied in Germany and at Oxford in 1914; wrote dissertation on F. H. Bradley in London, 1915–16. "The Love Song of J. Alfred Prufrock" published in *Poetry* in 1915. Married Vivien Haigh-Wood in June 1915. Taught grammar school, 1915–16; took up freelance writing and lecturing to alleviate financial demands of Vivien's chronic illnesses. *Prufrock and Other Observations* published in 1917. Worked at Lloyds Bank, 1916–25. Poetry collection *Ara Vos Prec* appeared in 1920. Published *The Sacred Wood* (1920), the first of many collections of critical essays; later criticism appeared in *Homage to John Dryden* (1924), *For Lancelot Andrewes: Essays on Style and Order* (1928), *After Strange Gods: A Primer of Modern Heresy* (1934), *The Idea of a Christian Society* (1939), and *Notes Towards the Definition of Culture* (1948). Suffered breakdown in 1921. Entrusted first draft of *The Waste Land* to Ezra Pound and subsequently incorporated most of Pound's proposed revisions. Founded journal *The Criterion* (1922–39); published *The Waste Land* in its first issue in October 1922. In 1925, left Lloyds Bank and joined publishing house Faber and Gwyer (later Faber and Faber). Published *Poems 1909–1925* (1925). Baptized into Anglican Church in 1927; became a naturalized British citizen that same year. Published *Ash-Wednesday* (1930) and *Selected Essays* (1932). Permanently separated from Vivien in 1932. Returned to Harvard as Charles Eliot Norton Professor of Poetry; Harvard lectures published as *The Use of Poetry and The Use of Criticism* (1933). Lectured at University of Virginia, Edinburgh, and Cambridge. Wrote verse dramas *Murder in the Cathedral* (1935) and *The Family Reunion* (1939), and *Old Possum's Book of Practical Cats* (1939), a collection of light verse. Published *Four Quartets* (1943), sequence of four poems written between 1935 and 1942. Received Nobel Prize for Literature and England's Order of Merit in 1948. His plays *The Cocktail Party* (1950) and *The Confidential Clerk* (1954) were successfully produced. Married Esme Valerie Fletcher, his secretary at Faber, in 1957. His last play, *The Elder Statesman*, was published in 1959.

Abbie Huston Evans (December 20, 1881–November 1983) b. Lee, New Hampshire. Attended public schools in Camden, Maine. Education interrupted by eye problems requiring surgery and long convalescence. After recovery, attended Radcliffe, receiving B.A. in 1913 and M.A. in 1918. Served with Red Cross in Europe during World War I, and afterward with overseas YMCA. Worked as social worker among Colorado miners and Pennsylvania steelworkers. Joined staff of Settlement Music School in Philadelphia in 1923, teaching dance, art, and drama. Encouraged as poet by Edna St. Vincent Millay, who was once her Sunday school pupil. First book of poems, *Outcrop*, published in 1928 with introduction by Millay. Won Guarantor's Prize from *Poetry* in 1931. Second book, *The Bright North*, published in 1938. Awarded Loines Prize for Poetry in 1960; collection *Fact of Crystal* published the following year. *Collected Poems* published in 1970.

Donald Evans (July 24, 1884–May 26, 1921) b. Philadelphia, Pennsylvania. Graduated from Haverford College. Began working in 1905 for the *Philadel-*

phia Inquirer. Moved to New York by 1912; wrote for *The New York Times.* First poetry collection, *Discords,* published in 1912. Founded Claire Marie Press, which published Evans' *Sonnets from the Patagonian* (1914) and Gertrude Stein's *Tender Buttons* (1914). Returned in 1915 to the *Inquirer,* enlisted in the army in 1917, reaching rank of sergeant. Married Esther Porter in 1918; they had two daughters. Published poems in magazines including *Rogue* and *Others;* his other collections were *Two Deaths in the Bronx* (1916), *Nine Poems from a Valetudinarian* (1916), and *Ironica* (1919). After his discharge from the army in 1919, worked as managing editor of *The Daily Garment News.* Died in Bellevue Hospital; believed to have committed suicide.

Arthur Davison Ficke (November 10, 1883–November 30, 1945) b. Davenport, Iowa. Attended Harvard, earning A.B. in 1904. Taught English while studying for law degree at University of Iowa. Married Evelyn Blunt in 1907. Published *From the Isles: A Series of Songs Out of Greece* (1907), *The Happy Princess* (1907), and *The Earth Passion, Boundary, and Other Poems* (1908). Joined father's law practice in 1908. Published poetry collections *The Breaking of Bonds* (1910), *Sonnets of a Portrait Painter* (1914), *The Man on the Hilltop* (1915), and *An April Elegy* (1917), verse drama *Mr. Faust* (1913), and *Chats on Japanese Prints* (1915). With Harvard friend Witter Bynner concocted parodistic verse school Spectrism; under pen names Anne Knish and Emanuel Morgan, they published *Spectra: A Book of Poetic Experiments* (1916). The group, which was joined by Marjorie Allan Seiffert (writing as Elijah Hay), was taken seriously until Bynner revealed the hoax in 1918. Became captain in U.S. Army in 1917. In France met Gladys Brown, an ambulance driver; divorced first wife in 1922 and married Brown in 1923. Later books included *Out of Silence* (1924), *Selected Poems* (1926), *Mountain Against Mountain* (1929), *The Secret* (1936), the novel *Mrs. Morton of Mexico* (1939), and *Tumultuous Shore* (1942).

John Gould Fletcher (January 3, 1886–May 10, 1950) b. Little Rock, Arkansas. Father was wealthy banker and cotton broker. Schooled at home and in private schools before attending Little Rock High School and Phillips Academy. Entered Harvard in 1903; left before graduation upon receiving legacy after father's death. Settled in London in 1909; published five volumes of poetry privately; met W. B. Yeats, H.D., and Ezra Pound. Quarreled with Pound over what he believed to be Pound's uncredited appropriation of some of his ideas. Formed association with Amy Lowell, who published his work in her anthologies of Imagist poetry. Returned to America in 1914. Published poetry collections *Irradiations* (1915), *Sand and Spray* (1915), and *Goblins and Pagodas* (1916). Married Daisy Arbuthnot, with whom he had been living for several years, in 1916; marriage dissolved within a year. Returned to Europe. Published poetry collections *Japanese Prints* (1918), *Parables* (1925), *Branches of Adam* (1926), and *The Black Rock* (1928), and biography *Paul Gauguin: His Life and Art* (1921). Became a contributor to *The Fugitive* and later met members of Fugitive group while lecturing in the South in 1927. *The Two Frontiers: A Study in Historical Psychology* appeared in 1930. Returned to Arkansas permanently in 1933. Founded Arkansas Folk Lore Society in 1935; wrote long poem "The Story of Arkansas" for the state's centennial. Married Charlie May Hogue Simon, a children's book author, in 1936. Later books of poetry included *XXIV Elegies* (1935), *South Star* (1941), and *The Burning Mountain* (1946). Drowned himself in a pool near his home.

Elsa von Freytag-Loringhoven (July 12, 1874–December 14, 1927) b. Else Hildegard Ploetz in Swinoujscie, a Baltic town in present-day Poland. Grew up in Berlin; had brief careers in theater and art. Felix Paul Greve, her third husband, was arrested for fraud soon after their marriage, and served a two-year prison sentence. Moved with husband to America in 1910; marriage broke up after a failed attempt at farming in Kentucky. Moved to New York; married the Baron von Freytag-Loringhoven on November 19, 1913, and settled at the Ritz. (The Baron returned to Germany at the outbreak of World War I, and later committed suicide.) Moved to Greenwich Village; worked as artist's model. Introduced in 1915 to Marcel Duchamp, under whose influence she began to sculpt and write poetry; her work was featured in *New York Dada* (1921), edited by Duchamp and Man Ray, and in *The Little Review*, 1920–23. Became notorious for outlandish appearance and extreme behavior. Met William Carlos Williams in 1918; after two violent altercations he had her arrested for assault. Returned to Europe in 1923, with funding partly provided by Williams. Appealed to friends and relatives in Berlin for financial support; Djuna Barnes offered to help her publish a volume of poetry. Admitted in 1925 to a charitable institution; transferred briefly to a mental hospital before being released. Maintained an apartment in Paris in 1926 paid for by American friends; died of asphyxiation when the gas was left on (according to some accounts, this was done deliberately by a former lover).

Robert Frost (March 26, 1874–January 29, 1963) b. Robert Lee Frost in San Francisco, California. First child of William Prescott Frost Jr. and Isabelle Moodie, both teachers. After father's death in 1885, family moved to Salem Depot, New Hampshire. Attended Lawrence High School, 1888–92; published poems in school magazine. After attending Dartmouth for one semester, left to take over mother's eighth-grade class in Methuen. Worked at Arlington Woolen Mill until February 1894; returned to Salem to teach elementary school. Worked as reporter for Lawrence *Daily American* and *Sentinel*. Married former classmate Elinor White in 1895; of their six children, four survived early childhood. Studied briefly at Harvard, 1897–99; took up poultry farming. Grandfather died in 1901, leaving small annuity and use of farm in Derry, New Hampshire. Published poems and stories in local journals; taught at Pinkerton Academy in Derry. Moved with family to Buckinghamshire, England, in 1912; published first book of poetry, *A Boy's Will* (1913), in England. Met Ezra Pound, H.D., William Butler Yeats, and other writers; formed close friendship with English poet Edward Thomas. Published *North* *of Boston* (1914); returned to America in 1915. First two books published in American editions; met Edwin Arlington Robinson and Louis Untermeyer. Moved family to farm in Franconia, New Hampshire. Elected to National Institute of Arts and Letters; published *Mountain Interval* (1916). Began teaching at Amherst College the following year. Committed sister Jeanie to mental hospital in Maine. Moved to South Shaftsbury, Vermont. *Selected Poems* published 1923; *New Hampshire* (1923) won Pulitzer Prize for Poetry. Accepted lifetime appointment at University of Michigan as Fellow in Letters in 1924, and divided time between Ann Arbor and Amherst. Participated in first Bread Loaf Writers' Conference in 1926. Published *West-Running Brook* and expanded *Selected Poems* (both 1928). *Collected Poems* (1930) won Pulitzer Prize; elected to American Academy of Arts and Letters. Daughter Marjorie died in 1934. *A Further Range* (1936) won Pulitzer Prize. Elinor died of heart failure in 1938. Son Carol committed suicide in 1940. *A Witness Tree* (1942) won fourth Pulitzer Prize, followed by *A Masque of Reason* (1945), *Steeple Bush* (1947), and *A Masque of Mercy* (1947). Committed daughter Irma to New Hampshire mental hospital in 1947. In 1957, joined T. S. Eliot, Ernest Hemingway, and Archibald MacLeish in petitioning attorney general to drop treason indictment against Ezra Pound. Appointed Consultant in Poetry at Library of Congress. Invited by John F. Kennedy to take part in 1961 inaugural ceremonies. Published *In the Clearing* (1962). Visited Russia in 1962; met poets Anna Akhmatova and Yevgeny Yevtushenko and Soviet Premier Nikita Khrushchev. Awarded Bollingen Prize four weeks before death.

Arturo Giovannitti (January 7, 1884–December 31, 1959) b. Arturo Massimo Giovannitti in Campobasso, Italy. Immigrated to United States in 1902. Studied theology at McGill University; ordained as Protestant evangelical minister. Moved to New York City around 1906; became secretary of Italian Socialist Federation (1908) and edited its newspaper, *Il Proletario*. Joined the Industrial Workers of the World in 1912; led immigrant workers in textile strike in Lawrence, Massachusetts; arrested on charges of being accessory to the murder of a striker. Wrote "The Walker" while awaiting trial; acquitted after spending ten months in jail. Translated Emile Pouget's *Sabotage* (1913). Poetry collected in *Arrows in the Gale* (1914), with a foreword by Helen Keller. Wrote antiwar play *As It Was in the Beginning* (1917). Co-founded the Anti-Fascist Alliance of North America in 1923. Served as general secretary of the Italian Chamber of Labor and of the Italian Labor Education Bureau. Published *Quando Canta il Gallo* (1957), collection of his poems in Italian. Suffered from paralysis of legs in later years. Was editing *The Complete Poems of Arturo Giovannitti* (1962) at the time of his death.

Samuel Greenberg (November 3, 1893–August 17, 1917) b. Samuel Bernard Greenberg in Vienna, Austria. Immigrated with parents and seven older siblings to New York City in 1900. Left school in seventh grade to work 12-hour days in factories. Mother died in 1910, father in 1911; lived afterward with various siblings. Began drawing and copying art at the Metropolitan Museum of Art, where he was encouraged by art critic William Murrell Fisher. Symptoms of tuberculosis appeared in 1913; spent remaining years in public hospitals, where he wrote poetry prolifically, completed a short play, and wrote his autobiography. Died in public hospital on Ward's Island. His manuscripts, consisting of more than 17 notebooks filled with poetry, prose, and drawings, were kept by Fisher, and later read and copied by Hart Crane, who adapted Greenberg's "Conduct" as "Emblems of Conduct." James Laughlin published a pamphlet of 22 poems by Greenberg in 1939, and Harold Holden and Jack McManis published *Poems by Samuel Greenberg* in 1947.

Angelina Weld Grimké (February 27, 1880–June 10, 1958) b. Boston, Massachusetts. Educated at several schools in Minnesota and Massachusetts before taking degree in physical education in 1902 from Boston Normal School of Gymnastics. Taught physical education at Armstrong Manual Training School (1902–7), and later at M Street High School, where she also taught English (1907–26). Published poems, stories, reviews, and sketches in *The Crisis* and *Opportunity*. Play *Rachel* performed in 1916 at Myrtilla Miner Normal School, and published in 1920. Published poems in anthology *Negro Poets and Their Poems* (1923) and in Countee Cullen's anthology, *Caroling Dusk* (1927). Moved to New York City in 1926.

Arthur Guiterman (November 20, 1871–January 11, 1943) b. Vienna, Austria, where parents were conducting business. Raised in New York. Attended City College of New York, where he participated in athletics and drama; graduated 1891. Worked as editor of trade journals. Began contributing poems and ballads to newspapers, attracting notice for patriotic poems during Spanish-American War. Worked on editorial page of *The New York Times*. Published *Betel Nuts* (1907), collection of short verses based on Asian proverbs. In 1909, married Vida Lindo, daughter of Venezuelan aristocrat. Published successful collections of light verse *The Laughing Muse* (1915) and *The Mirthful Lyre* (1918). Elected president of Poetry Society of America, 1925–26. Contributed over a hundred poems to *The New Yorker* beginning with its first issue. His many collections included *Chips of Jade* (1920), *Ballads of Old New York* (1920), *A Ballad Maker's Pack* (1921), *The Light Guitar* (1923), *A Poet's Proverbs* (1924), *Gaily the Troubadour* (1936), and *Lyric Laughter* (1939).

Hazel Hall (February 7, 1886–May 11, 1924) b. St. Paul, Minnesota. Family moved to Portland, Oregon, when she was a child, and she lived there for the rest of her life. Following an attack of scarlet fever at age 12, became paralyzed and was confined to a wheelchair. Lived with mother and sister and helped support family by working at fine needlework until her vision deteriorated. Began publishing poetry at age 30, and her work appeared in magazines including *Poetry*, *The Dial*, *The Literary Review*, and *Contemporary Verse*. Received Young Poet's Prize from *Poetry* in 1921. Poetry collected in *Curtains* (1921), *Walkers* (1923), and the posthumous *Cry of Time* (1928).

W. C. Handy (November 16, 1873–March 28, 1958) b. William Christopher Handy in Florence, Alabama; his parents were formerly slaves; father was Methodist minister. Studied music at Florence District School and organized a quartet which performed at the World's Columbian Exposition in Chicago in 1893. Toured the South with various bands, forming Mahara's Minstrels in 1896; traveled to Cuba and Mexico. Settled in Memphis, Tennessee. Married Elizabeth Price in 1898. Published many original compositions as well as adaptations of folk and popular material; the songs associated with him included "Memphis Blues," "St. Louis Blues," "Beale Street Blues," "Old Miss Rag," "A Good Man Is Hard to Find," and "Careless Love." Co-founded a successful music publishing firm, and in 1918 traveled to New York to make his first recordings. Lost his sight, then partially regained vision before being permanently blinded in an accident in 1943. Published his songs and transcriptions in *Blues: An Anthology* (1926); published other books including *Negro Authors and Composers of the United States* (1935), his autobiography *Father of the Blues* (1941), and *Unsung Americans Sung* (1944). Second marriage, at the age of 80, was to Irma Louise Logan. His 84th birthday was celebrated at the Waldorf-Astoria in New York at a reception attended by over 800 people. He died in Harlem.

Marsden Hartley (January 4, 1877–September 2, 1943) b. Edmund Hartley in Lewiston, Maine; parents were English; mother died when he was eight. Left school at 14 and worked in shoe factory. Joined his family in Cleveland, where he won scholarship to Cleveland School of Art. Continued training in New York City, at William Merritt Chase School and National Academy of Design. Spent summers in Maine, painting landscapes and writing poetry. Gave one-man exhibition in 1908 at Alfred Stieglitz's 291 Gallery in New York. Lived in Berlin, 1913–15; supported in his painting career by Karl von Freyburg; devastated by von Freyburg's death in the war. Published poems and essays in *The Dial, Poetry, The Little Review, Contact, Others*, and *American Caravan*. Lived in Taos, 1918–19. Essays collected in *Adventures in the Arts* (1921). Lived in Paris and Berlin, 1921–24; published *25 Poems* (1923). Exhibited paintings at Stieglitz's An American Place and Intimate galleries, and later with other New York art dealers. Received Guggenheim Fellowship in 1930; traveled to Mexico and Germany, 1932–33. The death in 1932 of Hart Crane, a close friend, prompted Hartley to compose several poems and a painting in tribute. Returned to America in 1934; published *Androscoggin* (1940) and *Sea Burial* (1941). Died in Corea, Maine.

Roy Helton (b. April 3, 1886) b. Roy Addison Helton in Washington, D.C. Graduated from University of Pennsylvania in 1908. Married Anne Watson in 1909. His books included *Youth's Pilgrimage* (1915), *Outcasts in Beulah Land* (1919), *Jimmy Sharswood* (1924), *The Early Adventures of Peacham Grew* (1925), *Lonesome Water* (1930), *Nitchey Tilley* (1934), *Sold Out to the Future* (1935), and *Come Back to Earth* (1946). He received the *Nation* poetry prize in 1923.

Joe Hill (October 7, 1879–November 19, 1915) b. Joel Emmanuel Haaglund, in Gavle, Sweden. Immigrated to the United States in 1902, living on the Bowery in New York. As an itinerant laborer, moved west through Chicago and worked in mines, the lumber industry, and as a longshoreman. Became member of the San Pedro, California, local of the Industrial Workers of the World (IWW) in 1910. His songs, including "Casey Jones—The Union Scab," "The Rebel Girl," "There Is Power in the Union," "Coffee an'," and "The Preacher and the Slave," were published in the IWW's *Little Red Song Book*. Participated in dock workers' strike in San Pedro and other labor actions; may have fought in Mexican revolution. Moved around 1913 to the Swedish community of Murray, Utah, where he worked at the Park City Mines. Accused in January 1914 of the murder of John A. Morrison, a Salt Lake City grocer; convicted and sentenced to death. Trial attracted international attention, including protest from Swedish government, on grounds of insufficient evidence and legal irregularity. While awaiting execution, sent telegram to IWW leader Bill Haywood that was widely disseminated: "Don't waste any time in mourning. Organize." Executed by a firing squad at the Utah State Prison in Sugar House, Utah.

Robinson Jeffers (January 10, 1887–January 20, 1962) b. John Robinson Jeffers, near Pittsburgh, Pennsylvania. Son of William Hamilton Jeffers, professor of Old Testament literature, and Annie Robinson Tuttle, church organist. Knew Latin and Greek by age ten; in 1898 entered first of five Swiss boarding schools. Entered University of Pittsburgh in 1902; studied German and French; transferred to Occidental College in Los Angeles. While in graduate school at University of Southern California, met Una Call Kuster, a married literature student with whom he began long affair. Studied at University of Zurich; enrolled in USC medical school in 1907; withdrew briefly to study forestry at University of Washington. Privately published early poems in *Flagons and Apples* (1912). Returned to Los Angeles; Kuster's husband became aware of affair and divorced her and she and Jeffers married in August 1913. Their daughter, born in May 1914, died shortly after birth. The couple moved in September to Carmel, California. Poetry collection *Californians* published 1916; twin sons born the same year. Working with local masons, Jeffers built stone cottage Tor House in Carmel overlooking the ocean; continued to add to house for many years, doing much of the work himself; built two-and-a-half story stone tower dedicated to Una. Published *Tamar and Other Poems* (1924), which interspersed short lyrics with long narrative poems; expanded as *Roan Stallion, Tamar, and Other Poems* (1925), the book became a critical and popular success. Subsequently he published *The Women at Point Sur* (1927), *Cawdor* (1928), *Dear Judas* (1929), *Descent to the Dead* (1931), *Thurso's Landing* (1932), *Give Your Heart to the Hawks* (1933), *Solstice* (1935), *Such Counsels You Gave to Me* (1937), and *Be Angry at the Sun* (1941). His adaptation of Euripides' *Medea* was produced on Broadway in 1947. Jeffers' poems criticizing American involvement in World War II and attacking political leaders by name prompted his publisher, Random House, to include a disclaimer in *The Double Axe* (1948). Una died in 1950. *Hungerfield* appeared in 1954; final poems collected in *The Beginning and the End* (1963).

Orrick Johns (June 2, 1887–July 8, 1946) b. St. Louis, Missouri. Father, George Sibley Johns, was longtime editor of *St. Louis Post-Dispatch*. Served as literary editor of *Reedy's Mirror*; helped found Players' Club of St. Louis. Moved to New York, where he became associated with Alfred Kreymborg's circle. Won the *Lyric Year* poetry prize in 1912. His books included poetry collections *Asphalt* (1917), *Black Branches* (1920), and *Wild Plums* (1926), novel *Blindfold* (1923), and memoir *Time of Our Lives: The Story of My Father and Myself* (1937). Worked as advertising copy writer. Moved to California in 1929; became active as labor organizer. During the 1930's was an associate editor of *New Masses* and an organizer of League of American Writers; served as director of Federal Writers' Project in New York City, 1935–36. Committed suicide by drinking poison.

Fenton Johnson (May 7, 1888–September 17, 1958) b. Chicago, Illinois. Attended University of Chicago, and later Northwestern University. Began writing poems and drama at an early age. Taught at State University at Louisville, 1906–7. Married Cecelia Rhone. First volume of poetry, *A Little Dreaming* (1913), published privately. Moved to New York and studied at Columbia University's Pulitzer School of Journalism. Published at his own expense two further collections, *Visions of the Dusk* (1915) and *Songs of the Soil* (1916). Returned to Chicago and published *The Champion*, 1916–17, monthly magazine detailing African-American achievements in theater, sports and music; after it failed, published *The Favorite Magazine* for just over two years. His free verse spirituals appeared in *Poetry* and in William Stanley Braithwaite's *Anthology of Magazine Verse* in 1918. Published book of essays, *For the Highest Good* (1920), and story collection *Tales of Darkest America* (1920). Represented in a number of anthologies, including James Weldon Johnson's *The Book of American Negro Poetry* (1922) and Alfred Kreymborg's *An Anthology of American Poetry: Lyric America, 1630–1930* (1930). Worked in the late 1930's for the Federal Writers' Project in Chicago, and completed unpublished collection of poems, "The Daily Grind: 41 WPA Poems."

Georgia Douglas Johnson (September 10, 1886–May 1966) b. Georgia Douglas Camp in Marietta, Georgia. Graduated Atlanta University in 1896; studied music at Oberlin Conservatory and Cleveland College of Music. Married Henry Lincoln Johnson, a lawyer, in 1903; they had two sons. Moved in 1910 to Washington, D.C., where husband established law firm and became involved in politics, serving as Recorder of Deeds in the administration of William Howard Taft. She began publishing poetry in magazines in 1916; her first book, *The Heart of a Woman*, appeared in 1918, followed by *Bronze* (1922) and *An Autumn Love Cycle* (1928). Established a literary salon at her home, where guests included Langston Hughes, Jean Toomer, Zora Neale

Hurston, Alain Locke, A. Philip Randolph, and Anne Spencer. After husband's death in 1925, supported herself and her sons as a teacher, civil-service clerk, librarian, and secretary for the Department of Labor. Traveled, giving lectures and poetry readings; wrote plays including *Blue Blood* (1926), *Plumes* (1927), *Frederick Douglass* (1935), and *William and Ellen Craft* (1935). Wrote syndicated newspaper column "Homely Philosophy," 1926–32. Her last poetry collection, *Share My World*, appeared in 1962. Awarded an honorary doctorate of literature by Atlanta University in 1965.

James Weldon Johnson (June 17, 1871–June 24, 1938) b. Jacksonville, Florida. Son of freeborn black father and Bahamian mother. Attended Stanton School, where his mother taught. Worked as secretary for Dr. Thomas Osmond Summers, and accompanied him on trips to New York and Washington. Entered Atlanta University, where he debated, sang, and began writing seriously. Taught at rural Georgia school for two summers. Upon graduation in 1894, became principal of Stanton School. Founded *The Daily American*, first African-American daily newspaper, publishing it for eight months. Studied law and was first black admitted to Florida bar. Spent summers in New York writing songs for Broadway shows with his brother J. Rosamond Johnson and lyricist Bob Cole, including the highly successful "Under the Bamboo Tree." Wrote "Lift Every Voice and Sing" (sometimes known as the "Negro National Anthem") with brother for celebration of Abraham Lincoln's birthday in 1900. Moved permanently to New York in 1902; began studying literature at Columbia University. Appointed U.S. consul in Venezuela (1906). Married Grace Nail. Transferred to Nicaragua in 1909. Anonymously published first novel, *The Autobiography of an Ex-Colored Man* (1912). In 1916, named field secretary for the National Association for the Advancement of Colored People (NAACP). In 1920, published series of articles, "Self-Determining Haiti," in *The Nation*. *Fifty Years*, collection of his poetry to date, published in 1917. Edited *The Book of American Negro Poetry* (1922), *The Book of American Negro Spirituals* (1925), and *The Second Book of American Negro Spirituals* (1926). Published *God's Trombones: Seven Negro Sermons in Verse* (1927). Contributed numerous essays to NAACP's journal *The Crisis*. Published historical study *Black Manhattan* (1930). Resigned from NAACP and accepted teaching position at Fisk University. Published autobiography *Along This Way* (1930), *Negro Americans, What Now?* (1934), and *St. Peter Relates an Incident: Selected Poems* (1935). Killed when his car was struck at a railroad crossing in Maine.

Joyce Kilmer (December 6, 1886–July 30, 1918) b. Alfred Joyce Kilmer, in New Brunswick, New Jersey. Attended Rutgers (1904–6) and graduated from Columbia University in 1908. Married Aline Murray in June 1908; they had five children. Taught Latin at high school in Morristown, New Jersey. Moved to New York City in 1909, joining staff of the *Standard Dictionary* and writing for magazines. Became literary editor of Catholic publication *The Churchman* in 1912; a year later joined staff of *The New York Times*. Served as poetry editor for *The Literary Digest* and *Current Literature*. First poetry collection, *Summer of Love,* appeared in 1911. "Trees," his most famous poem, was published in *Poetry* in August 1913 and was subsequently collected in *Trees and Other Poems* (1914). His other books were *The Circus, and Other Essays* (1916), *Main Street and Other Poems* (1917), *Literature in the Making* (1917), and *Dreams and Images* (1917). Was briefly in Columbia Officers' Training Corps; enlisted as a private in 7th regiment, New York National Guard, when U.S. entered World War I. Killed in action near Seringes, France; awarded Croix de Guerre posthumously.

Alfred Kreymborg (December 10, 1883–August 14, 1966) b. New York City. Did not finish high school; sold music rolls for player pianos; was a chess prodigy, and competed in state tournaments. Early writings collected in *Love and Life, and Other Studies* (1908). Managed journal *Musical Advance* (1913) for its publisher, Franklin Hopkins (Hopkins invented composite musical instrument the mandolute, on which Kreymborg later gave public performances). Met Man Ray at Alfred Stieglitz's 291 Gallery, and briefly co-published *Glebe* with him. Poetry collection *Mushrooms: A Book of Free Forms* appeared in 1916. Founded *Others* in 1917, with financial support from Walter Conrad Arensberg; published work by T. S. Eliot, William Carlos Williams, Carl Sandburg, Marianne Moore, Wallace Stevens, Mina Loy, and others. Divorced first wife, Christine, in 1918 and married Dorothy Bloom. Verse play *Lima Beans* was produced by the Provincetown Players with cast including Loy and Williams. Continued to write verse dramas, collected in *Plays for Poem-Mimes* (1918), *Plays for Merry Andrews* (1920), and *Puppet Plays* (1923); presented puppet plays with his wife. Poetry collection *Blood of Things* published 1920. Discontinued *Others* in 1920, and the following year became editor of Harold Loeb's *Broom*, published in Rome. Met Gertrude Stein, James Joyce, and others. Returned to America in 1923. Published *Less Lonely* (1923) and *Scarlet and Mellow* (1926), marking turn toward formal verse, and autobiography *Troubadour* (1925). Co-edited periodic anthology *The American Caravan*, of which five volumes appeared between 1927 and 1936. *Our Singing Strength* (1929), a history of American poetry, was followed by *Lyric America: An Anthology of American Poetry, 1630–1930*. Later works included *The Lost Sail* (1928), *The Planets* (1938), a radio play in verse, *The Selected Poems, 1912–1944* (1945), *Man and Shadow: An Allegory* (1946), and *No More War* (1950). Served as president of the Poetry Society of America, and was a regular judge for the Pulitzer Prize for Poetry.

William Ellery Leonard (January 25, 1876–May 2, 1944) b. William Ellery Channing Leonard in Plainfield, New Jersey. Worked his way through Boston University, earning a B.A. in 1898. Taught Latin at Boston University; received M.A. from Harvard in 1899. Went to Germany on a fellowship. Taught German in high school while working on Ph.D. dissertation, published as *Byron and Byronism in America* (1905). Worked as an editor for Lippincott's dictionary in Philadelphia. Published *Sonnets and Poems* (1906) and *The Poet* *of Galilee* (1909). Taught at the University of Wisconsin at Madison. Married Charlotte Freeman in 1909; she committed suicide two years later. Suffered from recurring bouts of "distance phobia" and refused to venture far from home. Published poetry collections *The Vaunt of Man* (1912) and *The Lynching Bee* (1920), and the plays *Glory of the Morning* (1912) and *Red Bird* (1923). Translation of Lucretius, completed in 1912, published in 1921 as *Of the Nature of Things: A Metrical Translation*. Married Charlotte Charlton, a former student, in 1914, and moved to a cottage on Lake Wingra. War poetry collected in *Poems 1914–1916* (1917). Privately published *Two Lives*, long autobiographical poem about his first marriage, in 1923 (trade edition appeared in 1926). Published translations of *Beowulf* (1923) and *Gilgamesh* (1934); memoir *The Locomotive-God* (1927), and poetry collection *A Son of Earth* (1928). Divorced second wife in 1934; married Grace Golden in 1935. Separated from Golden in 1937; remarried Charlton in 1940. *A Man Against Time* published posthumously in 1945.

Vachel Lindsay (November 10, 1879–December 5, 1931) b. Nicholas Vachel Lindsay in Springfield, Illinois. Family were adherents of Disciples of Christ, also known as Campbellites. Entered Campbellite Hiram College in 1897 with plans to enter ministry, but left in 1900 to study fine arts at the Art Institute of Chicago, then at the New York School of Art with William Merritt Chase and Robert Henri. Published two poetry broadsides in 1905 and sold them on the street. In 1906, began lifelong practice of "tramps" across large sections of America; walked from Florida to Kentucky, and then from New York to Ohio, often bartering for room and board with broadsides or recitations of his poems. Lived in family home in Springfield, 1908–12. Sent *The Village Magazine* (1910), collection of his poems and drawings, to poets and editors; received favorable responses from Witter Bynner, Upton Sinclair, and Hamlin Garland. Walk west from Springfield in 1912 ended in Wagon Mound, New Mexico. "General William Booth Enters into Heaven" published as lead poem in *Poetry* in January 1913; strong public response led to first trade book, *General William Booth Enters into Heaven* (1913). Began, at first through letters, courtship of Sara Teasdale, one of a series of infatuations habitual with Lindsay, sometimes involving women he barely knew (such as the movie actress Mae Marsh); saw Teasdale regularly in New York in 1914 and proposed marriage. Published poetry collection *The Congo* (1914) and *The Art of the Moving Picture* (1915), pioneering study of film. Became well-known for public readings that encouraged audience participation. Published *The Chinese Nightingale* (1917), *The Golden Whales of California and Other Rhymes in the American Language* (1920), *The Golden Book of Springfield* (1920), and *Collected Poems* (1923). Reading tours became increasingly exhausting, and Lindsay suffered mental and physical collapse in January 1923; sent to the Mayo Clinic for treatment, and was diagnosed with epilepsy. Taught at a women's college in Mississippi for two years. Moved to Spokane, Washington, where he met Elizabeth Conner; they were married in 1925. Later books, such as *Going-to-the-Sun* (1923) and *Going-to-the-Stars* (1926), were less popular than his earlier work. Published *Johnny Appleseed* (1928), poetry written for children. Suffered financial hardships; returned to Springfield in 1929, with wife, daughter, and infant son. Final walking tour cut short due to severe physical and mental strain. Committed suicide by swallowing lysol.

Haniel Long (March 9, 1888–October 17, 1956) b. Haniel Clark Long in Rangoon, Burma, where his father was a Methodist missionary. Returned with parents to the United States in 1891, settling in Pittsburgh. Enrolled at Exeter Academy in 1903. Attended Harvard 1907–10; studied with William James and George Santayana; formed friendship with Witter Bynner. Worked as a reporter for New York *Globe and Commercial Advertiser* (1909–10). Joined English faculty of Carnegie Technology School in Pittsburgh. Married Alice Knoblauch in 1912; son Tony born 1914. Published *Poems* (1920) and *Notes for a New Mythology* (1926). Settled permanently in Santa Fe in 1929. In 1933, founded Writer's Editions, Inc., which published poetry collection *Atlantides* that same year, and experimental prose work *Pittsburgh Memoranda* in 1935; later books included *Interlinear to Cabeza de Vaca* (1936), *Walt Whitman and the Springs of Courage* (1938), *Malinche (Doña Marina)* (1939), *Piñon Country* (1941), *French Soldier* (1942), *Children, Students, and a Few Adults* (1942), *The Grist Mill* (1945), and *A Letter to St. Augustine after Rereading His Confessions* (1950). Died following heart surgery, three days after his wife's death.

H. P. Lovecraft (August 20, 1890–March 10, 1937) b. Howard Phillips Lovecraft in Providence, Rhode Island. Father was committed to an asylum in 1893 and died five years later. Began reading Poe at age eight; wrote story "The Beast in the Cave" at 15. Attended public school in Providence; failed to graduate after nervous breakdown. Began writing astronomy column for *Pawtuxet Valley Gleaner* in 1906. Lived with mother until her death in 1921. Contributed to small magazines and journals; elected editor of United Amateur Press Association in 1920. Wrote many horror and fantasy stories and novellas, including "The Colour Out of Space," "The Dunwich Horror," "The Shadow Out of Time," and "At the Mountains of Madness"; "The Rats in the Walls" was the first of these to appear in *Weird Tales*, to which he became a frequent contributor. Corresponded extensively with other writers in the field, including August Derleth, Clark Ashton Smith, and Frank Belknap Long. Married Sonia Greene, a milliner, in 1924; they settled in Brooklyn. Rejected offer to become editor of *Weird Tales*. After Sonia left to work in the Midwest, moved back to Providence in 1926 to live with an aunt. Wrote "The Call of Cthulhu," first of cycle of related stories concerning extraterrestrial beings. Published study *Supernatural Horror in Literature* (1927) and novels *The Dream Quest of Unknown Kadath* (1927) and *The Case of Charles Dexter Ward* (1928). Divorced in 1929. Stories collected in *The Shadow Over Innsmouth* (1936); many other collections published posthumously. Many of his poems appeared originally in *Weird Tales*. *Collected Poems*, edited by August Derleth, was published in 1963.

Amy Lowell (February 9, 1874–May 12, 1925) b. Amy Lawrence Lowell in Brookline, Massachusetts. Siblings included astronomer Percival Lowell and Harvard University president Abbot Lawrence Lowell. Grew up on Sevenels, father's ten-acre estate. Educated at home; wrote stories with mother and sister Elizabeth, privately printed as *Dream Drops or Stories from Fairy Land by a Dreamer* (1887). Spent six months in Europe in 1896; traveled up the Nile in 1897. Purchased Sevenels after her father's death in 1900. Published first book, *A Dome of Many-Coloured Glass* (1912). Traveled to England in 1913 and again in 1914; met H.D., Ford Madox Ford, Ezra Pound, and D. H. Lawrence. Contributed to anthology *Des Imagistes* (1914); split with Pound and Ford over definition of Imagism. With support of John Gould Fletcher, H.D., and Richard Aldington, edited annual anthology *Some Imagist Poets* (1915–17). Later poetry collections included *Sword Blades and Poppy Seed* (1914), *Men, Women and Ghosts* (1916), *Can Grande's Castle* (1918), *Pictures of a Floating World* (1919), and *Legends* (1921). Published two critical works, *Six French Poets* (1915) and *Tendencies in Modern American Poetry* (1917). Collaborated with Florence Ayscough on volume of Chinese translations, *Fir-Flower Tablets* (1921). Published *John Keats* (1925), a biography. Died of a massive stroke. Ada Dwyer Russell, her companion from 1909 to 1925, oversaw posthumous publication of *What's O'Clock*, which won the Pulitzer Prize in 1926; other posthumous volumes were *East Wind* (1926) and *Ballads for Sale* (1927).

Mina Loy (December 27, 1882–September 25, 1966) b. Mina Gertrude Löwy in London, England. Studied painting with Angelo Jank at Künstlerinnenverein in Munich. Returned to London in 1901; exhibited her work in student shows. Moved to Paris in 1903, changed her last name to Loy, and married Stephen Haweis, a fellow art student. Attended salon of Gertrude Stein's brother Leo; met Guillaume Apollinaire and Pablo Picasso. Daughter Oda, born 1904, died on her first birthday. Moved to Florence in 1906. Daughter Joella born in 1907, son Giles in 1909. Became a Christian Scientist in 1909, after Joella became ill with polio. Closely involved in Italian Futurist literary circles; had affairs with writers F. T. Marinetti and Giovanni Papini. Separated from Haweis in 1913 (divorced 1917). Poems published in magazines *Camera Work, Trend, Others,* and *Rogue,* 1914–15. Worked as a nurse in surgical hospital during World War I. Sailed for New York in October 1916, leaving her children with a nurse. Welcomed into New York literary circles, especially Alfred Stieglitz's 291 Gallery and Alfred Kreymborg's *Others* group. Starred with William Carlos Williams in Kreymborg's play *Lima Beans,* staged at the Provincetown Playhouse. With Marcel Duchamp, published short-lived Dadaist journal, *The Blind Man.* Worked as fashion model; designed lampshades and dresses. Kreymborg devoted the April 1917 *Others* to Loy's long poem "Songs to Joannes." Married Arthur Cravan (born Fabian Avenarius Lloyd), Dadaist poet and prizefighter, in 1918 in Mexico City. Planned to travel by commercial ship to Valparaiso, with Cravan (who had visa problems) traveling the same route in a small private craft; on a trial voyage of his boat, he disappeared and was never seen again. Loy went to Buenos Aires, where their child, Jemima Fabienne (Fabi), was born in April 1919. Returned to Florence, but left in 1920 looking for news of Cravan in New York. Formed close friendships with Djuna Barnes and Robert McAlmon. Worked on long autobiographical poem "Anglo-Mongrels and the Rose," which appeared piecemeal in magazines but was not collected in book form during her lifetime. Reunited with daughters in Florence in 1921, after Giles was taken to his home in the Bahamas by Stephen Haweis earlier that year; Giles died in 1923. Lived in Paris with Joella and Fabi, 1923–36. Poems appeared frequently in *The Little Review* and *The Dial*. Published first book, *Lunar Baedeker* (1923), with McAlmon's Contact Editions. In 1925 her paper cutouts and painted flower arrangements appeared in New York in Madison Avenue shows and fashion windows. Wrote unpublished novel *Insel* in the early 1930's; worked as artists' agent and dealer, 1931–36, representing such painters as Salvador Dali, Max Ernst, and René Magritte on behalf of Julien Levy Gallery of New York. Returned to New York in 1936. Formed close friendship with Joseph Cornell; devoted herself to painting and sculpture. Became American citizen in 1946; moved to the Bowery in New York City in 1949. Moved in 1953 to Aspen, where her daughters were living. Her selected poems were published as *Lunar Baedeker & Time-Tables* by Jonathan Williams' Jargon Society Press in 1958, and her sculptures were exhibited at Bodley Gallery in New York in 1959. Died in Aspen.

Claude McKay (September 15, 1889–May 22, 1948) b. Festus Claudius McKay near Clarendon Hills, Jamaica, youngest of 11 children; from age six, his older brother assumed guardianship. Apprenticed to a cabinet maker; joined Jamaican Constabulary in 1909. Met English linguist Edward Jekyll, who fostered interest in writing poetry. Published two poetry collections, *Songs of Jamaica* and *Constab Ballads*, in 1912, both written in Jamaican dialect. Won prize which he used to enroll at Tuskegee Institute in Alabama. Moved to New York City in 1914. Lived in Harlem, working at odd jobs; married briefly to Eulalie Imelda Edwards. Under pseudonym Eli Edwards, published poems in *Seven Arts* in 1917. Poem "If We Must Die," written in response to American race riots, appeared in Max Eastman's *The Liberator* in 1919. Traveled to London in 1920, where he worked on radical *Workers' Dreadnought* and published poetry collection *Spring in New Hampshire*. Became an editor of *The Liberator*. *Harlem Shadows* published in 1922. Traveled to Moscow in 1922 and 1923; met Trotsky. Remained in Europe until 1934, settling in Marseilles. Published novels *Home to Harlem* (1928), *Banjo* (1929), and *Banana Bottom* (1933), and story collection *Gingertown* (1932). After return to America, married Ellen Tarry in 1938; during final years lived in Chicago, where he worked for the National Catholic Youth Organization.

Archibald MacLeish (May 7, 1892–April 20, 1982) b. Glencoe, Illinois. Attended Hotchkiss School in Lakeville, Connecticut. Enrolled at Yale in 1911;

wrote for *Yale Literary Magazine*. Graduated Phi Beta Kappa in 1915; entered Harvard Law School. Married Ada Hitchcock in 1916. Education interrupted while he served in World War I; advanced to the rank of captain. Published first poetry collection, *Tower of Ivory*, in 1917. Graduated at top of law school class in 1919; worked for the next two years as trial lawyer in Boston firm of Choate, Hall, and Stewart. Gave up legal career in 1923 and moved to France with his family to devote himself to writing. Published *The Happy Marriage* (1924), *The Pot of Earth* (1925), verse play *Nobodaddy* (1926), *Streets in the Moon* (1928), and *The Hamlet of A. MacLeish* (1928). Returned to America in 1928 and settled at Uphill Farm in Conway, Massachusetts. Published *New Found Land* (1930). Long poem about the conquest of Mexico, *Conquistador* (1932), won Pulitzer Prize. Worked as editor at *Fortune*, 1928–38. Published poetry collections *Frescoes for Mr. Rockefeller's City* (1933), *Public Speech* (1936), *America Was Promises* (1939), and *Colloquy for the States* (1943), and verse plays collected in *Panic* (1935), *The Fall of the City* (1937), and *Air Raid* (1938). Appointed Librarian of the Congress, 1939–44. Served as director of U.S. Office of Facts and Figures (1941–42), Assistant Director of the U.S. Office of War Information (1942–43), and Assistant Secretary of State (1944–45). Was Boylston Professor of Rhetoric and Poetry at Harvard, 1949–62. Instrumental in procuring release of Ezra Pound from St. Elizabeth's mental hospital. In addition to a number of collections of essays and speeches, published poetry collections *Actfive* (1948) and *Songs for Eve* (1954); *Collected Poems, 1917–1952* (1952) won Pulitzer Prize. He wrote a further series of verse plays, of which *J.B.* (1958) won his third Pulitzer Prize and was produced successfully on Broadway. Final collection *The Wild Old Wicked Man* was published in 1968.

Don Marquis (July 29, 1878–December 29, 1937) b. Donald Robert Perry Marquis in Walnut, Illinois. Wrote for local newspapers in his youth, and moved in 1900 to Washington, D.C., where he worked for the *Washington Times*; later wrote for the *Atlanta Journal*, 1902–9. Named associate editor at Joel Chandler Harris's *Uncle Remus's Home Magazine*, where he wrote book reviews and satirical pieces. Married Reina Melcher in 1909 and moved with her to New York. Novel *Danny's Own Story* published in 1912. Hired to write column "The Sun Dial" for New York *Sun*. Published poetry collection *Dreams and Dust* (1915), novel *The Cruise of the Jasper B.* (1916), and *Hermione and Her Little Group of Serious Thinkers* (1916) and *The Old Soak* (1921), featuring characters from his column. Wife died in 1923; remarried 1926. Light verse collected in *Noah an' Jonah an' Cap'n John Smith* (1921), *Sonnets to a Red-Haired Lady (by a Gentleman with a Blue Beard) and Famous Love Affairs* (1922), and *Love Sonnets of a Cave Man* (1928). His most successful book, *archy and mehitabel* (1927), was followed by the sequels *archys life of mehitabel* (1933) and *archy does his part* (1935). His many other books included *The Revolt of the Oyster* (1922), *The Almost Perfect State* (1927), *Chapters for the Orthodox* (1934), and the poetry collections *Poems and Portraits* (1922) and *The Awakening* (1924).

Edgar Lee Masters (August 23, 1868–March 5, 1950) b. Garnett, Kansas. Grew up in Illinois towns of Petersburg and Lewistown, near the Spoon River. Admitted to Illinois bar in 1891, and worked in father's firm; moved to Chicago. Married Helen Jenkins in 1898. Published *A Book of Verses* (1898) and *The Blood of the Prophets* (1905). Law partner of Clarence Darrow, 1903–11. Published *Songs and Sonnets* (1910) under pseudonym Webster Ford. Met Theodore Dreiser and William Reedy, editor of *Reedy's Mirror*. In May 1914, influenced by reading of ancient Greek epigrams, began writing free verse portraits of small-town characters; these were published under a pseudonym in *Reedy's Mirror*, and subsequently collected in book form under his own name as *Spoon River Anthology* (1915), which became a bestseller. Gradually abandoned legal career; published further poetry collections *Songs and Satires* (1916), *The Great Valley* (1916), *Toward the Gulf* (1918), *Starved Rock* (1919), *Domesday Book* (1920), and *The Open Sea* (1921); none of his later work enjoyed the critical or popular success of *Spoon River Anthology*. After divorce in 1923, moved to New York City. Published *The New Spoon River* in 1924 and made a cross-country speaking tour. Published *Selected Poems* (1925). Married Ellen Coyne in 1926; settled at Chelsea Hotel in New York in 1930. Subsequent collections of poetry included *The Fate of the Jury* (1929), *Lichee Nuts* (1930), *The Serpent in the Wilderness* (1933), *Invisible Landscapes* (1935), *Poems of People* (1936), *The Golden Fleece of California* (1936), *The Tide of Time* (1937), and *More People* (1939); also published novels, an autobiography, a collection of plays, and biographies of Abraham Lincoln, Vachel Lindsay, Walt Whitman, and Mark Twain. Received award from National Institute and American Academy of Arts and Letters (1942), Shelley Memorial Award (1944), and Academy of American Poets Fellowship (1946). Died in a Pennsylvania nursing home.

Edna St. Vincent Millay (February 22, 1892–October 19, 1950) b. Rockland, Maine. Parents divorced in 1900; mother took children to Camden, Maine, and worked as a nurse to support family. Submitted "Renascence," a long poem, to 1912 poetry contest of *The Lyric Year*; it came in fourth but was praised by Witter Bynner and Arthur Davison Ficke, establishing Millay's reputation. Attended Vassar, 1914–17. First poetry collection *Renascence* published 1917. Moved to Greenwich Village. Wrote and directed verse play *Aria da Capo* for Provincetown Players in 1919. Formed close friendship with Edmund Wilson. Published collections *A Few Figs from Thistles* (1920) and *Second April* (1921). Traveled in Europe, 1921–23. *The Ballad of the Harp Weaver* (1922) won Pulitzer Prize. Married Eugene Boissevain in New York in 1923. Bought farm ("Steepletop") in Austerlitz, New York. Awarded honorary doctorate from Tufts in 1925. Wrote libretto for Deems Taylor's opera *The King's Henchman* (1927). Later poetry collections included *The Buck in the Snow* (1928), *Fatal Interview* (1931), *Wine From These Grapes* (1934), *Conversation at Midnight* (1937), *Huntsman, What Quarry?* (1939), *Make Bright the Arrows* (1940), *Collected Sonnets* (1941), and *The Murder of Lidice* (1942). Elected to National Institute of Arts and Letters in 1929. With George Dillon, translated

Baudelaire's *Flowers of Evil* (1936). Received Gold Medal of Poetry Society of America in 1943. Her husband died in 1949. *Collected Poems* published posthumously in 1956.

Harriet Monroe (December 23, 1860–September 26, 1936) b. Chicago, Illinois. Graduated from Convent of the Visitation in Georgetown, D.C., in 1879. Spent summer of 1887 in New York City with mother and sister; met Robert Louis Stevenson, with whom she had previously corresponded. Lived in New York City with sister, 1888–89; frequently attended Sunday evening gatherings at home of Edmund Clarence Stedman, where she met William Dean Howells, Richard Watson Gilder, Elizabeth and Richard Henry Stoddard, and other literary figures; wrote drama criticism for the *Herald Tribune*. Returned to Chicago and in 1890 began writing art criticism for *Chicago Tribune*. In 1890 and 1897 toured Europe; met Henry James, Aubrey Beardsley, James McNeill Whistler, Thomas Hardy, and Alice Meynell; in Chicago, formed friendships with Albert Pinkham Ryder and Henry Blake Fuller. Published *Valeria and Other Poems* (1892). Received commission to write poem for World's Columbian Exposition in Chicago; poem recited by five thousand voices at dedication ceremony and published as *The Columbian Ode* (1893). In 1896 published biography of brother-in-law John Wellborn Root, architect who had been one of the chief designers of the Columbian Exposition. *The Passing Show: Five Modern Plays in Verse* appeared in 1903. Wrote long poem *The Dance of the Seasons* (1911). Raised money to launch *Poetry: A Magazine of Verse*; first issue published September 1912. Contributors during Monroe's editorship included Ezra Pound (who served initially as foreign editor), Wallace Stevens, William Butler Yeats, William Carlos Williams, Robert Frost, T. S. Eliot, H.D., Marianne Moore, Hart Crane, Vachel Lindsay, Edgar Lee Masters, Amy Lowell, Carl Sandburg, Robinson Jeffers, Langston Hughes, Louis Zukofsky, Basil Bunting, Kenneth Rexroth, W. H. Auden, and many others. Published poetry collections *You and I* (1914), *The Difference* (1924), and *Chosen Poems* (1935), and essay collection *Poets and Their Art* (1926); with Alice Corbin edited anthology *The New Poetry* (1917). Died of cerebral hemorrhage in Arequipa, Peru, while returning from literary conference in Buenos Aires. Autobiography published posthumously as *A Poet's Life: Seventy Years in a Changing World* (1938).

Marianne Moore (November 15, 1887–February 5, 1972) b. Marianne Craig Moore in Kirkwood, Missouri. Father suffered a nervous breakdown and died when Moore was seven; with mother and brother, lived with grandfather in Kirkwood, and subsequently in Carlisle, Pennsylvania. Enrolled in 1896 at Metzger Institute for Girls, where mother taught English. Studied at Bryn Mawr, majoring in biology and histology; published first poems in college literary magazine in 1907. Received A.B. degree in 1909; studied business at Carlisle Commercial College 1909–10. Taught secretarial skills, law, commercial English, and coached boys' sports teams at the United States Industrial Indian School in Carlisle. Contributed poems to Bryn Mawr alumnae magazine; from 1915 published poems in *The Egoist*, *Others*, *Poetry*, and other magazines. Moved with mother to Greenwich Village in 1918. First book, *Poems* (1921), was compiled without her knowledge by H.D. and Bryher and published in England. *Observations* (1924) received $2,000 award from Dial Press. Worked for the Hudson Park Branch of the New York Public Library; in 1925 became editor of *The Dial*. Moved to Brooklyn with mother in 1929, remaining there for nearly 40 years. With encouragement of T. S. Eliot, assembled *Selected Poems* (1935). Published *The Pangolin and Other Verse* (1936), *What Are Years* (1941), and *Nevertheless* (1944). Mother died in 1947. Spent nine years on translation of *The Fables of La Fontaine* (1954). *Collected Poems* (1951) won National Book Award, Pulitzer Prize, and Bollingen Prize. *Predilections* (1955) collected essays and reviews. Moved back to Greenwich Village in 1966.

John G. Neihardt (January 8, 1881–November 4, 1973) b. John Greenleaf Neihardt in Sharpsburg, Illinois (changed middle name to Gneisenau, after Prussian hero of Napoleonic wars). After father deserted the family, moved with mother to Wayne, Nebraska. While suffering from a high fever in 1892, underwent hallucinatory experience in which a voice told him to write poetry. Attended Nebraska Normal School, 1893–97. In 1898 wrote and at his own expense published *The Divine Enchantment* (1898), long poem influenced by Hindu theology; when no copies were sold, he bought back the books and burned them. In 1900 moved in with his mother near an Omaha Indian reservation in Bancroft, Nebraska. Over the next 15 years, wrote articles, book reviews, short stories, novels, drama, and five volumes of poetry, including *The Lonesome Trail* (1907), *A Bundle of Myrrh* (1909), and *Man-Song* (1910). Married Mona Martinsen, a sculptor, in 1908. In 1913, began lengthy poetic sequence *A Cycle of the West*. Published the cycle's first two books, *The Song of Hugh Glass* and *The Song of Three Friends* in 1915; named Poet Laureate of Nebraska and the Prairies by Nebraska state legislature in 1921. Published *The Song of the Indian Wars* (1925); became literary editor of the *St. Louis Post-Dispatch* in 1926. Met Lakota Sioux shaman Black Elk at Pine Ridge Reservation in South Dakota in 1930, and collaborated with him on religious memoir *Black Elk Speaks* (1932). *The Song of the Messiah* (1935) and *The Song of Jed Smith* (1941) completed the epic cycle, which was collected in one volume in 1949. Named poet in residence and lecturer at the University of Missouri at Concordia, where he remained until 1961.

Dorothy Parker (August 22, 1893–June 7, 1967) b. Dorothy Rothschild in West End, New Jersey. Mother died soon after she was born; attended a New York City convent school and Miss Dana's, finishing school in Morristown, New Jersey. Worked at *Vogue*, 1913–16. Married Wall Street broker Edwin Pond Parker II in 1917; he served in the military for two years just after their marriage. Staff writer for *Vanity Fair*, 1916–20; served briefly as magazine's chief drama critic until she was fired for writing scathing reviews of plays produced by *Vanity Fair* patrons. Subsequently wrote extensively for *The New*

Yorker, contributing fiction, poetry, drama criticism, and book reviews. Established herself as member of the Round Table at the Algonquin Hotel, an informal group of writers and artists including Robert Benchley, George S. Kaufman, and James Thurber; witticisms attributed to her became famous. Divorced in 1928. Married actor Alan Campbell in 1933; collaborated on film scripts including *A Star Is Born* (1937), *Saboteur* (1942), and *Smash-Up* (1947), and lived in Hollywood until Campbell's death in 1963. Poetry collected in *Enough Rope* (1926), *Sunset Gun* (1928), *Death and Taxes* (1931), and *Not So Deep as a Well* (1936); short fiction in *Laments for the Living* (1930), *After Such Pleasure* (1933), and *Here Lies* (1939). Wrote play *Ladies of the Corridor* (1953) with Arnaud d'Usseau. Died in New York City. Left most of her estate to Martin Luther King Jr.

Charlie Patton (1887–April 28, 1934) b. on Dockery Plantation in Ruleville, Mississippi. Made first recording in 1929; recorded 21 sides for Paramount, 1929–30. Some of his records were released under the pseudonym "The Masked Marvel." Settled in Holly Ridge, Mississippi. Recorded for Vocalion in New York in 1934 shortly before his death. His records included "Pony Blues," "Mississippi Boweavil Blues," "Screamin' and Hollerin' the Blues," "High Sheriff Blues," "Moon Going Down," "High Water Everywhere," "Revenue Man Blues," and "Hang It on the Wall."

Edwin Ford Piper (February 8, 1871–May 17, 1939) b. Auburn, Nebraska. Father raised cattle. Graduated from University of Nebraska in 1897, and received M.A. in 1900; studied at Harvard, 1903–4. Married Janet Pressley in 1927. Taught English at University of Nebraska and later at Iowa State University; conducted creative writing workshops for many years. Assembled extensive collection of American folk songs and ballads. His books included *Barbed Wire and Other Poems* (1917), *Barbed Wire and Wayfarers* (1923), *Paintrock Road* (1927), and *Canterbury Pilgrims* (1935).

Cole Porter (June 9, 1891–October 15, 1964) b. Peru, Indiana. Began composing songs at age ten. Valedictorian of Worcester Academy in Massachusetts. Attended Yale, where he wrote many of the school's football songs, several musical comedies, and led glee club. After graduation in 1913, toured Europe. Entered Harvard Law School; transferred to Harvard School of Music in 1914. Several of his songs, for which he wrote both music and lyrics, were used in Broadway musicals in 1915; Broadway show, *See America First*, opened the following year. Sailed for France in 1917 to work for Duryea Relief Organization; enlisted in French Foreign Legion. Married Linda Lee Thomas in 1919; they moved into her house in Paris, where Porter studied music theory at the Schola Cantorum. Contributed songs to numerous musicals, and traveled frequently in Europe. Broadway play *Paris* (1928), followed by *The New Yorkers* (1930), *Gay Divorce* (1932), *Anything Goes* (1934), *Jubilee* (1935), *Red, Hot and Blue* (1936), *Leave It to Me* (1938), and *Du Barry Was a Lady* (1939). Stayed in Hollywood, 1935–36, writing score for film *Born* *to Dance*. Both legs crushed in 1937 riding accident; underwent over 30 operations over next two decades to prevent amputation. Later musicals, many highly successful, included *Panama Hattie* (1940), *Let's Face It* (1941), *Something for the Boys* (1943), *Mexican Hayride* (1944), *Kiss Me, Kate* (1948), and *Can Can* (1953). Linda Porter died in 1954. Wrote scores for the films *High Society* (1956) and *Les Girls* (1957). Right leg amputated in 1958; frequently hospitalized during final years. His many songs included "Let's Do It" (1928), "Let's Misbehave" (1927), "What Is This Thing Called Love?" (1929), "Love for Sale" (1930), "Just One of Those Things" (1930), "Night and Day" (1932), "I Get a Kick Out of You" (1934), "You're the Top" (1934), "Anything Goes" (1934), "Begin the Beguine" (1935), "I've Got You Under My Skin" (1936), "In the Still of the Night" (1937), "Ev'ry Time We Say Goodbye" (1944), "So in Love" (1948), "Always True to You in My Fashion" (1949), "From This Moment On" (1950), "I Love Paris" (1953), and "All of You" (1954).

Ezra Pound (October 30, 1885–November 1, 1972) b. Ezra Loomis Pound in Hailey, Idaho. Family moved in 1889 to Philadelphia, where father worked at U.S. Mint. Entered University of Pennsylvania in 1901; formed lifelong friendship with medical student William Carlos Williams. Transferred to Hamilton College, where he studied five languages and completed Ph.B. in 1905; earned M.A. in Romance languages from University of Pennsylvania. Traveled to Spain on fellowship in summer of 1906 to study plays of Lope de Vega. Taught Romance languages at Wabash College in Crawfordsville, Indiana, in 1907; fired for allowing stranded actress to spend night in his room. Was briefly engaged to Hilda Doolittle (H.D.). Spent three months in Venice before moving to London. First poetry collection, *A Lume Spento* (1908), published at his own expense, followed by *A Quinzaine for This Yule* (1908), *Personae* (1909), and *Exultations* (1909). Through novelist Olivia Shakespear and poet W. B. Yeats, introduced to London literary circles; associated with younger poets including T. E. Hulme and F. S. Flint; formed close friendship with Ford Madox Ford. Published poetry collections *Provença* (1910), *Canzoni* (1911), and *Ripostes* (1912), and literary study *The Spirit of Romance* (1910). Coined poetic label "Les Imagistes," and achieved wide recognition as a founder of the Imagist school, although he soon disavowed the term. Named foreign editor of Harriet Monroe's *Poetry*; championed work of Williams, H.D., and Robert Frost. Met James Joyce, whose work he continued to promote, and for whom he helped arrange financial assistance. Became friend of sculptor Henri Gaudier-Brzeska. Formed friendship with painter and novelist Wyndham Lewis and coined term "Vorticism" to describe art movement with which he was associated; with Lewis, started *BLAST: A Review of the Great English Vortex*. Married Dorothy Shakespear (daughter of Olivia Shakespear) in April 1914. In September 1914, met T. S. Eliot and arranged publication of "The Love Song of J. Alfred Prufrock" in *Poetry*. Began lifelong study of Confucius. *Cathay*, adaptation of classical Chinese poetry, published 1915. As Ernest Fenollosa's literary executor, adapted Fenollosa's versions of Japanese No plays in the volumes *Certain Noble Plays of Japan* (1916) and *'Noh' or Accomplishment* (1916). Wrote *Gaudier-Brzeska: A Memoir* (1916) after his friend was killed in the war. In *Poetry* in 1916 published "Three Cantos," the first published sections of the long "poem including history" he had conceived as early as 1904. Became interested in the Social Credit theories of Major C. H. Douglas. Published prose collections *Pavannes and Divisions* (1918) and *Instigations* (1920); poetic sequence *Hugh Selwyn Mauberley* (1920); and poetry collection *Umbra* (1920). Left England in January 1921 and moved to France for three years. Collected subscriptions for publication of Joyce's *Ulysses*. Made extensive editorial changes in the manuscript of Eliot's *The Waste Land* (1922). Became lover of American violinist Olga Rudge. Published *Indiscretions* (1923), a family history, and *Antheil and the Treatise on Harmony* (1924). Moved to Italy in 1924, residing mostly in Rapallo. In 1925 Olga Rudge gave birth to Pound's daughter, Mary; the following year Dorothy Shakespear gave birth to a son, Omar. Collected poems published as *Personae* in 1926. Published *A Draft of XVI Cantos* (1925), *A Draft of the Cantos 17–27* (1928), *A Draft of XXX Cantos* (1930); *Ta Hio* (1928), a translation of Confucius; and four issues of *The Exile*. From 1930, spent summers in Venice with Rudge while Dorothy stayed in England. Had audience with Benito Mussolini in January 1933. Published *Eleven New Cantos: XXXI–XLI* (1934) and *The Fifth Decad of Cantos* (1937) as well as prose works *How to Read* (1931), *ABC of Economics* (1933), *ABC of Reading* (1934), *Jefferson and/or Mussolini* (1935), and *Guide to Kulchur* (1938). On a visit to United States in 1939, attempted to lobby officials in Washington on political and economic policy; had interviews with senators Burton Wheeler and William Borah; visited with E. E. Cummings, Louis Zukofsky, and Williams. Published *Cantos LII–LXXI* (1940). After Italy declared war on Britain and France in 1940, broadcast over Rome Radio pro-Fascist speeches marked by anti-Semitic invective and vilification of Roosevelt and other allied leaders; indicted in absentia for treason by federal grand jury. On May 3, 1945, Pound was captured by Italian partisans and taken to Genoa for interrogation by FBI agents; on May 24 he was confined in a military stockade, where he was held for nearly five months. Flown to Washington on November 18 and reindicted for treason. After a hearing in February 1946, a jury found him to be of unsound mind and he was committed to St. Elizabeth's mental hospital in Washington until he became fit to stand trial. *The Pisan Cantos* (1948), written during his confinement in Italy, won 1949 Bollingen Prize. During his hospitalization, Pound's visitors included Eliot, Marianne Moore, Cummings, Zukofsky, Charles Olson, Langston Hughes, H. L. Mencken, Elizabeth Bishop, and Archibald MacLeish. Published two further volumes of Chinese translations, *The Unwobbling Pivot & The Great Digest* (1947) and *The Classic Anthology as Defined by Confucius* (1954), an additional volume of cantos, *Section: Rock-Drill de los cantares* (1955), and a translation of Sophocles, *Women of Trachis* (1956). In 1957, MacLeish sent a letter, co-signed by Eliot, Ernest Hemingway, and Frost, to the attorney general, requesting that charges against Pound be dropped. In April 1958, the treason indictment was dismissed, and he returned to Italy. Published two final volumes of cantos, *Thrones de los cantares* (1959) and *Drafts and Fragments of Cantos CX–CXVII* (1969). Made last trip to the United States in 1969; died in Venice.

Ma Rainey (April 26, 1886–December 22, 1939) b. Gertrude Melissa Nix Pridgett in Columbus, Georgia. Her parents were entertainers; toured tent shows with them. Married William Rainey in 1904; they toured as "Rainey and Rainey, the Assassinators of the Blues." After separating from husband, toured with the Rabbit Foot Minstrels and other groups; formed her own group with backup band Georgia Jazz Band, featuring Thomas A. Dorsey on piano. Her first recording was released on Paramount in 1923, followed by nearly a hundred more over the next five years, including "See See Rider," "Slow Driving Moan," "Oh My Babe Blues," "Trust No Man," "Jealous Hearted Blues," "Sweet Rough Man," and "Slave to the Blues"; accompanists included Louis Armstrong, Coleman Hawkins, and Fletcher Henderson. Her career faded during the Depression, and she retired from performing in 1935. Settled in Columbus in her last years.

John Crowe Ransom (April 30, 1888–July 3, 1974) b. Pulaski, Tennessee. Father was a Methodist minister who preached in several towns in central Tennessee. Early education was at home; later enrolled at Bowen School near Vanderbilt University. Admitted to Vanderbilt at age 15 in 1903; studies interrupted for financial reasons; graduated at top of class in 1909. Taught at a private academy before going to Oxford as a Rhodes Scholar; took B.A. in 1913. Became an instructor at Vanderbilt; joined Nashville intellectual circle associated with Sidney Mttron Hirsch. Served for two years in field artillery during World War I. First poetry collection, *Poems About God*, appeared in 1919. After failed attempt to launch career as freelance journalist in New York, returned to Vanderbilt as assistant professor. Married Robb Reavill in 1920. Continued to meet with Nashville circle; participated in founding of *The Fugitive*, journal of poetry and criticism. Published two partly overlapping poetry collections, *Chills and Fever* and *Grace After Meat*, three months apart in 1924; a third collection, *Two Gentlemen in Bonds*, appeared in 1927. Published *God Without Thunder: An Unorthodox Defense of Orthodoxy* in 1930, and was one of "Twelve Southerners" who signed their names to *I'll Take My Stand*, a defense of agrarian values. Went to England on a Guggenheim Fellowship, 1931–32. Left Vanderbilt for Kenyon College in the late 1930's; was editor of *The Kenyon Review* for more than two decades. In later years devoted himself primarily to criticism and teaching; published heavily revised versions of earlier poetry. Received Bollingen Prize (1951), Academy of American Poets Fellowship (1962), and National Book Award for *Selected Poems* (1963).

John Reed (October 22, 1887–October 17, 1920) b. Portland, Oregon. Educated at Portland Academy (1898–1904), Morristown Academy (1904–6), and

Harvard University (1906–10), where he contributed to the *Lampoon* and was an editor of the *Monthly*. Moved in 1911 to New York City; worked at literary magazine *The American*. Published journalistic sketches and articles; became an editor of *The Masses*. Poetry collected in privately printed volumes *Sangar* (1912) and *The Day in Bohemia* (1913). Arrested for involvement in silk-workers' strike in Paterson, New Jersey. Traveled to Mexico in November 1913 to report for the *Metropolitan*; met Pancho Villa and was permitted to travel with a group of Villa's troops until their massacre by federal forces, from which he fled; covered Villa's assault on Torreón in March 1914. Articles on Mexico collected in *Insurgent Mexico* (1914). Reported coal-miners' strike in Ludlow, Colorado; interviewed Woodrow Wilson. Covered World War I for *Metropolitan*, reporting from Greece, Serbia, Romania, and Russia; articles collected in *The War in Eastern Europe* (1916). Spent summer of 1916 in Provincetown, involved in formation of theater group the Provincetown Players; married Louise Bryant the following November. Poetry collection *Tamburlaine* appeared in 1916. Traveled to Russia in 1917 and witnessed October revolution in Petrograd. Formed close associations with Lenin, Trotsky, Bukharin, and other Bolshevik leaders; worked as writer for Soviet Bureau of International Revolutionary Propaganda. Returned to New York to stand trial with *Masses* colleagues on charges of conspiracy to obstruct the draft; after two trials, charges were dismissed. Wrote *Ten Days That Shook the World* (1919), about experiences during October revolution. Active in New York Socialist Party; contributing editor of *Revolutionary Age*. Was a co-founder of Communist Labor Party and edited its journal, *Voice of Labor*. Along with other party leaders, was charged in absentia with anarchy in Illinois in January 1920. Traveled to Finland on a forged passport; was arrested and jailed for three months. Helped organize Second Congress of Communist International in Petrograd in July 1920. Contracted typhus and died in Moscow. Buried in Kremlin.

Lizette Woodworth Reese (January 9, 1856–December 17, 1935) b. Huntingdon (now Waverly), Maryland, a suburb of Baltimore. Father served as a Confederate soldier. After graduating Eastern High School she taught at various public and private schools in the Baltimore area; taught English at Western High School, 1901–21. Published first poem, "The Deserted House," in *The Southern Magazine* in 1874; first collection of verse, *A Branch of May*, appeared in 1887. Formed close friendship with poet and anthologist Edmund Clarence Stedman. Published *A Handful of Lavender* (1891), followed by *A Quiet Road* (1896), *A Wayside Lute* (1909), and *Spicewood* (1920). Sonnet "Tears," published in *Scribner's* in 1899, became widely known. Retired from teaching in 1921. Published verse collections *Wild Cherry* (1923), *Selected Poems* (1926), *Little Henrietta* (1927), *White April* (1930), *Pastures* (1933), and two volumes of prose memoirs, *A Victorian Village* (1920) and *The York Road* (1931). Narrative poem *The Old House in the Country* (1936) and unfinished novel *Worleys* (1936) appeared posthumously.

Lola Ridge (December 12, 1873–May 19, 1941) b. Rose Emily Ridge in Dublin, Ireland. At age 13, immigrated with her mother to New Zealand. Married briefly from 1895 to Peter Webster, manager of a gold mine. Studied painting in Sydney, Australia. Began writing poetry while studying with painter Julian Rossi Ashton. Moved to San Francisco and adopted first name Lola; published first poems in *Overland Monthly*. Moved to New York City, where she wrote advertising copy and sold fiction to popular magazines; published poetry in Emma Goldman's *Mother Earth*. Worked variously as factory worker, illustrator, and artist's model. Published *The Ghetto and Other Poems* in 1918. Married David Lawson in 1919. Active member of Alfred Kreymborg's group; became associate editor of *Others*. Briefly served as American editor of Harold Loeb's *Broom*; was a contributing editor to *New Masses* at its inception in 1926. Poetry collected in *Sun-Up* (1920) and *Red Flag* (1927). Active in protests against trial and execution of Sacco and Vanzetti; wrote *Firehead* (1929) in response to case. Traveled to the Middle East in 1931 and 1935–37 (as a Guggenheim fellow) to research a poem cycle that was never completed. Her last book, *Dance of Fire*, appeared in 1935.

Elizabeth Madox Roberts (October 30, 1881–March 13, 1941) b. Perryville, Kentucky. Attended private school in Springfield, where her family had moved in 1884; later boarded with relatives in Covington, Kentucky, while attending high school. Attended State College of Kentucky in 1900; withdrew after a year due to poor health and financial difficulties. In 1901 opened a private school in Springfield, where she taught until 1914. First volume of poetry, *In the Great Steep's Garden*, published 1915. Enrolled as freshman at University of Chicago in 1917. Published her work in *Poetry*. Earned Ph.D. in 1921; awarded Fiske Poetry Prize in 1922, and published second collection of poetry, *Under the Tree*. Enjoyed success with a series of novels including *The Time of Man* (1926), *My Heart and My Flesh* (1927), *The Great Meadow* (1930), and *Black Is My True Love's Hair* (1938). Her later poetry was collected in *Song in the Meadow* (1940).

Edwin Arlington Robinson (December 22, 1869–April 6, 1935) b. Head Tide, Maine. Raised in Gardiner, Maine. Studied at Harvard, 1891–93; published poems in *Harvard Advocate*. Worked in Boston and Gardiner for a number of years while devoting himself to poetry. Published *The Torrent and the Night Before* (1896) at his own expense, followed by *The Children of the Night* (1897). Worked in 1899 as confidential clerk to Harvard president Charles W. Eliot before moving to New York City. Held variety of jobs, including work as time checker for construction of IRT subway, 1903–4; began to drink heavily. Encouraged by Edmund Clarence Stedman, who anthologized a number of his poems; renewed friendship with Harvard acquaintance William Vaughn Moody. Published *Captain Craig* (1902). Continued to live in obscurity until President Theodore Roosevelt, an admirer of his poetry, offered him job in New York custom house, where he worked 1905-9. *The Town Down the River* (1910), dedicated to Roosevelt, and *The Man Against the Sky* (1916) won him wider attention ; published plays *Van Zorn* (1914) and *The Porcupine* (1915). From 1911 spent summers at MacDowell Colony in Peterborough, New Hampshire; assisted, beginning in 1916, by financial stipend donated anonymously by friends. *Merlin* (1917) was first of triptych of book-length Arthurian poems, followed by *Lancelot* (1920) and *Tristram* (1927). Won three Pulitzer Prizes, for *Collected Poems* (1921), *The Man Who Died Twice* (1924), and *Tristram*, which was a popular success. Other late books of poetry included *The Three Taverns* (1920), *Avon's Harvest* (1921), *Roman Bartholow* (1923), *Dionysus in Doubt* (1925), *Cavender's House* (1929), *The Glory of the Nightingales* (1930), *Matthias at the Door* (1931), *Talifer* (1933), *Amaranth* (1934), and *King Jasper* (1935).

Carl Sandburg (January 6, 1878–July 22, 1967) b. Carl August Sandburg in Galesburg, Illinois, son of Swedish immigrants. Left school at age 13; at 18, used father's railroad pass to visit Chicago. Jumped trains from Illinois to Colorado and back, working as farm hand, dishwasher, and at other odd jobs. Served in the Spanish-American War in Puerto Rico in 1898. Enrolled at Lombard College in Illinois. Encouraged to write by Philip Green Wright, Lombard professor who published Sandburg's first three books of poetry on his private press. Worked for Wisconsin's Social Democratic Party, 1907–12. Served as secretary to Milwaukee's Socialist mayor Emil Seidel; wrote for local newspaper, the *Social Democratic Herald*. Married Paula Steichen, an active Socialist and sister of photographer Edward Steichen, in 1908; they had two daughters. Moved to Chicago in 1912; wrote for Socialist newspaper the *Chicago Evening World*. Published six poems in *Poetry* in 1914. Met other Chicago writers including Theodore Dreiser and Edgar Lee Masters. Became well known for poetry collections *Chicago Poems* (1916) and *Cornhuskers* (1918). Served as Eastern European correspondent for the Newspaper Enterprise Association; later covered labor developments for Chicago *Daily News*. Lectured frequently and gave public performances of folk songs. Published poetry collections *Smoke and Steel* (1920) and *Slabs of the Sunburnt West* (1922), children's books *Rootabaga Stories* (1922) and *Rootabaga Pigeons* (1923), and journalistic report *The Chicago Race Riots* (1919). Worked for 17 years on multi-volume biography of Abraham Lincoln, published as *Abraham Lincoln: The Prairie Years* (1926) and *Abraham Lincoln: The War Years* (1939), which won Pulitzer Prize. Published poetry collections *Good Morning, America* (1928) and *The People, Yes* (1936). Edited *The American Song Bag*, anthology of folk songs; later books included *Home Front Memo* (1943) and novel *Remembrance Rock* (1948). Moved in 1945 to North Carolina. *Complete Poems* (1950) won Pulitzer Prize; memoir *Always the Young Strangers* appeared in 1953. Traveled widely throughout the 1950's and 1960's, lecturing, appearing on television, collaborating with Edward Steichen on photographic exhibit *The Family of Man*. Final volume of poetry, *Honey and Salt*, published 1963.

Alan Seeger (June 22, 1888–July 4, 1916) b. New York City. Moved with family to Mexico in 1900. Sent to Hackley School in 1902; in 1906 entered Harvard. Became an editor of the *Harvard Monthly*, where he published many poems. Went to live in Paris in 1912. After war broke out in 1914, enlisted in French Foreign Legion. Mortally wounded on July 4, 1916, during attack on Belloy-en-Santerre; awarded the Croix de Guerre and the Médaille Militaire. *Poems* (1916) published posthumously.

Wilbert Snow (April 6, 1884–September 28, 1977) b. Charles Wilbert Snow on White Head Island, St. George, Maine. Graduated Bowdoin College in 1907; later studied at Columbia. Worked in Council, Alaska, as teacher and government reindeer agent; published *Songs of the Neukluk*, written in collaboration with Ewen MacLellan. Taught briefly at University of Utah, Indiana University, and Reed College; became professor of English at Wesleyan, 1921–52. Married Jeannette Simmons in 1922; they had five sons. Was active in politics from 1912, when he campaigned for Woodrow Wilson. As a Democrat, served as lieutenant governor of Connecticut under Governor Raymond E. Baldwin, 1944–46; following Baldwin's resignation, served out last 13 days of his term as governor. Lectured for U.S. State Department in Europe and Asia, 1951–52. Helped found Middlesex Community College in 1966. Books included *Maine Coast* (1923), *The Inner Harbor* (1926), *Down East* (1932), *Before the Wind* (1938), *Maine Tides* (1940), *Spruce Head* (1946), and *Sonnets to Steve* (1957). His *Collected Poems* appeared in 1963. He published an autobiography, *Codline's Child*, in 1974. Died at his cottage on Spruce Island, Maine.

Anne Spencer (February 6, 1882–July 25, 1975) b. Annie Bethel Bannister, on plantation in Henry County, Virginia; only child of former slaves. Mother left father in 1886 and moved to Bramwell, West Virginia, where she placed Spencer in foster care with Mr. and Mrs. William Dixie, a prominent black couple. Educated at home until 1893, when she enrolled in the Virginia Seminary and Normal School in Lynchburg. Graduated at the top of her class in 1899; taught elementary school near Bramwell. In 1901, married high school classmate Edward Alexander Spencer; they had two daughters and a son. Established local chapter of National Association for the Advancement of Colored People in 1919 with help from James Weldon Johnson, who also arranged for the publication of Spencer's first poems. Her first published poem appeared in *The Crisis* in 1920; other poems were anthologized in Johnson's *Book of American Negro Poetry* (1922) and Louis Untermeyer's *American Poetry Since 1900* (1923). Worked as librarian at Dunbar High School in Lynchburg, 1924–46. Was a friend of Langston Hughes, Sterling Brown, Claude McKay, and W.E.B. Du Bois.

Leonora Speyer (November 7, 1872–February 10, 1956) b. Leonora Von Stosch in Washington, D.C. Father, Count Ferdinand von Stosch, had fought with Union army in Civil War; mother was American. Studied violin at Brussels Conservatory, taking first prize at age 16; toured Europe and U.S. as concert performer; performed with Boston Symphony Orchestra. After a first marriage ended in divorce, married Edgar Speyer, American banker who was chairman of the London Underground Railway and an important patron of the arts. Lived with her husband in Europe until his retirement in 1915, when they settled in New York. Her poetry collections included *A Canopic Jar* (1921), *Fiddler's Farewell* (1926), for which she won the Pulitzer Prize, *Naked Heel* (1931), *Slow Well: New and Selected Poems* (1939), and *Nor Without Music* (1946). Edited *American Poets: An Anthology of Contemporary Verse* (1923). Taught poetry at Columbia University beginning in 1937. Awarded Gold Medal of Poetry Society of America in 1955.

Gertrude Stein (February 3, 1874–July 27, 1946) b. Allegheny, Pennsylvania, youngest of five surviving children. After living in Austria and Paris, Stein's family settled in East Oakland, California, in 1880. Mother died in 1888. Left high school in 1889 without diploma. Brother Michael assumed guardianship of family after father's death in 1891. Went to Baltimore to live with sister Bertha in 1892. Enrolled at Radcliffe the following year (brother Leo attended Harvard), studying with George Santayana, William James, and others. Awarded B.A. in 1898. Entered Johns Hopkins School of Medicine in 1897; shared an apartment with Leo. Published two papers on psychology; left school in 1900 without medical degree. Traveled in 1903 to Paris, living with Leo, who was pursuing a painting career, in his apartment at 27, rue de Fleurus. Wrote novella *Q.E.D.* in 1903 and began *The Making of Americans* (completed 1911). With Leo, purchased paintings by Gauguin, Cézanne, and Renoir. Wrote *Three Lives* (published 1909). Introduced in 1905 to Matisse; formed close friendship with Picasso. Series of Saturday-night salons hosted by Stein and Leo began in 1906. Wide circle of acquaintances included Sherwood Anderson, Ford Madox Ford, Marsden Hartley, Ernest Hemingway, Jean Cocteau, and Man Ray. In 1907 met Alice B. Toklas, who became Stein's lifelong companion; she moved to rue de Fleurus residence in 1910. Quarreled with Leo, who moved out in 1913; they never spoke again. Published *Tender Buttons* (1914). During World War I, drove supply truck for American Fund for French Wounded; after armistice, participated in civilian relief in Alsace. *The Making of Americans* published by Contact Editions in 1925. Completed libretto, *Four Saints in Three Acts* (1927), for opera by Virgil Thomson. Published *Useful Knowledge* (1928). Founded Plain Edition press in 1930; initial publications included *Before the Flowers of Friendship Faded Friendship Faded*, *How to Write,* and *Operas and Plays. The Autobiography of Alice B. Toklas* (1933) became a bestseller in America; traveled to U.S. in 1934 for widely publicized lecture tour. Published *The Geographical History of America* (1936), *Everybody's Autobiography* (1937), children's book *The World Is Round* (1939), *Paris France* (1940), and *Ida: A Novel* (1941). Remained with Toklas in France during wartime; lived in Bilignin and Culoz, both under Vichy rule. After liberation of Culoz, made radio broadcasts to American troops before returning to Paris. Account of war years published in *Wars I Have Seen*

(1945). Collaborated with Thomson on opera *The Mother of Us All*, based on life of Susan B. Anthony. Died following surgery for stomach cancer.

George Sterling (December 1, 1869–November 17, 1926) b. Sag Harbor, New York. Oldest of nine children. For three years attended divinity school at St. Charles College in Ellicot City, Maryland, where he heard lectures by poet John Bannister Tabb, S.J. Sent to San Francisco in 1890 to work for his uncle's real-estate business; became active in local literary scene, and formed friendships with Frank Norris, Ambrose Bierce, and Joaquin Miller. Married Carrie Rand in February 1896. First book, *The Testimony of the Suns,* appeared in 1903. Formed close friendship with Jack London, who modeled character Russ Brissenden in 1909 novel *Martin Eden* on Sterling. Moved in 1905 to Carmel, California, where friends and visitors included Mary Austin, Bliss Carman, Upton Sinclair, and Witter Bynner. Published *A Wine of Wizardry* (1909), *The House of Orchids* (1911), and *Beyond the Breakers* (1914). After 1914 divorce, moved briefly to New York City before returning to San Francisco. Published two volumes of war poems, *The Caged Eagle* (1916) and *The Binding of the Beast and Other War Verse* (1917). Troubled by disappearance of Ambrose Bierce in 1914, death of Jack London in 1916, and suicide of Carrie in 1918. Honored at Panama-Pacific International Exposition in 1915. Published *Lilith: A Dramatic Poem* (1919); in *Robinson Jeffers: The Man and the Artist* (1926), championed Jeffers' work. Later books included *Rosamund* (1920), *Sails and Mirage* (1921), and *Selected Poems* (1923). Committed suicide by ingesting cyanide in his room at the Bohemian Club.

Wallace Stevens (October 2, 1879–August 2, 1955) b. Reading, Pennsylvania. Attended Reading Boys' School. Began three-year program at Harvard in 1897; friends included Witter Bynner and Arthur Davison Ficke; contributed poems and stories to Harvard magazines and became president of *Harvard Advocate*. Moved to New York in 1900, working night shift at *New-York Tribune*. Attended New York Law School 1901–3; in the decade after graduation worked for several firms in the New York area. Met Elsie Moll in Reading in 1904; they were married in 1909. Attended salon of Harvard friend Walter Conrad Arensberg; met William Carlos Williams, Mina Loy, Marcel Duchamp, Donald Evans, and others. Contributed poems to *Others, Rogue, Soil, Poetry,* and *The Little Review.* Joined Hartford Accident and Indemnity Company; traveled frequently on business. Verse play *Three Travelers Watch a Sunrise* (1916) won prize from *Poetry.* Made first of annual winter visits to Florida in 1922. First poetry collection, *Harmonium,* published in 1923. Daughter Holly born 1924. Moved to Hartford in 1932, and named vice-president of the Hartford Company two years later. Published *Ideas of Order* (1936), *Owl's Clover* (1936), *The Man With the Blue Guitar* (1937), *Parts of a World* and long poem "Notes Toward a Supreme Fiction" (both 1942). Delivered "Description Without Place" as Phi Beta Kappa poem at Harvard in 1945; named fellow of National Institute of Arts and Letters. Published *Transport to Summer* (1947). Received Bollingen Prize in 1950; published *The*

Auroras of Autumn, for which he won National Book Award in 1951. Essays collected in *The Necessary Angel* (1951). Read "The Sail of Ulysses" as Phi Beta Kappa poem at Columbia in 1954. Published *Collected Poems* (1954), which received National Book Award and Pulitzer Prize in May 1955.

Sara Teasdale (August 8, 1884–January 29, 1933) b. St. Louis, Missouri. Tutored at home; later attended private schools until 1903. Joined the Potters, a women's arts club, in 1904; published early writings in *Reedy's Mirror*. First poetry collection, *Sonnets to Duse* (1907), published at parents' expense, followed by *Helen of Troy* (1911). Attended meetings of Poetry Society of America in New York in 1911; visited Europe in 1912. Met Harriet Monroe, who published many of Teasdale's poems in *Poetry*. Began correspondence with Vachel Lindsay, who proposed marriage in 1914; in the same year, she married St. Louis businessman Ernst Filsinger. Published *Rivers to the Sea* (1915); moved with husband to New York in 1916. Edited anthology of women's poetry, *The Answering Voice* (1917); collection *Love Songs* (1917) won Columbia (later Pulitzer) Poetry Prize. Published *Flame and Shadow* (1920) and *Dark of the Moon* (1926); edited *Rainbow Gold* (1921), anthology of poems for children. Formed close friendship with Margaret Conklin, college student who admired her work and became her literary executor. Divorced her husband in 1929. Worked on an edition of Christina Rossetti's poetry. Devastated by news of Vachel Lindsay's suicide in 1931. Died in her New York apartment of an overdose of sleeping pills. Her late poems were published as *Strange Victory* (1933).

Edith Wharton (January 24, 1862–August 11, 1937) b. Edith Newbold Jones in New York City. Family moved to Europe in 1866, and lived successively in England, Italy, France, and Germany before returning to America in 1872. Educated at home; private edition of poems published at mother's expense in 1878. Married Edward Wharton in 1885; they traveled for several months every year in Europe. Published poems in *Scribner's*, *Harper's*, and *Century Magazine*; began publishing short stories. Bought New York townhouse and country estate; studied art and interior decoration, and co-wrote *The Decoration of Houses* (1897). Published story collections *The Great Inclination* (1899) and *Crucial Instances* (1901), and historical novel *The Valley of Decision* (1902). Built large house, The Mount, in Lenox, Massachusetts, in 1901. Divided time between Lenox and Europe; toured Sussex with close friend Henry James. Continued to publish fiction, including *The House of Mirth* (1905), *Madame de Treymes* (1907), *The Fruit of the Tree* (1907), *Ethan Frome* (1911), *The Reef* (1912), and *The Custom of the Country* (1913). Poems collected in *Artemis to Actaeon* (1909) and *Twelve Poems* (1926). In 1908 began affair with journalist William Morton Fullerton. The following year, husband admitted embezzling money from Wharton's trust funds; she was granted a divorce in 1913 on grounds of adultery. Traveled in North Africa and Spain in 1914. During World War I, established American Hostels for Refugees and organized Children of Flanders Rescue Committee; named Chevalier of the Legion of

Honor in 1916. Bought house in village of St. Brice-sous-Forêt outside Paris. Later fiction included *Summer* (1917), *The Marne* (1918), *The Age of Innocence* (1920), *The Old Maid* (1921), *The Glimpses of the Moon* (1922), *A Son at the Front* (1923), *The Mother's Recompense* (1925), *The Children* (1928), *Hudson River Bracketed* (1929), and *The Gods Arrive* (1932). In 1923 became first woman to receive honorary doctorate of letters from Yale. Autobiography *A Backward Glance* published 1934. Suffered a stroke in June 1937 and died two months later at St. Brice.

John Hall Wheelock (September 9, 1886–March 22, 1978) b. Far Rockaway, New York. Attended Morristown School in New Jersey. Entered Harvard in 1904; contributed to the *Harvard Advocate*, and named Class Poet for 1908; met Maxwell Perkins and Van Wyck Brooks. With Brooks, published first book of poetry, *Verses by Two Undergraduates* (1905). After graduating Phi Beta Kappa, continued studies in Europe; spent two years in Germany. Worked at Scribner's book store and publishing company in New York. Published second volume of poetry, *The Human Fantasy* (1911). Formed friendship with Sara Teasdale. After publishing *The Belovèd Adventure* (1912) and *Love and Liberation* (1913), won award from New England Poetry Society for *Poems, 1911–1936* (1936). Remained at Scribner's, where he ultimately became a senior editor. Married Phyllis de Kay in 1940. Initiated *Poets of Today* series in 1954. Later volumes included *Poems Old and New* (1956), *The Gardener* (1961), *What Is Poetry?* (1963), *Dear Men and Women* (1966), *By Daylight and in Dream: New and Collected Poems, 1904–1970* (1970), *In Love and Song* (1971), *This Blessed Earth: New and Selected Poems, 1927–1977* (1978), and *Afternoon: Amagansett Beach* (1978).

William Carlos Williams (September 17, 1883–March 4, 1963) b. Rutherford, New Jersey. Father, William George Williams, a cologne distributor, was English and had been raised in West Indies; mother, Raquel Hélène Hoheb Rose, was born in Puerto Rico. Spanish was dominant language at home; paternal grandmother Emily Dickinson Wellcome lived with family and taught the children English. Attended public school in Rutherford; in 1897 traveled with mother, living in Geneva and Paris; returned to New Jersey in 1899. Attended Horace Mann High School in New York City. Entered University of Pennsylvania school of dentistry in 1902, transferred to medical school a year later; while at Penn began lifelong friendship with Ezra Pound and met H.D. (Hilda Doolittle) and the painter Charles Demuth. Interned at two New York City hospitals, 1906–9. Published *Poems* (1909) at his own expense. Marriage proposal to Florence (Flossie) Herman accepted before he left for year of study in pediatrics at University of Leipzig. Visited Pound in London and met William Butler Yeats. Returned to Rutherford in 1910 and established medical practice. Married Flossie in 1912; they had two sons. With Pound's help published *The Tempers* (1913); contributed poems to Pound's anthology *Des Imagistes* (1914). Became acquainted with circle of writers and artists including Wallace Stevens, Mina Loy, Marcel Duchamp, and Alfred Kreymborg, editor of *Others*, to which Williams contributed regularly; frequented Walter Conrad Arensberg's salon and Alfred Stieglitz's 291 Gallery. Published *Al Que Quiere!* (1917), *Kora in Hell: Improvisations* (1920), *Sour Grapes* (1921), *The Great American Novel* (1923), and *Spring and All* (1923). Joined the Passaic General Hospital as a pediatrician in 1924; traveled to Europe with Flossie that same year, visiting Pound, H.D., James Joyce, and Ernest Hemingway. Published historical essays *In the American Grain* (1925) and *A Voyage to Pagany* (1928), novel based on European trip. Met Louis Zukofsky in 1928; Zukofsky included poems by Williams in February 1931 issue of *Poetry* devoted to "Objectivist" poets; Objectivist Press published Williams' *Collected Poems 1921–1931* (1934). Published prose collections *A Novelette and Other Prose* (1932) and *The Knife of the Times* (1932) and poetry collections *An Early Martyr* (1935) and *Adam & Eve & the City* (1936). Through Pound, met James Laughlin, publisher of New Directions, which published most of his subsequent books, beginning with novel *White Mule* (1937), story collection *Life Along the Passaic River* (1938), and *The Complete Collected Poems* (1938). Worked for many years on long poem *Paterson*, published between 1946 and 1958; also published collections including *The Broken Span* (1941) and *The Wedge* (1944). Suffered heart attack in 1948. Received National Book Award Gold Medal for Poetry for *Paterson* in 1950; shared 1953 Bollingen Prize with Archibald MacLeish. Suffered stroke shortly after appointment as Consultant to the Library of Congress in 1952; claims that Williams was a Communist sympathizer prompted an FBI investigation, suspended when the Library of Congress rescinded Williams' appointment on grounds of his health problems. Published *The Desert Music* (1954) and *Journey to Love* (1955). Met and corresponded with younger poets, including Robert Creeley, Denise Levertov, and Allen Ginsberg. Posthumously awarded Pulitzer Prize for *Pictures from Breughel* (1962). Later prose books included *The Autobiography of William Carlos Williams* (1951), *Selected Essays* (1954), and *Yes, Mrs. Williams* (1959).

Charles Erskine Scott Wood (February 20, 1852–January 22, 1944) b. Erie, Pennsylvania. Lived in Baltimore with maternal uncle while father, a U.S. Navy surgeon, served in Civil War. Educated at Baltimore schools; appointed in 1869 to U.S. Military Academy at West Point, where career was marked by numerous infractions of discipline. Commissioned as second lieutenant in 1874 and joined 21st Infantry in California. Worked as surveyor in northern California; served as judge advocate of the Department of the Columbia. Relieved from active military duty in 1877 to join Taylor Expedition to Alaska, of which he assumed leadership. Served in campaigns against Nez Percé Indians in 1877 and against Bannock and Piute, 1878; appointed aide-de-camp to General Oliver Otis Howard. Married Nannie Moale Smith in 1879. Entered Columbia University in 1881, where he met sculptor Olin Warner and painter Albert Pinkham Ryder; after graduating, returned to active military duty in Boise City, Idaho. Resigned from army in March 1884 after threat of court-martial; began successful legal practice in Portland, Oregon. Helped found

Portland Art Association in 1888. Defended Lazard Frères banking house, which held title to a large tract of land in Oregon, against U.S. government. Published *A Book of Tales, Being Myths of the North American Indians* (1901) and *A Masque of Love* (1904). Became contributor to *Liberty: The Pioneer Organ of Anarchism* and to Emma Goldman's journal *Mother Earth*. Met Lincoln Steffens in 1907, forming long friendship. Began lifelong affair with Sara Ehrgott, a journalist and feminist, in 1911. Worked on long poem later published as *The Poet in the Desert* (1915); other poetry collections included *Maia* (1918), *Circe* (1919), and *Poems from the Ranges* (1929). Settled in San Francisco with Ehrgott in 1918. Published series of satirical dialogues in *The Masses*, later collected as *Heavenly Discourses* (1927). Visited regularly in San Francisco by George Sterling, John Cowper Powys, and Genevieve Taggard. Spent later years at Los Gatos, California, where he became acquainted with Robinson Jeffers. *Too Much Government*, a collection of essays, published in 1931. Learned that he had been named as a Communist by House of Representative's Special Committee on Un-American Activities and wrote letter of protest to the committee's chairman, Martin Dies. Served on the Committee for the Defense of Trotsky. Appointed president of anti-fascist Association of Western Writers in 1936. Suffered heart attack in 1937.

Elinor Wylie (September 7, 1885–December 16, 1928) b. Elinor Morton Hoyt in Somerville, New Jersey. Attended Miss Baldwin's School for Girls, near Bryn Mawr, 1893–97. Family moved to Washington, D.C., where father was eventually appointed Counsellor of the State Department by Theodore Roosevelt. Attended Holton-Arms School. Married Philip Hichborn in December 1906; their son, Philip III, born the following year. Husband was diagnosed as suffering from acute mental illness. Met Horace Wylie, a Washington socialite, in 1908; they eloped on a boat from Canada to England in 1910. Remained in England with Horace because his wife refused to grant a divorce; changed their surname to Waring and lived in a cottage in Bournemouth. Philip Hichborn committed suicide in 1912. Poetry collection *Incidental Numbers* (1912) was privately printed. Returned to U.S. in spring of 1915. Married Horace after his divorce became final and settled with him in New York; moved to Washington a year later. Published four poems in April 1920 issue of *Poetry*. Poet William Rose Benét helped her publish *Nets to Catch the Wind* (1921). Accepted invitation in 1922 to MacDowell Colony in New Hampshire, where she worked on novel *Jennifer Lorn: A Sedate Extravaganza* (1923). Appointed literary editor of *Vanity Fair* in 1923. Divorced Horace Wylie and married Benét. Published poetry collection *Black Armour* (1923). Moved to New Canaan, Connecticut, in 1924. Published novels *The Venetian Glass Nephew* (1925), *The Orphan Angel* (1926), and *Mr. Hodge and Mr. Hazard* (1928), and poetry collection *Trivial Breath* (1928). Divided time between New York and Europe in her last years. Died of a stroke. *Angels and Earthly Creatures* (1928) published posthumously.

Note on the Texts

The choice of text for each of the poems selected for inclusion in this volume has been made on the basis of a study of its textual history and a comparison of editions printed during the author's lifetime. In general, each text is from the earliest book edition prepared with the author's participation; revised editions are sometimes followed, in light of the degree of authorial supervision and the stage of the writer's career at which the revisions were made, but the preference has been for the authorially approved book version closest to the date of composition. Texts from periodicals, anthologies, and posthumous sources have been used only when a poem was not printed in one of the author's books during his or her lifetime, or when such a book version is not authoritative. For song lyrics, collected editions (when available) have been preferred over sheet-music texts or new transcriptions.

The following is a list of the sources of all of the texts included in this volume, listed alphabetically by the authors of the poems.

Franklin P. Adams. If—: *So Much Velvet* (Garden City, N.Y.: Doubleday Page and Co., 1925).

Henry Adams. Prayer to the Virgin of Chartres: *Letters to a Niece and Prayer to the Virgin of Chartres* (Boston: Houghton Mifflin, 1920).

Conrad Aiken. Morning Song of Senlin: *The Charnel Rose* (Boston: The Four Seas, 1918). Tetélestai; And in the Hanging Gardens; The Room; Sea Holly: *Priapus and the Pool and Other Poems* (New York: Boni & Liveright, 1925). *from* Preludes for Memnon: *Preludes for Memnon* (New York: Charles Scribner's Sons, 1933).

Sherwood Anderson. American Spring Song: *Mid-American Chants* (New York: John Lane & Co., 1918).

Anonymous Ballads. White House Blues; Claude Allen; The Titanic: Duncan Emrich (ed.), *American Folk Poetry* (Boston: Little, Brown, 1974). Casey Jones; Midnight Special: Carl Sandburg (ed.), *The American Songbag* (New York: Harcourt, Brace, 1927).

Walter Conrad Arensberg. Voyage à l'Infini: *Idols* (Boston: Houghton Mifflin, 1916). Ing; Arithmetical Progression of the Verb "To Be"; Axiom; Theorem: Alfred Kreymborg (ed.), *Others: An Anthology of the New Verse* (New York: Alfred A. Knopf, 1917).

Mary Austin. The Grass on the Mountain: *The American Rhythm: Studies and Reexpressions of Amerindian Songs* (Boston: Houghton Mifflin, 1923).

Djuna Barnes. Portrait of a Lady Walking: *Conjunctions 31* (1998). The Walking-Mort: *The New Yorker*, May 15, 1971.

Irving Berlin. Slumming on Park Avenue: *Slumming on Park Avenue* (New York: Irving Berlin Music Corporation, 1937).

John Peale Bishop. Speaking of Poetry; In the Dordogne; Young Men Dead; Metamorphoses of M; The Return: *Now With His Love* (New York: Charles Scribner's Sons, 1933).

Maxwell Bodenheim. Death; Rear Porches of an Apartment Building; Interlude: *Minna and Myself* (New York: Pagan Publishing Co., 1917).

Anna Hempstead Branch. The Monk in the Kitchen: *Rose of the Wind and Other Poems* (Boston: Houghton Mifflin, 1910). In the Beginning Was the Word; *from* Sonnets from a Lockbox: *Sonnets from a Lockbox* (Boston: Houghton Mifflin, 1929).

Witter Bynner. Opus 2; Opus 17: *Spectra: A Book of Poetic Experiments* (New York: Mitchell Kennerley, 1916). The Wave; The Wall; Lightning; Horses; A Sigh; The Moon: *The Beloved Stranger* (New York: Alfred A. Knopf, 1919). Tiles: *A Canticle of Pan* (New York: Alfred A. Knopf, 1920). Wistaria; Donald Evans: *Caravan* (New York: Alfred A. Knopf, 1925). Driftwood: *Grenstone Poems*, revised edition (New York: Frederick A. Stokes, 1926). Lovers; A Foreigner; Idols: *Indian Earth* (New York: Alfred A. Knopf, 1929). Drinking Alone with the Moon: *The Jade Mountain* (New York: Alfred A. Knopf, 1929). Defeat: *Take Away the Darkness* (New York: Alfred A. Knopf, 1947). The Titanic: *Poetry*, February 1949. "All tempest"; "Any other time would have done"; "But for these apertures": *New Poems 1960* (New York: Alfred A. Knopf, 1960).

Skipwith Cannell. The King: Alfred Kreymborg (ed.), *Others: An Anthology of the New Verse* (New York: Alfred A. Knopf, 1917).

Badger Clark Jr. A Border Affair: *Sun and Saddle Leather* (Boston: R.G. Badger, 1915).

Sarah N. Cleghorn. Comrade Jesus; The Golf Links Lie So Near the Mill: *Portraits and Protests* (New York: Henry Holt and Company, 1917).

Adelaide Crapsey. November Night; Release; Triad; Snow; Anguish; Trapped; Moon-Shadows; Susanna and the Elders; The Guarded Wound; Night Winds; Arbutus; Amaze; The Warning; Niagara; On Seeing Weather-Beaten Trees; The Sun-Dial; Song; The Witch; The Lonely Death; Fragment; To a Hermit Thrush: *Verse* (Rochester, N.Y.: The Manas Press, 1915).

Donald Davidson. Sanctuary: *Lee in the Mountains and Other Poems* (New York: Charles Scribner's Sons, 1938).

Frances Densmore. I Am Walking; The Sound Is Fading Away; My Love Has Departed: *Chippewa Music* (Washington: Government Printing Office, 1910). The Song of Butterfly; A Song of Spring; The Sky Will Resound; I Have Found My Lover: *Chippewa Music—II* (Washington: Government Printing Office, 1913).

H.D. (Hilda Doolittle). Orchard; Oread; Sea Rose; Mid-Day; Evening; Garden; Sea Violet; Sea Poppies; Storm; Sea Iris: *Sea Garden* (London: Constable, 1916). Hippolytus Temporizes; At Baia; Song; The Whole White World; Egypt: *Hymen* (London: The Egoist Press, 1921). The Pool;

Helen; Lethe: *Heliodora and Other Poems* (London: Jonathan Cape, 1924). Fragment 113: *Collected Poems of H.D.* (New York: Boni & Liveright, 1926). Trance; Birds in Snow; *from* Songs from Cyprus; *from* Let Zeus Record; Epitaph; The Mysteries: Renaissance Choros: *Red Roses for Bronze* (London: Chatto & Windus, 1931). "If you take the moon in your hands"; "Now let the cycle sweep us here and there": Norman Holmes Pearson (ed.), *Selected Poems of H.D.* (New York: New Directions, 1957). "Are these ashes in my hand": Louis Martz (ed.), *Collected Poems 1912–1944* (New York: New Directions, 1983). *from* The Walls Do Not Fall: *The Walls Do Not Fall* (London: Oxford University Press, 1944). *from* Tribute to the Angels: *Tribute to the Angels* (London: Oxford University Press, 1945). *from* The Flowering of the Rod: *The Flowering of the Rod* (London: Oxford University Press, 1946).

W.E.B. Du Bois. The Song of the Smoke: *Horizon*, February 1907. A Litany at Atlanta: *Darkwater* (New York: Harcourt Brace, 1921).

Max Eastman. To John Reed; To Genevieve Taggard Who Called Me Traitor in a Poem: *Poems of Five Decades* (New York: Harper, 1954).

T. S. Eliot. The Love Song of J. Alfred Prufrock; Portrait of a Lady; Preludes; The Boston Evening Transcript; La Figlia Che Piange: *Prufrock and Other Observations* (London: The Egoist Press, 1917). Sweeney Among the Nightingales: *Poems* (London: Hogarth Press, 1919). Gerontion: *Poems* (New York: Alfred A. Knopf, 1920). The Waste Land: *The Waste Land* (New York: Boni & Liveright, 1922). Marina: *Marina* (London: Faber & Faber, 1930). Ash-Wednesday: *Ash-Wednesday* (London: Faber & Faber, 1930). Sweeney Agonistes: *Sweeney Agonistes: Fragments of an Aristophanic Melodrama* (London: Faber & Faber, 1932). Whispers of Immortality; The Hollow Men; Burnt Norton: *Poems 1909–1935* (London: Faber & Faber, 1935).

Abbie Huston Evans. Juniper; The Old Yellow Shop; Under Cover: *Outcrop* (New York: Harper and Brothers, 1928). Fringed Gentians: *The Bright North* (New York: Macmillan, 1938). Martian Landscape: *Collected Poems* (Pittsburgh: University of Pittsburgh Press, 1970).

Donald Evans. En Monocle; In the Vices: *Sonnets from the Patagonian* (Philadelphia: Nicholas L. Brown, 1914).

Arthur Davison Ficke. Opus 118; Opus 131: *Spectra: A Book of Poetic Experiments* (New York: Mitchell Kennerley, 1916).

John Gould Fletcher. Blue Symphony: *Goblins and Pagodas* (Boston: Houghton Mifflin, 1916).

Elsa von Freytag-Loringhoven. A Dozen Cocktails—Please: *Sulfur* 2:3 (1983). Klink-Hratzvenga (Deathwail): *The Little Review*, March 1920. Café du Dome: *transition*, October 1927.

Robert Frost. The Pasture; Storm Fear; Mowing; The Tuft of Flowers; Mending Wall; The Death of the Hired Man; Home Burial; After Apple-Picking; The Wood-Pile; The Road Not Taken; An Old Man's Winter Night; Hyla Brook; The Oven Bird; Bond and Free; Birches; Putting in the Seed; The Sound of Trees; 'Out, Out—'; A Star in a Stone-Boat; The

Witch of Coös; Nothing Gold Can Stay; Fire and Ice; Dust of Snow; Stopping by Woods on a Snowy Evening; For Once, Then, Something; The Onset; To Earthward; The Need of Being Versed in Country Things; Spring Pools; The Freedom of the Moon; Once by the Pacific; A Minor Bird; Bereft; Tree at My Window; Acquainted with the Night; West-Running Brook; The Investment; Two Tramps in Mud Time; A Drumlin Woodchuck; Desert Places; The Strong Are Saying Nothing; Neither Out Far Nor In Deep; Design; Unharvested; Provide, Provide; On a Bird Singing in Its Sleep; The Silken Tent; All Revelation; Come In; The Most of It; Never Again Would Birds' Song Be the Same; The Subverted Flower; Directive; A Cliff Dwelling; Choose Something Like a Star: *Complete Poems of Robert Frost 1949* (New York: Henry Holt and Company, 1949). A Cabin in the Clearing; One More Brevity; The Draft Horse; Questioning Faces: *In the Clearing* (New York: Holt, Rinehart and Winston, 1962).

Arturo Giovannitti. The Walker: *Arrows in the Gale* (Riverside, CT: Hillacre Bookhouse, 1914).

Samuel Greenberg. The Glass Bubbles; Secrecy; Etching; God; African Desert; To Dear Daniel: Harold Holden and Jack McManis (eds.), *Poems By Samuel Greenberg* (New York: Henry Holt and Company, 1947).

Angelina Weld Grimké. Dawn: Robert T. Kerlin (ed.), *Negro Poets and Their Poems* (Washington, D.C.: Associated Publishers, 1923). Dusk: *Opportunity*, April 1924. Grass Fingers; Tenebris; A Mona Lisa: Countee Cullen (ed.), *Caroling Dusk* (New York: Harper and Brothers, 1927). Epitaph on a Living Woman: Carolivia Herron (ed.), *Selected Works of Angelina Weld Grimké* (Oxford: Oxford University Press, 1991).

Arthur Guiterman. On the Vanity of Earthly Greatness: *Gaily the Troubadour.* (New York: E.P. Dutton, 1936).

Hazel Hall. Seams; The Listening Macaws: *Curtains* (New York: John Lane, 1921). Light Sleep; Woman Death: *Cry of Time* (New York: E.P. Dutton, 1929).

W. C. Handy. St. Louis Blues; Beale Street Blues: *Blues: An Anthology* (New York: Macmillan, 1925).

Marsden Hartley. Fishmonger: Alfred Kreymborg (ed.), *Others for 1919* (New York: Nicholas L. Brown, 1920). West Pitch at the Falls; This Crusty Fragment: *Androscoggin* (Portland, ME: Falmouth Publishing House, 1940). Indian Point; As the Buck Lay Dead: *Sea Burial* (Portland, ME: Leon Tebbetts Editions, 1941). "Lapping of waters"; Wingaersheek Beach; What Have We All—A Soliloquy of Essences: Gail R. Scott (ed.), *The Collected Poems of Marsden Hartley 1904–1943* (Santa Rosa, CA: Black Sparrow Press, 1987).

Roy Helton. Lonesome Water: *Lonesome Water* (New York: Harper & Brothers, 1930).

Joe Hill. The Preacher and the Slave: Joyce L. Kornbluh (ed.), *Rebel Voices: An I.W.W. Anthology* (Ann Arbor: University of Michigan Press, 1964).

Robinson Jeffers. Salmon Fishing; Shine, Perishing Republic; Granite and Cypress; Birds; Haunted Country; Hurt Hawks; Apology for Bad Dreams;

Tor House; The Bed by the Window; The Place for No Story; Love the Wild Swan; Rock and Hawk; Prescription of Painful Ends; For Una; Advice to Pilgrims; Cassandra; Animals; The Beauty of Things; Carmel Point; The Deer Lay Down Their Bones; Vulture; "I have been warned": Tim Hunt (ed.), *The Collected Poetry of Robinson Jeffers* (3 vols. San Francisco: Stanford University Press, 1987).

Orrick Johns. Salon des Vers; Invitation: *Black Branches* (New York: Pagan Publishing Co., 1920). Wild Plum: *Wild Plum* (New York: Macmillan, 1926).

Fenton Johnson. Tired; Aunt Hannah Jackson; The Minister: Alfred Kreymborg (ed.), *Others for 1919* (New York: Nicholas L. Brown, 1920).

Georgia Douglas Johnson. I Want To Die While You Love Me: *An Autumn Love Cycle* (New York: Harold Vinal, 1928).

James Weldon Johnson. O Black and Unknown Bards; To America; The White Witch; Sunset in the Tropics; Brer Rabbit, You's de Cutes' of 'Em All: *Fifty Years and Other Poems* (Boston: The Cornhill Co., 1917). The Creation; The Judgment Day: *God's Trombones: Seven Negro Sermons in Verse* (New York: Viking, 1927). Lift Every Voice and Sing: *Saint Peter Relates an Incident* (New York: Viking, 1935).

Joyce Kilmer. Trees: *Trees and Other Poems* (Garden City, N.Y.: Doubleday and Co., 1914).

Alfred Kreymborg. Ants; The Tree; Culture; Improvisation: *Mushrooms* (New York: John Marshall, 1916). Tiger Lily: *Mushrooms* (New York: Coward-McCann, 1928).

William Ellery Leonard. *from* Two Lives: *Two Lives* (New York: B.W. Huebsch, 1922).

Vachel Lindsay. General William Booth Enters into Heaven; The Eagle That Is Forgotten: *General William Booth Enters Into Heaven* (New York: Mitchell Kennerley, 1913). The Congo; Factory Windows Are Always Broken; Abraham Lincoln Walks at Midnight: *The Congo and Other Poems* (New York: Macmillan, 1914). Mae Marsh, Motion Picture Actress: *The Chinese Nightingale and Other Poems* (New York: Macmillan, 1917). Bryan, Bryan, Bryan, Bryan; The Daniel Jazz: *The Golden Whales of California and Other Rhymes in the American Language* (New York: Macmillan, 1920).

Haniel Long. Cobweb; In the Dark World; Day and Night: *Atlantides* (Santa Fe: Writers' Editions, 1933). A New Music; For Tony, Embarking in Spring: *The Grist Mill* (Santa Fe: Rydal Press, 1945). Daphnis and Chloe; Lightning; Our Spring Needs Shoveling: James H. Maguire (ed.), *My Seasons: Selected Poems* (Boise, ID: Asahta Press, 1977).

H. P. Lovecraft. The Well; Alienation: *Collected Poems* (Cassia, FL: Dragon-Fly Press, 1936).

Amy Lowell. The Pike: *Sword Blades and Poppy Seed* (Boston: Houghton Mifflin, 1914). Patterns; Thompson's Lunch Room—Grand Central Station: *Men, Women and Ghosts* (Boston: Houghton Mifflin, 1916). Spring Longing; Vernal Equinox; Venus Transiens; Bright Sunlight; The Weather-Cock Points South; Shore Grass: *Pictures of the Floating World* (Boston: Houghton Mifflin, 1919). Lilacs; Meeting-House Hill; Katydids: *What's*

O'Clock (Boston: Houghton Mifflin, 1925). New Heavens for Old;
Dissonance: *Ballads for Sale* (Boston: Houghton Mifflin, 1927).

Mina Loy. Songs to Joannes; Poe; Apology of Genius; Lunar Baedeker; Der
Blinde Junge; Brancusi's Golden Bird; Gertrude Stein; On Third Avenue:
Roger Conover (ed.), *The Lost Lunar Baedeker* (New York: The Noonday
Press, 1996).

Claude McKay. The Lynching; The Harlem Dancer; The Castaways; The
Tropics in New York; Harlem Shadows: *Spring in New Hampshire*
(London: Grant Richards, 1920). If We Must Die; The White City; Dawn
in New York; Africa; Outcast; Birds of Prey; Subway Wind; Jasmines:
Harlem Shadows (New York: Harcourt, Brace & World, 1922). Negro
Spiritual: *The Liberator*, May 1922.

Archibald MacLeish. Ars Poetica: *Streets in the Moon* (Boston: Houghton
Mifflin, 1926). Return; You, Andrew Marvell; Epistle To Be Left in the
Earth; Cinema of a Man: *New Found Land* (Paris: The Black Sun Press,
1930). Sentiments for a Dedication: *Poems 1924–1933* (Boston: Houghton
Mifflin, 1933). Voyage West: *Actfive and Other Poems* (New York: Random
House, 1948).

Don Marquis. *from* the coming of archy; the song of mehitabel; aesop revised
by archy; archy confesses: *archy & mehitabel* (Garden City, N.Y.:
Doubleday, Page and Co., 1927).

Edgar Lee Masters. *from* Spoon River Anthology: *Spoon River Anthology*
(New York: Macmillan, 1915).

Edna St. Vincent Millay. God's World; Afternoon on a Hill; Sorrow; "If I
should learn"; Bluebeard; Witch-Wife: *Renascence* (New York: Mitchell
Kennerley, 1917). Spring; Eel-Grass; Elegy; Passer Mortuus Est: *Second
April* (New York: Frank Shays, 1921). First Fig; Second Fig; "I think I
should have loved you presently"; "I shall forget you presently, my dear";
Recuerdo: *A Few Figs From Thistles* (New York: Harper and Bros., 1922).
The Wood Road; Scrub; Siege; "Euclid alone has looked on Beauty bare";
"What lips my lips have kissed, and where, and why"; "I, being born a
woman and distressed"; "Gazing upon him now, severe and dead"; Never
May the Fruit Be Plucked: *The Harp-Weaver and Other Poems* (New York:
Harper and Bros., 1923). Winter Night: *The Buck in the Snow* (New York:
Harper and Bros., 1928). "Love is not all; it is not meat nor drink": *Fatal
Interview* (New York: Harper and Bros., 1931). Rendezvous; Menses;
Sonnet: *Huntsman, What Quarry?* (New York: Harper and Bros., 1939).

Harriet Monroe. Radio: *Chosen Poems* (New York: Macmillan, 1935).

Marianne Moore. To an Intra-Mural Rat; To a Steam Roller; "He Wrote
the History Book"; To a Snail; Is Your Town Ninevah?; Critics and
Connoisseurs; Like a Bulrush; When I Buy Pictures; Silence; Bowls; A
Grave; Those Various Scalpels; Peter; To a Chameleon; An Egyptian Pulled
Glass Bottle in the Shape of a Fish: *Observations* (New York: The Dial
Press, 1924). The Past Is the Present; The Monkeys; Black Earth: *Selected
Poems* (New York: Macmillan, 1935). The Mind Is an Enchanting Thing:
Nevertheless (New York: Macmillan, 1944). The Fish; Poetry: *Collected*

Poems (New York: Macmillan, 1951). O To Be a Dragon: *O To Be a Dragon* (New York: Viking, 1957). Marriage; The Steeple-Jack; Smooth Gnarled Crape Myrtle; Bird-Witted; The Pangolin; He "Digesteth Harde Yron"; In Distrust of Merits; Tom Fool at Jamaica: *The Complete Poems of Marianne Moore* (New York: Viking, 1967).

John G. Neihardt. *from* The Song of the Messiah: *The Song of the Messiah* (New York: Macmillan, 1935).

Dorothy Parker. Résumé; One Perfect Rose; Ballade at Thirty-Five; Men; News Item; Observation; Symptom Recital: *Enough Rope* (New York: Boni & Liveright, 1926). The Red Dress; Bric-à-Brac; A Pig's-Eye View of Literature; Bohemia; Coda: *Sunset Gun* (New York: Boni & Liveright, 1928).

Charlie Patton. High Water Everywhere: Eric Sackheim (ed.), *The Blues Line* (New York: Grossman, 1969).

Edwin Ford Piper. Big Swimming; Indian Counsel: *Paintrock Road* (New York: Macmillan, 1927).

Cole Porter. I Get a Kick Out of You; Anything Goes; Just One of Those Things: Roger Kimball (ed.), *The Complete Lyrics of Cole Porter* (New York: Alfred A. Knopf, 1983).

Ezra Pound. Sestina: Altaforte; Planh for the Young English King: *Exultations* (London: Elkin Matthews, 1909). De Aegypto: *Canzoni* (London: Elkin Matthews, 1911). Portrait d'une Femme; The Seafarer; Of Jacopo del Sellaio; The Return: *Ripostes* (London: Stephen Swift, 1912). The River-Merchant's Wife: A Letter; Lament of the Frontier Guard; Exile's Letter: *Cathay* (London: Elkin Matthews, 1915). The Garden; A Pact; Les Millwin; The Study in Æsthetics; A Song of the Degrees; Liu Ch'e; Fan-Piece, For Her Imperial Lord; In a Station of the Metro; Papyrus; Tame Cat; Near Perigord: *Lustra* (London: Elkin Matthews, 1916). Alba: *Quia Pauper Amavi* (London: The Egoist Press, 1919). Hugh Selwyn Mauberley: *Poems 1918–1921* (New York: Boni & Liveright, 1921). *from* Homage to Sextus Propertius: *Personae* (New York: Boni & Liveright, 1926). Canto II, Canto IV, Canto XIII, Canto XVII: *A Draft of XXX Cantos* (New York: Farrar & Rinehart, 1933). Canto XXXVI: *Eleven New Cantos* (New York: Farrar & Rinehart, 1934). Canto XLV, Canto XLVII, Canto XLIX: *The Fifth Decad of Cantos* (New York: Farrar & Rinehart, 1937). Canto LXXXI: *The Pisan Cantos* (New York: New Directions, 1948). Canto XC: *Section: Rock-Drill* (New York: New Directions, 1956). Canto CXVI; *from* Notes for Canto CXVII et seq: *Drafts & Fragments of Cantos CX-CXVII* (New York: New Directions, 1969). *from* The Classic Anthology as Defined by Confucius: *The Classic Anthology as Defined by Confucius* (Cambridge: Harvard University Press, 1954). Choruses from *Women of Trakis*: *Women of Trakis, by Sophokles* (New York: New Directions, 1957).

Ma Rainey. Southern Blues: Eric Sackheim (ed.), *The Blues Line* (New York: Grossman, 1969).

John Crowe Ransom. Spectral Lovers; Bells for John Whitesides'

Daughter; Judith of Bethulia; Here Lies a Lady; Blackberry Winter; Nocturne; Philomela; Captain Carpenter: *Chills and Fever* (New York: Alfred A. Knopf, 1924). Piazza Piece; The Equilibrists; Janet Waking; Blue Girls: *Two Gentlemen in Bonds* (New York: Alfred A. Knopf, 1927). Painted Head: *Selected Poems* (New York: Alfred A. Knopf, 1945).

John Reed. *from* America in 1918: *New Masses*, October 15, 1935.

Lizette Woodworth Reese. Crows; Fog; Wind; The White Fury of the Spring: *White April* (New York: Farrar & Rinehart, 1930).

Lola Ridge, *from* The Ghetto: *The Ghetto* (New York: B.W. Huebsch, 1918). The Fifth-Floor Window; Kerensky: *Red Flag* (New York: Viking, 1927).

Elizabeth Madox Roberts. Evening Song; The Song of the Dove; An Old Love in Song; Disconsolate Morning: *Song in the Meadow* (New York: Viking, 1940).

Edwin Arlington Robinson. Calverly's; Shadrach O'Leary; How Annandale Went Out; Miniver Cheevy; For a Dead Lady: *The Town Down the River* (New York: Charles Scribner's Sons, 1910). Cassandra; Hillcrest; Eros Turannos; The Unforgiven; The Poor Relation: *The Man Against the Sky* (New York: Macmillan, 1916). The Mill; Souvenir: *The Three Taverns* (New York: Macmillan, 1920). Isaac and Archibald; Mr. Flood's Party: *Collected Poems* (New York: Macmillan, 1921). The Sheaves; Karma; Why He Was There: *Dionysus in Doubt* (New York: Macmillan, 1925).

Carl Sandburg. Chicago; The Harbor; Mag; Mamie; Fog; Under a Hat Rim; Nocturne in a Deserted Brickyard; Window; Harrison Street Court; Languages: *Chicago Poems* (New York: Henry Holt, 1916). Sunset from Omaha Hotel Window; Adelaide Crapsey; Bilbea; Portrait of a Motor Car; Cool Tombs: *Cornhuskers* (New York: Henry Holt, 1918). Galoots; Manual System; Cahoots: *Smoke and Steel* (New York: Harcourt, Brace, 1920). *from* The People, Yes: *The People, Yes* (New York: Harcourt Brace, 1936). On a Flimmering Floom You Shall Ride: *Complete Poems* (Harcourt, Brace and World, 1950).

Alan Seeger. I Have a Rendezvous with Death: *Poems* (New York: Charles Scribner's Sons, 1917).

Wilbert Snow. Advice to a Clam-Digger: *The Inner Harbor* (New York: Harcourt Brace, 1926).

Anne Spencer. At the Carnival: James Weldon Johnson (ed.), *The Book of Negro Poetry* (New York: Harcourt, Brace, 1922). Lines to a Nasturtium: *Palms*, October 1926.

Leonora Speyer. Witch!; To a Song of Sappho Discovered in Egypt: *Fiddler's Farewell* (New York: Alfred A. Knopf, 1926).

Gertrude Stein. *from* Tender Buttons: Objects; *from* Lifting Belly; Idem the Same.; *from* Stanzas in Meditation: Typescripts, The Yale Collection of American Literature, Beinecke Rare Book and Manuscript Library, Yale University. Susie Asado: *Geography and Plays* (Boston: The Four Seas, 1922). *from* The World Is Round: *The World Is Round* (New York: William R. Scott, 1939).

George Sterling. The Black Vulture: *The House of Orchids and Other Poems* (San Francisco: A.M. Robertson, 1911).

Wallace Stevens. Sunday Morning; Peter Quince at the Clavier; Thirteen Ways of Looking at a Blackbird; Nomad Exquisite; Infanta Marina; Domination of Black; The Snow Man; Tea at the Palaz of Hoon; The Emperor of Ice-Cream; Disillusionment of Ten O'Clock; To the One of Fictive Music: *Harmonium* (New York: Alfred A. Knopf, 1923). The Death of a Soldier; Sea Surface Full of Clouds: *Harmonium*, second edition (New York: Alfred A. Knopf, 1931). The Idea of Order at Key West; The Sun This March; Meditation Celestial & Terrestrial; A Postcard from the Volcano; Autumn Refrain: *Ideas of Order* (New York: Alfred A. Knopf, 1936). Poetry Is a Destructive Force; The Poems of Our Climate; Study of Two Pears; The Man on the Dump; Landscape with Boat; Phosphor Reading by His Own Light: *Parts of a World* (New York: Alfred A. Knopf, 1942). Notes Toward a Supreme Fiction; God Is Good. It Is a Beautiful Night; The Motive for Metaphor; Men Made Out of Words: *Transport to Summer* (New York: Alfred A. Knopf, 1947). The Auroras of Autumn; Large Red Man Reading: *The Auroras of Autumn* (New York: Alfred A. Knopf, 1950). To an Old Philosopher in Rome; Final Soliloquy of the Interior Paramour; The Rock; The Plain Sense of Things; The Planet on the Table; The River of Rivers in Connecticut; Not Ideas About the Thing But the Thing Itself: *The Collected Poems of Wallace Stevens* (New York: Alfred A. Knopf, 1954). A Discovery of Thought: *Imagi*, Summer 1950. The Course of a Particular: *Hudson Review*, Spring 1951. Reality Is an Activity of the Most August Imagination: *Perspective*, Autumn 1954. Of Mere Being: Typescript, Huntington Library, San Marino, California.

Sara Teasdale. The Shrine: *Helen of Troy and Other Poems* (New York: G.P. Putnam, 1911). The Look; At Night; Moods; I Shall Not Care; Enough; Summer Night, Riverside; After Love; Night Song at Amalfi: *Rivers to the Sea* (New York: Macmillan, 1915). Jewels; Wood Song: *Love Songs* (New York: Macmillan, 1917). The Broken Field; "A Little While"; "There Will Come Soft Rains"; The Unchanging; The Sanctuary: *Flame and Shadow* (New York: Macmillan, 1920). "I Shall Live To Be Old": *Dark of the Moon* (New York: Macmillan, 1926). Moon's Ending; Lines: *Strange Victory* (New York: Macmillan, 1933).

Edith Wharton. Terminus: R.W.B. Lewis, *Edith Wharton: A Biography* (New York: Harper & Row, 1976).

John Hall Wheelock. The Fish-Hawk: *The Black Panther* (New York: Charles Scribner's Sons, 1922). Afternoon: Amagansett Beach: *Poems Old and New* (New York: Charles Scribner's Sons, 1956). Earth, Take Me Back: *Dear Men and Women* (New York: Charles Scribner's Sons, 1966).

William Carlos Williams. Pastoral; Chicory and Daisies; Dawn; Spring Strains; Sympathetic Portrait of a Child; January Morning: *Al Que Quiero!* (Boston: The Four Seas, 1917). Romance Moderne; The Desolate Field; Thursday; Queen-Anne's-Lace; The Widow's Lament in Springtime; The Lonely Street: *Sour Grapes* (Boston: The Four Seas,

1921). *from* Spring and All: *Spring and All* (Paris: Contact Editions, 1923).
Young Sycamore; Hemmed-in Males; On Gay Wallpaper; This Is Just to
Say: *Collected Poems 1921–1931* (New York: Objectivist Press, 1934). Flowers
by the Sea; The Yachts: *An Early Martyr, and Other Poems* (New York:
Alcestis Press, 1935). Perpetuum Mobile: The City: *Adam & Eve & the
City* (Peru, VT: Alcestis Press, 1936). The Young Housewife; "There are
no perfect waves"; "The moon, the dried weeds"; Paterson: Episode 17;
These; Between Walls: *Complete Collected Poems* (Norfolk, CT: New
Directions, 1938). A Sort of Song; Paterson: The Falls; The Dance;
Burning the Christmas Greens: *The Wedge* (Cummington, MA:
Cummington Press, 1944). The Last Words of My English Grandmother:
Collected Earlier Poems (New York: New Directions, 1951). The Descent;
To Daphne and Virginia: *The Desert Music, and Other Poems* (New York:
Random House, 1954). To a Man Dying on His Feet: *Journey to Love*
(New York: Random House, 1955). The World Contracted to a
Recognizable Image: *Pictures from Breughel and Other Poems* (New York:
New Directions, 1962). The Predicter of Famine: Christopher Macgowan,
(ed.), *The Collected Poems of William Carlos Williams. Vol. 2: 1939-1962*
(New York: New Directions, 1988).

Charles Erskine Scott Wood. *from* The Poet in the Desert: *The Poet in the
Desert* (Privately printed: Portland, OR, 1915).

Elinor Wylie. Beauty; August; Wild Peaches; Village Mystery; Incantation:
Nets to Catch the Wind (New York: Harcourt Brace, 1921). Sonnet:
Bookman's, May 1922. Let No Charitable Hope; Preference; Self-Portrait;
Now That Your Eyes Are Shut; Parting Gift: *Black Armour* (New York:
George H. Doran, 1923). Confession of Faith: *Trivial Breath* (New York:
Alfred A. Knopf, 1928). Green Hair; Ejaculation: *Collected Poems* (New
York: Alfred A. Knopf, 1932).

The following is a list of pages where a stanza break coincides with the foot
of the page (except where such breaks are apparent from the regular stanzaic
structure of the poem): 70; 83; 91; 94; 111; 112; 113; 120; 127; 130; 142; 158; 163;
226; 230; 235; 249; 250; 263; 273; 274; 279; 283; 284; 286; 287; 289; 290; 291;
301; 310; 317; 372; 383; 395; 396; 402; 403; 405; 406; 407; 408; 418; 419; 435;
439; 441; 443; 445; 446; 454; 463; 464; 465; 466; 470; 477; 480; 488; 490; 518;
523; 525; 526; 528; 530; 541; 543; 544; 549; 551; 552; 570; 579; 595; 596; 603; 604;
606; 617; 640; 641; 656; 701; 723; 728; 730; 731; 747; 749; 760; 761; 762; 763;
766; 767; 768; 769; 770; 775; 784; 812; 818; 819; 821; 838; 865; 866; 869.

This volume presents the texts listed here without change except for the
correction of typographical errors; it does not, however, attempt to repro-
duce nontextual features of their typographic design. Cross-references have
been changed to correspond to the page numbers of this volume. Spelling,
punctuation, and capitalization are often expressive, and they are not al-
tered, even when inconsistent or irregular. The following is a list of typo-
graphical errors in the source texts that have been corrected, cited by page
and line number: 3.16, You're; 3.28, 'Cause; 227.6, That's want; 279.36, you.;

280.6, Mumbo; 280.7, "Mumbo; 379.7, indetermonably; 435.3, unforseen; 435.21, plung; 437.19, *Ann's*; 437.21, anemony; 440.11, then; 441.21, lilys; 442.1, Hate his; 442.8, azalia; 443.23, If; 444.24, anemonies; 456.26, *Hemmed in*; 461.18, feckless; 466.13, cream; 476.21, Sargossa; 505.4, I even; 522.4, Rihoku's; 522.16, Cire; 523.14, Rochechouart; 531.28, Cytharean; 532.15, Ἴδμεν; 534.2, γρωα; 534.2, θεὸν; 534.15, decor"; 541.4, *poèsie*; 541.14, NUK-TIS; 541.26, seive; 543.7, neo-Neitzschean; 553.16, Terreus; 568.18, Velasquez; 568.27, Alcazar; 569.21, budelle; 573.15, porportions; 611.5, back; 691.1, thoes; 691.9 to; 743.36, a a; 745.12, *Od*; 764.6, stye; 785.5, fixity.; 828.7, throught; 849.16, *Marvel.*

ACKNOWLEDGMENTS

Great care has been taken to trace all owners of copyright material included in this book. If any have been inadvertently omitted or overlooked, acknowledgment will gladly be made in future printings.

Franklin P. Adams. If—: Copyright © Franklin P. Adams. Reprinted with permission.

Conrad Aiken. Morning Song of Senlin; Tetélestai; And in the Hanging Gardens; The Room; Sea Holly; *from* Preludes for Memnon: From *Collected Poems*, 2nd Edition by Conrad Aiken, copyright © 1953, 1970 by Conrad Aiken. Used by permission of Oxford University Press, Inc.

Anonymous Ballads. Casey Jones; Midnight Special: From *The American Songbag*, copyright 1927 by Harcourt, Inc., renewed © 1955 by Carl Sandburg. Reprinted by permission of the publisher.

Djuna Barnes. Portrait of a Lady Walking; The Walking-Mort: From *The New Yorker*: Copyright © The Estate of Djuna Barnes. Reprinted with permission of the Authors League Fund.

Irving Berlin. Slumming on Park Avenue: Copyright 1937, © 1958 by Irving Berlin. International Copyright Secured. Reprinted with permission.

John Peale Bishop. Speaking of Poetry; In the Dordogne; Young Men Dead; Metamorphoses of M; The Return: Copyright 1948, renewed © 1976 by Charles Scribner's Sons. Reprinted with permission of Scribner, a division of Simon & Schuster from *The Collected Poems of John Peale Bishop*, edited by Allen Tate.

Witter Bynner. Wistaria; Donald Evans; Driftwood; Lovers; A Foreigner; Idols; Defeat; The Titanic; "All tempest"; "Any other time would have done": From *Selected Poems* by Witter Bynner, copyright © 1978 by the Witter Bynner Foundation for Poetry, Inc.; reprinted by permission of Farrar, Straus, & Giroux, LLC. "But for these apertures": Copyright © The Witter Bynner Foundation for Poetry, Inc.; reprinted with permission.

H.D. (Hilda Doolittle). Fragment 113; Helen; Lethe; Trance; Birds in Snow; The Mysteries; *from* Songs from Cyprus; *from* Let Zeus Record; Epitaph; *from* The Walls Do Not Fall; *from* Sigil; *from* Tribute to the Angels; *from* The Flowering of the Rod: From *Collected Poems 1912–1944*. Copyright © 1982 by The Estate of Hilda Doolittle. Reprinted by permission of New Directions Publishing Corp.

Max Eastman. To John Reed; To Genevieve Taggard Who Called Me Traitor in a Poem: Copyright © Max Eastman. Reprinted with permission of Yvette Eastman.

T. S. Eliot. Ash-Wednesday: From *Collected Poems 1909–1962*: Copyright 1930, renewed © 1958 by T. S. Eliot, reprinted by permission of Harcourt Brace & Company. Marina; Sweeney Agonistes; The Hollow Men: From *Collected Poems 1909–1962*, copyright 1936 by Harcourt, Inc., copyright © 1964, 1963 by T. S. Eliot; reprinted by permission of the publisher. Burnt Norton: From *Four Quartets*, copyright 1936 by Harcourt, Inc. and renewed © 1964 by T. S. Eliot; reprinted by permission of the publisher.

Abbie Huston Evans. The Old Yellow Shop; Under Cover; Juniper; Martian Landscape: From *Collected Poems* by Abbie Huston Evans, copyright © 1950, 1952, 1953, 1956, 1960, 1961, 1966, 1970. Reprinted by permission of the University of Pittsburgh Press. Fringed Gentians: From *Fact of Crystal*, copyright 1950 by Abbie Huston Evans, renewed © 1977 by George M. Kevlin; reprinted by permission of Harcourt Brace & Co.

Robert Frost. The Pasture; Storm Fear; Mowing; The Tuft of Flowers; Mending Wall; The Death of the Hired Man; Home Burial; After Apple-Picking; The Wood-Pile; The Road Not Taken; An Old Man's Winter Night; Hyla Brook; The Oven Bird; Bond and Free; Birches; Putting in the Seed; The Sound of Trees; 'Out, Out—'; A Star in a Stone-Boat; The Witch of Coös; Nothing Gold Can Stay; Fire and Ice; Dust of Snow; Stopping by Woods on a Snowy Evening; For Once, Then, Something; The Onset; To Earthward; The Need of Being Versed in Country Things; Spring Pools;

Haniel Long. Daphnis and Chloe; Lightning; Cobweb; In the Dark World; Day and Night; A New Music; For Tony, Embarking in Spring; Our Spring Needs Shoveling: Copyright © Haniel Long. Reprinted by permission of the Department of Special Collections, Charles E. Young Research Library, The University of California at Los Angeles.

H. P. Lovecraft. The Well; Alienation: Copyright © H. P. Lovecraft. Reprinted by permission of Arkham House Publishers, Inc., and JABberwocky Literary Agency, P.O. Box 4558, Sunnyside, NY 11104-0558.

Amy Lowell: Lilacs; Meeting-House Hill; Katydids; New Heavens for Old; Dissonance: Copyright © 1927, 1955 by Houghton Mifflin, Inc. Reprinted with permission.

Mina Loy. Apology of Genius; Der Blinde Junge; Brancusi's Golden Bird; Gertrude Stein; Songs to Joannes; Lunar Baedeker; On Third Avenue; Poe: From *The Lost Lunar Baedeker* by Mina Loy, edited by Roger Conover. Copyright © 1996 by the Estate of Mina Loy, edition copyright © 1996 by Roger Conover. Reprinted by permission of Farrar, Straus & Giroux, LLC.

Archibald MacLeish. Ars Poetica; Return; You, Andrew Marvell; Epistle To Be Left in the Earth; Sentiments for a Dedication; Voyage West: Copyright © 1985 by the Estate of Archibald MacLeish. Reprinted by permission of Houghton Mifflin, Inc., from *Collected Poems 1917–1982*. All rights reserved.

Don Marquis. *From* the coming of archy; the song of mehitabel; aesop revised by archy; archy confesses: Copyright © 1927 by Doubleday, a division of Bantam, Doubleday, Dell Publishing Group, Inc. Used by permission of Doubleday, a division of Random House, Inc.

Edna St. Vincent Millay. Winter Night: Copyright 1928, © 1955 by Edna St. Vincent Millay and Norma Millay Ellis. "Love is not all: it is not meat nor drink": Copyright 1931, © 1958 by Edna St. Vincent Millay and Norma Millay Ellis. Menses; Sonnet; Rendezvous: Copyright © Edna St. Vincent Millay and Norma Millay Ellis. All rights reserved. These poems reprinted by permission of Elizabeth Barnett, literary executor.

Marianne Moore. Black Earth: Reprinted with the permission of Simon and Schuster, Inc. from *Selected Poems of Marianne Moore*. Copyright 1935 by Marianne Moore; copyright renewed © 1963 by Marianne Moore and T.S. Eliot. Poetry; The Past Is the Present; Marriage; The Fish; The Monkeys; The Mind Is an Enchanting Thing; He "Digesteth Harde Yron"; Smooth Gnarled Crape Myrtle; The Pangolin; Bird-Witted; In Distrust of Merits: Reprinted with the permission of Simon & Schuster, Inc. from *The Collected Poems of Marianne Moore*. Copyright 1941, 1944 by Marianne Moore; copyrights renewed © 1969, 1972 by Marianne Moore. O To Be a Dragon: Copyright © 1957 by Marianne Moore, renewed by Lawrence E. Brinn and Louise Crane, Executors of the Estate of Marianne Moore; The Steeple-Jack: copyright 1951, © 1970 by Marianne Moore, copyright © 1979 by Lawrence E. Brinn and Louise Crane, Executors of the Estate of Marianne Moore; Tom Fool at Jamaica: Copyright © 1953 by Marianne Moore, from *The Complete Poems of Marianne Moore*. Used by permission of Viking Penguin, a division of Penguin Putnam Inc.

John G. Neihardt. *From* The Song of the Messiah. From *A Cycle of the West* by John G. Neihardt by permission of the University of Nebraska Press. Copyright © 1915, 1919, 1925, 1935, 1941, 1949 by the Macmillan Company. Copyright © 1943, 1946, 1953 by John G. Neihardt. Copyright © 1991 by the University of Nebraska Press.

Dorothy Parker. Résumé; News Item; One Perfect Rose; Men; Observation; Symptom Recital; Ballade at Thirty-Five; The Red Dress; Bric-à-Brac; A Pig's-Eye View of Literature; Bohemia; Coda: Copyrights 1926, 1928, renewed © 1954, 1956 by Dorothy Parker. From *The Portable Dorothy Parker* by Dorothy Parker. Used by permission of Viking Penguin, a division of Penguin Putnam Inc.

Cole Porter. I Get a Kick Out of You; Anything Goes; Just One of Those Things: Copyright © The Cole Porter Musical & Literary Property Trusts. Reprinted with permission.

Ezra Pound. *From* Homage to Sextus Propertius: From *Personae*, copyright © 1926 by Ezra Pound. Reprinted by permission of New Directions Publishing Corp. Canto II; Canto IV; Canto XIII; Canto XVII; Canto XXVI; Canto XLV; Canto XLVII; Canto XLIX; Canto LXXXI; Canto XC; Canto CXVI; *from* Notes for Canto CXVII et seq.: From *The Cantos of Ezra Pound*, copyright © 1934, 1938, 1948 by Ezra Pound. Reprinted by permission of New Directions Publishing Corp. From *The Classic Anthology as Defined by Confucius*: reprinted by permission of the publisher from *Shih-Ching: The Classic Anthology as Defined by Confucius* by Ezra Pound, Cambridge, Mass.: Harvard University Press, copyright © 1954, 1982 by the President and Fellows of Harvard College. Choruses from Women of Trakis: From *Women of Trakis*, copyright © 1957 by Ezra Pound. Reprinted by permission of New Directions Publishing Corp.

John Crowe Ransom. Blackberry Winter; Here Lies a Lady; Judith of Bethulia; Philomela; Nocturne; Bells for John Whitesides' Daughter; Spectral Lovers; Captain Carpenter; Janet Waking; Piazza Piece; Painted Head; The Equilibrists; Blue Girls: From *Selected Poems* by John Crowe Ransom, copyright 1924, 1927, 1934 by Alfred A. Knopf Inc., renewed © 1952, 1955, 1962 by John Crowe Ransom. Reprinted with permission of the publisher.

Lizette Woodworth Reese. Crows; Fog; Wind; The White Fury of the Spring: Copyright © Lizette Woodworth Reese. Reprinted by permission of Octagon Books, a division of Hippocrene Books, Inc.

Lola Ridge. The Fifth-Floor Window; Kerensky: Copyright © The Estate of Lola Ridge. Reprinted with permission.

Elizabeth Madox Roberts. Evening Song; Song of the Dove; An Old Love in Song; Disconsolate Morning: From *Song in the Meadow*, copyright 1940 by Elizabeth Madox Roberts, renewed © 1967 by Ivors S. Roberts. Used by permission of Viking Penguin, a division of Penguin Putnam Inc.

Edwin Arlington Robinson. The Sheaves; Karma; Why He Was There; Mr. Flood's Party: copyright 1925 by Macmillan Publishing Company, renewed © 1953 by Ruth Nivison and Barbara R. Holt. Reprinted with permission of Simon & Schuster from *The Collected Poems of Edwin Arlington Robinson*.

Carl Sandburg. *From* The People, Yes: From *The People, Yes*, copyright 1936 by Harcourt, Inc. and renewed © 1964 by Carl Sandburg, reprinted by permission of the publisher. On a Flimmering Floom You Shall Ride: From *The Complete Poems of Carl Sandburg*, copyright © 1970, 1969 by Lillian Steichen Sandburg, Trustee, reprinted by permission of Harcourt, Inc.

Wilbert Snow. Advice to a Clam-Digger: Copyright © 1963 Wesleyan University Press. Reprinted by permission of University Press of New England.

Leonora Speyer. Witch!; To a Song of Sappho Discovered in Egypt: From *Fiddler's Farewell* by Leonora Speyer, copyright 1926 by Alfred A. Knopf and renewed © 1954 by Leonora Speyer. Reprinted with permission.

Gertrude Stein. Susie Asado; *from* Lifting Belly; Idem the Same.; *from* Stanzas in Meditation; *from* The World Is Round: Copyright © The Estate of Gertrude Stein. Published with permission. From *Tender Buttons*: From *The Selected Writings of Gertrude Stein*, edited with introduction and notes by Carl Van Vechten, copyright © 1946 by Random House, Inc. Reprinted by permission of Random House, Inc.

Wallace Stevens. The Death of a Soldier; Sea Surface Full of Clouds; The Idea of Order at Key West; A Postcard from the Volcano; The Sun This March; Autumn Refrain; Meditation Celestial & Terrestial; Phosphor Reading by His Own Light; Landscape with Boat; The Man on the Dump; Study of Two Pears; Poetry Is a Destructive Force; The Poems of Our Climate; God Is Good. It Is a Beautiful Night; Notes Toward a Supreme Fiction; The Motive for Metaphor; Men Made Out of Words; Large Red Man Reading; The Auroras of Autumn; The River of Rivers in Connecticut; The Planet on the Table; The Plain Sense of Things; Final Soliloquy of the Interior Paramour; The Rock; Not Ideas About the Thing But the Thing Itself; To an Old Philosopher in Rome: Copyright © 1923, 1936, 1942, 1947, 1936, 1948, 1950, 1951, 1952, 1954, renewed © 1951, 1964, 1970, by Holly Stevens. From *Collected Poems* by Wallace Stevens, reprinted by permission of Alfred A. Knopf, Inc. The Course of a Particular; Of Mere Being; A Discovery of Thought; Reality Is an Activity of the Most August Imagination: Copyright © 1957, 1971 by Holly Stevens. Reprinted by permission of Alfred A. Knopf, Inc.

Sara Teasdale. The Solitary; "I Shall Live to Be Old": Copyright 1926, renewed © 1954 by Mamie T. Wheless. Reprinted with permission of Simon & Schuster from *The Collected Poems of Sara Teasdale*. Lines; Moon's Ending: Copyright 1933 by Macmillan Publishing Company, renewed © 1961 by Guaranty Trust Company of New York, Executor. Reprinted with permission of Simon & Schuster from *The Collected Poems of Sara Teasdale*.

Edith Wharton. Terminus: Copyright © The Estate of Edith Wharton. Reprinted by permission of the Estate of Edith Wharton and the Watkins/ Loomis Agency.

John Hall Wheelock. Afternoon: Amagansett Beach; Earth, Take Me Back: Copyright © 1956 by John Hall Wheelock. Reprinted with permission of Scribner, a division of Simon & Schuster from *Poems Old and New* by John Hall Wheelock.

William Carlos Williams. "The moon, the dried weeds"; "There are no perfect waves"; Perpetuum Mobile: The City; The Yachts; This Is Just to Say; Young Sycamore; Hemmed-in Males; Paterson: Episode 17; These; The Young Housewife; Flowers By the Sea; The Last Words of My English Grandmother; Between Walls: From *Collected Poems: 1909–1939*, copyright © 1938 by New Directions Publishing Corp. Reprinted with permission. A Sort of Song; The Predicter of Famine; To Daphne and Virginia; The Descent; The World Contracted to a Recognizable Image; Burning the Christmas Greens; To a Man Dying on His Feet; The Dance; Paterson: The Falls: From *Collected Poems: 1939–1962*, copyright © 1944, 1948, 1953, 1962 by William Carlos Williams. Reprinted by permission of New Directions Publishing Corp.

Elinor Wylie. Confession of Faith; Green Hair; Ejaculation: From *Collected Poems* by Elinor Wylie. Copyright 1928, 1932 by Alfred A. Knopf, renewed © 1956, 1960 by Edwina C. Rubenstein. Reprinted by permission of the publisher.

Notes

In the notes below, the reference numbers denote page and line of this volume (the line count includes titles). No note is made for material included in standard desk-reference books, such as *Webster's Ninth New Collegiate Dictionary* or *Webster's Biographical Dictionary*. Quotations from Shakespeare are keyed to *The Riverside Shakespeare* (Boston: Houghton Mifflin, 1974), edited by G. Blakemore Evans. References to the Bible have been keyed to the King James Version.

1.3   Zolgotz] Leon F. Czolgosz (1873–1901), the anarchist who assassinated President William McKinley at the Pan-American Exposition held in Buffalo, New York, on September 6, 1901, and who was later executed for the crime.

2.12   *Casey Jones*] Jones was engineer of a six-car Illinois Central Railroad train making a run from Memphis to Canton, Mississippi, on April 29–30, 1900. After a late departure, Jones made up the time by allegedly traveling at record speeds; he was fatally injured in a collision with a freight train at Vaughan, Mississippi.

4.1   *Claude Allen*] On March 13, 1912, after a Hillsville, Virginia, judge sentenced Floyd Allen to a year in prison for aiding in the escape of a prisoner (his nephew), Allen and other members of his family opened fire in the courtroom. In the ensuing gunfight, the judge, the local sheriff, and three others were killed; Floyd Allen and his brother Sidna were among those wounded. The Allens escaped the courtroom but eventually were captured and tried for the shootings. Floyd Allen and his son Claude were convicted and executed.

31.28   "Oh, why . . . be proud?"] First line of "Mortality" (1824) by William Knox.

36.16   "East Lynne"] Novel (1861) by English author Mrs. Henry Wood; its dramatized form was widely performed on the American stage.

60.10   *Mrs. Edward MacDowell*] Founder of the MacDowell Colony in Petersborough, New Hampshire, the artists' colony where Robinson spent many of his summers. "Hillcrest" was the name of the MacDowell farmhouse.

68.24   Tilbury Town] Fictional setting for many of Robinson's poems, based on his home town of Gardiner, Maine.

68.27   the poet says] Edward FitzGerald, in stanza 7 of *The Rubiyat of Omar Khayyam* (1859).

69.4   Roland] Hero of the medieval French poem *La Chanson de Roland*; mortally wounded in an ambush, he sounded his horn as a warning to Charlemagne.

74.3   *Lift Every Voice and Sing*] Written in February 1900 for a school commemoration of Lincoln's birthday held in Jacksonville, Florida, the poem was set to music by Johnson's brother J. Rosamond Johnson; it has sometimes been referred to as the "Negro National Anthem."

86.3   *Big Swimming*] "Big swimming" is a name for uncrossable water. [Piper's note.]

95.35   Acosta] Uriel da Acosta (1591–1640), Portuguese Jewish philosopher and theologian, a convert from Roman Catholicism, was excommunicated after his attacks on rabbinical Judaism.

119.34   the Hyla breed] Any of a breed of tree frogs, called spring peepers, which on spring nights sound like ringing bells.

120.11   *The Oven Bird*] A North American warbler, sometimes called a "teacher bird," whose dome-shaped nest resembles an oven and whose call sounds like "teacher, teacher."

124.13   'Out, Out—'] Shakespeare, *Macbeth*, V, v, 23.

125.12   *Stone-Boat*] A low, flat sled used for transporting stones.

127.10   Coös] Coos County in northern New Hampshire.

127.23   the Sioux Control] A U.S. agent in charge of the affairs of the Sioux Indian tribe.

137.28   *Put out the Light*] Cf. Shakespeare, *Othello*, V, ii, 7.

157.8   can't get saved . . . St. Mark] Cf. Mark 4:11–12.

158.12   Keats' Eremite] Cf. John Keats, "Bright Star": "Bright star, would I were steadfast as thou art— / Not in lone splendour hung aloft the night / And watching, with eternal lids apart, / Like nature's patient, sleepless Eremite . . . ."

168.23   *Venus Transiens*] The Transit of Venus.

191.6   *Susie Asado*] This portrait was suggested by Antonia Marce (1890–1936), a flamenco dancer known as "La Argentina."

224.14   Medea's wreath] In Euripides' play, Medea brings about the death of Creon's daughter by giving her a costume that catches fire when worn.

230.6   my dead wife] Leonard's first wife, Charlotte Freeman, committed suicide in 1911.

230.10   turned his Latian verse to mine] Leonard's translation of
Lucretius, completed in 1912, was published in 1921 as *Of the Nature of
Things: A Metrical Translation.*

238.10–11   Debussy's / *"Reflets dans l'eau."*] Orchestral work completed
in 1905, the first piece in the series *Images.*

247.23   Mark's wife] Isolde, in Arthurian legend.

248.4   *the coming of archy*] The poem, the first in a long series published
in the New York *Sun* and other newspapers, is prefaced by a prose narrative
which reads in part:

> "We came into our room earlier than usual in the morning, and discovered
> a giant cockroach jumping about upon the keys.
> "He did not see us, and we watched him. He would climb painfully upon
> the framework of the machine and cast himself with all his force upon a key,
> head downward, and his weight and the impact of the blow were just suffi-
> cient to operate the machine, one slow letter after another. He could not
> work the capital letters, and he had a great deal of difficulty operating the
> mechanism that shifts the paper so that a fresh line may be started. . . . After
> about an hour of his frightfully difficult literary labor he fell to the floor ex-
> hausted. . . .
> "Congratulating ourselves that we had left a sheet of paper in the machine
> the night before so that all this work had not been in vain, we made an ex-
> amination, and this is what we found:"

263.27   Petemen] Safe-crackers.

269.2–3   *testimony of the poet MacLeish*] During 1944 Senate Foreign
Relations Committee confirmation hearings on Roosevelt's appointment of
Archibald MacLeish as assistant secretary of state for cultural and public affairs,
MacLeish was questioned by Senator Bennett Champ Clark of Missouri. Clark
quoted from several of MacLeish's poems, and asked him, "since the new as-
sistant secretary is supposed to impose culture on the whole world," to "tell
us what they mean." In reply, MacLeish quoted Robert Browning: "When I
wrote that, God and I knew what it meant; but now God alone knows."

270.4   *"Sweet Bye and Bye"*] Hymn (1868) composed by Joseph P.
Webster.

272.4   The Blood of the Lamb] "Are You Washed in the Blood," hymn
composed by Elisha A. Hoffman.

276.17–18   Leopold's ghost . . . hand-maimed host] Leopold II of
Belgium established the Congo Free State under his personal authority in
1885, exploiting it for its rubber and ivory resources; under his administration,
widespread atrocities occurred, including severing the hands and feet of
African workers who failed to meet their quotas.

278.33   Jacob . . . golden stairs] Cf. Genesis 28:12.

282.1   *Mae Marsh*] American film actress (1895–1968) who appeared in many silent films, including D. W. Griffith's *The Birth of a Nation* and *Intolerance*.

283.11   silver Zion] William Jennings Bryan, a Nebraska Democrat, advocated expanding the currency through the "free and unlimited coinage of silver," with the value of silver to gold fixed at a 16 to 1 ratio.

287.3   Gibson Girl] Image of a fashionable young woman of the upper classes, based on the popular drawings of illustrator Charles Dana Gibson (1867–1944).

287.33–35   *"The people have a right . . . cross of gold."*] From Bryan's speech delivered at the 1896 Democratic Party Convention in Chicago.

296.24   *Peter Quince*] Carpenter and play director in Shakespeare's *A Midsummer Night's Dream.*

307.14   *C'était . . . mon âme.*] It was my child, my jewel, my soul.

308.3   *C'était . . . or.*] It was my celestial brother, my life, my gold.

308.22   *C'était . . . amour.*] It was my ecstasy and my love.

309.13   *C'était . . . divine.*] It was my faith, divine nonchalance.

310.3   *C'était . . . l'ignominie.*] It was my bastard spirit, shame.

314.23   Corazon] Heart.

316.3   Opusculum paedagogum] A small pedagogical work.

325.30   Schwärmerei] Gushing rapture.

331.29   là-bas] Over there.

372.18   *Emanuel Morgan*] A pseudonym for Bynner. With Arthur Davison Ficke (who wrote under the pseudonym "Anne Knish") Bynner invented the mock poetic school of "Spectrism," which was taken seriously by a number of poets and reviewers; the hoax was revealed in 1918.

378.11   the foreigner] D. H. Lawrence.

380.16   Justus Miles Forman] American novelist and playwright (1875–1915); he died in the sinking of the *Lusitania*, not, as stated by Bynner, the *Titanic*.

380.20   Charles Frohman] Theater producer (1860–1915) who died in the sinking of the *Lusitania*.

385.19–20   late delivered . . . of man] The Mariner 4 spacecraft photographed the Martian surface when it passed near the planet in 1965 and radioed the images back to Earth in a digital code.

392.24   porte-enfant] Baby carriage.

408.15   *Der Blinde Junge*] The blind youth.

408.19   Kriegsopfer] War victim.

415.3   Mauna Loa] Vine whose flowers are used for leis in Hawaii.

421.12   *Anne Knish*] See note 372.18.

431.26   Half Moon] Ship in which Henry Hudson sailed up the Hudson River to the vicinity of present-day Albany, New York, in 1609.

433.24   Park Avenue] In Rutherford, New Jersey, where Williams lived.

442.14   Hartley praises Miss Wirt] Marsden Hartley praised the circus equestrian May Wirth in *Adventures in the Arts* (1921).

442.25   grief of the bowmen of Shu] Cf. Ezra Pound's "Song of the Bowmen of Shu" (1915).

444.28   J. P. M.] J. Pierpont Morgan.

449.12   from her mouth] This line was deleted in later editions of the poem.

452.1   Elsie] Retarded nursemaid, hired from the state orphanage, who worked for Williams and his family at the time this poem was written.

455.13–15   What's . . . up—] These three lines were deleted in later editions of the poem.

457.8   W.C.T.U.] The Women's Christian Temperance Union.

457.14   Sullivan and Kilrain] Prizefighters John L. Sullivan (1858–1918) and Jake Kilrain (1859–1937) fought a bare-knuckles match for the heavyweight championship on July 8, 1889.

457.15   Pop Anson] Adrian "Pop" (or "Cap") Anson (1852–1922), baseball player and manager who spent most of his career in Chicago.

470.9   "the dying swan"] Dance solo made famous by Anna Pavlova (1882–1931).

505.3   *De Aegypto*] Of Egypt. This poem was originally titled "Aegupton" in *A Lume Spento* (1908). When collected in *Personae* (1926), its final two stanzas were omitted.

505.12   Manus animam pinxit] My hand painted my soul.

506.8   LOQUITUR] Speaker.

506.8   *En*] Sir.

506.9–10   Dante . . . strife] Cf. *Inferno*, Canto 28, lines 118–42.

508.1   *Planh*] Lament.

513.22   *Jacopo del Sellaio*] Florentine painter (1442–93).

515.7   "Slade"] London's Slade School of Art.

515.11   *Cleopatra*]   Diaghilev's one-act ballet *Cléopâtre*, first performed in Paris in 1909.

517.6   *guarda! ch' è be'a!*]   Look! She's beautiful!

517.17   *sta fermo!*]   Keep quiet!

520.11   RIHAKU]   Japanese reading of the name of the Chinese poet Li Po, as adopted by Pound from Ernest Fenollosa's usage.

522.4   Riboku]   Japanese form of Chinese general Li Mu.

522.12–13   *A Perigord . . . ab malh.*]   In *The Spirit of Romance* (1910), Pound translated these lines: "At Perigord near to the wall, / Aye, within a mace throw of it." "Perigord" is the Provençal town of Périgueux.

522.18   a fine canzone]   "Dompna Pois De Me No'us Cal," which Pound translated and published in 1914.

523.8   "that . . . lamp."]   Cf. *Inferno*, Canto 28, lines 121–22.

523.12   "counterpass."]   Cf. *Inferno*, Canto 28, line 142.

524.34   St. Leider . . . Polhonac]   The troubadour Guillaume de Saint-Leidier seduced Adelaide de Claustra, the wife of Héracle, Viscount of Polignac, after she agreed to accept him only at her husband's invitation. Héracle sang a love song composed by Guillaume for Adelaide and unwittingly assisted in the seduction of his wife.

525.1–2   *"Et albirar . . .* knew that]   In "Troubadours—Their Sorts and Conditions" (1913), Pound translated this line by Guston Phoebus, Count of Foix (1331–91): "And sing not all they have in mind."

525.12   *al* and *ochaisos*]   Rhyming words used in "Dompna Pois De Me No'us Cal."

526.17   *trobar clus*]   A hermetic style practiced by some Provençal poets.

526.18   "best craftsman"]   In *Purgatorio*, Canto 26, line 117, Dante calls Arnaut Daniel the "better craftsman" ("miglior fabbro").

527.4–9   *Surely I saw . . . counterpart."*]   Cf. *Inferno*, Canto 28, lines 118–23, 139–42.

527.12   *Ed eran . . . uno in due*]   And they were two in one and one in two.

532.1   *Hugh Selwyn Mauberly*]   In the 1926 Boni & Liveright edition of *Personae*, Pound added this note: "The sequence is so distinctly a farewell to London that the reader who chooses to regard this as an exclusively American edition may as well omit it and turn at once to page 205."

532.3   *Vocat æstus in umbram*]   The heat calls us into the shade.

532.5   *Ode . . . Sepulchre*]   "Ode for the Selection of His Tomb," an adaptation of the title of an ode by Pierre Ronsard. All other editions except for the Boni & Liveright *Poems 1918–1921* add the initials "E.P." to the beginning of the title.

532.15 ``Ἴδμεν γάρ τοι πάνθ᾽, ὅσ᾽ ἐνὶ Τροίῃ] *Odyssey*, XII, 189, from the sirens' song: "For we know all the toils that are in wide Troy."

532.24–25 *l'an . . . son eage*] "In the thirtieth year of his life"; adapted from the opening of Francois Villon's *Le Testament*.

533.24 τὸ καλόν] The beautiful.

534.2 τίν᾽ ἄνδρα, τίν᾽ ἥρωα, τίνα θεόν,] Cf. Pindar, *Olympian Odes*, II, 2: "What god, what hero, aye, and what man shall we loudly praise?"

534.7 pro domo] For the home.

534.15 pro patria . . . et decor] "For the fatherland, neither sweetly nor gloriously": Adaptation of Horace, *Odes*, III, ii, 13: "dulce et decorum est pro patria mori" ("It is sweet and glorious to die for one's fatherland").

535.12–13 When John Ruskin . . . Treasuries"] "Of Kings' Treasuries" was the opening chapter in Ruskin's *Sesame and Lilies* (1865).

535.15 Fœtid Buchanan . . . his voice] Robert W. Buchanan attacked the pre-Raphaelite poets in "The Fleshly School of Poetry" (1871). Dante Gabriel Rossetti's poem "Jenny" was singled out for attack.

535.19–22 The Burne-Jones . . . rhapsodize] Burne-Jones' painting *King Cophetua and the Beggar Maid*, in the Tate Gallery's collection since 1919.

535.30 "Ah, poor Jenny's case"] See note 535.15.

536.5 "Siena . . . Maremma"] "Siena made me; Maremma undid me": Dante, *Purgatorio*, Canto 5, line 134.

536.11 the Rhymers' Club] Group founded in the early 1890s by W. B. Yeats, Ernest Rhys, and T. W. Rolleston; its members included Ernest Dowson, Lionel Johnson, Victor Plarr, and Arthur Symons.

537.26 friend of Bloughram's] Gigadibs, literary hack in Browning's poem "Bishop Bloughram's Apology" (1855).

538.24–25 "Daphne . . . hands"] Translation of lines from Théophile Gautier's "Le Château du Souvenir" (1852).

539.15 "Which . . . nourished"] Translation of the first line of Jules Laforgue's "Complainte des Pianos" (1885).

540.16 *1920 (Mauberley)*] For *Personae* (1926), Pound added an epitaph adapted from Ovid, *Metamorphosis*, VII, 86: "Vacuos exercet aera morsus" ("His empty mouth snaps at the air").

540.18–19 "eau-forte . . . Jaquemart"] Etching by Jules Jacquemart (1837–80).

541.2–7 *"Qu'est-ce . . .* CAID ALI] "What do they know of love, and what can they understand? If they cannot understand poetry, if they have no feeling for music, what can they understand of this passion, in comparison with which the rose is gross and the perfume of violets a clap of thunder?" "Caid Ali" is a pseudonym for Pound.

541.8 diabolus in the scale] Medieval music theorists called the augmented fourth the "devil in music."

541.10 ANANGKE] Necessity.

541.14 NUKTOS AGALMA] Night's jewel.

541.25 TO AGATHON] The good.

545.20 Anadyomene] Foam-born (epithet of Aphrodite).

545.21 Reinach] Salomon Reinach (1858–1932), French art historian; his *Apollo* (1904) is a study of ancient sculpture.

546.3 "Sordello"] Title of long poem (1840) by Browning, based on the life of the 13th-century Italian troubadour and soldier.

546.5 Lo Sordels . . . Mantovana] Sordello is from Mantovana.

546.8 Lir] Celtic sea-god.

546.12 "Eleanor, ἑλέναυς and ἑλέπτολις!"] "Eleanor, ship-destroying and city-destroying," puns on Helen of Troy's name in Aeschylus' *Agamemnon,* line 689. Eleanor here refers to Eleanor of Aquitaine.

546.15–23 "Let her go . . . voices."] Adaptation of *Iliad,* III, 139–60.

546.20 Schoeney] Schoenus, father of Atalanta.

546.24 Tyro] Shade encountered by Achilles in *Odyssey,* XI, 235–39.

547.3–549.14 The ship landed . . . ivory stillness] Adaptation of Ovid, *Metamorposes,* III, 641–910.

548.19 Lyæus] Bacchus.

550.9 ANAXIFORMINGES!] "Lords of the lyre," from Pindar's second Olympian Ode.

550.9 Aurunculeia] Bride in *Collis o Helliconii,* the epithalamium of Catullus.

550.22 Ityn!] Itys, son of Tereus and Procne, king and queen of Thebes. Tereus raped his sister-in-law Philomela and cut out her tongue; in revenge, Procne killed Itys and served his flesh to Tereus. Philomela was transformed into a nightingale; her lament for Itys, "et ter flebiliter" ("and thrice with tears") is quoted from Horace, *Odes,* IV, xii, 5.

550.27 Cabestan] Guillem da Cabestanh, Provençal troubadour, who was said to have been murdered by Ramon of Chateau Roussilon, the jealous husband of Cabestanh's lover Seremonda. Ramon served Cabestan's cooked heart to Seremonda, who then committed suicide.

551.25   Vidal]   Provençal troubadour Peire Vidals.

552.4   Salmacis]   Water-nymph who attempted to rape Hermaphroditos; cf. Ovid, *Metamorphoses*, IV, 349–480.

552.6   *e lo soleils plovil*]   Phrase from Daniel's "Lancan son passat li giure"; Pound elsewhere translated the complete line as "To where the rain falls from the sun."

552.11–12   The pines at Takasago . . . Isé!]   Cf. the Japanese Noh play *Takasago*, in which the spirits of an aging couple inhabit two pine trees.

553.15   Gyges]   Lydian hidden by King Candaules in the queen's bedroom in order to admire her beauty; discovering Gyges, the queen ordered him to kill Candaules and marry her.

553.31   Kung]   Confucius. Canto XIII is a pastiche of statements attributed to Confucius, based on J.P.G. Pauthier's *Les Quatre Livres de philosophie morale et politique de la Chine* (1840).

555.29–30   A day . . . passing."]   When this Canto was published in *A Draft of XXX Cantos* (Hours Press, 1930), these lines were accidentally added by the typesetter, and were retained in later Farrar & Rinehart and New Directions editions of *The Cantos*. When the critic Hugh Kenner asked Pound about the lines in 1957, Pound replied, "Repeat in XIII sanctioned by time and the author, or rather first by the author, who never objects to the typesetter making improvements."

556.7   ZAGREUS!]   Bacchus.

557.37   Borso]   Borso d'Este (1431–71), Ferraran ruler and patron of the arts.

557.37   *i vitrei*]   The glassmakers.

558.38   Sigismundo]   Sigismundo Malatesta (1417–68), ruler of Rimini, warred against the forces of Pope Pius II; he was defeated and lost most of his territory.

559.2–561.13   A lady . . . company.]   Translation of Calvacanti's canzone "Donna mi priegha."

561.25   Sacrum . . . coitu]   Sacred, sacred, the illumination in coitus.

561.28   "Five castles!"]   Sordello was rewarded with five castles for his military services.

561.31   dye-works]   Sordello was rewarded with the town of Palena, known for its dye-works.

561.35–562.1   Dilectis miles . . . Thetis]   Most beloved and familiar sol-
dier . . . the fort of Mount Odorisio / Mounts San Silvestro, Pagliete and
Pila . . . / In the region of Thetis.

562.4   pratis nemoribus pascuis]   Meadows, woodlands, pastures.

562.9   Quan ben . . . pensamen]   When I think deep in my good thought.

563.7   'La Calunnia']   "The Slander," painting by Sandro Botticelli.

563.8   Ambrogio Praedis]   Ambrogio de Predis (?1455–?1506), Milanese
miniaturist.

563.9   *Adamo me fecit*]   "Adam made me": words inscribed on San Zeno
Church in Verona.

563.10–11   St Trophime . . . Saint Hilaire]   Provençal churches in Arles
and Poitiers.

564.3–5   *phtheggometha* . . . φθεγγώμεθα θᾶσσον]   Let us raise our
voices without delay: *Odyssey*, X, 228.

564.20–21   *Kai* . . . ADONIN]   And the fates Adonis. Adapted from
line 94 of Bion's "Lament for Adonis."

564.34   Molü]   Herb that Odysseus used as antidote for a potion of
Circe's. Cf. *Odyssey*, X.

564.39–565.13   Begin thy plowing . . . time.]   Adapted from Hesiod,
Works and Days, lines 383–91.

565.38   Apeliota]   The east wind.

567.24–27   K E I . . . K A I]   Japanese-style transliteration of a Chinese
poem attributed to Emperor Shun (2255–05 B.C.), translated thus by Pound:
"Gate, gate of gleaming, / knotting, dispersing, / flower of sun, flower of
moon / day's dawn after day's dawn new fire / Sun up . . . what is it?"

568.5–7   Hay . . . reliHion"]   They have a lot of Catholicism . . . and
very little religion.

568.8   Yo . . . desparecen"]   I believe that kings will disappear.

568.23   Bowers]   Claude Gernade Bowers (1879–1958), American ambas-
sador to Spain, 1933–39.

568.39   Basil]   The English poet Basil Bunting (1900–85).

569.10–11   André Spire . . . Agricole]   Spire (1868–1966), a French poet,
had served on the board of Crédit Agricole, a French bank.

569.21–22   "Te cavero . . . a te"]   "I'll cut your guts out." "And me,
your liver." Fragmentary citation of Canto X's argument between
Sigismondo Malatesta and Federigo d'Urbino during an unsuccessful peace-
making attempt by Borso d'Este.

569.27 Ἰυγξ. . . . . ʼεμὸν ποτί δῶμα τὸν ἄνδρα] Fragmentary phrases from Theocritus' second idyll, pertaining to the workings of a love charm: "Little wheel . . . man to my house."

570.2 Muss.] Mussolini.

570.6 and George Horace . . . (Senator)] George Horace Lorimer (1868–1937) was the only journalist allowed to interview Senator Albert Jeremiah Beveridge after Beveridge's trip to the Philippines in 1899.

570.18 Althea] Cf. Richard Lovelace's "To Althea from Prison."

571.4 Ed ascoltando al leggier mormorio] And listening to the light murmur.

571.14 Εἰδὼς] Knowing.

571.29 What . . . heritage] In the English editions of this canto published by Faber and Faber, this line is followed by the line: "What thou lov'st well shall not be reft from thee."

572.2 Paquin] Jeanne Paquin (1869–1936), French fashion designer.

572.20 Blunt] Wilfrid Scawen Blunt (1840–1922), English poet visited by Pound and Yeats in 1914.

572.25 faltered,] English editions of this canto published by Faber and Faber read "faltered."

572.27–30 Animus . . . procedit.] "The human soul is not love, but love flows from it, and it delights not in the idea of itself but in the love which flows from it": Richard of St. Victor (d. 1183), *Quomodo Spiritus sanctus est amor Patris et Filii.*

573.5 Templum aedificans] Building the temple.

573.18–19 Kuthera . . . sempiterna] Aphrodite the terrifying, Aphrodite everlasting.

573.20 Ubi amor, ibi oculus] Where love is, there is the eye: Richard of St. Victor, *Benjamin Minor.*

573.21 Vae . . . inutile] Woe to those who think without purpose.

573.22–23 quam . . . imago] From a sentence by Richard of St. Victor, translated in full by Pound as: "[The good things of will,] through which an image of the divine likeness [will be found] in us."

573.26 ἠγάπησεν πολύ] She loved much.

573.27 liberavit masnatos] He freed his slaves.

573.30 semina motuum] Seeds of motion.

574.1 m'elevasti] You lifted me up.

574.20   Juan Ramon]   Spanish poet Juan Ramón Jiménez (1881–1958).

574.36   Richardus]   Richard of St. Victor.

574.38   Gaio!]   Merry!

575.7   ac ferae]   And wild beasts.

575.8   cervi]   Deer.

575.10   Bagheera]   Panther in Kipling's *The Jungle Book*.

575.12   ἐπὶ χθονί]   Around the earth.

575.15   οἱ χθόνιοι]   Spirits of the underworld.

575.23   χελιδών, χελιδών]   Swallow.

575.39   Ἠλέκτρα]   Elektra.

576.27   Litterae nihil sanantes]   Writings that cure nothing.

577.6   "plus j'aime le chien"]   "The more I love dogs": half of the remark, "The more I know of men, the more I love dogs."

577.15   chi crescerà i nostri]   Who will increase our loves: cf. Dante, *Paradiso*, Canto 5.

577.17   third heaven]   The third heaven of Dante's Paradise, governed by Venus.

577.35–36   al poco . . . cerchio d'ombra]   At the dim daylight and to the large circle of shadow: first line of the first sestina of Dante's *Canzoniere*.

577.39–40   al Vicolo d'oro . . . (Tigullio)]   "The Lane of Gold in Rapallo"; Rapallo is on the Bay of Tigullio.

578.17–18   Rupe Tarpeia]   Rome's Tarpeian Rock, used for public executions in antiquity.

582.11   DAYSAIR]   Deianira, wife of Herakles.

591.20   nine Visigoth . . . Museum]   Nine gold crowns dating from 7th-century Spain, in the collection of the Musée de Cluny in Paris.

633.27   *I John . . . testify*]   Cf. Revelation.

634.7   *vas spirituale*]   Spiritual receptacle.

636.5–6   *to-day . . . in Paradise.*]   Luke 23:44.

639.6   *many waters . . . love's fire.*]   Cf. Song of Solomon 8:7.

648.7   sang]   Ginseng.

676.30–31   Tamar and Cawdor / and Thurso's wife]   Characters in Jeffers' narrative poems *Tamar* (1924), *Cawdor* (1928), and *Thurso's Landing* (1932).

680.13   *The Past*] Moore's notes for her poems are printed exactly as they appeared in *The Complete Poems of Marianne Moore* (1967) except for page numbers, which are keyed to this volume.

A NOTE ON THE NOTES

A willingness to satisfy contradictory objections to one's manner of writing might turn one's work into the donkey that finally found itself being carried by its masters, since some readers suggest that quotation-marks are disruptive of pleasant progress; others, that notes to what should be complete are a pedantry or evidence of an insufficiently realized task. But since in anything I have written, there have been lines in which the chief interest is borrowed, and I have not yet been able to outgrow this hybrid method of composition, acknowledgements seem only honest. Perhaps those who are annoyed by provisos, detainments, and postscripts could be persuaded to take probity on faith and disregard the notes.

M. M.

THE PAST IS THE PRESENT *(page 680)*
Lines 7–8: *"Hebrew poetry is prose with a sort of heightened consciousness."* Dr. E. H. Kellogg in Bible class, Presbyterian Church, Carlisle, Pennsylvania.

POETRY *(page 692)*
Diary of Tolstoy, p. 84: "Where the boundary between prose and poetry lies, I shall never be able to understand. The question is raised in manuals of style, yet the answer to it lies beyond me. Poetry is verse: prose is not verse. Or else poetry is everything with the exception of business documents and school books."
"Literalists of the imagination." Yeats, *Ideas of Good and Evil* (A. H. Bullen, 1903), p. 182. "The limitation of his view was from the very intensity of his vision; he was a too literal realist of imagination, as others are of nature; and because he believed that the figures seen by the mind's eye, when exalted by inspiration, were 'eternal existences,' symbols of divine essences, he hated every grace of style that might obscure their lineaments."

MARRIAGE *(page 695)*
Statements that took my fancy which I tried to arrange plausibly.
Lines 14–15: *"Of circular traditions . . ."* Francis Bacon.
Lines 25–28: *Write simultaneously.* "Miss A—— will write simultaneously in three languages, English, German, and French, talking in the meantime. [She] takes advantage of her abilities in everyday life, writing her letters simultaneously with both hands; namely, the first, third, and fifth words with her left and the second, fourth, and sixth with her right hand. While generally writing outward, she is able as well to write inward with both hands." "Multiple Consciousness or Reflex Action of Unaccustomed Range," *Scientific American,* January 1922.
Line 42: *"See her, see her in this common world."* "George Shock."
Lines 48–55: *"That strange paradise, unlike flesh, stones . . ."* Richard Baxter, *The Saints' Everlasting Rest.*
Lines 65–66: "We were puzzled and we were fascinated, as if by something feline, by something colubrine." Philip Littell, reviewing Santayana's *Poems* in *The New Republic,* March 21, 1923.

Lines 83–84: *"Treading chasms . . ."* Hazlitt: "Essay on Burke's Style."

Lines 91–97: *"Past states . . ."* Richard Baxter.

Lines 101–102: *"He experiences a solemn joy."* *"A Travers Champs,"* by Anatole France in *Filles et Garçons* (Hachette): *"Le petit Jean comprend qu'el est beau et cette idée le pénetre d'un respect profond de lui-méme. . . . Il goûte une joie pieuse à se sentir devenu une idole."*

Line 108: *"It clothes me with a shirt of fire."* Hagop Boghossian in a poem, "The Nightingale."

Lines 109–113: *"He dares not clap his hands . . ."* Edward Thomas, *Feminine Influence on the Poets* (Martin Secker, 1910).

Lines 116–117, 121–123: *"Illusion of a fire . . . ," "as high as deep . . ."* Richard Baxter.

Line 125: "Marriage is a law, and the worst of all laws . . . a very trivial object indeed." Godwin.

Lines 146–152: *"For love that will gaze an eagle blind . . ."* Anthony Trollope, *Barchester Towers.*

Lines 159–161: *"No truth can be fully known . . ."* Robert of Sorbonne.

Lines 167–168: *"Darkeneth her countenance as a bear doth."* Ecclesiasticus.

Line 175: *"Married people often look that way."* C. Bertram Hartmann.

Lines 176–178: "Seldom and cold . . ." Richard Baxter.

Line 181: "Ahasuerus' *tête-à-tête* banquet." George Adam Smith, *Expositor's Bible.*

Line 183: *"Good monster, lead the way."* *The Tempest.*

Lines 187–190: *"Four o'clock does not exist . . ."* Comtesse de Noailles, "Le Thé," *Femina,* December 1921. *"Dans leur impérieuse humilité elles jouent instinctivement leurs rôles sur le globe."*

Lines 194–196: *"What monarch . . ."* From "The Rape of the Lock," a parody by Mary Frances Nearing, with suggestions by M. Moore.

Lines 198–199: *"The sound of the flute . . ."* A. Mitram Rihbany, *The Syrian Christ* (Houghton, Mifflin, 1916). Silence of women—"to an Oriental, this is as poetry set to music."

Lines 200–204: *"Men are monopolists . . ."* Miss M. Carey Thomas, Founder's address, Mount Holyoke, 1921: "Men practically reserve for themselves stately funerals, splendid monuments, memorial statues, membership in academies, medals, titles, honorary degrees, stars, garters, ribbons, buttons and other shining baubles, so valueless in themselves and yet so infinitely desirable because they are symbols of recognition by their fellow-craftsmen of difficult work well done."

Lines 207–208: *"The crumbs from a lion's meal . . .":* Amos iii, 12. Translation by George Adam Smith, *Expositor's Bible.*

Line 211: *"A wife is a coffin."* Ezra Pound.

Line 223: *"Settle on my hand."* Charles Reade, *Christie Johnston.*

Lines 232–233: "Asiatics have rights; Europeans have obligations." Edmund Burke.

Lines 252–253: *"Leaves her peaceful husband . . ."* Simone Puget, advertisement entitled "Change of Fashion," *English Review,* June 1914: "Thus proceed pretty dolls when they leave their old home to renovate their frame, and dear others who may abandon their peaceful husband only because they have seen enough of him."

Lines 256–258: *"Everything to do with love is mystery . . ."* F. C. Tilney, *Fables of La Fontaine,* "Love and Folly," Book XII, No. 14.

Lines 286–287: *"Liberty and Union . . ."* Daniel Webster (statue with inscription, Central Park, New York City).

SMOOTH GNARLED CRAPE MYRTLE *(page 707)*
Lines 16–18: "Bulbul is a broadly generic term like sparrow, warbler, bunting. . . . The legendary nightingale of Persia is the white-eared bulbul, *Pycnotus leucotis*, richly garbed in black velvet, trimmed with brown, white, and saffron yellow; and it is a true bulbul; . . . Edward FitzGerald told what Omar meant: that the speech of man changes and coarsens, but the bulbul sings eternally in the 'high-piping Pehlevi,' the pure heroic Sanskrit of the ancient poets." J. I. Lawrence, *New York Sun*, June 23, 1934.
Lines 26–27: "Those who sleep in New York, but dream of London." Beau Nash, *The Playbill*, January 1935.
Lines 31–32: *"Joined in friendship, crowned by love."* Battersea box motto.
Lines 45–47: *"Without loneliness . . ."* Yoné Noguchi paraphrasing Saigyo, *The Spectator* (London), February 15, 1935.
Lines 49–51: "By Peace Plenty, by Wisdom Peace," framing horns of plenty and caduceus, above clasped hands, on the first-edition title page of Lodge's *Rosalynde*.

BIRD-WITTED *(page 709)*
Sir Francis Bacon: "If a boy be bird-witted."

THE PANGOLIN *(page 711)*
Line 9: *"The closing ear-ridge,"* and certain other detail, from "Pangolins" by Robert T. Hatt, *Natural History*, December 1935.
Lines 16–17: *"Stepping . . . peculiarly."* See Lyddeker's *Royal Natural History*.
Lines 23–24: Thomas of Leighton Buzzard's vine: a fragment of iron-work in Westminster Abbey.
Lines 65–66: *A sailboat was the first machine.* See F. L. Morse, *Power: Its Application from the 17th Dynasty to the 20th Century.*

HE "DIGESTETH HARDE YRON" *(page 714)*
"The estrich digesteth harde yron to preserve his health." Lyly's *Euphues*.
Line 5: *The large sparrow.* "Xenophon (Anabasis, I, 5, 2) reports many ostriches in the desert on the left . . . side of the middle Euphrates, on the way from North Syria to Babylonia." George Jennison, *Animals for Show and Pleasure in Ancient Rome.*
Lines 7, 17–18, 31: *A symbol of justice, men in ostrich-skins, Leda's egg,* and other allusions. Berthold Laufer, "Ostrich Egg-shell Cups from Mesopotamia," *The Open Court*, May 1926. "An ostrich plume symbolized truth and justice, and was the emblem of the goddess Ma-at, the patron saint of judges. Her head is adorned with an ostrich feather, her eyes are closed . . . as Justice is blindfolded."
Line 40: *Six hundred ostrich brains.* At a banquet given by Elagabalus. See above: *Animals for Show and Pleasure in Ancient Rome.*
Lines 43–44: *Egg-shell goblets.* E.g., the painted ostrich-egg cup mounted in silver gilt by Elias Geier of Leipzig about 1589. Edward Wenham, "Antiques in and about London," *New York Sun*, May 22, 1937.
Line 44: *Eight pairs of ostriches.* See above: *Animals for Show and Pleasure in Ancient Rome.*
Line 60: Sparrow-camel: στρουθιοκάμηλος.

TOM FOOL AT JAMAICA *(page 720)*
Line 6: *mule and jockey.* A mule and jockey by "Giulio Gomez 6 años" from a col-
lection of drawings by Spanish school children. Solicited on behalf of a fund-
raising committee for Republican Spain, sold by Lord and Taylor; given to me
by Miss Louise Crane.

Lines 8–9: *"There is submerged magnificence . . ."* The Reverend David C. Shipley,
July 20, 1952.
Line 9: *Sentir avec ardeur.* By Madame Boufflers—Marie-Françoise-Catherine de
Beauvau, Marquise de Boufflers (1711–1786). See note by Dr. Achilles Fang,
annotating Lu Chi's "Wên Fu" (A.D. 261–303)—his "Rhymeprose on Litera-
ture" ("rhymeprose" from "Reimprosa" of German medievalists): "As far as
notes go, I am at one with a contemporary of Rousseau's: 'Il faut dire en deux
mots / Ce qu'on veut dire'; . . . But I cannot claim 'J'ai réussi,' especially
because I broke Mme. de Boufflers' injunction ('Il faut éviter l'emploi / Du
moi, du moi.')." *Harvard Journal of Asiatic Studies*, Volume 14, Number 3,
December 1951, page 529 (revised, *New Mexico Quarterly*, September 1952).

Air: *Sentir avec ardeur*

Il faut dire en deux mots
Ce qu'on veut dire;
Les longs propos
Sont sots.

Il faut savoir lire
Avant que d'écrire,
Et puis dire en deux mots
Ce qu'on veut dire.
Les longs propos
Sont sots.

Il ne faut pas toujours conter,
Citer,
Dater,

Mais écouter.
Il faut éviter l'emploi
    Du moi, du moi,
    Voici pourquoi:

Il est tyrannique,
Trop académique;
    L'ennui, l'ennui
    Marche avec lui.
Je me conduis toujours ainsi
        Ici,
        Aussi
    J'ai réussi.

Il faut dire en deux mots
Ce qu'on veut dire;
    Les longs propos
    Sont sots.

Line 13: *Master Atkinson.* I opened *The New York Times* one morning (March 3, 1952) and a column by Arthur Daley on Ted Atkinson and Tom Fool took my fancy. Asked what he thought of Hill Gail, Ted Atkinson said, "He's a real good horse, . . . real good," and paused a moment. "But I think he ranks only second to Tom Fool. . . . I prefer Tom Fool. . . . He makes a more sustained effort and makes it more often." Reminded that Citation could make eight or ten spurts in a race, "That's it," said Ted enthusiastically. "It's the mark of a champion to spurt 100 yards, settle back and spurt another 100 yards, giving that extra burst whenever needed. From what I've seen of Tom Fool, I'd call him a 'handy horse.'" He mentioned two others. "They had only one way of running. But Tom Fool. . . ." Then I saw a picture of Tom Fool (*New York Times*, April 1, 1952) with Ted Atkinson in the saddle and felt I must pay him a slight tribute; got on with it a little way, then realized that I had just received an award from Youth United for a Better Tomorrow and was worried indeed. I deplore gambling and had never seen a race. Then in the *Times* for July 24, 1952, I saw a column by Joseph C. Nichols about Frederic Capossela, the announcer at Belmont Park, who said when interviewed, "Nervous? No, I'm never nervous. . . . I'll tell you where it's tough. The straight-away at Belmont Park, where as many as twenty-eight horses run at you from a point three quarters of a mile away. I get 'em though, and why shouldn't I? I'm relaxed, I'm confident and I don't bet."

In the way of a sequel, "Money Isn't Everything" by Arthur Daley (*New York Times*, March 1, 1955): " 'There's a constant fascination to thoroughbreds,' said Ted, '. . . they're so much like people. . . . My first love was Red Hay . . . a stout-hearted little fellow . . . he always tried, always gave his best.' [Mr. Daley: 'The same description fits Atkinson.'] 'There was Devil Diver, . . . the mare Snow Goose. One of my big favorites . . . crazy to get going. . . . But once she swung into stride . . . you could ride her with shoelaces for reins. . . . And there was Coaltown. . . . There were others of course, but I never met one who could compare with Tom Fool, my favorite of favorites. He had the most personality of all. . . . Just to look at him lit a spark. He had an intelligent head, an intelligent look and, best of all, was intelligent. He had soft eyes, a wide brow and—gee, I'm sounding like a lovesick boy. But I think he had the handsomest face of any horse I ever had anything to do with. He was a great horse but I was fond of him not so much for what he achieved as for what he was.' With that the sprightly Master Theodore fastened the number plate on his right shoulder and headed for the paddock."

Lines 14–15: *"Chance is a regrettable impurity."* The *I Ching* or *Book of Changes*, translated by Richard Wilhelm and Cary Baynes, Bollingen Series XIX (New York: Pantheon Books, 1950).

Line 29: *Fats Waller.* Thomas Waller, "a protean jazz figure," died in 1943. See *The New York Times*, article and Richard Tucker (Pix) photograph, March 16, 1952.

Line 31: *Ozzie Smith.* Osborne Smith, a Negro chanter and drummer who improvised the music for Ian Hugo's *Ai-Yé.*

Line 31: *Eubie Blake.* The Negro pianist in *Shuffle Along.*

O TO BE A DRAGON *(page 721)*

Dragon: see secondary symbols, Volume II of *The Tao of Painting*, translated and edited by Mai-mai Sze, Bollingen Series 49 (New York: Pantheon, 1956; Modern Library edition, p. 57).

Lines 1–2: Solomon's wish: "an understanding heart." I Kings 3:9.

683.15 *The Monkeys*] This poem appeared with the title "My Apish Cousin," in *Observations* (1924).

687.11 *Black Earth*] In *Collected Poems* (1951), this poem was re-titled "Melancthon."

701.25–26 demonstration . . . with the egg] At a banquet, Columbus was asked if he thought someone else would have discovered the New World had he not done so. In response, Columbus asked the guests to stand an egg on one end; when they failed, he crushed one end against the table and stood it on the flattened part.

705.29 salpiglossis] Herbaceous annual of Chilean origin, cultivated for its colorful, funnel-shaped flowers.

728.4–9 *S'io credesse . . . rispondo*] Dante, *Inferno*, 27, 61–67.

736.6 "dying fall"] Shakespeare, *Twelfth Night*, I, i, 4.

738.13 *La Figlia Che Piange*] The Weeping Girl.

739.7 ὤμοι, πέπηγμαι καίριαν πηλὴν ἔσω.] Agamemnon's words as he is murdered in Aeschylus' *Agamemnon* (line 1343): "Alas, I am struck a mortal blow within."

739.8–9 *Why . . . wrong.*] *The Reign of King Edward the Third* (1596, sometimes attributed in part to Shakespeare), II, i, 109–10.

741.27–29 *Thou hast nor youth . . . both.*] Shakespeare, *Measure for Measure*, III, i, 32–34.

744.1 *The Waste Land*] Later editions include the dedication, "For Ezra Pound, *il miglior fabbro.*" (See note 526.18.)

744.2–4   *Nam Sibyllam . . . ἀποθανεῖν θέλω.*] Petronius, *Satyricon*, Chapter 48: I myself saw the Sybil of Cumae hanging in a bottle, and when the boys asked her, "Sybil, what do you want?" she answered, "I want to die."

744.17   Bin . . . deutsch] I'm no Russian, I come from Lithuania, a true German.

745.1–4   *Frisch . . . du?*] Fresh blows the wind toward my homeland. Where are you waiting, my Irish child?

745.12   *Oed' und leer das Meer.*] The lake is barren and empty.

746.9   hypocrite . . . frère!] Hypocrite reader!—my double—my brother!

746.33–34   The change . . . rudely forced] See note 550.22.

749.32   *Et. . . .coupole!*] And, O the childrens' voices, singing in the dome!

756.8   *Poi s'ascose . . . affina*] He hid himself in the refining flame.

756.9   *Quando fiam ceu chelidon—*] When shall I be as the swallow.

756.10   *Le Prince . . . abolie*] The Prince of Aquitaine, with his ruined tower.

759.29–33   *Blick . . . Tränen*] *A Glimpse of Chaos:* Already half of Europe, already at least half of Eastern Europe, is on the way to Chaos, drives drunk with holy delusions on the edge of the abyss and sings drunken hymns the way Dimitri Karamazov sang. The bourgeois laughs at these songs; the saint and the seer listen with tears.

760.20   *penny for the Old Guy*] Children's cry on Guy Fawkes Day.

763.23   *Quis hic locus, quae regio, quae mundi plaga?*] Cf. Seneca, *Hercules Furens:* "What place is this, what kingdom, what region of the world?"

766.17–18   And God . . . bones live?] Cf. Ezekiel 37:3.

768.33   Sovegna vos] Cf. Dante, *Purgatorio*, Canto 26.

783.2–6   τοῦ λόγου . . . Herakleitos)] "Although the Word, the Logos, is universal, most people live as though they had their own special rules." . . . "The way up is the way down." . . . Diels: *The Fragments of the Presocratics* (Heraclitus).

785.17   *Erhebung*] Exaltation.

803.18   Procne . . . Itylus] See note 550.22.

811.3   *Senlin*] Protagonist of a series of poems by Aiken, collected in *Senlin: A Biography* (1918).

813.5   *Tetélestai*] It is finished: Christ's last words on the cross.

823.31   *Per aspidistra . . . ad astra*] From the aspidistra to the stars.

834.22   Missus Ned McLean] Wife of Edward B. McLean, publisher of *The Washington Post.*

834.27   Max Gordon] Broadway producer (1892–1978) whose many successful shows included *The Band Wagon* (1931), *The Cat and the Fiddle* (1931), *Roberta* (1933), and *The Great Waltz* (1934).

835.3–4   If Sam Goldwyn . . . in diction] The Russian actress Anna Sten (b. 1903) was signed to a contract by movie producer Samuel Goldwyn, who attempted to groom her for stardom; her films were unsuccessful and she became known as "Goldwyn's Folly." Goldwyn was notorious for his malapropisms.

835.7   Lady Mendl] Elsie de Wolfe (1865–1950), who after a first career as a professional actress (1890–1905) became a decorator and arbiter of taste.

835.19   Missus R] Eleanor Roosevelt.

848.12   Ernest] Ernest Hemingway.

859.18   *Passer Mortuus Est*] Catullus III, 1: The sparrow is dead.

Index of Titles and First Lines

Index of Poets

Library of Congress Cataloging-in-Publication Data

American poetry. The twentieth century.
    p. cm. — (The Library of America ; 115–116)
    Includes bibliographical references (p.) and index.
    ISBN 1–883011–77–9 (v. 1 : alk. paper) —
    ISBN 1–883011–78–7 (v. 2 : alk. paper)
    1. American poetry—20th century.   I. Series.
PS613.A4 2000
811'.50821—dc21   99–043721

THE LIBRARY OF AMERICA SERIES

The Library of America fosters appreciation and pride in America's literary heritage by publishing, and keeping permanently in print, authoritative editions of its best and most significant writing. An independent nonprofit organization, it was founded in 1979 with seed money from the National Endowment for the Humanities and the Ford Foundation.